1989 Which? Wi

1989 Which? Wine Guide

Edited by Roger Voss

Published by Consumers' Association
and Hodder & Stoughton

Which? Books are commissioned and researched by
The Association for Consumer Research and published by
Consumers' Association, 2 Marylebone Road, NW1 4DX and
Hodder & Stoughton, 47 Bedford Square, London WC1B 3DP

British Library Cataloguing in Publication Data

Which? wine guide. – 1989 –
1. Wines. Buyers' guides – Serials
2. Great Britain. Wines trades.
Directories – Serials
641.2'2'0294

ISBN 0 340 43064 8

Typography   Tim Higgins
Cover photograph   Trevor Melton
Cover typography   Fox + Partners
Illustrations   Diana Durant
Researcher   Charlotte Baker

Cartography by GEOprojects (UK) Ltd
Henley-on-Thames, Oxfordshire

Typesetting by Rowland Phototypesetting Ltd
Bury St Edmunds, Suffolk

Printed and bound in Great Britain
by Collins, Glasgow

Contents

Part I Where to buy

Part II What to buy

CONTENTS

Part III Wine away from home

Introduction

In the year when we in the United Kingdom drank over a billion bottles of wine for the first time, alcohol has received a poorer press than it has had for quite a while. Football hooliganism, riots in country towns, troubles on Spanish beaches: in every case, alcohol has been blamed. During this period, licensing hours in England and Wales have been relaxed, making it easier for people, if they so wish, to drink throughout the day.

Certainly, the consumption of alcohol is common to all these events, but it has been only one factor, and no more than that. The French and Italians drink much more than we do, yet they don't have the same reputation. It is much more a question of the attitude with which we in Britain still regard the consumption of alcohol. All too often, we see it as a means of getting drunk, of being macho, whereas in continental Europe, being drunk is considered socially demeaning at every level of society.

The longer there are those who adopt a puritanical attitude towards drinking – a movement that is gaining ground in this country as it has done in the USA – and the longer repressive attitudes are allowed to hold sway, the more likely we are to over-indulge when given the chance. If we're treated like adults, we'll behave like adults, and pass on responsible attitudes to our children.

The role of wine

Which is where, we feel, wine plays an important role. When was the last time a football riot was caused by people who had been drinking too much wine? Wine is much more a drink taken at meals or at least in association with food – and is therefore less likely to cause extreme, rowdy drunkenness.

And wine, as Jancis Robinson writes, both in her book *The Demon Drink* (Mitchell Beazley) and in her feature on page 15, can be positively beneficial. For example, it is widely agreed that alcohol in moderation may do you good both mentally and physically, and there is even some evidence that it may lessen the incidence of heart disease. And that is putting on one side the genuinely civilising effect of wine. It is no coincidence that wine has played an important part in much of the history of western culture, from its religious connections to its inspirational qualities.

Part of civilised life

While we would hestitate to claim such a significant role for *Which? Wine Guide*, we do like to see ourselves as encouraging an improvement in the standards of what we drink, which in turn should lead to our taking wine as part of a civilised life rather than as an excuse for consuming too much. The way in which we do this is essentially to indicate which wines would make for enjoyable drinking – and then where to buy them.

We are always concerned with value for money, but it would be a mistake to confuse value for money with cheapness. Customs duty is applied in fixed bands according to whether the wine is still, sparkling or fortified. This means that, for instance, if around 90p of the price of a bottle of still table wine is taken up by duty and VAT, a cheap wine will very often be poor value. It is much better to pay a little more, because the percentage of the price of the bottle representing the wine is then much higher. If a bottle of wine costs £2, nearly 50 per cent of that is duty and VAT; if it costs £3, only 33 per cent is duty and VAT, and so on.

And this simple economic fact is now dawning on us. We broke through what wine retailers regarded as the magic upper price limit of £2.50 some time ago; now, it seems, we are prepared to pay around £3 for a bottle of wine. It's all a far cry from the £1.99 Liebfraumilch, which is increasingly showing itself to be a loss leader to attract customers into the shop.

Paying more for extra service

Our buying habits have changed in other ways. We are also willing to pay a little more for our wine to get extra service. So while supermarkets continue to flourish, supplying us with much of what we drink, other wine retailers (including wine warehouses) are offering a wider service in the form of newsletters, wine tastings, delivery, advice – all the sorts of things that we might have thought would disappear in the highly price-competitive world of wine retailing.

But in fact competition has had exactly the reverse effect. Because there are now so many wine merchants of all sorts chasing our custom, we are being wooed assiduously. And very nice it is, too. The standards of service have improved considerably over the past two years, with a consequent rise in the number of merchants who are making it into the Guide.

The range widens

At the same time, wine retailers have also increased the range of what they sell. Australian wine is the most obvious example: every merchant now has a fair spread of what that lucky country produces. And while prices of her wines may never be quite so amazingly good as they were last year, we are still getting extremely good value for money.

Italy, Portugal and Spain are other such examples. Italian sections of merchants' lists have grown apace, not with two-litre bottles of plonk, but with representative selections of what is good and often great. Portugal, meanwhile, continues to come up with some superb bargains, especially in mature red wines, while Spain's contribution is of red and white wines from regions besides Rioja – from Penedès, Valdepeñas, Ribera del Duero, Toro.

And, of course, there is always France, which still supplies 39 per cent of what we drink. While Burgundy is expensive, and the Rhône is becoming more so, Bordeaux has some terrific bargains once you cut through the maze of Grands Crus and Grands Vins to reach the middle ranks; likewise, the Midi and the smaller French regions have more and more to offer.

Our Best Buys

We have introduced one new section to the Guide this year: our choice of the year's **Best Buys**. It is an eclectic, personal choice and reflects the editor's preferences. But it is also a reflection of the best value that wine merchants have to offer us in the coming months. We have arranged it by style – dry white, sparkling, light red, and so on – rather than by country of origin, but we continue to offer a range of Best Buys from each region after the appropriate entry in Part II.

Roger Voss

Consumers' Association and South African wine

A hallmark of consumers' associations world-wide is a commitment against discrimination of consumers on grounds of race, creed, gender or nationality. As a founder member and supporter of the International Organisation of Consumer Unions, Consumers' Association supports this policy of non-discrimination. We do not assess wine from South Africa as a matter of principle. So long as people are denied basic human and consumer rights by virtue of the colour of their skin, the Association believes that it must take a moral stand and signal its total abhorrence of such a régime. We regret having to exclude South African wines from *Which? Wine Guide* but the moral issue must be paramount.

How to use this Guide

Part I – Where to buy

This is our directory of the nation's top wine merchants all over the
United Kingdom (and, in one case, in the Republic of Ireland). We
include supermarkets, high street off-licences and wine warehouses as
well as individual wine merchants. They are in the Guide either
because they sell an exciting range of wines or because they offer
particularly good value. Generally they score well on both counts. We
always investigate many more wine merchants than we include in the
Guide. Many fail to make it because in our opinion they just do not
reach our high standards. Of course, a few merchants may have
slipped through our net – if you have a favourite merchant who is not
in the Guide, please let us know (there are report forms at the back of
the book).

Directory entries

Before the main text, a directory entry will give you the following
information:

1 Name of the firm – generally the name of the shop.

2 The address of the place where you can order or buy wine. For
chains with a number of branches, we give the head office only –
phone them for your nearest branch.

3 Any special awards that the merchant has won – see page 43.

4 Open and closed – the opening hours and the days on which the
shop or order office is closed.

5 Credit cards – which ones are accepted; whether you can open a
personal or business account. Most merchants operate on 30-day credit
if you have an account – but always read the small print in their list or
ask if you are planning to open an account. Some merchants now
charge interest on overdue accounts.

6 Discounts – what discounts are offered (generally on unmixed
cases). This information does not include any special offers a merchant
may make.

7 Delivery – what delivery terms the merchant offers. It pays to read
these closely, because even if a merchant seems expensive, free
delivery can make quite a difference to the final bill.

8 Glass hire – information on what you need to spend on wine in order to hire glasses free of charge. Always ask for details about payment for breakages.

9 Tastings and talks – whether the wine merchant organises tastings or talks and at what charge. Details of some merchants' tastings and talks are in the FIND OUT MORE ABOUT WINE section (see page 622).

10 Cellarage – whether a merchant will look after your wine for you if your cellar is not big enough, and how much he will charge.

11 An indication of whether the shop sells wine by the single bottle or by the case only. Wholesalers may not sell wine by the single bottle – they are indicated by the symbol ■ .

Part II – Guide to wines

The second main section is our review of the latest news from the world's vineyards. We start with our selection of the year's best buys. Then each regional entry is organised like this:

1 An introductory section giving up-to-date information on new styles of wine, new trends and what to watch for over the coming year.

2 A glossary of terms used in that region to describe wines.

3 A directory of principal producers, merchants and estates in the region, with information about particular stockists in this country.

4 Best buys – our choice of the wines we would buy over the next year from that region.

5 Specialist stockists – wine merchants who specialise in the wines of the region. Unless the address is printed there, details of the merchants will be found in the WHERE TO BUY merchants directory.

More help?

Other sections of the Guide are also designed to help you bring a wine and a merchant together or find a merchant in your area.

1 WHO'S WHERE – the gazetteer on page 47 – lists all the merchants in the WHERE TO BUY merchants directory by town or village and by county. Use this if you want to find a good local wine merchant. The gazetteer cannot, however, include all the branches of chains, high street off-licences or supermarkets – you will need to contact the head office for this information (see page 52).

2 The index of wines – if you want to find where a wine is mentioned in the WHAT TO BUY section, turn to page 640.

Wine is good for you

Is wine healthy? It certainly forms an essential part of our present civilisation. And JANCIS ROBINSON MW, *whose book on alcohol,* The Demon Drink, *was published earlier in 1988, argues that because it is the most natural form of alcohol, it can also – in moderation – be positively good for you.*

I could easily be accused of bias, but it does seem to me that of all alcoholic drinks, wine – quite apart from being the most delicious – is the least dangerous.

Those of us who love wine must acknowledge that it contains a substance, ethyl alcohol, which can damage our minds, our bodies and society in general if used unwisely. The alcohol contained in wine is, sadly, not of some magical non-liver-rotting sort and indeed is identical to the alcohol contained in, say, gin and lager. Continued over-enthusiastic consumption of alcohol in any form can lead to cirrhosis, hypertension and a host of other nasty conditions. The trick is to know how to master alcohol, and to keep a weather eye on our relationship with it.

Before examining some of wine's special qualities, it is important to stress that even alcohol per se can be beneficial. As we all know from delightful experience – even if we rarely stop to acknowledge the fact –

alcohol can be a great life enhancer. Taken in controlled doses, this wonderful substance lifts the spirits, inducing a state of mild euphoria and making the world seem a better place to be – although I suspect that *Which? Wine Guide* readers scarcely need me to point this out.

Moderate drinkers are healthier

Quite apart from this, alcohol's obvious attribute, however, there is convincing medical evidence that moderate drinkers are healthier than abstainers. More than fifteen independent and scrupulously objective research projects around the world have demonstrated that the incidence of coronary heart disease, our most serious killer, is lower in those who indulge in one or two drinks a day than in those who forgo this pleasure. And there is a similar pattern in research into hypertension, or high blood pressure: teetotallers tend to have higher blood pressure than moderate drinkers. (More is not merrier, however. Heavy drinkers are much more likely to suffer heart attacks and high blood pressure than abstainers.)

Alcoholic drinks of all sorts have also been shown to have strong therapeutic value in treating the elderly. (One Boston experiment showed that geriatric patients introduced to a cocktail hour were fully weaned off sedatives, were far more mobile and, puzzlingly, more continent.) Members of the medical profession have been using alcohol's sedative properties for decades, of course. Alcoholic drinks have been prescribed for all manner of patients – from pints of port for wounded soldiers to stout for nursing mothers, and alcohol is an active ingredient in gripewater and a number of other common paediatric remedies. Alcohol stimulates the appetite and has in its time been a useful painkiller and antiseptic – notably in societies without a reliable water supply.

One of the most frequently quoted exponents of this last quality was Saint Paul who advised in his first Epistle to Timothy: 'Be no longer a drinker of water, but use a little wine for thy stomach's sake and thine often infirmities.'

This illustrates nicely at least two of wine's unique qualities: its antiquity and its religious connotation. Wine was almost certainly man's first alcoholic drink, since all that was needed to make it was a bunch of grapes left lying in the sun in a container that would hold the resultant fermented juice. No other common ferment, even beer, is as simple to make, and man had to wait for distilled spirits until the work of Arab alchemists in the Middle Ages.

Wine has also been used as a sacrament for centuries, most notably in the Christian church as an integral part of Holy Communion. In predominantly Roman Catholic cultures, it is unthinkable that wine, daily transubstantiated into the blood of Christ, could be the fount of evil. (It is perhaps significant that these cultures include some of the world's major wine-producing countries.)

Wine more respectable

It is partly for these reasons that wine seems instinctively more 'respectable' than other alcoholic drinks, but it is for more solid reasons, because of the botanical nature of that magical plant the vine, that wine can in fact offer us so much intellectual stimulation. Any liquid containing fermentable sugars can be turned into an alcoholic drink, but the vine's fruit happens to be particularly juicy and sweet. But more than that it is a plant which is extremely adaptable – both genetically, which is why there are so many and different vine varieties, and environmentally, which is why the vine will grow in such an intriguing variety of soils and climates. All of this results in a range of sensations and significant production factors that is unparalleled in any other alcoholic drink. There are fascinating nuances of flavour and provenance in hand-crafted spirits and beers, but wine is surely the drink, very possibly the victual, which offers most in the way of connoisseurship. And a far higher proportion of wine than of beer, cider or any spirit I can think of is produced by skilled and opinionated artisans rather than industry.

This helps to explain why those of us who enjoy wine are reluctant to accept the argument that our tasting activity is merely an excuse for indulgence in alcohol.

Socially, it is difficult to argue that wine is not the most virtuous form of alcohol. Traditionally it has been drunk with food, the healthiest way to mitigate any damage done by alcohol. And traditionally in Britain, wine has been drunk by a fairly narrow social stratum. But even now that wine is much more widely drunk, and increasingly as an aperitif without food, in both this country and the United States, the most recent research shows that it is far from being associated with such alcohol-related misdemeanours as drunk driving offences or hooliganism. Just as wine has been synonymous with civilisation, wine still seems to be closely associated, if not necessarily synonymous, with civilised behaviour.

Valiant quantities

Medically, wine's virtues in relation to other alcoholic drinks are rather less clear. There are (unproven) theories that France's relatively low incidence of heart attacks could be related to the valiant quantities of wine still drunk by the average Frenchman. Some theorists have even posited a connection between wine (or alcohol) and a reduction in cholesterol levels but this is so far unproven, and olive oil and garlic are other candidates as explanations for the generally healthy state of the Mediterranean heart. Few are in any doubt, however, that the particularly high cirrhosis mortality rates in France, Portugal and Italy are related to their status as the world's top three wine-consuming countries. But that the highest cirrhosis mortality rate of all is among Hungarians, who are not great wine drinkers but sink formidable quantities of spirits, suggests that it may well be alcohol in general rather than wine in particular that is responsible for cirrhosis.

Wine contains more traces of minerals and vitamins than most spirits, but many beers can offer at least as useful a range of nutrients, notably riboflavin, niacin and folic acid, and some of the world's more homespun beers can be positively nutritious. The average glass of wine, however, does supply about 15 per cent of a man's daily recommended intake of iron and 10 per cent of a woman's, and there is considerable evidence to suggest that wine drunk with food helps the body to absorb any useful minerals such as calcium, phosphorus, magnesium and zinc that are in that food.

Wine has sometimes been drunk merely for nourishment: there was a time when agricultural workers around the Mediterranean might expect to find up to a third of their daily calories from their consumption of a drink that was so much more reliable than the local tapwater. Nowadays we tend to be more concerned to limit rather than maximise our calorific intake and on this basis dry wine, of either colour, is certainly not one of the most fattening ways to drink alcohol, but the sweeter and/or stronger the wine, the more calories are in it.

The medical profession has come up with a measure called a 'unit' of alcohol, which nowadays means 8gm pure alcohol (it was once a more indulgent 10gm) and is roughly equivalent to a half-pint of standard lager or bitter, a single measure of spirits with an alcoholic strength of 40% and a ninth of a bottle of 12% wine (or just under a seventh of a bottle of 10% wine, or a thirteenth of a bottle of 18% fortified wine).

On this basis, a unit of dry wine contains 60 calories, a unit of dry fortified wine such as a fino Sherry contains 70 calories and a unit of sweet fortified wine such as Port contains 165 calories, while a unit of standard lager contains 80 calories and a unit of gin or vodka 55 calories.

The latest medical Royal Colleges' reports on alcohol suggest that a safe weekly intake of alcohol is 21 units for men and 14 for women and that anything above 50 units a week for men and 35 for women may well be harmful. Unfortunately for members of the more gustatorily sensitive sex, the same amount of alcohol is more concentrated and therefore potentially more damaging in a woman than in a man, even of the same size, because of the fattier female childbearing form.

Individuals vary enormously in their capacity to react to alcohol and to withstand its medical ravages, but those who should be particularly wary include women who are pregnant or intending to conceive, anyone with high blood pressure, an ulcer, fatty heart muscle, diabetics, those on medication and who have had stomach surgery. Many doctors advise pregnant and pre-pregnant women to abstain altogether.

On the other hand, few of those of who have visited the world's wine regions can fail to have been struck by the fact that the typical vigneron appears to drink quantities of wine that the Royal Colleges might well classify as hazardous, yet usually live to a ripe old age. (It should be remembered that the typical French or Italian oenophile drinks wine exclusively with meals and never before or after, in contrast to his or her counterpart in this country.) Clearly this is just one aspect of one of the most fascinating substances regularly ingested by 90 per cent of British adults on which more research is needed.

Do's and don't's

Meanwhile, a few tips on drinking and serving wine sensibly:

● Never drink wine to quench thirst: always drink water as well.

● Try not to drink on an empty stomach.

● Give the liver a rest by regular abstention for at least a day.

● Never force drinks on others, especially when they are driving; always provide a non-alcoholic alternative.

● Monitor your alcohol intake.

● Be extra careful when on medication.

● Be particularly wary of fortified wines (drinks between 15 and 30% alcohol enter the system most rapidly).

● Inform yourself about alcohol, respect it, and be sure to enjoy it.

(Jancis Robinson's book, *The Demon Drink*, is published by Mitchell Beazley at £9.95.)

Jancis Robinson **MW** *is a regular television broadcaster on wine and has written many books on the subject, including* The Wine Book, The Great Wine Book, Masterglass *and* Vines, Grapes and Wines.

Wine and food – forget the rules

White wine with fish, red wine with meat, they used to say in all the etiquette books. Well, that's nonsense, says DAVID WOLFE. *Much more important, he believes, is to trust your own tastebuds to match flavours, and he passes on some of his personal observations on how to do it.*

In recent years I have enjoyed many tastings of food and wine together. This, added to years of experimenting with food and wine matching, has led me to three conclusions. First, of course you can drink whatever you like with any food. However, for someone with a discriminating palate who is aiming for a perfect gastronomic match, there are rules. Some of them are not absolutely unbreakable, nor equally applicable to all palates.

Second, many oft-repeated maxims turn out to be false. For instance, white wine need not always accompany fish, but nor can you automatically assume that any white wine will match any fish.

Third, the unfashionable is easily overlooked: for example, dry fortified wines – primarily Sherry, but dry Marsala too. They can complement many foods, especially at the start of a meal.

But to begin at the beginning. The simplest way of finding the perfect gastronomic match is to leave it to chance. There are parallels in other arts. The ballet 'Le Jeune Homme et Mort' was choreographed to specially composed music. At the final rehearsal, its creator, Jean Cocteau, found that it did not work, so on the first night he substituted music by Bach. The ballet was a phenomenal success, and critics praised the 'inspired' moments when music and movement coincided.

So the last bottle from the cellar with the last can from the storecupboard or the last packet from the freezer may combine to make a superb meal. Making the business less risky, you could apply the geographical approach. In theory, wine and food from the same country always go well together. Grilled fish, goats' cheese salad and retsina can make a fine lunch on the beach in Greece. But sometimes the success of certain wine and food combinations fades out of context and on a winter's evening at home, a powerful white Rioja or a fine single-vineyard Soave might be even more enjoyable.

It is no surprise to find that wine from its birthplace, the Middle East, tends to match the food of the region. Most red wines go well with the cuisines of the Lebanon, Egypt, Iran, even Armenia, provided they are not too clean and classical. In other words, fine claret, Burgundy and Rhône are less suitable than Provençal, southern Italian and 'old-style' wines from Spain and Eastern Europe.

Sometimes it is almost impossible to improve on the local combination. Arcachon oysters with little garlicky chipolatas (one to every six oysters) are best matched in Bordeaux with a dry Entre-Deux-Mers or Graves. Even so, a Bordelais, until recently at least, would be as likely to offer an Alsace wine. Likewise, after a few days in Champagne one returns to a red wine region, or home, with relief. A Champenois, in an unguarded moment, may grant that still red wine is needed with the meat at dinner. He may go even further and admit that the red wine of Bouzy, amusing as its name may be, is not as good with lamb as a red Bordeaux – or, in these enlightened times, a New World Cabernet Sauvignon.

Flavour matching

The crux of the matter is finding complementary tastes, not colours. The old maxim of red wine with red meat, white wine with white meat is nonsense. Consider rabbit, a 'white meat'. Stewed in cider with tomatoes, bacon, onions and apples, it calls for an acid wine, so a Muscadet or a Loire Sauvignon would be possibilities, or a crisp young pink from the Rhône, and my preference would be for a red Loire, a Chinon, a Bourgueil or a Saumur-Champigny. Flavour matching can be very precise. If the rabbit is roast or sautéed with mushrooms, everything depends on the mushrooms. With flat field mushrooms, ceps, morels or truffles, a red wine would be best. In the same order I would suggest Rhône, claret, fine claret or Burgundy, great Rhône or Burgundy. With button mushrooms my choice would be Beaujolais;

with girolles a white wine, a fresh tangy Savoie, or a Condrieu from the northern Rhône. (Please take it as read that New World or other European equivalents could be substituted for most of the French classics.)

Take another meat that is traditionally regarded as 'white' – chicken. The Burgundian wine grower shows off his greatest red with a simply roast poulet de Bresse. A lesser, less delicate red, deserves only coq au vin.

Still in Burgundy, there is another colour paradox – snails, which though dark brown to black count as 'white meat' for historico-religious reasons: since they were defined as white they could be eaten on fast days. They are usually accompanied by a crisp, young white wine, but a fruity young Beaujolais is good, too. The same wines go well with jambon persillé – does that make Burgundian ham red, white or pink?

One of the best examples of complementary tastes is demonstrated by the relationship of red Burgundy to beef marmite, marmite referring to the burnt crust which forms on the skin of, and underneath, joints of roast beef. In trying to define the taste of red Burgundy I have often made this comparison, which is understood by both wine and beef lovers. It is no coincidence that the match of roast beef and red Burgundy is one of the greatest gastronomic miracles.

Flavour contrasts

But the perfect combination of wine and food need not be a case of like and like. Flavour contrasting is just as much of an art. A match that works by contrast is that of white wine with fatty meat or an oily sauce. It works not because the wine is white, but because it is acid, and acidity cuts fat. That being so, an acidic red should go equally well, yet with buttery snails I like Chablis, and with fatty rillettes de porc, a white Loire.

Chinese food goes with most wines: so I concluded at a tasting at which twelve wine merchants and wine writers each brought two or three bottles. There were thirty-one wines in all, of all colours and varied origins. Sparkling wines, especially chalky Spanish cavas, went well, because their acidity and hardness cut through the oiliness of Chinese dishes. But my conclusion was that thirty wines would have been enough: the type of wine I find unsympathetic to Chinese food is the one most often recommended. 'Spicy' wines, and particularly Gewürztraminers, are for me totally irrelevant: the spiciness is of a different order.

Sauternes is often served with foie gras – as a match or a contrast? My theory is that it is actually a contrast between the blandness of the goose-liver and – no, not the sweetness of the wine, but its saltiness. That is the key to its co-existence with foie gras. This saltiness of Sauternes also explains why it goes with Roquefort, the saltiest of cheeses, and why attempts to match Sauternes with other cheeses, even other blues, are doomed to failure.

In the rest of the cheese world, good matches include mature Cheddar with a big red wine, Cheshire and claret, Stilton and Port, matured Gouda or Parmesan with almost any red, fine cheese of the Gruyère family – especially Appenzeller – with almost any light red or white. Burgundian cheese, whether fresh and creamy, or fermented, is perfect with Burgundy wine. But what wine goes with Camembert? It might be worth reverting to geography and trying Calvados.

Fashion

Fashion also plays a part in flavour matching, and who can argue against it? The old rule of white wine with fish usually holds good because the tannin in red wine and the iodine in fish, crustaceans and molluscs are irreconcilable enemies who fight on the palate. But red wine with fish could not be more fashionable. It enables the 1989-wise chef or wine writer to show his or her readiness to get rid of the mystique of wine and silly old rules.

The one fish, which to my knowledge has always come in a red wine sauce, at least in France, is the lamprey. The wine is St-Emilion and is also drunk with the strange creature. I tested it in the case of sole Colbert. The main part of the backbone of a whole Dover sole is removed and the cavity filled with maître d'hôtel butter, before being deep-fried in batter. I once replaced it with beurre marchand de vin, made with red wine and shallots, and in this case, a strong lamb-based glaze. The meaty butter was good with the fish, and it seemed natural to match it with red wine. (But in fact nothing matched the sole so well as a white Burgundy.)

Even if you do subscribe to the conventional view of white wine with fish, you can't just plump for any old white. Salmon is a tricky case: 'with salmon' is too vague. If it is poached, much depends on the poaching medium. This was proved when a panel was asked to judge wines with a fish poached in a court-bouillon in which the absence of carrots had been over-compensated by extra onions. No wine could stand up to the oniony fish.

More skilfully poached salmon calls for moderately fruity wine. Even young white Burgundy of the highest class may overpower delicately flavoured fish (yes, salmon is, or should be, delicate) so I prefer to retreat to the lower ranks. Monthélie, Auxey-Duresses, Montagny or Rully are a few possibilities. A rich sauce can be matched by a powerful Mâcon blanc (today often as rich as Meursault used to be) or cut by the acidity of Beaujolais blanc, or Pouilly Fuissé. Light Chardonnays from the Loire and Ardèche or Northern Italy should also go well.

The wine killers

To the conundrum of what to serve with those well-known 'wine killers' – eggs, asparagus, artichoke and chocolate. It all depends on how you treat them. Eggs in the form of a soufflé, especially cheese soufflé, are a perfect background for the finest of clarets, but fried eggs with a red wine sauce – oeufs meurette – call for red Loire or Burgundy. If the eggs are scrambled the appropriate wine likewise must suit the other ingredients – truffles or smoked fish may be less in quantity, but they determine the flavour.

The wine-killing vegetables, artichoke and asparagus, yet again depend on how they are done. In a Spanish-style casserole, any good Spanish red is suitable; or any full-bodied red, provided it is not too classically restrained. Valpolicella Recioto Amarone would be preferable to simple Valpolicella, however good the latter might be, and Australian Shiraz better than Cabernet Sauvignon. Simpler cooking requires something lighter. Pinot Grigio is a good accompaniment to both vegetables if there is no more than a little tomato in the recipe.

With chocolate, you cannot cut the fat so it must be matched. Málaga is a perfect marriage – surprisingly, because some people describe Málaga as liquid chocolate. But I have enjoyed Sauternes, and even St-Emilion – on odd occasions.

Or take Indian food. Everyone knows that Indian food kills fine wine and that lager or lassi complement and even enhance it. Yet on a cold day, sitting by a window of an Indian restaurant with a view of a blizzard, I enjoyed a St-Emilion with my meal.

The one real killer is Japanese food. The problem here is the effect on the palate of the raw fish which is the glory of that cuisine. It may be the fault rather of its sauce and pickled ginger. Whatever the cause, sashimi is fatal to the taste of wine, and a sushi lunch may even spoil the wine at dinner.

But the point of all these observations is that there is no substitute – and no more fun – than constant experimentation to come up with the very best combinations that appeal to your individual palate. The thrill of finding that perfect combination – like the moment when a dancer seems suspended in mid-air – justifies much effort.

David Wolfe used to own a restaurant before he took up journalism full-time. He is restaurant critic for Decanter *and regularly joins their tasting panels. He also writes on food and wine for* London Portrait *and many other magazines.*

A glass of something sweet and sticky

Dessert wines – pudding wines – remain resolutely unfashionable among many wine drinkers. Dry is healthy, less fattening and smarter. That's sad, believes STEPHEN BROOK, *who has a passion for the sweet and sticky and wants to share it. Here, he explains how the great sweet wines come about, and where they come from.*

Ten years ago a guest thirsty for a sweet wine at the end of a meal stood little chance of being offered one. An occasional glass of Port was as much as one could hope for. Gradually, this lamentable situation began to improve, as dimpled bottles of delicate orange Muscat de Beaumes de Venise rapidly became the standard post-prandial tipple. Very delicious, too, and when properly chilled it could prove a most refreshing way to conclude a dinner party. This sudden vogue may have inspired some wine lovers to explore the extraordinary range of sweet wines now available in this country, but they still seem under-appreciated.

There are two main reasons for this. Most people buy wines to drink with food, and it remains generally true that dry wines accompany food better than sweet ones. It strikes many people as superfluous, not to say extravagant, to open a bottle for the plain pleasure of drinking the wine on its own. The second reason is that many of the more affordable sweet wines available in Britain are fairly disgusting. Spanish Sauternes, first consumed by me at college parties, put me off sweet wines for over a decade. I would not be surprised if unhappy encounters with cheap, sugary, cloying imitations of Sauternes or even cheaper and more sickly Spätlesen and Auslesen are having a similarly off-putting effect on younger wine drinkers today.

The recipe

However, plenty of extremely good sweet wines are available at reasonable prices. My definition of 'good' is simple enough: to be palatable, a sweet wine must be a balanced wine. The sugar content, which gives the wine its sumptuous character, must be balanced by a level of acidity that both keeps the wine fresh and prevents it tasting cloying, especially on the finish. If you want sweetness alone, drink golden syrup, not wine. Any idiot can make sweet wine: all he needs to do is pick very ripe grapes and stop the fermentation before the natural grape sugars have been consumed by the yeasts and turned into alcohol. If that doesn't produce the desired effect, he can always stir in some syrup of figs . . .

To make good, not to mention great, sweet wine, on the other hand, is extremely difficult. It's not enough to pick very ripe grapes, for the sweetness routinely obtained in grapes grown in very hot climates (such as central California or southern Italy) will almost certainly lack that redeeming acidity. Growers can be guaranteed more satisfactory acidity levels in more northerly climates (such as the Loire or the Rhine), but the grapes are less likely to attain the required degrees of sweetness. The winning combination of perfect climatic conditions and correctly ripened fruit is rare. Good vintages for sweet wines are infrequent, yields tend to be low, the vinification process is slow and laborious. Not surprisingly, the successful wines tend to be expensive. What is remarkable is that they are not far more expensive.

The role of botrytis

Not that Ch d'Yquem, admittedly, is exactly cheap. But its closest rivals, in terms of quality, are about a quarter of the price or less. Sauternes, of which Yquem remains the supreme example, is especially costly to make because good examples of the wine cannot be made unless a repellent fungus called botrytis (noble rot) makes its appearance. Botrytis spores swoop only if specific climatic conditions obtain: a combination of misty nights and sunny days. The effect of botrytis is to shrivel the grapes, concentrating both their sweetness and acidity and imparting an irresistible honeyed flavour to the wine. Inferior producers of Sauternes will pick their grapes when ripe, whether botrytis-infected or not, because they are not prepared to risk losing the crop by waiting for the noble rot, which either may not arrive at all or may be preceded by ruinous frost, hail and rain.

Top-quality Sauternes, therefore, cannot be made in every vintage, and even in good vintages only the most scrupulous producers will make outstanding wines. Fortunately, recent vintages have been good. The great vintages of 1975 and 1976 are now rare and costly, but excellent wines from 1980 and 1983 are readily available. Generic Sauternes should invariably be avoided but inexpensive wines in the Sauternes style are also made in Bordeaux, and some of those from Ste-Croix-du-Mont or Loupiac or Cérons can be excellent value. It's advisable to try a bottle before buying on a larger scale, since variations between vintages and between individual producers can be marked. Top Sauternes can age and improve for 20 years or more, though most of the wines are deliciously approachable at five years old.

If you are in the habit of serving foie gras to your dinner guests, you might try a glass of Sauternes as an accompaniment. My limited researches confirm that the combination is first-rate, and Sauternes is also a match for the flavour of Roquefort cheese. (*For the reasons why this should be, see the feature on Wine and Food – Editor.*)

Beyond Sauternes

There are other wines from France that, being less unctuously sweet than Sauternes, can be served with a greater variety of foods or drunk as an aperitif. The much maligned Chenin Blanc grape produces lovely delicate moelleux wines along the Loire, from Vouvray and the slopes south of Angers. The generic appellation for the latter is Coteaux de Layon, but it's worth looking out for the only marginally more costly Chaume, Quarts de Chaume, and Bonnezeaux. A lingering, apple-fresh acidity sustains these elegant wines, and in certain vintages they can age indefinitely. Indeed, that's part of the problem, for these wines require about ten or fifteen years in bottle before they begin to show their quality. Fortunately, older bottles can be found at a reasonable price.

Another attractive sweet wine of France is Jurançon, made from Manseng grapes grown on the foothills of the Pyrenees. Picked in late November, the grapes are not botrytis-affected. The wine has a unique tangy, spicy flavour. Despite very limited production, it is undervalued and relatively easy to find in Britain (for instance, Marks & Spencer have just introduced a medium-sweet example). Jurançon's high acidity makes it suitable as either an aperitif or a refreshing after-dinner glass.

German wines remain resolutely unfashionable, and anyone who has tasted a range of the cheaper stuff that finds its way into supermarkets and off-licences can see why. This factor, harnessed to the low popularity of sweet wines, means that German sweet wines, usually made from the Riesling grape, are foolishly disparaged. This is good news for the consumer, however, for it is possible to find superb bottles of honeyed 1975 and 1976 Auslese wines at absurdly low prices. At their best, these wines have a clean acidity to counter the lushness of nobly rotten Riesling grapes. It would be best to seek advice from merchants on which wines to buy, as there are some tired and flabby German wines in the shops alongside the finest examples. For sheer elegance, these wines are hard to match. Unlike Sauternes, they are delicate and low in alcohol: perfect sweet wines for summer drinking.

At the top end of the scale are the magnificent Beerenauslesen and Trockenbeerenauslesen (made from carefully selected nobly rotten grapes), but these can cost well over £20. However, very reasonably priced bottles in these styles from neighbouring Austria are beginning to come back into the shops after that country's fall from grace, and some of them are certainly worth trying.

Also worth investigating are New World attempts to make wines in these styles. Until recently, the Californians were more successful with Riesling wines, the Australians with Sauternes-style wines. This rule of thumb is becoming less firm, since the absence of an appellation system frees New World winemakers to experiment with different styles. Some of the best Californian 'botrytised' Rieslings are almost as pricey as their German models, though the less expensive wines are often just as good. In blind tastings, some of these New World wines have been thrown in as 'ringers' in order to fool tasters, and successfully too.

Pockets of sweet wines

One of the charms of sampling sweet wines is that they are often very localised: freak micro-climatic conditions and obscure viticultural traditions result in some unique wines, such as the Jurançon mentioned earlier. This is also true of Tokay, a rich and alcoholic sweet wine made from the Furmint grape and exclusive to a small region in eastern Hungary. The wine attains its special character both because of the peculiar method of vinification (a paste made from pressed botrytis-affected grapes is added to Furmint must or wine so as to induce a second fermentation, giving sweetness and alcoholic strength to the final wine) and because of ageing, which takes place for up to six years in small barrels. The wine is allowed to oxidise gently, giving it both its distinctive flavour and its capacity to age in bottle indefinitely. Two centuries ago Tokay was as highly prized as any wine in the world. Now less fashionable, it is available at ridiculously low prices. You either love it or hate it. If you love it, you will find it hard to question the producers' claim that its high mineral extract gives the wine miraculous medicinal properties.

Italy is another region of very localised production. Many of the most splendid wines, especially from southern Italy and the islands, are not exported, though fortunately one of the finest of them all, a marvellously rich unfortified Muscat called Bukkuram, is available here. Many Italian sweet wines are made by the passito method, which involves sun-drying the grapes before pressing them. This desiccating process increases the sugar content to very high levels. As long as the bunches are carefully selected to weed out rotten grapes, passito wines can be impressively concentrated.

The most exciting sweet wines of Italy are, in fact, red. Made from the same grapes that produce Valpolicella, Recioto is a passito wine made in two styles. One, called Amarone, is fermented dry, and is an intimidating wine of 16 per cent alcohol or more. The ordinary Recioto, perhaps more complex, contains a small amount of residual sugar, so that the wine is slightly sweet on the palate but finishes, miraculously, completely dry. The sheer concentration of fruit in a great Recioto is unsurpassed by any other wine. These wines are good substitutes for Port at the end of a meal: they are every bit as complex and are less likely to induce a hangover. Commercial Recioto can be merely hefty and coarse. Fortunately, a few enterprising British merchants have laid their hands on bottles from the very best producers.

Indeed, the growing band of lovers of sweet wines is increasingly well served by the British wine trade. Buy and enjoy them now, before the word spreads and these delectable and often very rare wines vanish from the shelves.

Stephen Brook is the author of Liquid Gold, Dessert Wines of the World *(Constable, £14.95).*

On page 579, we list wine merchants who have a good selection of sweet wines.

It's all down to service

The growth of wine sales at supermarkets and wine warehouses and the dominance by sheer numbers of high street off-licences have both suggested that the end of the traditional wine merchant may be nigh. Not a bit of it, as readers of this Guide will know and as CHARLES METCALFE *endorses. Here he explains why.*

John Drinkwell & Sons, wine merchants to the gentry, established in 1872, are having a pretty tough time at the moment. Asco have opened a huge new supermarket on the outskirts of town, with a delicatessen counter the envy of the county and a wine section stocking every wine in their Vintage Choice range; Peter Barnett have just unveiled a pilot wine shop, Spirit of the Vine, on one of the best sites in the High Street, resplendent with Art Nouveau decor and smoked glass shelving; and Oddlots have bought Drinkwell's ailing competitors, Alfred Boosey, and crammed the large premises with attractively displayed wines from every country under the sun, especially Australia and Chile. How is a conservative, family-owned country wine merchant to respond to these challenges? Can John Drinkwell survive?

In the real world, the answers are 'in various ways' and 'yes'. The Drinkwells of this world may be muttering about impossible competition and tightening belts, but the reality is that the best amongst them *have* evolved ways of ensuring the continued support of their customers, and it's all good news for us, the consumers.

The notion of service

It comes down to service. A customer does not go into a hotel to be sneered at, or a restaurant to be insulted, or a wine merchant to be embarrassed. We British may not find that courteous yet dignified service comes to us easily, but it is something we have to learn in an economy increasingly dominated by service industries. And this is nowhere more true than in the business of selling wine. No longer do you have to step into a wine shop to be condescended to by an assistant whose only qualifications for the job are absence of chin and impeccable suiting.

The very look of John Drinkwell & Sons can put the casual shopper off. It may be only two steps up into the shop, but they represent quite a climb for a shopper worried about getting value for money. So, the greeting inside is friendly, not overbearing, and at least some of the prices compare well with those at local branches of off-licence chains.

Price is far from being the only factor in the equation, however, and it is usually the one that worries the new breed of wine merchants least of all. They take the view that if they cannot woo and keep customers by other aspects of their service, they might as well sell up to Oddlots, Peter Barnett, or whoever. And because they are small in comparison with the large, brewery-owned chains, the Drinkwells and their like can effect changes much faster in the wines they stock, the look of their shops and the behaviour of their staff.

Old-fashioned virtues

While on the subject of the large brewery-owned off-licence chains (Victoria Wine Company, Peter Dominic/Bottoms Up and Thresher, in order of size), it's a good moment to focus on a select group of wine merchants owned by smaller, family-controlled brewery companies. Adnams, Eldridge Pope, and Thos Peatling (formerly Peatling & Cawdron) have three of the best-looking wine lists in the country, and make much of the old-fashioned virtues of finding and buying the best, then keeping the wines until they are ready to drink before selling them. Simon Loftus of Adnams, in particular, has steered outspokenly clear of the Bordeaux 'en primeur' market, seeing its 'in it for a quick return' aspect as the antithesis of a traditional wine merchant's role. Lay & Wheeler and Tanners fit into this élite group as well, although neither is brewery-owned – but both are wine merchants who make a very useful part of their annual turnover from local distribution agencies for beers, soft drinks and spirits.

From all these, you can expect to find lists of well-cellared clarets,

Ports and other long-lived wines to rank against any others in the country, as well as fine wines ferreted out from single estates all round the world. Each company will have its own particular speciality, and in the Burgundy, Italian and German sections, single property wines bottled on the estate are likely to be more characterful than the blander offerings often available.

The wine lists of some of these companies can be attractions in themselves. Lay & Wheeler and Eldridge Pope both produce well-researched and illustrated lists, but Adnams' is the most enjoyable. It is written by Simon Loftus, whose passionate enthusiasm for wine and finely crafted prose make each year's list as much of a pleasure to read as to scan for the year's wine discoveries.

Regional evangelism

Simon Loftus's passion about wine in general is a pointer to another breed of wine merchant, the evangelist for a particular region. Many of these are based outside London, and some have been in business long enough to claim responsibility for discovering estates now revered as the top in their field. Robin Yapp, of Yapp Brothers in Wiltshire, is a good example, ex-dentist and shipper of the great and good from the Rhône and the Loire. For a long time his dentistry co-existed with the wine business, but eventually the wine won. Barry Kettle, of Arriba Kettle, Spanish wine specialists, still occasionally practises as an architect (ARIBA, geddit?). John Hawes, founder of another prestigious Spanish wine importer, Laymont & Shaw in Cornwall, works in the local china clay industry.

Spain, in fact, has a remarkably wide collection of merchant enthusiasts all over Britain (a spin-off from the Great British Summer Holiday, perhaps). Moreno Wines in London, Martinez Fine Wine in Harrogate, Ilkley and Leeds, Mi Casa in Buxton and Sherborne Vintners in Dorset all make Spanish wines a speciality on their lists. Other countries and regions seem to have attracted fewer fervent preachers, or, at least, fewer from whom the wine lover can buy direct. Italy has Millevini in Stockport, whose list of fine Italian wines grows more impressive each year; the smaller estates of Beaujolais are well served by Roger Harris, a Norfolk farmer when he isn't importing wines; the wines of Bulgaria and Hungary are assiduously, and cheaply, promoted by Wines of Westhorpe; Sookias and Bertaut is the result of holidays in the South-West of France by two couples who now import an excellent selection of wines from 14 different regions in that corner of France; the Great American Wine Company and Douglas Henn-Macrae specialise in American wines, the GAWC from all over the States, Henn-Macrae from the less well-known wine states, Oregon, Washington and Texas; as well as the American wines, Douglas Henn-Macrae (who also teaches German and sings in the choir of Rochester Cathedral) is one of the few merchants who specialise in lesser-known German areas, particularly for red wines; and, finally, Domaine Direct sell nothing but red and white Burgundies from some of the finest estates in that notoriously unpredictable region.

That may seem a long list, but it represents very many of the merchants in the country who have chosen to specialise in one particular field, and whose wines are available to the ordinary consumer. Other merchants renowned for their range of wines from a particular area sell their speciality in the context of a larger list. Even Robin Yapp has expanded from his original Rhônes and Loires to include wines from Provence, Alsace and Champagne as well.

Some wine merchants have personal or business reasons for areas of specialisation. The Sookias and Bertaut families have houses in south-west France. The wife of the sales director of J C Karn in Cheltenham, stockists of more New Zealand wines than anyone else in Britain, comes from New Zealand. Majestic Wine Warehouses list far more California wines since they bought the California-based Liquor Barn chain. Others have anticipated new trends and fashions in winemaking and consumption, or sometimes scrambled aboard an already moving bandwagon. 'New World' and organic wines are just two such categories that have made the reputations of several wine merchants.

Adding up the specialists

In fact, you can tell how well a region's, or country's, wines are selling in the UK by totting up the number of active specialists. Germany is in the doldrums at the moment: there is no one established merchant who makes a living exclusively out of German wines. Certain merchants (such as Peter Green of Edinburgh, O W Loeb of London and Henry Townsend of Beaconsfield) have excellent selections of classic German wines, but none would claim to make much money out of them.

The wines of Australia, California and New Zealand, however, have made (and are still making) names and money for fairly young companies such as Alex Findlater, Ostlers and Windrush Wines, while the recent vogue for organic wines has benefited, for instance, Vintage Roots and West Heath Wine.

Another phenomenon of the last decade, buying wine (especially claret) 'en primeur', long before it is actually shipped, has contributed significantly to the cash flows of many wine merchants. The money comes into their accounts well before they have to settle up with the merchants in Bordeaux, and the more they sell 'en primeur', the less stock they need to finance to fulfil their future requirements. 'Not the role of the traditional wine merchant,' some may say, but buying 'en primeur', provided you have the cellar space and trust your merchant's judgement, is a way of planning a cellar that few wine lovers ever regret.

The notion of trust

But you have to trust your merchant, and that's just as true if all you're buying is a bottle of own-label claret. It is a relationship rarely possible in an off-licence, and has led to the emergence of a new breed of wine merchant. These are often country-based, often refugees from large and impersonal organisations, sometimes experts in a certain country's wines, and always prepared to work ridiculous hours to ensure the survival of their business by satisfying their customers. Men and women like Francis Murray of the Barnes Wine Shop, Tony Chaplin of Chaplin & Son, Michael Slinger of Chesterford Vintners, Alex Findlater of Alex Findlater, Richard Harvey of Richard Harvey Wines, Ronnie Hicks and Robin Don of Hicks & Don, Nick Davies of Hungerford Wine Company, Christopher Piper of Christopher Piper Wines, Zubair Mohamed of Raeburn Fine Wines and Foods, Derek Smedley of Smedley Vintners, Barry and Debbie Ralph of the Upper Crust, Helen Verdcourt of Helen Verdcourt Wines and Mark Savage of Windrush Wines will assure the survival of John Drinkwell & Sons throughout the country. By selecting good wines, dispensing sound and unpompous advice, selling the wines at reasonable prices, delivering them at unreasonable hours, and never falling prey to the English embarrassment at giving good service, these sorts of John Drinkwells should build the kind of loyal following happy to buy wine from the family firm for generations to come.

Charles Metcalfe is wine correspondent of Today *and associate editor of* Wine *magazine.*

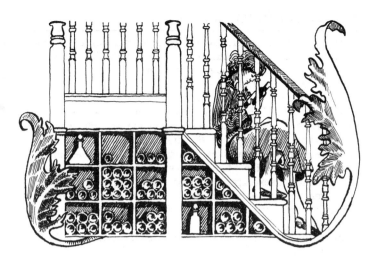

But I don't have a cellar . . .

Your house may not have a cellar, and you may not want to buy the top clarets and Ports, but a few bottles of wine put on one side in a dark place will ensure great drinking pleasure in months and years to come. NICHOLAS DAVIES *gives some practical advice on organising a cellar, and suggests some affordable wines to lay down.*

Just because you don't have a cellar, don't think this doesn't apply to you. Everyone would be advised to lay down wine, whether they have a cellar or not, for two main reasons: to ensure future stocks of mature wine, and also as a financial investment.

In the past the only people who laid down wine were importers, wine merchants, clubs/hotels/large restaurants, and wealthy owners of large houses. The last two categories still maintain the practice, but wine merchants and importers now work on such low margins in a very competitive market that many cannot afford the cost of financing stocks for such a long time.

So, if you wish to ensure you will have stocks of a wine when it is mature, it's a good idea to mature it yourself. As you will have been in charge of the wine's storage, you will know that it has not been changing hands frequently and so have a better guarantee that the wine will be in good condition when you come to drink it.

An added bonus is that certain types of wine (principally fine claret and vintage Port) have increased in value in the past, often substantially. Many people have made significant financial gains by buying such wines en primeur and then selling them five to ten years later. A word of caution, though – like any investment, the value of wine can decrease as well as increase.

So you don't have a cellar? Don't worry, you can still benefit from laying down wine. For relatively short-term storage (say up to three or four years) and for small quantities of each wine, an improvised cellar at home is more than adequate. For longer-term storage, and case quantities or more, the facilities offered by a reputable wine merchant may be a better solution. Many store tens of thousands of cases for their customers in excellent conditions in cellars 80 ft underground with a near-constant temperature of 50/51°F. Obviously, it is almost impossible for individuals to do similarly unless they have a very deep and well-insulated cellar.

For shorter-term storage at home the following conditions are desirable:

- A fairly constant temperature (50–60°F throughout the year) without any sudden fluctuations. Rooms with radiators or windows should be avoided
- Darkness
- Lack of vibration – the further away from roads, railways or often-used corridors, the better.

Various rooms in the average house can be used, but the cupboard under the stairs is often the best. However, a small, seldom-used box room could be insulated (polystyrene tiles will do) and the windows shuttered. Don't keep the wine in the kitchen – the temperature fluctuation is far too great – unless for consumption very soon.

A number of types of racking are available, the best being the traditional metal and wood type which looks like a grid from the front. These can be made to measure (most wine merchants will be happy to supply whatever you need) and are very sturdy. The plastic, expandable systems are good, if fairly expensive, but the self-construction bins available in many hardware shops tend to be flimsy and are unlikely to last. One DIY system that can work well is clay land drainage pipes stacked on top of each other.

For the more ambitious, various temperature-controlled cabinets are highly efficient but not cheap, or the Spiral Cellar, a sort of nuclear fall-out-shelter-cum-dovecote, which is sunk into the ground with pigeonholes for bottles all the way down its spiral staircase (details from the company of the same name – 037 284 2692).

Whichever system you adopt, it's important to keep the bottles labels up, so that the wine can be more easily identified, the labels themselves don't get scuffed, and, if the wine is old, or will be kept for a long time, the sediment will always gather in one place: on the inside opposite the label.

Organisation

A matrix system is one of the best ways of setting up a cellar. The horizontal rows are coded A to Z (then AA to ZZ etc), and the vertical rows by number. A typical layout might look like this:

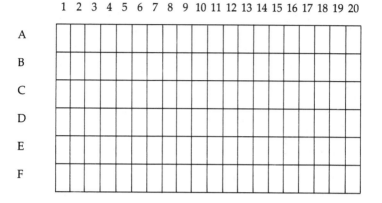

It you have sutticient space, organisation is made simpler by having several racks, or allocating different parts of racks to a specific type of wine: one for Bordeaux, one for Rhône, a quarter of a rack for Champagne, half a rack for Port, and so on.

Ideal for keeping clear records of the contents of your cellar is a loose-leaf file. Each new wine can be recorded on the same page as others of its type (clarets, Champagnes, sweet whites, light reds, or however else you find it useful).

Wherever you put the new bottle, whether within the allocated section or just in the next hole that is available, you will be able to see at a glance from your loose-leaf system where it is. The advantage is that you don't have to reorganise your bins and unsettle the wines every time you buy a new bottle.

Under your main headings of claret, sweet white and so on, each bottle will have a line to itself across the page, with headings covering the following information: the exact location (D5, J9); the date you bought the wine and from whom; its vintage, name and colour; its cost (of particular interest in years to come); then you could note down an idea of when you should be drinking the wine, such as 'from 1990 to 1998?' or 'now' or 'must drink by end of 1989'. Finally, columns can be devoted to the date you actually drink the wine, and tasting notes as succinct or verbose as you feel inclined.

Wines for keeping

So what sorts of wines are for keeping? Most people think of claret, Burgundy and Vintage Port but there are many others which will improve with age, some of them white.

Alsace Top-quality Alsace (Gewürztraminer, Riesling, Muscat and Tokay) from the best producers takes on a unique richness and depth of flavour with age. The best (with descriptions like Grand Cru, Réserve Personnelle, Vendange Tardive, Cuvée Spéciale, Sélection de Grains Nobles) will last for 20 years and more. Producers to look out for include Hugel, Trimbach, Beyer, Preiss-Zimmer, Kreydenweiss, Gisselbrecht and others, and good recent vintages include 1986, 1985 and 1983.

Champagne Even the cheapest non-vintage Champagne will improve dramatically after six months to a year in a cellar (make a note on the case or bottle when you bought it if you're not keeping a cellar book). But top vintage Champagnes have surprisingly long keeping abilities. My favourites include Krug (Grande Cuvée and vintage), Dom Pérignon, Henriot, Perrier-Jouët, Roederer, Bollinger and Heidsieck Monopole. The top wines from these houses will improve over 15 to 20 years, developing a lovely biscuity and nutty flavour as well as losing some acidity. Most vintages are worth laying down, although unless you like a really mature style it's not worth laying down anything older than 1978.

The Loire Most people don't even consider the Loire when thinking about laying down wine, but the sweet, semi-sweet and dry wines from Vouvray, Savennières and Coteaux du Layon will improve dramatically over 10–20 years. Top red Chinon and Bourgueil will soften attractively over ten years, and even a top Sancerre or Pouilly-Fumé from a good vintage can improve for up to 15 years – I recently enjoyed a delicious bottle of Pouilly-Fumé de Ladoucette 1970! The best recent vintage to lay down is 1986.

Beaujolais Crus (from top vintages) Very good single vineyard Beaujolais can improve for up to ten years (sometimes more), and 1985s and some 1986s like Fleurie, Juliénas, Morgon and Moulin-à-Vent will certainly get better until 1995. Even the ubiquitous Beaujolais Nouveau will improve for a year or two if it is from a reputable producer – it's worth paying more for a good one.

Rhône reds These are tremendous value and are well worth laying down. Even lesser wines like Côtes du Rhône Villages from a top producer like Paul Jaboulet Aîné can benefit from up to ten years' cellaring. And the top wines like Hermitage la Chapelle, Côte Rôtie Les Jumelles (both from Jaboulet), Hermitage from Chave or Sorrel, or

Guigal's Côte Rôtie can last for many decades and still be magnificent. Crozes-Hermitage can be great value. There are also some very good Châteauneuf-du-Pape wines which will improve, including those from Mont Redon, Beaucastel, Chante-Cigale, Vieux Télégraphe and Château Rayas. Recent Rhône vintages worth laying down are 1985, 1983, 1982 and 1978.

South-West France and the Midi Many Corbières and Madiran producers are now making their wines in a lighter style, but if you can find a heavy, tannic example of either, or a very good Côtes-du-Roussillon Villages, it should improve for six or eight years.

Burgundy This is not an area for the thrifty. At the lower end of the scale, good 1985 Bourgogne Rouge or Blanc can be worth laying down for a few years – wines from Leroy, Constant and Jadot amongst others have been impressive recently. And there are some very decent wines from the Côte Chalonnaise which won't break the bank – producers to watch out for include Juillot, Cogny, Constant, Villaine, Bernard Michel and Thénard. But to lay down top Burgundy (and it's worth it) you have to dig deep in your pocket. It depends very much on the producer, so a very much abbreviated selection might read (*for red and whites*): Jadot, Dubreuil-Fontaine, Hospices de Beaune, de Vogüé, Constant, Rodet; (*for reds*): Domaine de la Romanée-Conti, Trapet, Pousse d'Or, Burguet, Drouhin-Larose, Rousseau, Dujac, Jayer, Roty, Tollot-Beaut, Lafarge, Roumieu; (*for whites*): Niellon, Sauzet, Leflaive, Javillier, Morey, Lafon, Gagnard-Delagrange, Latour, Jaffelin, Delarche. Vintages to go for are 1986, 1985, 1983 (with very careful selection), some 1982s, some 1980s and 1978s if obtainable.

Bordeaux This is the classic wine to lay down. Many of the top reds are now out of reach of the average pocket, so I would recommend various Crus Bourgeois and less expensive classed growths (lay them down for 10–20 years) like Châteaux Chasse-Spleen, Monbrison, Haut-Bages-Libéral, Fombrauge, Cissac, Labégorce-Zédé, Léoville-Barton, Potensac, Larmande, Marquis de Terme and d'Angludet. If money is no object Mouton-Rothschild, Margaux, Cheval-Blanc, Ducru-Beaucaillou, Ausone, Pichon-Lalande, Cos d'Estournel and Domaine de Chevalier would be supreme choices. Top recent vintages for laying down are 1986, 1985, 1983, 1982 and 1978. Dry white Graves are also worth laying down (although they are very expensive) and can improve for 20 years or more. The best include Domaine de Chevalier, Haut Brion Blanc, de Fieuzal, Malartic-Lagravière, Smith-Haut-Lafitte and Rahoul. Buy only recent vintages – 1987, 1986 and 1985 are all good.

For those with a sweet tooth it would be well worth laying down some Sauternes, Barsac, Monbazillac or Ste-Croix du Mont. The last two should be kept for only ten years, but top Sauternes or Barsac can last for decades. The best value châteaux include Doisy-Daëne, Rieussec,

Lafaurie-Peyraguey, Rabaud-Promis and Nairac. Go for the 1985 or 1983 vintages.

Spain Rioja and Ribera Duero reds (forget the whites, apart from occasional odd-style Riojas) will improve dramatically with keeping up to 20 years and more. Favourites include Viña Real, Imperial, Viña Ardanza, Berberana, Muga, Marqués de Murrieta, Vega Sicilia and Bodegas Ribera Duero.

Portugal Some of the top Dãos and Bairradas can age remarkably well (up to 25 years), and one favourite, Perequita from J M da Fonseca, can profitably be kept for up to 15 years in a good vintage. Colares and Garrafeira wines would also be worth keeping.

New World I have yet to see evidence that Australian and California reds improve significantly with age and my advice would be – just buy them for current drinking. Some of the sweet wines, however, are worth keeping. (*Note from Editor: this is a very personal opinion – others would disagree.*)

Germany I confess to not being a German wine fan, although I have drunk some delicious old bottles. Every cellar should have at least a few bottles. Go for better single estate wines of Spätlese quality and up. The top Auslesen and Beerenauslesen can last for decades and are not necessary expensive for their quality. The best recent vintages are 1980 and 1985, although if you see a 1976 for less than £15 a bottle, snap it up!

Vintage Port The classic in anyone's cellar. In the past, wealthy parents and godparents used to lay down pipes of Port for their young. A pipe is roughly 58 cases and so in today's terms represents a considerable investment – over £8,000 for a pipe of one of the better 1985 Ports. But there's no need to go to extremes – a bottle, or a case or two will suffice! It's worth buying the best, and shippers whose wines I find consistent include Dow, Warre, Taylor, Fonseca, Graham, Quinta do Noval and Churchill. Recent vintages worth buying are 1985, 1983, and 1977. But remember, they need a long time in the cellar – 20 years after the vintage is when they are best for drinking.

Nicholas Davies is managing director of the Hungerford Wine Company and the Galloping Crayfish wine bar, both of which appear in this Guide.

Part I

Where to buy

What to buy

1989 Which? Wine Guide awards

Awards are made on the basis of the quality of the wines sold, the range of the list, the prices of the wines and the service offered. This year, we have four four-symbol and sixteen three-symbol award winners – all achieving, in our view, the high standards we have set.

Key to symbols

🐷 **Low mark-up on wine** Awarded to merchants who are more modest than most in their pricing of lower and middle price ranges in particular (*not* to those who offer poor wines at cheap prices).

❀ **Wine quality** Awarded to merchants whose wines are of a consistently good quality across their range.

▱ **Wine range** Awarded to merchants with an unusually wide choice of good wines, whether from one country or the whole world.

☞ **Service** Awarded to merchants who give exceptional service.

	Low mark-up	Wine quality	Wine range	Service
Addison Avenue Wine Shop		❀		
Adnams Wine Merchants		❀	▱	☞
James Aitken & Son			▱	
Alastair's Grapevine	🐷			
H Allen Smith		❀		
Asda	🐷			
Averys of Bristol				☞
David Baillie Vintners			▱	☞
Nigel Baring		❀		
Barnes Wine Shop		❀	▱	
Berry Bros & Rudd				☞
Bibendum	🐷	❀	▱	☞
Bin 89 Wine Warehouse	🐷			

	Pig	Flower	Glass	Hand
Bordeaux Direct			✦	
Bordeaux Direct Taste Shops			✦	
Buckingham Wines		✿		
The Butlers Wine Cellar			✦	
Anthony Byrne Fine Wines		✿		☞
D Byrne & Co			✦	
The Champagne House		✿		
Chesterford Vintners				☞
Christopher & Co			✦	
Claridge Fine Wines				☞
College Cellar		✿		
Corney & Barrow		✿		☞
Restaurant Croque-en-Bouche			✦	
Curzon Wine Company		✿		☞
Davisons Wine Merchants				☞
Domaine Direct		✿	✦	
Peter Dominic	🐷		✦	
Eldridge Pope		✿	✦	
Farr Vintners		✿		
Farthinghoe Fine Wine & Food				☞
Alex Findlater		✿	✦	☞
Fine Vintage Wines		✿		
Friarwood		✿		
Goedhuis & Co		✿		
Andrew Gordon Wines			✦	
Grape Ideas Wine Warehouse	🐷			
Great American Wine Company			✦	
Great Northern Wine Company			✦	
Peter Green	🐷	✿	✦	☞
Green's	🐷	✿		☞
Gerard Harris		✿	✦	☞
Roger Harris			✦	
Richard Harvey Wines			✦	
Haynes Hanson & Clark		✿		☞
Hicks & Don	🐷	✿	✦	
High Breck Vintners	🐷			☞

	🐷	❀	🍾	☞
George Hill of Loughborough	🐷			
J E Hogg	🐷		🍾	
Hungerford Wine Company		❀		☞
G Hush	🐷			
Ilkley Wine Cellars			🍾	
Ingletons Wines		❀		
S H Jones		❀	🍾	
Justerini & Brooks		❀		☞
Kurtz & Chan Wines		❀		
Lay & Wheeler		❀	🍾	☞
Laymont and Shaw		❀	🍾	
Laytons		❀		☞
O W Loeb		❀	🍾	☞
Lorne House Vintners	🐷			
Majestic Wine Warehouses	🐷		🍾	☞
The Market		❀	🍾	
Market Vintners			🍾	
Marks & Spencer		❀		
Martinez Fine Wine			🍾	☞
Master Cellar Wine Warehouse	🐷		🍾	
Andrew Mead Wines	🐷			
Millevini			🍾	
Moreno Wines			🍾	
Morris & Verdin		❀		
Morrisons	🐷			
Le Nez Rouge	🐷	❀	🍾	
Nickolls & Perks		❀		
The Nobody Inn			🍾	
Oddbins	🐷	❀	🍾	☞
Orpheus & Bacchus		❀		
Ostlers		❀	🍾	
Pavilion Wine Company		❀		
Thos Peatling			🍾	☞
Christopher Piper Wines		❀	🍾	☞
Premier Wine Warehouse	🐷			
Arthur Rackhams	🐷		🍾	

	🐷	❀	◁	☞
Raeburn Fine Wines and Foods	🐷	❀	◁	☞
Reid Wines		❀		
La Reserva Wines			◁	
La Réserve		❀		☞
William Rush	🐷			
J Sainsbury	🐷		◁	
Paul Sanderson Wines	🐷		◁	
Seckford Wines			◁	
Selfridges		❀	◁	
Edward Sheldon		❀		
Sherborne Vintners			◁	
Sookias and Bertaut			◁	☞
Stapylton Fletcher	🐷			
Tanners Wines		❀	◁	☞
Tesco	🐷			
Philip Tite Fine Wines		❀		
Henry Townsend		❀	◁	
T & W Wines		❀	◁	
Ubiquitous Chip			◁	
The Upper Crust			◁	☞
Valvona & Crolla		❀		
Helen Verdcourt Wines			◁	☞
La Vigneronne		❀	◁	☞
Waitrose	🐷		◁	
Wessex Wines	🐷			
Willoughbys				☞
Windrush Wines		❀	◁	☞
Winecellars	🐷	❀	◁	
Wine Growers Association			◁	
The Wine Society		❀	◁	☞
The Wine Spot	🐷			
Wines from Paris	🐷			
Wizard Wine Warehouses	🐷			
Peter Wylie Fine Wines		❀		
Yapp Brothers		❀	◁	☞
Yorkshire Fine Wine Company		❀		☞

Who's where

This is a gazetteer of individual wine stockists listed in the Guide. See also the directory of chains and supermarkets on page 52.

London

E2
Balls Brothers 68
Four Vintners 127

EC1
Cantina Augusto 90
Corney & Barrow 102
Market Vintners 174
Old Street Wine
  Company 194
Ostlers 196

EC2
Corney & Barrow 102
City Wine Shop 127
Pavilion Wine
  Company 198

EC3
Champagne and
  Caviar Shop 91
Green's 139
Russell & McIver 212

EC4
Corney & Barrow 102

N1
Bretzel Foods 255
The Market 174

N6
Bottle and Basket 81
The Market 174

N7
Le Nez
  Rouge/Berkmann
  Wine Cellars 189

N8
Haywood Wines 121

NW1
Bibendum 74
Laytons 169
Prestige Vintners 203

NW3
H Allen Smith 60
Richard Kihl 165
The Market 174
Le Provençal 174
Madeleine Trehearne
  Partners 236

NW4
Amazing Grapes 62

NW6
Grape Ideas 135

NW8
Alex Findlater 124

NW10
Wine Growers
  Association 257

SE1
Clink Street Wine
  Vaults 100
Davys of London 108
O W Loeb 171
Mayor Sworder 179
Quintet Wines 204

SE10
Wines Galore

SW1
Berry Bros & Rudd 73
Ellis Son & Vidler 120
Farr Vintners 122
Harrods 143
John Harvey & Sons 144
Justerini & Brooks 163
Kurtz & Chan 166

Morris & Verdin 188
André Simon 222
Stones of Belgravia 227

SW3
H Allen Smith 60
Bibendum 74
Buckingham Wines 83
College Cellar 101
La Réserve 210
André Simon 222

SW5
Buckingham Wines 83

SW6
Friarwood 128
Harbottle Wines 151
Haynes, Hanson &
  Clark 146
The Market 174
Premier Wine
  Warehouse 202

SW7
Jeroboams 161
La Vigneronne 242

SW9
Ad Hoc 55

SW10
Viticulteur 205

SW11
Goedhuis & Co 132

SW12
The Market 174

SW13
Barnes Wine Shop 69

SW15
Drunken Mouse 116
Sookias and Bertaut
  224

SW18
Supergrape 228
Winecellars 255

W1
H Allen Smith 60
Les Amis du Vin Shop 97
Buckingham Wines 83
Christopher & Co 97
Curzon Wine Company 106
English Wine Shop 121
Esprit du Vin 231
Fortnum & Mason 126
Selfridges 219
André Simon 222
Wine Society 261

W2
Nigel Baring 68
Champagne House 92
Continental Wine House 102
The Market 174
Moreno Wines 186
La Réserve 210

W4
Chiswick Wine Cellar 95
Philip Tite Fine Wines 232

W8
Buckingham Wines 83
Haynes, Hanson & Clark 146
The Vintner 205

W9
Moreno Wines 186
The Winery 97

W11
Addison Avenue Wine Shop 53
Buckingham Wines 83
Corney & Barrow 102

W14
Queens Club Wines 204

WC1
H Allen Smith 60
Domaine Direct 114

Great American Wine Company 136

WC2
Findlater Mackie Todd 125
Kiwifruits 165
Studio 50 198

England

Avon

Bath
Sainsbury Bros 214

Batheaston
Luxembourg Wine Company 172

Bristol
Averys 66
John Harvey & Sons 144

Hallatrow
Reid Wines 208

Bedfordshire

Houghton Conquest
Bedford Fine Wines 72

Lilley
Smedley Vintners 223

Luton
Wines of Westhorpe 265

Berkshire

Eton
M & W Gilbey 130

Hungerford
Hungerford Wine Company 157

Maidenhead
David Alexander 59
Helen Verdcourt Wines 241

Mortimer
Nalders Wine Agency 151

Reading
Bordeaux Direct 79
Vintage Roots 244

Sunninghill
Marske Mill House 177

Whitchurch
Col G P Pease 151

Buckinghamshire

Amersham
Demijohn Wines 110

Aston Clinton
Gerard Harris 141

Beaconsfield
Magnum Opus Wine Company 176
Marlow Wine Shop 176
Henry Townsend 235

Gerrards Cross
William Rush 212

Marlow
Marlow Wine Shop 176

Cambridgeshire

Cambridge
Barwell & Jones 71
Oxford & Cambridge Fine Wine 198

Cottenham
Pond Farm Wines 202

Ramsey
Anthony Byrne Fine Wines 85

Cheshire

Alderley Edge
Eaton Elliot Winebrokers 117

Chester
Classic Wine Warehouses 99
George Dutton 253

Hale
Cadwgan Fine Wine Merchants 87

Nantwich
Rodney Densem Wines 111

Stockport
Millevini 183

Wilmslow
Willoughbys 253

Cornwall
St Austell
Del Monico's Famous
Wine Emporium 109

Truro
G M Vintners 131
Laymont & Shaw 168
Market Wine Stores 131

Cumbria
Alston
Alston Wines 61

Burgh-by-Sands
B H Wines 74

Carlisle
Rattlers Wine
Warehouse 207

Grange-over-Sands
A L Vose 245

Kendal
Frank E Stainton 225

Penrith
Cumbrian Cellar 105

Derbyshire
Buxton
Mi Casa Wines 182

Devon
Doddiscombsleigh
Nobody Inn 191

Exeter
David Baillie Vintners
67
White Hart Vaults 264

Marsh Barton
G M Vintners 131

Ottery St Mary
Christopher Piper
Wines 200

Plymtree
Peter Wylie Fine
Wines 267

Dorset
Bridport
Wessex Wines 249

Christchurch
Christchurch Fine
Wine Co 96

Dorchester
Weatherbury Vintners
247

Leigh
Sherborne Vintners
221

Shillingstone
C C G Edwards 118

Wimborne Minster
Richard Harvey Wines
145

Essex
Chelmsford
Welbeck Wine 248

Chigwell
Classic Wines 99

Coggeshall
Peter Watts Wines 247

Colchester
Lay & Wheeler 167
Snipe Wine Cellars 224

Great Chesterford
Chesterford Vintners
94

Maldon
Ingletons Wines 160

Gloucestershire
Cheltenham
J C Karn 164
Rose Tree Wine Co 211

Cirencester
Windrush Wines 254

Tetbury
Thomas Panton 197

Greater Manchester
Chadderton
Willoughbys 253

Didsbury
Merrill's 182

Stockport
Wine Spot 2 262

Urmston
Wine Spot 262

Hampshire
Basingstoke
Wine Shop 73

Hartley Wintney
Horseshoe Wines 67

Headley
High Breck Vintners
151

Winchester
Godrich & Petman 132
Lockes 170
Winchester Wine
Company 254

Hereford & Worcester
Cleobury Mortimer
Hopton Wines 155

Hereford
Tanners Wines 229

Honeybourne
Arriba Kettle 62

Kidderminster
Touchstone Wines 233
Wine Schoppen 259

Malvern Wells
Croque-en-Bouche 104

Hertfordshire
Bishop's Stortford
Hedley Wright 147

Odsey
Pennyloaf Wines 200

St Albans
Desborough & Brown
112

Stevenage
Wine Society 261

Ware
Sapsford Wines 216

Kent
Eccles
Douglas Henn-Macrae
149

Hawkenbury
Claridge Fine Wines
98

Maidstone
Stapylton Fletcher 226

Sevenoaks
Reid Wines 208

Lancashire
Clitheroe
D Byrne & Co 86
Whiteside's 251

Lancaster
Mitchells Wine Bin 184

Morecambe
Mitchells Wine Bin 184

Preston
E H Booth 78

Samlesbury Bottoms
Borg Castel 80

Tunstall
Redpath & Thackray
207

Leicestershire
Ashby-de-la-Zouch
A H Colombier 101
David's of Ashby 106

Leicester
G E Bromley 82

Loughborough
George Hill 153

Lincolnshire
Spalding
G E Bromley 82
J H Measures 181

Merseyside
Liverpool
Thomas Baty 253
Hilbre Wine Company
152
David Scatchard 217

Norfolk
Beeston St Lawrence
Beeston Hall Cellars
151

Elmham
Hicks & Don 149

Harleston
Barwell & Jones 71

King's Lynn
Snipe Wine Cellars 224

Norwich
Barwell & Jones 71

Thetford
T & W Wines 236

Weston Longville
Roger Harris 142

Northamptonshire
Earls Barton
Summerlee Wines 227

Farthinghoe
Farthinghoe Fine
Wine and Food 122

Titchmarsh
Ferrers le Mesurier 123

Northumberland
Hexham
Alston Wines 61

Rothbury
Alston Wines 61

Wooler
Graham MacHarg Fine
Wines 161

Nottinghamshire
Askham
Askham Wines 65

Keyworth
Plumtree Wines 201

Newark
Ian G Howe 156

Oxfordshire
Banbury
S H Jones 162

Blewbury
Sebastopol Wines 217

Oxford
Fine Vintage Wines
126
Grape Ideas 135

Oxford & Cambridge
Fine Wine 196

Thame
Hampden Wine
Company 140

Wallingford
Lamb Wine Company
166

Shropshire
Bridgnorth
Tanners Wines 229

Lilleshall
William Addison 54

Newport
William Addison 54

Shrewsbury
Tanners Wines 229

Somerset
Bishop's Lydeard
Châteaux Wines 94

Staffordshire
Stafford
William Addison 54

Suffolk
Felixstowe
The Grosvenor 71

Hadleigh
Hadleigh Wine Cellars
140

Halesworth
Alex Findlater 124

Ipswich
Barwell & Jones 71
Burlington Wines 84
Champagne de
Villages 91
Wines of Interest 265

Long Melford
Old Maltings Wine
Company 193

Martlesham Heath
Seckford Wines 218

Needham Market
Snipe Wine Cellars 224

Newmarket
Linford Wines 193
Old Maltings Wine
  Company 193

Southwold
Adnams 56

Woodbridge
Cross Inn 71

Surrey

Buckland
Ben Ellis and
  Associates 119

Cranleigh
A & A Wines 53
Lorne House Vintners
  172

Croydon
Master Cellar Wine
  Warehouse 179

Dorking
Andrew Gordon
  Wines 133

East Horsley
Upper Crust 239

Guildford
Orpheus & Bacchus
  195

Pirbright
West Heath Wine 250

Richmond
Richmond Wine
  Warehouse 210

Sutton
The Market 174

Wallington
Wine House 258

Sussex (East)

Alfriston
English Wine Centre
  121

Brighton
Butlers Wine Cellar 84

Lewes
Cliffe Cellars 120

Sussex (West)

Billingshurst
Charles Hennings 148

Haywards Heath
Rex Norris 192

Midhurst
Duras Direct 166

Petworth
Charles Hennings 148

Pulborough
Charles Hennings 148

Rudgwick
J Dudley 151

Worthing
A G Barnett 151
Chaplin & Son 93

Tyne & Wear

Newcastle upon Tyne
Dennhöfer Wines 110
Richard Granger 135

Warwickshire

Leamington Spa
Alastair's Grapevine
  58

Shipston-on-Stour
Edward Sheldon 220

West Midlands

Stourbridge
Greenwood & Co 190
Nickolls & Perks 190

Walsall
Whittalls Wines 252

Wiltshire

Devizes
Sherston Wine
  Company 221

Mere
Yapp Brothers 268

Salisbury
Hungerford Wine
  Company 157

Sherston
Sherston Wine
  Company 221

Westbury
Hicks & Don 149

Yorkshire (North)

Harrogate
Martinez Fine Wine
  178

Nun Monkton
Yorkshire Fine Wine
  Company 269

Oswaldkirk
Patrick Toone 77

York
Cachet Wines 87

Yorkshire (South)

Rotherham
Bin Ends 77

Sheffield
Bin 89 Wine
  Warehouse 76
Michael Menzel 181
Wine Schoppen 259

Stainforth
Wine Warehouse 259

Yorkshire (West)

Huddersfield
Grapehop 209
Pennine Wines 199

Ilkley
Ilkley Wine Cellars 159
Martinez Fine Wine
  178

Leeds
Cairns & Hickey 88
Great Northern Wine
  Company 137
Martinez Fine Wine
  178
Vinceremos Wines 244

Linthwaite
La Reserva Wines 209

Shelf
Classic Wines 259

Scotland

Ayr
Whighams 250

51

Dundee
James Aitken 57

Edinburgh
Peter Green 138
J E Hogg 154
G Hush 158
Irvine Robertson
    Wines 161
Justerini & Brooks 163
Raeburn Fine Wines
    and Foods 206
Paul Sanderson Wines
    216
Valvona & Crolla 240
Whighams, Young &
    Saunders 250
Wine Emporium 256
Wines from Paris 263

Elgin
Gordon & MacPhail
    134

Glasgow
Barrel Selection 70
Ubiquitous Chip Wine
    Shop 237
Wine Emporium 256

Moffat
Moffat Wine Shop 185

Perth
Matthew Gloag & Son
    130

Thurso
Wine Shop 260

Wales

Hawarden
Ashley Scott 64

Presteigne
Andrew Mead Wines
    180

Welshpool
Tanners Wines 229

Channel Islands

St Brelade, Jersey
Victor Hugo Wines
    156

St Helier, Jersey
Bath Street Wine
    Cellar 156
Victor Hugo Wines
    156

St Saviour, Jersey
Victor Hugo Wines
    156

Northern Ireland

Belfast
Direct Wine
    Shipments 113
Duncairn Wines 113

Coleraine
Wine and Ale House
    113

Republic of Ireland

Dublin
Mitchell & Son 184

CHAINS AND SUPERMARKETS

Space does not permit us to list the addresses of all the branches of each chain, but details at the head of the entry include the address and telephone number of the company's head office, from whom you will be able to find out your nearest branch.

Asda 63
Blayneys 78
Bordeaux Direct Taste
    Shops 80
Bottoms Up 115
Davisons 107
Peter Dominic 115
Eldridge Pope 118
Fullers 129
Majestic 173

Marks & Spencer 175
Morris's Wine Stores
    187
Morrisons 189
Oddbins 192
Thos Peatling 198
Arthur Rackhams
    205
Safeway 213
J Sainsbury 214

Tesco 230
Thresher 231
J Townend & Sons
    234
Unwins 238
Victoria Wine
    Company 241
Waitrose 246
Wizard Wine
    Warehouses 266

A & A Wines

Smithbrook Kilns, nr Cranleigh,   TEL (0483) 274666
Surrey GU6 8JJ

OPEN Mon–Fri 9.30–5.30   Sat 10–12   CLOSED Sun, public holidays
CREDIT CARDS None accepted; personal and business accounts
DISCOUNTS Quantity discounts negotiable   DELIVERY Free within 12-mile
radius and for 5+ cases in London, Home Counties, Surrey, Sussex, Hampshire;
otherwise £1–£1.50 per case   GLASS HIRE Free with 1-case order
TASTINGS AND TALKS Monthly tastings in cellars; to groups on request
CELLARAGE Not available   ■

Spain and Italy are the main reasons for this firm's first appearance in
the Guide. Riojas from Campo Viejo, Bodegas Riojanas and Bodegas
Franco Españolas sit alongside smaller bodegas such as Marqués del
Puerto and Felix Azpilicueta (who make Siglo Saco, the rather good
wine in the atrocious sack-covered bottle), while in Penedès, there are
wines from the ubiquitous and talented Torres family, the Palacio de
León collection and excellent value Jumilla wines (Campo Seco Tinto
Reserve 1980, £2.99). Sherries come from Bobadilla.

Turning to Italy, we find Chiantis from Pagni and La Pagliaia
(including the Sherry-like Vin Santo at £7.25), Soave and Valpolicella
from Tedeschi and Boscaini and Barolo from Borgogno and La Brenta
d'Oro.

There is also some interest in French country wines (look for the red
Roussillon Domaine de Montariol 1986 at £2.75), a few old garrafeiras
from Portugal and wines from Wente in California – plus Australian
wines from McWilliams and Wyndham Estate.

Best buys

Graves, Château Coucheroy 1983, £4.75; Barolo 1979, La Brenta d'Oro
1979, £4.85; Chianti Classico 1986, La Pagliaia, £3.50; Rioja Faustino
Martinez, Faustino V Reserva 1983, £4.35

Addison Avenue Wine Shop

8 Addison Avenue, London W11 8QS   TEL 01-603 6340

OPEN Mon, Tue, Wed, Fri 10–7.30   Thur 10–9   Sat 10–6   CLOSED Sun, public
holidays   CREDIT CARDS Access, Amex, Visa; personal and business
accounts   DISCOUNTS 5% on unmixed cases   DELIVERY Free in London W2,
W11 and W14 (min 1 case) and central London for orders over £100; otherwise at
cost; mail order available   GLASS HIRE Free with case order
TASTINGS AND TALKS 2–3 tastings monthly in-store; to groups on request
CELLARAGE £4 per case per year

This list continues to be strong primarily in Bordeaux and Burgundy,
although selections from other areas also offer some interest and
quality. There is a big range of bin ends and small quantities of fine
wines.

The Bordeaux section is sensibly divided into wines for drinking and wines for laying down. Under those for current drinking we find petit château wines from recent vintages (two well-priced examples are Ch Moulin de Landry, Côtes de Castillon 1982 at £3.95 and Ch Haut-Peyruguet 1985, Bordeaux at £3.60). More prestigious names take the list back to 1966. For wines to lay down, current vintages available in a wide range include 1985, 1983 and 1982, with smaller selections back to 1975.

The same division is applied to white Burgundy, with a mix of domaine wines and those from some top négociants such as Louis Latour and Joseph Drouhin. Look especially for the wines of Chartron et Trébuchet in the laying down section. Red Burgundies are much less impressive.

Elsewhere the list shortens considerably, but attractions include Châteauneuf-du-Pape from Ch de Beaucastel, and St-Joseph from Jaboulet and, outside France, Chianti from Badia a Coltibuono and Antinori, the Cabernet Sauvignon-based Marqués de Griñon 1983 from Spain (£7.75), a few Australian wines, and a good selection of Robert Mondavi wines from California.

Best buys

Fitou 1985, Jean Cassignol, £2.95; Champagne Eugène Clicquot, £9.35; Delegats New Zealand Sauvignon Blanc 1987, £6.21; Coltibuono Rosso 1983, Badia a Coltibuono, £3.75

William Addison (Newport)

HEAD OFFICE AND THE WAREHOUSE	TEL (0952) 670200
Village Farm, Lilleshall, Newport,	(24-hour answering
Shropshire TF10 9HB	service (0952) 670300)
67 High Street, Newport, Shropshire TF10 7AU	TEL (0952) 810627
35 Mill Street, Stafford, Staffordshire	TEL (0785) 52735
ST16 2AJ	

OPEN Mon–Sat 9–5 CLOSED Wed pm (Stafford), Mon (Newport), Sun, public holidays CREDIT CARDS Visa; personal and business accounts DISCOUNTS Available DELIVERY Free in Shropshire and Staffordshire (min 1 case); elsewhere at cost; mail order available GLASS HIRE Free with wine order TASTINGS AND TALKS Occasional in-store tastings; to groups on request CELLARAGE £3.45 per case per year

---

This is a fairly conservative range, which means that it is strongest on the old classics of Bordeaux and Burgundy.

In Bordeaux, there are good selections from most of the recent fine vintages – look especially for the good value 1981s and 1983s, as well as 1982s and 1985s. Among stocks of older vintages, William Addison also carry a few mature 1976s for drinking now.

In Burgundy, the reliance is mainly on négociant wines – from Antonin Rodet, Louis Latour and Chanson. A few mature whites from the 1980 vintage join some better value 1985 and 1986 Mâcon wines. In reds, the best value is from the Côte Chalonnaise, such as Rully 1985, Chandesais at £5.69 (prices in the list do not include VAT but we have added it here), and Bourgogne Rouge Vieilles Vignes 1985, Antonin Rodet (£5.74).

In the Rhône, good buys would be the wines of the Perrin family (Ch de Beaucastel in Châteauneuf-du-Pape, Côtes du Rhône Cru de Coudoulet, La Vieille Ferme). On the Loire, look for Muscadet from Ch de Cléray and the Quincy of Félicien Brou, and in Alsace wines from Louis Sipp. There are plenty of grande marque Champagnes, including some large sizes.

Outside France, Germany could be good, but the list vouchsafes no producers, so we don't know. Spain has Marqués de Cáceres Riojas, plus the excellent value Cerro Anon Gran Reserva 1975 at £6.61. The other highlight is Australia, which now boasts wines from Rouge Homme, Brown Brothers, Lindeman's and Mildara. Over the water are New Zealand wines from Nobilo. Look, too, for the range of vintage Ports.

Best buys

Beaujolais from Duboeuf; Minervois 1985, Ch Villerambert, £3.21; Settesoli Bianco and Rosso, Italian vino da tavola, £2.59

Ad Hoc Wine Warehouse

363 Clapham Road, London SW9 9BT   TEL 01-274 7433
OPEN Mon–Fri 9–7.30 Sat 10–7.30 Sun 11–6 CLOSED Public holidays
CREDIT CARDS Access, Visa; personal and business accounts DISCOUNTS Not available DELIVERY Free in Greater London and Home Counties (min 5 cases); elsewhere at cost GLASS HIRE Free with 1-case order
TASTINGS AND TALKS Tastings approximately every 2 months; to groups on request CELLARAGE Not available

We've had some good reports of this wine warehouse since its opening in 1987. Particular strengths are Portugal, Spain and Italy, and it is for these countries' wines – rather than the French sector – that Ad Hoc gets into the Guide.

Italy is especially good: Barolos from Fontanafredda, Franco Fiorina and Guiseppe Cortese; Bolla Valpolicella; Campo Fiorín, the super vino da tavola from Masi; Chiantis from Rocca delle Macie, Fizzano and Antinori; Brunello from Fattoria dei Barbi; Morellino di Scansano 1983 Riserva with its cherry fruit (£7.26), Tiefenbrunner Südtirol wines and Regaleali wines from Sicily – plus many more.

In Spain, we find serried ranks of Reserva and Gran Reserva Riojas – the oldest dating from 1971; Torres wines from the Penedès in profusion; Marqués de Griñon Cabernet Sauvignon; Raimat wines and Vega Sicilia. In Portugal, it is the great firm of J M da Fonseca which stars.

Other countries which get a good showing include Bulgaria and Australia (with Brown Brothers, Orlando and Rosemount). In France, things are less exciting: the strongest areas are Bordeaux, with some good petits châteaux and French country wines (especially in the South-West).

Best buys

Côtes du Marmandais Cave de Cocument, red and white, £2.45; Vino da Tavola Bianco, Antinori, £3.54; Periquita 1978, J M da Fonseca, £3.15; Bulgarian wines; Viña Albali, Valdepeñas 1981, £2.72

Adnams Wine Merchants ❀ ▭ ☞

The Crown, High Street, Southwold, Suffolk IP18 6DP	TEL (0502) 724222
The Cellar & Kitchen Store, Victoria Street, Southwold, Suffolk IP18 6JW	TEL (0502) 724222
The Wine Shop, South Green, Southwold, Suffolk IP18 6EW	TEL (0502) 722138

OPEN (The Crown) Mon–Fri 9–1, 2–5 (mail order); (Cellar & Kitchen Store) Mon–Sat 10–6.30; (Wine Shop) Mon–Sat 10–1, 2.15–7.30 CLOSED Sun, public holidays CREDIT CARDS Access, Visa; business accounts DISCOUNTS 5% on 1 case DELIVERY Free in UK mainland except Highlands and Islands (min 2 cases); 1 case £2.99; elsewhere at cost; mail order available GLASS HIRE Free with 1-case order TASTINGS AND TALKS 30+ bottles always available in Cellar & Kitchen Store; large annual tasting held locally; to groups on request CELLARAGE £3.16 per case per year

---

We are not quite sure which is the luckier – Adnams the wine merchants, for having one of the few family breweries left to back them up; or Adnams the brewers, for having such a top-flight wine merchant working in association with them. Unlike so many big brewery-owned wine merchants, the combination actually works in Southwold – and both beer drinkers and wine drinkers are the better for it.

We are quite sure that the wine side has expanded over the past year – but we've lost count of the bottles. A splendid cellar shop has opened at the back of the Crown restaurant and hotel, which are Adnams' main offices. Prices here are on a cash and carry basis, and are therefore cheaper than the mail order operation.

The list itself is mammoth. From its opening with fortified wines (Sherries from Hidalgo, Madeira from Cossart Gordon and Marsala from de Bartoli) to its close – winewise at least – with the Indian sparkler Omar Khayyam (much better than it sounds), Adnams' director Simon Loftus steers you through a wealth of fascinating wines with his firmly opinionated commentary, making this lavish production a wonderful bedtime read as well as a wine list.

From an almost impossibly deep range of wines, we can pick out only a few particular strengths: Burgundy, for a huge selection of domaine wines, each one bought with obvious care and research; the Rhône, for its array of wines from Jaboulet Aîné and Guigal; the Loire, for its outstanding selection of mature sweet Vouvrays from Huet and Foreau Clos Naudin.

Italy is likewise a treasure trove. We commented in past years on Adnams' enthusiasm for the Veneto – the Reciotos of Valpolicella in particular. But Piedmont is also especially well favoured (such as Barolos from Renato Ratti and Conterno, as well as the Barbera of Damonte). In an age when German wines are unfashionable, Adnams maintain a strong listing of estate bottles, including a few still from the great 1976 vintage.

Over in the New World, California is represented by Trefethen, Ridge, Saintsbury (look for their Pinot Noir 1984 at £8.63), and Heitz, among other great names. Australia has inevitably expanded (Penfolds, Brown Brothers, Andrew Mitchell in Clare Valley and Moss Wood in Western Australia), as has New Zealand, with Matua Valley and Cloudy Bay.

Other highlights include Tokay from Hungary, the Ribera del Duero Pesquera from Spain, and an interesting range of early landed Cognacs.

Best buys

Vin de Pays de l'Hérault, Marsanne Domaine du Bosc, £3.28; Ch Thieuley 1987, Bordeaux Clairet (rosé), £4.14; Cantone Vin de Corse Calvi Discala, £4.03; Côtes du Rhône 1987, Ch du Grand Moulas, £3.62; Vouvrays from Clos Naudin

---

James Aitken & Son

53 Perth Road, Dundee DD1 4HY   TEL (0382) 21197

OPEN Mon–Fri 8.30–5.45   Sat 8.30–5   CLOSED Sun, some public holidays
CREDIT CARDS None accepted; personal and business accounts
DISCOUNTS 5% on 1 unmixed case or 2 mixed cases (mail order)
DELIVERY Free in city of Dundee; otherwise 50p outside city boundary; mail order available   GLASS HIRE Free   TASTINGS AND TALKS To groups on request   CELLARAGE Free for wines purchased from premises

---

We continue to admire the reliability of the wine selection from this family grocer and wine merchant, and we approve of the way that they have kept pace with the expansion of the wine world's horizons.

France remains a mainstay of the list. There seem to be few corners of the country into which they do not go: among regional wines from the South, Corbières Ch de Jonquières 1986 red (£2.97) is a good value example, and in the South-West, look for the sweet Jurançon Moelleux of Clos Guirouilh (£4.85). There are the Alsace wines of Dopff au Moulin and Dopff et Irion and a big range of Rhônes from Jaboulet Aîné.

These join the solid list of clarets (with vintages back to 1971 and including some decent value petit château wines), red Burgundies – many from the négociant firm of Faiveley – and white Burgundies, including domaine-bottled wines from Sauzet and Chablis from Louis Michel.

Other countries display a similar width of choice. Germany has some estate wines from top producers like von Buhl, Bürklin-Wolf and the State Domaine in the Mosel; Italy goes in for Chiantis from Brolio and Fizzano, plus the single vineyard Orvietos from Bigi; Australia's pride is a collection from Brown Brothers; and Portugal's range is getting bigger and better (look for the two Douro reds from Quinta do Cotto). There's even a surprisingly big selection of Greek wines – the reds of probably more interest than the whites.

Best buys

Vin de Pays des Côtes de Gascogne, Domaine Tariquet, £3.15; Côtes de Bergerac 1985, Ch Grand Conseil, £3.79; Durkheimer Abstfrohnhof Riesling Spätlese 1983, Ritter, £4.85; Valdepeñas Armonioso, Bodegas los Llanos, £3.15; Bairrada 1980, Luis Pato, £5.35

Alastair's Grapevine

2 Upper Grove Street, Leamington Spa,   TEL (0926) 39032
Warwickshire CV32 5AN

OPEN Mon–Fri 9.30–6.30   Sat 9.30–5.30   CLOSED Sun, public holidays
CREDIT CARDS Access, Visa   DISCOUNTS 5% on 1 case   DELIVERY Free
within 30-mile radius (min 1 case) and for 6+ cases elsewhere; otherwise £5 per case; mail order available   GLASS HIRE Free with minimum £50 order
TASTINGS AND TALKS Two main tastings annually; occasional in-store promotional tastings; to groups on request   CELLARAGE Not available

---

Alastair MacBrayne likes to send us jolly pictures of what he gets up to – of the charity team which entered the Beaujolais run, for example, and a George Goulet Champagne dinner in Birmingham. Our inspectors tell us that this sense of fun extends to a very pleasing atmosphere in his shop.

There has been a gradual change towards importing more wines directly, which has helped keep prices quite competitive. The list starts off with some well-priced French regional wines – for example, the Coteaux du Quercy of Christian Laur at £3.49, a Cahors-style red, or Domaine d'Ormesson Vin de Pays d'Oc (unaccountably under white wines on the list when it is definitely a red) at £3.75.

In the better-known region, we find Louis Gisselbrecht Alsace wines, and some good single estate bottles from the Loire and Beaujolais (the Beaujolais Villages of André Colange 1987 is £4.83). There are small selections of Burgundies (look for the domaine wines of Chantal Lescure and René Manuel). On the Rhône, comparisons would be fascinating between four sweet Vins Doux Naturels, as well as some good quality reds. The Bordeaux section is short but to the point.

Other areas of interest include Germany (but a lack of producers makes this area difficult to follow), and Italy (Franciacorta red, white and sparkling are a feature here, as well as wines from the Isonzo area of Friuli). Spain offers Riojas from Faustino Rivero and a dry white from Galicia (reminiscent in style to Vinho Verde from neighbouring Portugal). New to the list are Australian wines from Wyndham Estates, while there are boutique wines from Yarra Yering, Mount Barker and Sutherland.

Sherries are from Barbadillo, Ports from Offley Forrester, Madeiras from Rutherford and Miles, Champagne from George Goulet.

Best buys

Franciacorta Rosso 1987, Contessa Camilla Maggi Martinoni, £3.75; Minervois 1986, Ch de Fabas, £2.99; Bairrada Tinto 1980, Frei João, £3.40; Rioja 1987, Faustino Rivero, £3.19; Rutherford and Miles Reserve Madeiras, £7.99

David Alexander

69 Queen Street, Maidenhead,   TEL (0628) 30295
Berkshire SL6 1LT

OPEN Mon–Thur 10–8.30   Fri, Sat 10–9   Sun 12–2   CLOSED Public holidays
CREDIT CARDS Access, Diners, Visa; personal and business accounts
DISCOUNTS 5% for 1 case   DELIVERY Free in Maidenhead and West London
(min £10 order); otherwise at cost   GLASS HIRE Free with order
TASTINGS AND TALKS In-store tastings most Saturdays; to groups on request
CELLARAGE Approximately £5 per year

Verdict: a wide-ranging list, with a little from everywhere. That said, the concentration now seems to be on the New World, with a marked increase in wines from Australia (including the Pirramimma wines from McLaren in South Australia) and from California (Mark West, Clos du Val, Monticello, Dry Creek and Buena Vista) all fresh to the list.

A sensibly priced range of clarets (Ch du Breuil 1981 at £7, Prieur du Meyney 1982 at £6.50) are not matched in quantity by the rest of France, although look for Rhône wines from Delas Frères and the Sancerre and Pouilly Fumé of Guy Saget. Champagne is promising, including large bottles of Laurent-Perrier.

Italy's list is surprisingly badly annotated but hides some treats – try the Chianti Classico La Quercia at £4.79 or the Cannonau di Alghero Roana from Sardinia at £3.49. Other highlights are a good range of

---

Prices were current in summer 1988 to the best of our knowledge but can only be a rough indication of prices throughout 1989.

Riojas, wines from Torres, Bulgarian wines at rather high prices and a
small selection of Ports and Sherries.

Best buys

Milion Merlot, Yugoslavia, £2.05; Geoffrey Roberts California red and
white, £2.99; Prieur du Ch Meyney 1982, £6.50; Côtes du Marmandais
Rouge 1986, £2.79

H Allen Smith

24–25 Scala Street, London W1P 1LU	TEL 01-637 4767/0387
56 Lamb's Conduit Street, London WC1N 3LW	TEL 01-405 3106
29 Heath Street, London NW3 6TR	TEL 01-435 6845
26 Old Church Street, London SW3 5BY	TEL 01-352 4114

OPEN Mon–Fri 9.30–7 (NW3 10–8) Sat 10–1 (NW3 10–8) CLOSED Sun,
public holidays CREDIT CARDS All accepted; personal and business accounts
DISCOUNTS 5% on 1 case DELIVERY Free in central London (min 1 case) and
in outer London postal districts (min 3 cases); otherwise £2 for under 3 cases;
mail order available GLASS HIRE Free with 1-case order
TASTINGS AND TALKS Wines always available in-store; large annual tastings;
smaller tastings every 1–2 months; to groups on request CELLARAGE £3.45 per
case per year

While H Allen Smith's reputation is for Spanish, Portuguese and
Italian wines, this year they have been widening their French range.
For instance, a very useful range of clarets has been built up 'for
current drinking' (Ch Ségur 1985, Haut-Médoc at £4.95 and Ch Haut
Millet 1983, Premières Côtes de Blaye at £3.95 are good examples).
Other strong French areas are Alsace wines from the Co-operative of
Turckheim, and some useful and good-value vins de pays (Vin de Pays
de Loire Atlantique, a Muscadet-type wine, is £1.99). Joseph Perrier
Champagnes (Brut nv at £11.95) would be a change from the house
Champagne at £9.95.

Turning to Italy, we move to the agency side of the business. Here,
H Allen Smith are the principal importers of the wines of
Tiefenbrunner in the Alto Adige/Südtirol and of Aldo Conterno in
Piedmont (look for the Barbera d'Alba at £6.95). Also try the Tuscan
wines of Castello San Polo in Rosso, and the excellent value
Montepulciano d'Abruzzo of Cantina Tollo (£2.95). In Portugal,
H Allen Smith import the considerable wines of the top firm,
J M da Fonseca.

In Spain, Riojas come from Marqués de Cáceres, Bodegas Lan and
Muga, while the inexpensive Navarra wines of Monte Ory are worth
trying (Monte Ory Crianza 1983, £3.35). From Ribera del Duero are
Bodegas Ribera Duero (the co-operative) 1986 at £3.45 and Protos Gran
Reserva 1980 at £8.50, while Vega Sicilia 1976 is £32.50. Rueda provides
Marqués de Griñon white as well as red. Don't forget the Torres wines
from Penedès, or H Allen Smith's own imports from Cavas Hill.

More imports from the New World: Hardy's in Australia, and the good-value (for California) Pinot Noir at £5.25 and Zinfandel (NV) at £4.35 from Mountain View Vineyards.

Best buys

South Australian Shiraz Nottage Hill 1985, Thomas Hardy, £4.65; Schloss Böckelheimer Burgweg Kabinett 1986, £2.65; Chianti Rufina 1985, Villa di Monte, £2.95; Mont Marçal 1977 Reserva (white), Cavas Hill, £4.65; Quinta da Camarate 1982, J M da Fonseca, £3.95

Alston Wines

Front Street, Alston, Cumbria CA9 3HU	TEL (0498) 81800
Hencotes, Hexham, Northumberland NE46 2EQ	TEL (0434) 602637
Peacehaven, Town Foot, Rothbury,	TEL (0669) 2095
Northumberland NE65 7SP	

OPEN (Alston) Mon–Thur 9.30–5.30   Fri, Sat 9.30–7   public holidays 10–4; (Hexham) Mon–Sat 9–6; (Rothbury) Mon–Wed 10–6   Thur–Sat 10–8   public holidays 10–4   CLOSED Good Friday, Chr Day, Boxing Day, New Year's Day   CREDIT CARDS Access, Amex, Diners, Visa; personal and business accounts   DISCOUNTS 5% on ½ case, 10% on full case   DELIVERY Free within 10-mile radius of each shop (min 1 case); elsewhere approx £5 per case; mail order available   GLASS HIRE Free with 1-case order   TASTINGS AND TALKS In-store tastings most Saturdays; Alston Wine Appreciation Club; to groups on request   CELLARAGE Not available

Although the Durham branch of this enterprising wine merchant has closed, there are now three branches instead of last year's two: the original in Alston, another in Hexham and a third in Rothbury.

In an area which has been something of a blank in our gazetteer, this is encouraging news because owner Mac Brown has put together an attractive list, covering some unusual corners of the wine world. For example, he offers three Rumanian wines – almost a record – as well as the Algerian red Coteaux de Mascara (£3.90) and Greek red wines from the co-operative of Nemea.

Mainstream wines include a range of clarets, all ready to drink, which move in price from Ch la Barde 1983, Côtes du Bourg at £4.30 up to Ch Cissac 1979, Haut Médoc at £12.90. Burgundies also cover a good spread, while in Beaujolais we find wines from Duboeuf and Sarrau. On the Loire, look for the organic wines of Guy Bossard in Muscadet, and in Alsace the wines of Louis Gisselbrecht. Jacquesson supplies the Champagne.

Two strong sections are Spain (CVNE Riojas) and Italy, which turns up Chiantis from Fattoria di Ripanera (1985 vintage at £5), Barolo from Borgogno, Venegazzù White Label and the Vernaccia of San Quirico (1985 vintage at £4.85) among a good, sound selection. Look, too, for Australia's offering – Orlando, McWilliams, Taltarni, Peter Lehmann and Rosemount wines. New Zealand shows off with Babich wines.

Best buys

Bairrada 1982, Co-operative of Mealhada, £2.95; Chianti Classico 1982, Villa Cerna, £4.60; Taltarni Victorian Shiraz 1982, £5; Palacio de León white and red NV, £2.85

Amazing Grapes

94 Brent Street, Hendon, London NW4 2ES   TEL 01-202 2631

OPEN Mon–Fri 9.30–6   Sun, public holidays 10–2   CLOSED Sat
CREDIT CARDS Visa; personal and business accounts
DISCOUNTS Approximately 8% on 1 case   DELIVERY Free locally (NW4, NW11, N2) (min 1 case); otherwise at cost; mail order available
GLASS HIRE Free   TASTINGS AND TALKS To groups on request
CELLARAGE Not available

This firm reaches the Guide on the strength of its short but useful range of wines made under Kosher supervision, from France, Italy and California as well as Israel.

French wines move from Bordeaux (St-Emilion 1986, Ch de Chevalier Bayard at £6.95), through Coteaux du Tricastin Cellier du Grand Roi (£3.20) to Sancerre 1986 of Alphonse Mellot (£7.75). The California wines include a Chardonnay and Chenin Blanc. In Israel itself, the list concentrates on the familiar Carmel range and the wines from the young good quality vineyards of Gamla and Yarden on the Golan Heights.

Best buys

Gamla and Yarden Israeli wines

Les Amis du Vin

See Christopher & Co.

Arriba Kettle

MAIL ORDER Buckle Street, Honeybourne,   TEL (0386) 833024
Nr Evesham, Hereford & Worcester WR11 5QB

OPEN 24-hour telephone answering service   CREDIT CARDS None accepted; business accounts accepted   DISCOUNTS From £1.50 on 3 cases to £2.75 on 11+ cases; £1 per case collected   DELIVERY Free on UK mainland (min 2 cases)
GLASS HIRE Free in West Midlands, North Cotswolds and Central London
TASTINGS AND TALKS For mail order customers in November held in Birmingham and north Cotswolds; to groups on request
CELLARAGE Not available   ■

Spanish wines are the raison d'être of Arriba Kettle. Over the years, owner Barry Kettle (who also practises as an architect), has developed a number of exclusive agencies alongside wines that are available elsewhere (and a handful of Ports from over the border).

His particular strength lies in the Rioja. Wines from Bodegas Alavesas (Solar de Samaniego) and Cosecheros Alaveses (Atardi) are the two exclusive wines in this section, but bottles from a number of small bodegas – Castillo de Cuzcurrita, Viña Salceda and the single estate Remelluri – don't have much wider distribution. Other Riojas come from most of the famous names.

Elsewhere in Spain, we alight on Penedès, with wines from the Bodegas of Manuel Sancho (including a range of the sparkling cava Mont Marçal – the Brut is £5.20), and those from Torres and Masía Bach. Other Spanish regions covered include Navarra, Valdepeñas and Ribera del Duero. Look also for Sherries from Bodegas Orleans-Borbon (the old Amontillado Ataulfo is £3.99) and Almacenista Sherries from Lustau.

Best buys

Atardi Blanco and Tinto, Cosecheros Alaveses, £3.13; Ataulfo Amontillado, Bodegas Orleans-Borbon, £3.99; Cava Mont Marçal Nature and Rosado, £4.72; Rioja Viña Salceda 1982, £3.97

Asda

HEAD OFFICE Asda House, South Bank,   TEL (0532) 435435
Great Wilson Street, Leeds, West Yorkshire LS11 5AD
120 licensed branches nationwide

OPEN (Generally) Mon–Wed, Sat 9–8   Thur, Fri 9–8.30   CLOSED Sun (except Scotland), public holidays   CREDIT CARDS Access, Visa; personal and business accounts   DISCOUNTS, DELIVERY, GLASS HIRE Not available
TASTINGS AND TALKS Regular in-store tastings; occasionally to groups on request   CELLARAGE Not available

Like most of the more adventurous supermarket groups, Asda has a two-tier system of wines. All the own-label wines are available in all stores; finer wines from the Wine Rack can be bought in 80 or so of the larger branches.

Judging by recent tastings of their wines, Asda are scoring very well indeed in both their range and quality. In the own-label selection, there is a strong collection of French vins de pays (look for the Vin de Pays de Vaucluse red at £1.89, and the white from the Côtes de Gascogne at £1.99). Other own-label wines we have enjoyed are the Rioja at £2.69; Côtes du Rhône at £2.29; and Soave at £2.09. They have also hit upon a surprisingly good value white Burgundy at £3.49. (Bear in mind, though, that when we went to press, all Asda own-label wines were still in 70cl bottles. In accordance with EEC directives, this must change on 1 January 1989, so prices may rise.) Asda Champagne at £7.45 (in a 75cl bottle) has rated well in recent tastings.

In the Wine Rack selection, there are some very good things indeed, such as Ch la Cardonne 1980 at £4.99 or Ch le Gardéra 1983 at £4.25, both clever buys. Spain does well, with Riojas from Faustino and the Raimat Abadía at £3.79, among others. There's a good choice of sweet white Bordeaux, and a fairly priced selection of Burgundy. Italy's Franciacorta Longhi-de Carli is £3.49, while Chile's Viña Linderos Cabernet Sauvignon is £3.29.

Best buys

Asda White Burgundy, Alain Combard, £3.49; Asda Elegant Dry Fino Sherry, £2.99; Asda Rioja, Bodegas Castillo de Fuentoro, £2.69; Cabernet Sauvignon Vin de Pays des Pyrénées Orientales, £1.99; Asda Crémant de Bourgogne, £4.99.

Ashley Scott

P O Box 28, The Highway, Hawarden,   TEL (0244) 520655
Deeside, Clwyd CH5 3RY   (answering machine out of hours)

OPEN Mon–Sat 8.30–6   CREDIT CARDS None accepted; personal and business accounts   DISCOUNTS 5% on 1 unmixed case   DELIVERY Free in North Wales, Cheshire, Merseyside, Lancashire (min 1 case); elsewhere at cost; mail order available   GLASS HIRE Free with 1-case order   TASTINGS AND TALKS Annual tasting in November by invitation (available on request); to groups on request CELLARAGE Available   ▪

Look away from France for the real interest of this list. In Germany, there are estate wines from Louis Guntrum and Adolf Huesgen. In Italy, there are wines from Quintarelli in the Veneto, Mascarello's Barolo, Chianti from Le Torri and Vino Nobile di Montepulciano from Piccini. In Portugal, Caves Aliança supply a range of very good value wines from Bairrada. In Spain, there are Sherries from Delgado Zuleta, and in the New World, Cook's New Zealand wines and Wyndham Estate wines from Australia.

In France, highlights include the Mas de la Dame Coteaux des Baux en Provence wines (1984 red at £4.45), a good selection of Sauternes and Beaujolais from Thorin. House Champagne is Beaulieu (Brut NV at £8.95), Alsace wines are from Muré – and there's English wine from Biddenden.

Best buys

Palacio de León Tinto NV, £2.45; Delgado Zuleta Sherries; Ch de Bayle 1985, Bordeaux, £3.25; Coteaux des Baux en Provence, Mas de la Dame Rouge, £4.45; Sauvignon Vin de Pays du Jardin de la France, £2.75

Wine in bag-in-box ages and spoils quicker than in bottle. Drink up one box before you buy the next, and don't keep boxes hanging around in a cupboard because they will lose their freshness. Used or unopened, a wine box will keep better if you store it tap downwards, keeping wine, not air, in the valve.

Askham Wines

Askham, via Newark,   TEL (077 783) 659
Nottinghamshire NG22 0RP

OPEN Mon–Fri 9–5   Sat 9–1   CLOSED Sun, public holidays
CREDIT CARDS None accepted; personal and business accounts
DISCOUNTS Variable   DELIVERY Free within 50-mile radius and mainland UK
(min £50 order); mail order available   GLASS HIRE Free with 2-case minimum
order   TASTINGS AND TALKS Two main tastings a year; to groups on request
CELLARAGE Not available   ∎

This is not a long list. The attraction of it is that each wine has a
purpose, so that there is no padding. The quality of the wines is good,
too – a great bonus.

So don't expect to find hundreds of clarets, for example. What you
will find, though, is a sensibly priced selection that gives you Ch de
Palanquey, Côtes de Castillon 1983 at £4.40 up to Ch la Lagune 1978 at
£20.60. In Burgundy domaine wine comes from Pierre Boillot and
Chablis from Michel Remon, while Beaujolais features Sylvain Fessy.
The Loire has the excellent Touraine varietal wines from the Confrérie
des Vignerons de Oisly-et-Thésée, while the Champagne is that of
Billecart-Salmon.

In Spain, look for the top-class Riojas of La Rioja Alta (the Viña
Ardanza 1980 is £5.37), and in Portugal for the wines of J M da Fonseca
and its associated company, João Pires. In California, there's a nice
clutch of wineries (Round Hill, Hawk Crest, Cuvaison), and Columbia
winery in Washington State. Rouge Homme wines represent
Australia, and Delegat's New Zealand.

Best buys

Fino Bandera, Gil Luque, £3.93; Round Hill Chardonnay 1985, Napa
Valley, £4.95; Côtes du Lubéron 1986, Ch Val Joanis Blanc, £4.05; Von
Buhl Riesling 1986, Rheinpfalz, £4.31

Astral Wines

See Morris's.

Averys of Bristol ☞

7 Park Street, Bristol, Avon BS1 5NG   TEL (0272) 214141

OPEN Mon–Fri 9–6 Sat 9–5 CLOSED Sun, public holidays
CREDIT CARDS Access, Visa; personal and business accounts
DISCOUNTS Available DELIVERY Free on UK mainland (min 1 case within
5-mile radius of Bristol, 2 cases elsewhere); otherwise £5.50 for under 2 cases;
mail order available GLASS HIRE Free with refundable deposit
TASTINGS AND TALKS Daily tastings in-store; annual tasting; to groups on
request CELLARAGE £2.50 per case or part-case per year

This long-established wine merchant is now bringing together the Old
World and the New in a very satisfactory blend. Clarets and
Burgundies are strong and Averys have extended their range of New
World wines (of which they were one of the pioneers in this country).

In California, they are importers of Alexander Valley in the Russian
River Valley and Freemark Abbey and Rutherford Hill in Napa. There
are also a number of wines from Robert Mondavi. In Australia, the
featured wineries are Tyrrells in the Hunter (the producers of the
strangely named Long Flat Red and White – both good value at £3.94),
Rouge Homme in Coonawarra and Tim Knappstein in Clare. From
across the Tasman Sea come the wines of Nick Nobilo (who makes one
of the best Pinot Noirs in New Zealand – the 1984 vintage is £5.80), but
more of a curiosity, perhaps, are the Inniskillin wines from Niagara in
Canada.

In the Old World, on a surprisingly traditional list the range of
clarets goes back to 1970, with big showings from the vintages of the
early 1980s (Ch Haut-Sociondo 1983, Premières Côtes de Blaye at £4.72
and Ch Puy Castéra 1982, Haut Médoc at £6.75 are both good buys). In
Burgundy, many of the reds come from Remoissenet and Averys' own
bottlings, but there are also domaine wines, especially in the whites.

Outside France, strong areas include German estate bottles,
particularly on the Mosel, with wines from the Friedrich Wilhelm
Gymnasium (Graacher Domprobst Riesling Kabinett 1985 at £6.40), but
a few wines from the superb 1976 vintage can also be drooled over.
Italy and Spain have a few stars, Portugal none, while Sherries and
Ports are mainly Averys' own bottlings.

Regular special offers to mailing list customers, plus daily tastings in
their Bristol shop, are added attractions to dealings with this firm.
There are plans to open a shop in London towards the end of 1988.

Best buys

Rouge Homme Coonawarra Shiraz 1984, £4.92; Averys Champagne,
£9.53; Rutherford Hill Napa Valley Chardonnay 1984, £5.24; Utiel
Requena Tinto 1982, Casa lo Alto, £3.36

David Baillie Vintners ☞ ☞

At the Sign of the Lucky Horseshoe,   TEL (0392) 221345
Longbrook Street, Exeter, Devon EX4 6AP
ASSOCIATED OUTLET
Horseshoe Wines, 10 Heathside Way,   TEL (025 126) 5102
Hartley Wintney, Hampshire RG27 8SG

OPEN Mon–Sat 9–6   CLOSED Sun, public holidays   CREDIT CARDS Access, Amex, Visa; personal and business accounts   DISCOUNTS 5% on 1 unmixed case   DELIVERY Free on UK mainland (min 2 cases); otherwise at cost; mail order available   GLASS HIRE Free   TASTINGS AND TALKS Monthly tastings; to groups on request   CELLARAGE £2 per case per year

This year we have noticed one major change as well as steady improvement in this excellent West Country wine merchant's list.

Last year we commented that the Italian section was rather dull. Now famous names parade past – Contratto Barolos, Chianti from Vicchiomaggio and Antinori, Rubesco di Torgiano from Lungarotti, the southern Italian whites from Mastroberadino (Greco di Tufo at £6.42) and Südtirol wines from Tiefenbrunner.

More traditional areas of interest are the Rhône (wines from Jaboulet Aîné dominate here), Chablis (with wines from Lamblin et Fils) and Burgundy (look for domaine-bottled wines by Bruno Clair in Marsannay, Jacques Germain in Chorey-lès-Beaune and Jean-Claude Monnier in Meursault, among many others). Bordeaux offers house wines from Nathaniel Johnston (Claret at £3.48) and a rather more pricey section of château wines – no real bargains here. But good value can be had from other French regions – the Corbières of Domaine St-Julien de Septime at £2.79; and Ch la Jaubertie Bergerac at £3.89.

Other highlights include estate-bottled wines from Germany, Torres wines from Spain, Clos du Val from California and a rapidly-expanding Australian section – Rosemount, Hill-Smith Estate, Quelltaler, Taltarni, Brown Brothers, Rothbury Estate. There's a good wood Port from Martinez-Gassiot (Finest Old Tawny at £6.55); Almacenista Sherries from Lustau; and a rare range of early landed Cognacs.

Best buys

Chianti Classico Riserva 1982, Castello Vicchiomaggio, £5.20; Champagne René Lancier, £9.77; Lustau Almacenista Sherries; Ch de Rivière 1986, Minervois, £2.69; Columbia Crest Washington State Sauvignon Blanc 1986, £4.68

Balls Brothers

Balls Brothers Wine Centre,   TEL 01-739 6466
313 Cambridge Heath Road, London E2 9LQ

OPEN Mon–Sat 10–6   CLOSED Sun, public holidays   CREDIT CARDS Access,
Visa   DISCOUNTS Not available   DELIVERY Free on UK mainland
(min 2 cases); mail order available   GLASS HIRE Free by arrangement
TASTINGS AND TALKS Constant tastings in Wine Centre; large annual tasting in
May; to groups on request   CELLARAGE £1.56 per case per year

This City-based group of wine bars also has a wine merchant side,
aimed mainly at City business. Perhaps not surprisingly, it is still a
pretty conservative list. Clarets are a strong section, with a good price
spectrum from Ch de Brondeau 1985, Bordeaux Supérieur at £3.70, up
to the more rarified heights of Ch Ducru-Beaucaillou 1983 at £31.50.
In Burgundy, négociants like Geisweiler, Chanson Père et Fils and
Faiveley are there, as are a few domaine wines from Henri Germain
and Nicolas Servant. Beaujolais is from Loron; Alsace from Trimbach
and Blanck; the Rhône pages include the good value Côtes du Rhône of
Ch du Grand Moulas (the 1987 vintage is £3.65), plus wines from
Guigal and Jaboulet Aîné; more value is to be had in the Loire with the
Sauvignon de Touraine of Domaine du Grand Moulin at £3.45.

After this, the list shortens considerably, but quality is kept up in the
few Australians (from Tyrrells and Stanley Leasingham), Riojas from
La Rioja Alta, Italian wines from Antinori, Concha y Toro from Chile.
There's plenty of Champagne, as might be expected (Vicomte d'Almon
is the house brand at £9.25), and the same goes, equally naturally, for
Ports. (See also the WINE BAR section.)

Best buys

Ch Combe des Dames 1985, Bordeaux, £3.45; Domaine Ste-Eulalie,
Minervois, £3.15; Rioja 1979, Remelluri, £4.75; Gold Cap Very Fine Old
Tawny Port, £8.55; Coteaux d'Aix-en-Provence 1986,
Ch de Fonscolombe Blanc, £3

Nigel Baring

11 Stanhope Place, London W2 2HH   TEL 01-724 0836

OPEN Mon–Fri 9–5   CLOSED Sat, Sun, public holidays   CREDIT CARDS None
accepted; personal and business accounts   DISCOUNTS Quantity discounts
DELIVERY Free in central London (min 5 cases); elsewhere £2.50 plus VAT; mail
order available   GLASS HIRE Not available   TASTINGS AND TALKS Annual
tasting for existing clients   CELLARAGE £4 per case per year   ■

Although the bulk of this merchant's list is fine claret, including some
old vintages, there are other areas of interest as well. Look, for
example, for Lost Hills and La Crema wineries in California, red
Burgundy from Louis Jadot, white Burgundy from Leflaive. There are

good things on the Rhône, too, including a good selection of Côtes du
Rhône Cairanne, Hermitage from Bernard Faurie, Crozes-Hermitage
from Tardy & Ange, Condrieu from Georges Vernay. Vintage Ports
back to 1963 and Champagnes round off a definitely fine wine
selection.

Best buys

Crozes-Hermitage 1985, Tardy & Ange, £3.71; fine clarets;
Ch Beaumont 1986, Haut-Médoc, £3.58 (before duty and VAT);
Côte Rôtie 1982, Bernard Faurie, £6.62

Barnes Wine Shop

51 Barnes High Street, London SW13 9LN   TEL 01-878 8643
OPEN Mon–Sat 9.30–8.30   Sun 12–2   CLOSED Public holidays
CREDIT CARDS Access, Visa; personal and business accounts   DISCOUNTS 5%
on 1 case; larger discounts negotiable   DELIVERY Free in central London (min 1
case); charges elsewhere negotiable; mail order available   GLASS HIRE Free
with 2-case order   TASTINGS AND TALKS In-store tastings available on request;
to groups on request   CELLARAGE £2.60 per case per year

This may not be the longest list in this Guide, but there are few where
every wine seems to serve a particular purpose so well or where every
wine is of such high quality in its particular style and area.

It's also a sensibly arranged list – a simple segregation of red, white
and rosé wines, plus a special sub-division for pudding wines, of
which the shop has a splendid collection. To start with these, we
perceive an obvious affection for the Muscat grape (look for the Muscat
from Quady in California – half-bottles are £5.45), coupled with some
fine Late Harvest wines from California and Australia, Ch la Salle,
again from California, plus Jurançon Moelleux from France and the
rare and wonderful Madeira-style Verdello from Bleasdale in
Langhorne Creek, South Australia (6-year-old, £8.45).

On the dry side strengths lie in Australia – again not in terms of
quantity but for the quality of such smaller boutique wineries as Capel
Vale, Yarra Yering, Middlebrook, Huntington Estate, Sutherland and
Brokenwood – all making small amounts of very fine wines. The same
is true of California – Cuvaison, Acacia, ZD, Sonoma Cutrer,
Bouchaine.

In Europe, areas of particular interest include the Alsace wines from
the Turckheim co-operative, the Jermann wines from Friuli in Italy,
Beaujolais from Louis Tête, Riojas from Olarra. From the other end of
the Mediterranean, there are six vintages of Ch Musar from the
Lebanon. And don't forget Sherries from Lustau, Barbadillo and Don
Zoilo, Fonseca Ports and plenty of Champagnes.

Best buys

Valdepeñas Reserva 1981, Señorio de los Llanos, £3.49; Tokay d'Alsace 1986, Cave Co-opérative de Turckheim, £3.95; Côtes du Ventoux 1985, Domaine des Anges, £3.49; Moscato d'Asti Granduca d'Asti, £4.95; Verdello 6-year-old, Bleasdale, South Australia, £8.45

Barrel Selection

St Georges Cross, Glasgow G20 7PY   TEL 041-332 1040

OPEN Mon–Fri 10.30–8   Sat 10.30–6   Sun 12–6   CLOSED Chr Day, Boxing Day, New Year's Day   CREDIT CARDS Access, Amex, Visa; business accounts DISCOUNTS Available   DELIVERY Free in Glasgow area (min £100+ order); otherwise £1 per case for orders of £50+, £2.50 per case for orders under £50; elsewhere at cost   GLASS HIRE Free   TASTINGS AND TALKS To groups on request   CELLARAGE Not available ▪

A new entry in the Guide, this merchant runs a wine warehouse in Glasgow's West End. There's a definite sense of humour about the business, but also a more serious side in a good range of wines.

Most of the wine world is covered in the regular list, supplemented by bin-ends and small parcels of fine wines from Bordeaux, Burgundy, Germany and of Vintage Port. No one area is stronger than another, but we like the sound of a good set of wines from the South of France (Faugères 1986, Resplandy at £2.69; Chancel Vin de Pays Blanc at £2.65). There's only a small selection of Burgundy, but look for Jaboulet Aîné Rhône wines and Alsace from P & E Dopff. House Champagne is the good value Marcel Rouet (NV) at £8.89.

Other European countries containing some interest include Italy (Chianti Classico Machiavelli 1982 at £4.09 is a bargain), Spain (Rioja Campo Viejo 1984, £3.25) and Portugal (Reguengos de Monsaraz 1985, £2.79). Sherry is from Burdon and Ports are from Ramos Pinto.

Outside Europe, look for Australian wines from Mildara and Wente Brothers wines from California.

Best buys

Melnik Damianitza 1978, Bulgaria, £2.75; Chianti Classico Machiavelli 1982, £4.09; Australian Barrel Selection table wines, £2.55; Faugères 1986, Resplandy, £2.69

The Wine Development Board is a small organisation with the responsibility of encouraging more people to drink wine. They may be able to supply literature and general promotional material. Contact them at: PO Box 583, Five Kings House, Kennet Wharf Lane, Upper Thames Street, London EC4V 3BH; TEL 01-248 5835.

Barwell & Jones

HEAD OFFICE 24 Fore Street, Ipswich, Suffolk IP4 1JU	TEL (0473) 231723
118 Sprowston Road, Norwich, Norfolk NR3 4QH	TEL (0603) 484966
70 Trumpington Street, Cambridge, Cambridgeshire CB2 1RJ	TEL (0223) 354431
3 Redenhall Road, Harleston, Norfolk IP20 9EN	TEL (0379) 852243
94 Rushmere Road, Ipswich, Suffolk IP4 4JL	TEL (0473) 727426
MANAGED HOUSE WITH OFF-LICENCE	
The Cross Inn, 2 Church Street, Woodbridge, Suffolk IP12 1DH	TEL (03943) 3288
The Grosvenor, 25/29 Ranelagh Road, Felixstowe, Suffolk IP11 7HA	TEL (0394) 284137

OPEN Hours vary from branch to branch CREDIT CARDS Access, Visa; personal and business accounts DISCOUNTS Negotiable DELIVERY Free in East Anglia and London; mail order available GLASS HIRE Free TASTINGS AND TALKS Occasional in-store tastings; to groups on request CELLARAGE Available; charges negotiable

This small group of shops offers a good all-round range of wines, without being particularly strong in any one area. In fact, the best sections of the list – apart from Italian wines – are in the classic areas of France.

In a good range of Burgundies – many from négociant Jaboulet Vercherre, others from Coron – are interspersed a few domaine wines. It's good to see mature red Burgundy as well. In Alsace, the wines come from Pierre Sparr, while Domaine des Dorices is the source of the Muscadet. Among the clarets, petit château wines from the 1983 vintage come at good prices (Ch Beau-Site, Premières Côtes de Bordeaux, £4.47), as well as some top classed growths.

In the South of France, Barwell & Jones' speciality is the fine Coteaux d'Aix-en-Provence of Commanderie de la Bargemone (Rouge 1985 at £4.22). Moving east to Italy, we come across some fine wines from Guerrieri-Rizzardi who operate an organic vineyard in the Veneto (if you buy the superb Amarone Valpolicella 1985 at £7.74, give it several years before drinking). Other Italians worth noting are Brunellos from Col d'Orcia and Barolo and Dolcetto from Giacosa Bruno.

Spain has Riojas from Bodegas Montecillo (the red 1985 is £3.92), and there are a few New World wines (California from Mondavi and Clos du Bois). Look, too, for the good value lighter style Ports of Burmeester.

Best buys

Soave Costeggiola Classico 1987, Guerrieri-Rizzardi, £4.55; Côtes du Ventoux 1985, Domaine les Grand'terres, £3.47; Vino Nobile di

Montepulciano Riserva 1982, Fognano, £5.48; Montecillo Cumbrero
Rioja 1985, £3.92

Thomas Baty & Sons

See Willoughbys.

Bedford Fine Wines

The Knife and Cleaver, Houghton Conquest,   TEL (0234) 740387
Bedford, Bedfordshire MK45 3LA

OPEN Mon–Fri 10–4   Sat 10–1   CLOSED Sun, public holidays
CREDIT CARDS Access, Visa; personal and business accounts   DISCOUNTS 3%
on mixed cases, 5% on unmixed cases   DELIVERY Free within 15-mile radius of
Bedford (min 2 cases), Luton, St Albans, North and central London (min 5
cases); elsewhere at cost; mail order available   GLASS HIRE Free with 1+ case
order   TASTINGS AND TALKS Regular monthly tastings in-store; to groups on
request   CELLARAGE Not available

This year, Bedford Fine Wines have expanded their Italian and Spanish
sections, although the heart of the list remains in Bordeaux.

In Italy, in addition to a good selection of wines from Frescobaldi
(look for Tenuta di Pomino 1986 at £4.85 and Chianti Rufina Castello di
Nipozzano 1982 at £5.75), there are now wines from Guerrieri-Rizzardi
in Valpolicella, from Lungarotti in Torgiano and from Pio Cesare in
Piedmont. In Spain, while Torres dominates, Berberana, Montecillo
and Marqués de Riscal also feature, as well as the Ribera del Duero
Pesquera 1985 (£10.55).

In France, clarets are a well-balanced range (including the house
claret Le Bordeaux Prestige of Peter Allan Sichel at £5.25); a smaller
selection of Burgundies presents wines from Moillard, Faiveley, Jean
Gros and Bouchard Père, while there is a mixed bag from Alsace
(Schlumberger, Dopff au Moulin, Kuentz-Bas). The sweet Quarts de
Chaume of Jean Baumard on the Loire and some good value from the
south of France are other interesting pockets. Sherries are mainly from
Barbadillo and Lustau, Madeiras from Rutherford and Miles.

Best buys

Minervois 1986, Ch de Pouzols, £2.72; Hautes Côtes de Beaune 1984,
Carré, £4.80; Ch Timberlay 1985, Bordeaux, £3.80; Valpolicella Classico
Superiore 1985, Guerrieri-Rizzardi, £3.60

Berkmann Wine Cellars

See Le Nez Rouge.

Berry Bros & Rudd ☞

3 St James's Street,   TEL 01-839 9033
London SW1A 1EG   (answering machine 01-930 1888)
The Wine Shop, Hamilton Close, Houndmills,   TEL (0256) 23566
Basingstoke, Hampshire RG21 2YH

OPEN Mon–Fri 9.30–5 (London)   9–5 (Basingstoke)   Sat 9–1 (Basingstoke)
CLOSED Sat (London), Sun, public holidays   CREDIT CARDS Access, Diners,
Visa; personal and business accounts   DISCOUNTS 3% on 1–5 cases, 5% on
5–10 cases, 7.5% on 10+ cases   DELIVERY Free on UK mainland (min 1 case);
mail order available   GLASS HIRE Available with wine order within delivery
area   TASTINGS AND TALKS Bi-annual tasting (June and November) in
Basingstoke cellars; to groups on request   CELLARAGE £3.31 per case per year

To those accustomed to the wine list from Berry Bros, designed to fit
neatly into a waistcoat pocket, the sight of the 1988 edition must have
come as something of a shock. To delve inside its unrecognisably large
pages and then to find wines from Australia alongside the familiar
clarets – what is the world coming to?

In fact, Berry Bros, like any good wine merchant, is moving with the
times, despite the venerable image of its London office, a complete
contrast to the modernity of its wine shop in Basingstoke. So while
there are still plenty of clarets, many with the familiar tiny label which
significs that they have been bottled in England (often offering very
good value), and still plenty of vintage Ports, we now find small but
well-chosen sections of Italian, Spanish and California wines alongside
the Australian.

Apart from claret, France has a firm stratum of Burgundy, now
balanced nicely between domaine and négociant wines, a rather
disappointing collection of Loire bottles, Alsace wines from Trimbach,
Rhônes from Chapoutier and Guigal and a shortish range of
Champagnes.

Germany offers a splendid selection of very serious estate wines
(Wegeler-Deinhard, Landgraf von Hessen, Geheimrat Aschrott, von
Buhl, Bert Simon). Italy has wines from Boscaini, Lungarotti, Ceretto
in Piedmont, Lageder in the Südtirol; Spain has Riojas from CVNE.
Then, in the New World, the innovation of Australia introduces
Hill-Smith, Brown Brothers, Yalumba and Rosemount among others,
as well as California's Monticello, Iron Horse and Trefethen.

Berry Bros sampling cases are a good way of getting an overview of a
region. Look, too, for special offers, and lists of wines for laying down.

Best buys

Bourgogne Pinot Noir, Berry Bros, £4.65; Côtes du Ventoux 1985,
Ch Crillon, £3.70; Berry Bros bottlings of claret; German estate wines;
vintage Madeiras

B H Wines

Boustead Hill House, Boustead Hill,   TEL (0228 76) 711
Burgh-by-Sands, Carlisle, Cumbria CA5 6AA

OPEN 'All reasonable hours' – 24-hour answering machine
CREDIT CARDS None accepted   DISCOUNTS Negotiable   DELIVERY Free
within Carlisle area (min 1 case); otherwise by negotiation; mail order possible
GLASS HIRE Free with 1-case order   TASTINGS AND TALKS Free tastings twice
yearly; to groups on request   CELLARAGE Not available   ■

Nice for a change to see a list organised in the way we tend to drink
wine – by colour rather than geography. So the red wines, in
alphabetical order, kick off with Argentina and an Andean Vineyard
Cabernet Sauvignon 1979 at £4.27.

There are also red wines from Leasingham, Brown Brothers and
Orlando in Australia, from Mondavi and Clos du Bois in California,
and from Viña Linderos in Chile. In France, look for the Coteaux des
Baux en Provence of Domaine de Trévallon 1984 at £6.29, or the
Rasteau Côtes du Rhône Villages 1984 at £3.71, among a range which
takes in small selections from classic areas as well as the French
regions. Italy lists Chianti from Brolio and Fattoria dell'Ugo (the 1985
vintage is £3.06), plus the organic wines of the Fugazza sisters in
Oltrepò Pavese (the 1981 vintage comes at £4.21).

Turning to white wines, Australia comes up with the unique Dry
Muscat of Brown Brothers (the 1986 vintage is £4.19), followed by
Alsace wines from Muré, a few German examples, Südtirol wines from
Schreckbihl and the Frascati of Villa di Catone, plus the old-style white
Rioja Monopole from CVNE.

Sherries are from Garvey, Champagne from Bricout (Carte Noir Brut
Réserve at £10.99) and Ports from Ramos Pinto.

Best buys

Chianti Putto 1985, Fattoria dell'Ugo, £3.06; Palacio de León, £2.59;
Montilla Iberia Dry, £2.25; Vin de Pays Charentais Caberlot 1985, £2.25;
Spring Gulley Rhine Riesling 1984, Leasingham, £3.59

Bibendum

113 Regent's Park Road, London NW1 8UR   TEL 01-586 9761
81 Fulham Road, London SW3 6RE   TEL 01-584 3577

OPEN (NW1) Mon–Sat 10–8   Sun 11–6; (SW3) Mon–Sat 9.30–6   CLOSED Sun
(SW3); public holidays   CREDIT CARDS Access, Visa; personal and business
accounts   DISCOUNTS Negotiable   DELIVERY Free within London postal
districts (min 1 mixed case); elsewhere £3.95 per consignment; mail order
available   GLASS HIRE Free with 1 mixed case order
TASTINGS AND TALKS Wines always available for tasting at NW1; range of
wines available every weekend; major theme tastings several times a year;
to groups on request   CELLARAGE £3.50 per case per year

Since the last Guide was produced, this wine merchant, one of our top award winners, have opened a branch at the Conran-owned Michelin building in South Kensington, which operates more as a conventional shop (in that you can buy single bottles) than the splendid warehouse in Primrose Hill (case purchases only), but has the same range of wines.

Apart from that, their collection goes from strength to strength. It's eclectic, wide-ranging, and packed with unusual finds, wines from producers who have not exported before, wines from lesser regions. But the underlying strength continues to be a large investment in fine wines from classic areas, particularly claret and vintage Port, which visitors to the warehouse will see stacked enticingly in their wooden boxes.

Among a wealth of wines, we can pick out only a few from some of the particularly strong areas. Rhônes come from many of the top producers: Marc Sorrel in Hermitage, Emile Florentin of St-Joseph, Noël Versat in Cornas, Domaine les Pallières in Gigondas, Châteauneuf-du-Pape from Clos des Papes, Crozes-Hermitage from Tardy & Ange. Special Rhône offers are made regularly.

In Burgundy, there is a similar richness. Nearly all the wines are domaine-bottled, many of them top names, and not all at silly Burgundy prices either (Mâcon Villages from Jean Berger is £4.61; Rully 1986, Duvernay is £7.71). Good petit château wines from Bordeaux set the great wines in their wooden boxes in perspective. Champagne from Albert Beerens is a very acceptable house Champagne at £8.91, but Bibendum stock grandes marques as well. Alsace is supplied by Rolly Gassmann, and the Loire includes the wines of Gaston Huet in Vouvray.

Outside France, the German range is short but entirely based on estates (with Max Ferdinand Richter in the Mosel a highlight), while Italy is another focus, bursting with family firms and great names: the Viniatteri wines, Barolo from Giacomo Conterno, Viticola Suavia in Soave, Chianti from Fattoria Monsanto.

Australia scores well, particularly in the smaller wineries – Coriole in McLaren Vale, Tim Adams in Clare, Leconfield in Coonawarra, Yarra Burn in Yarra Valley. From California, there are wines from Heitz, Stag's Leap Wine Cellars and Clos du Bois as well as Mondavi and Acacia in Carneros.

Best buys

Vin de Pays de l'Aude, Cuvée de St-Eugène, £2.10; St-Pourçain-sur-Sioule 1986, Domaine Ray, £3.57; Beaujolais, Union des Vignerons de Bully, £3.25; Montepulciano d'Abruzzo 1986, Cantina Tollo, £2.78; Champagne Veuve Delaroy, £8.43; Chardonnay del Veneto 1987, Floriano, £2.97; Vinho Verde, Paco de Texeiro, £3.74

Bin 89 Wine Warehouse

89 Trippet Lane, Sheffield,   TEL (0742) 755889
South Yorkshire S1 4EL

OPEN Tue–Fri 11–6   Sat 10–1   CLOSED Mon, Sun, public holidays
CREDIT CARDS None accepted; personal and business accounts
DISCOUNTS 5% on 5 cases (min)   DELIVERY Free in Sheffield and parts of
Derbyshire (min 2 cases); elsewhere at cost; mail order available
GLASS HIRE Free with 1-case order   TASTINGS AND TALKS Two in-store
tastings by invitation per year; to groups on request   CELLARAGE £3 per case
per year

There's a definite feeling of excitement in Bin 89's list, and the
enthusiasms generally seem justified by the quality of the wines.

The most recent enthusiasm is for Italy, so we find Bianco di Custoza
from Portalupi at £3.85 for the 1986 vintage; the Malbec-based Torre
Quarto Rosso from the deep south of Puglia at £4.15 for the 1981
vintage; Barolo from Gemma, Soave from Pieropan: all good quality.

The same goes for Australia, with some top-flight wines from
smaller wineries: Tamburlaine in the Hunter Valley, Pirramimma in
McLaren Vale, Anglesey in South Australia, Mount Helen Estate in
Victoria. California, by comparison, is dull.

The French section is a fair hotchpotch of wines, some good, some
less interesting. We like the selection of good value wines from the
south of France, the Côtes du Rhône of the Celliers du Dauphin, the
Listel wines, the Muscadet of Guy Bossard and the Pouilly Fumé of
Didier Dagueneau. There's a short list of keenly-priced clarets, a dull
list of German wines, Delahaye Champagne (Brut at £8.95), and some
attractive tawny Ports.

The opening of a wine bar was planned for around Christmas 1988.

Best buys

Alsace Gewürztraminer 1985, Charles Grass, £3.75; Côtes du
Roussillon 1985, Ch de Couchous, £2.85; Barbera d'Alba 1983,
Prunotto, £4.75; Torre Quarto Rosso 1981, £4.15

Bin Ends

Toone House & Cellars,   TEL (0709) 367771
83–85 Badsley Moor Lane, Rotherham,
South Yorkshire S65 2PH
ASSOCIATED OUTLET
(By the case only)
Patrick Toone Personal Wine Merchant,   TEL (04393) 504
Pavilion House, Oswaldkirk, York, North Yorkshire YO6 5XZ

OPEN (Bin Ends) Mon–Fri 10–5.30 Sat 9.30–12.30 CLOSED Sun, public
holidays CREDIT CARDS None accepted; personal and business accounts
DISCOUNTS 5% on 1 unmixed case, 7.5% on 3 mixed cases DELIVERY Free
within 25-mile radius (min 1 case); elsewhere by negotiation; mail order on
request GLASS HIRE Free with 1-case order
TASTINGS AND TALKS Three-day tasting every four months; bottle open most
days; to groups on request CELLARAGE £2 per case per year

There is a double act in operation here. Bin Ends act as the retail outlet,
while Patrick Toone sells by the case only. Both use the same list.

That list – all good quality stuff – has grown very satisfactorily since
last year. For a start, Australia has put in an appearance in the form of
wines from Rosemount, Brown Brothers and de Bortoli (we
particularly like Brown Brothers' Muscat wines). The range of fortified
wines – Sherries from Garvey and Barbadillo and Ports from Fonseca
and Kopke – has also grown impressively. There are old vintages of
Barolos from Borgogno (the 1947 is £39 a bottle, the 1979 £7.30). Still in
Italy, look for Regaleali, Sicily's top wine, and the Chianti Classico of
Pagliarese. Spain offers Riojas from CVNE. It's a pity the list still
doesn't let on who makes the German wines.

In France, the selection starts with Alsace from Dopff au Moulin and
Beaujolais from Paul Sapin (try his Chénas 1985 at £5.29). In Bordeaux,
good value petit château wines are thin on the ground, but there's a
reasonable selection over £5. Burgundy perhaps suffers from an
over-emphasis on négociant wines, although those from Faiveley are
of considerable class. Chablis has domaine wines from Laroche.
Champagne features three houses – Beaumet, De Meric and Bollinger –
as well as the house Champagne from André Simon (Brut NV, £8.99).

Best buys

Beaujolais Chénas 1985, Paul Sapin, £5.29; Ch Canteloup 1983,
St-Estèphe, £4.95; Sherries from Garvey and Barbadillo; Cabernet Vino
da Tavola, £2.60

Blayneys Wine Merchants

HEAD OFFICE Riverside Road,   TEL 091-548 4488
Sunderland, Tyne & Wear SR5 3JW
175 branches in the North

OPEN Generally Mon–Sat 10–10   Sun, public holidays 12–2, 7–10
CLOSED Chr Day   CREDIT CARDS Access, Visa; personal and business
accounts by arrangement   DISCOUNTS 5% on 1 case   DELIVERY Free from
selected branches only   GLASS HIRE Free   TASTINGS AND TALKS Occasional
in-store tastings   CELLARAGE Not available

This group of off-licences has been expanded in the past two years
with the takeover of Dickens Wine Houses in Yorkshire and some
branches of Agnews. Encouragingly their range of wines has begun to
improve.

While they still go in for aberrations like a big range of British
Sherries, we also find the Real Thing in Barbadillo Manzanilla (£3.95)
and Gonzalez Byass Caballero (£3.95). They have assembled a good
range of Ports, too, including some vintage wines.

Moving to table wines, we find the same mix of the boring and the
interesting. Clarets are good and well balanced (only the wine
warehouses stock the full range of classed growths, but most branches
carry a selection of the petit château wines). Italy, for example, is a
disaster area; but then Spain does well with Faustino Riojas and Torres
Gran Coronas. Germany is a write-off, made up for in the New World
by a good splurge of Brown Brothers in Australia, and Cooks and
Montana in New Zealand.

Best buys

Champagne de Clairval Brut, £8.25; Alsace Riesling 1985, Kuehn,
£4.85; Beaujolais Villages 1986 Regnié, Loron, £3.69; Ch les Ormes de
Pez 1983, £6.59; Rioja Gran Reserva, Faustino I 1981, £5.25; Manzanilla,
Barbadillo, £3.95

E H Booth

HEAD OFFICE 4–6 Fishergate, Preston,   TEL (0772) 51701
Lancashire PR1 3LJ
22 branches in Cumbria and Lancashire

OPEN (Generally) Mon–Fri 8.30–5.30   Sat 9–5   CLOSED Sun, Good Friday,
some public holidays   CREDIT CARDS Access, Visa   DISCOUNTS By
arrangement   DELIVERY Free on UK mainland (min 5 cases); otherwise £2 per
case; mail order available   GLASS HIRE Free   TASTINGS AND TALKS Tastings
available in-store; to groups on request (max 50 people)   CELLARAGE Not
available

Booths stores run two lists: a standard one, and another of fine wines
available on order and at the Fishergate, Preston branch. It is for this
fine wine list that Booths make it into the Guide.

The list is strong in traditional areas: Ports, clarets (with some mature vintages) and domaine-bottled and négociant Burgundy. But there is a nod in the direction of new trends, with Australian wines, some good mature Barolos and Brunellos from Italy and some California wines.

Best buys

Booths Gigondas 1983, £4.29; Mainzer Domherr Bacchus Kabinett, Guntrum, £3.49; Booths Rioja 1983, £2.69

Bordeaux Direct   ⊏⊐

New Aquitaine House, Paddock Road,   TEL (0734) 481711
Reading, Berkshire RG4 0JY
Bordeaux Direct, New Aquitaine House,   TEL (as above)
Paddock Road, Reading, Berkshire RG4 0JY

OPEN 7 days a week (answering service outside office hours)
CLOSED 24 Dec–1 Jan   CREDIT CARDS All accepted; business accounts
DISCOUNTS Available on wines on special offer   DELIVERY Free nationally
(min £50 order); mail order available   GLASS HIRE Not available
TASTINGS AND TALKS Regular tastings in Wine Club Shop; to large groups on
request   CELLARAGE £? per case per year

Bordeaux Direct is the mail order arm of the Sunday Times Wine Club (also known as the Wine Club). Their retail arm is the Taste Shop. All three names operate from a continually varying list, following a policy of buying parcels of wines from lesser-known areas or discovering new producers or new regions of the world. You need to be a member to buy from them.

Certain names nevertheless remain stable. They are an eclectic bunch, including Martinez Bujanda Riojas, Jekel Vineyards in California, Columbia Winery in Washington State, Los Vascos Estate in Chile, Tomas Abad Sherries, the Co-operative of Kitzenheim in Alsace and Hunters Estate in New Zealand.

A recent list also came up with Barolo and Dolcetto from Voerzio, Bruno Paillard Champagne, some good domaine-bottled Burgundy, German estate wines, and Côtes du Forez from the upper reaches of the Loire. Bulgarian wines continue to be good value, and there are plenty of sample cases to help try out new discoveries.

It seems a pity, though, to have to report complaints from club members about poor and slow service. We would be grateful for more reports, please.

Most wine merchants will hire out glasses free of charge, provided they are collected and returned clean, and that you are buying enough wine to fill them! In most cases, it's first come, first served, so get your order in early to ensure supply.

WHERE TO BUY

Best buys

Corbières 1986, Cave Embres et Castelmaure, £3.25; Los Vascos Cabernet Sauvignon 1985, Chile, £3.99; Tomas Abad Fresh Dry Fino, £5.39; Rioja Gran Reserva 1975, Conde de Valdamar, £6.99

Bordeaux Direct Taste Shops ⊨

HEAD OFFICE 9 Ashmere Terrace,   TEL (0734) 393277
Loverock Road, Reading, Berkshire RG3 1DZ
10 shops in Berkshire, Buckinghamshire, Hertfordshire, Oxfordshire and Surrey

OPEN Mon–Wed, Fri 12–7 Thur 12–9 Sat 9–6 CLOSED Sun, public holidays CREDIT CARDS All accepted; personal and business accounts DISCOUNTS Available DELIVERY Free on UK mainland (min £50 order); otherwise £3.50 per address; mail order available GLASS HIRE Free with min 6 bottle purchase TASTINGS AND TALKS Wines available in-store every day; theme tastings Thur evenings, to groups on request CELLARAGE Not available

These Taste Shops are associated with Bordeaux Direct (see the previous page), and likewise operate from a constantly changing list. All that can be guaranteed is that somewhere in the list will be a new discovery, somehow the hallmark of this organisation.

As illustration, on a recent version, we find a new range of Portuguese wines (Douro 1986, Adega Cooperativa d'Alijo, £2.99; Bairrada Cave de Souseleas 1985, £3.49); Riojas from Bodegas Martinez Bujanda; and the owner's own Bordeaux Ch la Clarière of Tony Laithwaite (the 1985 vintage at £5.95).

Best buys

Los Vascos Chilean Cabernet Sauvignon, £3.99; Jurançon Grains Nobles, Cave de Gan, £3.39; Fino Sherry, Tomas Abad, £5.39; Cariñena Gran Ducay 1984, Bodega San Valero, £3.99

Borg Castel

Samlesbury Mill, Goosefoot Lane,   TEL (025 485) 2128
Samlesbury Bottoms, Preston, Lancashire PR5 0RN

OPEN Mon–Wed, Fri 10–5 Thur 7–9.30 Sat Possible 1st Sun of each month CLOSED Sun, except as above, some public holidays CREDIT CARDS None accepted; personal and business accounts DISCOUNTS Quantity discounts available DELIVERY Free within 30-mile radius (min 1 case); elsewhere negotiable; mail order available GLASS HIRE Free with case order TASTINGS AND TALKS In-store tastings every Thur evening and first Sun each month; 2 annual tastings by invitation; to groups (30–50 people) on request CELLARAGE Negotiable

Two lists operate at this merchant. One, a fine wine list, takes in some mature vintages of claret, some old red Burgundies (mainly négociant wines), a few Sauternes and some Vintage Ports.

The other covers more everyday wines, but with some good clarets (and plenty of petit château wines), négociant Burgundy from Vallet Frères, a good range of Alsace from Caves Tradition at Turckheim (in particular, the Tokay Pinot Gris 1986 at £4.10). Some interest occurs on the Loire, too, with Savennières Domaine de la Bizolière 1985 at £4.38 and Sancerre from Gitton Père et Fils.

There are German estate wines, some from Plettenberg on the Nahe, others from Deinhard, but many, on the list at least, from unknown producers. Italy has what could be an interesting range of wines – but, again, no producers. In Spain, look for wines from CVNE in Rioja.

Best buys

Ch Laroche 1981, Premières Côtes de Bordeaux, £4.66; Marcilly Selection NV, French Vin de Table, £3.48; Alsace wines from the Turckheim co-operative

Bottle and Basket

15 Highgate High Street, London N6 5JT   TEL 01-341 7018

OPEN Mon–Fri and bank holidays 11–3, 5–9   Sat 11–9   Sun and religious holidays 12–2, 7–9   CLOSED Chr Day   CREDIT CARDS Access, Visa DISCOUNTS 5% on 1 case collected   DELIVERY Free within 2-mile radius excluding the City (min 1 case); elsewhere not available   GLASS HIRE Free with reasonable order   TASTINGS AND TALKS Occasional in-store tastings on Saturdays   CELLARAGE Not available

Spain calls the tune here but treats elsewhere would also make a visit to this small shop in Highgate Village worthwhile.

Taking Spain first: there's an excellent range of Riojas, with some old vintages (Tondonia Gran Reserva 1973, £11.78), coupled with newer, lighter sin crianza wines (Señor Burgues 1985, £2.66). Other Spanish reds are mainly from Penedès (and Torres) but also include Vega Sicilia and some less expensive wines from Ribera del Duero. In whites, look for the old-style Riojas of Tondonia (1981 at £5.80), or, in Sherries, for the Don Zoilo range.

Following the fashion, Australia has arrived, bringing wines from Tyrrell's, Hardy's, Wolf Blass and Brown Brothers. New Zealand's advent is marked by bottles from Stoneleigh Vineyards. There are also Israeli wines from the Golan Heights (Yarden Sauvignon, £6.27).

In France, the main strengths are Alsace wines from Willm and Dopff au Moulin and some interesting regional labels – Nielluccio from Corsica (the 1986 vintage is £3.47) or varietal wines from Chantovent in the South of France. Bordeaux is rather pricey, and Burgundy is better in Beaujolais than in Burgundy proper. There's a good range of Champagne.

Best buys

Rioja 1981, Solar de Samaniego, £3.57; Quinta de Santo Amaro 1985, João Pires, Portugal, £3.04; Ruffino Chiantis; Cava Freixenet Brut Nature 1984, £4.94

Bottoms Up

See Peter Dominic.

Bretzel Foods

See Winecellars.

G E Bromley

London Street, Leicester, Leicestershire LE5 3RH	TEL (0533) 768471
271 Leicester Road, Wigston Fields, Leicester, Leicestershire LE8 1JW	TEL (0533) 882057
J H Measures & Sons, The Crescent, Spalding, Lincolnshire PE11 1AF	TEL (0775) 2676

OPEN (Leicester) Tue-Fri 10–1, 5–9.30   Sat 10–1, 6–10   Sun 12–2, 7–9.30; (Wigston) Mon–Sat 10–1, 5–10   Sun 12–1.30, 7–10; (Spalding) Mon–Sat 9–6 CLOSED Sun, most public holidays (Spalding) CREDIT CARDS Access, Visa; personal and business accounts   DISCOUNTS 2.5% on 5 cases, 5% on 12+ cases   DELIVERY Free in Lincoln, Boston, Holbeach, Peterborough, Wellingborough, Rugby, Nuneaton, Ashby, Derby, Nottingham and Newark (min 3 cases); otherwise 1 case £3.45, 2 cases £2.30; elsewhere at cost; mail order available   GLASS HIRE Free with 1-case order   TASTINGS AND TALKS In-store tastings; to groups on request   CELLARAGE £2.40 per case per year

While perhaps too many dull branded wines figure on this list, there is also some good, solid stuff. Much of it is French-based, but we perceive an increasing interest in Australia, and some fine bottles from Spain.

Starting in the depths of the French countryside, there's good basic red and white Vin de Pays de la Vallée du Paradis from near Narbonne (£2.98), Vin de Pays des Côtes de Gascogne, Ch de Fonscolombe Coteaux d'Aix-en-Provence and the Minervois of Domaine Ste-Eulalie. Moving to Bordeaux, G E Bromley & Sons have unearthed some good petit château wines as well as crus bourgeois, with vintages back to 1970 for the top classed growths (Ch Haut-Batailley 1970 at £25.07).

Burgundy provides mainly négociant wines (Chanson predominating) while on the Rhône, wines from Guigal and Jaboulet Aîné in the north, and Châteauneuf-du-Pape from Ch de Beaucastel and Domaine du Vieux Télégraphe in the south, would all make for enjoyable drinking. Also look for the Côtes du Rhône 1986, Ch du Grand Moulas. Alsace comes from Pierre Blanck, while house Champagne is from Baron de Beaupré (£8.39).

Star areas outside France number some good German estate wines, especially in the Rheinpfalz, and Torres wines from Spain, plus a few goodies in Portugal (Garrafeira 1974, Caves Velhas at £3.89). Then to Australia, and we find Rosemount, Tisdall, Brown Brothers, Rouge Homme and Renmano among other fine names.

Best buys

Minervois 1985, Domaine Ste-Eulalie, £2.99; Tyrrell's Long Flat Red 1984, Hunter Valley, £3.79; Reiler vom Heissen Stein Riesling und Müller-Thurgau Kabinett 1985, Rudolf Müller, £3.21; Chianti Rufina 1985, Villa di Vetrice, £3.16

Buckingham Wines

157 Great Portland Street, London W1N 5FB	TEL 01-580 1622
98 Holland Park Avenue, London W11 3RB	TEL 01-727 5148
6 Fulham Road, London SW3 6HG	TEL 01-584 1450
282 Old Brompton Road, London SW5 9HR	TEL 01-370 4402
71 Abingdon Road, London W8 6AW	TEL 01-937 3996

OPEN Mon–Fri 9–7.30   Sat 10–7.30 (W1); Mon–Sat 10–9.30   Sun 12–2, 7–9 (W11 & SW3); Mon–Sat 10.30–10.30   Sun 12–2, 7–9 (SW5); Mon–Sat 10.30–8.30 (W8)   CLOSED Sun, public holidays (W1 and W8) CREDIT CARDS Access, Visa; personal and business accounts   DISCOUNTS 5% on 1 case collected   DELIVERY Free within 1-mile radius of each store (min 1 bottle); elsewhere variable; mail order available   GLASS HIRE Free with appropriate case order   TASTINGS AND TALKS Six+ bottles normally open at all times in-store; to groups on request   CELLARAGE Charges negotiable

Although this small group of shops, with smart addresses in west and central London, is strongest in Bordeaux and Champagne, it manages to wander from the straight and narrow into some interesting byways.

The main source of pride is the clarets, particularly attractive for their strong showing of old vintages – something only a few wine merchants can offer – with plenty from 1970, 1966, even 1961 and 1945, and much in between. Obviously, these wines are not cheap, but prices here are comparable with those found at auction.

Champagne is a must for a wine merchant in such yuppie neighbourhoods. Buckinghams have stocked up on plenty of wines from the major grande marque houses, as well as their house Champagne (Jean Lemoine at £8.95).

Although the rest of the list is leaner, items of interest include some good pudding wines from Bordeaux; Schoech and Trimbach wines from Alsace; Tiefenbrunner and Lageder wines from the Italian Südtirol; German estate wines; some good Riojas (look for Viña Real, and Caves Oro Vales Gran Reserva at £5.50); Concha y Toro Chilean wines; and Brown Brothers wines from Australia. Even a Russian Crimean wine puts in an appearance. Whiskies are pretty good, too.

Best buys

Monte Nero, Caliga (Greece), £3.95; Caves Oro Vales Gran Reserva, Rioja, £5.50; Las Lomas Tinto (Utiel Requena, Spain), £3.15; old vintages of claret

Burlington Wines

46 Burlington Road, Ipswich, Suffolk IP1 2HS   TEL (0473) 50242

OPEN Mon–Fri 9–5.45   Sat 9–1   CLOSED Sun, public holidays
CREDIT CARDS None accepted; business accounts   DISCOUNTS 5% on orders of £200 and 4 unmixed cases   DELIVERY Free in City of London and central Ipswich and elsewhere for 6+ cases; otherwise London postal district £1.50 per case, elsewhere £1.95 per case, with a minimum of £5 per delivery; mail order available   GLASS HIRE Free   TASTINGS AND TALKS Wines always available in-store; to groups on request   CELLARAGE £1.50 per case per year   ■

This is the wholesale side of Wines of Interest (*q.v.*).

The Butlers Wine Cellar

247 Queens Park Road, Brighton,   TEL (0273) 698724
East Sussex BN2 2XJ

OPEN Mon–Fri 9–5.30   Sat 9–1   CLOSED Sun, public holidays
CREDIT CARDS Visa; business accounts   DISCOUNTS Not available
DELIVERY Free within 15-mile radius (min 1 case); mail order available
GLASS HIRE Free with 1-case order   TASTINGS AND TALKS, CELLARAGE Not available

Owner Geoffrey Butler runs a rapidly-changing list of bin-ends, many of them mature clarets and Burgundies, and regular customers get sent anything between eight and ten updates a year. Prices are keen.

On a recent list, for example, clarets go back to 1961 in quantity, with a few even older examples, such as 1928 Ch Bel-Orme-Tronquoy-de-Lalande at £85 a bottle. There are an encouraging number of half-bottles of these older wines, as well. Red Burgundies go back to 1962 and whites to 1968.

But the range of bin-ends doesn't stop with these two classic areas – there are good numbers of Rhône wines (although these tend to be younger), of German wines from the classic 1976 vintage (again a good number of halves), and, at a more mundane level, an attractive set of French regional wines. The Portuguese section on this particular issue had the excellent red Reguengos de Monsaraz 1986 at £3.25, while there were old soleras of Valdespino Sherries and Lomelino Madeiras. The changing list of old vintage Ports is an enjoyable read, too.

Best buys

Mature clarets

Anthony Byrne Fine Wines

SALES OFFICE Kingscote House, TEL (0487) 814555
Biggin Lane, Ramsey, Cambridgeshire PE17 1NB
WINE WAREHOUSE 88 High Street, TEL (as above)
Ramsey, Cambridgeshire PE17 1BS
OPEN Mon–Fri 9–6 Sat 9–5.30 CLOSED Sun, public holidays
CREDIT CARDS Access, Visa; personal and business accounts DISCOUNTS 5%
on mixed cases, 10% on unmixed cases DELIVERY Free in UK (min 2 cases
which may be mixed) GLASS HIRE Free with 1-case order
TASTINGS AND TALKS Programme of tastings throughout the year at various
locations CELLARAGE £1.95 per case per year

While the heart of Anthony Byrne's list remains in Burgundy and
Beaujolais, much is to be found elsewhere. The company imports
directly from individual growers and gradually develops a region or a
country as buyers visit that area.

This, for example, is what has happened in Italy. We now find wines
from Maculan in Breganze in the Veneto near Vicenza (try the Pinot
Nero 1986 at £5.52), or the Vinattieri wines made by the formidable
combination of Burton Anderson, Maurizio Castelli and Alois Lageder
in Tuscany and the Südtirol.

The Loire is likewise now an area of some importance. Apart from
old favourites such as the top quality Pouilly Fumé of Didier
Dagueneau and the Muscadets of Sauvion, there's Sancerre from
Vincent Pinard, Lucien Crochet and Serge Laloue, and Ménétou-Salon
from no fewer than three producers, plus the terrific value of the wines
from the Touraine co-operative of Oisly-et-Thésée. Alsace, too, comes
in for a strong showing, with a huge range of wines from Zind
Humbrecht, while Champagne is from André Drappier (Carte d'Or
NV, £11.52).

To Burgundy. Here is a roll call of many of the top names in the
region, and it is obvious that it needs constant visits to the area to build
up a list of this quality. Bernard Bachelet is a favoured name, but he is
joined by Tollot Beaut, Gagnard Delagrange, Domaine Arnoux,
Armand Rousseau, Clerget, Charles Viénot. From just further south,
the Beaujolais is from Georges Duboeuf, and there are cuvées here
which no other merchant stocks.

The Bordeaux list is less interesting, although we would recommend
the house clarets and the old vintages of the Sauternes Ch Gilette.
The Rhône manages another, but shorter, roll call of names: Guigal,
Jaboulet Aîné, Domaine des Entrefaux in Crozes-Hermitage, Clos
St-Jean in Châteauneuf-du-Pape.

A series of tastings keeps customers fully occupied, and if you have
problems finding a wine for your dinner party, Anthony Byrne has a
computer programme which matches wine and food.

WHERE TO BUY

Best buys

Wines from the Confrérie of Oisly-et-Thésée; Sauvion Muscadets; Cuvée Duboeuf Rouge, £2.91; Bourgogne Passetoutgrain 1985, Domaine Arnoux, £4.85; Ch Trinité Valrose 1985, Bordeaux Supérieur, £4.55

D Byrne & Co   ✉

12 King Street, Clitheroe,   TEL (0200) 23152
Lancashire BB7 2EP

OPEN Mon, Wed, Sat 9–6   Thur, Fri 9–8   CLOSED Sun, public holidays
CREDIT CARDS None accepted; personal and business accounts
DISCOUNTS £1 on mixed case, £1.20 on unmixed case, 5% on orders over £250
DELIVERY Free within 50-mile radius of Clitheroe; otherwise £4 for 1 case, £3.50
per case for 2 cases, 3 cases free; mail order available   GLASS HIRE Free with
1-case order   TASTINGS AND TALKS Regular in-store tastings; to groups on
request   CELLARAGE Free

We still suspect that this formidable list of wines would be off-putting to most people – just a mass of names with hardly any comment, and doing little justice to its encyclopaedic nature.

But to begin at the beginning: clarets go back to 1978, with some occasional bargains (Ch Victoria, a cru bourgeois, is £5.19 for the 1982 vintage; or Ch Pontet Canet 1983 is £9.45). Burgundy still tends to be dominated by Chanson wines, but there are treats like the wines from Tollot Beaut or Armand Rousseau in reds and the Chablis of Henri Laroche. Rhône wines feature Chapoutier, plus a wealth of Châteauneuf-du-Papes (including Ch Fortia or Ch de Beaucastel). Beaujolais is weighty with Georges Duboeuf wines and Alsace has an enormous selection from big names like Hugel, Trimbach, Louis Gisselbrecht, Dopff et Irion and Dopff au Moulin.

The comprehensive nature continues beyond France. A wide span of German estate wines covers plenty of famous names – Dr Weil, Deinhard and Bürklin-Wolf in the Rhine vineyards; von Schubert and Bischöfliches Konvikt on the Mosel.

Then we move through a good collection of Riojas, Alto Adige wines from Tiefenbrunner, Chiantis and Barolos, and some rarities from Italy such as the Breganze di Breganze of Maculan in the Veneto (£4.09) and wines from Nera in the Valtellina.

Then on to the New World. The Australian collection continues to be a *Who's Who* – Hardy's, Rosemount, Brown Brothers, Orlando, Rothbury Estate . . . California, too, is encouragingly strong on Chardonnay and Cabernet Sauvignon.

Best buys

German estate wines; Viña Linderos Cabernet Sauvignon 1982 (Chile), £3.69; Inferno 1982, Nino Negri, £3.35; Chardonnay 1985, Tiefenbrunner, £3.55; Alsace wines

Cachet Wines

61–65 Heworth Road, York, TEL (0904) 425853
North Yorkshire YO3 0AA

OPEN Mon–Sat 10–6 CLOSED Sun, public holidays CREDIT CARDS None
accepted; personal and business accounts DISCOUNTS 5% on 1 unmixed
case DELIVERY Free within 30-mile radius (min 1 case); otherwise £3 in
Yorkshire; elsewhere at cost GLASS HIRE Free TASTINGS AND TALKS To
groups on request CELLARAGE £1.50 per case per year

French wines are the central theme of this list, but there are plenty of
excursions to Italy (for Chianti Classico from Villa Cerna and Barolos
from Oddero), to Spain (for CVNE Riojas), to Portugal (for João Pires
wines – Palmela Dry Muscat at £3.80), and further afield to California
(an interesting range which includes Sanford and Mark West wines)
and Australia (for Orlando, Jacob's Creek and Rosemount).

   Back to France: on the Loire are wines from the Confrérie des
Vignerons de Oisly-et-Thésée (Sauvignon de Touraine at £4.25) and
Muscadet from Domaine l'Ebaupin (the 1987 vintage is £2.99). Alsace
has wines from Willy Gisselbrecht, while Burgundy has domaine
wines from Jean Pascal (Bourgogne Chardonnay 1986 at £5.80) and
Domaine Parent. On the Rhône, there are wines from the Perrin family
of Cru de Coudoulet (Côtes du Rhône) and Ch de Beaucastel
(Châteauneuf-du-Pape), as well as La Vieille Ferme wines. The
Bordeaux list offers some good value – the Bordeaux Supérieur of
Ch Parenchère 1981 is £3.85, Ch de Cruzeau 1981, Graves is £4.30.

   In the area of fortified wines, Ramos Pinto is the featured Port
house, Garvey the Sherry firm. Georges Gardet is the featured
Champagne (Brut Spécial NV at £8.75).

Best buys

Ch Parenchère 1981, Bordeaux Supérieur, £3.85; Champagne Gardet
Brut Spécial NV, £8.75; Côtes de St-Mont 1986, Producteurs de
Plaimont, £2.16; Côtes du Lubéron 1987, La Vieille Ferme Blanc, £2.65;
Jacob's Creek red and white, £2.65

Cadwgan Fine Wine Merchants

152A Ashley Road, Hale, Altrincham, TEL 061-928 0357
Cheshire WA15 9SA

OPEN Mon–Fri 11–8 Sat 9–8 CLOSED Sun, public holidays
CREDIT CARDS Access, Visa DISCOUNTS 5% on 1 unmixed case
DELIVERY Free within 10-mile radius from shop (min 2 cases); elsewhere at cost;
mail order available GLASS HIRE Free within 1-case order
TASTINGS AND TALKS Monthly tastings by arrangement; bi-monthly tastings at
local hotel; to groups on request CELLARAGE Not available

This is still very much a French-based list, although both Spain and
Italy have well thought out contributions.

The French section is strongest in classic areas. A major interest is Champagne, with wines from Aubry (Brut NV at £9.41), De Castellane, Pol Roger, Louis Roederer, Bricout, Alfred Gratien and Krug (Brut Vintage 1976 at £38.60) – a good range of prices and qualities. Then we turn to a mixed bag of Burgundies, with plenty of basic wines (Bourgogne Pinot Noir 1983, Vallet Frères at £6.85) as well as some domaine bottles, mainly from négociants. In Bordeaux, there are wines stretching back to the 1966 vintage, with the main concentration around 1983 (good buys from 1981).

The Loire features Savennières and Quarts de Chaume from Jean Baumard and Vouvray from Gaston Huet, and the Rhône has Côtes du Rhône Villages from the Rasteau co-operative. In Spain, the list homes in on CVNE Riojas and Torres wines (and Garvey Sherries), while in Italy, Soave from Pieropan and the Montefalco d'Arquata of Adanti (as well as Carema White Label) are good choices. German estate wines are from Deinhard. New World wines concentrate on Montrose in Australia, the fortified stickies of Baileys of Glenrowan and Babich New Zealand wines.

Two new branches are planned for this firm, both due to be open by the end of 1988.

Best buys

Champagne Aubry NV, £9.41; Savennières 1986, Jean Baumard, £4.99; Alsace wines from Cave des Vignerons de Turckheim; Rasteau Côtes du Rhône Villages 1985, £3.80; Bianco di Custoza 1987, Portalupi, £3.85

Cairns & Hickey

17 Blenheim Terrace, Woodhouse Lane,   TEL (0532) 459501
Leeds, West Yorkshire LS2 9HN

OPEN Mon–Fri 9–6   Sat 9–1   CLOSED Sun, public holidays
CREDIT CARDS None accepted; personal and business accounts
DISCOUNTS 5% on wine case lots   DELIVERY Free within 25-mile radius of Leeds; elsewhere at cost; mail order available   GLASS HIRE Free within suitable wine order   TASTINGS AND TALKS Wines always available in-store; to groups on request   CELLARAGE £2.50 per case per year

French wines – and classic French wines at that – are the main strengths of this list. While Cairns & Hickey dip a toe into Germany (with estate wines from Deinhard), another into Spain (with some good Reserva and Gran Reserva Riojas), Italy (just) and the New World (only just), everything really revolves around claret and Burgundy.

'Some sound wines but with few excitements' is our verdict. In Burgundy, among the négociant wines from Louis Latour, Chanson and Bouchard Père, we also find some good basic Pinot Noir Bourgogne Rouge (Louis Latour at £4.70 or Charles Viénot at £4.90). Next door is Chablis from William Fèvre and Domaine Laroche (Chablis Grand Cru Blanchots 1984 at £12.50).

In Bordeaux, the list tends to get to classed growths too quickly, with not enough wine in the middle and lower price ranges. But in the upper echelons you will find a range of wines from the 1982 and 1983 vintages, back to an excellent selection of the classics from 1961. Other vintages and wines appear on the bin-end lists (issued six times a year). Other French areas are covered more perfunctorily – Guy Saget and Jean Baumard on the Loire; Hugel and Dopff et Irion in Alsace. Outside France, look for the interesting range of Vintage Ports.

Best buys

Faugères 1985, Cuvée Jules Gaston, £2.55; Rioja 1985, Campo Viejo, £2.95; Colares 1974, Real Vinícola, £3.30; Champagne Charles Diss, £8.25; Vintage Ports

Alistair Cameron

6 Stradbroke Road, London N5 2PZ

As we went to press, Alistair Cameron closed his business and can now be found at the Kensington Park Road branch of Corney & Barrow.

Cantina Augusto

91–95 Clerkenwell Road, London EC1R 5BX   TEL 01-242 3246
OPEN Mon–Thur 9–6   Fri 9–6.30   Sat mornings in Dec   CLOSED Sun, public
holidays   CREDIT CARDS Access, Visa; personal and business accounts
DISCOUNTS Approximately 10% on 1 case   DELIVERY Free in London (min
£100 order), £2 charge for orders under £50, £1 charge for orders £50–£100;
elsewhere at cost; mail order possible   GLASS HIRE Free with order
TASTINGS AND TALKS Regular promotional tastings; to groups on request
CELLARAGE Not available

Despite an increase in the range of French wines, and some interesting
developments in Portugal (try the Garrafeira Particular 1978 of Caves
Borlido at £4.80), the main interest here still centres on Italy.

Tuscany has received some recent attention: on the one hand are
whites from Antinori and Carla Guarnieri (Bianco della Lanciola 1986,
£3.50), and on the other reds from the Chianti Classico Le Chiantigiane
co-operative and Ruffino, as well as Vino Nobile di Montepulciano of
Tenuta Santa Agnese and Brunello from La Poderina. Look also for the
super vino da tavola of Guarnieri, called Terricci (the 1983 vintage is
£8.40).

Other regions to fare well are Sicily (Regaleali and Corvo wines),
Piedmont (Barolo from Pio Cesare and Prunotto) and the Südtirol
(Niedermayer Weissburgunder 1986 at £3.70). Look, too, for rarities
like Neri's Inferno at £4.40, and Friuli wines of Angoris, or the
Mastroberardino Taurasi 1983 at £8.85.

Best buys
Südtirol Chardonnay 1987, Niedermayer, £3.85; Pinot Nero 1985,
Angoris, £3.95; Freisa 1987, Damilano, £3.45; Sangiovese di Romagna
1986, Coltiva, £1.99

C C Enterprises

See the Wine Schoppen.

Special awards

🐷 means bargain prices (good *value* may be obtained from merchants
without this symbol, of course, if you are prepared to pay for service)

🏵 means that the wines stocked are of consistently high quality

▱ means that the merchant stocks an above-average range

☞ means that extra-special service is offered: helpful advice, informative
lists and newsletters, tastings etc.

Champagne and Caviar Shop

18 Leadenhall Market, London EC3U 1LR   TEL 01-626 4912

OPEN Mon–Fri 9–6   CLOSED Sat, Sun, public holidays
CREDIT CARDS Access, Amex, Visa; personal and business accounts
DISCOUNTS 5–10% (min 1 case)   DELIVERY Free in the City (min £50 order)
and central London (min £100 order); otherwise £1.50 in the City; £3.50 in central
London, £4.50 in Greater London, £5.50 within M25; mail order available
GLASS HIRE Free   TASTINGS AND TALKS Occasional in-store tastings
CELLARAGE Free

Life is very simple here – if also dwelling on its finer points. It's
Champagne (and caviar) all the way, and Grande Marque Champagnes
only, at that. Prices – perhaps considering the location – tend not to be
the cheapest around.

From Ayala (Brut NV at £13.50) through the alphabet to Veuve
Clicquot (Yellow Label Brut at £15.75), there are wines from 27
producers, generally two or three from each, including a non-vintage,
a vintage and a luxury cuvée, plus plenty of half-bottles for those who
want to lessen the strain on their wallets.

Best buys

Mercier Brut Réserve, £10; Ruinart Brut NV, £15.75; Canard-Duchêne
Brut NV, £12

Champagne de Villages

Park House, 29 Fonnereau Road, Ipswich,   TEL (0473) 56922
Suffolk IP1 3JR

OPEN Mon–Fri 9–5.30   CLOSED Sat, Sun, public holidays
CREDIT CARDS Access; personal and business accounts   DISCOUNTS Available
(min 5 cases)   DELIVERY Free within 10-mile radius of Ipswich (min 1 case) and
for orders of 5+ cases; otherwise £6.30 per case; mail order available
GLASS HIRE Free with 1-case order   TASTINGS AND TALKS Regular tastings
held for customers; to groups on request   CELLARAGE £3.50 per case per year ■

As is right and proper, Champagne remains the most interesting part
of this list, although other areas of France are covered too.

The Champagne pages present an unusual range of wines from
growers, many from the top vineyard areas in the region. Look out for
the wines of Michel Labbé in Chaméry or Pierre Arnould in Verzenay,
both in the Montagne de Reims and both making wines entirely from
the Pinot Noir for which the Montagne is most famous. Or, as a
contrast, there are the 100 per cent Chardonnay wines of Georges
Lilbert – his lower pressure Crémant is particularly enjoyable (£12.02 –
prices do not include VAT on the list, but we have included it here).

Champagne de Villages also stock still Champenois wines – the
Rouge from Raymond Davilliers, the white from Georges Lilbert, and

the Rosé de Riceys of Alexandre Bonnet, from the village of that name, which is made only in tiny quantities in favourable years (£13.86).

The philosophy of buying from owner/producers is applied to the rest of France, so Ch Caillou of Jean Bernard is the featured château in Barsac, while Ch Perron represents Lalande de Pomerol (the 1981 vintage is £7.99). There are pricier offerings from Domaine du Chevalier and Ch Laville-Haut-Brion (the 1983 vintage is £50.48 a bottle).

In other areas, look for the Burgundies of Delaunay and the domaine white wines of Jean Pascal in Puligny-Montrachet. Other pockets of interest are the wines of Michel Bahuaud in Muscadet and of Masson-Blondelet in Pouilly Fumé, country wines from Cahors and Bergerac and some estate wines from the south.

Best buys

Champagne Vieille Réserve Brut, Jean-Paul Arvois, £10.23; Ch Perron 1981, Lalande de Pomerol, £7.99; Quincy 1987, P et J Mardon, £4.89; Côtes de Bergerac Rouge 1985, Ch Grand Conseil, £4.14

The Champagne House

15 Dawson Place, London W2 4TH   TEL 01-221 5538

OPEN Mon–Thur 9.30–6   CLOSED Fri, Sat, Sun, public holidays
CREDIT CARDS None accepted   DISCOUNTS Negotiable (min 3 cases)
DELIVERY Free in Kensington, Chelsea, Westminster, City of London (min 1 case); elsewhere at cost; mail order available   GLASS HIRE Free with 1-case order   TASTINGS AND TALKS Tutored tastings for established customers; to selected groups on request   CELLARAGE Not available   ■

This is probably the most comprehensive range of Champagnes in the Guide, and certainly one of the best. The list is also immensely informative about Champagne in general and about the producers from whom they buy in particular.

Some of the producers are small firms, making wines from their own vineyards as well as acting as négociants (Robert Driant, Roland Fliniaux). Others are some of the top grande marque houses (Krug, Pol Roger, Bollinger). The best prices appear in the first category.

In both are to be found a variety of vintage and non-vintage wines and also some of the cuvées prestige from the top firms, such as Bollinger's Vieilles Vignes or Perrier-Jouët's Belle Epoque. Look, too, for the still white Coteaux Champenois or go for a tasting case (£150).

Best buys

Albert Le Brun Cuvée Réserve, NV, £9.90; Roland Fliniaux, Les Années de Folie, NV, £12.50; Gosset 1982, £17.94

Chaplin & Son

35 Rowlands Road, Worthing,   TEL (0903) 35888
West Sussex BN11 3JJ

OPEN Mon–Sat 8.45–1.15, 2.15–5.30   CLOSED Sun, public holidays
CREDIT CARDS Access, Visa; business accounts   DISCOUNTS 5% on 1 mixed
case   DELIVERY Free within 10-mile radius (min 1 case); elsewhere at cost; mail
order available   GLASS HIRE Free with appropriate order
TASTINGS AND TALKS Frequent in-store tastings; to groups on request
CELLARAGE Not available

Chaplins will be 100 years old in 1989, and they promise tastings and
celebrations. Their list continues to be sound and workmanlike, with a
sensible range of wines in most areas. We particularly like their range
of fortified wines – especially their Sherries (the house Sherries are Tio
Carlos – Fino £3.39), but there's also a range from other top producers.
The same goes for Champagnes (the house Champagne is their
own-label Charles Balachat at £8.45).

Moving on to table wines, clarets from vintages back to 1978 are
presented in price rather than vintage order, so we start with
Ch Faurie-Pascaud 1984 at £3.13 and move on to Ch la Conseillante
1982 at £30. Bordeaux prices have remained pretty constant since last
year – some have even gone down. Beaujolais is from Loron, and there
are Burgundies from Labouré-Roi and Antonin Rodet. Jaboulet Aîné
wines are the stars from the Rhône, but Chaplins offer surprisingly
small selections from the Loire and Alsace. Listel wines from the south
of France (Domaine du Bosquet 1982, £3.35) represent good value.

Outside France, Germany is passed over quickly, but Italy comes up
with some top wines at good prices (Barolo Riserva 1980, Borgogno at
£5.99; Frascati Colli di Catone 1986 at £3.29). A big range of the
admirable Torres wines from Spain contrasts with the less demanding
California offerings by Paul Masson. Look for a full range of Penfolds
Australians (including Grange Bin 95 1978 at £23.69 – regarded by
many as Australia's finest wine). The New Zealand selection has
expanded this year, although 1985 vintages of Sauvignon on their list
are probably past their best – stick to the Chardonnays of older
vintages. On the other hand the choice of malt whiskies seems to have
shrunk since last year, but Chaplins say they will order.

Best buys

Médoc, Nathaniel Johnston, £2.99; wines from Listel; Vinho Verde
Quinta da Aveleda, £3.29; CVNE Rioja Viña Real 1982, £3.59;
Champagne Charles Balachat, NV, £8.45; Tio Carlos Sherries

The symbol ■ indicates that wine is sold only by the case. However, most
wholesalers are usually happy to sell mixed cases.

Châteaux Wines

11 Church Street, Bishop's Lydeard, Taunton, TEL (0454) 613959
Somerset TA4 3AT

OPEN Mon–Fri 9–5.30 Sat most mornings until 12.30 CLOSED Sun, public
holidays CREDIT CARDS Access, Visa; personal and business accounts
DISCOUNTS Negotiable DELIVERY Free on UK mainland (min 1 case);
elsewhere at cost; mail order available GLASS HIRE Not available
TASTINGS AND TALKS Occasional in-house tastings; promotional tastings to
customers on request; to groups on request CELLARAGE £4 per case or
part-case per year for wines purchased from premises   ■

The name of this firm reflects the fact that, apart from their
Champagne, they buy almost exclusively from French estates rather
than from négociants. The majority of the French wines are bought
direct, and prices are good.

Perhaps contrary to expectation, Burgundy rather than Bordeaux is
the strong area. Look for the wines of Robert Ampeau in Beaune and
Volnay and the Chablis of Simmonet. The house Burgundy,
Proprietor's Reserve, is good value (white at £6.98, red at £5.94).
Champagne, from Laurent Perrier, covers a wide range.

Outside France, there are the Lebanese wines of Ch Musar (1979
vintage at £5.14, 1981 at £5.42), while Australian wines are from
Rosemount and Californian from Clos du Val.

Best buys

Proprietor's Reserve red Burgundy, £5.94; Ch St-Bonnet 1981, Médoc,
£4.75; Ch Musar 1979, £5.14; Laurent Perrier Champagnes

Chesterford Vintners   ☞

The Old Greyhound, Great Chesterford, TEL (0799) 30088
Saffron Walden, Essex CB10 1NY
Tempest, Slinger & Co
Town and Country Vintners
(address as above)

OPEN Mon–Wed 9.30–5.30 Thur–Fri 9.30–7.30 Sat 9–5 CLOSED Sun,
public holidays CREDIT CARDS Access, Visa; personal and business accounts
DISCOUNTS Quantity discounts DELIVERY Free within 25-mile radius of Great
Chesterfield and within central London (min 2 cases) and UK mainland (min 10
cases); otherwise single bottles–1 case £4.80 per consignment, 2–4 cases £2.80
per case, 5–9 cases £1.20 per case; mail order available GLASS HIRE Free with
order TASTINGS AND TALKS In-store tastings 3–4 times per year; to groups on
request CELLARAGE Possible; £5 per case per year

This is essentially a French list, where the rest of the world impinges
but lightly, but it's none the worse for that. All areas offer plenty of
choice. At the start we find growers' Champagnes (Alex de St-Ives
Grand Cru Champagne de Mesnil is £9.80) as well as more familiar

grande marque wines – and the rare still Coteaux Champenois wines as a bonus.

Then we move to a short but good value list of clarets (most under £8), a small range of Burgundies – again with an emphasis on value (try the Beaujolais-style Coteaux du Lyonnais of François Descôtes at £4.20 as more than a curiosity). The Loire choice is good, including the rarely seen wines of Cheverny (try the bone dry Romorantin from Cazin at £3.89), while there's another unusual, but good, set of wines from the region of Die, better known for the sparkling Clairette de Die (Chesterford have an example of this at £5.56).

On the Rhône, the search for the less familiar continues. Go for the Côtes du Rhône of Ch des Vallonnières (the 1987 vintage is £4.30) or the varietal wines of the Vignerons Ardéchois. Up in the Alps are the refreshingly crisp Savoie wines of Quenard.

Once we're past the Coteaux d'Aix wines of Ch la Coste and Trimbach Alsace wines, the list shortens. But there are still some good moments, with Italy offering Antinori wines (Castello della Salla from the Orvieto area at £5.98) and Brolio Chianti, and Torres wines from Spain. The climax comes with Sherries – from Delgado Zuleta, Gonzalez Byass and Domecq.

Best buys

Sauvignon de Cheverny 1987, Bernard and François Cazin, £3.89; Syrah Vin de Pays des Coteaux de l'Ardèche, Vignerons Ardéchois, £2.69; Gamay de Pays de la Drôme, Cellier Hannibal, £2.66

Chiswick Wine Cellar

84 Chiswick High Road, London W4 1SY   TEL 01-994 7989

OPEN Mon–Sat 10–10   Sun 12–2   CLOSED Public holidays
CREDIT CARDS None accepted   DISCOUNTS Available   DELIVERY Free in Chiswick and Hammersmith (min 1 case); otherwise at cost
GLASS HIRE Available   TASTINGS AND TALKS In-store tastings at the end of every month   CELLARAGE Not available

A wide-ranging selection of wines which particularly homes in on Italy. Look for Gavi dei Gavi 1985 of Villa Spanina at £5.49; Terre di Cortona 1986 from the great Montepulciano producer Avignonesi at £6.29; and mature vintages of Sassicaia, as well as the more everyday offerings. Elsewhere, there are Torres wines from Spain and Bulgarian wines.

Best buys

Jacob's Creek Australian red, £2.79; Bulgarian wines

Cellarage is generally provided at the rates quoted only when the wines have been bought from the merchant concerned.

Christchurch Fine Wine Co

1–3 Vine Lane, High Street, Christchurch,   TEL (0202) 473255
Dorset BH23 1AE

OPEN Mon–Sat 10–5   CLOSED Sun   CREDIT CARDS Visa   DISCOUNTS 5%
for Christchurch Fine Wine Club members   DELIVERY Free in Bournemouth
area (min 1 case); otherwise at cost; mail order available   GLASS HIRE Free with
1-case order   TASTINGS AND TALKS Club tastings every 3 weeks; to local
groups on request   CELLARAGE Not available

This is a new entry in our Guide, although readers of *The Good Food
Guide* will know the company under their Splinters Restaurant hat.
They have turned an old stable block into a retail shop, and have
started a wine club, a monthly newsletter and tutored tastings.

Their wine list lives up to this promising introduction. It begins with
a fine array of Champagnes – Jacquesson, Deutz, three vintages of
Dom Pérignon, Veuve Clicquot, Perrier-Jouët and De Venoge. Then
we move into a very strong range of mature clarets going back to 1961,
some at very good prices (it's a pity the list appears to be in no order at
all) – look for the range of Ch Cantemerle and Ch La Lagune. As befits
a restaurant, there are a good number of sweet white Bordeaux,
including half-bottles.

In Burgundy, we find more of the same quality and range of mature
vintages of reds. There's a mix between négociant wines (Prosper
Maufoux, Labouré-Roi) and domaine bottlings (Clair-Daü, Jacques
Prieur), and a big range from the Hospices de Beaune selection. On the
Loire, stars include Muscadet from Chereau and Quarts de Chaume
from Rochais, while the Rhône produces Chapoutier Côte Rôtie,
Châteauneuf-du-Pape Vieux Télégraphe and even the rare Ch Grillet
(at appropriately rare prices). Alsace wines are from Kuentz Bas and
Dopff au Moulin.

The estates of Germany may be well represented, too, but the list
does not reveal makers' names, so it is difficult to judge. Taylor's and
Fonseca Ports are much to the fore, plus a couple of Sherries from
Lustau.

Best buys

Mature clarets; Gigondas 1985, Aujoux, £4.85; Ch de Breuil 1982,
Médoc, £5.15; Beaujolais Villages 1986, Domaine Chapitre, £3.60

The Wine & Spirit Education Trust is an educational charity, approved by
the Department of Education and Science, whose object is the education
and training of all those (over the age of 18) who are connected with some
aspect of the drinks industry, and for those who intend to enter these
trades. The courses are run at three levels – Certificate, Higher Certificate
and Diploma – all on a part-time basis. Contact the Trust at: Five Kings
House, Kennet Wharf, Upper Thames Street, London EC4V 3AJ;
TEL 01-236 3551.

Christopher & Co

MAIL ORDER 19 Charlotte Street,   TEL 01-636 4020
London W1P 1HB
Les Amis du Vin Shop, 51 Chiltern Street,   TEL 01-487 3419
London W1M 1HQ
The Winery, 4 Clifton Road, London W9 1SS   TEL 01-286 6475

OPEN (Les Amis) Mon–Fri 10.30–7   Sat 10.30–5   (Winery) Mon–Fri
10.30–8.30   Sat 10–6   CLOSED Sun, public holidays   CREDIT CARDS Access,
Amex, Diners, Visa; business accounts   DISCOUNTS 5% on 1 unmixed case,
12.5% on 10+ cases   DELIVERY Free on UK mainland (min 2 cases or £75
order); otherwise £5; mail order available   GLASS HIRE Available through Les
Amis du Vin Shop   TASTINGS AND TALKS Tastings through Les Amis du Vin
Club; to groups on request   CELLARAGE £4.83 per case per year

There have been complicated changes at Christopher's in the past year.
First they were absorbed by Les Amis du Vin, then the whole
organisation was taken over by Trusthouse Forte. The Christopher's
name now relates to the wine retailing side while Les Amis du Vin has
become the wine club (see under WINE CLUBS for more details).

The result of all this has been to create a much more interesting list
than the two entities managed to achieve in recent years. It may start in
France but there is much to please from many parts of the wine world,
including plenty of half-bottles, especially in dessert wines.

In France, it's not the two classic areas which speak loudest,
although Burgundy presents a good range. It's the smaller corners –
like the Beaujolais of Ch de Corcelles, Touraine wines of Plouzeau or
the Sancerre of Michel Thomas – that demand more attention. Then
there's the range of French regional wines – look for the Vin de Pays
des Côtes de Gascogne 1987, Domaine des Landes, £2.95; and the
varietal Syrah Vin de Pays des Collines Rhodaniennes from the
co-operative of Tain l'Hermitage.

In Italy, the top quality Tuscan wines of Frescobaldi are out in force;
Spain has Torres wines and CVNE Riojas; there are Concha y Toro
wines from Chile. Then we arrive in the star areas of Australia (with
wines from top-flight producers such as Pewsey Vale, Yalumba,
Rothbury, Katnook, Petaluma) and California (Mondavi, Dry Creek,
Ch St Jean, Iron Horse, Clos du Bois, Trefethen, Joseph Phelps – and
many others). Two fascinating sparkling wines caught our attention –
Yalumba D from Australia (£10.35) and Schramsberg wines from
California (Blanc de Blancs 1984 at £12.10).

Best buys

Touraine Sauvignon, Domaine de Garrelière, £3.39; Cabernet Vin de
Pays de l'Aude, £2.99; Christopher's Australian Red Shiraz, £2.99;
Pomino Rosso 1983, Frescobaldi, £6.05; Chardonnay Jeunes Vignes
1986, Ch Fuissé, M Vincent, £5.25

City Wine Shop

See the Four Vintners.

Claridge Fine Wines   ☞

Boarden Farm, Hawkenbury,   TEL (0580) 893303/893292
nr Staplehurst, Kent TN12 0EB

OPEN Mon–Fri 9–12.30 (for collection of goods) (office open 9–5)   Sat 9–12.30
CLOSED Sun, public holidays CREDIT CARDS None accepted; personal and
business accounts DISCOUNTS Available DELIVERY Free in Kent, East
Sussex, London, Essex (min 1 case) and elsewhere (min 3 cases); otherwise £5
per case; mail order available GLASS HIRE Free with case order
TASTINGS AND TALKS Occasional tastings on the farm; to groups on request
CELLARAGE £3.45 per case per year   ■

Somebody who writes in their wine list: 'Rosé – one of the world's
underrated wine styles', deserves to be encouraged. Tracy Leigh
Claridge, owner of the eponymous firm, goes on to recommend a rare
rosé Côtes de Thongue Vin de Pays from the South-West of France
(£2.80) and the more familiar Ch Val-Joanis Côtes de Lubéron (£3.35),
both good dry examples of how delicious rosé wines can be.

Apart from rosés, one of the major strengths of this list is a big range
of Australian wines, some from small boutique wineries with high
reputations, such as Pirramimma in McLaren Vale (look for the
Cabernet Sauvignon 1984 and the mature, rich 1982 vintage), or the
small Heathcote Winery in Victoria (especially good for white wines).
Other wineries are perhaps more familiar – Seppelts, Rosemount,
Tisdall, Brown Brothers among them. They also stock a good range of
the fabulous liqueur Muscats of Rutherglen and Glenrowan in
northern Victoria.

Back on European soil, we find an interesting range of vintages of
Ch Clarke in Listrac, owned by Edmond de Rothschild whose wines
are acquiring a rapidly increasing reputation (the 1985 at £10.80 is good
value). There is a small but well-chosen selection from the Loire and,
on the Rhône, the Châteauneuf-du-Pape of Boisson at Domaine
Elisabeth Chambellan. Burgundy has wines from Faiveley (including
their 'monopole' of Clos de la Maréchale in Nuits St-Georges). And, at
more down to earth prices, there is an attractive regional collection,
wines from Adam in Alsace, and Riojas from CVNE and Lopez de
Heredia (look for their old-style, wood-aged whites). Madeiras are
from the family firm of Henriques and Henriques.

Plans are afoot for a retail outlet for this firm.

Best buys

Cabardes 1987, Ch de Rayssac, £2.80; wines from Ch Val-Joanis, Côtes
du Lubéron; Tisdalls Rosbercon Cabernet/Merlot 1987, £4.80; Peter

Lehmann Queen of Clubs Dry Semillon 1987, £4.20; CVNE Rioja, Viña Real 1984, £3.80

Classic Wines

181 High Road, Chigwell, Essex IG7 6NU   TEL 01-500 7614

OPEN Mon–Fri 9–6   CLOSED Sat, Sun, public holidays   CREDIT CARDS None accepted; personal and business accounts   DISCOUNTS Negotiable
DELIVERY Free on UK mainland (min 6 cases); mail order available
GLASS HIRE Not available   TASTINGS AND TALKS Occasional in-store tastings; to groups on request   CELLARAGE Not available   ■

The name of this merchant says it all. They concentrate on fine clarets, Burgundies, white Bordeaux (a big range of Ch d'Yquem back to 1948 on the current list) and Vintage Ports. Inevitably, with a range such as this, small supplies run out quickly, so the list is updated every couple of months.

There's always plenty of choice. A recent issue offered Ch Lafite 1948 at £145, magnums of Ch Ducru-Beaucaillou 1983 at £200 for six bottles, a number of 1955 Vintage Ports and some mature vintages of Dom Pérignon Champagne.

Classic Wines (near Halifax)

See the Wine Schoppen.

Classic Wine Warehouses

Unit A2, Stadium Industrial Estate,   TEL (0244) 377876
Sealand Road, Chester, Cheshire CH1 4LU

OPEN Mon–Fri 8–6   Sat 9–5   CLOSED Sun, public holidays
CREDIT CARDS All accepted; personal and business accounts
DISCOUNTS Negotiable   DELIVERY Free within 5-mile radius (min 1 case); otherwise £2 per case in Lancashire, Cheshire, Clwyd and Merseyside and £5 per case elsewhere; mail order available   GLASS HIRE Free with 1-case order
TASTINGS AND TALKS Monthly in-store tastings; to groups on request
CELLARAGE Not available

Gentle expansion of this firm's range of wines over the past year has been enough to bring them into the Guide for the first time since 1986.

It may still not be the most exciting collection, but there are some good points, including some middle-price cru bourgeois from Bordeaux – look for Ch Coufran 1983 Haut-Médoc at £7.98 or Ch Verdignan 1979 at £9.34 (prices do not include VAT but we have included it here). There are some decently priced white Burgundies, but the Loire is very dull. Hugel represents Alsace, and some old favourites in French country wines are Fitou Mme Parmentier (£3.03) – but beware this wine is now non-vintage – and the Faugères Jules

Gaston 1986 (£2.68). They make a thing of Lanson Champagnes, including their second marque of Massé.

Outside France, interest focuses on occasional treats from Germany, Campo Viejo Riojas, Fontanafredda wines from Italy (also look for the varietal wines from Aquíleia in Friuli) and Lindemans wines from Australia.

Best buys

Champagne Massé NV, £7.50; Alsace Pinot Blanc 1985, Hugel £3.99; Ch Thieuley Bordeaux Cépage Sauvignon 1987, £4.20; Bernkasteler Badstübe Riesling 1984, Friedrich Wilhelm Gymnasium, £5.09

Cliffe Cellars

See Ellis Son & Vidler.

Clink Street Wine Vaults

Crown House, Clink Street, London SE1 9DG   TEL 01-403 4669

OPEN Mon–Fri 9–5.30 Sat (am) by appointment CLOSED Sat (except as above), Sun, public holidays CREDIT CARDS All accepted; personal and business accounts DISCOUNTS Quantity discounts DELIVERY Free locally (min 5+ cases) GLASS HIRE Free TASTINGS AND TALKS To groups on request CELLARAGE Not available ∎

This merchant lurks in the darkest corners of ancient Southwark, not far from the Cathedral. There they have put together a useful range of wines covering most areas of the wine world.

The list starts firmly in France, with Muscadet from Marquis de Goulaine and Sancerre from de Ladoucette; Rhône wines from Jaboulet Aîné and Chapoutier; a small collection of clarets including some good value petit château wines (Ch Lalène 1985, Bordeaux Supérieur, £4.12); Burgundies from André Morey; and Alsace wines from Hugel. There's plenty of Champagne (house Champagne is Pannier Brut NV at £8.58).

Other countries of Europe to get a showing are Spain, with Riojas from Montecillo and Cotto, plus the ubiquitous Torres wines; and Italy, with Brunello di Montalcino from Col d'Orcia and Chianti Classico of Lilliano. Fortified wines include Sherries from de Terry and Harvey's 1796 range. Other parts of the world get only brief nods: Australia with Peter Lehmann and Montrose wines, New Zealand with Nobilo, and California with Alexander Valley.

Best buys

Ch Lalène 1985, Bordeaux Supérieur, £4.12; Rioja Reserva 1982 Cotto de Imaz, £5.11; Torres Coronas 1984, £3.93; de Terry Sherries

College Cellar

56 Walton Street, London SW3 1RB   TEL 01-584 9855 and
                                                          01-581 0250

OPEN Mon–Fri 9.30–5.30 CLOSED Sat, Sun, public holidays
CREDIT CARDS Access, Visa; personal and business accounts DISCOUNTS Not
available DELIVERY Free in London (min 1 case); elsewhere at cost; mail order
available GLASS HIRE Not available TASTINGS AND TALKS In-store tastings
held every Saturday CELLARAGE Not available   ■

This is the fine wine associate of La Réserve (*q.v.*). Here you will find a
glorious selection of claret vintages back to 1938 (on the current list –
stocks of such fine wines inevitably vary all the time), some beautifully
mature sweet white Bordeaux, and Burgundy. Featured estates in
Burgundy include Albert Morot, Chandon de Briailles, Tollot-Beaut,
plus some of the top négociant names.

Look, too, for some mature northern Rhône wines, and vintage Port
back to the fabled 1927 vintage.

Best buys

Old vintages of claret, Port and Rhône wines

A H Colombier

51 Moira Road, Ashby-de-la Zouch,   TEL (0530) 412350
Leicestershire LE5 6GB

OPEN Mon–Fri 8.30–5 Sat on request CLOSED Sun, some public holidays
CREDIT CARDS None accepted; personal and business accounts
DISCOUNTS Quantity discount DELIVERY Free in central Midlands
(for reasonable quantity); elsewhere at cost GLASS HIRE Not available
TASTINGS AND TALKS To customers on request CELLARAGE May be
arranged   ■

Gradual expansion of the list at these merchants now justifies their
appearance in the Guide for the first time. Beware that prices on the list
do not include VAT – we have added it here.

Mind you, some areas are less than interesting – the Rhône, for
example (despite the Châteauneuf-du-Pape of Paul Avril) and the
Loire, and Germany exists mainly in a vacuum without producers'
names. But Italy has been expanded with some good varietal wines
from Orsini in the Veneto, Barolo from Orsola and wines from Rubini
in Colli Orientale del Friuli.

Of the two classic areas of France, Burgundy fares better. There are
domaine wines from Patrick Javillier and Jean-Louis Moretaux, as well
as good value basic wines from the Mâconnais and Côte Châlonnaise.
In Bordeaux, there are few petit château wines and prices are on the
high side – the best bargains are to be found among the red Graves.

Best buys

Ch Latour 1985, Bordeaux Supérieur, £4.80; Mâcon Supérieur Rouge 1986, Jean Marie, £3.50; Côtes du Rhône 1986, Domaine Maby, £3.77; Champagne Leclerc Briant Blanc de Noirs NV, £9.21

Continental Wine House

25 Edgware Road, London W2 2JE   TEL 01-262 2126

OPEN Mon–Sat 10–10.30   Sun, public holidays 12–2, 7–10   CLOSED Chr Day   CREDIT CARDS Access, Amex, Diners, Visa; personal and business accounts   DISCOUNTS Available on full cases (unmixed and cash on delivery)   DELIVERY Nominal charge of £1.50 within 3-mile radius; elsewhere at cost   GLASS HIRE Free (with refundable deposit)   TASTINGS AND TALKS Regular in-store tastings   CELLARAGE Not available

Italian wines remain the reason for this merchant's inclusion in the Guide. Look for Barbaresco from Oddero (£5.35); Cannonau del Parteolla from Sardinia, Chiantis from Pagliarese (Riserva, £5.95), the red super vino da tavola from Coltibuono, wines from Cirò in Calabria and Corvo and Regaleali in Sicily, the Tenuta di Pomino white from Frescobaldi and Valpolicellas from Bolla.

From the rest of the world, there are some good Reservas and Gran Reservas Riojas; some rather pricey cru Beaujolais; and Hardy's wines from Australia.

Best buys

Cirò Rosso Classico, £3.70; Barbera d'Asti, Brugo, £3.65; Inferno, Valtellina Superiore, £4.85

Copyhold Farm Shop

See Goedhuis & Co.

Corney & Barrow

12 Helmet Row, London EC1V 3QJ   TEL 01-251 4051
118 Moorgate, London EC2M 6UR   TEL 01-638 3125
44 Cannon Street, London EC4N 6JJ   TEL 01-489 8409
194 Kensington Park Road, London W11 2ES   TEL 01-221 5122

OPEN Mon–Fri 9–7 (City), 10.30–8 (Kensington)   Sat 10.30–8 (Kensington)   CLOSED Sat (City), Sun, Chr Day, bank holidays   CREDIT CARDS Access, Visa, Corney & Barrow Account Card; personal and business accounts   DISCOUNTS Negotiable   DELIVERY Free in central London (min 2 cases) and UK mainland (min 3 cases); mail order available   GLASS HIRE Free with order   TASTINGS AND TALKS In-store tastings on demand in Kensington (Sat am); to groups on request   CELLARAGE £4.14 per case per year

Corney & Barrow don't like to be thought of just as City wine merchants – although of course they do own a string of wine bars and restaurants in the Square Mile.

They are, nevertheless, very fine wine merchants with a serious list, homing in on Bordeaux and Burgundy, and bringing together some of the finest wines of each region. But they also have a lighter side – their shop in west London (now managed by Alistair Cameron whose own business used to be in the Guide) operates from its own list, buying in different (and good value) wines (for details, contact the shop direct).

Corney & Barrow's City list plunges straight into fine clarets. They have close links with the Bordeaux négociant and vineyard-owning firm of J-P Moueix, part-owners of the fabled Ch Pétrus and of a string of top estates in Pomerol and St-Emilion, and these form the heart of the range. The firm also produces some good petit château wines – try Ch Bel Air Bordeaux Supérieur 1986 at £3.75 (prices for single bottles do not include VAT, which we have added here, although case prices do include the tax) or Ch Montdespic Côtes de Castillon 1986 at £3.85. There are clarets from the Médoc as well, plus older vintages of the classed growths back to 1961.

In Burgundy, the bulk of wines are from domaines: Marquis d'Angerville, Domaine Trapet, Domaine Dujac, Domaine Daniel Senard, Domaine Newman, Domaine Matrot. There are also white Burgundies from Olivier Leflaive, a négociant firm associated with Domaine Leflaive.

The rest of the world needs to be pretty good in such exalted company. And it is. Jaboulet Aîné is the preferred producer in the Rhône, while Alsace wines come from Heydt. There's the top quality Vin de Pays of Mas de Daumas Gassac in the Hérault (plus some excellent vins de pays from the rest of France). In Spain, there are CVNE Riojas, Marqués de Griñon Cabernet Sauvignon and the highly acclaimed Ribera del Duero Pesquera, plus Vega Sicilia. Italy shows well with wines from Antinori and Lungarotti, and there are short but high quality ranges of German estate wines, Simi wines from California, Pokolbin Chardonnay from Australia and Cloudy Bay Sauvignon Blanc from New Zealand. Look, too, for a big range of Vintage Ports, and an excellent house tawny (Corney & Barrow 10-year-old Tawny £8.05).

Best buys

Cabernet Sauvignon 1986, Domaine du Puget, £2.58; Cellaro Bianco 1986, Sambuca di Sicilia, £3.08; Corney & Barrow 10-year-old Tawny, £8.05; Ch de Montdespic 1986, Côtes de Castillon, £3.85; Ch Bertin 1985, Montagne St-Emilion, £4.95

Restaurant Croque-en-Bouche ✉

221 Wells Road, Malvern Wells,   TEL (06845) 65612
Hereford and Worcester WR14 4HF

OPEN Any reasonable time, by arrangement   CREDIT CARDS Access, Visa
DISCOUNTS Not available   DELIVERY Free locally (min 2 cases); otherwise £8
for 3 cases, £10 for 4 cases, 5+ cases free; mail order available   GLASS HIRE Not
available   TASTINGS AND TALKS Not available   CELLARAGE Small quantities,
free   ■

Don't be misled by the short list which Croque-en-Bouche calls its
Retail Wine List. Behind proprietor Robin Jones's most popular wines
lies a cellar of a thousand others, all available in the restaurant, but also
all for sale retail at £3 less.

Mr Jones's indulgences seem to be the Rhône and Vouvray, old
vintages of claret and California. There's even a Russian wine if you are
curious. He helpfully arranges the list by colour – white wines first,
then reds.

The Rhône seems to be the most favoured place. On the retail list,
look for the Châteauneuf-du-Pape of Domaine de Beaucastel and their
Côtes du Rhône Cru de Coudoulet (the 1985 vintage is £5.70). The
main list includes eight wines from Côte Rôtie and three from Cornas –
definitely something of a record. Elsewhere in France, Alsace is well
served, as are sweet pudding wines from Bordeaux (after all this is a
restaurant list as well), while red Bordeaux has wines going back to the
1955 vintage (Ch Léoville Las Cases 1955, £54, or, more prosaically,
Ch Lassalle 1982 at £5.90 on the retail list).

Outside France, explore the good ranges from California, Australia
and New Zealand (Morton Estate Chardonnay 1986 is £6.70). Italy
comes up with some top reds from Tuscany (Chianti Classico 1978,
Badia a Coltibuono, £11.60), and there are some well-matured Reservas
from Rioja (and Vega Sicilia 1976 at £24.40). For after dinner,
Croque-en-Bouche offers a tempting clutch of eaux-de-vie and
brandies.

Anyone bewildered by the amazing range of treats could try the
sample cases which home in on Spain and a number of French regions.

Best buys

Côtes du Rhône 1983, Guigal £5.90; Morton Estate Chardonnay 1987,
£6.70; Sauvignon du Haut-Poitou 1986, £3.20; Touraine Cabernet 1983,
Domaine Châtoire, £3.90; Colares Reserva 1974, Real Vinícola, £3.80

Please write to tell us about any ideas for features you would like to see in
next year's edition or in *Which? Wine Monthly*.

Cumbrian Cellar

1 St Andrew's Square, Penrith,   TEL (0768) 63664
Cumbria CA11 7AN

OPEN Mon–Sat 9–5.30   CLOSED Sun, Chr Day, Boxing Day, Good Friday
CREDIT CARDS Access, Visa; personal and business accounts   DISCOUNTS 5%
on 1 case   DELIVERY Free in Cumbria (min 1 case); elsewhere at cost; mail order
available   GLASS HIRE Free with 1-case order
TASTINGS AND TALKS Occasional in-store tastings and for customers wishing to
sample before buying; small groups, larger groups £1.50–£3.50 according to
subject   CELLARAGE £3 per case per year

In competition with the national high street off-licences, the Cumbrian
Cellar sensibly concentrates on areas in which the big groups are less
interested. The classic French areas and German wines are covered,
but the shop is best at Spain (including Sherries), Italy and Australia.

Spain takes in a good number of Riojas, from CVNE, La Rioja Alta,
Faustino and the familiar Marqués de Cáceres, plus a selection of
Freixenet Cava to add a little sparkle, not to mention a big and
enjoyable range of Sherries from Valdespino, Osborne, Williams &
Humbert and Duke of Wellington. Ports are from Kopke.

Italy offers some good value wines (Chianti Classico Rocca delle
Macie 1986 is £3.95), plus some top names such as the Montepulciano
d'Abruzzo of Illuminati (the 1981 vintage at £7.15) and the superbly
named Inferno of Nino Negri (the 1982 vintage at £4.70).

In other parts of Europe, look for Greek wines including Ch Carras
and plenty of Bulgarian wines (although these are a little pricey,
reflecting the problems of a one-branch business). In France, best are
the regional wines (Jurançon from Clos Guirouilh) and the Alsace
wines from Muré.

Cumbrian Cellars has homed in a number of big names in the New
World – Lindeman's, Mildara, Rosemount, Tisdall and Orlando and, a
particular treat, Jim Barry's Clare Valley wines in Australia; Cooks and
Babich wines from New Zealand; and Concha y Toro and Cousiño
Macul from Chile. The Indian sparkling Omar Khayyam (£10.85),
Flame Lily wines from Zimbabwe, and a couple of Russian wines are
novelty postscripts.

Best buys

Sherries from Valdespino and Duke of Wellington; Cerasuolo Rosato
1986, Illuminati, £4.05; Rioja CVNE Viña Real 1982, £4.15; Cava
Marqués de Monistrol Brut, £4.90

Why not club together with friends to enjoy volume discounts and free
delivery?

Curzon Wine Company

11 Curzon Street, London W1Y 7FJ   TEL 01-499 3327

OPEN Mon–Fri 10–7   Sat 10–6   CLOSED Sun, public holidays
CREDIT CARDS All major cards accepted; personal and business accounts
DISCOUNTS 5% on 1 case   DELIVERY Free in central London (min 1 case);
elsewhere at cost; mail order available   GLASS HIRE Free with 1-case order
TASTINGS AND TALKS Regular monthly tastings; to groups on request
CELLARAGE Negotiable

This is a well-heeled collection of wines, reflecting the neighbourhood
in which this shop finds itself, and it includes several bottles not easily
found elsewhere: for instance, Jura Ch Chalon, Réserve Catherine Rye
1976 at £18.35, some top-quality older vintages of claret (back to 1961),
and old vintages of Ch Nairac in Barsac.

The strongest areas on the well-balanced list are Bordeaux (with the
older vintages), Burgundy (a sound range of domaine wines from
producers like Jacques Prieur, Marcel Amance, Dujac, Ponsot) and
Champagne: apart from a hoard of Perrier-Jouët and Laurent-Perrier,
most of the top names are there, including a fascinating pair of Krug
Collection vintages (1953 at £130.35 a bottle).

At a more everyday level, prices are rather high, but we would
recommend the Berberana Riojas, or the unusual selection from
Piedmont (Carema White Label 1983 of Ferrando is £8.30) or the
Reichsrat von Buhl wines from the Rheinpfalz in Germany. In France,
there are Alsace wines from Léon Beyer and Sancerre from Guy Saget,
while the New World offers Brown Brothers and Quelltaler wines from
Australia and Te Mata wines from New Zealand. Vintage Ports in a
recent list included a 1896 Taylors at £172.45 – to reserve for its
centenary, perhaps?

Best buys

Curzon Sauvignon, £3.45; Berberana Rioja, Carta de Oro 1983, £4.70;
Alsace Pinot Blanc 1986, Léon Beyer, £4.75; Ch les Douves de Francs
1985, Côtes de Francs, £5.45

David's of Ashby

1–3 Mill Lane Mews,   TEL (0530) 415704
Ashby-de-la-Zouch, Leicestershire LE6 5HP

OPEN Mon, Tue, Thur, Fri 9–5   Wed 9–1   Sat 8.30–5   CLOSED Sun, public
holidays   CREDIT CARDS Access; personal and business accounts
DISCOUNTS 5% on 1 case   DELIVERY Free locally (min 1 case); elsewhere £8.63
minimum charge up to 8 cases; transport cost of £1.15 per case; mail order
available   GLASS HIRE Free with 1-case order
TASTINGS AND TALKS Fortnightly tastings on selected wines; to groups on
request   CELLARAGE (Min annual charge £5) 5p per case per week (includes
insurance)

It's the nuggets in this list that make it interesting: for example, the wines of Pio Cesare and Ruffino in the Italian section, those of Mas de la Dame in Baux en Provence, and the range of Pol Roger Champagnes.

Otherwise, it's a workmanlike, sensibly priced range of wines from the major French areas. Bordeaux is well supplied with some good petit château wines, and a feature is the wine of Ch le Fournas Bernodette in the Haut-Médoc, enabling comparisons to be made of vintages back to 1973. In Burgundy, many of the wines come from Thorin (as they do in Beaujolais). Neither the Loire nor the Rhône are of interest.

Outside France, look for the wines of Faustino in Rioja and of Caves Aliança in Portugal (especially their 1978 Garrafeira red at £5.90). Sherries are from Savory and James, Madeiras from Antonio Henriques, Ports from Niepoort.

Best buys

Côtes du Frontonnais 1985, Les Celliers de Léopold, £3.29; Caves Aliança Garrafeira Particular Tinto 1978, £5.90; Ch Bel Air 1985, Bordeaux, £3.95; Chianti Classico Ruffino Aziano 1986, £4.70

Davisons Wine Merchants

HEAD OFFICE 7 Aberdeen Road, Croydon,   TEL 01-681 3222
Surrey CR0 1EQ
Approx 80 branches in London and Home Counties
OPEN Mon–Sat 10–2, 5–10   Sun 12–2, 7–9   CREDIT CARDS Access, Amex
(some branches), Visa; personal and business accounts   DISCOUNTS 8.5%
on 1 mixed case of wine   DELIVERY Free within 5–10 miles radius of shop
(min 1 case); mail order available through Master Cellar Wine Warehouse
GLASS HIRE Free   TASTINGS AND TALKS Regular tastings in some branches
CELLARAGE Not available

This chain of wine merchants continues to amaze with the depth of its range of mature claret and Burgundy. Being a family firm, they say, they are prepared to afford the cost of cellaring these wines until they are ready to drink – would that more merchants offered the same service.

They have been expanding their business in the country towns of the Home Counties while cutting down on the number of smaller off-licences in London – in other words, they are becoming more and more the proper wine merchant.

You can find on their list Ch Latour 1970 at £69 (remember, this is a group of around 80 branches – so not all shops will have this wine) at one end of the scale, and at the other, some very acceptable petit château wines (Ch Macquin St-Georges 1982, St-Georges St-Emilion at £3.99; Ch La Tour St-Bonnet 1983 at £3.99; Ch Villars, Fronsac, 1983 at £6.49). In the same vein, Davisons stock plenty of mature Sauternes.

Moving to Burgundy, red comes from 1982 and 1983 and is a mix of domaine and négociant wines, and white is from 1984 onwards. Elsewhere in France, look for regional wines such as the Minervois Domaine de Ste-Eulalie 1986 at £2.99 or Sancerre Le Grand Chemarin from Roger and Alsace from Hugel.

Davisons have at last expanded beyond France as well. Their Spanish section contains Torres wines and Marqués de Murrieta Riojas, Italy boasts Zenato Soave and Ruffino and Machiavelli Chianti. Bulgarian wines are all present at their usual amazing prices (Plovdiv Cabernet Sauvignon 1983, £2.45). There are German wines from Huesgen, and Australian from Jacobs Creek, Rosemount, Lindeman's and Wolf Blass, with New Zealand from Cook's and Montana.

In the same generous vein as the clarets, Davisons have cellared a fine collection of Vintage Ports (currently back to 1960) which are available on special order.

Best buys

Soave Classico 1987, Zenato, £3.99; Bulgarian wines; mature clarets; Cahors Carte Noire 1986, £3.65; Champagne Ellner Brut, £8.75; Rioja 1985, Laturce, £2.99

Davys of London

151 Borough High Street, London SE1 1HR   TEL 01-407 1484
OPEN Mon–Fri 10–6   CLOSED Sat, Sun, public holidays
CREDIT CARDS Access, Visa, Davys of London; personal and business accounts   DISCOUNTS 5% on 1 case; quantity discounts   DELIVERY Free in central London (min 2 cases); otherwise £2.50 per 6 bottles; mail order available
GLASS HIRE Free   TASTINGS AND TALKS Monthly in-store tastings during autumn; to groups on request   CELLARAGE Not available

This is the retail side of the group of wine bars (see the WINE BARS section) which now boasts around 40 in London and eight or so more in the south of England. The whites are traditional but of a high standard.

It's a Bordeaux, Burgundy and Port list. There are some very good prices for well-known names (Ch la Dominique, St-Emilion 1981 at £9.25; Ch Gruaud-Larose 1977 at £11.60). Davy's basic claret, drunk by the case-load every day in the wine bars, is of a very decent quality (£3.25). Other Bordeaux are available in smaller quantities.

Burgundy comes mainly from négociants – Bouchard Aîné, Faiveley, Louis Latour – while Beaujolais is from Loron. There are some mature reds (from the 1979 vintage) plus whites from 1983.

Champagne is the other French wine of significance: Veuve Clicquot (the wine bars' house Champagne) is a bargain £12.45 a bottle, while Bollinger and Pol Roger are the other two featured grandes marques. There's much less from other parts of the world – although look for Brown Brothers' Australian wines, a good basic Rioja (£3.55) and

Bulgarian wines (Oriahovitza Cabernet Sauvignon Reserve 1980, £2.85).

Fortified wines include a good range of Vintage Ports as well as some vintage Madeiras and some reliable own-label Sherry (Manzanilla No 1, £4.50).

Best buys

Davys Claret NV, £3.25; Veuve Clicquot Champagne NV, £12.45; Davys Rioja 1983, £3.55

Del Monico's Famous Wine Emporium

23 South Street, St Austell, Cornwall PL25 5BH   TEL (0726) 73593

OPEN Mon–Sat 9–6   Sun (Aug only) 12–2   CLOSED Sun (except Aug), some public holidays   CREDIT CARDS Access, Visa; personal and business accounts   DISCOUNTS Negotiable   DELIVERY Free within 20-mile radius of St Austell   GLASS HIRE Free with order   TASTINGS AND TALKS Some wines opened in-store for customers to try; larger tasting in May (Sat only); to groups on request possible   CELLARAGE Free

'Any changes?' we asked David del Monico. 'None,' he replied, 'apart from revamping the shop exterior, but it's just as grotty inside.' Well, we agree, it's not the most beautiful shop in this Guide, but there are plenty of choice wines to take your mind off the decor.

Nuggets are scattered throughout a French-dominated list: wines from Listel in the Midi, Ch la Coste wines from Provence, a good Alsace selection, plus a shortish list of clarets which moves smartly from house claret to some classed growths.

Moving to Italy brings Regaleali Sicilian wines, Chianti from Mellini and Veneto wines from Bolla, while across in Iberia, there's Rioja from CVNE and Olarra Cerro Anon in Spain and the excellent value Quinta de Abrigada Garrafeira 1976 (£5.89) in Portugal. The Australian list has expanded to take in some Penfold's wines, while the fortified section includes a number of 10-year-old tawnies and Sherries from Osborne.

Best buys

Bulgarian Cabernet Sauvignon, £1.98; Listel wines; Cava Freixenet Cordon Negro, £4.85; Wolf Blass Australian Chardonnay 1986, £4.85

The Delicatessen (North Berwick)

See J E Hogg.

Demijohn Wines

Penn Street, nr Amersham,   TEL (0494) 715376
Buckinghamshire HP7 0PX

OPEN Tue–Fri 12–7 Sat 11–7 CLOSED Mon, Sun, public holidays
CREDIT CARDS Access, Visa; personal and business accounts
DISCOUNTS 2.5% on 1 unmixed case, 7.5% on 5 cases DELIVERY Free within
5-mile radius (min 1 case); elsewhere at cost; mail order available
GLASS HIRE Free with 1-case order TASTINGS AND TALKS Bottles always
open in shop; occasional 8-wine regional tastings; to groups on request within
10-mile radius CELLARAGE Not available   ■

Italy remains the highlight of Demijohn's list. French wines are still of
limited interest, and prices for these are better elsewhere, but 'a new
Australian wine' is promised each month. Already wines from Hardys
and the unique Dry Muscat Blanc from Brown Brothers (1986 vintage at
£4.56) have joined the list.

In Italy plenty of good names present a strong front. From
Piedmont, there is Barbaresco from Cortese and Barolo from Marchesi
di Barolo; from Tuscany, the lighter style Brunello from
Castelgiocondo, and Chianti Classico from Badia a Coltibuono,
Poggiarello, Riecine and San Polo in Rosso. Look, too, for the
Montepulciano d'Abruzzo of Cornacchia (the 1985 vintage is £3.59) and
the basic Settesoli Rosso from Sicily (£2.68).

White Italian stars include Tiefenbrunner's Chardonnay from the
Südtirol, and the Coltibuono Bianco from Tuscany (£3.98). And try the
dessert Sherry-style Vin Santo della Toscana 1978 of Aiola at £7.48.

Best buys

Barbaresco Rabaja 1986, Cortese, £5.79; Moscato Spumante La Verra,
£4.29; Settesoli Bianco and Rosso, £2.68; Cerasuolo d'Abruzzo 1986,
Cornacchia, £3.51

Dennhöfer Wines

47 Bath Lane, Newcastle upon Tyne,   TEL 091-232 7342
Tyne & Wear NE4 5SP

OPEN Mon–Fri 9–6 Sat 10–2 CLOSED Sun, public holidays
CREDIT CARDS Access, Amex, Visa; personal and business accounts
DISCOUNTS 5–10% (min 1 case) DELIVERY Free in North-East (min 1 case);
elsewhere £5.75 per case plus £1 per additional case; mail order available
GLASS HIRE Free TASTINGS AND TALKS Occasional in-store tastings; monthly
tastings in restaurant; to groups on request CELLARAGE Up to 5 cases free;
over 5 cases £1 per case per year

Since we have commented in the past on the lack of information on
Dennhöfer's list, we must now praise them for remedying the situation
in the latest one. Now we are told who makes the wines and even
learn a little bit about them.

The list has undergone some expansion as well. In the range of clarets, for example, appear a good bunch from the 1981 vintage (Ch Potensac, £8.23) and 1982, plus offerings from 1978 and 1979 (Ch Talbot 1979, £10.99). In Burgundy, the excellent co-operative of Buxy supplies the basic wines, and more expensive wines come from Labouré-Roi and Charles Viénot. Beaujolais is from Pierre Dupond. The featured house Champagne is Yves Pascal (Brut NV at £8.90), while Veuve Clicquot and Bollinger are also available.

In keeping with the firm's name, there is a strong German section, especially in the varietal wines from Clusserath Math Jos in the Mosel. Other wines are supplied by Deinhard and the Staatsweingut in Eltville on the Rheingau. Italy is enlivened by Chiantis from Brolio, Spain by Riojas from CVNE and Garvey Sherries. A new arrival are Australian wines from Wyndham Estates.

Best buys

Saulheimer Holle Auslese 1985, Johann Flick, £3.91; Alsace Pinot Blanc 1986, Ringenbach Moser, £3.38; Bourgogne Rouge 1985, Labouré-Roi, £3.95; Cabernet Sauvignon 1985, Wyndham Estate, £4.35

Rodney Densem Wines

OFFICE AND WHOLESALE Stapeley Bank, London Road, Nantwich, Cheshire CW5 7JW   TEL (0270) 623665 (for both addresses)   RETAIL 4 Pillory Street, Nantwich, Cheshire CW5 5BB

OPEN Mon–Fri 10–6 (closed Wed pm)   Sat 9–5.30   CLOSED Sun, public holidays   CREDIT CARDS Access, Visa; personal and business accounts DISCOUNTS 5% on 1 case   DELIVERY Free within 20-mile radius (min 1 case); elsewhere at cost; mail order available   GLASS HIRE Free with 1-case order TASTINGS AND TALKS 6–8 tastings annually by invitation; to groups on request   CELLARAGE Not available

It is the retail shop's rapidly changing range of bin-ends and fine wines (including old clarets and Ports) that gives Rodney Densem Wines a firm place in the Guide. Because of the nature of bin-ends, no printed list is available but visits or phone calls to the shop should elicit plenty of helpful information.

The printed wholesale list, though less interesting, does have some worthwhile sections: Spain with Torres wines; Australia with Lindeman's and Brown Brothers bottles. Look, too, for a good range of Champagnes, Alsace wines from Hugel, Pouilly Fumé from Masson-Blondelet and Sancerre from H Bourgeois, as well as German estate wines from Louis Guntrum.

Best buys

Le Chant de la Treille, Ch Lamothe, £3.30; Alsace Pinot Blanc 1986,
Co-operative of Gueberschwihr, £3.37; Côtes du Rhône, Domaine de la
Baume 1986, £3.79

Desborough & Brown Fine Wines

21 George Street, St Albans,   TEL (0727) 44449
Hertfordshire AL3 4ES

OPEN Tue–Fri 10–3, 4–7 Sat 9–6   Public holidays 12–2   CLOSED Mon, Sun
CREDIT CARDS All accepted; personal and business accounts
DISCOUNTS Available   DELIVERY Free within 15-mile radius of St Albans (min
1 case)   GLASS HIRE Free with any case order   TASTINGS AND TALKS Plans to
hold tastings every two weeks on Saturdays   CELLARAGE Not available   ■

The Fine Wine Shop opened in June 1988 and has very much the same
wines as the wholesale side of the business.

Strengths lie in the French regions. The Loire has a particularly good
selection, with dessert wines from Anjou, Savennières from Yves
Soulez, Ménétou-Salon and Sancerre from Jean-Max Roger, red – and a
rare white – Chinon Domaine de la Noblaie and Pouilly Fumé,
Domaine de la Tuilerie.

There are similar treats in the South-West of France. Producteurs
Plaimont – one of the best co-operatives in the area – provide
Pacherenc du Vic Bilh and Madiran as well as the fresh white Vin de
Pays des Côtes de Gascogne (£2.89), while the equally good Caves des
Vignerons Réunis de Buzet provide a whole range of Côtes de Buzet
wines. Bergerac comes from Henri de Dietrich.

Elsewhere in France, look for Alsace wines from Willy Gisselbrecht,
Champagne from the co-operative of Mailly (Brut Réserve NV at
£10.95), a big range of the varietal wines of the Unions des
Co-opératives in Ardèche (all under £3 and very good value) and
Beaujolais from Auguste Lafont.

Wines from the rest of the world are fewer on the ground:
Frescobaldi wines from Italy, CVNE and Olarra Riojas, Portuguese
selections from João Pires and J M da Fonseca. The New World is
represented by Fetzer, Tjisseling and Pine Ridge in California; Cousiño
Macul in Australia; Drayton and Elderton wines (both small boutique
wineries) in Australia; and Matua Valley in New Zealand.

Best buys

Chardonnay 1987, Cousiño Macul, £4.29; varietal wines from the
Ardèche; Côtes de Buzet 1985, Ch de Gueyze, £4.65; Sauvignon Blanc
1987, Matua Valley, £5.95

Prices are correct to the best of our knowledge in summer 1988.

Direct Wine Shipments

5/7 Corporation Square, Belfast,	TEL (0232) 238700/243906
Co Antrim BT1 3AJ	

ASSOCIATED OUTLETS

Duncairn Wines, 555 Antrim Road, Belfast,	TEL (0232) 370694
Co Antrim BT15 3BU	
Wine and Ale House, 18 Abbey Street,	TEL (0265) 2113/4031
Coleraine, Co Londonderry BT6 8LL	

OPEN Mon–Fri 9–5.45 (8pm Thur) Sat 10–5 CLOSED Sun, public holidays
CREDIT CARDS Access, Visa; personal and business accounts DISCOUNTS 5%
on 1 case DELIVERY Free in Belfast (min 1 case) and Northern Ireland (min 3
cases); mail order available GLASS HIRE Arranged through local glass-hire
company TASTINGS AND TALKS Wine evenings arranged; tastings held
monthly on Saturdays CELLARAGE Not available

Strengths from this – the only Northern Ireland wine merchant in the
Guide – are Bordeaux, Burgundy, Spain and Bulgaria.

In Bordeaux, we find an increased range of petit château wines,
some at very good prices (look for Ch la Rose de By 1985, Médoc at
£4.30 or Margaux Private Reserve 1983 from Ch Kirwan at £6.89. In
Burgundy, Direct Wine Shipments act as local agents for Louis Latour,
Loron, Mommessin, Chanson Père and the co-operative of the Hautes
Côtes de Beaune. They also stock Chablis from Henri Laroche. Other
well-covered French areas are Alsace (with Hugel and Gustave Lorentz
wines) and the Rhône (Chapoutier).

While Italy still suffers from a two-litre bottle approach (except for
the excellent range from Antinori in Tuscany and the Cirò wines from
Calabria), and the only flicker of eminence in Germany is Dr
Bürklin-Wolf in the Rheinpfalz, Spain is well served: Torres wines in
profusion, Marqués de Cáceres Riojas, wines from Ribera del Duero
(including Vega Sicilia) and Viña Albali from Valdepeñas.

There is a comprehensive listing of Bulgarian wines at competitive
prices, and other good choices would include Mondavi and Firestone
wines from California, and Brown Brothers wines from Australia.
Sherries are from Lustau, Ports from Quinta do Noval.

Best buys

Bulgarian wines; Ch St-Estève, Coteaux Varois, £2.09; Viña Sol 1987,
Torres, £2.75; Vin de Pays de l'Hérault Blanc, £1.79; Protos 1976, Ribera
del Duero, £5.80; Rioja 1978, Marqués de Cáceres Reserva, £4.95

Most wine merchants will hire out glasses free of charge, provided they are
collected and returned clean, and that you are buying enough wine to fill
them! In most cases, it's first come, first served, so get your order in early to
ensure supply.

Domaine Direct

29 Wilmington Square, London WC1X 0EG   TEL 01-837 3521/1142
OPEN Mon–Fri 9–6   Sat 9–1   CLOSED Sun, public holidays
CREDIT CARDS None accepted; personal and business accounts
DISCOUNTS Not available   DELIVERY Free in central London (min 1 case) and
UK mainland (min 3 cases); otherwise 1 case £5.75, 2 cases £8.05; mail order
available   GLASS HIRE Free   TASTINGS AND TALKS Major annual tasting;
2–3 other tastings annually; theme tastings; to groups on request (limited)
CELLARAGE £3.45 per case per year   ∎

The Domaines in the name of this merchant are all in Burgundy and
Chablis, a whole galaxy of famous names.

Sensibly, Domaine Direct don't just go for the top wines, but provide
a good cross-section of what Burgundy has to offer, so we get
Bourgogne Passetoutgrains 1985 under their own name at £4.89, or,
in whites, Bourgogne Aligoté from Bernard Michel at £5.46 (prices on
this list do not include VAT, but we have added it here).

Moving up a notch, the Côte Châlonnaise and the Mâconnais
provide more good value (in Burgundian terms, that is). Look for
Mercurey 1984 of Michel Juillot at £8, and Domaine Corsin's white
St-Véran 1986 at £7.47. Then we plunge into big names – Simon Bize,
Domaine de Montille, Domaine de la Pousse d'Or, Roux Père et Fils,
Alain Michelot, Comte Lafon. In Chablis, wines come from Jean Durup
and René Dauvissat.

There are wines also from Burgundy or Chablis satellites –
Sauvignon de St-Bris, Bourgogne Irancy, a few Beaujolais and plenty of
half-bottles. Regular customers should latch on to the new cellar
scheme to help them 'build up a core of excellent Burgundies'.

Best buys

Mâcon-Viré 1986, André Bonhomme, £6.33; Montany Coères 1986,
Bernard Michel, £6.84; Bourgogne Passetoutgrains 1986, Domaine
Direct, £4.89; Bourgogne Aligoté 1986, J P Ragot, £5.06

Special awards

🐷 means bargain prices (good *value* may be obtained from merchants
without this symbol, of course, if you are prepared to pay for service)

❀ means that the wines stocked are of consistently high quality

▭ means that the merchant stocks an above-average range

☞ means that extra-special service is offered: helpful advice, informative
lists and newsletters, tastings etc.

Peter Dominic

HEAD OFFICE Vintner House, TEL (0279) 26801
Templefields Industrial Estate, Harlow,
Essex CM20 2EA
ASSOCIATED OUTLETS Bottoms Up
Approx 800 outlets nationwide

OPEN Varies from store to store; majority open 7 days a week, Mon–Fri 10–9
CREDIT CARDS Access, Amex, Diners, Visa; personal and business accounts
accepted from Grand Metropolitan cardholders DISCOUNTS 5% (min 1 mixed
case) DELIVERY Free within 35-mile radius of branch (min £25 order);
elsewhere charges negotiable; mail order available via Wine Mine Club of Gift
Express GLASS HIRE Free with order TASTINGS AND TALKS Tastings in 120
Wine Centres every weekend; promotional tastings in branches; to groups on
request; Wine Mine Club tastings CELLARAGE £3.75 per case per year or
part-year

Of all the national high street off-licence groups, Peter Dominic has put
together one of the best wine lists. While others may concentrate more
on cigarettes, this group (which also takes in Bottoms Up shops) has
maintained the quality as well as the countrywide distribution of its
wines (although the smallest branches may not have a complete
selection).

It's a wide-ranging list, too, sensibly steering away from expensive
Burgundy and towards, for instance, a good Italian section (look for
the Nebbiolo d'Alba of Borgogno at £4.25 or the Carmignano Villa di
Capezzana at £5.35). Other attractions are in Spain (Riojas from La
Rioja Alta and CVNE as well as wines from Torres or the Cabernet
Sauvignon from Jean León at £7.99). The same quality is not always
kept up at house wine level – the Lagunilla Riojas are rather dull, as are
some of the branded French vins de table such as Monsieur le Patron or
the ubiquitous Piat d'Or.

More interestingly, California wines are from Firestone, Robert
Mondavi and Inglenook, or you could go for the Chilean Cabernet
Sauvignon of Viña Linderos (£3.85). Appealing Australian bottles
include wines from Hill-Smith, Rosemount, Brown Brothers and Berri
Estates. New Zealand is represented by Cooks.

Peter Dominic carry a good clutch of Bulgarian wines, still around
the £2 mark, and Red Infuriator from Algeria – not as bad as it sounds –
at £2.55. In France, the house Champagne is Lambert at £8.59, and
there's claret from good middle-range châteaux such as Ch Greysac
(the 1983 vintage at £5.85) and Ch la Cardonne (the 1985 vintage at
£5.35) as well as pricier bottles. In fortified wines look for Ports from
Croft and Morgan, and an attractively priced collection of Madeiras.

Best buys

Lambert Grande Réserve Champagne, NV, £8.59; Torres Sangre de Toro 1985, £3.75; Rosso Cònero CaSal di Serra 1982, £3.45; Yalumba Rhine Riesling 1987, £3.99; Serradayres Tinto, Portugal 1984, £2.79

Drunken Mouse

195–7 Lower Richmond Road, London SW15 1HJ   TEL 01-785 2939
OPEN Mon–Sat 10.30–9   Sun 12–2   Public holidays 12–2, 7–9
CLOSED Chr Day, New Year's Day   CREDIT CARDS Access, Diners, Visa
DISCOUNTS Available   DELIVERY Free within 3-mile radius (min 1 case); elsewhere at cost   GLASS HIRE Free with 1-case order
TASTINGS AND TALKS Weekly tastings (Sat)   CELLARAGE Not available

Come to this wine merchant for their Australian wines, of which they have put together a very good range, sensibly grouped in price brackets. Under £5, we find Orlando RF Cabernet Sauvignon (£4.19), Yalumba Signature Reserve Shiraz/Cabernet Sauvignon (£4.99) and Penfolds Semillon/Chardonnay 1985 (£4.39).

Moving up to the £5–£10 bracket, there are wines from Rouge Homme, Cape Mentelle, Wolf Blass, Richard Hamilton in Wilunga, a good sparkler in the shape of Yellowglen Brut (£6.99), and the marvellous Petersons Chardonnay 1986 (£8.99). Top of the range is the 1980 vintage of Grange Hermitage at £21.50.

The rest of the world is rather insignificant in comparison, but look for Duboeuf Beaujolais, some good-value petit château Bordeaux, and Rhône wines from Vidal Fleury. Elsewhere in Europe, there are Torres wines from Spain, plus Freixenet Cava (Cordon Negro at £4.39).

Best buys

Wyndham Estates Bin 555 Shiraz 1984, £3.89; Orlando RF Chardonnay 1986, £4.19; Beaujolais Villages 1986, Georges Duboeuf, £3.79; Alsace Pinot Blanc Cuvée Réserve 1986, Louis Gisselbrecht, £3.99

Duncairn Wines

See Direct Wine Shipments.

Duras Direct

61 Elmleigh, Midhurst, West Sussex GU29 9HA   TEL (073 081) 4150
OPEN Mon–Fri 9–6   Sat, Sun, public holidays 9–1   CLOSED Chr Day
CREDIT CARDS None accepted; personal and business accounts
DISCOUNTS Negotiable   DELIVERY Free within 10-mile radius of Midhurst (min 1 case); otherwise charges negotiable; mail order available
GLASS HIRE Free   TASTINGS AND TALKS To invited guests and to groups on request   CELLARAGE Not available   ∎

A short list, specialising in wines from the South-West of France. From Duras itself, we find wines from three estates – Domaine Amblard, Domaine les Brugues-Mau Michau and Domaine de Ferrant. Prices are keen – the most expensive red is Domaine de Ferrant 1985 at £4.07. They also import Domaine de Fages, a top-quality Cahors.

As an aside, the company also offer a small selection of Loire wines – Muscadet Domaine les Roitelières and Sancerre and Pouilly Fumé.

Best buys

Cahors Domaine de Fages 1985, £3.98; Duras, Domaine les Brugues-Mau Michau 1982, £3.98

George Dutton & Son

See Willoughbys.

Eaton Elliot Winebrokers

15 London Road, Alderley Edge, Cheshire SK9 7JT   TEL (0625) 582354/584851

OPEN Mon–Sat 9–7   CLOSED Sun, public holidays   CREDIT CARDS All accepted; personal and business accounts   DISCOUNTS 5% on 1 case, 10% on 6 cases   DELIVERY Free within 30-mile radius of Alderley Edge (min 1 case); elsewhere £7.50 per consignment (depending on size); mail order available GLASS HIRE Free with 1-case order   TASTINGS AND TALKS 2 annual tastings; to groups on request   CELLARAGE Not available

This is a high quality list, with strengths in the French regions and in Italy. Under the first heading, we would include the Loire (look for the organic Muscadet of Guy Bossard, the Bourgueil of Caslot-Galbrun and Sancerre from Vacheron); we would also add the Alsace wines from the Cave Co-opérative of Turckheim, and the superb Jura wines of Ch d'Arlay (Vin Jaune de Gard, £18.45). From the South-West of France, there are the Jurançon wines of Henri Ramonteau and Madiran from Denis de Robillard.

Of the classic areas, Burgundy fares better than Bordeaux. There is Pouilly Fuissé from Domaine Corsin, Chablis from the La Chablisienne co-operative and Ch Thivin Beaujolais. Champagne is from Nicolas Feuillatte.

Italy is the strongest area outside France, with wines from Duca d'Asti in Piedmont, from Santa Sofia in the Veneto (look for their Bianco di Custoza at £3.30), and from Castello di Volpaia in Chianti. German wines come from Langguth Erben, while the New World is represented by Schug Cellars in California – look for their Pinot Noir – and by Rosemount in Australia. Sherries are Lustau, Ports are Churchill.

Best buys

Vin de Pays des Côtes de Gascogne, Domaine Tariquet 1987, £2.95;
Bourgueil 1986, Caslot-Galbrun, £4.50; Côtes du Rhône Domaine
Mistral 1986, £2.99; Bianco di Custoza 1986, Santa Sofia, £3.45

C C G Edwards

Burlton, Shillingstone, Dorset DT11 0SP   TEL (0258) 860641

OPEN Any time by appointment or mail order   CLOSED August
CREDIT CARDS None accepted   DISCOUNTS Available   DELIVERY Free in
England and Wales (min 1 case); otherwise at cost; mail order available
GLASS HIRE Free   TASTINGS AND TALKS Informal tastings with each new
shipment   CELLARAGE Not available

This is a short list of organically produced wines from France, Italy,
Germany and England. Only wines from one or two vineyards are
shipped each year. A new listing is of Ch la Croix Simon in
Entre-Deux-Mers (the 1987 vintage of the red is £4.60, the 1987 of the
white is £4.20).

Eldridge Pope

HEAD OFFICE Weymouth Avenue,   TEL (0305) 251251
Dorchester, Dorset DT1 1QT
10 branches (1 called Godrich & Petman) and 2 Reynier Wine Libraries

OPEN Generally Mon–Sat 9–1, 2–5.30 (varying ½ days)   (Reynier) Mon–Fri
11–2.30, 5–7.30   CLOSED Sun, public holidays   CREDIT CARDS Access,
Visa   DISCOUNTS Available   DELIVERY Free within 20-mile radius (min 1
case), otherwise £3.45; elsewhere 1 or part-case £3.45, 2–3 cases £5.75; 4+ cases
free; mail order available   GLASS HIRE Available with order
TASTINGS AND TALKS Occasional in-store tastings; to groups on request
CELLARAGE £2 per case per year

This is one of the major lists in this Guide. Its greatest strengths are
evident in fortified wines, in Germany and in France – especially
Bordeaux. Beyond Bordeaux, parts of France to get some serious
coverage include the Loire, with the great Anjou wines of Jean Baumard
(Coteaux du Layon Clos de Ste-Catherine 1985 at £4.72) and a fine
collection of Moulin Touchais mature dessert wines (the 1947 vintage at
£26.50, the 1981 at £6.21). In Alsace, too, there is a big range from the
house of Dopff et Irion, including some of the rich Sélection de Grains
Nobles as well as 1985 and 1983 vintage wines. Considerable attention
is paid to vins de pays as well – plenty of good value from the Midi and
Provence.

But the heart of the list lies in Bordeaux – both in size and quality. On
a recent list, vintages went back in relatively small numbers to 1928,
but after 1953 there is plenty to choose from, whether in bottle,
magnum or half-bottle, and even selections from the 1970s, before a
positively gargantuan range from 1982 and 1985. There is also much to

delight in sweet white Bordeaux – all part of this merchant's continuing interest in dessert wines.

Burgundy has a mixture of négociant and domaine wines. Beaujolais comes from Pierre Ferraud, and some mature red Burgundies go back to 1970. Quite a few wines are bought at the Hospices de Beaune. In this area – as in many others on the list – Eldridge Pope's Chairman's range provides good quality.

Fortified wines are another major strength: a string of mature vintage Ports – back to 1917 – and a good range of crusted Ports (Gould Campbell 1980, £6.83). Madeiras are a splendid set, including old vintages (Terrantez 1899 – from a rare grape variety – at £91.05).

The third big section is Germany. Here Eldridge Pope are agents for the prestigious estate of Schloss Vollrads on the Rheingau, but they also have wines from other major producers – Schloss Reinhartshausen, von Buhl, Reichsgraf von Kesselstatt.

While neither Italy nor Spain (apart from Riojas from Muga) get much of a look in, the Luxembourg wines from Bernard Massard are a curiosity. California is represented by Gundlach Bunschu and Grgich Hills. This is probably the last list in the country without an Australian wine (although a couple have infiltrated in the past).

See also Reynier Wine Bar in the WINE BARS section.

Best buys

Chairman's range of wines; Ménétou-Salon 1986, Morognes, Jean-Max Roger, £4.89; Alsace Tokay Pinot Gris 1985, Dopff et Irion, £3.92; Faugères Collection, Vignerons les Crus Faugères, £2.88; Schloss Vollrads German wines; Penedès Tinto, Jaume Serra, £2.94

Ben Ellis and Associates

The Harvesters, Lawrence Lane, Buckland,　　　　TEL　(073 784) 2160
Betchworth, Surrey RH3 7BE

OPEN 'All hours' – 24-hour answering machine　CREDIT CARDS None accepted; personal and business accounts　DISCOUNTS Not available
DELIVERY Free in Surrey and central London (min1 case), elsewhere 5 cases; otherwise at cost; mail order available　GLASS HIRE Free with 1-case order
TASTINGS AND TALKS Bi-annual tastings; regular tutored tastings; to groups on request　CELLARAGE Only by special arrangement　　　　　　■

Germany, Spain and the New World may all put in an appearance on the Ben Ellis list, but France is really the order of the day.

And Bordeaux is the heart. Best served are the 1985, 1983 and 1981 vintages, with good value to be found in the ready-to-drink wines of 1981. What is good about this strong range is that they do not just concentrate on the obvious châteaux, but delve into a few byways to find good value as well as quality. We would certainly recommend Ch Laniote in St-Emilion, Ch Siran in Margaux and Ch des Annereaux in Lalande de Pomerol as current good buys.

In Burgundy, many wines come from Labouré-Roi, but the estate wines from René Manuel and Hubert Guyot should not be ignored. Good value is to be found in the Côte Chalonnais wines of Emile Voarick (Mercurey Rouge 1985 at £6.92) and Paul Sapin (Mâcon-Lugny Blanc 1986, £4.40). Paul Sapin is also the source of Beaujolais. On the Rhône, look for the Châteauneuf wines of Domaine du Vieux Télégraphe, and in Alsace the wines of Muré. The Loire features the Vouvrays of Marc Brédif.

Best buys

Ch Segonzac 1983, Premières Côtes de Blaye, £4.57; Sancerre Côte de la Roche 1986, Michel Block, £5.74; Chilean Cabernet Sauvignon 1983, Viña Linderos, £3.44; Churchills Crusted Port, bottled 1980, £9.56

Ellis, Son & Vidler

57 Cambridge Street, London SW1V 4PS   TEL 01-834 4101
Cliffe Cellars, 12/13 Cliffe Estate, Lewes,   TEL (0273) 480235
East Sussex BN8 6JL

OPEN Mon–Fri 9.30–5.30 (London), 9–5 (Lewes)   CLOSED Sat, Sun, public holidays   CREDIT CARDS Access, Visa; personal and business accounts DISCOUNTS 5% on 10 cases; £1.80 per case collection allowance DELIVERY Free within 35-mile radius (min 3 cases or £84 order) and nationally (min 10 cases); otherwise 1 case £6.77, 2 cases £3.50 per case, 3–5 cases £2.40 per case, 6–10 cases £1.55 per case; £3.60 local charge for 1–2 cases; mail order available   GLASS HIRE Free with 3-case order   TASTINGS AND TALKS 3 annual tastings and on request   CELLARAGE £3.50 per case per year including insurance.

This is still very much a Bordeaux-based list, and other wines are fitted around it. What they have is a good range starting with some petit chateau wines (Ch Combe des Dames 1985 at £4.03, Ch Pitray 1983, Côtes de Castillon £4.14). Vintages go back to 1978, and there are plenty of top claret names, but prices are not particularly cheap.

The other major area of interest on this list is fortified wines. Their association with Cossart Madeiras means there is a good range of these, and there are plenty of Vintage Ports (back to 1955). Sherries are less exciting apart from the odd bottle of Almacenista Sherry.

Other parts of the wine world fare more briefly. Best areas are some good Sauternes from Ch Guiraud, Riojas from Berberana, German wines from Max Ferd Richter and a good value selection of French country wines (look for Ch Boudigand 1986, Côtes de Bergerac at £3.86 or the House Sauvignon from the Loire at £2.66.

Best buys

Ch Pitray 1983, Côtes de Castillon, £4.14; Madeiras from Cossart Gordon; Rioja 1985, Carta de Plata, £3.91; Geoffrey Roberts Reserve California red and white, £3.09

English Wine Centre

Drusilla's Corner, Alfriston,　　　　　　　TEL (0323) 870532
East Sussex BN26 5QS

OPEN Mon–Sun 10.30–5　CLOSED 24–26 Dec, 1 Jan　CREDIT CARDS Access,
Amex, Visa; personal and business accounts　DISCOUNTS Variable (min 1
case)　DELIVERY Free within 15-mile radius (min 1 case); elsewhere 1 case
£9.50, 2 cases £4.75 per case, 3–5 cases £3.12 per case, 6–10 cases £2.12 per case;
mail order available　GLASS HIRE Free with 1-case order
TASTINGS AND TALKS Promotional tastings may be possible; to groups on
request　CELLARAGE Limited

Cuckmere, Breaky Bottom, Carr Taylor, Nutbourne Manor,
Lamberhurst, Biddenden, Penshurst, Hambledon – just a few of the
many top names to feature in the English Wine Centre's gazetteer. For
those spoilt for choice, try the introductory tasting case at £57.50.

Best buys

Sussex County, £4.45; Drusilla's English Wine, £3.99; Wootton
Müller-Thurgau 1983, £3.95

English Wine Shop

3 Harcourt Street, London W1H 1DS　　　　TEL 01-724 5009
HEAD OFFICE Heywood Wines,　　　　　　　TEL 01-340 9635
9 Montenotte Road, London N8 8RL

OPEN Tue–Fri 11.30–6.30　Sat 10–3　CLOSED Sun, Mon, public holidays
CREDIT CARDS Access; business accounts　DISCOUNTS 9/10% on 1 case
DELIVERY Bottles at cost; cases by carrier at cost; 4+ cases in London area free;
4+ cases on UK mainland by quotation; mail order available　GLASS HIRE Free
with 1-case order　TASTINGS AND TALKS Monthly in-store tastings; to groups
on request　CELLARAGE Not available

If you want a wide choice of English wines, this is the place to come.
The English Wine Shop have assembled a fine collection from familiar
and less familiar vineyards, many from the 1984 vintage, but probably
moving on to the 1985 by the end of 1988.

　　Particularly worth looking out for are the Pilton Manor wines, the
dry white from Michaelmas House in Essex, the interesting
Chardonnay and Seyval Blanc Hambledon 1984 (£3.65), and the
Müller-Thurgau and Seyval Blanc dry blend from Wraxall. There are a
few older vintages, and the Carr-Taylor sparkling wine at £7.75. Prices
– considering the heavy excise duties imposed on English wine
producers – are good.

Best buys

Michaelmas House Dry 1984, £3.65; Pilton Manor 1986, £3.85; Wraxall
Dry 1984, £3.60

Esprit du Vin

See Thresher.

Farr Vintners

154 Tachbrook Street, London SW1V 2NE   TEL 01-630 5348
(mail/phone order only)

OPEN Mon–Fri 9–6   CLOSED Sat, Sun, public holidays   CREDIT CARDS None
accepted; personal and business accounts   DISCOUNTS Not available
DELIVERY At cost; mail order available   GLASS HIRE Not available
TASTINGS AND TALKS Regular tutored tastings; to groups on request
CELLARAGE £2.50 per case per year   ■

Farr Vintners bulge with what the wine auctioneers like to call 'the
finest and rarest' wines: great classics from Bordeaux and Burgundy,
old vintages of Port and Rhône wines – and even (it just shows how
quickly a wine becomes a classic) the original vintages of the
Mondavi/Rothschild Opus One from California.

With such a selection, largely made up of small parcels of wines, the
list changes quickly, so it's best to consult Farr Vintners before
ordering. They also specialise in old wine and large bottle sizes, and
have a constantly moving bin end list. Occasionally, they are asked to
sell a complete cellar: such lists make fascinating reading.

Best buys

Fine wines of old vintages

Farthinghoe Fine Wine and Food

The Old Rectory, Farthinghoe, Brackley,   TEL (0295) 710018
Northamptonshire NN13 5NZ

OPEN By arrangement   CREDIT CARDS None accepted; personal and business
accounts   DISCOUNTS Quantity discounts (min 2 cases)   DELIVERY Free on
UK mainland (min 1 case); offshore islands by arrangement; mail order
available   GLASS HIRE £2 per case of 48   TASTINGS AND TALKS Regular
evening tastings with supper; to groups on request   CELLARAGE £3.16 per case
per year (in bond only)

As its name implies, this firm is a very successful double act. On the
food side, Nicola Cox gives demonstrations in Farthinghoe's
well-equipped lecture theatre as well as travelling the country giving
lectures. Visiting lecturers here have included Prue Leith. There is also
a shop selling useful kitchen items.

On the wine side, Simon Cox has been boosting the list, which stays
mainly in France, but also ventures to Italy with Chianti Classico Badia
a Coltibuono, to Australia with Brown Brothers wines and to a number
of California wineries (Trefethen, Carmenet, Firestone, Stag's Leap).

In France, Champagne makes a festive start to the list. Louis Krémer and George Goulet are the featured houses. Alsace is highly favoured – look for wines from Louis Gisselbrecht, Trimbach, Théo Faller, Rolly Gassmann and Hugel, and try the mixed case if you find decision-making difficult. There's more this year from the Loire (such as the Jean Baumard Savennières and the Sancerre le Grand Chemarin of Balland), but lack of demand has forced a cut in the range of German wines.

In Bordeaux, we find some good petit château wines as well as some very pricy top classed growths, while the Rhône has Hermitage la Chapelle of Jaboulet Aîné, and some top estate Châteauneuf-du-Papes.

Best buys

Alsace wines from Louis Gisselbrecht; Ch du Martouret 1986, Bordeaux Supérieur, £3.85; Cuvée Christopher Tatham et Corsin NV, Vin de Table Blanc, £6.45

Ferrers le Mesurier

Turnsloe, North Street, Titchmarsh,   TEL (08012) 2660
Kettering, Northamptonshire NN14 3DH

OPEN All hours, but telephone first if outside normal hours
CREDIT CARDS None accepted   DISCOUNTS By arrangement   DELIVERY Free generally within 50-mile radius of Titchmarsh (min 1 case); London, Cambridge and Norwich (min 1 case); elsewhere at cost   GLASS HIRE Not available
TASTINGS AND TALKS Annual Cambridge tasting; other tastings by arrangement   CELLARAGE Free if wine purchased from premises ■

While still taking an interest in Burgundy, this merchant has deliberately cut down on his buying until prices are more sensible. So, although there are still some 1983 reds around, only one 1985 is in evidence (Bourgogne Pinot 1985, Roulot, £6.32). Likewise, fewer white wines are available than in previous years, although they are well priced.

Instead, the range of Bordeaux has expanded at the level of petit château wines (look for Ch St-Jacques Bordeaux Supérieur 1983 at £4.31), and there are more wines from the Loire – a new addition is Reuilly 1987, C Lafond at £4.60 – which include two Vouvrays from Gaston Huet, Beaujolais from Loron and Colonge, George Goulet Champagne (Brut NV at £11.50) and Alsace wines from Louis Gisselbrecht are other interesting bottles.

Best buys

Reuilly 1987, C Lafond, £4.60; Ch St-Jacques 1983, Bordeaux Supérieur, £4.31; Beaujolais Villages 1987, A Colonge, £4.31

Send us your views on the report forms at the back of the book.

Alex Findlater

OFFICE Heveningham High House, Halesworth,   TEL (0986 83) 274
Suffolk IP19 0EA
SHOP 77 Abbey Road, London NW8 0AE   TEL 01-624 7311
OPEN Mon–Fri 10–1, 2–9 Sat 10–9 CLOSED Sun, public holidays
CREDIT CARDS Access, Visa; personal and business accounts DISCOUNTS 5%
on 1 case DELIVERY Free on UK mainland (min 3 cases); otherwise at cost; mail
order available GLASS HIRE Free with 2-case order
TASTINGS AND TALKS Australian Wine Festival every June; to groups on
request CELLARAGE £3.45 per case per year

There are really two complete ranges at this merchant: one is of
Australian and New Zealand wines, the other covers the rest of the
world. Both are extensive and full of high quality things.

Alex Findlater have by far the longest listing of Antipodean wines in
the country. Virtually every Australian winery which exports is
represented here, and much the same is true of New Zealand.
Amplified by excellent introductory notes, the list is a veritable
compendium, full of interest and information.

The range of wines beyond Australasia is pretty good in many areas.
In France, apart from fine ranges of Bordeaux (vintages back to 1961)
and Burgundy (good domaine wines as well as wines from Louis
Latour), strengths are apparent in vins de pays and the South of
France, with wines such as Coteaux d'Aix-en-Provence of Ch la Coste
and Listel wines. Look, too, for Rhône wines from Jaboulet Aîné. The
Loire is extensively treated: Olga Raffault's Chinon, the wines from the
Confrérie d'Oisly-et-Thésée, and Savennières from Ch de la Roche aux
Moines. In Alsace, we find Kuentz-Bas as the main supplier along with
Schlumberger, Trimbach and Muré.

Across the Rhine the range of German estate bottlings is enormous,
with plenty in all areas. A featured producer is Loosen Prüm Erben's
Weingut St Johannishof in the Mosel, while on the Rheingau the same
role falls to Langwerth von Simmern. Old vintages are worth perusing.

Another country to come out well is Italy, particularly Piedmont
with its Barolos from Pio Cesare and Contratto; in Tuscany, look for
Badia a Coltibuono Chianti and the Carmignano of Villa di Capezzana,
plus wines from Antinori and Frescobaldi. Maculan wines from
Breganze and Bardolino from Portalupi emphasise the concentration
on top names.

Spain is a little more obvious, but good anyway: Torres wines,
Beronia Riojas, and a number of vintages of Vega Sicilia. Portugal
brings in the Douro wines of Champalimaud as well as J M da Fonseca.
In fortified wines, the best area is Sherry: Barbadillo, Gonzalez Byass,
Valdespino and Sandeman. Madeiras are from Henriques &
Henriques.

Best buys

Most Australian wines; Côtes de Duras 1985, Ch la Pilar, £2.95;
German wines from Langwerth von Simmern; Quinta do Cotto 1982,
Montez-Champalimaud, £4.15; Monterey Classic California red and
white, £3.55; Sherries

Findlater Mackie Todd

Findlater House, 22 Great Queen Street,   TEL 01-831 7701
London WC2B 5BB

OPEN Mon–Fri 9–6   Sat only during December   CLOSED Sun, public
holidays   CREDIT CARDS All accepted; personal and business accounts
DISCOUNTS 7.5% on 10 cases   DELIVERY Free on UK mainland (min 1 case);
Northern Ireland and offshore (excluding Isle of Wight) £3.50 per case; mail
order available   GLASS HIRE Available   TASTINGS AND TALKS Occasional
in-store tastings; to groups on request   CELLARAGE £3.50 per case per year

After 64 years in Wigmore Street, Findlater Mackie Todd have moved
to new premises in Covent Garden. They continue to offer wines from
a standard list, but also send out regular special offers to customers on
their mailing list. On another level, the Inner Cellar range consists of
fine wines, mainly mature and old clarets.

The standard list contains many areas of interest   fortified wines
(the Findlater range of Sherries like Dry Fly is well known), a big
showing of clarets from recent vintages, Burgundy from Louis Latour,
Lupé Cholet and Moillard, and Chablis from Moreau, Alsace from
Hugel. On the Rhône, look for the Gigondas Domaine du Grand
Montmirail and on the Loire the Muscadet Clos des Orfeuilles. Charles
Heidsieck Champagnes are out in force.

Outside France, the best areas on this standard list are Germany,
with estate wines from Bassermann-Jordan and J J Prüm, and Italy,
with Chiantis from Ruffino and Veneto wines of Santa Margherita
(look also for this producer's Alto Adige Luna dei Feldi white 1985 at
£5.64). Spain has Riojas from Faustino and the inexpensive Señor
Burgues.

Best buys

Regular special offers; Findlater Sherries; Italian wines from Santa
Margherita and Ruffino

Special awards

⬡ is for bargain prices   ⬜ is for a very good range of wines

✿ is for high quality wines   ⬜ is for exceptional service

Fine Vintage Wines

3/5 Hythe Bridge, Oxford,   TEL (0865) 724866/791315
Oxfordshire OX1 2EW

OPEN Mon–Sat 10–7   Sun 11–2   CLOSED Most public holidays
CREDIT CARDS Access, Visa; personal and business accounts (by prior
arrangement)   DISCOUNTS 5% on 1 case   DELIVERY Free within 10-mile
radius in Oxford and 5-mile radius in London (min 1 case); otherwise minimum
charge of £6.50 per case on UK mainland; mail order available
GLASS HIRE Free with 1-case order   TASTINGS AND TALKS Regular Saturday
morning promotions; to groups on request   CELLARAGE 5p per case per week

This merchant is associated with Grape Ideas Wine Warehouse (*qv*).
Both operate from the same premises in Oxford, and are also linked
with David Scatchard (*qv*) in Liverpool.

Their range of wines is very much what the name suggests. It's
strong on areas such as mature clarets (with a good price range),
domaine-bottled Burgundy (including reds from the early 1970s), a big
range of mature Vintage Ports – and a fascinating collection of old
vintage Madeiras (with what must be one of the oldest wines in this
guide – a 1795 Terrantez from Companhía Vinícola da Madeira at a
mere £376).

Other areas are less well represented, but Rhône wines from Roger
Combe in Gigondas and from Jaboulet Aîné and Chapoutier (plenty
from the superb 1983 vintage), Alsace wines from Faller and
Champagne from Louis Roederer are all attractive. In Italy, there are
some interesting bottles from producers like Colacicchi (Torre
Ercolana), Caparzo (Ca del Pazzo) and Sella e Mosca in Sardinia.
Australia offers wines from the Katnook Estate, while Preston
Vineyards wines come from California.

Best buys

Mature clarets; Grumello 1982, CVEV, £4.90; Rioja Tinto 1978 CVNE,
£3.55; old solera Madeiras

Fortnum & Mason

181 Piccadilly, London W1A 1ER   TEL 01-734 8040

OPEN Mon–Fri 9–5.30   CLOSED Sun, public holidays   CREDIT CARDS All
accepted; personal and business accounts   DISCOUNTS 5–10% (min 1 case)
DELIVERY Free in Greater London (min £10 order); otherwise at cost; mail order
available   GLASS HIRE Not available   TASTINGS AND TALKS Occasional
promotional tastings   CELLARAGE Not available

Horizons have suddenly broadened at this most famous of London
grocers. The New World has been discovered – as have Italy, Spain
and Portugal – so the list is looking in much better shape than it did last
year. However, bear in mind that prices are high.

Mind you, some things don't change, such as the huge range of

Champagnes – one of the best around. And Bordeaux still numbers some really mature vintages (such as 1929 and 1945) as well as more recent ones. The nature of this list can be divined from the vintages of Ch d'Yquem in Sauternes, and from the fact that nearly all the clarets are classed growths.

There's a smaller selection from Burgundy – but, again, some classy (and pricy) stuff – from négociants and domaines alike. On the Loire the greatest interest is in Sancerre and Pouilly Fumé (although the mature Quarts de Chaume 1971 of Jean Baumard at £25 would be delicious now). A good range of Alsace wines, and a few regional wines (like Domaine Ott in Provence), are likewise at the expensive end of the spectrum.

Then we come to the changes. Spain has CVNE Riojas and Torres wines, plus Vega Sicilia; Italy has Veneto wines from the Guerrieri-Rizzardi estate, wines from Bigi in Orvieto, Chiantis from Rocca delle Macie and others from Antinori. Portugal offers examples from João Pires and J M da Fonseca. In the New World we now find California wines from Acacia, Firestone, Ridge, Jordan and Joseph Phelps; Rouge Homme, Leo Buring, Petersons, Petaluma, Montrose, Rothbury and Penfold's from Australia; Matua Valley, Babich and Cloudy Bay from New Zealand. There are Sherries from Don Zoilo and Barbadillo; and a good collection of Vintage Ports.

Best buys

Montepulciano d'Abruzzo 1986, Illuminati, £4.30; Ch Pavie, St-Emilion 1978, £20; Ch Millet 1982, Graves, £10.95; Leo Buring Chardonnay 1987, South Australia, £6.50

The Four Vintners

HEAD OFFICE AND CELLARS   TEL (Order Office) 01-739 7335
7–9 Kingsland Road, London E2 8AA
City Wine Shop, 2 Mitre Court,   TEL 01-606 2959/2909
off Wood Street, London EC2V 7JB
8 other branches in London, Middlesex, Essex and Surrey

OPEN Mon–Fri 9–5.30   CLOSED Sat, Sun, public holidays
CREDIT CARDS Access, Amex, Diners, Visa; personal and business accounts
DISCOUNTS 10% on 1 case   DELIVERY Free in London and Home Counties
(min 3 cases); elsewhere at cost; mail order available   GLASS HIRE Free with
1-case order   TASTINGS AND TALKS Held regularly at branches; tasting for
customers in 16th-century dungeons by invitation; to groups on request
CELLARAGE Free for wines purchased from premises

This is a traditional list – long on the classic French areas, but still lumping together much else under 'wine from other countries': Faustino Riojas from Spain, Clos du Bois and Firestone from California and McWilliams Hanwood from Australia . . .

On French soil, this list offers a reasonable range of clarets (including some petit château wines), back to 1962 in the case of the current list, with a few mature sweet white Sauternes (1971 Ch Coutet at £28.50). In Burgundy, we find Labaume Aîné as the main supplier, while Chablis comes from Domaine Long Depaquit, Tremblay and Moreau.

There's some interest in the French regions (Ch de la Condamine 1986, Corbières is £3.19; Côtes du Ventoux, Michel Bernard is £2.85), and the Loire has Muscadet from Pichon-Potiron and Sancerre from Bernard Balland. Other observations are a range of grande marque Champagnes, a rather dire Italian section, not much from Germany and plenty of mature Vintage Ports, plus Lustau Sherries.

Best buys

Hanwood Chardonnay 1986, New South Wales, £4.75; Côtes du Frontonnais 1985, Ch Bellevue la Forêt, £3.85; Ch Plagnac 1981, Médoc, £5.50; Champagne Jules Ferraud, £8.99

Friarwood

26 New Kings Road, London SW6 4ST   TEL 01-736 2628
OPEN Mon–Sat 9–7   Sun by appointment   CLOSED Chr Day, Boxing Day, Easter Day   CREDIT CARDS All accepted; personal and business accounts
DISCOUNTS Negotiable   DELIVERY Free in London (min 3 cases) and rest of UK (min 6 cases); otherwise at cost; mail order available
GLASS HIRE Available   TASTINGS AND TALKS To groups on request
CELLARAGE 8p per case per week (inc insurance)   ■

This remains a single-minded list. Top-quality Bordeaux and Burgundy are the theme, and if other areas do put in an appearance, it is essentially to complement rather than to move in a new direction.

In Bordeaux, we find a big selection of classed growth wines from the 1986 vintage (which is on offer en primeur) back to the great 1970 vintage, as well as sweet white Bordeaux, again from the top estates. In Burgundy, the pattern is repeated, with domaine wines from some pretty serious names (Billard-Gonnet, Fontaine-Gagnard, Domaine Guyot, Romanée-Conti, Patrick Javillier). Reds here go back to 1969. Many Burgundies are exclusive to Friarwood.

Elsewhere, the operation is on a smaller scale, but wines are mostly domaine bottles, whether Sancerre, Pouilly Fumé, Beaujolais or the Rhône. Featured Champagnes are Alfred Gratien and Abel Lepitre, as well as Friarwood's own-label.

Best buys

1981 clarets; Champagne Friarwood, £8.24

Prices are only a rough indication, and were current in summer 1988.

Fullers (Fuller, Smith & Turner)

HEAD OFFICE Griffin Brewery,   ·   TEL 01-994 3691
London W4 2QB
60 shops in West London and Thames Valley

OPEN (Usually) Mon–Sat 10–9   Sun 12–2, 7–9   CLOSED Some public
holidays   CREDIT CARDS Access, Visa; personal and business accounts
DISCOUNTS Up to 10% (min 1 case)   DELIVERY Free within reasonable radius
of shop and in Greater London for wholesale orders; otherwise £1.60 per case
GLASS HIRE Free   TASTINGS AND TALKS Regular tastings in some shops; to
groups on request (min 25 people)   CELLARAGE Available

The range at this chain of shops has become much better than even two
years ago. They have succeeded in searching out interesting and good
value wines in most of the major areas.

One big plus is that on the whole they have avoided the brands, but
instead have put together a good selection of petit château wines.
There is also an enlarged range of good Burgundies, a mix of négociant
and domaine wines (look for Hautes Côtes de Beaune 1985 of Domaine
Michel Plait, or Sorin's Sauvignon de St-Bris 1986). While the Loire
selection is short, Muscadets from Chéreau-Carré and Ch du
Cléray are sound, and the Rhône has wines from Jaboulet Aîné. The
French country wines take in varietal vins de pays from the Ardèche,
and the Cépage Merlot Vin de Pays des Côtes de Thongue, plus wines
from Ch la Jaubertie in Bergerac and from Listel.

Of the other European countries, the best served seems to be Italy,
with Veneto wines from Guerrieri-Rizzardi, Antinori Chianti, Barbera
from Fontanafredda, Chardonnay from Tiefenbrunner. In Spain, there
are Torres wines, Domecq Riojas and Raimat Abadía from Catalonia.
Australia and New Zealand have come on as well – look for Cook's
from New Zealand and Brown Brothers from Australia, while William
Wheeler is the winery from California.

In a final burst, the list reveals a range of Sherries from many of the
major producers, and a big collection of Vintage Ports.

Best buys

Bergerac Blanc 1987, Ch la Jaubertie, £3.95; Côtes du Ventoux 1986,
Jaboulet Aîné, £2.99; Alsace Pinot Blanc 1985, St-Odile, £2.99; petit
château clarets

Gare du Vin

See Victoria Wine Company.

Most wine merchants will supply wine for parties on a sale or return basis.

M & W Gilbey

Eton Wine Bar, 82/83 High Street,   TEL (0753) 854921/855182
Eton, Windsor, Berkshire SL4 6AF

OPEN 7 days a week CREDIT CARDS None accepted; personal and business accounts DISCOUNTS Not available DELIVERY Free in UK (min 5 cases); mail order available GLASS HIRE, TASTINGS AND TALKS, CELLARAGE Not available ■

This fairly short list is very sensibly divided up into styles – dry white, red, rosé, and so on, rather than by country, and arranged in price order.

This means that you find a clutch of white Burgundies from Chanut Frères (who supply some of the red Burgundies as well) mingling with Ménétou-Salon from Pellé (the 1987 vintage at £4.79), building up to Puligny-Montrachet and Chablis Montée de Tonnerre from Domaine Servin. In reds, the base line is Beaujolais from Chanut Frères, but on the way to more top-flight Burgundy, there's Côtes de Castillon 1985, Ch Lagrange Monbadon at £4.04, and a good Côtes du Rhône, Domaine Martin 1983 at £3.34. A few German wines and Magenta house Champagne at £8.68 round off the list. (See also the Eton Wine Bar in the WINE BARS section.)

Best buys

Alsace Sylvaner 1986, Caves de Hunawihr, £3.12; Ardèche Merlot 1986, Domaine de Bournet, £3.50; Ch le Fage 1986, Bergerac Sauvignon Blanc, £3.17; Côtes de Castillon 1985, Ch Lagrange Monbadon, £4.04

Matthew Gloag & Son

Bordeaux House, 33 Kinnoull Street,   TEL (0738) 21101
Perth, Perthshire PH1 5EU

OPEN Mon–Fri 9–5 CLOSED Sat, Sun, some public holidays
CREDIT CARDS Access; personal and business accounts DISCOUNTS Available for Club members only DELIVERY Free in mainland Scotland (min 1 case); otherwise £2.20 on mainland England and Scottish Islands; mail order available GLASS HIRE Free with nominal case order
TASTINGS AND TALKS Regular tutored tastings through club; to groups on request CELLARAGE 3.45 per case per year

---

After last year's disappointments, when Matthew Gloag's list seemed to be shrinking almost to nothing, we are delighted to report a certain expansion, as well as a new Wine Club offering discount prices.

The main changes seem to be in the French regions, Spain and the New World, but they have also rounded up a number of less expensive clarets (although none of them is actually really good value). Vintages go back to 1970. In Burgundy, we find wines from Delaunay, Mazilly and Domaine André Nudant, while Beaujolais is from Louis

Deschamps. The Loire section is still tiny, but Alsace is much better (with wines from Dopff et Irion), and the Rhône has a good range from Jaboulet Aîné.

Other French regions boast the excellent Côtes du Lubéron wines of Ch Val-Joanis, Côtes du Marmandais of Cave du Cocumont and the Cabardes of Ch la Seigne 1986 (£3.20). Beyond France, look for Torres wines in Penedès, plus the Pesquera Ribera del Duero 1985 at £13.50. Italy can only really offer Chianti Machiavelli. German wines come from Deinhard.

In Australia, we now get a range which includes the normally good value Jacob's Creek (although here at a ridiculously high price) and wines from Mildara, while Selaks wines come from New Zealand. A few mature Vintage Ports and Sherries from Barbadillo complete the selection.

Best buys

Ch Beauséjour 1983, Fronsac, £4.75; Cabardes 1986, Ch la Seigne, £3.20; Barbadillo Sherries

G M Vintners

7 Wellington Terrace, George Street, Truro, Cornwall TR1 3JA	TEL (0872) 79680
3 Alphinbrook Road, Marsh Barton, Exeter, Devon EX2 8RG	TEL (0392) 218186
Market Wine Stores, Lemon Street Market, Truro, Cornwall TR1 1QD	TEL (0872) 41446

OPEN Mon–Sat 9–5   CLOSED Sun, public holidays   CREDIT CARDS Access; personal and business accounts   DISCOUNTS Not available   DELIVERY Free within Cornwall, Devon and Somerset (min 1 case within own area, 6 cases outside)   GLASS HIRE Available   TASTINGS AND TALKS Monthly during season; to groups on request   CELLARAGE Negotiable

The group of shops which trades under the G M Vintners banner includes two wine warehouses and a retail outlet in Truro. Their prices do not include VAT (we have added it on here) but nevertheless remain sensibly affordable.

On a sound rather than an exciting list, the Loire, as last year, is one of the best represented areas, with refreshing Muscadet from Ch de Coing de St-Fiacre at £4.12, and the remarkable dry Savennières of Ch d'Epire at £5.19. Less pricy wines include the clean Sauvignon de Touraine of Les Vins Touchais at £2.78. Beaujolais is from Loron, Burgundy from Chanson Père, and domaine-bottled Chablis from Domaine du Colombier. Pommery supplies the Champagne, and there's a small selection of claret (look for the Ch de la Rivière 1982 at £7.77).

Italy is well treated with wines from Bolla in the Veneto, Pighin in Friuli and Melini in Chianti, plus the top estate wines of Regaleali in

Sicily. Portugal is represented by table wines from João Pires and Ports
from da Souza. Australia chips in with a good range of Penfolds reds
(including Grange 1980 at £24.18 and Dalwood Shiraz/Cabernet 1984 at
£3.83).

Best buys

Wines from Listel; Ménétou-Salon 1987, Domaine de Chatenoy,
£4.51; Forster Bischofsgarten Kerner Spätlese 1983, Bonnet, £5.84;
Ch Mondetour 1985, Entre-Deux-Mers (red), £3.67

Godrich & Petman

9A Parchment Street, Winchester,   TEL (0962) 53081
Hampshire SO23 8AT
ASSOCIATED WITH Eldridge Pope,   TEL (0305) 251251
Weymouth Avenue, Dorchester, Dorset DT1 1QT
12 branches in South and South-West

OPEN Mon–Fri 9–5.30 Sat 9–5 CLOSED Sun, public holidays
CREDIT CARDS Access, Visa; personal and business accounts DISCOUNTS Not
available DELIVERY Free in Andover, Basingstoke, Southampton and
Winchester (min £20 order); mail order available GLASS HIRE Free with some
case orders TASTINGS AND TALKS Monthly in-store tastings (evenings) and
special offers; to groups on request CELLARAGE Free

This chain of stores operates from the same list as Eldridge Pope (*qv*).

Goedhuis & Co

101 Albert Bridge Road, London SW11 4PF   TEL 01-223 6057

OPEN Mon–Fri 9.30–5.30 CLOSED Sat, Sun, public holidays
CREDIT CARDS Access, Visa; personal and business DISCOUNTS Only for
corporate clients DELIVERY Free in London (min 3 cases) and UK (min 5
cases); otherwise £2.87 in London and £5.75 in rest of UK; mail order available
GLASS HIRE Free TASTINGS AND TALKS Two major annual tastings
CELLARAGE £3.68 per case per year   ∎

Although not long – even if the longest yet from this firm – this is a list
of high quality, with careful buying evident in every area.

While it still concentrates on classic French areas, there's more from
other countries than last year. Australia is developing into a very good
range, quite compact but with wines from smaller boutique wineries
not otherwise seen over here – Basedow, Hollick Coonawarra and
Frasers. Similarly in New Zealand we get Yates and Judd Estate as well
as the more familiar Cook's. In Europe, the good value Señorio de los
Llanos from Valdepeñas has made an appearance, and Champagne
now includes wine from Barnaut as well as various grande marque
houses.

And so to Bordeaux. What is encouraging about this list is the
number of good value petit château wines, including vintages back to

1978, as well as clarets from 1985 and 1986 for laying down. In
Burgundy, there's a good roll call of domaine wines, and on the Loire
we find the Ménétou-Salon of Henri Pellé as an antidote to the pricier
Sancerre and Pouilly Fumé. The Rhône has a big range of wines from
Guigal, Chave and Ch de Beaucastel, while Alsace wines are from the
award-winning Rolly Gassmann.

Best buys

Sauvignon les Martinières 1987, Domaine Michaud, £3.60; Ch Gourran
1981, Premières Côtes de Bordeaux, £5.20; Mâcon-Prissé 1986, Cave
Co-opérative de Prissé, £4.60; Bourgogne Passetoutgrain 1986, Henri
Jayer, £5.70

Andrew Gordon Wines

Glebelands, Vincent Lane, Dorking,   TEL (0306) 885711
Surrey RH4 3YZ

OPEN Mon–Fri 9–5.30   Sat 9–4   CLOSED Sun, public holidays
CREDIT CARDS Access; personal and business accounts
DISCOUNTS Available   DELIVERY Free in Surrey (min 1 case) and London area
(min 6 cases); otherwise 1–11 cases £1.25 per case, 12–21 cases £1 per case, 21+
cases free   GLASS HIRE Free   TASTINGS AND TALKS Occasional in-store
tastings; to groups on request   CELLARAGE Not available   ■

This is the firm that offers you a share of a French vineyard in the Côtes
de Duras, with a guarantee of 30 cases of the wine a year. But just in
case 30 cases of the same wine don't appeal – or in case you want
something else as well – there are plenty of other goodies on this
wide-ranging list.

Andrew Gordon's interest in the French regions extends to more
than just the Côtes de Duras: for instance, a considerable range from
the Midi and the South-West and from more far-flung areas such as
Savoie and Sauvignon de St-Bris. In Bordeaux, there's some good
value in the petit château wines as well as more serious stuff that on a
recent list went back to the 1962 vintage. In Burgundy, Mr Gordon has
very sensibly gone for lesser appellations and offers us some good (in
Burgundian terms) bargains in the process. Other French areas to do
well are the Rhône (especially in the south with Côtes du Rhône), and
Alsace wines from Victor Preiss.

Over the Alps in Italy, the list remains as good as last year, with
some good value Chianti from Grati, Valpolicella from Castello d'Illasi
and Lugana Ca' dei Frati as good buys. Other countries are treated
more briefly – but consider Monte Ory Gran Reserva 1978 from
Navarra in Spain (£3.45), or a pair of hearty Tunisian reds, or
Australian wines such as the superb Peterson Hunter Valley
Chardonnay (the 1985 vintage is £7.65). Fortified wines – especially
Ports and Madeiras – are good, too.

Best buys

Cabardes 1986, Domaine St-Roch, £2.25; Ch la Tour de Bessan 1985, Margaux, £6.99; Bourgogne Blanc 1987 Oak Aged, Les Vignes de la Croix, £5.25; Chianti Classico 1985, Isole e Olena, £3.85

Gordon & MacPhail

58–60 South Street, Elgin, Moray IV30 1JY   TEL (0343) 45111

OPEN Mon–Fri 9–5.15   Sat 9–5   CLOSED Wed pm (Jan, Feb, March, May, Oct to mid-Nov), Sun, public holidays   CREDIT CARDS Access, Visa; personal and business accounts   DISCOUNTS 5% on 6 bottles, 10% on 12 bottles   DELIVERY Free within 20-mile radius (min 1 bottle) and elsewhere (min 1+ cases); mail order available   GLASS HIRE Free   TASTINGS AND TALKS,   CELLARAGE Not available

If you manage to surface from the huge range of malt whiskies, you will find a useful rather than exciting range of wines, which is strongest in fairly traditional areas – Bordeaux, Burgundy, Germany and Vintage Ports.

Vintage Ports are there from most of the post-war vintages, including a number of the most recent 1985s. In Bordeaux, there's an equally strong showing from 1985, with wines from 1986 just available. Prices for the petit château wines are competitive. Burgundy is a mix of négociant wines (Chanson and Ropiteau) and domaine wines, and Beaujolais is from Paul Bocuse, one of the brand names of Georges Duboeuf.

There are good things in Germany – estate wines from the State Domaine in the Nahe, wines from Langwerth von Simmern on the Rheingau and Bürklin-Wolf in the Rheinpfalz. Italy and Spain are disappointments, but Portugal offers wines from J M da Fonseca. In the New World, Australian wines come from Tyrrell's, New Zealand from Cook's and Montana.

Best buys

Ch de Brondeau 1985, Bordeaux Supérieur, £4.60; Paul Bocuse Beaujolais; Côtes du Ventoux 1986, Domaine des Anges, £3.32; Kreuznacher Mollenbrunnen Riesling Kabinett Halbtrocken 1985, P Anheuser, £4.73

The Wine Development Board is a small organisation with the responsibility of encouraging more people to drink wine. They may be able to supply literature and general promotional material. Contact them at: PO Box 583, Five Kings House, Kennet Wharf Lane, Upper Thames Street, London EC4V 3BH; TEL 01-248 5835.

Richard Granger

West Jesmond Station, Lyndhurst Avenue,   TEL 091-281 5000
Newcastle upon Tyne, Tyne & Wear NE2 3HH

OPEN Mon–Fri 8.30–6.30 Sat 8.30–1 CLOSED Sun, public holidays
CREDIT CARDS Access, Visa; personal and business accounts DISCOUNTS Not
available DELIVERY Free within 15-mile radius; otherwise negotiable; mail
order available GLASS HIRE Available TASTINGS AND TALKS Regular
in-store tastings; to groups on request CELLARAGE Not available

This is a short list, but the prices are good, with a fair sprinkling of
wines from right round the world, apart from a good showing in
France.

The clarets are sensibly priced, with some good value at the lower
end (Ch le Gardéra 1983 at £4.50; or Ch Graves de By 1983 at £3.25).
Beaujolais is from Duboeuf (he also provides Mâconnais white
Burgundy), while the Rhône has Côte Rôtie and Crozes-Hermitage
from Chapoutier. On the Loire, Pouilly Fumé is from de Ladoucette,
and Hugel and Trimbach wines represent Alsace.

Outside France, look for estate German wines from Deinhard,
Spanish Torres wines and Australian bottles from Leasingham and
Orlando. Viña Linderos Cabernet Sauvignon 1983, is a Chilean bargain
at £3.45, and the half-bottles of the De Bortoli Botrytised Semillon 1982
from New South Wales will be stunners (£8.70).

Best buys

Ch le Gardéra 1983, £4.50; Champagne Granger Private Cuvée, £8.30;
Viña Linderos Cabernet Sauvignon 1983, Chile, £3.45; Taylors
10-year-old Tawny Port, £8.45

Grapehop

See La Reserva Wines.

Grape Ideas Wine Warehouse

3/5 Hythe Bridge Street, Oxford,   TEL (0865) 722137
Oxfordshire OX1 2EW
2A Canfield Gardens, Swiss Cottage,   TEL 01-328 7317
London NW6 3BS

OPEN Mon–Sat 10–7 Sun 11–2 CLOSED Most public holidays
CREDIT CARDS Access, Visa; personal and business accounts (by
arrangement) DISCOUNTS Quantity discounts up to 5% DELIVERY Free
within 10-mile radius in Oxford and 5-mile radius in London (min 1 case);
otherwise minimum charge of £6.50 per case; mail order available
GLASS HIRE Free with 1-case order TASTINGS AND TALKS Regular Saturday
morning tastings; to groups on request CELLARAGE 5p per case per week

Grape Ideas have expanded over the past year, with the opening of a branch in north London. They are linked to Fine Vintage Wines (*qv*), and together provide a wide range of wines.

The Grape Ideas list tends to concentrate on the everyday wines, but even so, the list contains some classy numbers as well as some good value. For instance, in the Bordeaux section alongside some good petit château wines we find classed growths from 1978. In turn, they rub shoulders with an attractive selection of wines from the French regions – Bergerac from Fleury, Ch Fonscolombe Coteaux d'Aix-en-Provence, wines from Listel, and Côtes de Duras from Poulet.

In Burgundy, there are a few domaine wines (with many more under the Fine Vintage Wine list). Guy Saget is the supplier of some good Loire wines – Sancerre, Quincy and Pouilly Fumé, while on the Rhône look for wines from Jaboulet Aîné. Plenty of good bottles pop up in the Champagne section – Garnier, Henriot, Louis Roederer.

Beyond France, highspots occur in Spain (Torres wines), Bulgaria (some terrific value) and Italy (Frescobaldi wines). There are the good quality Yarden and Gamla wines from Israel, New Zealand wines from Cooks and Australian from Leasingham, Katnook and Rosemount. This is one of the few merchants to stock an Argentine wine (Andean Vineyards Cabernet Sauvignon, £3.95). Back in Spain, Sherries are from Osborne.

Best buys

Osborne Fino Quinta Sherry, £4.15; St-Simon Champagne, £7.30; Monterey Classic California red and white, £3.75; Sauvignon du Haut-Poitou 1986, £3.09; Chilean Cabernet Sauvignon 1983, Viña Linderos, £3.55

Great American Wine Company

BCM, Box 150, London WC1N 3XX   TEL 01-407 0502

OPEN 24 hours a day   CREDIT CARDS None accepted; personal and business accounts   DISCOUNTS Quantity discounts negotiable   DELIVERY Nationwide (min 1 case)   GLASS HIRE Not available   TASTINGS AND TALKS Occasional tastings for clients   CELLARAGE Not available   ■

This is as good a list as any in this Guide for discovering that American wine is not just from California. Here you will find Oregon wines from Knudsen Erath, Sokol Blosser and Yamhill Valley (now there's a set of names to conjure with), while in Washington the Hogue Cellars are prominent. Across the continent are New York State wines from Gold Seal on the Finger Lakes, and Hargrave Vineyard and Pindar Vineyards on Long Island.

After these excursions, California seems almost like home. There's some good value here – Patrick Dore and Fetzer wines are inexpensive for California, as are wines from Bel Arbres. At the top end, look for the wines of ZD, Bouchaine and Tjisseling. (Prices on this merchant's list are given without VAT – we have added it below.)

Best buys

Fetzer Vineyards NV red and white, £2.84; Bouchaine White Label Pinot Noir 1985, £4.85; Bel Arbres Sauvignon Blanc 1986, £3.96

Great Northern Wine Company

The Dark Arches, Leeds Canal Basin,   TEL (0532) 461200
Leeds, West Yorkshire LS1 4BR

OPEN Mon–Fri 9–6.30 Sat, public holidays 10–5.30 CLOSED Sun, 25 & 26 Dec, 1 Jan CREDIT CARDS Access, Visa; personal and business accounts DISCOUNTS Variable (min 1 case) DELIVERY Free within 30-mile radius of Leeds (min 1 case) and 4+ cases; otherwise at cost; mail order available GLASS HIRE Free TASTINGS AND TALKS Monthly tastings offered to customers; to groups on request CELLARAGE £2.75 per case per year

---

This is developing into an attractive, well-balanced list, with plenty of interest in all areas.

It starts firmly in France, with a good range of country wines (look for the sweet Jurançon Moelleux 1984 of Clos Guirouilh at £5.15, or the spectacular Collioure Cuvée les Piloums, Domaine du Mas Blanc at £7.89, or the Listel Cabernet Vin de Pays d'Oc at £3.38). Staying in the south, you might also choose the Côtes du Ventoux, La Vieille Ferme of the Perrin family (£3.55) and good wines from Côtes du Rhône and Châteauneuf.

The Loire produces some attractive Muscadet (Ch des Gautronnières at £3.90), while the source of Alsace is Louis Sipp. A short list of clarets goes back to 1979 (Ch la Duchesse Canon Fronsac 1979 is £6.15). Burgundy comes from négociant houses such as Antonin Rodet, Louis Latour, Ropiteau, Chablis from Alain Geoffroy, and among the Champagnes is the good-value version of André Drappier.

Other European vineyards supply interest, too. While Germany is relatively neglected, Torres and Raimat represent Spain, as well as Riojas from Berberana and Campo Viejo, and J M da Fonseca is the Portuguese celebrity. A few star reds from Italy include Valpolicella Classico 1983 Vigneti di Marana, Boscaini, £4.10 and Cannonau 1981, Sella e Mosca, £4.15.

Australia is out in force with Brown Brothers, Rosemount, Orlando, Wirra Wirra, Leasingham, Brokenwood (and the Morris Liqueur Muscat at £8.30). New Zealand has Selaks wines, there are Sherries from Valdespino, Garvey and Don Zoilo, and some of the excellent tawny Ports from Ramos Pinto.

Best buys

Bonchalaz Blanc and Rouge, Henri Maire, Jura, £2.99; Cahors 1983, Ch St-Didier Parnac, £3.55; Riesling 1986, Guntrum, £3.19; Shiraz 1982,

Taltarni, £4.85; Pemartin Solera 1914 Rare Manzanilla, £4.95;
Rutherford & Miles Madeiras

Peter Green

37a/b Warrender Park Road,   TEL 031-229 5925
Edinburgh EH9 1HJ

OPEN Mon–Fri 9.30–6.30   Sat 9.30–7   CLOSED Sun, public holidays
CREDIT CARDS None accepted; personal and business accounts
DISCOUNTS 5% on unmixed cases   DELIVERY 50p per trip in City of
Edinburgh; mail order available   GLASS HIRE Free
TASTINGS AND TALKS Annual tasting in October by invitation; to groups on
request   CELLARAGE Not available

Peter Green's wines never cease to amaze us. Partner Michael Romer
tells us that his aim as a wine merchant is 'never to drink the same wine
twice', which perhaps explains why the list expands every year.

What is so interesting about the range is that it avoids the easy
options of a huge directory of claret and Burgundy. Instead, it
branches out around the world, concentrating just as much on Italy,
Spain and Portugal as on France. It makes for a very balanced list at all
price levels, and gives this merchant the full four awards yet again.

With such a wealth of wines, we can only pick out areas which are
even better than the rest. One such is Alsace, where 1983 and 1985
wines from many of the major producers abound. On the Loire, there
are sweet wines from Quarts de Chaume and Bonnezeaux as well as
some reasonably priced Sancerres (for Sancerre, that is). The Rhône
has Hermitage from Chapoutier and also plenty of good value from the
Côtes du Rhône. The rest of France is expanding as well, with plenty
under £3 from the Midi. The range of Champagnes concentrates on
vintage wines.

The span of German estate wines is exemplary and includes plenty
of Auslesen as well as the Kabinett wines for everyday drinking
(there's even a Liebfraumilch at £1.99). And then we come to Italy: a
wonder of a list and a roll-call of names at all price levels: you can get
basic good quality Chianti from Amici Grossi at £2.89, you can get
seven different Recioto Valpolicellas, six different vintages of
Colombini Brunello di Montalcino, wines from Mastroberardino near
Naples, wines from Sella e Mosca in Sardinia – and many many more.

The same pictures emerges in Spain, with a big selection of Gran
Reserva Riojas to go alongside an even bigger set of more everyday
Riojas, against four vintages of Jean León's Cabernet Sauvignon and
three vintages of Torres Gran Coronas Black Label. There are wines
from Galicia, Ribera del Duero and Valdepeñas, and plenty of Sherries
as well. Portugal is served well by wines from Champalimaud in the
Douro and the ubiquitous and good wines from J M da Fonseca as well
as a Colares 1981 at £4.25 – give this wine another ten years. Look, too,
for five-year-old and ten-year-old Madeiras. There's a range from

Greece which includes the good-quality Ch Carras and Calliga Ruby.

In the New World, things are surprisingly restrained: a good range of Australian wine balances with the rest of the list but doesn't go overboard on the fashions. New Zealand has a sensible representation as well – wines from Montana, Babich, Stoneleigh Vineyards and Matua Valley. In America, there's Trefethen, Carneros and Mondavi – and wines from Texas and Oregon as well. Chile brings in Cousiño Macul, Concha y Toro, Santa Rita and Torres.

And don't forget the range of malt whiskies.

Best buys

Chilean Cabernet Sauvignon 1981, Antiguas Reservas, £3.99; Alsace Pinot Blanc 1986, Schlumberger, £4.70; Bourgueil 1987, Domaine Audemont, £3.75; Orlando RF Australian Cabernet Sauvignon 1985, £4.19; Duke of Wellington Sherries; Chianti 1987, Amici Grossi, £2.89

Green's

34 Royal Exchange, London EC3V 3LP   TEL 01-929 1799

OPEN Mon–Fri 9–6 CLOSED Sat, Sun, public holidays
CREDIT CARDS Access, Visa; personal and business accounts DISCOUNTS Not available DELIVERY Free in London postal district (min 1 case); elsewhere £5.75 per consignment, mail order available GLASS HIRE Nominal charge
TASTINGS AND TALKS Regular tastings given and also on request
CELLARAGE £5.75 per case per year (including insurance and free London delivery)

Although no longer under the same management as Bibendum, Green's still buy through them and operate from a shorter version of their list (see the Bibendum entry for details), offering the same good value. Green's also have access to a fine wine list run by Collins Wines, weighty with clarets and Ports.

In addition, there are still a few items from the days before Green's was sold to Bibendum. These include the Floquet Champagne (£9.49 a bottle), Burgundies from Raoul Clerget and Chassagne Montrachet from Jean-Marc Morey and Bernard Morey.

Best buys

Crozes-Hermitage 1986, Domaine des Entrefaux, £4.77; Cabernet Sauvignon Vin de Pays de l'Aude, Les Vignerons de Val d'Orbieu, £2.67; German wines from Max-Ferd Richter; Chianti Rufina 1986, Gratti, £2.97; Ch Dubraud 1983, Bordeaux, £3.77

Greenwood & Co

See Nickolls & Perks.

Hadleigh Wine Cellars

Eastgate Street, Bury St Edmunds, TEL (0284) 750988
Suffolk IP33 1YQ

OPEN Mon–Fri 9–1, 2–5.30 Sat 9–2.30 Good Friday morning CLOSED Sun,
public holidays CREDIT CARDS Access, Visa; personal and business
accounts DISCOUNTS 8% on 1 mixed case DELIVERY Free locally (min 1
mixed case); elsewhere at cost; mail order available GLASS HIRE Free with
order TASTINGS AND TALKS Bottles always open in-store; Spring and Autumn
tastings; to groups on request CELLARAGE Not available

The move to these larger premises may herald an expansion of this
merchant's current range. Not that it misses out on any areas at the
moment, and in many sections of the list prices are good.

Value is best outside the classic French areas (although look for petit
château wines from the 1985 vintage). Other clarets include classed
growths back to 1961. Burgundy offers a good value basic Pinot Noir
1986 from Loron at £3.75, plus pricier examples. Loron is also supplier
of the Beaujolais, while Rhône wines come from Jaboulet Aîné. The
Loire range includes an unusual bone dry white Cheverny 1986 at
£2.75, while Alsace wines come from Muré.

There's an extensive range of French country wines – varietal wines
from the Ardèche, the wordy Merlot Vin de Pays des Coteaux de la
Cité de Carcassonne of Domaine de Sautes la Bas at £2.95, Jurançon
from the Caves de Gan.

Outside France, the list shortens. Italy has the good value Chianti of
Rocca delle Macie (1986 at £3.73) and the Rosso Cònero of Bianchi at
£4.30. There are Riojas from Bodegas Artacho, Australian wines from
Orlando and Tisdall, New Zealand from Montana and Delegats,
Sherries from Osborne and a small selection of Vintage Ports.

Best buys

Côtes du Rhône Villages Valréas 1986, J P Brotte, £4.50; Champagne
Rasselet NV Brut, £8.95; Ch Trinité-Valrose 1986, Bordeaux Supérieur,
£3.80; varietal wines from the Ardèche; Picola Estate Red, Tisdall,
Goulburn Valley, Victoria, £4.28

Hampden Wine Company

8 Upper High Street, Thame, TEL (084 421) 3251
Oxfordshire OX9 3ER

OPEN Mon, Tue, Thur, Fri 9.30–5.30 Wed 9.30–1 Sat 9–5 CLOSED Sun,
public holidays CREDIT CARDS Access, Visa; personal and business
accounts DISCOUNTS 5% on 1 case; quantity discounts negotiable
DELIVERY Free in Thame and district (min 2 cases); elsewhere at cost
GLASS HIRE Free with 1 case order TASTINGS AND TALKS Wines available
in-store every Saturday and occasionally during the week; to groups on
request CELLARAGE Free for customers only (space limited)

This new firm has put together an ambitious first list, full of good things and obviously taking recognition of areas which are up and coming in the wine world.

One such is Portugal – they have gone further than just the high quality but fairly widely distributed wines of João Pires and J M da Fonseca, by finding the rich, meaty red Reguengos de Monsaraz 1987 at £2.70 from the Alentejo and a top Bairrada from Luis Pato (1985 vintage at £5.60). Similarly, in Australia, they have not gone just for the big names, but have included some smaller wineries (Rouge Homme, Cape Mentelle) and, in New Zealand, have picked out Nobilo's Gisborne Chardonnay (1986 vintage at £7.05).

But the list still places France in the forefront. Alsace wines come from Rolly Gassmann, and include older vintages and Sélection de Grains Nobles wines. On the Loire, the chosen Muscadet is the organically produced wine of Guy Bossard. Both Bordeaux and Burgundy are pricey, but look for the fine wines of Henri Jayer – his Bourgogne Passetoutgrains 1986 at £5.40 is excellent. The sole Beaujolais is from Michel Gutty (Beaujolais Villages 1987 at £4.25). In Provence, the best value is the Mas de Gourgonnier 1985, Coteaux des Baux en Provence at £4.95.

Moving to Spain, we find Riojas from CVNE and Valdepeñas from Felix Solis, while in Italy, there are wines from Lungarotti in Umbria, Antinori in Tuscany and Guerrieri-Rizzardi in the Veneto. A German section is promised later.

Best buys

Periquita 1982, J M da Fonseca, £3.50; Blanc de Blancs, Guy Bossard, £2.95; Domaine de Callory, Vin de Pays du Comté Tolosan, £2.95; Valdoro Valdepeñas Blanco 1987, Bodegas Felix Solis, £2.80

Gerard Harris

2 Green End Street, Aston Clinton,   TEL (0296) 631041
Aylesbury, Buckinghamshire HP22 5HP

OPEN Mon–Sat 9.30–8; limited morning service during public holidays
CLOSED Sun   CREDIT CARDS Access, Visa; personal and business accounts
DISCOUNTS 10% for 1 case (except for fine clarets, Ports etc in limited stock)
DELIVERY Free within 20-mile radius of Aston Clinton (min 1 case); otherwise
£5.75 per consignment; mail order available   GLASS HIRE Free with 1-case
order   TASTINGS AND TALKS Three major tastings annually; to groups on
request   CELLARAGE £4.30 per case per year (inc VAT)

Watching a merchant's list getting better and better is very enjoyable, as with Gerard Harris's portfolio, which is associated with the Bell Inn at Aston Clinton. This is building on previous strengths, such as Germany and Bordeaux, and expanding widely through the rest of Europe and into New World areas.

This is probably the only list in the Guide to start with Germany.

Although the selection is shorter than it used to be (a sad reflection on the lack of interest in fine German wines), there is still much to enjoy. Particularly strong are estate wines on the Mosel (with wines from Deinhard, von Hövel, Reichsgraf von Kesselstatt and J J Prüm) and on the Rheingau (Nägler, Staatsweingut of Eltville, Schloss Reinhartshausen).

Bordeaux next, and here we are treated to a parade of wines back to 1961. The best vintage selections are from 1982 (going from Ch Peyraud, Côtes de Blaye, at £4.85 up to Ch Beychevelle at £19.55). Also worth looking for are the magnums from top estates in many vintages, and some attractive Sauternes back to 1970.

In Burgundy, among a good mix of domaine and négociant wines, Faiveley, Joseph Drouhin and Louis Latour are among the favoured négociants, Romanée-Conti, Armand Rousseau and Gagnard Delagrange among the domaines. There are magnums here as well – an unusual sight. While the Loire and the Rhône are shorter, Gerard Harris includes some treats nevertheless. In Alsace, the wines come from Léon Beyer and Hugel, and French regional wines come from areas as far apart as the Jura and Cahors.

The Italian section remains small but beautiful with the Tenuta di Pomino of Frescobaldi, Chianti Classico from Badia a Coltibuono and Brunello from Tenuta Il Poggione. Spain has Torres wines as well as CVNE Riojas.

In the New World, Brown Brothers wines from Australia make their mark, along with Moss Wood, Taltarni and Wynns. There are the Cloudy Bay wines from New Zealand, and Trefethen wines from California (Eshcol red and white at £5.32). Not least, look for Sherries from Hidalgo and Diez Hermanos and a small number of Vintage Ports.

Best buys

German estate wines; Ch Fonroque 1983, St-Emilion, £6.90; Chiroubles Domaine de la Grosse Pierre 1987, £4.80; Côtes du Ventoux 1985, Jaboulet Aîné, £3.45; Lustau Palo Cortado Sherry, £4.25

Roger Harris ✉

Loke Farm, Weston Longville,   TEL (0603) 880171
Norfolk NR9 5LG

OPEN Mon–Fri 9–5   CLOSED Sat, Sun, public holidays   CREDIT CARDS All accepted; personal and business accounts   DISCOUNTS 2 cases £1 per case, 5+ cases £2 per case   DELIVERY Free on UK mainland (min 1 case); otherwise at cost; mail order available   GLASS HIRE Not available
TASTINGS AND TALKS In-store tastings on request; to groups on request
CELLARAGE Not available   ■

It's Beaujolais Beaujolais all the way with this list – and what a feast it is. Mr Harris collects producers and has put together a fascinating range of wines that represent the whole gamut of Beaujolais production. The new-look list tells us everything we need to know about this beautiful region.

The range moves from the comparatively large-scale operations of the co-operatives (Beaujolais from the Cellier des Samsons is £3.85 – prices on this list include case delivery to anywhere in mainland Britain) through to the small family farms like that of Ernest Aujas in Juliénas (their Juliénas 1983 is £6.10).

Every cru is here, including the less familiar ones such as Chénas and Côte de Brouilly, and there is a good range of basic Beaujolais as well as Beaujolais Villages. In addition, Mr Harris has a rare white Beaujolais and a Beaujolais Rosé, as well as a red Gamay wine from the small neighbouring region of Coteaux du Lyonnais (Cave des Vignerons de Sain-Bel 1987 at £3.80), an increasing range from the Mâconnais (so that he can offer white as well as red wines, we suspect) and Champagne from Ruelle-Pertois, a small grower in Moussy.

Best buys

Beaujolais 1987, Cave Co-opérative de Saint-Verand, £4.20; Beaujolais Villages 1987, Jean-Charles Pivot, £4.75; Chénas 1986, Henri Lespinasse, £5.65; Coteaux du Lyonnais Rouge 1987, Cave Vignerons de Sain-Bel, £3.80

Harrods

Knightsbridge, London SW1X 7XL   TEL 01-730 1234

OPEN Mon, Tue, Thur–Sat 9–6   Wed 9.30–7   most public holidays 10–5 CLOSED Sun   CREDIT CARDS All accepted; personal and business accounts DISCOUNTS Available on full cases (excluding Harrods party wines, de luxe Champagnes, Cru Classé Bordeaux, vermouths, aperitifs and Vintage Ports) – 12 bottles for price of 11   DELIVERY Free within 25-mile radius of Knightsbridge for account customers; elsewhere 1 case £7.50, additional cases £4 per case; mail order available   GLASS HIRE Not available   TASTINGS AND TALKS Frequent in-store tastings   CELLARAGE Not available

This is a range of wines that, although good, has been overtaken by events. By that we mean that plenty of other merchants now keep just as fine a collection, but at much lower prices and with equally good service.

The one possible exception to this is the Champagne section, which is very good indeed at the top, grande marque level, with plenty of de luxe cuvées (but a sign of their prices is that their house Champagne, Eugène Laroche, is £12.85, the price of grande marque wines in other merchants).

Bearing prices in mind, other strengths of Harrods' list are the mature clarets (and equally mature Sauternes), and a rapidly expanding Italian section, which now takes in a number of the super vini da tavola as well as wines from Antinori and Frescobaldi in

Tuscany, Prunotto in Barolo and Mastroberardino near Naples.

Spain, too, offers a good range – wines from Torres, from CVNE and Marqués de Murrieta in Rioja and Raimat. Australia has been given a boost with wines from Rosemount and Brown Brothers, Penfold's and Leeuwin Estate, and there are some top-quality wines from California. Other countries get walk-on parts, but there are plenty of Vintage Ports.

Best buys

Mixed case selections; Harrods Claret, Sélection Louis Vialard, £3.60; Coltibuono Rosso 1986, £4.20; Viña Albina Rioja Tinto 1982, Bodegas Riojanas, £4.20

John Harvey & Sons

HEAD OFFICE Harvey House,   TEL (0272) 836161
Whitchurch Lane, Bristol, Avon BS14 0JZ
27 Pall Mall London SW1V 5LP   TEL 01-839 4685
12 Denmark Street, Bristol, Avon BS1 5DQ   TEL (0272) 273759

OPEN Mon–Fri 9.30–5.30   CLOSED Sat, Sun, public holidays
CREDIT CARDS All accepted; personal and business accounts
DISCOUNTS Quantity discounts   DELIVERY Free on UK mainland (min 1 case); elsewhere £2 per case; mail order available   GLASS HIRE Free within Bristol and London delivery area   TASTINGS AND TALKS Regular in-store tastings; to groups on request   CELLARAGE £2.50 per case per year

Clarets, along with Ports and Sherries, continue to be the mainstays of this list. The clarets are dominated by a full range of Ch Latour, for which Harveys are British agents, balanced at the other end of the spectrum by petit château wines.

Ports are from Cockburn, which is owned by Harveys – look especially for the excellent aged tawnies and Vintage Ports. Harveys' own Sherries form the backbone of this section, and stars here are the 1979 range and the Old Bottled Sherries (ones which are matured in bottle rather like Vintage Ports, developing great character).

Elsewhere, interest centres on a good range of 1983 Sauternes and Barsac, on a new selection of Mosel wines from the 1986 vintage, on Australian wines from Brown Brothers and Orlando and in Châteauneuf-du-Pape of Domaine de Marcoux. Prices do not include VAT, but we have added it below.

Best buys

Les Forts de Latour 1979, £13.71; Bernkasteler Badstübe Riesling Halbtrocken 1986, Dr Loosen, £3.50; Harveys Hunting Port, £6.82; Harveys Old Bottled Sherries

Richard Harvey Wines　　　　　　　　　　　　　📨

The Old Court House, Wimborne Minster,　　　TEL (0202) 881111
Dorset BH21 1LT

OPEN Mon–Fri 9.30–5.30　Sat 9.30–1　CLOSED Sun, public holidays
CREDIT CARDS Visa; personal and business accounts　DISCOUNTS 2½% for 1
unmixed case, 5% on 6 unmixed cases; larger quantities negotiable
DELIVERY Free within 15-mile radius of Wimborne (min 1 case); free in Dorset,
Hampshire, Avon, Wiltshire, Somerset, Devon, Berks and central London (min
3 cases), rest of UK (min 6 cases); otherwise 1–2 cases £5.75 per case (£3.45 in
areas above), 3–5 cases £3.45 per case; mail order available　GLASS HIRE Free
with reasonable order　TASTINGS AND TALKS Two major annual tastings; to
groups on request　CELLARAGE £4.60 per case per year　　　　　　■

Richard Harvey's business exhibits all the virtues of not being too
large. He is able to home in on estate wines, single vineyards and
producers of high quality who don't have vast quantities to sell.

Mind you, the business is expanding. In last year's Guide, we
reported a move to a new shop; this year, Richard Harvey has not only
merged with another local wine merchant but is planning to open a
warehouse in Bournemouth in the winter of '88/'89.

The list starts firmly in France, with a good selection of regional
wines (look for the Cahors of Rigal & Fils at £3.70; or the good-value
Côtes du Ventoux of Domaine des Anges at £2.75). Then we move to
the classic areas – a sensibly small selection of claret going back to the
1978 vintage but focusing on 1983. Burgundy is dominated by domaine
wines – René Leclerc in Gevrey-Chambertin, Tollot-Beaut in Savigny
and Corton-Charlemagne, Domaine Leflaive in Bâtard-Montrachet.
Prices are good for what these wines are.

The Loire is well treated with Chinon from Pierre Ferrand and
Sancerre from Bernard Reverdy. Rhône wines are supplied by Jaboulet
Aîné, Guigal and Clos des Papes in Châteauneuf-du-Pape, while
Alsace stars the wines of Rolly Gassmann. The house Champagne is by
Alexandre Bonnet at £9.95.

In Italy, the estate wine philosophy continues to hold good: Ca' del
Monte makes the Valpolicella, Barolo is from Rocche di Manzoni
(Barolo 1982 at £13.50), Chianti is from Volpaia and Badia a Coltibuono.
German estate wines cover the major growing areas in a small list of
famous names (Balthasar Ress, Bassermann-Jordan, Friedrich-Wilhelm
Gymnasium). Well-chosen Ports rub shoulders with Sherry from
Barbadillo and Madeira from Cossart Gordon.

Best buys

Ch Potensac 1984, £5.75; Côtes du Ventoux 1984, Domaine des Anges,
£2.75; Bourgogne Rouge 1985, Henri Jayer, £8.95; Valpolicella Classico
Superiore 1984, Ca' del Monte, £3.20

Haynes Hanson & Clark

17 Lettice Street, London SW6 4EH	TEL 01-736 7878
36 Kensington Church Street, London W8 4BX	TEL 01-937 9732

OPEN Mon–Fri 9.15–7 (SW6); Mon–Sat 9.30–7 (W8)   CLOSED Sat (SW6), Sun, public holidays   CREDIT CARDS None accepted; personal and business accounts   DISCOUNTS 10% on 1 unmixed case   DELIVERY Free in central London and on regular van-delivery runs (Thames Valley and East Anglia) (min 1 case); elsewhere 1 case £3.80, 2 cases £2.80 per case, 3–4 cases £1.20 per case, 5+ cases free on UK mainland; mail order available   GLASS HIRE Free with 1-case order   TASTINGS AND TALKS Regular in-store tastings at Kensington Shop; regular tastings for customers by invitation; to groups on request   CELLARAGE Can arrange on customers' behalf

If this firm is always associated with Burgundy, that's probably because one of the directors (Anthony Hanson) has written the definitive book on the subject – and as a consequence tends to know from whom to buy in this tortuous area (he has also lived there, which helps even more).

But Haynes Hanson & Clark are also pretty good in Bordeaux. They've built up a good range of wines from the five vintages before 1987 and are particularly strong in 1985 and 1983, although there's plenty back to 1979. Prices climb from the middle of the range upwards, but are not expensive for what the wines are.

In Burgundy, too, they have been buying from past vintages – particularly 1985. During the summer of 1988, they made an opening offer of 1986 wines, but continue to stress the quality of 1985. Look for the best (not necessarily the best-known) names in Burgundy – Simon Bize, Jean-Pierre Meulien, Pascal Prunier, Michel Clerget, Jacques-Frédéric Mugnier, Jacqueline Jayer . . . so the list goes on. Every Burgundy here can be recommended – a rare accolade for a wine merchant.

If the rest of the list seems an anti-climax, one must remember that everything is relative, for there is much to delight in on the Loire and the Rhône (top names such as Jaboulet Aîné, Guigal, Domaine du Vieux Télégraphe). We always enjoy the Pierre Vaudon Champagne (£9.95) a rare Blanc de Noirs made from black grapes only.

Outside France, peruse the German estate wines, and the New World section including Mount Barker in Australia and Stoneleigh Vineyards in New Zealand. To stock the California Saintsbury Pinot Noir is a high recommendation from a Burgundy expert (£8.65).

Best buys

Burgundies; Champagne Pierre Vaudon, £9.95; California Pinot Noir 1986, Saintsbury, £8.65; Beaujolais Villages 1987, François Crot, £4; Ch les Rivaux 1985, Bordeaux Supérieur, £3.95

Hedley Wright

The Country Wine Cellars, Twyford Road, TEL (0279) 506512
Bishop's Stortford, Hertfordshire CM21 2YT

OPEN Mon–Fri 9–5 Sat 9.30–5 CLOSED Sun, public holidays
CREDIT CARDS Access, Visa; personal and business accounts
DISCOUNTS Negotiable on 5+ cases DELIVERY Free on UK mainland (min 1
case); mail order available GLASS HIRE Free with 1-case order
TASTINGS AND TALKS In-store tastings every Saturday; 2 major annual tastings;
to groups on request CELLARAGE £3.95 per case per year

After a year's delay Hedley Wright have finally moved to new and
larger premises in Bishop's Stortford from their original home in
Sawbridgeworth. At the same time, they seem to have expanded their
range of wines, especially outside France.

The Italian section seems to have sprung from nowhere, and now
includes a good representation of what is happening in that country
(San Jacopo Chianti Classico, Castello Vicchiomaggio 1985 at £4.35;
white Torbato di Alghero NV from Sella e Mosca in Sardinia at £4.50).
Australia and New Zealand have also put in an appearance (New
Zealand with Babich and Matua Valley wines; Australia with Leo
Buring, Mitchelton and Berri Estates). So has Chile, with an exclusive
purchase of wines from Santa Helena (Siglo de Oro Cabernet
Sauvignon 1986 at £2.99). Spanish wines stay firmly with Torres.

On their more traditional French home ground, Hedley Wright's
basic house claret is Nathaniel Johnston's Country Gentleman's
Reserve Claret, £3.65; other good solid items on the list are wines from
the Domaine Fougeray de Beauclair in Burgundy (Marsannay Rouge
1986 at £5.60), Beaujolais from Maurice Geoffray, Rhône wines from
Jaboulet Aîné (and Châteauneuf-du-Pape from Domaine Elisabeth
Chambellan) and Louis Gisselbrecht Alsace wines.

Best buys

Crusted Port (Bottled 1986), Churchill, £9.25; Domaine de Mirabeau
Rouge, Vin de Pays des Collines de la Maure, £2.60; Chardonnay Vin
de Pays de l'Hérault 1987, Domaine de la Source, £3.60; The Country
Gentleman's Reserve Claret NV, Nathaniel Johnston, £3.65

Special awards

🐷 means bargain prices (good *value* may be obtained from merchants
without this symbol, of course, if you are prepared to pay for service)

❀ means that the wines stocked are of consistently high quality

▱ means that the merchant stocks an above-average range

☞ means that extra-special service is offered: helpful advice, informative
lists and newsletters, tastings etc.

Charles Hennings

London House, Pulborough,	TEL (079 82) 2485
West Sussex RH20 2BW	
10 Jenger's Mead, Billingshurst,	TEL (040 381) 3187
West Sussex RH14 9TB	
Golden Square, Petworth,	TEL (0798) 43021
West Sussex GU28 0AP	

OPEN Mon–Thur, Sat 9–1, 2–6 Fri 9–7.30 CLOSED Sun, public holidays
CREDIT CARDS Access, Visa; personal and business accounts DISCOUNTS 5%
on 1 case DELIVERY Free within 20-mile radius of Pulborough (min 3 cases);
otherwise at cost GLASS HIRE Free with equivalent case order
TASTINGS AND TALKS Weekly in-store tastings; one Summer and Christmas
tasting CELLARAGE Not available

Rather than being awash with good things, this is a list in which to find
nuggets of excitement. Perhaps surprisingly for a traditional wine
merchant, as this firm is described by its owner, the nuggets are not to
be found in France but in other European countries and in Australia.

Spain is probably the most interesting of the European sections, with
Faustino Riojas, CVNE Imperial, Campo Viejo Gran Reserva 1978
(£5.95 – a bargain), the Contino single vineyard Rioja, Marqués de
Cáceres, Marqués de Riscal and Torres Gran Coronas and Coronas.
Look, too, for the Jean Perico and Freixenet cavas.

By contrast, Italy is virtually ignored, but Germany produces wines
from Rudolf Müller and J J Prüm. Local patriotism dictates the presence
of wines from the nearby vineyard of Nutbourne Manor.

The south of France provides some good value (Cahors Domaine du
Colombie 1983 at £3.79 or Les Fenouillets Côtes du Roussillon Villages
1983 at £2.59). Bordeaux, by contrast, seems to have too many branded
or generic wines, and not enough good value from petits châteaux,
while Burgundy comes mainly from négociants (Chanson, Antonin
Rodet, Labouré-Roi).

Robert Mondavi in California, Penfolds reds in Australia and some
single estate wines from New Zealand are the best of the New World
bottles.

Best buys

Mildara Cabernet Sauvignon/Merlot 1984, Australia, £3.99; Fitou 1985,
Caves de Fitou, £2.85; Rioja Gran Reserva 1978, Campo Viejo, £5.95;
Ockfener Bockstein Riesling Kabinett 1983, Rudolf Müller, £4.35

Prices were correct to the best of our knowledge as we went to press. They,
and ranges of wines stocked, are likely to change during the course of 1989,
and are intended only as a rough indication of an establishment's range
and prices.

Douglas Henn-Macrae

81 Mackenders Lane, Eccles, Maidstone,   TEL (0622) 70952
Kent ME20 7JA
(Not a shop)

OPEN Mon–Sat (any reasonable hour up to 10 pm)   CLOSED Sun, Chr &
Easter   CREDIT CARD Visa   DISCOUNTS 5% on unmixed cases
DELIVERY Free on UK mainland (min 3 cases); otherwise £5.75 per order; mail
order   GLASS HIRE Not available   TASTINGS AND TALKS Tastings available;
to groups on request   CELLARAGE Not available   ■

Douglas Henn-Macrae, new to the Guide, has decided to concentrate
on two completely disparate areas – the other states of America (not
California, that is) and Germany. And he's doing both proud.

This is the merchant who told us that he had just bought up the
entire stock of one Texan vineyard (in fact, the Texas Vineyards of
Ivanhoe, Texas) – all 6,000 cases of it – and was shipping them all to
Britain. Wines from Fall Creek Vineyards and Sanchez Creek
Vineyards are also both from the Lone Star State. In Oregon, Mr
Henn-Macrae has wine from Adelsheim Vineyard; and in Washington,
he stocks a full range from Stewart Vineyards (especially late harvest
dessert wines).

The German side of the business likewise concentrates on wines
from less familiar areas: from the Nahe, from the tiny vineyards of the
Hessische Bergstrasse (probably the only merchant to import wines
from here), from Württemberg and – much more familiar – from the
Rheinpfalz and Mosel. Large ranges from one or two producers are the
norm in all these areas.

Best buys

Dessert wines from Stewart Vineyards, Washington State;
Schlossböckelheimer Burgweg Riesling Auslese 1976, Weingut
Berthold Pleitz, £7.20; Schwaigerner Grafenberg Trollinger 1986,
Heuchelberg Kellerei, £4.67

Hicks & Don

4 The Market Place, Westbury,   TEL (0373) 864723
Wiltshire BA13 3EA
Park House, Elmham, Dereham,   TEL (0362) 81571
Norfolk NR20 5AB

OPEN Mon–Fri 9–5.30   Sat by appointment (mornings only)   CLOSED Sun,
public holidays   CREDIT CARDS Access, Visa; personal and business
accounts   DISCOUNTS 5% on 5 cases   DELIVERY Free on UK mainland and Isle
of Wight (min 3 cases); £1 for Northern Ireland (min 3 cases); mail order
available   GLASS HIRE Free   TASTINGS AND TALKS To groups on request
CELLARAGE £1.84 per case per year (excluding insurance)

Hicks and Don won all our four awards last year, but in the wake of some recent complaints from our readers about a strange lack of availability of service, we have had to drop that particular award.

We hope that the lapse is only temporary, because the range of wines and their quality remains as good as ever. Last year's good balance in the list – with no one area really dominating – continues. If we had to pick out particularly strong areas, we would suggest the French regions (as they rightly say, 'France is still one of the best sources for good value off the beaten track'). So look for instance for the fresh Chardonnay Vin de Pays du Jardin de la France (£3.25) or Cahors Domaine Eugénie 1985 (£4.07).

The Alsace section is highly enjoyable, with good value from Jean Maurer and prestige from Hugel. Burgundy is getting bigger – the domaine wines from Domaine Parent, Madeleine Boillot and Daniel Chanzy caught our eye. Bordeaux has plenty of petit château wines, plus suggestions of wines for laying down. New with the 1987 vintage was a big range of Beaujolais, all from small domaines, which we hope will be repeated with the 1988 wines.

Outside France, there are good things in Italy (Rapitalà wines from Sicily, Chianti Classico from Castello dei Rampola, Rubesco from Lungarotti and the wines of the Vinattieri consortium), from Spain (Torres wines, Olarra Rioja), Greece (from John Calliga and Ch Carras) and now Australia – Rosemount, Hill-Smith Mountadam and Brown Brothers. The California listing is good as well – Mondavi, Firestone, Mark West. The range of German wines, too, takes in some good estate names.

The Champagne section looks hard at Joseph Perrier, Port is from various top shippers, and a very fine range of Sherries has been marshalled from Barbadillo and Pedro Rodriguez. English wines from Hicks & Don's own Elmham Park vineyard join others from local Norfolk estates.

Best buys

Domaine Beaujolais; Ch Thieuley Sauvignon 1986, £4.15; Ch des Tours 1985, St-Croix du Mont, £4.70; Vin de Pays de Vaucluse, Domaine de la Grange Blanche, £3.25; Waldracher Romerlay Riesling Spätlese 1983, Peter Scherf, £5.49

The Wine & Spirit Education Trust is an educational charity, approved by the Department of Education and Science, whose object is the education and training of all those (over the age of 18) who are connected with some aspect of the drinks industry, and for those who intend to enter these trades. The courses are run at three levels – Certificate, Higher Certificate and Diploma – all on a part-time basis. Contact the Trust at: Five Kings House, Kennet Wharf, Upper Thames Street, London EC4V 3AJ; TEL 01-236 3551.

High Breck Vintners   ⌂ ☞

Spats Lane, Headley, nr Bordon,	TEL (0428) 713689
Hampshire GU35 8SY	

ASSOCIATED OUTLETS

Nalders Wine Agency, Street House,	TEL (0734) 332312
The Street, Mortimer, Berkshire RG7 3NR	
Harbottle Wines, 27 Perrymead Street,	TEL 01-731 1972
London SW6 3SN	
Sir Ronald Preston, Beeston Hall Cellars,	TEL (0692) 630771
Beeston St Lawrence, nr Norwich, Norfolk NR12 8YS	
A G Barnett, 17 Windsor Road, Worthing,	TEL (0903) 32629
West Sussex BN11 2LU	
Col G P Pease, Milverton Cottage,	TEL (07357) 2624
Whitchurch, Pangbourne, Berkshire RG8 7HA	
J Dudley, Dukes Cottage, Rudgwick,	TEL (040372) 2357
Horsham, West Sussex RH12 3DF	

OPEN Mon–Fri 9.30–6 Sat 10–1 Sun, public holidays by appointment
CLOSED Chr Day CREDIT CARDS None accepted; personal and business
accounts DISCOUNTS 2.5% on 10 cases or on £600 per year, 3.75% on 20 cases
or on £1,200 per year, 5% on £2,000+ per year DELIVERY Free on UK
mainland and Isle of Wight (min 3 cases); elsewhere at cost; mail order
available GLASS HIRE Free with 1+ case order TASTINGS AND TALKS 5 6
tastings annually CELLARAGE £3.45 per case per year (space limited) ■

This is a very good list, rarely straying outside France (except for Ports
and Sherries) but bringing together a fine range from most parts of that
country. It is full of commentary and arranged by colour of wine –
white, sweet white, rosé and red.

Areas in which High Breck show extra interest include Alsace (with
wines from the high-quality firm of Wiederhirn in Riquewihr – look for
Vendange Tardive wines), the Loire (with Sancerre and Pouilly Fumé
from Gitton Père et Fils); dessert wines from Coteaux du Layon
Chaume and Bonnezeaux; and Bourgueil from Domaine des
Raguenières), and Beaujolais (with a super range from Les Eventails
des Producteurs).

The claret selection concentrates sensibly on mid-priced wines and
has plenty from the 1985 and 1982 vintages, while further east, we find
wines from Henry Ryman's Ch la Jaubertie in Bergerac. Outside
France, the main excursion is to Taylor and Noval Ports and an
excellent range of Sherries from Lustau.

Best buys

Atlantic Tawny, Taylor, £7.14; Alsace wines from Widerhirn; Coteaux
du Layon Chaume 1983, J-P Tijou, £4.88; St-Chinian Rouanet, £2.73;
Beaujolais from Les Eventails

Hilbre Wine Company

Gibraltar Row, Pierhead, Liverpool L3 7HJ   TEL 051-236 8800
OPEN Mon–Fri 8.30–5.45   Sat 9.30–12.30   CLOSED Sun, public holidays
CREDIT CARDS None accepted; personal and business accounts
DISCOUNTS Available   DELIVERY Free within Cumbria, Clwyd, Greater
Manchester, Lancashire, Manchester, Merseyside and North Staffordshire (min
1 case); elsewhere at cost; mail order available   GLASS HIRE Free with 1-case
order   TASTINGS AND TALKS Regular in-store tastings; to groups on request
CELLARAGE By arrangement (at the Liverpool Warehousing Co)

In this sound, still quite traditional list, it is worth recording the new
excursions first: a good range of wines from Lindemans (Cabernet
Sauvignon Bin 45 1985, and Semillon/Chardonnay Bin 77 1987, both
£4.91); also Montana wines from New Zealand, Inglenook wines from
California and plenty from Bulgaria.

Together with Germany, which offers some interesting estate wines,
France is the main focus. Clarets are well chosen, with some good
value in the Early Drinking wines (Ch Haut-Gaussens at £3.20);
vintages go back to 1980 in some quantity. While the Rhône list
remains short, there is now a good sprinkling of domaine-bottled
wines from Burgundy among the négociant wines of Patriarche (look
for Armand Rousseau, Domaine Laroche Chablis and Domaine du
Château de Meursault).

In the Loire, interest centres on the Muscadet Le Master de
Donatien and the Pouilly Fumé of Serge Dagueneau, while Alsace
contributes the wines from Dopff et Irion. House Champagne from
Lambert is good value at £8.29, among a good selection.

This year has witnessed a welcome increase in French regional wines
– try Les Quatre Coteaux Côtes du Roussillon red at £3.04 or the Blanc
de Blancs Caves St-André Vin de Pays Charentais white at £2.51.

Best buys

Les Quatre Coteaux, Côtes du Roussillon, £3.04; Ch Haut-Gaussens
1986, Bordeaux, £3.20 (also in magnums and halves); Schloss Vollrads
Riesling Blaugold Kabinett 1983, £7.74; Champagne Lambert Extra
Dry, £8.29

George Hill of Loughborough

The Wine Shop, 59 Wards End,   TEL (0509) 212717
Loughborough, Leicestershire LE11 3HB

OPEN Mon–Sat 9–6   CLOSED Sun, public holidays   CREDIT CARDS All
accepted; personal and business accounts   DISCOUNTS Approximately 10% on
1 case   DELIVERY Free within 30-mile radius (min 1 case); otherwise dependent
on area and quantity required; mail order possible   GLASS HIRE Free with
1-case order   TASTINGS AND TALKS In-store tastings every fortnight; large
annual tasting; to groups on request   CELLARAGE £2.50–£3 per case per year

This is a range of wines that has been slowly but usefully expanding
over the years. The latest areas to get a boost are Australia and the
French regions.

Taking the French regions first, there is a sound selection of
well-known names from smaller areas: Domaine des Terres Blanches
from Coteaux des Baux en Provence, for example, and the luscious
sweet Ch de Rey, Muscat de Rivesaltes (£6.45). Good red table wine
comes from Georges Duboeuf (Cuvée de l'Amitié at £3.29), plus wines
from Côtes de Duras, Pacherenc du Vic-Bilh and Fitou. New Australian
arrivals include wines from Peter Lehmann, Orlando and Montrose
(look for the Pinot Noir 1985 at £5.80).

In between these two contrasting areas, we find a solid range of
more classic wines. The Burgundy section is quite short, followed by
Beaujolais from Benoit Lafont and Georges Duboeuf. Rhône wines
include some from Jaboulet Aîné and Gabriel Meffre, or there's Pouilly
Fumé from Ladoucette at Ch de Nozet and Alsace from Kuentz-Bas
and Victor Preiss. In Bordeaux, a sensible selection covers vintages
back to 1966 – not large, but not too expensive either, such as Ch la
Tour St-Bonnet 1979 (£7.78) and Margaux Private Reserve 1983
(£7.38).

Spain (with Riojas from Bilbainas and CVNE and Torres wines) is
better served than Italy (although look for the Masi Veneto wines).
Sherries are from Valdespino, Domecq and Gonzalez Byass; Ports from
Taylors and Smith Woodhouse.

Best buys

Côtes de Duras Blanc 1986, Ch la Pilar, £2.99; Ch Plagnac 1978, Médoc,
£5.50; Shiraz/Cabernet Sauvignon 1983, Peter Lehmann, £4;
Champagne Jacques Meyer Private Cuvée, £9.95

Find the best new wine bargains all year round with our newsletter, *Which?
Wine Monthly*, available for £15 a year from: Dept WG89, Consumers'
Association, FREEPOST, Hertford SG14 1YB – no stamp is needed if posted
within the UK.

J E Hogg

61 Cumberland Street, Edinburgh EH3 6RA   TEL 031-556 4025

OPEN Mon, Tue, Thur, Fri 9–1, 2.30–6   Wed, Sat 9–1   CLOSED Sun, local
public holidays   CREDIT CARDS None accepted   DISCOUNTS Not available
DELIVERY Free in Edinburgh (min 6 bottles), smaller orders 50p; otherwise £3.80
per case; mail order available   GLASS HIRE Free with order
TASTINGS AND TALKS To groups on request   CELLARAGE Not available

To say that James Hogg's printed list is economical with space would
be an understatement. On four closely typed pages, he manages to
pack in an enormous span of wines and, of course, malt whiskies.
Within this range, his chosen areas of specialisation are the French
classic areas, Italy, Spain, California and Australia. In other words, he
is one of the group of Edinburgh wine merchants that are making this
city such a good place for wine lovers.

Alsace is a strong area, with wines from many of the major
producers and plenty of mature wines, such as Vendange Tardive
wines from 1973 and 1976. Featured producers are Kuentz Bas, Hugel,
Dopff au Moulin, Dopff et Irion and Trimbach. James Hogg shows an
interest in some good value petit château clarets as well as more pricey
classed and bourgeois growths (vintages back to 1975). The Rhône is a
high spot – look for wines from Jaboulet Aîné, Guigal, Chapoutier –
and for mature vintages of Hermitage and Côte Rôtie.

Italy makes for enjoyable reading: there's Barolo from Fontanafredda
(including single vineyard cru wines), the rare Sfursat wines from
Lombardy, Chianti from Antinori and Ruffino and Brunello di
Montalcino from Colombini, wines from Lungarotti and from Livio
Felluga in the Collio region of Friuli. In Germany, we find a fine set of
estate wines – with plenty of Spätlesen and Auslesen. Spain has Torres
wines and Riojas from Faustino. Mr Hogg's focus on the New World
has brought in Penfold's red wines, plus Idyll Vineyards, Pewsey Vale
and Petaluma. And back in Europe there's a good range of Sherries
including some dry amontillados and olorosos from Lustau.

Best buys

Alsace Tokay Pinot Gris 1985, Dopff et Irion, £3.77; Ch la Tour
St-Bonnet 1983, £4.85; Beaujolais from Louis Tête; Cornas 1977,
Jaboulet Aîné, £8.57; Chianti Riserva Ducale 1983, Ruffino, £4.55;
Penfold's Kalimna Bin 28 Shiraz, £4.84

We have tried to make the *1989 Which? Wine Guide* as comprehensive as
possible, but we should love to hear from you with commonts on any other
wine merchants you feel deserve an entry, or on existing entries. Write to
us either by letter or using the report forms supplied at the back of the
book.

Hopton Wines

Hopton Court, Cleobury Mortimer,   TEL (0299) 270482
Kidderminster, Hereford & Worcester DY14 0HH

OPEN Mon–Fri 9–5.30   CLOSED Sat, Sun, public holidays
CREDIT CARDS None accepted; personal and business accounts
DISCOUNTS Available   DELIVERY Free within 30-mile radius of Cleobury
Mortimer; elsewhere 1 case £7.50, 2 cases £6.50 per case, 3+ cases free; mail
order available   GLASS HIRE Free with 1-case order
TASTINGS AND TALKS Spring, Summer and Autumn tastings; to groups on
request   CELLARAGE Negotiable

This remains a short list, but there is much to please. Of particular
interest is red Bordeaux, with a sensible range from petit château wines
(Ch Lavergne 1983, Côtes de Castillon at £3.77) up to classed growths
from 1970 and 1966 (Ch Beychevelle 1966 at £80.43 a bottle). Another
area of interest is Burgundy – look here for some good domaine
bottlings, as well as some good-value (for Burgundy) generics.

The list remains fairly firmly in France for much of its length: a good
range of Pol Roger Champagnes (includes some large bottles); there are
Rhône wines from Ch de Montmirail in Vacqueyras and Châteauneuf
of Bosquet des Papes, while Alsace offers wines from Pierre Sparr.

Outside France, Hopton Wines have rounded up a few good
Chiantis from Fattoria la Casaccia, Cooks wines from New Zealand and
Yalumba from Australia. Ports are from Delaforce, Sherries from
Domecq.

Best buys

Domaine de Terrefort 1982, Bordeaux Supérieur, £5.62; Ch Thieuly
1987, Bordeaux Blanc, £4.67; Chianti Riserva 1978, Fattoria la Casaccia,
£4.70; Bourgogne Rouge, Christian de Marjan, £5.11

Hornsea Wine Market

See J Townend & Sons.

Horseshoe Wines

See David Baillie Vintners.

House of Townend

See J Townend & Sons.

If your favourite wine merchant is not in this section, write and tell us
about him or her. There are report forms at the back of the book.

Ian G Howe

35 Appleton Gate, Newark,   TEL (0636) 704366
Nottinghamshire NG24 1JR

OPEN Mon–Sat 9.30–7   Good Friday 12 noon–2, 7–9   CLOSED Sun
CREDIT CARDS Access, Visa; personal and business accounts
DISCOUNTS 2.5% for 1 case (may be mixed), 3.5% for 3 cases   DELIVERY Free
within 20-mile radius (min 1 case); elsewhere by arrangement
GLASS HIRE Free with 1-case order   TASTINGS AND TALKS Regular
'single-wine' in-store tastings (Saturday morning); quarterly regional tastings by
invitation; to groups on request   CELLARAGE Not available

'We have an enthusiasm for French wines – perhaps from the less
classic areas,' writes Ian Howe of his range of wines.

One of the stars is the wine from Mas Chichet Vin de Pays Catalan,
named by Gault et Millau as a Vigneron de l'Année (the red and rosé
are both £2.99, while the Cabernet Sauvignon red is £4.65). There are
other treats from down south as well – try the Collioure wines of Parcé
et Fils from Roussillon, or the Faugères of Domaine de Coudougno.

Other French areas are not neglected. The Côtes du Rhône of
Domaine de Réméjeanne is recommended, as are the varietal wines
from the Ardèche. Look also for Alsace wines from Laugel, the
Burgundies from Domaine Parent, and the Saumur from
Bouvet-Ladubay.

Outside France, the increase in the range of Ports is encouraging,
with Churchill's Vintage Character and Crusted Port being particularly
fine wines of their type.

Best buys

Vin de Pays de Gascogne 1987, Colombard, £2.65; Côtes du Ventoux
1986, Caves des Vignerons de Beaumes-de-Venise, £2.95; Coteaux du
Layon 1986, Renou, £3.95; Mas Chichet Vin de Pays Catalan, Paul
Chichet, £2.99

Victor Hugo Wines

HEAD OFFICE Tregear House,   TEL (0534) 70532
Longueville, St Saviour, Jersey   (order office)
The Stables, Belmont Place, St Helier, Jersey   TEL (0534) 78173
8B Quennevais Precinct, St Brelade, Jersey   TEL (0534) 44519
3 Stopford Road, St Helier, Jersey   TEL (0534) 23421
Bath Street Wine Cellar, 15 Bath Street,   TEL (0534) 20237
St Helier, Jersey

OPEN Mon–Sat 9–5.30   CLOSED Sun, public holidays   CREDIT CARDS None
accepted; personal and business accounts   DISCOUNTS 10% on wine case lots
DELIVERY Free in Jersey (min 1 case); mail order sometimes   GLASS HIRE Free
with 2-case order   TASTINGS AND TALKS Various in-house promotions; to
groups on request   CELLARAGE Available

This is really a list for French wine drinkers. The selections from other countries are really just spots on a generally classic Bordeaux, Burgundy, Rhône and Loire canvas. Of course, with low duty and no VAT, Jersey prices make those of fine wines seem very good value indeed to those of us from mainland Britain.

So shoppers at Victor Hugo should look for a fine selection of clarets (including mature wines from the 1970s), Beaujolais from Pasquier-Desvignes (who also supply many of the Rhône wines), a good mix of domaine and négociant Burgundies (better in whites than reds – perhaps to appeal to Jersey's fish restaurateurs?) and Loire wines (which include Muscadet from Marquis de Goulaine and Ch de Cassemichère). Champagne houses featured are Laurent Perrier and Perrier-Jouët. Look too, for Alsace wines from Hugel, Schlumberger and Dopff et Irion.

Outside France, the best bits are German estate wines, Italian wines, including Valpolicella from Santi and Rocca delle Macie Chianti Classico, and Osborne Sherries. There are good Vintage Ports, too.

Best buys

Garrafeira Reserva Particular 1974, Paulo da Silva, £3.94; Ch la Croix 1978, Pomerol, £10.95; Muscadet de Sèvre-et-Maine sur lie, Ch de Cassemichère, £2.78

Hungerford Wine Company

OFFICE 128 High Street, Hungerford,   TEL (0488) 83238
Berkshire RG17 0DL

24 High Street, Hungerford,   TEL as above
Berkshire RG17 0NF

21 Queen Street, Market Square, Salisbury,   TEL (0722) 332038
Wiltshire SP1 1EY

OPEN Mon–Fri 9–5.30 Sat 9.30–5 CLOSED Sun, public holidays
CREDIT CARDS All accepted; personal and business accounts
DISCOUNTS Negotiable DELIVERY Free within 15-mile radius of shops (min 1 case) and on UK mainland (min 5 cases); otherwise £7 per consignment; mail order available GLASS HIRE Free with 1-case order
TASTINGS AND TALKS Wines always available in-store; regular tastings at the Galloping Crayfish wine bar; to groups on request CELLARAGE £3.91 per case per year (including insurance)

Expansion has been in the air at this enterprising company. They have moved into larger premises in Hungerford, opened the Galloping Crayfish (see the WINE BARS section) and acquired a new branch in Salisbury (formerly Bamptons).

As always, the core of their list is Bordeaux. Hungerford were one of the few firms to make an en primeur offer of clarets with the 1987 vintage, but, equally importantly, they have a huge range of fine clarets stretching back over the years. They keep a fascinating list of large bottles, particularly double magnums (four bottles) and impériales (eight bottles). Look, too, for their list of the second wines of the great châteaux which often offer a taste of the Grands Vins at a fraction of the price.

While claret dominates, other areas are not neglected. Burgundy has undergone a rapid expansion, especially in reds, and there are plenty of top-flight domaine wines (inevitably at top-flight prices). On the Rhône, Jaboulet Aîné is the featured producer, while in Champagne a solid list of grande marque wines backs up an excellent house Champagne at £8.95.

The best area outside France is Spain, with wines from the Peñafiel co-operative in Ribera del Duero and Riojas from CVNE. Italy, we are told, will improve – watch this space.

Best buys

Ch Lasserre 1983, Bordeaux Supérieur, £4.15; Duke of Palmella 1980, Torres Vedras, £2.50; The Hungerford Wine Co House Champagne, £8.95; Ch le Bon Pasteur 1984, Pomerol, £9.20

G Hush   🐷

235 Morningside Road, Edinburgh EH10 4QT   TEL 031-447 4539

OPEN Mon–Thur 10–1, 2.30–7.30   Fri 10–1, 2.30–9.30   Sat 9 am–9.30 pm CLOSED Sun, public holidays   CREDIT CARDS None accepted; business accounts   DISCOUNTS 5% on unmixed cases   DELIVERY Free within 3-mile radius for reasonable order; otherwise at cost   GLASS HIRE Free with case order   TASTINGS AND TALKS, CELLARAGE Not available

---

G Hush is one of the many merchants that make Edinburgh such a lucky city for wine. Their main interest lies not in the classic areas of France (although these are good enough) but in the French regions, Italy and the New World: if you are looking for Texas wines, look no further.

The range of French regional wines is very fine – wines from the Charentais (including a Loire red lookalike Sornin Cabernet Merlot at £2.79; the varietal wines from the Ardèche; and Buzet Cuvée Napoléon 1984 at £3.59). All the varietal wines from Haut-Poitou are present, plus Rhône wines from Jaboulet Aîné and Champagne from Palmer (Brut NV at £9.79).

In Italy, the range includes Chiantis from Ruffino, Capezzana and Rocca delle Macie as well as Soave from Tedeschi and Alto Adige Chardonnay (Chardonnay di Appiano 1986, £3.35). Germany has wines from Huesgen and Deinhard, while there are Torres wines and Marqués de Murrieta Riojas from Spain. J M da Fonseca is the producer of many of the Portuguese wines (as are Caves Aliança), and G Hush carry a big selection of the higher quality Bulgarian wines. Sherries include Barbadillo and Bobadilla, while there are Taylor tawny Ports.

The New World offers a small selection of Australian wines – Rosemount, Brown Brothers, Hardy's, Hill-Smith – alongside Babich and Montana wines from New Zealand. In America, Texan wines from Sanchez Creek and Llano are much better than you might expect and there are also Adelsheim wines from Oregon.

Best buys

Varietal wines from the Ardèche; wines from Haut-Poitou; Vin de Pays des Côtes de Gascogne 1986, Domaine du Tariquet, £2.65; Chianti 1986 Fattoria dell'Ugo, £2.69; Garrafeira Particular 1978, Caves Aliança, £3.95

Ilkley Wine Cellars

52 The Grove, Ilkley,   TEL (0943) 607313
West Yorkshire LS29 9BN

OPEN Mon–Thur 10–6.30　Fri 10–7　Sat 9–7　CLOSED Sun, public holidays
CREDIT CARDS All accepted　DISCOUNTS 5% for 1 case　DELIVERY Free on
UK mainland (min 4+ cases); otherwise at cost　GLASS HIRE Free with order
TASTINGS AND TALKS Occasional tastings; to groups on request
CELLARAGE Available

The Loire is the place to start. We find some fascinating wines: the Coteaux du Layon Chaume from Pierre-Yves Tijou, Savennières from Yves Soulez, a rare Coteaux d'Ancenis from just up-river of Muscadet, Sancerre from Gitton Père et Fils, Vouvray from Gaston Huet. There's good basic Sauvignon de Touraine and Muscadet and a good red Chinon (Domaine Raffault at £5.98) and St-Nicholas de Bourgueil.

While this is a star area, other French areas also do well. Look for the Champagnes of Grandin and Bricout, a pricey but attractive selection of Burgundies (with wines from Vallet Frères much to the fore), a good range of petit château clarets, and Côtes du Rhône Villages from the co-operative of Rasteau (the 1986 vintage is £3.59). Alsace is from the Turckheim co-operative.

Ilkley Wine Cellars maintain an interest in Italy, too, with the excellent Frascati Villa Catone (the 1986 vintage is £4.55) and Chianti from Villa Cafaggio and Rosso di Montalcino Tenuta Caparzo. In Portugal, we find reds from Carvalho, Ribeiro & Ferreira, plus wood-aged Ports from Niepoort and Amandio.

Beyond Europe, the stars must be the full complement of wines from Montrose in Mudgee, New South Wales, with Babich wines from New Zealand close behind.

Best buys

Ménétou-Salon Domaine de Châtenoy 1987, £5.75; Muscadet de Sèvre-et-Maine 1987, Ch d'Amour, £3.95; Frascati Superiore Villa Catone 1986, £4.55; Montrose Australian wines; Niepoort 1952 Colheita Vintage Port, £29.50

Ingletons Wines

Station Road, Maldon,   TEL (0621) 52421 (office)
Essex CM9 7LF   (0621) 52433 (cash & carry)

OPEN Mon–Fri 9–5 (cash & carry), 8–4 (warehouse), 8–5 (office) Sat 9–4.30
(cash & carry) CLOSED Sun, public holidays CREDIT CARDS None accepted;
personal and business accounts DISCOUNTS Not available DELIVERY Free
within 150-mile radius of Maldon (min 6 cases); elsewhere charges on request;
mail order available GLASS HIRE Available TASTINGS AND TALKS To groups
on request CELLARAGE Not available

Ingletons are dedicated to Burgundy. They make forays into other
French areas, but hardly venture outside France.

Theirs is one of the most extensive Burgundy listings in the Guide.
It starts off in the north, in Chablis, with domaine wines from Jean
Bègue, Pierre Rétif and de Grenouille. Then it moves in stately
progress down south to a succession of whites and reds from many of
the top domaine names in Burgundy. Villages are listed together, and
it's good to see some less familiar communes (and therefore some less
high prices) as well as the great names. For value, look for Ladoix,
Rully, St-Romain and Savigny-lès-Beaune. Jean Bedin represents
Beaujolais, just to the south.

As sideshows, the Rhône wines (Côtes du Rhône from the Enclave
des Papes), Sancerre from Brochard et ses Fils (Chavignol 1987 at
£5.23), a small selection of clarets and a solid selection of German estate
wines all provide entertainment. Alsace is from the Hunawihr
co-operative, and there's a good series of half-bottles. Prices on the
printed list do not include VAT, but we have added it here.

Best buys

Domaine de Fournery 1986, Côtes de Malepère, £2.35; Sauvignon de
St-Bris 1986, Luc Sorin, £3.48; Côtes de Beaune Villages 1985 Les
Fussières, René Monnier, £5.63; Côtes du Rhône 1986, Coloubrière,
£2.85

Special awards

🐷 means bargain prices (good *value* may be obtained from merchants
without this symbol, of course, if you are prepared to pay for service)

🏵 means that the wines stocked are of consistently high quality

🍾 means that the merchant stocks an above-average range

☞ means that extra-special service is offered: helpful advice, informative
lists and newsletters, tastings etc.

Irvine Robertson Wines

10/11 North Leith Sands, Edinburgh EH6 4ER   TEL 031-553 3521
ASSOCIATED OUTLET Graham MacHarg Fine Wines,   TEL (06685) 274
Fowberry Tower, Wooler, Northumberland NE71 6ER

OPEN Mon–Fri 9–5.30   CLOSED Sat, Sun, Chr and New Year
CREDIT CARDS None accepted; personal and business accounts
DISCOUNTS Available   DELIVERY Free throughout the UK (min 3 cases except
local deliveries); otherwise £4.02 per consignment; mail order available
GLASS HIRE Free   TASTINGS AND TALKS To groups on request
CELLARAGE Not available   ■

There have been few changes in the past year from this Leith wine
merchant: they continue to offer a well-balanced list with some good
value, which avoids being top-heavy in any area.

The best value is actually to be found in the clarets. From a shortish
selection, we would pick out Ch Belair 1985 at £3.37 (prices do not
include VAT, but we have added it here) or Ch Belcier 1983, Côtes de
Castillon at £3.83 as good buys. House claret comes from Nathaniel
Johnston. In Burgundy, prices for domaine bottlings from Jacques
Prieur, Mongeard Mugneret and Michel Voarick have remained very
stable.

On the Rhône, the wines from the Hermitage co-operative in the
north have been joined by Domaine Maby wines from Lirac and Tavel
in the south, while the Loire has the good value Ménétou-Salon of
Henri Pellé and Muscadet from Donatien Bahuaud. Heim are the
suppliers of Alsace wines.

The rest of Europe continues to be rather dull (apart from Riojas from
La Rioja Alta and Marqués de Murrieta), but wines from California
(Philip Togni, Round Hill, Stag's Leap and Hawk's Crest), Australia (a
big selection of Penfold's wines – look especially for the reds) and New
Zealand (Cook's) indicate a healthy interest in the New World.

Best buys

Churchills Crusted Port (bottled 1985), £8.22; Rioja Vega Tinto Reserva
1980, Bodegas Muerra, £4.47; Ch la Rèze 1986, Minervois, £2.74;
Nathaniel Johnston Reserve Claret NV, £2.99; House Cabernet NV,
Round Hill, Napa Valley, £4.58

Jeroboams

24 Bute Street, London SW7 3EX   TEL 01-225 2232

OPEN Mon–Fri 9–7   Sat 9–6   CLOSED Sun, public holidays
CREDIT CARDS Access, Amex, Visa; personal and business accounts
DISCOUNTS 5% on 1 case   DELIVERY Free in central London (min 1 case);
elsewhere at cost; mail order available   GLASS HIRE Free with 1-case order
TASTINGS AND TALKS Monthly in-store tastings; wine and cheese tastings; to
groups on request   CELLARAGE Not available

If you want to know which wines go with which cheeses, Jeroboams is the place to find out. They keep a fascinating list of the seasons in which proper unpasteurised cheeses are available, and which wines they have found match them. They then proceed to some fairly serious wines, mainly from France, which quite properly include some jeroboams.

The main part of the list is of clarets – vintages back to 1945 on a recent version, and mainly of classed growths. Burgundy tends to come from négociants. House wines are the red and white La Vieille Ferme from the Rhône. Other areas of interest include Champagne (some still Coteaux Champenois as well), Ch de Beaucastel Châteauneuf-du-Pape, Badia a Coltibuono wines from Tuscany, and some mature Vintage Ports – to go with the blue cheeses.

Best buys

La Vieille Ferme red and white, £3.50; Ch le Videau 1978, Côtes de Bourg, £3.99; Coltibuono Rosso 1985, £3.99

S H Jones

27 High Street, Banbury,　　　　　　　　　　　TEL (0295) 51178
Oxfordshire OX16 8EW
WHOLESALE WAREHOUSE/CASH & CARRY
Unit 1, Tramway Road Industrial Estate,　　　　TEL (0295) 51177
Banbury, Oxfordshire OX16 8TD

OPEN (High Street) Mon, Tue 8.30–1, 2–5.30　　Wed–Fri 8.30–5.30　　Sat 9–1
CLOSED Sun, public holidays　CREDIT CARDS Access, Visa; personal and business accounts　DISCOUNTS 5% on 1 mixed case, 7.5% on 10+ cases, 10% on 20+ cases　DELIVERY Free in Banbury and district and along main wholesale delivery routes inc Oxford City (min 2 cases); elsewhere at cost; mail order limited but on request　GLASS HIRE Free with suitable wine order
TASTINGS AND TALKS Continuous in-store promotional tastings; annual wine tasting (Nov); to groups on request　CELLARAGE £2.90 per case per year

S H Jones are long-established wine merchants who have managed to keep pace with changes in the wine world. Their wines are full of interest at all levels: the strengths are in the two classic French areas, certainly, but they have also moved further afield to keep up with the Rhône and the Loire and, outside France, with Germany and Italy.

In Bordeaux, we find some useful petit château wines, and a useful range of half-bottles (Ch Batailley 1970, £12.50). Vintages in this area go back from 1983 to 1966, and there's good sweet white Bordeaux as well. Burgundy consists of a good mix of domaine wines as well as those from négociants. Beaujolais is from Sarrau and Loron. French country wines provide some useful bargain drinking (such as Minervois Domaine Ste-Eulalie 1986, £2.99).

The Rhône is a star area, with a good line in Côtes du Rhône Villages from Domaine de la Fourmone, Châteauneuf-du-Pape from Domaine du Vieux Télégraphe and Ch de Beaucastel and northern Rhône wines from Guigal and Jaboulet Aîné. Look also for white Hermitage from Chave and Condrieu.

German estates are covered in some depth, featuring wines from 1983 and 1981 as well as 1985. Italy has Tuscan wines from Frescobaldi and Barolo from Fontanafredda, while Spain has Añares and Marquès de Murrieta Riojas. The New World has Buena Vista wines from California and Ch Tahbilk from Australia.

Best buys

Bulgarian Reserve Cabernet Sauvignon, £2.95; half-bottles of claret; Ch de Brondeau 1982, Bordeaux Supérieur, £4.45; Ch St-Estève, Coteaux Varois, £2.40; Alsace Pinot Blanc 1986, Blanck Frères, £3.45

Justerini & Brooks

61 St James's Street, London SW1A 1LZ   TEL 01-493 8721
39 George Street, Edinburgh EH2 2HN   TEL 031-226 4204

OPEN (London) Mon–Fri 9–5.30   Sat mornings in Dec; (Edinburgh) Mon–Fri 9–6   Sat 9.30–1   CLOSED Sun, public holidays   CREDIT CARDS Access, Amex, Diners, Visa, Grand Metropolitan Shareholders Card, Simpsons (Piccadilly) Card; personal and business accounts   DISCOUNTS 7.5% on 24–59 bottles, 10% on 60–95 bottles, 12.5% on 96+ bottles   DELIVERY Free in UK mainland (min 5 cases); otherwise 1–6 bottles £3.50, 7–59 bottles £2.50 in London and £6 elsewhere   GLASS HIRE Free with 1-case order
TASTINGS AND TALKS Regular in-store tastings for small groups; to existing customer groups on demand   CELLARAGE £3.75 per case per year (inc insurance)

This is a heavyweight list, full of quality things and not designed for everyday drinking. It's replete with wines from classic French areas – Bordeaux, Burgundy and the Rhône. J & B are also strong on providing a cellaring service and organising a buying policy of wines for laying down on behalf of customers. Visitors to both shops will notice considera▸le refurbishment.

The selection of clarets is strong on recent vintages but also has an interesting list of mature and old wines, the oldest on a recent list dating from 1945 (Ch Lafite at £420 a bottle). Equally interesting are the old Vintage Ports and Madeiras, some from 1900.

Burgundy cannot produce anything quite so venerable, but there are a wealthy of domaine wines and a few négociant wines from Jean Germain. The Domaine de la Tour Vaubourg represents Chablis, while Beaujolais offers some unusual single vineyard wines (look for Domaine de Raousset). The third strong area, the Rhône, comes up with a big selection of famous names from the northern end of the region (including some nearly mature Côte Rôtie and Hermitage 1979 of Guigal), and more recent vintages of southern Rhône wines (plus older vintages of Ch de Beaucastel Châteauneuf-du-Pape).

A good range of Alsace wines comes from both Hugel and Kuentz-Bas, and there's an impressive set of top-flight Champagnes. German estate wines include those from Bürklin-Wolf and Baron von Brentano, as well as the good value Bernkastel co-operative. When we move to Italy, we find Barolo and Barbaresco from Bruno Giacosa and Chianti Classico from Castello di Querceto. The Spanish list has expanded to include the Pesquera Ribera del Duero as well as Torres wines and Riojas from La Rioja Alta.

Mondavi, Wente and Beaulieu Vineyards are the California producers on this list, while Australia has Penfold's (including Grange Hermitage 1980 at £27), Brown Brothers, Rothbury Estate and Rosemount. England can hold up her head with Lamberhurst and Bodenham wines.

Best buys

Justerini's White Burgundy, £4.80; Ch Potensac 1983, Médoc, £8; Chiroubles 1986, Ch de Raousset, £6.60; Ch Trinité Valrose 1985, Bordeaux Supérieur, £4.05; Côtes du Rhône 1984, La Haie aux Grives, £4.45

J C Karn

Cheltenham Cellars, 7 Lansdown Place, Cheltenham, Gloucestershire GL50 2HU   TEL (0242) 513265

OPEN Mon–Fri 9.30–6   Sat 9.30–1.30   CLOSED Sun, public holidays
CREDIT CARDS None accepted; personal and business accounts
DISCOUNTS 5% on 1 case   DELIVERY Free within Gloucestershire (min £30 order); elsewhere negotiable; mail order available   GLASS HIRE Free with 1-case order   TASTINGS AND TALKS To groups on request
CELLARAGE Charges negotiable

Although much of this range of wines is safely middle-of-the-road, J C Karn have suddenly sprouted a whole new arm which brings them into the Guide for the first time.

New Zealand is that arm. While their claim to have the largest selection in the northern hemisphere is hard to prove, certainly the choice is considerable. Wines from the big boys – Cooks and Montana – sit alongside some smaller family wineries, such as Babich, Nobilo, Morton Estate, Ngatawara, Matua Valley and more. Newcomers to the list are the Corbans Stoneleigh Vineyard wines. Prices from £3.39 to £8.59 speak for themselves in terms of good value.

Elsewhere, the excitement subsides, but J C Karn has gathered together some well-priced clarets, a gradually increasing representation from other French wine regions, a few interesting German estate wines among a lot that are not, the occasional Italian and Spanish star (Torres wines, for example) and a big range of Sherries from Garvey and Domecq, among others.

Best buys

Babich New Zealand wines; Garvey Sherries; Dopff au Moulin Perle d'Alsace, £3.75; Rioja 1981, Muga, £4.60

Richard Kihl

164 Regent's Park Road, London NW3 8XN   TEL 01-586 5911

OPEN Mon–Fri 9–5.30 (trading mainly by telephone/telex/fax); orders may be also given through the Wine Accessories shop at the same address Mon–Fri 9.30–5   Sat 11–5   CLOSED Sat, Sun, public holidays   CREDIT CARDS None accepted; personal and business accounts   DISCOUNTS Not available   DELIVERY Free in London (min 1 case); mail order available   GLASS HIRE Not available   TASTINGS AND TALKS Regular in-store tastings   CELLARAGE £4 approx per case per year   ■

There are two sides to this merchant. One is a shop full of wine accessories and antique wine paraphernalia. The other is wine proper, operating mainly by mail order.

The wine side is definitely of the finest and rarest variety – old clarets, vintage Champagnes, old vintages of Port, old Burgundies (including wines from Domaine de la Romanée-Conti in profusion). But there are also plenty of more recent vintages as a foil to these rare bottles. The list changes rapidly as small parcels are purchased Half-bottles are an interesting specialisation.

Best buys

Mature clarets; half-bottles of fine wines

Kiwifruits

25 Bedfordbury, Covent Garden,   TEL 01-240 1423
London WC2N 4BL
(mail order only)

OPEN Mon–Fri 10–6.30   Sat 10–6   CLOSED Sun, public holidays   CREDIT CARDS All accepted; business accounts   DISCOUNTS Not available   DELIVERY Free in inner London (min 6 cases); elsewhere £9 per case, 1 bottle £3, 2 bottles £3.50, 4 bottles £4.50, 6 bottles £5   GLASS HIRE, TASTINGS AND TALKS, CELLARAGE Not available

Kiwifruits specialise in a number of the smaller New Zealand wine producers, mainly family concerns: Matua Valley, Brookfields, St Nesbit, Ngatarawa, Bellamour and Delegats. Quality of all these wines is high and any one of them would be worth buying. We would suggest, however, buying only those names not readily available elsewhere, as prices are not particularly cheap.

Prices were current in summer 1988 to the best of our knowledge but can only be a rough indication of prices throughout 1989.

Best buys

Mission Semillon-Sauvignon 1987, £5.85; Matua Valley Chardonnay
1986, Yates Estate, £7.65; Ngatarawa Cabernet Sauvignon 1987, Stables
Red, £6.75

Kurtz & Chan Wines

1 Duke of York Street, London SW1Y 6JP   TEL 01-930 6981

OPEN Mon–Fri 9.30–8   CLOSED Sat, Sun, public holidays
CREDIT CARDS None accepted; personal and business accounts
DISCOUNTS Not available   DELIVERY Free in London postal area (min 5 cases);
otherwise at cost; mail order available   GLASS HIRE, TASTINGS AND TALKS,
CELLARAGE   Not available   ■

If you want to buy probably the only jeroboam of Ch Pétrus 1945 left in
the world, this is where to come. It will cost you £25,000 and it's just a
part of one of the most extensive collections of mature Ch Pétrus we
know of. If you want something a little younger, you can also buy a
case of magnums of Ch Pétrus 1982 for £2,200 (before duty and tax).

All of which goes to indicate that these merchants concern
themselves with fine and mature wines. A recent list – everything,
being available in very limited quantities, changes rapidly – had
Ch Lafite from 1895, as well as considerable quantities of younger
clarets (in other words, from 1970 onwards), some interesting vintages
of mature white Bordeaux, serious things in red Burgundy, and some
more recent wines from the northern Rhône (including from the 1978
vintage). Large bottles of claret are a fascinating – if pricey –
specialisation.

Best buys

Mature clarets and Burgundies

Lamb Wine Company

P O Box 38, Wallingford,   TEL (0491) 35842
Oxfordshire OX10 8ED

OPEN 7 days a week (24-hour answerphone)   CREDIT CARDS None accepted;
business accounts   DISCOUNTS Available on 3+ cases   DELIVERY Free within
15-mile radius of Wallingford (min 1 case); otherwise at cost; mail order
available   GLASS HIRE Free   TASTINGS AND TALKS 2 annual tastings; to
groups on request   CELLARAGE Not available   ■

This is a small range of wines with points of interest in many areas,
particularly in France.

Look for Bergerac from Ch le Fage (Sauvignon Blanc 1986 at £3.75),
varietal wines from the Ardèche and Beaujolais from Chanut Frères.
Then there are small selections of Burgundy and Bordeaux and
Champagne from George Goulet (NV Brut at £11.71). In addition,

Ménétou-Salon of Henri Pellé from the Loire, Châteauneuf-du-Pape of
Domaine de Montpertuis and Coteaux des Baux en Provence Terres
Blanches would all be worth considering. And there's a fine range of
Ports from Ramos Pinto.

Best buys

Ch Beauval 1985, Bordeaux, £3.92; Cheverny 1987 white and red,
Domaine de Salvard, £3.99; Quinta da Ervamoira 10-year-old tawny
Port, Ramos Pinto, £10

Lay & Wheeler

HEAD OFFICE AND WINE SHOP 6 Culver Street   TEL (0206) 67261
West, Colchester, Essex CO1 1JA
Wine Market, Gosbecks Road, Colchester,   TEL as above
Essex CO2 9JT

OPEN (Wine Shop) Mon–Sat 8.30–5.30   (Wine Market) Mon–Sat 8.30–8
CLOSED Sun, public holidays   CREDIT CARDS Access, Visa; personal and
business accounts   DISCOUNTS Available   DELIVERY Free in Essex and South
Suffolk (min 1 case) and on UK mainland (min 2+ cases); otherwise £3.97 per
delivery; mail order available   GLASS HIRE Free with order
TASTINGS AND TALKS Wines available daily for customers; monthly tastings on
specific regions; major tutored workshops held quarterly; approx. 4 wine
workshops per month; to groups on request   CELLARAGE £3.17 per case per
year

This is one of the benchmark ranges in this Guide, which other wine
merchants would do well to study. They are not necessarily pricey
wines, either – one of Lay & Wheeler's main strengths is their choice of
middle-priced bottles.

    The classic areas of France feature strongly: for instance, an
exceptional span of domaine Burgundies and fine clarets (vintages here
go back to 1970) with the bonus of plenty of magnums of claret. Areas
of France in which there is also obvious interest are Alsace, the Loire
and the Rhône. In Alsace we find current vintages from Schlumberger,
Trimbach, Dopff au Moulin and Hugel, as well as some older wines.
On the Loire, treats include plenty of sweet Vouvrays and Montlouis,
plus the excellent Pouilly Fumé of Didier Dagueneau. On the Rhône,
look for a wealth of big names from both the north and south – Jaboulet
Aîné, Chave, Albert Dervieux, Domaine de Raspail in Gigondas.

    On leaving France, the selection is particularly strong in Germany
(plenty of estate wines here), and in Italy, which includes plenty of
Frescobaldi wines, and the wines of Mastroberardino in Campania,
and of Lungarotti in Umbria (although the Veneto is strangely rather
neglected). Spain has Riojas from CVNE and Murrieta to add to Torres
and Jean León wines from the Penedès. Look, too, for the Sherries of
Hidalgo. Portuguese table wines are somewhat neglected, but there
are plenty of Ports.

Australia is another commanding area, homing in on great things from the Hunter Valley (Sutherland, Allanmere, Murray Robson, Peterson), and from South Australia (Woodstock in McLaren Vale, Mitchell in Clare), plus Brown Brothers wines from Victoria. The interest here lies particularly in the smaller estate wines.

If this plethora of wines is all too much, try looking through the personal selections from the company's directors for inspiration.

While a visit to Lay & Wheeler's shop or the Wine Market is very enjoyable, we also recommend joining the mailing list just to get the splendid list twice-yearly, plus the succession of special offers.

Best buys

Vin de Pays des Côtes de Gascogne Colombard 1987, £2.63; Chardonnay 1986, Robson, Hunter Valley, £7.94; Saarburger Rausch Riesling Kabinett 1985, Forstmeister Geltz Zilliken, £5.87; Gran Colegiata Tinto 1985, Bodegas Porto, £4.01

Laymont & Shaw

The Old Chapel, Millpool, Truro,   TEL (0872) 70545
Cornwall TR1 1EX

OPEN Mon–Fri 9–5   CLOSED Sat, Sun, public holidays   CREDIT CARDS None accepted; personal and business accounts   DISCOUNTS 3–4 cases £1.50 per case, 5–9 cases £1.75 per case, 10+ cases £2 per case   DISCOUNTS Free on UK mainland (min 2 cases); mail order available   GLASS HIRE Free
TASTINGS AND TALKS To groups on request   CELLARAGE Not available   ■

The map of Spain on the cover of this merchant's list says it all, and fascinating reading the contents make.

This is the firm that imports Riojas from La Rioja Alta, Valdepeñas from Bodegas de los Llanos, Jean León wines from Penedès and the most famous of all Spanish wines, the Vega Sicilia from Ribera del Duero. But there's much more than just their agency lines on this list.

It kicks off with Ribera del Duero, and includes a new discovery – the wines from Yllera (Tinto Fino 1983 at £6.55) as well as Pesquera and the Peñafiel co-operative. Rioja has wines from many of the major names – La Rioja Alta, Lopez de Heredia, Muga, CVNE, Murrieta and the single estate Remelluri among others. Prices of these wines may be creeping inexorably upwards, but there's still good value from other Spanish areas.

Valdepeñas and Navarra – especially the former – are good places for bargain hunters. Laymont & Shaw stock the Bodegas los Llanos Reserva 1981 at £3.05 and the Gran Reserva 1978 at £3.69. In Navarra, look for the wines of Julián Chivite, while the star from Penedès is Jean León, although there are also plenty of wines from Torres. Cavas, also from Penedès, include the top rank Cava Juve y Camps at £7.95.

There are wines from many other areas – Málaga (Scholtz Hermanos), Lerida, Jumilla, Cariñena, Galicia and Rueda. Sherries also

168

form a comprehensive section – Diez Hermanos, Emilio Lustau, Barbadillo, Garvey and Gonzalez Byass.

Best buys

Valdepeñas 1978, Señorio de los Llanos Gran Reserva, £3.69; Navarra 1985, Gran Feudo, Julián Chivite, £3.11; Vega Sicilia Unico 1962, £33; Laymont & Shaw Rare Dry Fino, £3.99

Laytons

20 Midland Road, London NW1 2AD   TEL 01-388 5081

OPEN Mon–Fri 9–6   Sat 10–4   CLOSED Sun, public holidays
CREDIT CARDS Access, Amex, Visa; personal and business accounts
DISCOUNTS Negotiable   DELIVERY Free on UK mainland (min £100 order); otherwise £5.75; mail order available   GLASS HIRE 50p per dozen; delivery free for orders over £100   TASTINGS AND TALKS Regional and tutored tastings; free talks and tastings for existing clients on request   CELLARAGE £3.45–£5.75 per case per year depending on quantity ∎

While Laytons' great strength is in the classic French areas – and very good at them they are too – they have branched out this year to California with a Sauvignon, a Chardonnay and a Merlot from the small Newton Winery in the Napa Valley. It's also good to see a fully mature example of the Cabernet Sauvignon, the 1982 vintage (£9.20).

Apart from this far-flung excursion, most interest centres on Burgundy and Bordeaux, with Burgundy the star. These fine wines are mainly domaine-bottled but some come from the small quality négociant firm of Chartron et Trébuchet. Look particularly for red wines from the Côte de Beaune and whites from Chassagne-Montrachet and Puligny-Montrachet. Current vintages are 1985 for reds and 1986 for whites.

In Bordeaux, a well-balanced selection starts with some bargains (Ch des Vergnes 1985 at £3.54; Ch Carbonnieux 1984 at £8.43). Vintages go back to 1970 in smaller numbers and there are a few large bottles. In white Bordeaux, Ch Liot 1983 Sauternes is good value at £8.24.

Other regions of France are served more briefly. Champagne is an exception – Laytons hold the British agency for the house of Deutz. The Loire section includes some interesting wines – the Cheverny Sauvignon of Domaine Tessier at £3.75, for example – while in the Rhône, wines from Jaboulet Aîné, Delas Frères, the Vacqueyras Cuvée des Templiers of Domaine Clos du Cazeaux (1985 vintage at £4.98) and Châteauneuf from Mont-Redon and Vieux Télégraphe offer a strong front. There's a small selection from Italy and a big range of the Robertson's Rebello Valente Ports (including the top-rated 1985 vintage at £13.89).

Laytons also act as buyers for the André Simon shops (*qv*).

Best buys

Domaine-bottled Burgundy; Chardonnay Domaine des Hauts de
Sanziers, Vin de Pays du Jardin de la France, £3.35; Mâcon Pierreclos
Rouge 1986, Domaine Guffens-Heynen, £7.28; Jolly Good Claret NV,
£2.82

Linford Wines

See The Old Maltings Wine Company.

Lockes

5 Jewry Street, Winchester,   TEL (0962) 60006
Hampshire SO23 8RZ

OPEN Mon–Sat 9–5.30   CLOSED Sun, public holidays
CREDIT CARDS Access, Visa; business accounts   DISCOUNTS 5% on 1 case
(may be mixed)   DELIVERY Free delivery locally may be possible; elsewhere at
cost; mail order available   GLASS HIRE Free with reasonable case order
TASTINGS AND TALKS In-store tastings most Saturdays; tutored tastings
monthly; to groups on request   CELLARAGE Not available

Even though this is *Which? Wine Guide*, it would be impossible to avoid
mention of the restaurant to which the wine shop is attached – or of the
scrumptious delicatessen items in the shop itself. Lockes often
combine all aspects in tutored tastings and gourmet meals.

To the wines themselves. It is an attractively eclectic collection, not
vast but with every wine pulling its weight. It starts in the French
countryside with considerable interest in the shape of a Vin de Pays
des Côtes de Gascogne Cuvée Bois (matured in wood) at £5.45, tasting
almost like a Burgundian Chardonnay. Then it moves to more classic
French areas, with Alsace from Rolly Gassmann and Louis
Gisselbrecht, red Sancerre from Vacheron (probably the best in the
area), red Burgundy from Henri Jayer and Tollot Beaut, and white
Burgundy from Domaine des Colombiers and the over-priced but
superb Ch de Fuissé. Beaujolais is well served by Pierre Ferraud, Jacky
Janodet and Ch des Tours.

The other high spot in France is the northern Rhône (look for
Alphonse Desmeure and Albert Dervieux). Elsewhere there are
Deinhard wines from Germany, Fonseca, Champalimaud and João
Pires wines from Portugal, Sherries from Lustau, Chianti from Volpaia
and Australian wines from Rothbury Estate. A good range of
half-bottles as well.

Best buys

Blanc de Blancs NV, Guy Bossard, £2.99; Vin de Pays des Côtes de
Gascogne 1987, Domaine du Tariquet, £2.99; Côtes du Rhône Séguret
1981, La Fiole du Chevalier d'Elbène, £4.75; Vinho Verde 1986, Paco de
Texeiro, £3.95

O W Loeb

64 Southwark Bridge Road, London SE1 0AS   TEL 01-928 7750

OPEN Mon–Fri 9–5.30 CLOSED Sat, Sun, public holidays
CREDIT CARDS None accepted; personal and business accounts
DISCOUNTS 5% on 1–5 cases, 10% on 6–10 cases, wholesale prices on 10+
cases DELIVERY Free in central London (min 1 case); otherwise 1–2 cases
£11.50 per consignment, 3–5 cases £3.45 per consignment, 6+ cases free; mail
order available GLASS HIRE Not available TASTINGS AND TALKS To groups
on request CELLARAGE £4 per case per year or part year (only available under
bond)

A very fine range of wines from the two classic French areas of
Bordeaux and Burgundy is joined here by a superb range of Rhône
wines and one of the best German lists in the country.

There are other treats as well: the Alsace wines of Théo Faller is one,
Jura wines from Jean Bourdy another; O W Loeb also keep a fascinating
collection of Loire wines from A Foreau Clos Naudin in Vouvray, and
Beaujolais from Jacques Dépagneux. This year, Australian wines from
Tolleys and a lone California wine from S Anderson in the Napa Valley
have been added to what was, until now, an exclusively European list.

Bordeaux offers mainly wines from recent vintages – 1985, a few
from 1984, 1983 and 1982 and then selections back to 1960. Look for
sweet white Bordeaux from Ch de Fargues in Sauternes. In Burgundy,
domaine wines make a fine sight (Armand Rousseau, Dujac,
Tollot-Beaut, Etienne Sauzet) while Chablis is from Louis Michel.

Then we arrive at the Rhône. O W Loeb are agents in this country for
Jaboulet Aîné, and while this firm's wines crop up in many, many
merchants' lists, here is the most comprehensive range of recent
vintages. Look also for Châteauneuf-du-Pape from Ch Rayas.

Then to the biggest section – German estate wines. O W Loeb, now
British, was originally German (and in fact owns a merchant house of
the same name in Trier), so they ought to know a thing or two about
German wines. It shows, with plenty of famous names from all regions
(including Franconian wines from the Juliusspital in Würzburg).

Best buys

Alsace wines from 1985 and 1983 vintage; Ch Malescasse 1985,
Haut-Médoc, £6.53; Beaujolais from Jacques Dépagneux; St-Joseph
1984, La Grande Pompée, Jaboulet Aîné, £6.71

Special awards

🗁 is for bargain prices   🗎 is for a very good range of wines

❀ is for high quality wines 🗗 is for exceptional service

Lorne House Vintners ⌐⊐

Unit 5, Hewitts Industrial Estate,   TEL (0483) 271445
Elmbridge Road, Cranleigh, Surrey GU6 8LW

OPEN Mon–Fri 9–5.30   Sat 9–1   CLOSED Sun, public holidays
CREDIT CARDS None accepted; personal and business accounts
DISCOUNTS Collection discount of £1 per case   DELIVERY Free within 25-mile
radius of Cranleigh (min 2 cases) and UK mainland (min 10+ cases); otherwise
£5 per consignment; mail order available   GLASS HIRE Free with 1-case order
TASTINGS AND TALKS Last weekend of each month in-store (except Dec &
Aug)   CELLARAGE Not available   ■

The keynote in this range of wines continues to be value, and that
value is spreading wider as Lorne House's list enlarges.

They are still strong in areas like the Loire (Muscadet sur lie Domaine
de Louvetrie, Cuvée Prestige 1987 at £4.75; Sauvignon de Touraine
1987, Domaine Guénault at £2.90); also in Burgundy, where they have
unearthed some very good bargains (Côte de Beaune Villages 1986,
C Drapier at £5.05 is one); and the southern Rhône (Lirac wines from
Domaine Maby). Other French finds include Chardonnay from Jean
Germain in the Arbois at £3.90, some good value petit château claret
and house Champagne Blin at £8.10.

Outside France, they stock the Penedès wines of Jaume Serra and
Toro wines from the main producer there – Bodegas Farina (Gran
Colegiata 1982 at £4.50 is a bargain). There are a couple of new
discoveries from Portugal, and Trentino and Veneto wines of Tomassi
in Italy, plus an expanding German list (including
Zimmermann-Graeff and Paul Anheuser).

Best buys

Dolcetto d'Alba 1987, Terre da Vino, £4; Colegiata wines from Toro;
Chardonnay d'Arbois 1983, Jean Germain, £3.90; Ch Belcier 1983,
Côtes de Castillon, £3.75

Luxembourg Wine Company

80 Northend, Batheaston, Bath   TEL (0225) 858375
Avon BA1 7ES

OPEN Mon–Sun, public holidays 8–8   CREDIT CARDS None accepted; personal
and business accounts   DISCOUNTS Negotiable   DELIVERY Free on UK
mainland (min 3 cases); mail order available   GLASS HIRE Available
TASTINGS AND TALKS To groups on request   CELLARAGE Not available   ■

This firm does just what its name suggests. The wines come from two
of Luxembourg's major producers – Vinsmoselle and the Caves
Co-opératives of Wormeldange – which are now joined together in one
organisation. All the wines on the list are white: we would recommend
the Rieslings, the Elbling (1985 vintage at £2.40) and the Pinot Blanc

Grand Premier Cru 1986 at £3.55. Look, too, for the sparkling Le Comte de Wormeldange at £4.95, made by the Champagne method.

Best buys
Pinot Blanc 1986, £3.55; Riesling Nussbaum 1985, £4.50; Le Comte de Wormeldange Vin Mousseux, £4.95

Graham MacHarg

See Irvine Robertson.

Magnum Opus Wine Company

See Marlow Wine Shop.

Majestic Wine Warehouses

HEAD OFFICE 421 New Kings Road, London SW6 4RN   TEL 01-731 3131

23 branches in London, Birmingham, Bristol, Cambridge, Gloucester, Guildford, Ipswich, Norwich, Oxford, Poole, Salisbury and Swindon

OPEN (Generally) Mon–Sat, bank holidays 10–8 Sun, religious holidays 10–6; (Battersea branch 10–10 every day) CLOSED Chr Day, Boxing Day, New Year's Day CREDIT CARDS Access, Amex, Diners, Visa, Majestic Wine Charge Card; personal and business accounts DISCOUNTS Not usually
DELIVERY Free within 5-mile radius of any branch and for 10+ cases; elsewhere negotiable; mail order available GLASS HIRE Free with suitable order TASTINGS AND TALKS Wines always available in-store; specialised tastings most months; to groups on request CELLARAGE Not available   ■

Things are not quite what they were at Majestic. Maybe it's because they are now part of the largest wine retailers in the world (they bought the California chain of Liquor Barn), which has made them just too big. Maybe it's because the bosses are now in the States. We don't know for sure, but the effect has been that the former confident buying, with every wine a winner, has faltered during the past year. We have tasted wines that would have been rejected in the old days but are now stacked high in the wine warehouses.

That said, of course, there is still much to admire. Majestic keep adding wines, and many of them are excellent of their type. Not always bargains, mind you – we have found that other retailers sometimes sell the same wines more cheaply.

However, plenty of pleasure is to be found in their Bordeaux bargains (Ch Méaume 1984 at £3.49 continues to be terrific value), and also much further up the price scale. In Burgundy, they have hit on some wines under £3 (Labouré-Roi's Bourgogne Rouge at £2.99). The Rhône continues to feature Jaboulet Aîné, and the interest in the Loire has shifted to some new reds. Majestic have also gathered together an

173

enjoyable and inexpensive range of French country wines, and piles of Champagne, too, with de Telmont Grande Réserve Brut at £7.95 a perennial favourite.

There's more outside France – an expanded selection of German wines, Antinori and Lungarotti wines from Italy, Penfold's wines from Australia (look for their own-label Coromandel wines) and Cook's wines from New Zealand. And, with the California link, there are new arrivals all the time from the West Coast, many unavailable elsewhere – and here the prices are definitely good.

Best buys

Bulgarian wines; Ch Méaume 1984, Bordeaux Supérieur, £3.49; Côtes du Rhône 1985, Domaine du Mont Redon, £3.49; Ch la Pilar 1986, Côtes de Duras, £2.39; Vega Sicilia Valbuena 1983, £11.99; Coromandel Rhine Riesling 1987, Australia, £2.65

The Market

12 Craven Road, London W2 3PX	TEL 01-723 6965
165 Haverstock Hill, London NW3 4QT	TEL 01-722 6521
213/215 Upper Street, London N1 1RL	TEL 01-359 5386
700/702 Fulham Road, London SW6 5SA	TEL 01-736 4348
32/34 Highgate High Street, London N6 5JG	TEL 01-348 2422
14/17 Regent Parade, Brighton Road, Sutton, Surrey SM2 5BQ	TEL 01-643 5284
53/55 Balham Hill, Clapham South, London SW12 9DR	TEL 01-675 6901
Le Provençal, 167 Haverstock Hill, London NW3 4QT	TEL 01-586 7987

OPEN Hours vary from store to store, but generally 9–9

This group of shops continues to provide one of the best selections from any supermarket. They use the same buying team and list as Winecellars (*qv*), and although not all wines are stocked in the supermarkets they can be ordered.

Market Vintners

11–12 West Smithfield, London EC1A 9JR   TEL 01-248 8382

OPEN Mon–Fri 8.30–6   CLOSED Sat, Sun, public holidays
CREDIT CARDS Access, Visa; personal and business accounts
DISCOUNTS Trade only   DELIVERY Free in central London (min 1 case); elsewhere at cost; mail order available   GLASS HIRE Not available
TASTINGS AND TALKS In-store tastings quarterly – 'The Marketeers'; to groups on request   CELLARAGE £12 per year

For a firm supplying supposedly staid City businessmen, this firm has a remarkably wide-ranging list. So although there is certainly a good selection of claret (and more on a separate fine wine list), and now a vastly expanded range of domaine-bottled Burgundies, wines from areas that could be considered unlikely are also available.

Italy is one: with Barolo from Oddero, Bardolino from Portalupi, Venegazzù, Reciotos from Allegrini, Arneis from Castello di Neive, this is definitely a collection that shows what is happening in the Italian wine world. Spain is treated more briefly (although look for Almacenista Sherries), there are a few Ports (Warre's Late Bottled Vintage 1974 at £12.95 is very good). Fashionably, of course, Australia (Moss Wood and Tisdall) and California (Mountain View and Saintsbury) are here.

In France, apart from the classic two areas, we find Champagne from Bruno Paillard, some Rhône wines from Chapoutier and Jaboulet Aîné, plus a feature of wines from Guigal, and a few country wines (Cahors Domaine des Grauzils 1985 at £3.98).

Best buys
Ch Villars 1983, Fronsac, £6.90; Côtes du Rhône 1985, Cru de Coudoulet, £5.40; Carneros Pinot Noir 1986, Mountain View, £4.95

Market Wine Stores

The retail shops of G M Vintners (*qv*).

Marks & Spencer

Michael House, 47–67 Baker Street,   TEL 01-935 4422
London W1A 1DN
263 licensed branches nationwide

OPEN Varies from store to store (Thur late night shopping)   CLOSED Sun, public holidays   CREDIT CARDS Marks & Spencer Chargecard   DISCOUNTS 12 bottles for the price of 11   DELIVERY, GLASS HIRE, TASTINGS AND TALKS, CELLARAGE Not available

Marks & Spencer are now doing with their wine what they have for some time done with their food. They have deliberately distanced themselves from supermarkets, and have pushed their range of wines up-market. In doing so, they have come up with a very fine range – not large, but showing some shrewd buying of fine wines at good prices.

Take two releases during the summer of 1988 – a St-Julien 1985 (which happens to be the second wine of Ch Léoville-Barton) at £7.50. Or, from just down the road, Pauillac 1985 from Ch Pichon-Longueville at £8.50. They've done the same with large purchases of Chablis (they claim to sell more Chablis than anyone else in this Guide) and with the introduction of a fine vintage Champagne (St-Gall 1983 at £10.99) from Union Champagne.

Of course, there are more basic wines as well. There is now an expanded Loire list which includes a good value Cheverny at £2.75;

plus plenty of Lambrusco (including a dry white) and litre bottles of vin de table. But they're all good quality, even at this level – and, deliberately, we suspect, not the cheapest around.

This year has seen an innovation – a range of ten Australian wines, mainly from Hill-Smith and Yalumba, all (except the sparkling) under £4 – and all of excellent quality. Go particularly for the **Best buys**, but all will be enjoyable.

Best buys

St Michael South Australian Shiraz/Cabernet Sauvignon 1986, £3.75; St Michael Barossa Valley Semillon 1986, £3.75; Jeunes Vignes, La Chablisienne, £4.99; St-Julien 1985, Ch Léoville-Barton, £7.50; Vin de Pays des Bouches du Rhône, £2.25

Marlow Wine Shop

Anglers Court, Spittal Street, Marlow,   TEL (0628) 890001
Buckinghamshire SL7 1DB
HEAD OFFICE Magnum Opus Wine Company,   TEL (04946) 4742
1 The Highway, Beaconsfield, Buckinghamshire HP9 1QD

OPEN Mon–Sat 9–7 CLOSED Sun, public holidays CREDIT CARDS All accepted; personal and business accounts DISCOUNTS 5% on 1 case DELIVERY Free within 20-mile radius of Marlow; otherwise at cost; mail order available GLASS HIRE Free with wine order TASTINGS AND TALKS Selection of wines always available in-store; monthly evening tastings; to groups on request CELLARAGE £4 per case per year

This new full entry to the Guide is the result of the acquisition of the Marlow Wine Shop by the Magnum Opus Wine Company. Their list, while not long, is well put together and puts forward a few wines from every area which are worth considering.

There's a strong showing of Champagnes (Georges Gardet Brut Spécial at £10.70), a few good petit château clarets and some attractive-looking domaine Burgundies (Emile Voarick, Domaine Servin, Phillippe Bouzereau). Sylvain Fessy is the Beaujolais representative, Muré the one from Alsace. The Rhône has the excellent Ch du Grand Moulas Côtes du Rhône 1986 at £4.60.

There are short selections from Germany (including two wines from the Friedrich Wilhelm Gymnasium on the Mosel), Frescobaldi wines from Italy, and Olarra Riojas from Spain. There's a good value Colares 1981 Riserva from Portugal at £4.25 – but keep it for a good few years yet. Australia shows wines from Rothbury Estate, California from Robert Mondavi, New Zealand from Morton Estate. Ports include tawnies from Quinta do Noval.

Prices are only a rough indication, and were current in summer 1988.

Best buys

Ch Fonscolombe red, white and rosé, Coteaux d'Aix-en-Provence, £3.80; Ch Theulet 1986, Bergerac Blanc, £3.20; Rioja 1983, Añares Tinto, £3.95

Marske Mill House

London Road, Sunninghill, Ascot, Berkshire SL5 0PN

TEL (0990) 22790

OPEN Telephone enquiries or orders 7 days per week – open all hours
CREDIT CARDS None accepted   DISCOUNTS Available   DELIVERY Free
(delivery included in list price) on UK mainland (min 1 case); mail order
available   GLASS HIRE Not available   TASTINGS AND TALKS To groups on
request   CELLARAGE Not available ■

Still only eleven wines, still the shortest list in the Guide. But Marske Mill House stays because it offers good-quality wines not available elsewhere.

All the wines are from Umbria: wines from car-maker-turned-vigneron Lamborghini near the marshy lake of Trasimeno; the Montefalco wines of Arnaldo Caprai (including a white Grechetto, proof that it is the Grechetto grape which boosts the quality of wines like Orvieto – the 1985 vintage of Grechetto dell'Umbria is £4.12); the Altotiberini wines of Carlo Polidori; and a single wine from Fiametta (also by the lake of Trasimeno) – 'very much a hand-made wine', we are told, since it is organic, made from Sangiovese and Gamay grapes.

Best buys

Colli Altotiberini Rosso 1983, Carlo Polidori, £3.79; Grechetto dell'Umbria 1985, Arnaldo Caprai, £4.12

Martinez Fine Wine ⊑ ☞

36 The Grove, Ilkley,	TEL (0943) 603241
West Yorkshire LS29 9EE	
Corn Exchange Cellars, The Ginnel,	TEL (0423) 501783
Harrogate, North Yorkshire HG3 4JS	
60 Street Lane, Leeds,	TEL (0532) 668310
West Yorkshire LS8 2DQ	

OPEN Mon–Fri 9.30–6.30 Sat 9–6 Sun 10.30–4 (Ilkley) CLOSED Chr, Good Friday CREDIT CARDS Access, Amex, Visa; personal and business accounts DISCOUNTS 5% on 1 case DELIVERY Free in Yorkshire and parts of Lancashire (min 1 case); elsewhere 1–4 cases £2.50 per case, 5–9 cases £1.75 per case, 10+ cases free (England and Wales); mail order available GLASS HIRE Free with 2-case order TASTINGS AND TALKS Tastings 3/4 per year for customers on mailing list and through own wine club; to groups on request CELLARAGE £2.50 per case per year

This year Mr Martinez has opened cash and carry sections in his shops at Harrogate and Ilkley, offering a 10 per cent discount for unbroken case sales. An additional interest is his regularly changing fine wine list.

There's plenty to choose from, even more than last year. That expansion includes plenty from Australia – look for Penfold's wines and those from Wyndham Estate and Rosemount. From New Zealand, there are wines from Stoneleigh Vineyard as well as Cook's and Montana.

In Europe, we find a strong claret section, with some good petit château wines as well as some top classed growths. Burgundy comes from Jaffelin, while Alsace wines are from Willy Gisselbrecht. House Champagne is Claude Lallement at £9.50. The South of France consists of Listel wines and a small selection of country wines.

In southern Europe, while Spain offers a powerful range of Riojas (Tondonia, Berberana, CVNE), Torres wines and the good value Castillo de Alhambra white and red (£2.25), Italy has become even stronger with Valpolicella from Santa Sofia, Chianti Classico from Villa Cerna, Venegazzù and the excellent Chardonnay di Mezzocorona of Bollini (£4.75).

In fortified wines, the Spanish influence is again evident with Garvey and Delgado Zuleta Sherries, while in Port we find Churchill Vintage Character and tawnies from Souza and Quinta do Noval as well as vintage wines.

Best buys

Castillo de Alhambra red and white, £2.25; Tidon Rioja red and white, £2.50; Ch Capet Guillier 1983, St-Emilion, £6.75; Alsace Pinot Blanc NV, £3.20; Cahors 1983, Ch St-Didier Réserve Spéciale, £4.10

Master Cellar Wine Warehouse 🗩 🖃

5 Aberdeen Road, Croydon, Surrey CR0 1EQ   TEL 01-686 9989
OPEN Mon–Fri 10–8   Sat–Sun 10–6   CLOSED Public holidays
CREDIT CARDS Access, Visa   DISCOUNTS 2.5% on 10 cases   DELIVERY Free
locally; elsewhere 1 case £7, 2–5 cases £5 per case, 6–9 cases £4, 10+ cases free;
mail order available   GLASS HIRE Free with order
TASTINGS AND TALKS Wines for tasting always available; monthly tutored
tastings; to groups on request   CELLARAGE Not available   ■

This is the wine warehouse operated by the same company as
Davisons off-licences (*qv*), so it is no surprise to find that the greatest
strengths here are claret and Vintage Ports.

As we have commented in the past, the biggest plus is that very
many of these wines are ready to drink. Owners J T Davies are one of
the few merchants around who are willing to bear the cost of cellaring
until the wines are mature. Costly, but a real customer service.

Beyond the French classic areas, this list is much more expansive
than that of Davisons shops. There are Hugel Alsace wines, Beaujolais
from Georges Duboeuf, German estate wines from Huesgen and
Deinhard, and plenty of interest in Italy (including Chianti
Machiavelli, Bola single vineyard wines, Barolos from Ceretto) and in
Spain (especially Torres wines).

Australia is a big section, and prices are good. There are Penfold's,
Orlando and Brown Brothers wines and others from smaller wineries
such as Jeffrey Grosset. Then we come to the huge range of Vintage
Ports (again mature in many cases), and end up on a celebratory note
with the bargain Champagne Ellner at £7.49.

Best buys

Champagne Ellner Brut, £7.49; Sauvignon Blanc Semillon 1987, Tisdall,
£5.10; Chilean Cabernet Sauvignon 1983, Viña Linderos, £3.85;
Montana New Zealand Chardonnay 1987, £3.99; Ch la Tour St-Bonnet
Médoc 1983, £4.30

Mayor Sworder & Co

21 Duke Street Hill, London SE1 2SW   TEL 01-407 5111
OPEN Mon–Fri 9–5.30   CLOSED Sat, Sun, public holidays
CREDIT CARDS None accepted; personal and business accounts
DISCOUNTS Quantity discounts   DELIVERY Free in London and Home
Counties; elsewhere at cost; mail order available   GLASS HIRE Free with order
TASTINGS AND TALKS Annual tasting in June; to groups on request
CELLARAGE £3 per case per year

The printed list isn't everything here. In addition to what they describe
as 'substantial stocks' of fine wines – mature clarets and Vintage Ports –
Mayor Sworder also make frequent special offers of small parcels of
wine. Regular customers obviously need to scan their mail.

The list itself contains wines from many French producers which the company import direct. These include the Muscadet of Domaine de la Hautière, Chablis from André Vannier, Sancerre from Millet-Roger in Clos du Grand Chemarin and country wines such as Clos Bagatelle in St-Chinian and Domaine du Bosc in Gaillac.

Since they supply many City firms, Mayor Sworder sport a fine array of clarets (including some petit château wines), while Burgundy seems to consist mainly of négociant wines. Alsace wines from J Becker are to be recommended, as is the range of Rhône wines (look for Châteauneuf-du-Pape from Ch la Nerthe).

There is also a fine selection of German estate wines, but the rest of Europe hasn't got off the ground. Further afield, though, we find a star attraction in Idyll Vineyards from Geelong in Victoria. (Prices on the list do not include VAT, but we have added it in the **Best buys** below.)

Best buys

Clos Bagatelle 1983, St-Chinian, £3.50; Crozes-Hermitage 1983, Bégot, £6.21; Sworder's Mature Claret, £3.56; Serriger Scharzberg Kabinett 1982, Bert Simon, £3.74

Andrew Mead Wines

Shovelstrode, Presteigne, Powys LD8 2NP   TEL (05476) 268

OPEN By appointment only   CREDIT CARDS None accepted   DISCOUNTS Not available   DELIVERY Free within 15-mile radius of Presteigne, elsewhere 3 cases free, £4 for smaller orders   GLASS HIRE Free for regular customers   TASTINGS AND TALKS Very occasional tastings for regular customers   CELLARAGE Only exceptionally   ■

Don't come to Andrew Mead Wines for anything other than French and German wines (and a good range of vintage Ports). What you will find, though, is a fascinating collection of lesser-known wines from France, as well as plenty of famous names. Mr Mead starts his list with wines under £3 – what he calls his Daily Drinking section (Domaine de Tariquet 1987, Vin de Pays des Côtes de Gascogne, £2.80; Syrah Vin de Pays de l'Ardèche, £2.65). The German section is much less adventurous, apart from the Piesporter Goldtropfchen Mosel wines of Bollig-Lehnert.

When we move into higher realms, the buying shows up well. Mr Mead has gathered together a good selection of domaine-bottled Burgundies (the reds better than the whites) from growers such as Michel Colin, Tollot-Beaut, Jean Chauvenet and René Leclerc. In the Rhône, wines are from Guigal in the north and Domaine du Vieux Télégraphe in Châteauneuf-du-Pape. Sound clarets go back to 1973 (including a good value Ch Notton 1973 at £5.65, to prove that not everything from this year is now past its best). Prices of 1982 wines are particularly good.

The wines of Jean Cros in Gaillac, and an interesting Blanc de Blancs

Champagne from Le Mesnil produced by a number of growers as a joint venture (£10.20) provide other pockets of interest.

Best buys

Vin de Pays de l'Aude rouge, Domaine Herbe Sainte 1986, £2.80; Piesporter Goldtropfchen Auslese 1983, Bollig-Lehnert, £7.50; St-Pourçain Blanc 1987, Jean et François Ray, £3.35; Ch Patache d'Aux 1982, Médoc, £5.85; Bourgogne Passetoutgrains 1986, Henri Jayer, £4.75

J H Measures & Sons

The Crescent, Spalding, Lincolnshire PE11 1AF   TEL (0775) 2676

OPEN Mon–Sat 9–6   CLOSED Sun, public holidays   CREDIT CARDS Access, Visa; personal and business accounts   DISCOUNTS Approx 5% on 1 case DELIVERY Free in South Lincolnshire and East Midlands (min 1 case); elsewhere at cost; mail order available   GLASS HIRE Free with case order TASTINGS AND TALKS Frequent in-store tastings; major annual tasting in October at local venue; to groups on request   CELLARAGE Not available

This merchant operates from the same list as G E Bromley & Sons (*qv*).

Michael Menzel

297/299 Ecclesall Road, Sheffield,   TEL (0742) 683557
South Yorkshire S11 8HX

OPEN Mon–Sat 10–9   Sun 12–2, 7–9   CLOSED Public holidays CREDIT CARDS Access, Amex, Diners, Visa; personal and business accounts DISCOUNTS Available (min 1 case)   DELIVERY Free in Sheffield (min 1 case) and surrounding area (min 5 cases); elsewhere at cost; mail order available GLASS HIRE Free with 1-case order   TASTINGS AND TALKS In-store tastings for regular customers   CELLARAGE Not available

From an amazingly muddled list – with, for example, Vintage Ports sandwiched between white Bordeaux and Baden wines from Germany, it is possible to extract some interesting wines.

The interest is strongest outside France. In Italy, we find wines from some top names such as Masi in the Veneto, Frescobaldi in Tuscany, Pio Cesare and Giacosa Bruno in Piedmont, Badia a Coltibuono Chianti Classico and wines from Mastroberardino in Campania.

Spain, too, has good things to offer: Torres wines, Faustino and CVNE Riojas and a 1976 Vega Sicilia at the remarkably good price of £25.99, while in Australia, Brown Brothers, Hill Smith and Penfold's are the suppliers.

In France, Jaboulet Aîné wines from the Rhône, Hugel Alsace wines, Beaujolais and Burgundies from Joseph Drouhin and Louis Jadot and some mature clarets are the high spots. Good Champagnes, too.

Best buys

Côtes du Rhône 1985, Jaboulet Aîné, £3.78; Sangiovese de Toscana
1986, £3.33; English Müller-Thurgau 1983, Bruisyard St Peter, £3.44;
Raimat Abadía Reserva 1983, £3.55

Merrill's Wine Merchants

677 Wilmslow Road, Didsbury,   TEL 061-445 3261
Manchester M20 0RA

OPEN Mon–Sat 10–10.30   Sun, public holidays 12–2, 7–10.30
CREDIT CARDS Access, Visa; personal and business accounts   DISCOUNTS 5%
on a mixed case   DELIVERY Free in city centre, South Manchester and Cheshire
(min 1 case)   GLASS HIRE Free   TASTINGS AND TALKS Always in-store
tastings   CELLARAGE Not available.

A new merchant in the Guide, this firm offers a number of areas of
interest. One is Alsace, with wines from the co-operative of Turckheim
(including Vendange Tardive wines), and, while Burgundy languishes
in the hands of négociants, Beaujolais has a good set of wines from
Louis Tête and Jacques Dépagneux. In Bordeaux, vintages go back to
1979, with a good showing of 1985 and 1983 wines, while on the
Rhône, there's Côtes du Rhône from the Rasteau co-operative,
Crozes-Hermitage from Tardy et Ange and Châteauneuf-du-Pape of
Domaine Chante Cigale.

In Italy, worth considering are wines from Fontanafredda in
Piedmont, Veneto wines of Santi and the Orvietos of Bigi. Spain offers
a big selection: Torres wines and Riojas from Beronia, Bilbainas and
Marqués de Càceres. Australian wines come from Lindeman's,
Orlando and Hardy's (as well as Geoff Merrill) and New Zealand wines
from Babich.

Best buys

Torres Gran Viña Sol 1987, £4.79; Lindeman's Cabernet Sauvignon
1985, Australia, £4.99; Teroldego Rotaliano 1986, Ca' Donini, £3.69

Mi Casa Wines

77 West Road, Buxton, Derbyshire SK17 6HQ   TEL (0298) 3952

OPEN Mon–Fri 3–10   Sat 11–10   Sun, Good Friday 12–2, 7–10   Chr Day 12–1
(other public holidays as normal days)   CREDIT CARDS None accepted;
business accounts   DISCOUNTS 5% on 1 case   DELIVERY Free within 10-mile
radius of Buxton (min 1 case)   GLASS HIRE Free with 1-case order
TASTINGS AND TALKS To groups on request   CELLARAGE Not available

Besides a few German and French wines, it is Spain that is the real
interest here – and Spain in some depth, as well.

So we find plenty of Riojas, from Campo Viejo 1984 at £3.25 up to
Berberana Gran Reserva 1970 at £16.55, with a good number of Reserva

wines on the way. Across on the Mediterranean coast, there are Cavas from Freixenet and Conde de Caralt as well as the top Juve y Camps. Torres wines are here in profusion. Other areas are not neglected – Protos from the co-operative of Ribera del Duero, Marqués de Alella Blanco, Málaga and Cariñena. Sherries come from Beresford, De Soto and Cabrera, and there are Spanish brandies with wonderful names like Fabuloso.

Best buys

Monte Plane Gran Reserva 1978, Navarra, £3.90; Rioja Gran Reserva 1978, Campo Viejo, £5.45; Rioja 1981, Contino Reserva, £5.25; Valdepeñas Valdoro red and white, £2.65

Millevini

3 Middlewood Road, High Lane, Stockport,   TEL   (0663) 64366
Cheshire SK6 8AU

OPEN 7 days a week (answering service after 3 pm on weekdays)
CREDIT CARDS None accepted; business accounts   DISCOUNTS Up to 15%
(min 1 unmixed case)   DELIVERY Free within 20-mile radius of shop (min 1
case) and elsewhere (min 6 cases); otherwise £5; mail order only
GLASS HIRE Free with 1+ case order   TASTINGS AND TALKS To groups on
request   CELLARAGE Not available   ■

This Italian-only list is heavyweight stuff, full of great names, and demonstrating a fascinating cross-section of what is happening in this most diverse of wine countries.

Going north to south, the list kicks off in Piedmont, with Barbarescos from Barale and Castello di Neive, Barolo from Mascarello and Giacomo Conterno, Ghemme and Gattinara from Brugo, Gavi from La Chiara. In Lombardy, we find Franciacorta from Fugazza and Longhe-de Carli, while the Trentino–Alto Adige has wines from Tiefenbrunner and Zeni.

In the Veneto, the story is repeated: Bardolino from Portalupi, Valpolicella of Tedeschi, Venegazzù and Chardonnay from Loredan, Prosecco di Valdobbiadene. Friuli wines are from Collavini, Abruzzi wines further south from the top man, Valentini.

In Tuscany, look for Chianti of Pagliarese and the super vino da tavola Morellino di Scansano Le Pupille, while in Latium, there is the superb Torre Ercolana 1981 of Colacicchi. Apulia's pride is the Torre Quarto Malbec-based wine, Basilicata's the Aglianico del Vulture of di Angelo. Cirò wines from Calabria, Corvo from Sicily and some of Sella e Mosca's wines from Sardinia complete this excellent line up.

Best buys

Montepulciano d'Abruzzo 1985, Barone Cornacchia, £3.65; Valpolicella Classico Valverde 1985, Tedeschi, £4.81; Barolo 1979, Gemma, £7.01

Mitchell & Son

21 Kildare Street, Dublin 2,   TEL (0001) 760766
Republic of Ireland

OPEN Mon–Fri 10.30–5.30 Sat 10.30–1 CLOSED Sun, public holidays
CREDIT CARDS All accepted; personal and business accounts DISCOUNTS 5%
on 1 case DELIVERY Free within 45-mile radius of Dublin city (min 2 cases);
otherwise 1 case £IR3.80, 2 cases £IR4.20, 3 cases £IR5.40, 4 cases £IR6.80; 5+
cases free; mail order available GLASS HIRE Free with 2-case order
TASTINGS AND TALKS Tastings of new wines for customers by invitation; to
groups on request CELLARAGE Not available

This is certainly the most useful range of wine that we have found in
the Republic of Ireland. United Kingdom readers will realise how lucky
they are when they compare prices that Mitchells have to charge (to
take in duty and Irish VAT) with those in the UK.

New this year to this soundly based list are the Sherries of Emilio
Lustau (including some Almacenistas). After these and a selection
of Fonseca Ports, the list moves smartly to classic French areas.

A small selection of clarets from recent vintages is well chosen
across a wide price range (from Ch de la Tour 1985 at £IR8.40 to
Ch Rausan-Ségla 1982 at £IR29.95. Then we cross to Burgundy, where
négociants Mommessin and Prosper Maufoux are the main suppliers.
The rest of France is strangely sparse, though, apart from
Laurent-Perrier Champagne and a few Dopff au Moulin Alsace wines.

In Germany, things perk up again with Deinhard estate wines, but
the only star from Italy is the Chianti Classico of Vicchiomaggio.
Australia boasts Hardy's wines and California bottles from Christian
Brothers and Sequoia Grove. And then we're into Irish whiskey . . .

Best buys
João Pires Palmela 1986, £IR6.25; Siglo Rioja 1984, £IR5.95; Fonseca
1980 Vintage Port, £IR13.65

Mitchells Wine Bin

9 Moor Lane, Lancaster,   TEL (0524) 63773
Lancashire LA1 1QB
ASSOCIATED OUTLET Morecambe Soft Drinks   TEL (0524) 410491
Cash and Carry, Alice Street, Morecambe,
Lancashire LA4 5NH

OPEN Mon, Tue, Thur, Fri, Sat 9–5.30 Wed 9–12.30 CLOSED Wed from
12.30, Sun, public holidays CREDIT CARDS Access, Visa; personal and
business accounts DISCOUNTS 5% for 1 case; negotiable on monthly accounts
and larger quantities DELIVERY Free within 20-mile radius (min 1 case);
elsewhere negotiable; mail order available GLASS HIRE Free with reasonable
order TASTINGS AND TALKS Occasional in-store tastings; quarterly organised
tastings; to groups on request CELLARAGE Negotiable

Mitchells claim their specialities to be Western Australia, New Zealand and Oregon, an esoteric mix, we feel, which bodes well for customers coming to this wine shop in Lancaster.

There are other surprises as well: a good selection of English wines (Breaky Bottom Seyval Blanc 1986 and Staple St James Müller-Thurgau 1985, both at £5); and a rare seam of German estate wines taking in some big names (Deinhard, Bürklin-Wolf, Crusius, the State Domaines, von Schubert), going back to 1979 and including some Auslesen and Beerenauslesen.

More famous names appear in Spain, such as Torres, Jean León, the white Riojas from Marqués de Murrieta, and the classic great wines from Vega Sicilia. The star Italian buys are from Tiefenbrunner in the Südtirol and the Chiantis of Pagliarese.

France is an unusual disappointment although Burgundy offers the reliable wines of Joseph Drouhin, and clarets (pricey on the whole) go back to the occasional 1973. The best French section is Alsace represented by Hugel.

And so to those areas of specialisation. From Western Australia, look for the wines of Tim Knappstein in Clare, South Australia as well as those from Moss Wood and Cape Mentelle. Cape Mentelle's sister estate of Cloudy Bay provides some appealing New Zealand wines, while there are Oregon samples from Tualatin and Eyrie Vineyards.

Best buys

Harveys Hunting Port, £5.90; Rioja 1981, Carta de Oro, Berberana, £3.55; Chianti Classico 1983, Pigiatello, £3.45; Falkensteiner Hofberg 1985, Friedrich Wilhelm Gymnasium, £3.75

Moffat Wine Shop

15 Well Street, Moffat,   TEL (0683) 20554
Dumfriesshire DG10 GDP

OPEN Mon–Sat 9–5.30   CLOSED Sun   CREDIT CARDS Amex, Visa
DISCOUNTS 5% on 1 case   DELIVERY Free in Dumfriesshire (min 1 case);
elsewhere approximately £4 per case by parcel post; mail order available
GLASS HIRE Free   TASTINGS AND TALKS Autumn and Spring tastings at local hotel; to groups on request   CELLARAGE Free

We've had good reports about this shop, particularly about the service, not just within Scotland, but also to Sassenachs south of the Border. Praise has also been forthcoming for the increasing range of wines.

They've certainly increased the selection in areas such as Chile and the USA – even Switzerland. There are more half-bottles as well – a definite plus. All these sit alongside an immense hoard of whiskies.

Starting in France, we find a short selection of Bordeaux – well chosen and at good prices – but much less from the Loire and Burgundy, although some good domaine bottlings look attractive.

They've also moved out to the regions – look for the Fitou of Mont Tauch (1983 vintage at £3.25) and the Gaillac of Jean Cros.

Across the Rhine, Germany offers a few estate wines, while elsewhere in Europe, good things emerge in Italy, such as Frascati Colli di Catone; Chianti Classico Serristori and Machiavelli; Masi Valpolicella; Alto Adige wines from Lageder and Tiefenbrunner. Spain has CVNE Riojas and Torres wines from the Penedès, and there's a big selection from Bulgaria, too.

Torres pops up again in Chile. Wines from Peter Lehmann, Hardy's and Orlando have joined the Australian section, while New Zealand names include Montana, Babich and Stoneleigh Vineyard.

Best buys

California Zinfandel 1983, Wente, £4.89; Periquita 1982, J M da Fonseca, £3.39; Fitou 1983, Mont Tauch, £3.25; Chianti Classico 1983, Machiavelli, £2.99

Moreno Wines

11 Marylands Road, London W9 2DU   TEL 01-286 0678/9029
2 Norfolk Place, London W2 1QN   TEL 01-723 6897 and 724 3813

OPEN Mon–Fri 9–9 (W9), 10–8 (W2)   Sat 10–9 (W9), 9.30–8 (W2)   Sun 12–2 (W9)   CLOSED Sun (W2), public holidays   CREDIT CARDS Access, Visa; personal and business accounts   DISCOUNTS 5% on 1 case   DELIVERY Free on UK mainland (min 3 cases); otherwise 1 case £5.75, 2 cases £3.75 each; mail order available   GLASS HIRE Free with 1-case order   TASTINGS AND TALKS Plans for in-store tastings being made; own wine club meets monthly (exc Dec); to groups on request (depends on subject matter)   CELLARAGE Not available

Moreno Wines are one of the largest stockists of Spanish wines in the country, with nearly 500 examples widely chosen to reflect the country's whole spectrum. They are one of the few merchants to carry the fresh, light wines from Galicia in the North-West, and have also built up a big range of Spanish dessert wines (including Málagas). Naturally, their mineral water is also Spanish (Cabrei).

Rioja is a major strength, with an abundance of top named bodegas, a particular attraction being the number of older wines (including Gran Reservas from the 1970s).

Other areas of Spain are equally well served: Penedès (Torres and Conde de Caralt featuring strongly), Navarra (Bodegas Carricas's Mont-Plane wines), the wines of Bodegas Marqués de Sernan and Bodegas Campante in Galicia, wines from León, Jumilla, Priorato, Cariñena, Valdepeñas. Another of Spain's major areas, Ribera del Duero is also well represented.

Moreno's stock also includes wines from the Peñafiel co-operative (look for their Protos Gran Reserva for an old-style red, or for the younger vintages for a more modern approach) and from the fabled Vega Sicilia.

Completing this wide range are sparkling cavas (including the top-quality Juve y Camps at £5.07), Sherries and Montillas, and Málagas from Antonio Barcelo and Scholtz Hermanos.

There has been one departure from Spain this year – to Chile's high-quality Santa Rita bodega, whose wines are extremely good value (Chardonnay 1986 at £3.99 and Cabernet Sauvignon 1985 at £4.89).

Best buys

Chilean Sauvignon Blanc 1986, Viña Santa Rita, £3.99; Conde de Caralt Tinto 1984, £2.95; Navarra Teobaldo Tempranillo, Mont-Plane, £2.95; Jumilla Condestable Tinto 1985, £2.52; Ribera del Duero Tinto 2nd Year 1986, £3.32

Morris's Wine Stores

HEAD OFFICE Stirling Road,   TEL 021-704 3415
Cranmore Industrial Estate, Shirley, Solihull,
West Midlands B90 4XD
26 branches in the West Midlands (4 known as Astral Wines, 1 as Woodleys Wine Stores and 1 as W R Wines)

OPEN Every day; opening hours vary   CREDIT CARDS Access, Amex, Visa; personal and business accounts   DISCOUNTS Available   DELIVERY Free within 30-mile radius of Head Office (min 4 cases); £3 per case for 1–3 cases; mail order available   GLASS HIRE Available   TASTINGS AND TALKS Regular programmes of in-store tastings   CELLARAGE Not available

---

This is a useful list, with much of interest in all areas. Not all the wines are available in all the shops, but can be ordered.

It starts traditionally, with a good house claret from Peter Sichel at £3.44 (prices on the wholesale list do not include VAT, but we have added it here), and clarets in limited quantities from vintages back to 1967. Red and white Burgundy take in wines from Armand Rousseau, Domaine Dujac and Domaine Roumier as well as négociants Prosper Maufoux and Louis Latour. Beaujolais from Trenel Fils are worth considering (especially the wines from the 1985 vintage). Champagnes are good and represent a fair cross-section of grande marque houses.

From Germany come estate wines from Deinhard, while the list offers Bulgarian wines at good prices. Italy has wines from Frescobaldi and Valpolicella from Santi, while in Spain we find a growing range of Riojas (look for the Faustino I Gran Reserva 1981 at £6.14. In the realm of fortified wines, there are Sherries from many of the major houses and Ports which include Taylor's aged tawnies as well as a number of LBV wines.

New to the list are Australian wines from Tyrrell's and Lindeman's, while there is continued interest in Cooks New Zealand wines.

Best buys

1985 Beaujolais from Trenel Fils; Bulgarian wines; Côtes du Rhône

1987, Ch du Grand Moulas, £3.70; Wynns Coonawarra Estate Rhine Riesling 1983, £4.19; Chianti Rufina Villa Vetrice, £2.86

Morris & Verdin

28 Churton Street, London SW1V 2LP   TEL 01-630 8888

OPEN Mon–Fri 9.30–5.30   Sat 10–3   CLOSED Sun, public holidays
CREDIT CARDS None accepted; personal and business accounts
DISCOUNTS Available   DELIVERY Free in London and Oxford (min 1 case); otherwise £8.50 per consignment; mail order available   GLASS HIRE Free with case order   TASTINGS AND TALKS Regular informal Saturday morning tastings; to groups on request   CELLARAGE £4.60 per case per year (inc insurance)   ∎

It has been a year of consolidation at Morris & Verdin. They have widened their range from Burgundy (always a favourite here) and Alsace, and gone deeper into the New World.

Burgundy remains at the heart. A fine range of Chablis from producers like Louis Michel and Louis Pinson stretches out alongside white Burgundies from Comte Lafon and Pitoiset Uréna. Red Burgundies are even more extensive, with producers like Monthélie Douhairet, Girard Vollot, Comte Lafon, and – extensively – Daniel Rion all featured. While most prices inevitably reflect the high price of Burgundy, the Bourgogne Passetoutgrains 1985 of Daniel Rion, almost entirely Pinot Noir, is good value at £5.10; the wines from Savigny also represent value for money.

The estate wines of André Ostertag from the Alsace section are impressive, and, on the Loire, proof that not all Anjou Rouge is light stuff is put forward with the Vieilles Vignes 1986 of J Boivin (£4.50) – try his sweet Bonnezeaux as well. Look also for the Ménétou-Salon red and white of Henri Pellé. In other parts of France, we would recommend the Côtes de Provence of Domaine St-André de Figuières, the Cru de Coudoulet and Ch de Beaucastel wines from the southern Rhône and Champagne from André Jacquart.

The New World gets a look in, too, with Matua Valley in New Zealand, Moss Wood and Cape Mentelle in Western Australia and Cousiño Macul in Chile.

Best buys

Alsace Pinot Blanc, Ostertag, £4.10; Côtes du Ventoux 1986, La Vieille Ferme, £3.20; Bourgogne Passetoutgrains 1985, Domaine Rion, £5.10; Blanc de Blancs, Morris & Verdin, £2.10

Most wine merchants will hire out glasses free of charge, provided they are collected and returned clean, and that you are buying enough wine to fill them! In most cases, it's first come, first served, so get your order in early to ensure supply.

Morrisons

OFFICES/WAREHOUSE Wakefield 41 Industrial   TEL (0924) 822996
Estate, Wakefield, West Yorkshire WF2 0XF
43 branches in Cheshire, Cumbria, Derbyshire, Durham, Lancashire,
Lincolnshire, Merseyside, Northumberland and Yorkshire

OPEN (Generally) Mon, Tue, Sat 8.30–5.30   Wed, Thur, Fri 8.30–8
CLOSED Sun, some public holidays   CREDIT CARDS Access, Visa
DISCOUNTS, DELIVERY Not available   GLASS HIRE Free in selected stores
TASTINGS AND TALKS Regular in-store tastings   CELLARAGE Not available

This supermarket group continues to offer very good value for money.
Morrisons operate a wide-ranging list in well laid out wine and spirit
sections. They tend not to go in for own-label wines, and at the
cheaper levels rely on familiar brands.

In fact, the main interest lies in the fine wine section, which is
available in the larger stores (also look for a special list at the Enterprise
5 store in Idle, Bradford). This takes in some good petit château clarets,
Burgundies from Chanson, Ropiteau, Chauvenet; Beaujolais from
Duboeuf; Fontanafredda Barolo and Firestone California Merlot.
Again, prices are good.

In the standard range, some areas are well served, despite the
brands. There are good French vins de pays, Listel wines from the
Midi, Chianti and Galestro from Rocca delle Macie, Veneto wines from
Santi, Campo Viejo Riojas and a recently arrived bunch of New World
wines – Cooks from New Zealand, Orlando and Wyndham Estate
from Australia. In the realm of sparkling wines, look for Freixenet
Cavas and Massé NV Brut Champagne (£8.05).

Best buys

Sauvignon de St-Bris 1986, Sorin, £3.89; Cahors 1982, Clos Camp
d'Auriol, £2.99; Chianti Classico 1986, Rocca delle Macie, £3.19; Rioja
1983, Campo Viejo Reserva, £3.59; Bin 555 Shiraz, Wyndham Estate,
New South Wales, £3.19; Massé NV Champagne, £8.05

Le Nez Rouge/Berkmann Wine Cellars

12 Brewery Road, London N7 9NH   TEL 01-609 4711

OPEN Mon–Fri 9–5.30   Sat 10–4 (except Sat preceding public holidays)
CLOSED Sun, public holidays   CREDIT CARDS Access, Visa
DISCOUNTS 2½% for 1 unmixed case (£2 per case collected for members only)
DELIVERY Free to London postal districts (min 1 case) and mainland England
and Wales (min 5 cases); otherwise 1 case £4.50, 2 cases £2.50 per case, 3–4 cases
£1.50 per case; mail order available   GLASS HIRE Free with 2-case order
TASTINGS AND TALKS Informal tastings on Saturdays; tutored tastings monthly
on average; to groups on request   CELLARAGE £3.75 per case per year or part
year (unmixed cases purchased through club only)

Le Nez Rouge is the club arm of Berkmann Wine Cellars, who act as UK agents for a number of major producers, particularly in France. They have also branched out to take in the New World – Morton Estate in New Zealand and Petersons in the Hunter Valley of Australia (Chardonnay 1986, £7.80).

The heart of the list, though, is in Burgundy and Beaujolais. Burgundy is dominated by a huge collection of domaine wines from some of the top growers: Etienne Sauzet in Puligny-Montrachet, Albert Morey in Chassagne-Montrachet, Jacques Parent, Tollot-Beaut, Michel Lafarge. What is particularly interesting is the way in which the range takes in wines from lesser-known and therefore good value villages, such as Ruchottes-Chambertin, Fixin, Santenay (Grand Clos Rousseau 1984 of Albert Morey is £8.35).

In Beaujolais, Berkmann are the agents for Mr Beaujolais himself – Georges Duboeuf – and they carry the basic wines, a selection of cru wines and some single vineyard wines for which the Duboeuf company do the wine-making and bottling. Quality is high throughout.

If Bordeaux by comparison is rather more perfunctory, other famous firms for which Berkmann act as agents are Jean Sauvion in Muscadet, Gaston Beck in Alsace, Les Maîtres Vignerons in St-Tropez on the Côte d'Azur, Vidal-Fleury on the Rhône and the new star Champagnes of Bruno Paillard. They also sell the very Portuguese-style Ports – light and elegant tawnies – from Ramos Pinto. Prices for all the wines are very competitive, and members of Le Nez Rouge get special prices (we quote non-members' prices here).

Best buys

Ch Hervé Laroque 1983, Fronsac, £5.15; Tokay Pinot Gris 1986, Gaston Beck, £4.60; Muscadet les Découvertes de Sauvion et Fils 1987, £3.90; Chénas 1987, Georges Duboeuf, £4.50; Fitou Terre Natale 1985, Cave des Producteurs, £3.40

Nickolls & Perks

37 High Street, Stourbridge,   TEL (0384) 394518/377211
West Midlands DY8 1TA

ASSOCIATED COMPANY
Greenwood & Co, 178 High Street,   TEL (038 482) 2217
Lye, Stourbridge, West Midlands DY9 8LH

OPEN Mon–Sat 9–10 CLOSED Sun, public holidays CREDIT CARDS Access, Amex, Visa; personal and business accounts DISCOUNTS 10% on 1 case DELIVERY Free service negotiable GLASS HIRE Free with order TASTINGS AND TALKS Approximately six in-store tastings annually; to groups on request CELLARAGE £5 per case for 10+ cases, £10 per case on sliding scale

---

This is a very grand and huge list, full of treats, almost exclusively aimed at the fine wine market.

Old vintages abound. Bordeaux is especially well off, since this firm is one of the few sources of wines from vintages like 1945, 1953 and 1959. The Burgundy list concentrates on reds, and mainly on wines from négociants, although there are a few old domaine-bottled wines as well. The extensive section of vintage Ports makes fascinating reading, taking in as it does occasional wines from companies which no longer exist (Tuke Holdsworth 1955 at £50 a bottle or Mackenzie Vintage 1945 at £85), as well, of course, as the more familiar names.

A departure this year is a number of less expensive wines from areas such as the Loire, Bergerac and Cahors. We are told that the policy is now to increase the number of middle-priced wines at Nickolls & Perks and to have the more inexpensive wines at the associated shop of Greenwood & Co.

Best buys

Old vintages of claret and Port

The Nobody Inn

Doddiscombsleigh, nr Exeter, Devon EX6 7PS   TEL (0647) 52394

OPEN Mon–Sat 11–11   Sun 12–10.30   CREDIT CARDS Access, Visa; personal and business accounts   DISCOUNTS 5% for 1 case   DELIVERY At cost; mail order available   GLASS HIRE Free   TASTINGS AND TALKS Monthly tutored tastings between October and March; to groups on request   CELLARAGE Not available

---

Two of the strengths of this list are those which a restaurant ought to show – plenty of pudding wines and plenty of half-bottles. Perhaps other restaurateurs should read Mr Borst-Smith's list for ideas on how to do it properly.

Also sensibly for his customers, he divides his list up between white and red wines, starting with a favourite restaurant wine area – Alsace. Already a full section, more are promised from the 1983 and 1985 vintages, both great to drink at the moment. In Burgundy, the list is shorter – a reflection of prices – but alongside good bottles from the Rhône – wines from Auguste Clape in Cornas, and Châteauneuf from Ch de Beaucastel, Ch Rayas and Chante-Cigale – crops up Ch Grillet (the 1983 vintage is £26). Other curiosities are scattered right through this list – a Rancio from Rasteau, a Sherry-style wine from the Rhône, for example.

The star attraction in French reds, though, is the claret list, with wines back to the 1961 vintage, and good selections from 1978 and 1982.

Outside France, we turn first to Germany, with plenty of estate wines. Italy's list is rather short, but good Riojas as well as Torres wines make for a sound Spanish section.

California does pretty well (with wines from Clos du Bois, Dry Creek and Heitz) and Idaho and Oregon get a look in also, but Australia has the edge, offering wines from Moss Wood, Hill Smith, Wynns, Allendale and the luscious sweet botrytis Semillon of De Bortoli (the 1982 vintage is £9.72 for a half-bottle).

Whisky aficionados should head for the vast range of malts.

Best buys

Pudding wines; half-bottles; Joseph Phelps Syrah 1980, £5.98; Matua Valley Brownlie Bay View Estate Sauvignon Blanc 1986, £5.49; old vintages of Torres Gran Coronas Black Label

Rex Norris

50 Queens Road, Haywards Heath,   TEL (0444) 454756
West Sussex RH16 1EE

OPEN Mon–Thur 9–5.30   Fri 9–7.30   Sat 9–4.30   CLOSED Sun, public holidays   CREDIT CARDS Access, Visa; personal and business accounts   DISCOUNTS 10% on 1 case of mixed wine   DELIVERY Free in mid-Sussex   GLASS HIRE Free   TASTINGS AND TALKS Occasional in-store tastings   CELLARAGE Not available

A constantly changing list at this merchant can, at any one time, offer 25 Australian wines, 25 Spanish, a good array of German Eisweins and Trockenbeerenauslese wines – more than 250 in total. There is no list – so enquiries at the shop are the order of the day.

Best buys

Domaine de la Roncière, Costières du Gard, £2.75; Toro Colegiata Tinto 1985, £3.50; Rouge Homme Coonawarra Chardonnay 1986, £6.75; Marqués de Casa Concha 1979, Concha y Toro (Chile), £4.59

Oddbins

HEAD OFFICE 31–33 Weir Road,   TEL 01-879 1199
Durnsford Industrial Estate, London SW19 8UG
142 branches

OPEN (Generally) Mon–Sat 10–8   Sun, public holidays 12–2, 7–9   CLOSED Chr Day   CREDIT CARDS Access, Amex, Visa, Oddbins Credit Card; personal and business accounts   DISCOUNTS 5% on unmixed cases; quantity discounts possible   DELIVERY Free within locality of shop (min 1 case)   GLASS HIRE Free with reasonable case order   TASTINGS AND TALKS Weekend tastings in-store (except Scotland); to groups on request   CELLARAGE Not available

Oddbins are getting better and better. Since the improvements last year, they have started to do for countries such as Portugal what they've already done for Australia.

They are now the biggest retailers of Australian wines in the country: the range is enormous, and the prices very good. Barossa Valley Estates form the basic – but highly enjoyable, in most cases – range.

The Oddbins treatment of Portugal is now also supplying good value in abundance – look for the red Quinta da Abrigada at £3.49 or the white Dry Moscato 1987 of João Pires at £3.49, or the top red Reserva Especial of Ferreira, makers of the legendary Barca Velha, at £7.99. While the Spanish section is quite short, the Italian list, too, is lengthening: try the red Bonarda Oltrepò Pavese at £3.69 or the excellent value Spanna del Piemonte of Brugo at £2.99, or the white Orvieto Torricella of Bigi at £3.99. There has even been some growth in Germany – a neglected area which deserves the Oddbins treatment. The California list, though, is much smaller.

The French shelves buckle under a variety of treats: clarets and some good things from the Rhône (look for Jaboulet Aîné, or the Ch de Beaucastel Châteauneuf-du-Pape). The French regions come up with the Cahors wines of Rigal, and the newly introduced Oddbins Red, a very quaffable Vin de Pays des Côtes Catalans. On the Loire, there are the varietal Touraine wines from the co-operative of Oisly-et-Thésée, and Alsace has wines from Kuentz-Bas and the Turckheim co-operative.

Other sections worth considering are the full range of Bulgarian wines, a big selection of Champagnes (including plenty of vintage wines and de luxe cuvées) and an interesting bunch of fine old Sherries (Amontillado Viejo del Duque of Gonzalez Byass is £7.99).

Best buys

Champagnes; Barossa Valley Estate Rhine Riesling, £2.49; Barossa Valley Estate Shiraz/Cabernet, £2.69; Quinta da Abrigada Portuguese red 1984, £3.49; Castillo di Alhambra Spanish red and white, £1.99; Oddbins Red Vin de Pays des Côtes Catalans, £2.49

The Old Maltings Wine Company

The Old Maltings, Long Melford, Sudbury, Suffolk CO10 9JB	TEL (0787) 79638
Linford Wines, Belvoir House, High Street, Newmarket, Suffolk CB8 8DM	TEL (0638) 662068

OPEN Mon–Sat 9–1, 2–5 (Sudbury); Mon–Sat 8.30–5.30 (Newmarket)
CLOSED Sun, public holidays   CREDIT CARDS None accepted; personal and business accounts   DISCOUNTS 5–10% (min 1 case, may be mixed)
DELIVERY Free in London and South-East England (min 1 case); elsewhere at cost; mail order available   GLASS HIRE Free   TASTINGS AND TALKS In-store tastings every Sat, occasionally during the week; to groups on request
CELLARAGE £1.70 per case per year (under bond and duty paid)

This firm, back in the Guide after a year's absence, now owns Linford Wines in Newmarket. Their list has grown, too – embracing California, the French regions and Italy. Prices still seem on the high side, although some have certainly fallen, and a free delivery service for London and southern England may well compensate.

We start in France, on the Loire, with the Savennières of Yves Soulez (who also supplies a good Anjou Rouge – much better than usual), Moulin Touchais and Chinon from Drouet Frères. In Bordeaux, the house claret is from Nathaniel Johnston (rather pricey at £3.83) and there is a good range of petit château wines from recent vintages, plus classed growths back to 1970. The best wines from Burgundy are the Chablis of Simmonet-Febvre, while in Beaujolais look for Beaujolais Villages Ch du Carra 1987 at £4.80.

The northern Rhône lists Guigal, who also supplies a good Côtes du Rhône, while Alsace is from Willm. The Old Maltings have got together a good range of French regional wines, such as Gaillac Domaine Jean Cros Rouge at £4.29.

In Italy, look for wines from Bigi in Umbria, Chianti from Rocca delle Macie, and wines from Antinori, as well as Carmignano from Villa di Capezzana. Spain has wines from Torres, Portugal those from J M da Fonseca, Australia Hill-Smith and Brown Brothers, New Zealand Cooks and Stoneleigh Vineyard.

Best buys

Corbières 1985, Ch de la Condamine, £3.56; Ch la Harque 1987, Entre-Deux-Mers, £4.40; Côtes de Duras Sauvignon Blanc 1987, £3.88; Alsace wines from Willm

Old Street Wine Company

309 Old Street, London EC1V 6LE · · · · · · · · · · TEL 01-729 1768
OPEN Mon–Fri 12–7 Sat 11.30–1.30 CLOSED Sun, public holidays
CREDIT CARDS None accepted; personal and business accounts
DISCOUNTS 5% on 1 case DELIVERY Free in central London (min 1 case) and outer London (min 3 cases); otherwise at cost; mail order available
GLASS HIRE Free with 1-case order TASTINGS AND TALKS Monthly in-store tastings; to groups on request (min 15/20 people) CELLARAGE Not available

No longer part of Prestige Vintners, the Old Street Wine Company now operates from its own list.

It is particularly strong on the Loire, with wines from Coulée de Serrant, Ch de la Roche aux Moines, Quarts de Chaume of Ch de Belle Rive and Bonnezeaux of Domaine Godineau. There's Chinon from Couly-Dutheil and Domaine René Couly as well as Bourgueil from Domaines des Chesnaies, Sancerre from Bourgeois, Pouilly Fumé from Dagueneau. Smaller quantities of Loire bin-ends are also available.

A small listing of clarets includes some good petit château wines, and there is a nice clutch of Ch Rieussec Sauternes back to 1981. Burgundy is good on domaine-bottled whites. The South-West has Cahors Domaine du Single and Bergerac from Ch de Fayolle.

Outside France, look for Torres wines from Spain, Valdespino Sherries, and Drayton's Australian wines from the Hunter Valley.

Best buys

Touraine Gamay 1987, Hubert Sinson, £3.98; Gros Plant sur lie
Domaine des Croix, £2.98; Bergerac Rouge 1985, Ch de Fayolle, £3.59;
Rioja 1984 Bodegas Santiago, £3.85

Orpheus & Bacchus

3 Chapel Street, Guildford, Surrey GU1 3UH   TEL (0483) 576277

OPEN Mon–Wed, Fri 9.30–6   Thur 9.30–8   Sat 9.30–7   CLOSED Sun, public
holidays   CREDIT CARDS Access, Visa; personal and business accounts
DISCOUNTS 5% on 1 case, 10% on 5+ cases   DELIVERY Free locally; elsewhere
at cost   GLASS HIRE Free with wine purchased from premises
TASTINGS AND TALKS In-store tastings from time to time (Saturdays); to groups
on request   CELLARAGE Free for wine purchased from premises

Something of what marketing men might call a 'unique proposition',
this classical music shop cum wine merchant opened in June 1988.
Alongside the wines, you will find records, CDs and cassettes, scores
and sheet music.

The wine list is pretty serious, and while nothing is cheap, there are
some very fine bottles. We start with a big range of old and mature
clarets (the first list had Ch Calon-Ségur 1911 at £85 as its oldest
inhabitant). There is a section of cru bourgeois and petit château wines
for those who don't want to spend quite that much. Burgundy
continues in the same vein – Domaine de la Romanée-Conti, Emile
Voarick, Jacques Prieur, with Febvre Chablis. Pierre Sparr wines from
Alsace are reasonably priced, and Commanderie de la Bargemone from
Coteaux d'Aix-en-Provence.

Fine wines continue with old Barolos from Borgogno and top names
throughout the rest of Italy, Deinhard estate wines from Germany, and
old vintages of Torres Gran Coronas Black Label from Spain. In
California, look for Phelps and Firestone wines, and Lindeman's in
Australia. Hostomme Champagne is £9.65, and there are a few mature
Vintage Ports.

Best buys

Ch Calon-Ségur 1978, £14.95; Crozes-Hermitage 1983, Jaboulet
Vercherre, £3.65; Côtes du Frontonnais 1983, Ch Montauriol, £3.65;
Rioja Gran Reserva 1975, CVNE Imperial, £7.75

We have tried to make the *1989 Which? Wine Guide* as comprehensive as
possible, but we should love to hear from you with commonts on any other
wine merchants you feel deserve an entry, or on existing entries. Write to
us either by letter or using the report forms supplied at the back of the
book.

Ostlers

63A Clerkenwell Road, London EC1M 5NP   TEL 01-250 1522
Studio 50, 50 Strand, London WC2N 5LW   TEL 01-925 0751
(South Australian Wines & Crafts)

OPEN Mon–Fri 9.30–7   Sat 10–4 (Studio 50: Mon–Fri 10–5)   CLOSED Sun,
public holidays   CREDIT CARDS None accepted; personal and business
accounts   DISCOUNTS Negotiable   DELIVERY Free locally (min order
negotiable); elsewhere charges vary; mail order on request   GLASS HIRE Free
with case order   TASTINGS AND TALKS Regular Sat lunchtime in-store tasting;
extensive range of tastings held throughout the year; to groups on request on
premises   CELLARAGE £46 per bin per year

The opening of Studio 50 in the Strand has widened the horizons of
Ostlers while keeping them firmly at the forefront as one of the major
suppliers of Antipodean wines.

Studio 50 will concentrate on South Australian wines – after all, the
shop is leased from the South Australian government – and Ostlers
will continue to take in the broad spectrum of Australian winemaking.
Expect to find all the names, big and small, with special offers
highlighting different producers throughout the year.

Don't forget to look to Ostlers also for New Zealand wines (a recent
offer had Matua Valley, Hermann Siefried and Delegats). In Europe,
they have built up a collection of older clarets, Vintage Ports and
Madeiras and wines from Italy. They also sell American wines from the
list of Great American Wine Company (*qv*). Regular tastings are
arranged and a chatty newsletter goes out to mailing list customers.

Best buys

Le Chardonnay, Vin de Pays du Jardin de la France, Paul Boutinot,
£3.30; Yallum Ridge 1984, Cabernet/Shiraz, £4.75; Brands Laira Shiraz,
£5; regular special offers

Oxford & Cambridge Fine Wine

48 Clifton Road, Cambridge,   TEL (0223) 215274
Cambridgeshire CB1 4FQ

OPEN Mon–Fri 9–5.30   Sat 9–12.30   CLOSED Sun, public holidays
CREDIT CARDS Access, Visa; personal and business accounts   DISCOUNTS 5%
on 1 case, 7.5% on 6 cases, 10% on 12 cases   DELIVERY Free within 30-mile
radius of Oxford and Cambridge, and London postal districts (min 1 case);
elsewhere £4.50 on 1–4 cases, 5+ cases free; mail order available
GLASS HIRE Free with reasonable order   TASTINGS AND TALKS To groups on
request   CELLARAGE £3.15 per case per year

This is very much a traditional list aimed at the university trade, and
should be viewed in that light. The company operates mainly from a
warehouse in Cambridge, and in Oxford has a mail or telephone order
service only (0865–57734), but does run a daily delivery service in both cities

Being traditional, they do traditional things best: good own-label wines such as College Claret, the College Sherries and two good value wood Ports. There is a useful selection of other clarets, including petit château wines as well as classed growths, Beaujolais from Thorin and domaine and négociant Burgundies. Alsace comes from the excellent co-operative of Turckheim – a big range from here. There are also French country wines (Ch Mayragues of Gaillac is £3.25), Sancerre from Gitton and Ménétou-Salon of Jacky Rat at £4.90 – all good value.

Highlights beyond France include CVNE and Añares Riojas, a few German estate wines and Australian wines from Basedow, Brown Brothers and Hill-Smith.

Best buys

Alsace wines; Côtes du Roussillon, Domaine du Mas Sibade, £2.69; Sauvignon Vin de Pays du Jardin de la France, £2.95; College Claret, £3.30

Thomas Panton

The Wine Warehouse, Hampton Street,   TEL (0666) 53088
Tetbury, Gloucestershire GL8 8JN

OPEN Mon–Fri 9.15–1, 2.15–5.30 Sat 10–1, 2.30–5.30 CLOSED Sun, public holidays CREDIT CARDS Visa; personal and business accounts
DISCOUNTS 5% for 1 case DELIVERY Free within 60-mile radius of Tetbury (min 5 cases); mail order available GLASS HIRE Free (max 6 cases of glasses)
TASTINGS AND TALKS Not available CELLARAGE Charges negotiable

This firm, operating from a delightful Cotswold stone shop, returns to the Guide after an absence of six years. The list has become larger and is strongest in the classic areas of France, but has some nice surprises elsewhere, particularly in Italy.

But we start with Bordeaux. The oldest vintage is 1975, but there is a sensible selection from 1979 and 1983 and a much larger one from 1985 (Ch Maquin St-Georges, St-Emilion, £6.34). In Burgundy, look for Mâconnais wines from Pierre Ferraud; the same firm supplies the Beaujolais. Rhône wines are dominated by La Vieille Ferme (Côtes du Ventoux 1986, £3.39), while Alsace wines are by courtesy of Muré.

Italy comes up with some treats, with organically produced single vineyard wines from Guerrieri-Rizzardi in the Veneto (Bianco San Pietro, a Soave-style Vino da Tavola, £4). In Piedmont, look for the wines of Livio Pavese (Barbera Monferrato 1983 at £3.81), and in Tuscany, it would be fun to compare the vintages of Badia a Coltibuono Chianti Classico. Friuli wines from Tenuta Santa Anna and Trentino wines from Longariva are other enticements.

Best buys

Côtes du Ventoux 1986, La Vieille Ferme, £3.39; Soave Classico 1987, Guerrieri-Rizzardi, £4.10; Fino Sherry, Duke of Wellington, £3.85

Pavilion Wine Company

Finsbury Circus Gardens, Finsbury Circus,   TEL 01-628 8224
London EC2M 7AB

OPEN Mon–Fri 9–8   CLOSED Sat, Sun, public holidays
CREDIT CARDS Access, Amex, Visa; personal and business accounts
DISCOUNTS 2% for 6–11 cases   DELIVERY Free on UK mainland (min 3 cases);
mail order available   GLASS HIRE Free   TASTINGS AND TALKS Not available
CELLARAGE £5.75 per case per year (inc insurance)   ∎

From their elegant pavilion wine bar (see the WINE BARS section),
restaurant and shop in the centre of Finsbury Circus, this merchant
continues to offer a careful selection of wines, mainly from classic areas
in France, but with a firm nod in the direction of other parts of the wine
world.

By comparison with the small selection of clarets, there's much more
in Burgundy, with an interesting range of St-Aubin wines from Hubert
Lamy, Rully from Jean Daux, Meursault from Pitoiset-Uréna, Chablis
from Georges Verret. On the Loire, rarities include Jasnières of Joël
Gigou and Côtes Roannaises VDQS from Domaine du Picatier (a
Gamay-based wine produced near to the source of the Loire). Rhônes
come from Ch de Beaucastel Châteauneuf-du-Pape and Hermitage La
Chapelle from Jaboulet Aîné. The Pavilion Wine Company also pick
out the superb Mas de Daumas Gassac Vin de Pays de l'Hérault: the
1985 vintage is £8.62 (prices on the list do not include VAT, but we have
added it here).

Beyond France, the highlights are the Balgownie wines of Stuart
Anderson in Bendigo, Victoria.

Best buys

Côtes Roannaises 1986, Domaine du Picatier, £3.30; Côtes du Ventoux
1985, Domaine des Anges, £2.86; Jasnières 1985, Clos St-Jacques, £5.60;
Balgownie Estate Shiraz 1986, £5.22

Thos Peatling ▱ ☞

HEAD OFFICE Westgate House,   TEL (0284) 755948
Bury St Edmunds, Suffolk IP33 1QS
32 branches in Cambridgeshire, Essex, Hertfordshire, Lincolnshire,
Norfolk, Northamptonshire and Suffolk

OPEN Hours vary from branch to branch   CREDIT CARDS Access, Amex,
Diners, Visa; personal and business accounts   DISCOUNTS 5% on unmixed
cases   DELIVERY Free in East Anglia (min £20 order); elsewhere 1 case £4.44,
2 cases £8, 3 cases £9.50, 4 cases £11, 5+ cases free; mail order available
GLASS HIRE Free with corresponding order   TASTINGS AND TALKS Occasional
in-store tastings; to groups on request   CELLARAGE Free

Thos Peatling is not in fact a new name for a familiar face, Peatling & Cawdron, but a reversion to the name they started out with back in 1826. Plans are afoot to refurbish all the stores.

What doesn't change, we are delighted to report, is the quality of the wine list. The biggest concentration remains in Bordeaux and Burgundy, but other parts of the world are increasingly being noticed, and throughout there is a good balance between top flight and everyday wines.

This is especially true of Bordeaux, where Thos Peatling have assembled an enormous array of petit château wines at good prices. They follow the traditional role of the wine merchant in maturing wines until they are ready to drink, so you will also find plenty from vintages of the 1970s and beyond. In this section, as in every other in their smartly printed list, a helpful tasting note is offered.

In Burgundy, we are in the realm of pricier offerings, simply from the nature of the region. But even here there is plenty to choose from at all levels, and domaine and négociant wines mix happily. Things look slimmer on the Loire, but it would be worth considering the Ménétou-Salon of Jacky Rat as a good alternative to Sancerre. The Beaujolais is well served, with some attractively mature wines. The Rhône section is short, Alsace much more interesting.

Beyond France, we find a good range of Bulgarian wines, a big selection of German estate bottles, a rather old-fashioned view of Spain, a much more interesting set of wines from Italy and, further afield, a growing interest in Australia and New Zealand. Ports are good, Sherries less so.

Best buys

Vin de Table, Cuvée Vincent, £4.99; Franciacorta Rosso 1986, Camilla Martinoni, £4.50; petit château clarets from the 1979 and 1978 vintages; Alsace Riesling Caves de Bennwihr 1986, £3.79

Pennine Wines

7 Station Street, Huddersfield,	TEL (0484) 25747
West Yorkshire HD6 2NN	
ASSOCIATED OUTLET Wine Schoppen,	TEL (0742) 365684
1 Abbeydale Road South, Sheffield,	
South Yorkshire S7 2QL	

OPEN Mon–Sat 9.30–5 (closed Wed pm)   CLOSED Sun, public holidays
CREDIT CARDS All accepted; personal and business accounts   DISCOUNTS Up to 7% on case rates   DELIVERY Free in Huddersfield/Brighouse district (min 2 cases); elsewhere at cost   GLASS HIRE Free with 2-case order
TASTINGS AND TALKS Pre-Christmas tasting; to groups on request
CELLARAGE Not available

This shop offers the same list as The Wine Schoppen (*qv*).

Pennyloaf Wines

96 Station Road, Odsey, Ashwell, Hertfordshire SG7 5RR	TEL (046 274) 2725

OPEN Most of the time; advisable to telephone before calling
CREDIT CARDS None accepted; personal and business accounts
DISCOUNTS Variable   DELIVERY Free within 10-mile radius (min 1 case);
elsewhere at cost   GLASS HIRE Free with 1-case order
TASTINGS AND TALKS Various tastings held, usually on Saturdays; to groups on
request   CELLARAGE £1.75 per case per year   ∎

A short list, which specialises in wines from the South-West of France and the Loire. There's also a strong sideline of Beaujolais from Georges Duboeuf.

From the South-West, we find Cahors from Ch du Cayrou and Rigal, Bergerac from Domaine de Fraysse, Pécharmant from Domaine des Bertranoux (the 1986 vintage is a bargain at £4.91 a bottle – VAT is not included on the list, but we have added it here), Madiran from Alain Brumont at Ch Montus. The Loire offers good things in the form – among other treats – of Vouvrays of Gaston Huet, St-Nicolas de Bourgueil reds from Jean-Paul Mabileau, Muscadet of Sauvion et Fils and Saumur-Champigny of Ch de Chaintres. Look, too, for sweet wines from Coteaux du Layon.

Best buys

Clairette de Die Tradition, £4.97; Gaillac 1986, Ch Laroze, £4.19; St-Nicolas de Bourgueil wines of J-P Mabileau; Pécharmant 1986, Domaine des Bertranoux, £4.91

Christopher Piper Wines

1 Silver Street, Ottery St Mary, Devon EX11 1DB	TEL (0404 81) 4139/2197

OPEN Mon–Fri 9–6   Sat 9–5   CLOSED Sun, public holidays
CREDIT CARDS Access, Visa; personal and business accounts   DISCOUNTS 5%
on 1 mixed case, 10% on 3 mixed cases   DISCOUNTS Free on UK mainland (min
4 cases in South-West England, 6 cases elsewhere); mail order available
GLASS HIRE Free with 1-case order   TASTINGS AND TALKS In-store tastings
every Saturday; three major tastings annually; to groups on request
CELLARAGE £3.60 per case per year

Not many wine merchants can stick a photograph of their own French vineyard on the cover of their list, but Christopher Piper can. He is the owner of Ch des Tours in Brouilly, and, of course, his wines feature among the Beaujolais. It comes as no surprise that his greatest strengths lie in Beaujolais and Burgundy.

There is a regular treasure trove of Burgundies, mainly from well-known domaines (Michel Maillard, Dubreuil, Michel Lafarge, Chantal Lescure, Albert Morey) but also from the négociant house of

Labouré-Roi. Vintages are 1983, 1984 and 1985 for reds, 1985 and 1986 for whites. In Beaujolais, a range of Georges Duboeuf wines (including some single vineyard wines) joins Ch des Tours.

Other areas, especially in France, are not neglected. The Rhône benefits from a well-balanced assemblage (from Côtes du Rhône of Georges Duboeuf at £3.38 right up to Côte Rôtie Vidal-Fleury Brune et Blonde 1985 at £14.02). On the Loire, look for the Pouilly Fumé of Masson-Blondelet and Muscadet from Sauvion. In Provence, good bottles include the Maîtres Vignerons de St-Tropez (£4.16 for rosé and red), plus the famous Mas de Daumas Gassac (1984 vintage at £8.64). Champagne is that of George Goulet. Alsace that of Louis Gisselbrecht.

Beyond France, Germany has good estate wines, Italy some stars from Frescobaldi, Spain CVNE Riojas, and Portugal wines from J M da Fonseca. Safe names in the New World include Brown Brothers in Australia, Montana in New Zealand and Robert Mondavi in California.

Don't forget the huge range of half-bottles – many of them pudding wines.

Best buys

Half-bottles; Ch Roquevieille 1983, Côtes de Castillon, £4.78; Côtes du Rhône Villages Vacqueyras 1986, Domaine le Sang des Cailloux, £4.65; Brown Brothers Australian wines

Plumtree Wines

8 Normanton Lane, Keyworth,   TEL (06077) 5615
Nottinghamshire NG12 5HA

OPEN Every day (including public holidays) 9–9   CLOSED Chr Day
CREDIT CARDS None accepted; personal and business accounts
DISCOUNTS 5–10% on 1 case minimum   DELIVERY Free in Nottingham,
Leicester, Derby, Loughborough (min 1 case); elsewhere at cost; mail order
available   GLASS HIRE Free   TASTINGS AND TALKS Occasional in-store
tastings; to groups on request   CELLARAGE Not available   ■

This is an expanding list of wines which avoids the French classic areas but concentrates on Spain and, more recently, Australia.

In Spain, go for the Palacio de León wines of Vinos de León, Rioja Ramona from Bodegas Artacho and the Viña Solric Penedès wines of Josep Ferret. Australia has Hardy wines (including the good value Birds Series), Taltarni from Moonambel in Victoria and the Anglesey Estate in South Australia.

France manages a couple of good offerings from Côtes du Roussillon, Beaujolais from Loron and some good value Mâcon Villages. English wines are from Lamberhurst. The list prices do not include VAT, but we have added it for the **Best buys** below.

Best buys

Côtes du Roussillon Villages 1985, £2.92; Champagne Brut, Maurice

Delahaye, £9.08; Taltarni Shiraz 1982, £4.60; Palacio de León Tinto 1984, £2.59

Pond Farm Wines

120 High Street, Cottenham,　　　　　　　　TEL　(0954) 51828/51314
Cambridge, Cambridgeshire CB4 4RX
ASSOCIATED OUTLET　Wines of Argentina
(at same address as above)

OPEN Mon–Sat 9.30–7 (in winter), 9.30–8 (in summer)　Sun 12–2
CLOSED Some public holidays　CREDIT CARDS None accepted; personal and
business accounts　DISCOUNTS 1–4 cases 2.5%, 5–8 cases 5%, 9+ cases 7.5%
DELIVERY Free locally (approx 15-mile radius) (min 1 case); elsewhere at cost;
mail order available　GLASS HIRE Free with 1-case order
TASTINGS AND TALKS Occasionally by invitation; to groups on request
CELLARAGE Not available

This newcomer to the Guide offers a short list whose highlights include wines from the Bodegas Goyenechea in San Rafael, Argentina; wines from Concha y Toro and Cousiño Macul in Chile; the Riojas from Bodega Santa Daria, at the co-operative of Cenicero under the Valdemontan label; and Sherries from Lustau.

Elsewhere, there is Beaujolais from Thomas la Chevalière, a few domaine-bottled Burgundies, and Ports from Ramos Pinto.

Best buys

Argentine Cabernet Sauvignon 1982, Bodegas Goyenechea, £3.35; Alsace Riesling 1986, Jean Ziegler, £3.65; Rioja 1981, Valdemontan, £3.30

Premier Wine Warehouse

3 Heathmans Road, London SW6 4TJ　　　　　TEL　01-736 9073

OPEN Mon–Fri 11–8　Sat 10–7　Sun 11–4　CLOSED Public holidays
CREDIT CARDS Visa; personal and business accounts　DISCOUNTS Negotiable
(trade only)　DELIVERY Free within 2/3 mile radius (min 1 case) and Greater
London (min 4 cases); elsewhere at cost; mail order available　GLASS HIRE Free
with 1-case order　TASTINGS AND TALKS Theme tastings every 6–8 weeks; to
groups on request　CELLARAGE Not available　　　　　　　■

The French regions and Spain continue to be the strong points at this Parsons Green warehouse. The listing is very sensibly arranged in price order, and starts with some good bargains: Sauvignon de Touraine of André Besnard (£2.59) and Côtes du Ventoux 1984, Domaine des Anges (£2.69). More French bargains feature at higher price levels – in a recent list the 1978 vintage of the second wine of Ch Brane-Cantenac, was £8.99.

Spanish wines, too, come at attractive prices, starting with basic wines from León (Palacio de León red is £2.39) and La Mancha and moving up to some fine Riojas, taking in Torres wines on the way. Valdepeñas Señorio de los Llanos 1978 Reserva at £3.25 is remarkable value. Look out for the old-style Riojas from Tondonia (Tondonia Blanco 1981 at £4.75 is yet another bargain).

Other countries are treated more briefly, but there are some interesting wines from Australia (the de Bortoli sweet Botrytised Semillon and the Yarra Yering Cabernet Sauvignon 1982), Chile (more Torres wines here) and New Zealand (Babich). Champagnes offer a good choice (the house Champagne, Comte de Lisseuil Brut is £7.49), and the warehouse is proud of an exotic selection of beers from around the world.

Best buys

Ch du Gazin 1982, Canon Fronsac, £4.85; Sauvignon de St-Bris 1985, Luc Sorin, £4.25; Torres Coronas 1983, £3.17; Tondonia Blanco 1981, Lopez de Heredia, £4.75; Cava Conde de Caralt Brut NV, £4.25; Palacio de León, £2.39

Prestige Vintners

15 Stucley Place, London NW1 6NS   TEL 01-485 5895

OPEN Mon–Fri 10–6   Sat, Sun, public holidays by appointment
CREDIT CARDS None accepted; personal and business accounts
DISCOUNTS 5% on 6+ cases   DELIVERY Free in central London (min 1 case); otherwise 1 case £6.90, 2 cases £3.91 per case, 3–5 cases £2.76 per case, 6–9 cases £2.07 per case; mail order available   GLASS HIRE Free with case order
TASTINGS AND TALKS To groups on request   CELLARAGE Available at cost   ■

Come to this merchant for individual estate wines. They have a strong line in wines from the Loire and the South-West of France, as well as growers' wines from elsewhere (such as Balthasar Ress in the Rheingau in Germany and Tardy et Ange in Crozes-Hermitage on the Rhône).

In the Loire, a very fine selection of wines includes good-quality Anjou from Domaine Richou, Savennières Ch d'Epire, Quarts de Chaume Ch Belle-Rive, Chinon from Domaine Couly-Dutheil and Bourgueil from Lamé Delille-Boucard, Vouvray from Gaston Huet, Sancerre from Jean-Max Roger (and also Ménétou-Salon) and Muscadet from Guilbaud Frères.

Down in the deep South-West, there's a similar parade of wines. Gaillac from Ch Lastours is joined by Buzet from Les Vignerons des Côtes de Buzet (Baron d'Ardeuil 1985 at £4.20), Jurançon of Ch Joly and Cahors Ch de Chambert (the 1983 vintage is £5.50).

Other points of interest on this list are Champagnes from Louis Roederer, Krug, Taittinger and Bollinger; and Ports from Martinez Gassiot.

Best buys

Cahors 1983, Comte André de Monpezat, £3.65; Sauvignon de Touraine Vieilles Vignes 1987, Preys et Sinson, £3.39; Gaillac Rouge 1986, Ch Lastours, £3.50; Martinez Crusted Port (bottled 1986), £7.20

Queens Club Wines

2 Charleville Road, London W14 9JZ   TEL 01-385 3582

OPEN Mon–Sat 10.30–10.30 Sun 12–2, 7–9 CREDIT CARDS None accepted; personal and business accounts DISCOUNTS 5% on unmixed cases DELIVERY Free locally (min 1 case); otherwise at cost GLASS HIRE Not available TASTINGS AND TALKS Occasional tastings on Sunday mornings (8 per year) CELLARAGE Not available

No list here but an ever-changing range of wines which avoids the classic French areas ('too pricey', they say) but instead offers plenty from Germany, the New World, Portugal and Spain. There's a wine bar, too, just along the road, with jazz to go with the wines.

Best buys

Tinto da Anfora, Portugal, £4.40; Vin de Pays des Côtes de Gascogne, £2.60; house claret Grangeneuve, £3.50

Quintet Wines

136/142 New Kent Road, London SE1 6TU   TEL 01-703 3568

OPEN Mon–Fri 10–4 (callers by appointment only) CLOSED Sat, Sun, public holidays CREDIT CARDS None accepted; personal and business accounts DISCOUNTS By arrangement (min 1 case) DELIVERY Free in London (min 1 case); elsewhere at cost GLASS HIRE Not available TASTINGS AND TALKS Occasional in-store tastings; to groups on request CELLARAGE Not available   ■

For a company set up only in 1987, this list is perhaps surprisingly conventional. Some well-known names crop up in Burgundy: look for the wines of Machard de Gramont (the La Vierge Romaine Bourgogne Blanc at £6.42 is good basic white Burgundy – prices on the list do not include VAT but we have added it here), for Roux Père et Fils in St-Aubin or Luc Sorin in Sauvignon de St-Bris (the 1987 vintage is £4.07), or for Simon Bize in Savigny-lès-Beaune. There's also a big range of wines from Mommessin.

Other French still wine areas tend to get more perfunctory treatment (although it's nice to see some second wines from Bordeaux châteaux). But in Champagne, a big choice of wines from Grande Marque houses is very exciting. Sherries from Valdespino and Sandeman Ports are good value, alongside Riojas from Bodegas Santiago.

Best buys

Muscadet de Sèvre et Maine sur lie, Ch du Coing de St-Fiacre 1985, £5.65; Vin de Pays de l'Hérault Rouge, Les Terres Noires, £2.72; Alsace Pinot Blanc 1986, Willy Gisselbrecht, £3.35

Arthur Rackhams

HEAD OFFICE AND CELLARS
Winefare of London, Winefare House,   TEL (09323) 51585
5 High Road, Byfleet, Surrey KT14 7QF
12 branches in London, Staines and Surrey
The Vintner (fine wines),   TEL 01-229 2629
66 Kensington Church Street, London W8 4BY
Viticulteur, 391 King's Road,   TEL 01-352 6340
London SW10 0LP

OPEN Some outlets Mon–Sat 10–8   Sun, public holidays 12–2; other outlets Mon–Sat 10–10   Sun, public holidays 7–9   CREDIT CARDS All accepted; personal and business accounts   DISCOUNTS Members' Club discount (The Vintner Wine Club)   DELIVERY Free on UK mainland (min 3 cases); mail order available   GLASS HIRE Free   TASTINGS AND TALKS Tastings in-store every weekend; tutored tastings every weekend at Viticulteur; to groups on request   CELLARAGE Not available

Three lists are in operation here. One is of wines that can be bought in the shops; the second is of wines available through the Vintners Wine Club (see under WINE CLUBS); the third is an expansion of the range of wines from some producers on the main list, covering only domaines in France, and this selection is available only at the Viticulteur shop. While many wines overlap, there are differences, and prices are lower through the club. This entry looks at the wines in the Arthur Rackhams shops only.

It's not many wine merchants who start their list with Champagnes, but one look at the enormous range here shows that this is no ordinary selection. While many grande marque firms are listed, star place goes to Alfred Gratien – with mature vintages, large bottles, and the non-vintage Réserve at £10.99, while the basic house Champagne is Charles de Muret at £7.99.

The move to Bordeaux maintains a similar level, with plenty of good value petit château wines, pricier wines for laying down, and some more mature wines from 1979 and 1978. In Burgundy, there's some good value with basic Bourgogne AC wines from good producers, while on the Loire, look for the Muscadet of Donatien Bahuaud and the rare Cheverny from Phillippe Tessier.

Other points of interest include a small selection of estate German wines, some good Italians (Soave and Valpolicella from Zenato, and super vini da tavola from Monte Vertine in Tuscany), while in Spain we find a good cross-section of Riojas. Elsewhere, things are briefer –

Wyndham Estate wines from Australia, good value Bulgarians, and Stag's Leap wines from California.

Best buys

Champagne Domaine Charpentier Brut, £8.99; Beaujolais Villages Domaine Dalicieux 1987, £4.65; Soave Classico Zenato 1987, £3.69; Rioja 1985 CVNE Tinto, £3.49; Côtes de Provence, Ch du Berne Blanc 1985, £3.99

Raeburn Fine Wines and Foods

23 Comely Bank Road, Edinburgh EH4 1DS   TEL 031-332 5166
OPEN Mon, Tue, Thur, Fri, Sat 9–8.30   Wed 10.30–8.30   Sun, public holidays 9–7 (not open for alcoholic drinks on Sun)   CREDIT CARDS None accepted   DISCOUNTS 5% on unmixed cases, 2.5% on mixed cases
DELIVERY Free in Edinburgh (min 1 case); elsewhere at cost; mail order available   GLASS HIRE Free with wine order   TASTINGS AND TALKS To groups on request   CELLARAGE £2.50 per case per year (under bond)

This list gets better and better. It's even more extensive than last year's, but more importantly it no longer seems like a random collection of fine names. Now, more and more, it represents wines which Raeburn ship directly and, often, for which Raeburn are the only outlet in Scotland.

This policy is particularly true of wines from many estates in France and a number of the Italian producers. The first sign of this is with French regional wines – where Cahors wines from Burc et Fils at Domaine de la Pineraie and Clos Triguedina of Baldès et Fils, and Bergerac wines of Ch de Sanxet, are estates in which Raeburn has a special interest. In Burgundy, too, they are now shipping direct from a range of domaines – Domaine Vincent, Domaine de la Folie in Rully, Comtes Lafon in Meursault, Tollot-Beaut, Pernin-Rossin in Vosne-Romanée. Look, too, for Chablis from Jean-Paul Droin and Louis Pinson.

In Bordeaux, Raeburn are following the fortunes of a good range of cru bourgeois estates (Ch Sociando-Mallet, Ch Malartic-Lagravière, Ch le Pin in Pomerol). But there are recent vintages from many other middle-ranking estates as well.

There's a fine list of Rhône wines, with, again, some top estates – Emile Florentin in St-Joseph is one (and look, too, for Domaine de la Fourmone in Vacqueyras and Gigondas), while on the Loire, we would home in on the Vouvrays of Gaston Huet, and sweet wines from the Coteaux du Layon. Alsace has the wines of Rolly Gassmann in profusion. Champagne is from the co-operative of Le Mesnil-sur-Oger.

In Germany, the list continues with wines in depth from some great estates, and in Spain it looks at wines from Marqués de Murrieta and Torres. On to Italy, and here the estates again proliferate: Quintarelli in

Valpolicella, Chianti Classico Il Poggio, Barolo from Maria Feyles and Franciacorta from Ricci Curbastro.

Over the oceans, we find Australian wines from Moss Wood, Cape Mentelle and Redgate in Western Australia; Balgownie in Victoria; and a good range of the unique dessert Muscats from Rutherglen.

There are plenty of half-bottles as well.

Best buys

Bourgogne Passetoutgrains 1986, Henri Jayer, £5.30; Ch Notton 1973, Margaux, £5.99; Vin de Pays du Jardin de la France, Cépage Grolleau, Domaine des Saulaies, £2.99; Vin de Pays du Comte Tolosan, Domaine de Callory Rouge, £2.99; Coteaux du Layon Moelleux 1967, Beaulieu, £10.40

Rattlers Wine Warehouse

Arch No 5, Viaduct Estate, Carlisle,   TEL (0228) 43033
Cumbria CA5 2BN

OPEN Mon–Fri 10.30–5.30   Sat 10.30–6.30   CLOSED Sun, public holidays
CREDIT CARDS Access, Visa; personal and business accounts
DISCOUNTS Negotiable   DELIVERY Free within 30-mile radius of Carlisle (min 1 case); otherwise £1.65; mail order available   GLASS HIRE Free with wine order   TASTINGS AND TALKS Regular in-store tastings   CELLARAGE Charges negotiable

After a move to new premises, a new list was being prepared as we went to press. We can nevertheless recommend the wines below which give some idea of Rattler's enthusiasms.

Best buys

Ch Belcier de Castillon 1983, Côtes de Castillon, £4; Señorio de Sarria Gran Reserva 1981, Navarra, £4; Joseph Phelps Syrah 1980, California, £5.89; Stoneleigh Vineyard Chardonnay 1987, New Zealand, £5.79

Redpath and Thackray Wines

WAREHOUSE AND OFFICE Thurland Castle,   TEL (046 834) 360
Tunstall, via Carnforth, Lancashire LA6 2QR

OPEN Office hours   CREDIT CARDS None accepted; personal and business accounts   DISCOUNTS 5% on 5 cases   DELIVERY Free nationwide (min 1 case); mail order available   GLASS HIRE Not available   TASTINGS AND TALKS Not available as we went to press   CELLARAGE Charges negotiable ■

A move from Cambridge to Lancashire (and closure of their retail outlet) has been the main change at this merchant this year. A new list is being prepared which was not available as we went to press. Reports, please.

Reid Wines

The Mill, Marsh Lane, Hallatrow, Nr Bristol BS18 5EB	TEL (0761) 52645
Reid Wines Warehouse, Unit 2, Block 3, Vestry Trading Estate, Otford Road, Sevenoaks, Kent TN14 5EL	TEL (0732) 458533

OPEN Mon–Fri 9.30–5.30 Sat, Sun, public holidays by arrangement
(Hallatrow); Mon–Fri 9.30–6 Sat 9.30–1 (Sevenoaks) CLOSED Sun and public
holidays (Sevenoaks) CREDIT CARDS Access, Visa (Sevenoaks only); none
accepted at Hallatrow; some personal and business accounts at Hallatrow
DISCOUNTS 5% on orders over £250 at Sevenoaks only DELIVERY Free in
central London and within 25 miles of Hallatrow and Sevenoaks; elsewhere
1 bottle £2.87, 1 case £8.05, 5 cases free; mail order available GLASS HIRE Free
with 1-case order TASTINGS AND TALKS By arrangement; monthly in-store
tastings at Sevenoaks CELLARAGE £4.02 per case per year

Reid Wines are the firm to have brought you the Ronald Searle
cartoons of wine – but the wines themselves are much more serious.

The main Hallatrow list is one of the best for what auctioneers call
'finest and rarest' – half-bottles of 1934 Ch Montrose (at £15) or the
single bottle of Ch Latour 1950 (£85). Occasionally even older vintages
wing their way here.

Reid Wines' business involves buying small quantities of fine
wines, either at auction or from people selling the contents of their
cellars, or else from two jointly owned Australian/American wineries
(Taltarni and Clos du Val). Inevitably with this approach, the list is in
continual flux, so it is essential to enquire what they have got at the
moment rather than peruse any particular list.

The Sevenoaks warehouse stock is perhaps more conventional, with
a more regular supply of wine (although they, too, run special offers of
the contents of cellars). But it is all fine stuff, with claret and Burgundy
and the other major French regions predominating. Vintages are more
recent, though, and prices represent good value.

Best buys

Old and rare wines; Taltarni Australian wines; Ch Carras 1985, Greece,
£4.55

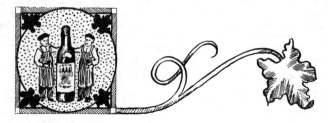

La Reserva Wines ⊜

Unit 6, Spring Grove Mills, Manchester Road, TEL (0484) 846732
Linthwaite, Huddersfield,
West Yorkshire HD7 5QG
ASSOCIATED OUTLET
Grapehop, 17 Imperial Arcade, TEL (0484) 533509
Huddersfield, West Yorkshire HD1 2BR

OPEN Mon–Sat 9–5.30 CLOSED Sun, Chr CREDIT CARDS Access, Visa;
personal and business accounts DISCOUNTS 10% on 1 mixed case
DELIVERY Free within 15-mile radius (minimum order depends on distance);
elsewhere £5 per case; mail order available GLASS HIRE Free with 1-case
order TASTINGS AND TALKS Bottles occasionally open on Saturdays; tastings
every 2 months by invitation; to groups on request CELLARAGE Not available

We are promised more Italians, and there are already Australian wines
(Orlando, Cape Mentelle, Lindeman's, Redgate, Mildara) and New
Zealand wines (Babich, Cooks, Stoneleigh Vineyard, Cloudy Bay).
But it is still to Spain, Chile and Portugal that we turn at La Reserva
Wines.

In Spain, the collection of Riojas is very fine, encompassing plenty of
wines – from sin crianza to Gran Reserva – from each bodega. Nearly
all the major producers, and many smaller ones, are here. In Navarra,
look for the wines of Señorio de Sarria, while Rueda has the top-flight
Marqués de Griñon. In Catalonia, it is Torres, Conde de Caralt, Raimat
and René Barbier. Plenty of sparkling Cavas, too.

There are wines from Galicia, Ribera del Duero (Vega Sicilia,
Pesquera, Bodegas Peñalba), Cariñena, Valdepeñas, León. And then
we get to an enormous hoard of Sherries – from Jose de Soto, Lustau,
Don Zoilo, Williams and Humbert, Bobadilla, Sanchez Romate, Garvey
– all great names making what La Reserva calls 'real Sherry'.

Chile proffers wines from Concha y Toro, Cousiño Macul, Torres
and Santa Rita (look for the Sauvignon Blanc 1986 at £4.69). Portugal
offers wines from J M da Fonseca, João Pires, dry Vinho Verde and
some good Bairradas.

Best buys

Rioja 1986, Señor Burgues Tinto, £3.20; Rioja Gran Reserva 1978,
Berberana, £6.85; Rioja Reserva 1981, Monte Real, £5.50; León Reserva,
Don Suero Tinto, £3.45

Special awards

🐷 is for bargain prices   ⊜ is for a very good range of wines

❀ is for high quality wines   ↘ is for exceptional service

La Réserve

56 Walton Street, London SW3 1RB — TEL 01-589 2020
47 Kendal Street, London W2 2BU — TEL 01-402 6920

OPEN Mon, Tue 10–7 Wed 9.30–8 Thur, Fri 9.30–7 Sat 9.30–5.30
CLOSED Sun, public holidays CREDIT CARDS Access, Visa; personal and
business accounts DISCOUNTS 10% on house wine, 5% on all others (min 1
case) DELIVERY Free in London (min 1 case); otherwise at cost; mail order
available GLASS HIRE Free with 1-case order TASTINGS AND TALKS In-store
tastings every Saturday; regular evening tastings; to groups on request
CELLARAGE Can arrange elsewhere

Here we are definitely in fine wine land, and very satisfying it is, too.
La Réserve is the retail side of College Cellar (*qv*) and the concentration
there on claret and Burgundy rubs off very nicely.

That's particularly true of Burgundy, of which there is an extensive
range, especially in whites. Many of the domaines are featured in
considerable depth – look for Chandon de Briailles, Rougeot, Olivier
Leflaive, Morot. The current list includes cru Beaujolais from Jacky
Janodet (Moulin-à-Vent 1986 at £7.90).

The Rhône is another star area. Hermitage and Châteauneuf-du-
Pape are featured – look for Hermitage wines from Guigal, Jaboulet
Aîné and Sorrel, and Châteauneuf wines from Ch Rayas, Ch Fortia and
Ch de Beaucastel.

Plenty of other attractions are strewn through the list: Alsace has
vendange tardive wines from a number of producers; there's plenty of
Champagne (including old vintages), and old Barolos from Borgogno.
The New World is showing up well with Clos du Bois, Mondavi and
Acacia from California; Hill Smith and Rosemount from Australia; and
Cloudy Bay from New Zealand. Vintage Ports go back to 1924 and
there are Valdespino Sherries.

Best buys

Vinho Verde Solar das Boucas, £4.65; Pécharmant 1983, Ch la
Renaudie, £4.55; Côtes du Ventoux 1985, La Vieille Ferme, £3.45;
Sauternes 1973, Ch Lafaurie-Peyraguey, £10.95

Richmond Wine Warehouse

138c Lower Mortlake Road, Richmond, — TEL 01-948 4196
Surrey TW9 2JZ

OPEN Mon–Thur, Sat 10–7 Fri 10–8 CLOSED Sun (except Dec), public
holidays CREDIT CARDS Access DISCOUNTS Discretionary DELIVERY Free
locally (min 2 cases); otherwise £5 per case, extra case £2.50 GLASS HIRE Free
with 2-case order TASTINGS AND TALKS Every Saturday in-store
CELLARAGE Not available ■

Greatly expanded sections of Australian and Spanish wines are the
biggest change at this merchant. They keep Wyndham's, Lindeman's,

Brown Brothers and Hardy's Ch Reynella from Australia; and Bodegas
Lagunilla, Bodegas Berberana and Bodegas Faustino from Spain.

Otherwise, a shortish list of fine clarets (some from vintages of the
1970s), a big range of Beaujolais, Chanson Burgundies, and some large
bottles of Champagne are the form.

Best buys

Ch Puyfromage 1985, Bordeaux Supérieur £3.99; De Souza Wood Port
1978, £7.75; Chianti Classico 1986, Antinori, £3.85; Champagne Brut
NV, Petitjean, £8.30

C A Rookes

This merchant is moving premises in January 1989 and no details of
their new address were available as we went to press.

The Rose Tree Wine Co

15 Suffolk Parade, Cheltenham,   TEL (0242) 583732
Gloucestershire GL50 2AE

OPEN Mon–Sat 9–7   CLOSED Sun, public holidays   CREDIT CARDS Visa;
personal and business accounts   DISCOUNTS 5% on 1 case   DELIVERY Free
within 30-mile radius (min 1 case); otherwise 2–5 cases £1.45 per case, 1 case £4;
mail order available   GLASS HIRE Free with 1-case order
TASTINGS AND TALKS Regular in-store tastings; to groups on request
CELLARAGE £1.78 per case per year

This new company, started in October 1987, is already offering a range
of wines characterised by a fair balance and some good prices.

They are best in France. Bordeaux shows well with some good petit
château wines, such as Ch Segonzac 1983 at £4.99 (prices on the list do
not include VAT, but we have added it here), or Ch Jouanin 1985, Côtes
de Castillon (£3.81). There are some good sweet white Bordeaux from
Sauternes, Barsac and Cadillac. In Burgundy, the catalogue of
domaine-bottled wines (Bruno Clair, Emile Voarick, William Fèvre in
Chablis, Armand Rousseau) is a pleasure to read. Beaujolais comes
from Robert Sarrau.

Other French areas have star turns as well. On the Loire, look for
some good red Chinon, and the superb Vouvray Moelleux 1971, Clos
du Bourg of Gaston Huet (£11.13). The Rhône is less interesting, but
the Turckheim co-operative comes up with some good value in Alsace.

While Germany shows off good wines from Franz von Metternich,
and Spain the popular Berberana Riojas, Italy is a bit of a disaster area
(apart from the Nebbiolo d'Alba of Livio Pavese at £4.71). Australia is
strong (with Brown Brothers, Tisdall and Cullens Margaret River),
while Clos du Val represents California, and Concha y Toro speaks for
Chile. Also available: Perrier-Jouët Champagne, Don Zoilo Sherries
and Smith Woodhouse Ports.

WHERE TO BUY

Best buys

Ch Thieuley Blanc 1987, £3.90; Ch Segonzac 1983, £4.99; Côtes du
Rhône 1986, Delas Frères, £3.16; Bodegas Ribera del Duero Tinto 1985,
£3.89; Cousiño Macul Antiguas Reservas 1981, £4.38; Smith
Woodhouse Ports

William Rush

Tecklewood, Uplands Close, Gerrards Cross,   TEL (0753) 882659
Buckinghamshire SL9 7JH

OPEN Every day, at any reasonable hour   CREDIT CARDS Access; personal and
business accounts   DISCOUNTS 5% on unmixed cases (cash payment)
DELIVERY Free within 15-mile radius of Gerrards Cross (min 1 case); otherwise
£7 per case   GLASS HIRE Free with minimum case order
TASTINGS AND TALKS Wines always open for tasting; to groups on request
CELLARAGE Not available   ∎

David Rush sticks firmly to his belief in Burgundy as the source of the
finest red and white wines in the world, impressively managing to
keep pretty much to his self-imposed upper selling price of £10.

In reds, we find wines from Chauvenet and domaine wines
produced by Emile Voarick (Mercurey 1985 at £7) and Fixin from Gelin
et Molland. In whites, there are Sauvignon de St-Bris of André Sorin
(1986 vintage at £4.16), St-Véran from Norbert Pauget and wines from
Yves Marceau and Larue.

Despite Mr Rush's predilections, he also ventures to other parts of
France, assembling a small selection of Beaujolais and Rhônes,
including a Châteauneuf-du-Pape 1984 of Domaine de la Ferme Michel
(£8.15). Bordeaux offers a good mix of middle-range clarets, a few
Sancerres, and Champagne Desmoulins at £10.40. There are also
offerings from Spain, Australia and England, plus some of Churchill's
Ports.

Best buys

Sauvignon de St-Bris 1985, André Sorin, £4.16; Beaujolais le Clos 1986,
Vivier-Merle £4.65; Mâcon Rouge 1985, Chauvenet £3.95

Russell & McIver

The Rectory, St Mary-at-Hill,   TEL 01-283 3575
London EC3R 8EE

OPEN Mon–Fri 9–5.30   CLOSED Sat, Sun, public holidays
CREDIT CARDS None accepted; personal and business accounts
DISCOUNTS By arrangement   DELIVERY Free on UK mainland (min 1 case in
London, 5 cases elsewhere); otherwise £4.60 per consignment; mail order
available   GLASS HIRE Free   TASTINGS AND TALKS Tastings organised
around the country particularly for private customers; to groups on request
CELLARAGE £3.45 per case per year

Russell & McIver's is a splendidly produced list, strong in Bordeaux, Burgundy, the Rhône and – appropriately for a City wine merchant which boasts an ex-Lord Mayor on its Board of Directors – fortified wines, especially Ports and Madeiras.

The firm make a point of their house wines – look for the two ranges under their own name and the Gresham brand. In Bordeaux, they have not only fine classed growths, but a sensible collection of petit château wines (Ch Gromel Bel Air 1983 Bordeaux Supérieur at £3.68; or, for mature petit château wine, try Ch de Parenchère 1982, Bordeaux Supérieur, £4.54).

In Beaujolais and Burgundy, there are some good domaine wines, again with reasonable prices (such as Bourgogne Pinot Noir 1986 of Domaine Talmard at £5.18). There are a few good southern country wines (look for the vins de pays under their own label), Rhône wines, which include good value Lirac from André Mejan, Sancerre and Pouilly Fumé from André Dezat on the Loire. Germany has estate wines from Max-Ferd Richter and Rudolf Müller, while Australia newly boasts Hunter Estate and Penfold's, and England the award-winning Biddenden Ortega 1986.

The fortified wine range includes the Tarquinio range of Madeiras from Lomelino, a good choice of wood Ports and mature vintages, and some of the excellent Sherries of Diez Hermanos.

Best buys

Russell & McIver Syrah Rosé 1987, Vin de Pays des Coteaux de l'Ardèche, £2.99; Ch Bonnet 1984, Bordeaux, £4.31; Ch de Valcombe, Costières du Gard, £2.76; Ramos Pinto 10-year-old tawny, Quinta Ervamoira, £9.43; Tarquinio range of 5-year-old Madeiras

Safeway

HEAD OFFICE Argyll House,   TEL 01-848 8744
Millington Road, Hayes, Middlesex UB3 4HY
Approximately 200 branches

OPEN Varies from store to store   CREDIT CARDS None accepted   DISCOUNTS,
DELIVERY Not available   GLASS HIRE Free with 1-case order   TASTINGS AND
TALKS, CELLARAGE Not available

The range of wines at this group of supermarkets is being re-vamped and details were not available as we went to press.

The Wine Development Board is a small organisation with the responsibility of encouraging more people to drink wine. They may be able to supply literature and general promotional material. Contact them at: PO Box 583, Five Kings House, Kennet Wharf Lane, Upper Thames Street, London EC4V 3BH; TEL 01-248 5835.

Sainsbury Bros

3 Edgar Buildings, George Street,   TEL (0225) 60481
Bath, Avon BA1 2EG

OPEN Mon–Fri 10–6   Sat 10–5.30   CLOSED Sun, public holidays
CREDIT CARDS Access, Visa; personal and business accounts
DISCOUNTS Available   DELIVERY Free in Bath, Bristol, Swindon and Taunton
(min 1 case); elsewhere on application   GLASS HIRE Free with 1-case order
TASTINGS AND TALKS Tastings held in cellars for customers; to groups on
request   CELLARAGE £3.45 per case per year

Despite a takeover, the list from this merchant remains much as it was.
It is a safe rather than an exciting range, but one or two changes this
year suggest that more may be round the corner.

One is the bigger range of Australian wines from Penfold's. There
are more Italian wines, too, such as the Veneto wines from Bolla and
Chianti from Mellini. There's a good line in Alsace wines from the
Pfaffenheim co-operative and Beaujolais from Loron. Bordeaux has
Fronsac from Ch de la Rivière (1981 vintage at £6.99 – prices on the list
do not include VAT, but we have added it here) and there are some
good petit château wines. From Champagne come Perrier-Jouët and
Pommery, and Torres wines from Spain.

Best buys

South Australian Dalwood Shiraz/Cabernet 1984, Penfold's, £3.54;
Valpolicella Classico 1985, Jago, Bolla, £3.48; Beaujolais Villages Cuvée
Grange Chartron 1986, Loron, £4.28

J Sainsbury   🐷 ✉

HEAD OFFICE Stamford House,   TEL 01-921 6000
Stamford Street, London SE1 9LL
280 licensed branches; 6 licensed SavaCentres

OPEN Varies from store to store; generally all open from 8.30 with late-night
shopping Tue–Fri   CLOSED Sun, public holidays   CREDIT CARDS None
accepted   DISCOUNTS Regular special offers   DELIVERY, GLASS HIRE,
TASTINGS AND TALKS, CELLARAGE Not available

It has been a year of consolidation at this, Britain's largest wine retailer.
While there have been no dramatic developments, a few wines have
been swelling the ranks each month. There are now over 200 wines in
the own-label range, and around 60 others in the Vintage Selection,
which is available in nearly 200 of the stores; nearly 100 stores carry the
full range. A scheme of discounts on multiple purchases of the same
wine has just been introduced.

The range continues to have its greatest successes in France. There
is, for example, an excellent choice in good value wines from the
South of France – Corbières and Minervois – and in the South-West –

Bergerac and Gaillac. Bordeaux, too, fares well: apart from the generic wines like Sainsbury's Claret, there are some good petit château wines – Ch de Bousquet Côtes de Bourg 1986 at £3.85 and Ch Tourteau-Chollet Graves 1985 at £4.95, for instance – as well as some top growths in the Vintage Selection (Ch Mouton Baronne Philippe 1980 at £8.75 was a recent bargain).

Burgundy, bearing in mind the prices of the wines at source, inevitably receives shorter shrift. But there are some good things from the Loire, a sound basic range of Alsace wines, a mix of simple quaffing wines and some more serious stuff on the Rhône, and always good value Champagnes.

Other parts of the world which Sainsbury's do proud are Italy, with some fine Chianti – San Polo in Rosso 1983 at £4.75, for instance – and a top Vernaccia from San Quirico; and Portugal, with the famous Quinta da Bacalhôa Cabernet Sauvignon 1985 (£3.95) and terrific value Arruda (£1.98). Recognition of the New World occurs in wines from Orlando, Wyndham's, Rosemount and Tyrrell's from Australia. Ports and Sherries include a few vintage wines as well as own-label brands.

Best buys

Sainsbury's Arruda, Portugal, £1.98; Sainsbury's Sauvignon de Touraine, £2.25; Sainsbury's Alsace Gewürztraminer 1986, £3.59; Vernaccia di San Gimignano, San Quirico 1987, £3.55; Ch Barreyres 1985 Haut-Médoc, £4.45

Paul Sanderson Wines

67/69 Main Street, Davidsons Mains,   TEL 031-312 6190
Edinburgh EH4 5AD

OPEN Mon 2–7 Tue–Thur 10–7 Fri, Sat 10–8 CLOSED Sun, Chr Day, Boxing Day, 1 & 2 January CREDIT CARDS None accepted; personal and business accounts DISCOUNTS 5% on 1 case (may be mixed) DELIVERY Free in Edinburgh (min 1 case); otherwise at cost; mail order available GLASS HIRE Free (if wine is bought from shop) TASTINGS AND TALKS To groups on request CELLARAGE Not available

Mr Sanderson's range of wines spans the world and his prices continue to give pleasure.

The country which provides the greatest interest, however, is Spain: Riojas from Berberana, Campo Viejo, Faustino, Coto, Marqués de Murrieta – with plenty of Reservas and Gran Reservas. There are Torres wines from Penedès, as well as Cavas Hill, and mature vintages of Vega Sicilia and its second wine Valbuena, and the Señorio de Sarria wines from Navarra. Sherry, too, does well – Garvey, Lustau Almacenistas, Gonzalez Byass and Hidalgo, among others.

Other wine regions which provide particular interest are Bordeaux with some fairly priced bottles; Italy (wines from Guerrieri-Rizzardi in the Veneto and Chianti from Castello Vicchiomaggio); estate German wines; Oregon wines from Adelsheim; and Australian wines from Rosemount, de Bortoli and Ch Reynella.

Best buys

Rioja Reserva 1981, Domecq Domain, £3.79; Raimat Reserva 1982, £3.99; Ribera Duero 1983, Bodegas Ribera del Duero, £3.69; Chianti Fattoria dell'Ugo, £2.99

Sapsford Wines

33 Musley Lane, Ware,   TEL (0920) 67040
Hertfordshire SG12 7EW

OPEN 'All hours' CREDIT CARDS Access; personal and business accounts DISCOUNTS 2.5–5% (min 5 cases) DELIVERY Free within 10-mile radius of Ware (min 1 case); elsewhere 1–4 cases £3 per case, 5+ cases free; mail order available GLASS HIRE Free with 3-case order TASTINGS AND TALKS Regular tastings at a local hotel; to groups on request CELLARAGE £6.90 per case per year ∎

The Loire is the mainstay of this list – an impressive range, nowhere more so than in Touraine, where Vouvray and Montlouis, reds from Chinon and wines from Cheverny (including the unusual Romorantin bone dry wines) all rub shoulders. In Anjou, we find Savennières Coulée de Serrant, sweet Coteaux du Layon, red Saumur Champigny and good, straightforward Anjou Rouge. Producers' names on this list would help customers.

Other interests include Italy's organic wines of Guerrieri-Rizzardi from the Veneto, Australia's Hardy's wines, and de Soto Sherries.

Best buys

Sweet wines from the Coteaux du Layon

SavaCentre

See J Sainsbury.

David Scatchard

The Wine Shop, 4 Temple Court,   TEL 051-236 6468
Liverpool L2 6PY

OPEN Mon–Fri 9.30–6 Sat 10–1 CLOSED Sun, public holidays
CREDIT CARDS Access, Visa; personal and business accounts DISCOUNTS 5% on 1 case; quantity discounts DELIVERY Free locally (min 2 cases) and nationwide (min 6 cases); Isle of Wight and Isle of Man £2 per case; mail order available by arrangement GLASS HIRE Free with case order
TASTINGS AND TALKS Occasional in-store tastings; private evening tastings by invitation; tutored tastings on Spanish wine for groups (min 60 people)
CELLARAGE Not available

David Scatchard is now associated with Fine Vintage Wines and Grape Ideas Wine Warehouse (both *qv*), but details of new wines were not available as we went to press.

However, they do list Riojas from Campo Viejo (Marqués de Villa Magna, Viña Alcorta and Marqués de Monistrol), Sherries from de Soto, Cava from Marqués de Monistrol and Montilla from Bodegas de Montealto. Vintages of Gran Reserva Riojas go back to 1959.

Best buys

Castillo de Tiebas Reserva, 1975, £3.55; Fino Soto 16.5, £3.49; Rioja 1982, Campo Viejo, £2.87; Wyndham Estate Cabernet Sauvignon Bin 444, £3.19

Sebastopol Wines

Sebastopol Barn, London Road, Blewbury,   TEL (0235) 850471
Oxfordshire OX11 9HB

OPEN Tue–Thur 10.30–5.30   Fri 10.30–6.30   Sat 10.30–5.30   Good Friday 10.30–6.30 CLOSED Sun, Mon CREDIT CARDS Access, Visa; business accounts DISCOUNTS 5% on 1 unmixed case; collection discount of £1 on unmixed case DELIVERY Free within 10-mile radius of Blewbury (min 1 case); elsewhere 1 case £5, 2 cases £4.50 per case, 3 cases £4 per case, 4+ cases free; mail order available GLASS HIRE Free with 1-case order
TASTINGS AND TALKS At least once a month on Saturdays; to groups on request CELLARAGE Not available   ■

Sebastopol Wines' well-balanced list may not be particularly long, but each wine is attractive in its own right.

Certain gaps are apparent – in Italy, for example, and Germany – but not in France. A good range of French regional wines, including the top Vin de Pays de l'Hérault Mas de Daumas Gassac (the 1985 vintage is £10.42), also takes in the good-value Madiran 1985 from the Producteurs Plaimont (£3.85). The Loire is of major interest – Vouvray from Prince Poniatowski and Marc Brédif and Savennières from Yves Soulez. The Rhône has Hermitage la Chapelle from Jaboulet Aîné, and the Côtes du Ventoux of La Vieille Ferme; also look for the Côtes du Rhône and Gigondas of Cartier as well.

On to Bordeaux: a small section, this, but sensibly divided into wines for drinking and wines for laying down. Burgundy goes in for domaine wines (Simon Bize, Leflaive, Clerget, Dujac), Alsace has Hugel wines, and Champagne is by Laurent Perrier.

For us, Spanish interest focuses on the Pesquera Ribera del Duero (the 1985 vintage is £10.32) and the Valdepeñas Señorio de los Llanos Gran Reserva 1978 (£3.98). Australia has grown this year, with wines from Penfolds (including the top Magill Estate), Brown Brothers and Cape Mentelle. Almacenista Sherries from Lustau and Churchill's Ports are good fortified choices.

Best buys

Madiran 1985, Producteurs Plaimont, £3.85; Savennières 1983, Domaine de la Bizolière, £4.99; Valdepeñas 1978, Señorio de los Llanos Gran Reserva, £3.98; Vin de Pays des Côtes de Gascogne 1987, Cépage Colombard, Producteurs Plaimont, £2.87

Seckford Wines ⊠

2 Betts Avenue, Martlesham Heath,   TEL (0473) 626072
Ipswich, Suffolk IP5 7RH

OPEN Tue–Sat 10–6 Sun 10–1 CLOSED Mon, public holidays
CREDIT CARDS Access, Visa; personal and business accounts DISCOUNTS 5%
on 1 unmixed case DELIVERY Free within 15–20-mile radius; mail order
available by arrangement GLASS HIRE Free with 1-case order
TASTINGS AND TALKS 5–6 weekend tastings annually CELLARAGE By
arrangement   ■

This firm claims to have the largest selection of Australian wines in the country. Certainly it is big and impressive, and doesn't concentrate on the obvious firms but goes out of its way to winkle out small wineries. That means that as well as Brown Brothers, Orlando, Wyndham Estate, De Bortoli, we find the boutique people as well: Yarra Yering, Rouge Homme, Jeffrey Grosset, Pipers Brook. The house wines from the Water Wheel Vineyard in Victoria (£3.99 for Cabernet Sauvignon 1985 or Shiraz 1985) offer good value.

In Europe, the greatest interest centres on the Rhône and in

Bordeaux in particular. The Rhône has Châteauneuf-du-Pape from Ch de Beaucastel, Côtes du Rhône Sablet from Cartier, Côte Rôtie from Guigal, while in Bordeaux there are some good cru bourgeois (often the best value in Bordeaux). Look for Ch la Tour St-Bonnet 1983 at £5.25 or the Moueix Bordeaux Supérieur 1982 (£3.85).

Other spots of interest are a few Spanish stars – Marqués de Griñon Cabernet Sauvignon 1982 at £7.95 and Campo Viejo 1982 Rioja at £3.37 – and the good-value Soave and Valpolicella of Tesdeschi.

Best buys

Côtes du Ventoux 1986, La Vieille Ferme, £2.99; Champagne François Delarge Brut, £6.99; Water Wheel Vineyards Cabernet Sauvignon 1985 and Shiraz 1985, £3.99; Spanna del Piemonte 1984, Agostino Brugo, £2.99

Selfridges

400 Oxford Street, London W1A 1AB   TEL 01-629 1234

OPEN Mon–Wed, Fri, Sat 9–6   Thur 9–8   CLOSED Sun, some public holidays   CREDIT CARDS All accepted; Sears Gold Card; personal and business accounts   DISCOUNTS Available on full cases   DELIVERY Free in central London (min £10 order); mail order available   GLASS HIRE Not available TASTINGS AND TALKS In-store tastings most weekends   CELLARAGE Not available

A completely new wine department has been designed to accommodate the excellent range of wines that this Oxford Street store now offers. What is especially interesting is that although there is plenty from Bordeaux and Burgundy it is the range from other areas of the wine world that give the list its character.

Champagne is a major section, covering non-vintage, vintage and de luxe brands in considerable depth. Another good French section is the Loire (look for Sauvignon de Touraine, Domaine Octavie, £4.15; and Quincy, Domaine de la Maison Blanche, £5.95). Bordeaux has vintages back to 1945, Burgundy a more emphatic presence of reds than whites.

Italy provides some tip-top wines – Chianti from Antinori, Veneto wines from Guerrieri-Rizzardi, Friuli wines from Jermann, Barolo from Ceretto, Montepulciano d'Abruzzo of Illuminati. Hungary offers a good range of Tokays, and Spain some excellent Sherries (Barbadillo, Domecq, Gonzalez-Byass, Sandeman, Don Zoilo). The California shelves have lengthened to house some fine wines – Mondavi, Trefethen, Clos du Bois, Paso Robles. In Australia, look for Penfold's reds, Sutherland and Rosemount whites, and plenty in between.

Best buys

Ch Millet 1986, Graves Blanc, £5.95; Galestro 1986, Antinori, £3.80; Anglesey South Australian Cabernet/Shiraz 1983, £4.65; Ch de Francs

1985, Côtes des Francs, £6.95; Donnafugata Rosso 1984, Sicily, Contessa Entellina, £4.95

Edward Sheldon

New Street, Shipston-on-Stour, Warwickshire CV36 4EN   TEL (0608) 61409/61639/62210

OPEN Mon–Fri 8.30–1, 2–5.30   Sat 8.30–1   CLOSED Sun, public holidays
CREDIT CARDS All accepted; personal and business accounts   DISCOUNTS 5% on 1 case, 10% on 6 cases   DELIVERY Free to certain areas of Cotswolds, Avon, Oxfordshire, Birmingham, Gloucestershire, Northamptonshire, Warwickshire, Shropshire, Staffordshire and London (min 1 case); otherwise 1 case £6, 2–5 cases £3 per case, 6–10 cases £2 per case, 11+ cases free; mail order available
GLASS HIRE Free   TASTINGS AND TALKS Annual Spring and Autumn tastings; to groups on request   CELLARAGE £3.45 per case per year

The backbone of Edward Sheldon's list remains firmly in classic wines: clarets, Burgundies and Vintage Ports. It is encouraging to see a good selection of half-bottles right through the list and, for those with money to spend, plenty of magnums, too.

The list starts with fortified wines, particularly Vintage Ports (with more unlisted because they are available only in small quantities). Vintages on the current list go back to 1955. Then we move to another good section, with a spread of vintage and non-vintage Champagnes.

The claret list is expansive, running back from 1985 to 1964, with especially good representation in 1983, 1982 and 1981. Both here and in the Burgundy section do we find many half-bottles and magnums. Burgundy has plenty of domaine wines and (in reds) vintages back to 1969.

Other areas worth looking at on this list are Spain (with Riojas from Marqués de Murrieta and La Rioja Alta) and Germany (with some fine estate wines, including a few examples from the 1976 vintage).

Best buys

Ch Haut Sociondo 1985, Premières Côtes de Blaye, £4.44; Bourgogne Pinot Noir 1985, Marion Frères, £4.79; Beaujolais St-Amour 1985, P Thévenin, £6.17; Oestricher Lenchen Riesling Auslese 1976, Deinhard, £16.22

Special awards

⟨⟩ is for bargain prices   ⟨⟩ is for a very good range of wines

✸ is for high quality wines   ⟨⟩ is for exceptional service

Sherborne Vintners

The Old Vicarage, Leigh, Sherborne,   TEL (0935) 873033
Dorset DT9 6HL   (0935) 872222 (orders 24 hours)

OPEN Every day 9–8   CREDIT CARDS None accepted; personal and business accounts   DISCOUNTS 6–10 cases £1 per case, 11+ cases £2 per case
DELIVERY Free within 20-mile radius of Sherborne (min 1 case) and UK mainland (min 2 cases); elsewhere £3.45 per case; mail order available
GLASS HIRE Free with 1-case order (locally)
TASTINGS AND TALKS Approximately 6 tastings a year; to groups on request
CELLARAGE 25p per case per month   ■

While Spain certainly takes up a considerable proportion of the list from this one-man band, there is plenty also from Portugal, France and Australia.

In Spain, Riojas in profusion include Gran Reservas back to the 1960s (Marqués de Murrieta Gran Reserva 1960 is £18.11). From neighbouring Navarra, we find wines from Señorio de Sarria, Chivite and Monte Ory, and from Valdepeñas the Señorio de los Llanos and the dry white Armonioso. La Mancha offers Marqués de Griñon Cabernet Sauvignon. From Ribera del Duero are the wines of Peñalba, the Ribera co-operative and Pesquera as well as Vega Sicilia. Penedès has a good few Cavas as well as wines from Torres, Masía Bach and Jaume Serra. Sherries are from Valdespino and Gonzalez Byass.

In Portugal, there are wines from J M da Fonseca and Churchill Graham. Australia offers Wyndham's, Wynns, Wolf Blass and Taltarni, while France is particularly strong in Bordeaux with petit château wines and on the Loire with a good cross-section of wines from Touraine.

Best buys

Valdepeñas Gran Reserva 1978, Señorio de los Llanos, £3.77; Seaview South Australian Shiraz, £3.55; Toro 1985, Gran Colegiata, £3.66; João Pires Quinta de Santa Amaro 1985, £3.25

Sherston Wine Company

HEAD OFFICE 1 Church Street,   TEL (0666) 840644
Sherston, Malmesbury, Wiltshire SN16 0LA
4 Sidmouth Parade, Sidmouth Street,   TEL (0380) 5545
Devizes, Wiltshire SN10 1LG

OPEN (Sherston) Mon, Tue, Wed, Sat 10–6   Thur, Fri 10–7.30   Sun 12–2;
(Devizes) Mon–Fri 10–8   Sat 9–8   Sun 12–2   CLOSED Public holidays
CREDIT CARDS Access, Visa; personal and business accounts   DISCOUNTS 5%
on 1 case   DELIVERY Free locally (min usually 3 cases); elsewhere at cost; mail
order available   GLASS HIRE Available   TASTINGS AND TALKS Frequent
in-store tastings; annual autumn tasting; for customers and groups on request
CELLARAGE Not available

Following the break-up of the original grouping of franchised shops under this name, this merchant now has a shop in Malmesbury (the original one) and a new place in Devizes.

This firm has always been strong in Spain, but they've branched out further now, resulting in a well-balanced list with plenty of interest from many areas.

Spain first. Here we find a good range of Riojas, nicely balancing aged wines with young wines, and with a good selection of Gran Reservas at rather high prices. There is Navarra wine from Bardon and Señorio de Sarria, Penedès Cavas from Conde de Caralt and Freixenet as well as Torres wines, and the Señorio de los Llanos Gran Reserva 1978 from Valdepeñas (£4.19).

The French collection is much less interesting, although things improve with some (rather pricey) French country wines. Germany is a write-off, but Italian successes include wines from Guerrieri-Rizzardi in the Veneto and Tenuta di Capezzana and Castello di Volpaia in Tuscany. There is a good range of reds from Portugal, plus the Niepoort colheita (wood-aged Vintage) Ports. Australia has wines from Wyndhams's, Orlando and McWilliams, next door to a lone Montana wine from New Zealand.

Best buys

Rioja con crianza 1984, Martinez Lacuesta, £3.50; Champagne Hostomme 1982, £14.99; Serradayres 1982, Portugal, £3.35

André Simon

14 Davies Street, London W1Y 1LJ	TEL 01-499 9144
50/52 Elizabeth Street, London SW1W 9PB	TEL 01-730 8108
21 Motcomb Street, London SW1X 8LB	TEL 01-235 3723
66 Fulham Road, London SW3 6HH	TEL 01-589 1238

OPEN Mon–Sat 9.30–8.30   CLOSED Sun, public holidays
CREDIT CARDS Access, Visa; personal and business accounts   DISCOUNTS Not available   DELIVERY Free in central London; elsewhere at cost; mail order on application   GLASS HIRE Free   TASTINGS AND TALKS Weekly in-store tastings   CELLARAGE £3 per case per year

The range of wines at André Simon's four shops changes as often as the buying team of the associate company, Layton (*qv*), travels to France and Italy to seek out new parcels of wine. The published list can therefore only indicate the general strengths.

These include some fine names: Antinori in Tuscany, CVNE Riojas, Joseph Drouhin and Chartron et Trébuchet Burgundies, Champagne Deutz and Robertson's Rebello Valente Ports. The clarets likewise change regularly, and there are some decent basic house wines from Bordeaux and the Côtes du Marmandais. In a departure from Europe, Newton Vineyard wines in the Napa Valley present some Californian interest.

Best buys

Ch le Breuil 1983, Côtes de Bourg, £5.25; Contino Rioja Reserva 1982, £8.50; Côtes du Marmandais Rouge 1985, £3.25; Robertson's Pyramid 10-year-old tawny Port, £7.90

Smedley Vintners

Rectory Cottage, Lilley, Luton,   TEL (046 276) 214
Bedfordshire LU2 8LU

OPEN Mon–Sat 8–9 Sun, public holidays 10–9 CREDIT CARDS None accepted; personal and business accounts DISCOUNTS Available
DELIVERY Free within 50-mile radius of Lilley (min 1 case); otherwise £3.50 per case; 5+ cases free; mail order available GLASS HIRE Free
TASTINGS AND TALKS In-store tastings 4 days a year; to groups on request
CELLARAGE Not available   ■

Since last year, Smedley Vintners have concentrated on bringing in a much larger range of wines from the New World. California is now represented by the super Trefethen and Firestone wines, and Australia by Rosemount, as well as Anglesey Estate in South Australia and Plantagenet Winery in Western Australia (especially good reds).

But the well-balanced list kicks off among the country wines of France. We find some good whites (always more difficult than reds), including the Vin de Pays des Côtes de Gascogne of Pierre Grassa at £2.68 and Bergerac Blanc Domaine de Grandschamp of Henry Ryman at £3.86. Best bet in the reds is probably the Côtes du Marmandais 1986 of Domaine de Beroy (£3.22).

The Loire and Alsace get fairly brief treatment, but there's a sensible range of clarets (especially in 1982 and 1983), some at good prices. In Burgundy, Bouchard Père is the source of négociant wines, and there's some good top Chablis.

In Italy, wines from Antinori in Tuscany and Umbria and from Lungarotti in Umbria are the most interesting, matched in Spain by CVNE Riojas and Torres wines from Penedès.

Last but not least are Ports from Quinta do Noval and Madeiras from Rutherford & Miles.

Best buys

Gaillac Rouge 1985, Domaine de Cassagnols, £3.22; Vin de Pays des Côtes de Gascogne 1987, Pierre Grassa, £2.68; Trefethen Eshcol Red, £4.50; Rubesco di Torgiano 1983, Lungarotti, £4.60

Find the best new wine bargains all year round with our newsletter, *Which? Wine Monthly*, available for £15 a year from: Dept WG89, Consumers' Association, FREEPOST, Hertford SG14 1YB – no stamp is needed if posted within the UK.

Snipe Wine Cellars

87 High Street, Needham Market, Suffolk IP6 8DQ	TEL (0449) 721943
34 North Station Road, Colchester, Essex CO1 1RQ	TEL (0206) 578171
11 Littleport Street, King's Lynn, Norfolk PE30 1PP	TEL (0553) 766714
WAREHOUSE A93 Cowdray Centre, Cowdray Avenue, Colchester, Essex CO1 1BG	TEL (0206) 67670

OPEN Mon–Sat 10–9 (closed Mon am)   Sun 12–2   Some public holidays
CREDIT CARDS Access, Visa; personal and business accounts   DISCOUNTS 5%
on 6 bottles, 10% on 1 case   DELIVERY Free in most of East Anglia (min 2 cases);
mail order available   GLASS HIRE Free   TASTINGS AND TALKS Regular
in-store tastings; to groups on request   CELLARAGE Not available

This is a good value range of wines, concentrating principally in
France. A new warehouse at King's Lynn has expanded their audience
in the past year. More information about producers on their list would
help their customers.

In France, look for the good selection of regional wines, most of
them under £3, while in Bordeaux there are some good value petit
chateau wines. The Loire has a good sur lie Muscadet from Pommeraye
(1986 vintage at £3.89) there's Beaujolais from Sarrau, basic Burgundies
from Bersan et Fils, Alsace from the Ribeauvillé co-operative.

Further afield, there are McWilliams wines from Australia and
Montana and Stoneleigh from New Zealand. While the local vineyards
of Nevards and Silver Snipe offer some English-grown productions.

Best buys

Ch Castellot 1986, Bergerac Rouge, £3.72; Nathaniel Johnston Special
Reserve Claret NV, £3.43; Coteaux du Lyonnais red, Sarrau, £3.32;
McWilliams Inheritance Cabernet/Shiraz 1985, £3.88

Sookias and Bertaut

The Cottage, Cambalt Road, Putney Hill, London SW15 6EW	TEL 01-788 4193

OPEN Tue–Fri 10–6   Sat 10–1   CLOSED Mon, public holidays, 1 weekend of
Aug   CREDIT CARDS Access, Visa; personal and business accounts
DISCOUNTS 2½% for 1 unmixed case; £1 per case collected   DELIVERY Free
within central and south-west London (min 1 case); otherwise £5.50 per UK
consignment; mail order available   GLASS HIRE Free locally with 1-case order
TASTINGS AND TALKS Free monthly tastings; to groups on request
CELLARAGE Not available

Sookias and Bertaut – the firm's name comes from the two families
who not only run it but do everything – are specialist wine merchants

par excellence. Their love affair with the wines of the South-West of France blossomed into such a business that their list now contains some of the most fascinating and unusual tastes you will find anywhere in France.

Of course they have wines from some of the best firms in the more familiar south-west areas, such as Ch Court-les-Mûts in Bergerac, and Clos Triguedina in Cahors (the 1982 vintage is £5.75). But they've also discovered some of the smaller areas – Marcillac, with wines from the only producer of any size, Laurens-Teulier (Marcillac Rouge 1986 is £3.85); Entraygues et du Fel VDQS white from Jean-Marc Viguier; Gaillac wines from Jean Cros; Madiran from Ch d'Arricau Bordes (the 1983 vintage is £5.35 – also available in magnums). And if you want to know what the taste of Tursan is like, try the powerful Domaine de Pécharde-Pourruchot 1986 of Dulucq at £4.20.

Best buys

Côtes du Frontonnais, 1986, Ch Flotis, £3.50; Jurançon Sec 1987, Domaine Cauhape, £4.95; Pécharmant 1985, Ch de Tiregand, £5.30

Frank E Stainton

3 Berry's Yard, Finkle Street,   TEL (0539) 31886
Kendal, Cumbria LA9 4AB

OPEN Mon–Sat 8.30–6   CLOSED Sun, public holidays   CREDIT CARDS Access; personal and business accounts   DISCOUNTS 5% on 1 case (mixed)
DELIVERY Free in South Lakeland to North Lancashire (min 1 case); elsewhere at cost; mail order available   GLASS HIRE Free with 1-case order
TASTINGS AND TALKS Wines available in-store every Saturday; to groups on request   CELLARAGE Not available

This remains a sensibly balanced list, providing a sound cross-section of wines in an area which is still short of good wine merchants.

Clarets offer some good value at the lower end as well as a few top classed growths (so look for Ch Citran 1983 at £5.68 or Ch Canteloup 1985 at £3.93). Burgundy names include Prosper Maufoux and Joseph Drouhin, and Beaujolais is from Georges Duboeuf. In Alsace, we find the wines of Kuentz-Bas, while house Champagne is by Guy Beauregard (£9.10). (Prices on the wholesale list do not include VAT, but we have added it here.)

The German selection remains good, with wines from Guntrum and Deinhard. In Italy, we like the look of the Chianti Classico Brolio and the Venegazzù Black Label Cabernet Sauvignon, while Spain comes up with Torres wines and Riojas from CVNE. The Californian section has been revamped to bring in a good-value California Reserve red and white at £2.59, and in Australia, there are wines from Hill-Smith and Orlando. Sherries are a comprehensive range from Garvey.

Best buys

Hill-Smith Semillon 1985, £4.80; Bairrada Frei João 1980, £3.50; Louis
Guntrum Riesling 1986, £3.50; California Reserve red and white, £2.59

Stapylton Fletcher

3 Haslemere, Sutton Road, Maidstone,   TEL (0622) 691188
Kent ME15 9NE

OPEN Mon–Fri 8–6   Sat 8.30–5   CLOSED Sun (except in summer and
pre-Christmas), some public holidays   CREDIT CARDS Access, Diners, Visa;
personal and business accounts   DISCOUNTS £1.15 per case on 6+ cases
DELIVERY Available; mail order available   GLASS HIRE Free
TASTINGS AND TALKS Monthly programme of in-store tastings; two tastings in
November; to groups on request   CELLARAGE £2.30 per case per year   ■

Stapylton Fletcher's new warehouse has more room than before, and
even if it lacks the character of the former premises in an oast house,
more important character remains in the wines. Cash and carry prices
are still keen.

France continues as the main interest, and it is encouraging to see
more regional wines displayed. We would certainly recommend the
wines from the Haut-Poitou co-operative (Sauvignon Blanc at £2.98),
and the interesting variety from the South-West (especially Gaillac and
the rare Côtes de Thongue, Vin de Pays red, Domaine de l'Arjolle at
£2.65).

Other more classic areas do pretty well, too. Here good prices really
show: Ch Troplong Mondot 1985, St-Emilion at £8.10 or the Fronsac
wines of Ch Mayne-Vieil 1982 at £5.05 are two good-value clarets.
Good examples of 1987 Beaujolais are from Delaunay and Les
Producteurs Eventail, and Delaunay reappears in the Burgundy
section (look for a terrific value Mâcon Rouge at £2.95). On the Loire,
Félicien Brou in Quincy and Vouvray go well with the Ménétou Salon
of Jean-Max Roger (1986 Le Petit Clos at £4.86), while there are reds
from Couly-Dutheil.

Outside France, look to Italy for the Chiantis of Rampolla and some
good Antinori whites. Equivalent value in Portugal is to be found in
the Tuella Douro table wines. An interesting New World case could be
made up of wines from Tyrrells and Rouge Homme in Australia, from
Nobilo, Stoneleigh Vineyard and Matua Valley in New Zealand, and a
bottle or two from Washington State in the USA.

Best buys

Syrah Vin de Pays de l'Ardèche 1986, £2.35; Tuella Tinto 1985,
Portugal, £2.42; Ch Lavergne 1985, Côtes de Castillon, £3.62;
Ch Larroze Rouge de Garde, Gaillac, Jean Cros, £3.92; Sherries
from Gil Luque

Stones of Belgravia

6 Pont Street, London SW1R 9EL   TEL 01-235 1612/4133
OPEN Mon–Fri 9.30–8.30   Sat 10–8   CLOSED Sun, public holidays
CREDIT CARDS Access, Amex, Visa; personal and business accounts
DISCOUNTS Available   DELIVERY Free in central London with suitable order;
elsewhere at cost; mail order available   GLASS HIRE Free with order
TASTINGS AND TALKS Occasional in-store tastings   CELLARAGE Not available

This is a deeply conventional range of wines and, inevitably, given the
address, the prices are high. But it's still worth visiting this shop –
recently completely refitted – for its clarets and Vintage Ports.

The claret listing is exhaustive, with wines on a recent list back to
1905, and a considerable number of vintages after 1978. Most of the
wines are classed growths or their equivalent. While Burgundy still
languishes in the arms of négociants, good Champagne is to be had
here (including large bottles and a few halves). On the Rhône, look for
wines from Guigal, Chave and Chapoutier in Hermitage and Côte
Rôtie (there's nothing in Côtes du Rhône). Alsace has wines from Léon
Beyer, Trimbach and Dopff au Moulin.

Italy is neglected, but Spain has a small but well thought out set of
Riojas. Australia and California look like burgeoning. And then we're
into Vintage Ports which span 40 years or so, from 1945 to 1982.

Best buys

Bergerac Sauvignon, Ch la Jaubertie, £4.25; Stones Champagne NV,
£8.95; Stones Bordeaux Rouge, £3.35; Crozes-Hermitage 1983,
Domaine de Clairmonts, £6.50

Studio 50

See Ostlers.

Summerlee Wines

Summerlee Wine Centre, 64 High Street,   TEL (0604) 810488
Earls Barton, Northamptonshire NN6 0JG

OPEN Mon–Fri 9–6   CLOSED Sat, Sun, public holidays   CREDIT CARDS None
accepted; personal and business accounts   DISCOUNTS Available; quantity
discounts   DELIVERY Free locally, London, Oxford and Cambridge (min 2+
cases); otherwise £5 per consignment   GLASS HIRE Free with wine bought from
premises   TASTINGS AND TALKS Occasional in-store tastings; tastings through
Summerlee Wine Society; to groups on request   CELLARAGE Available

A new entry to the Guide brings together some fine estate wines from
Beaujolais, Burgundy and Germany as well as Italy.

In Beaujolais, the négociant wines of Joannes Desmoulin are
complemented by the cru domaine-bottled wines of Domaine
Delachanal in Côte de Brouilly and Ch Chénas (confusingly) in Fleurie.

In Burgundy proper there are wines from Patrick Javillier in Meursault (who also supplies the Chablis), plus a good value Pinot Noir Bourgogne Rouge 1986 from Sorin-Defrance (£4.15).

Germany's star attraction are the Mosel estate wines of Max Ferd Richter, while on the nearby Saar, there is similar quality from Dieter Ebert of Schloss Saarstein. Italian wines from Roberto Anselmi in the Veneto and Chianti Classico Valiano are likewise from fine producers.

In addition, Summerlee Wines have got together a sound range of clarets, including examples from more recent vintages; also Loire wines from Louis Aubac and Domaine du Bois Semé in Muscadet and Balland in Sancerre; Côtes du Rhône from Domaine de la Chartreuse and Penedès wines from Josep Ferret (Viña Laranda Tempranillo 1986, £2.99).

Best buys

Beaujolais Villages 1986, Domaine de la Croix Jacques, £3.99; Côtes du Rhône 1987, Domaine de la Chartreuse, £3.35; German estate wines from Max Ferd Richter

Supergrape

81 Replingham Road, Southfields,   TEL 01-874 5963
London SW18 5LU

OPEN Mon–Fri 10–2, 5–9.30   Sat 10–9.30   Sun, public holidays 12–2, 7–9
CREDIT CARDS Access, Visa   DISCOUNTS Negotiable; minimum of 5%
discount for Club members   DELIVERY Free locally (min 1 case); otherwise at
cost   GLASS HIRE Free with appropriate order
TASTINGS AND TALKS Frequent in-store tastings; to groups on request
CELLARAGE Not available

A move to new premises has meant an expansion of Supergrape's list. They still have good clarets (with enough petit château wines to balance the classier stuff), Burgundy from more producers than before (plus Duboeuf Beaujolais), Alsace wines from Gisselbrecht – and plenty of Champagne.

What's new is a greatly expanded Australian list, with some good examples from smaller wineries, and a very fine range from New Zealand (Morton Estate, Delegats, Cloudy Bay, Matua Valley, Selaks). There are good things from Spain (Torres wines and Raimat), Italian wines which include Carmignano from Villa di Capezzana and a small selection of fine Vintage Ports.

Best buys

Australian Semillon and Shiraz, £2.95; Raimat Chardonnay, £4.50; Australian Liqueur Muscats from Rutherglen; Ch la Gardéra 1983, Bordeaux, £5.50

Tanners Wines   ❀ 🖃 ☞

26 Wyle Cop, Shrewsbury,	TEL (0743) 232400
Shropshire SY1 1XD	
72 Mardol, Shrewsbury,	TEL (0743) 66389
Shropshire SY1 1PZ	
39 Mytton Oak Road, Shrewsbury,	TEL (0743) 66387
Shropshire SY3 8UG	
36 High Street, Bridgnorth,	TEL (07462) 3148
Shropshire WV6 4DB	
4 St Peter's Square, Hereford,	TEL (0432) 272044
Hereford & Worcester HR1 2PG	
The Old Brewery, Brook Street, Welshpool,	TEL (0938) 2542
Powys	

OPEN (Wyle Cop) Mon–Sat 9–6; (Mardol) Mon–Sat 9–5.30; (Mytton Oak Road) Mon–Wed 9–6   Thur, Fri 9–7   Sat 9–5.30; (Bridgnorth and Hereford) Mon–Sat 9–5.30; (Welshpool) Mon–Fri 9–5.30   Sat 9–12 noon   CLOSED Sun, public holidays   CREDIT CARDS Access, Visa; personal and business accounts DISCOUNTS Available   DELIVERY Free on UK mainland (min £50 order); mail order available   GLASS HIRE Free if wine purchased from shop TASTINGS AND TALKS Series of wine tastings and wine tasting evenings; to groups on request   CELLARAGE Not available

Expansion is in the air at Tanners as they open a wine market at their Bridgnorth branch and quadruple the size of the Hereford shop. This means that customers wanting to take advantage of their discounted wine market prices (anything up to 10 per cent off the list price) will now have much more opportunity to do so.

Whether they will be able to make up their minds is another matter, because Tanners' list is strong in so many areas – claret, Burgundy, the Rhône, fortified wines, Italy, Australia. And in virtually every other area of the wine world, they have good, sensible, high quality representation.

If we start with France, we find a very attractive section of French regional wines, from Minervois and Languedoc, from Ch de Fonscolombe in Coteaux d'Aix-en-Provence, from Jurançon, Gaillac and Madiran in the South-West, plus many vins de pays throughout the Midi. Both claret and Burgundy are major sections with plenty of choice in price and vintage. The Loire is strongest on sweet wines and mature Vouvray, but the Rhône range is generous with Jaboulet Aîné and Guigal in the north and a number of top names in the south. Champagne has large bottles and half-bottles in good numbers – we know which we would prefer.

The list also has much of interest in Italy: Barolo from Ratti, Tiefenbrunner in the Alto Adige, Santi in the Veneto, Frescobaldi in Tuscany. Spain's offerings, though fewer, include wines from Peñalba Lopez in Ribera del Duero and Riojas from Lopez Heredia, plus wines from Torres. Fortified wines from both Spain and Portugal (especially Sherries) are a major strength.

In the New World, we find Australian wines from Hill-Smith and Brown Brothers as well as wines from smaller top quality wineries, while in New Zealand, Cook's are the source of some good value wines.

Best buys

Tanners Australian white and red, £3.75; Tanners Mariscal Sherries; Vin de Pays des Collines de la Moure, Abbaye de Valmagne 1985, £3.50; Madiran 1983, Domaine Pichard, £5.42; Saarburger Antoniusbrunnen Riesling Kabinett 1985, R Müller, £4.43

Tempest, Slinger & Co

See Chesterford Vintners.

Tesco

HEAD OFFICE New Tesco House, P O Box 18, Delamare Road, Cheshunt, Hertfordshire EN8 9SL   TEL (0992) 32222

For wine enquiries write to: HEAD OFFICE   TEL as above
Bentley House, Pegs Lane, Hertford,
Hertfordshire SG13 8EG
Approx 350 licensed branches

OPEN Varies from branch to branch   CREDIT CARDS Access, Visa
DISCOUNTS, DELIVERY, GLASS HIRE Not available
TASTINGS AND TALKS Occasional in-store tastings   CELLARAGE Not available

As more and more Tesco stores are of the mega rather than the mini size, so the availability of the full – or most of – the wine range increases. This is good, because the components of this continually expanding range are generally good, even if sometimes less than exciting. During the year, the display of the wines has improved, with more shelf cards and the use of style indicators (eg sweet or dry white, full or light red).

As with many supermarkets, Tesco run a two-tier system: a standard range of wines – many of them own-label and available, to a greater or lesser degree, in all the licensed branches; and a collection of fine wines, available only in the largest stores.

While France is definitely the strongest source, there are nuggets from other parts of the world. The Italian and Spanish sections have expanded to good effect – Italy has good own-label Barbaresco, Lago di Caldaro and Valdadige Bianco as well as a few pricier wines, while Spain offers a good own-label Reserva Rioja as well as Torres wines. Germany goes in for some good estate wines, but beyond Europe, there is still little to excite.

In France, go for the vins de pays (especially from the Côtes de

Gascogne), the Domaine des Baumelles from Ch Val-Joanis in the Côtes du Lubéron (£2.69), wines from the Loire and – pricier and in the fine wine section only – some fine clarets and Burgundies. Tesco also have one of the best low-alcohol wines around – Escoubes Light at £2.29.

Best buys

Muscadet sur lie 1987, Domaine de la Huperie, £3.25; Les Terres Fines Syrah 1986, Vin de Pays de l'Hérault, £2.69; Tesco Crémant de Bourgogne, £5.49; Tesco Bianco di Custoza, £2.49; Rioja Reserva 1980, £3.59

Thresher

HEAD OFFICE Sefton House, 42 Church Road,   TEL (0707) 328244
Welwyn Garden City, Hertfordshire AL8 6PJ
964 branches nationwide

ASSOCIATED OUTLET
Esprit du Vin, 51A Upper Berkeley Street,   TEL 01-723 1713
London W1H 7PN

OPEN Hours vary from branch to branch but generally Mon–Sat 10–10 Sun 12–2, 7–9 CLOSED Chr Day CREDIT CARDS Access, Visa; personal and business accounts DISCOUNTS Available DELIVERY Free in selected areas GLASS HIRE Free with party orders TASTINGS AND TALKS Occasional in-store tastings; to groups on request CELLARAGE Not available

Threshers purchased Gough Brothers during 1988 and now run a 900-strong empire of branches nationwide. Branches, they say, vary in what they stock according to local needs. They have also opened an experimental up-market shop called Esprit du Vin in London's West End.

There has been a definite improvement in the range and quality of wines offered through this chain of High Street off-licences. They seem to have made determined efforts to smarten up what was sometimes a rather dowdy wardrobe of wines. If they have not been entirely successful yet it's because – as in the consumer checks which we have run at *Which? Wine Monthly* – they don't seem to have shaken off all problems of stocking old, tired and badly stored wines. Not all the time, mind you, but we would suggest you go to branches with a high turnover, rather than the shop just round the corner which probably sells more beers and cigarettes than wines anyway.

To the wines themselves. While some areas remain dull – Germany, for example, is still in the era of Liebfraumilch and Piesporter, and neither the Loire nor the Rhône in France contain much of excitement yet – others have come on apace. Italy is rather good now, especially with the wines from Antinori in Tuscany. Spain has a few well-chosen wines, Australia and New Zealand are both here, and there are two terrific value wines from Chile (from the unpronounceable bodega of Errazuriz Panquehue, a red and white at £2.99).

In France, there's interest in the regions – a good Coteaux d'Aix-en-Provence white at £3.29, wines from Listel, an enjoyable own-label Côtes du Rhône at £2.59. In Bordeaux, Thresher's own-label claret is generally very acceptable (£2.75), plus some petit château wines as well as more classy names. Ports are from the top Portuguese-owned house of Ferreira, while house Champagne Descombes is £8.99.

Best buys

Thresher Côtes du Rhône Rouge NV, £2.59; Coteaux d'Aix-en Provence Blanc 1986, Domaine du Paradis, £3.29; Ch Monichot 1983, Côtes du Bourg, £3.95; Ferreira 10-year-old tawny Port, Quinta do Porto, £8.99; Vin de Pays des Coteaux de l'Ardèche red and white, Vignerons Ardéchois, £1.99

Philip Tite Fine Wines

73 Whitehall Park Road, London W4 3NB   TEL 01-995 0989

OPEN Mon–Fri 7.30–5   CLOSED Sat, Sun, public holidays   CREDIT CARDS All accepted   DISCOUNTS Not available   DELIVERY Free in London and Home Counties (min 1 case); otherwise £5 per case; 5+ cases free; mail order available GLASS HIRE Free with 5-case order   TASTINGS AND TALKS Not available CELLARAGE £4.60 per case per year

The wines are certainly fine at Philip Tite – a plethora of clarets, plus a good sprinkling of the finest and rarest from the rest of the wine world.

Clarets make serious reading. As we write, the current list starts at 1926 and goes onwards and upwards. Once we come to the 1970s, things expand right up to the mid-1980s and on to 1986. There are some top dry white Bordeaux and some mature Sauternes and Barsac wines.

Burgundy is not so exciting, despite some mature reds, but Philip Tite nurtures a particular interest in Chablis. Champagne is from some grande marque houses and from Renaudin (Brut Reserve NV at £10.23 – prices on the list do not include VAT, but we have added it here). There is a very fine range of Rhône wines, including plenty of the superb 1978s.

Elsewhere, Italy plays a star role, with some fine old Barolos from Borgogno and La Quercia and Chianti Classico Badia a Coltibuono from as far back as 1974. Vega Sicilia from Spain, old Madeiras from Henriques & Henriques and a large bunch of California wines from the 1974 vintage complete a very satisfying list.

Best buys

Mature clarets; mature Rhône wines

Patrick Toone

See Bin Ends.

Touchstone Wines

ORDER OFFICE 14 Vine Street,   TEL (0562) 746978
Kidderminster, Hereford & Worcester DY10 2TS

OPEN Mon–Fri 9.30–6.30   CLOSED Sat, Sun, public holidays
CREDIT CARDS None accepted; personal and business accounts
DISCOUNTS Available   DELIVERY Free within 50-mile radius of Birmingham
(min 1 case); otherwise 5+ case free, 1–4 cases at cost; mail order available
GLASS HIRE Free with 1+ case order within 50-mile radius
TASTINGS AND TALKS Monthly tastings at Brockencote Hall, nr Kidderminster
and Stafford; to groups on request   CELLARAGE Not available   ■

If you want to find out more about Rumanian wines, this is where to
come. Likewise, look no further if Montenegro in Yugoslavia is your
passion.

Touchstone import a fine range of Rumanian wines, many with
names that are completely unfamiliar in the UK. The Muscats and
other sweet wines (look for Pietroasele-Tamiioasa Romaneasca 1979 at
£2.75 for a half-bottle as a classic style) are probably the most
interesting from this country. From Yugoslavia, a couple of beety reds
from Montenegro attract attention.

But you would be wrong to assume that Touchstone is concerned
only with Eastern Europe. Highspots in the lesser Spanish areas
include the Gran Colegiata Toro wines from the Duero Valley west of
Valladolid (Gran Colegiata 1982 is a bargain £4.35); or the even newer
Denominacion de Origen of Somontano in the foothills of the Pyrenees.
Just across the border in Portugal, look for the wines from Quinta do
Cotto in the Douro Valley, or wines from João Pires (Catarina 1985,
which includes some Chardonnay in its blend, is £3.99).

Things seem rather more ordinary in France, lifted here and there by
stars such as the sweet Loire wines of Jean Baumard or the Cahors of
Domaine Eugénie (a good range with reserve vintages), Fitou from
Cave Pilote or Faugères from Domaine de Coudougno (1985 Faugères
Collection in litres at £2.99). Look, too, for the varietal wines of
Domaine de Ravanes, high quality wines under a lowly appellation of
Vin de Pays des Coteaux de Murviel.

Best buys

Rumanian wines; Toro Gran Colegiata 1982, £4.35; Cousiño Macul
Antiguas Reservas 1980, Chile, £3.99; Faugères Collection, £2.99 (litre);
Somontano Macabeo, £2.99

Prices are correct to the best of our knowledge in summer 1988.

J Townend & Sons

HEAD OFFICE Red Duster House,   TEL (0482) 26891
101 York Street, Hull, Humberside HU2 0QX
The Wine Cellars, Oxford Street, Hull,   TEL as above
Humberside HU2 0QX
16 branches (House of Townend, Townend Wine Centre, Willerby
Wine Market, Hornsea Wine Market) in Humberside and Yorkshire

OPEN Mon–Fri 9–5.30 Sat (Dec only) 9.30 am–12.30 pm CLOSED Sun, public
holidays CREDIT CARDS Access, Visa; personal and business accounts
DISCOUNTS Negotiable DELIVERY Free within 50-mile radius of Hull (min 1
mixed case); elsewhere at cost; mail order available GLASS HIRE Available
TASTINGS AND TALKS Regular tastings in retail outlets; large annual tasting in
October; monthly tastings at Willerby Wine Market; to groups on request
CELLARAGE £2.99 per case per year

J Townend & Sons are at the hub of this rather confusing
conglomeration; the Wine Cellars in Hull and many of the 16 branches
of House of Townend, Townend Wine Centre, Willerby Wine Market
and Hornsea Wine Market carry their full range, while others operate
from a pared down version.

It's a traditional list, strong in most French areas, less so in Italy and
Germany, and almost non-existent in Spain and Portugal. Clarets
major in recent vintages (particularly 1983 and 1982) and the selection
spans the price bridge (on one side Ch de Brondeau, a Bordeaux
Supérieur, is £2.61 for 1982 and £3.75 for 1983; on the other Ch Pétrus
1982 is £230).

In Burgundy, wines come from négociants like Chanson, Faiveley
and Geisweiler, and also from domaines (Machard de Gramont and
Buisson). Beaujolais is a star area, with a good number (including
single vineyard wines) from Georges Duboeuf and the Duboeuf
sous-marque of Paul Bocuse. Champagnes, too, do well (the House
Champagne, Baron de Beaupré is £8.85), and J Townend & Sons
have assembled an attractive range of French regional wines
(Ch Fonscolombe Coteaux d'Aix-en-Provence is £2.93). Alsace
wines are from Paul Blanck.

The German portfolio includes a number of estate wines (Erben,
von Simmern, Schloss Vollrads, Bürklin-Wolf), and in Italy, wines
from Frescobaldi in Tuscany and Tiefenbrunner in the Südtirol would
make for enjoyable drinking. Australia homes in on Brown Brothers'
wines, New Zealand on Cook's, and California on Mondavi. If Sherries
(from Wisdom and Warter) are not your scene, the choice of vintage
Ports goes back to 1970.

Best buys

Champagne Baron de Beaupré, £8.85; Tyrrell's Long Flat White and
Red, £3.41; Chardonnay Grave del Friuli 1987, Tenuta Santa Anna,
£3.63; Paul Bocuse and Georges Duboeuf Beaujolais

Henry Townsend

OFFICE York House, Oxford Road, TEL (049 46) 78291
Beaconsfield, Buckinghamshire HP9 1UJ

OPEN Mon–Fri 9–5.30 1st Sat in month 9–12.30 (other Saturdays by
arrangement) CLOSED Sun, public holidays CREDIT CARDS None accepted;
personal and business accounts DISCOUNTS 5% on 1 unmixed case
DELIVERY Free to South Buckinghamshire, Ascot and Windsor area,
Berkhamsted area, Chinnor and Bicester area, central London, City of London,
Hampstead, Highgate, London NW, W and SW (min 1 case); elsewhere 1–3
cases £5, 4+ cases free; mail order available GLASS HIRE Free with 1-case
order TASTINGS AND TALKS Series of tastings on Saturday mornings in
Coleshill and London; Summer and Autumn tastings held over 4 days; to wine
societies on request CELLARAGE £3.75 for 1st year and £3.25 for subsequent
years ■

There are some very fine things on this list. While it is certainly strong
in the classic French areas, the German section, the Australian range
and, increasingly, other European countries such as Italy are becoming
important. Also good reading are the ideas for wines to lay down, and
interesting offers such as the one in 1988 for Champagne and smoked
salmon.

Bordeaux is the first high spot. The vintages roll back to 1966, with
classed growths appearing only when Henry Townsend consider that
the wines are ready to drink. There are also good things in the realms
of sweet white Bordeaux. Over in Burgundy, the domaine wines are
heavily to the fore, with even more interest in white than red. The
Rhône lists wines from Guigal and Jaboulet Aîné as well as the great
white Hermitage of Chapoutier.

The one weak spot in France is the Loire, but Beaujolais from Les
Eventails, Alsace from Rolly Gassmann and Champagnes from Bruno
Paillard are all great names from their areas. Then we go to Germany:
this is one of the top lists of German estate wines in the Guide. It's
particularly strong on the Mosel-Saar-Ruwer, but fine names abound
throughout.

Spain has Riojas from La Rioja Alta, Penedès wines from Torres, and
Peñalba wines from Ribera del Duero. Italy has suddenly blossomed:
look for wines from Antinori, Lungarotti, Zenato and Contratto's
Barolo 1983 (£6). Chile's contribution is made up of wines from Concha
y Toro and Cousiño Macul.

In Australia, Henry Townsend have eschewed the familiar big
names and gone for some boutique wineries – Jim Barry and Tim
Adams in Clare Valley, Middlebrook and Pirramimma in McLaren
Vales, Bleasdale in Langhorne Creek.

On the fortified wine side, pleasurable purchases would be Sherries
from Hidalgo, good vintage Ports back to 1960 and Cossart Gordon
Madeiras.

Best buys

German estate wines; Chianti Putto 1986, Fattoria dell'Ugo, £3.70; Churchill's Finest Vintage Character Port, £6.30; Langhorne Creek Malbec 1984, Bleasdale, £5

Madeleine Trehearne Partners

20 New End Square, London NW3 1LN   TEL 01-435 6310

OPEN '24 hours, 7 days a week' CREDIT CARDS None accepted; personal and business accounts DISCOUNTS Available DELIVERY Free in NW3, NW6 and most of London (min 1 case); elsewhere by arrangement; mail order available GLASS HIRE Free with case order TASTINGS AND TALKS 4 tastings a year for mailing list; to groups on request CELLARAGE Minimal charge ∎

This is a new name for an old favourite. Ian and Madeleine Trehearne have renamed their business because, as they say, it is Madeleine who does all the work.

The Loire stays as the focal point in this short but well-chosen list. Berger Frères in Montlouis provide dry, sweet and sparkling wines, balanced by the lusciously elegant Quarts de Chaume 1982 of Ch de Belle Rive (£6.40). Of red interest is the Chinon 1986 of Raymond Desbourdes at £5.55.

There are smaller selections from Burgundy, Alsace (a delicious Gewürztraminer Vendange Tardive 1983 from Leiber at £13.50), Bordeaux and the Rhône. And honey, too.

Best buys

Ménétou Salon Blanc 1987, Bernard Clément, £5.45; Bourgogne Grand Ordinaire 1986, G Verret, £3.80

T & W Wines

51 King Street, Thetford,   TEL (0842) 765646
Norfolk IP24 2AU

OPEN Mon–Fri 9.30–5.30 Sat 9.30–5 Sun, public holidays on request CREDIT CARDS Access, Amex, Diners, Visa; personal and business accounts DISCOUNTS Not available DELIVERY Free within 15-mile radius of Thetford (min 1 case) and elsewhere (min 4 cases); otherwise 1–3 cases £9.77, 3–4 cases £6.63; mail order available GLASS HIRE Free with order TASTINGS AND TALKS In-store tastings; tastings organised in hotels and restaurants CELLARAGE £3.40 per case per year

From their attractively displayed shop in Thetford, T & W Wines continue to offer a staggering range – they claim 3,200 wines (we haven't actually counted) – which maintains a high quality throughout. That's equally true for everyday drinking (Ch Val Joanis 1986, Côtes du Lubéron at £4.43; or Glen Oaks Classic White from California at £4.37) or at the level of fine clarets, Burgundies and Vintage Ports.

One source of pride is the panoply of mature clarets, with vintages back (on a recent list) to 1950, and a mouthwatering range of mature Sauternes. In Burgundy, we find Domaine de la Romanée-Conti in profusion along with other famous names. There is a roll-call of grande marque Champagnes (including probably more old vintages of the Krug Collection than they have in Reims itself). There's Alsace from Hugel, Trimbach and Léon Beyer, German Beerenauslese and Trockenbeerenauslese from 1976 and before, and Vintage Ports back to the famous 1927.

Outside Europe, they have put together an exclusive range of California boutique wineries – Flora Springs, Silver Oak Cellars, Costello Vineyards, Dunn Vineyards, Duckhorn, St Clement.

One further encouragement is the array of half-bottles and – in Bordeaux – of large bottles.

Best buys

Sauternes 1982, Ch Briatte, £8.34; Souza wood-aged Colheita Port 1966, £5.17; Bourgogne Chardonnay 1986, Roux Père et Fils, £6.84; Silver Oak California Cabernet Sauvignon 1982, £14.66; Champagne Krug 1959, £97.75

Ubiquitous Chip Wine Shop

12 Ashton Lane, Glasgow G12 8SJ   TEL 041-334 7109

OPEN Mon–Fri 12–10   Sat 10–10   CLOSED Sun, 25 Dec, 1 Jan
CREDIT CARDS Amex, Diners, Visa; personal and business accounts
DISCOUNTS 5% on 1 case   DELIVERY Free within 10-mile radius of Glasgow (min 3 cases); elsewhere negotiable; mail order available   GLASS HIRE Free with 1-case order   TASTINGS AND TALKS Tutored wine dinners; occasional Sunday tastings in-store; private tastings by arrangement   CELLARAGE Not available

Still a benchmark restaurant for our colleagues on *The Good Food Guide*, the Chip's wine shop next door has altered its sights quite considerably over the past year.

Gone is the heavy reliance on France, and in its place comes a wide-ranging selection that looks carefully at most wine areas of the world and comes up with some goodies. (For aficionados, we must also mention the huge range of malt whiskies.)

While there is still a selection of clarets and Burgundies, interest in France now focuses just as much on the Rhône (with some good value Côtes du Rhône as well as more serious things from Jaboulet Aîné), the Loire (top Pouilly Fumé from de Ladoucette), the Rolly Gassmann Alsace wines and some good French country wines.

Italy likewise has more of interest: Venegazzù of Conte Loredan Gasparini, Brunello from Col d'Orcia and Chianti from Santa Caterina among others. From Portugal come the achievements of João Pires and J M da Fonseca, and Spain has good Gran Reserva Riojas. German Kabinett estate wines from the 1983 and 1985 vintages are from some

top names. In the New World, look for California wines from
Firestone, Mondavi and Clos du Val; in New Zealand, Stoneleigh
Vineyard and Cook's; and in Australia, Brown Brothers and
McWilliams.

Best buys

João Pires Palmela, £3.25; Rosso Cònero 1983, Vigneto San Lorenzo,
£3.75; California Chardonnay 1983, Concannon Vineyard, Livermore,
£3.35; Ribera del Duero 1984, Pesquera, £8.40

Unwins Wine Merchants

HEAD OFFICE Birchwood House,   TEL (0322) 72711
Victoria Road, Dartford, Kent DA1 5AJ
Approx 300 branches in South-East England

OPEN Mon–Fri 10–2, 4–10   Sat 10–10 Sun, public holidays 12–2, 7–9.30
CREDIT CARDS All accepted; personal and business accounts   DISCOUNTS 5%
on mixed case of sparkling wine, 10% on mixed case of table wine
DELIVERY Free in South-East England (min case lots); mail order available
GLASS HIRE Free   TASTINGS AND TALKS Occasional tastings in selected stores;
occasionally to groups on request   CELLARAGE Not available

This is a range of wines which seems to find it difficult to satisfy
everyday drinking requirements, but has a very good selection of such
classics as fine claret, Port and, especially, Champagne. Is the normal
Unwins customer after such wines?

Anyway, Unwins have looked further afield than last year: in the
middle of a dull listing of mediocre branded wines, we find occasional
treats. In Italy, for example, there are Ruffino Chiantis and wines from
Frescobaldi lurking amongst litre bottles of Valpolicella. In Spain, amid
12 different styles of branded plonk, there is Rioja from Faustino and
Domecq Domain.

Other areas worth looking at are Australia (with the normally good
value Renmano Chairman's Selection wines – although Unwins
continue to have higher prices than many merchants), Beaujolais from
Loron, Muscadet from Domaine du Cléray (although not the 1985
vintage listed in mid-1988) and some German estate wines from 1976.
Ports are good, Sherries less so.

Best buys

Rioja 1981, Domecq Domain, £4.25; Chilean Cabernet Sauvignon 1984,
Concha y Toro, £3.49; Californian Chardonnay 1983, Robert Mondavi,
£3.79; Lamberhurst Müller-Thurgau Dry 1984, England, £3.99

The Upper Crust

3–4 Bishopsmead Parade, East Horsley, Surrey KT24 6RT	TEL (04865) 3280

OPEN Mon–Sat 9–9   Sun 12–2, 7–9   Public holidays 10–1, 6–8   CLOSED Chr Day   CREDIT CARDS Access, Visa; certain personal and business accounts
DISCOUNTS 5% for 1 case of wine, 2½% for 1 case of Champagne
DELIVERY Free within local weekly 20-mile radius run (min 1 case); elsewhere at cost; mail order available   GLASS HIRE Free with order
TASTINGS AND TALKS Approx twelve tastings held annually; informal tastings held on Sats; tastings held for customers   CELLARAGE £3.50 per case per year

The Upper Crust moves fast. Barry and Debbie Ralph's shop arrived in the Guide for the first time last year, and already their list has increased by leaps and bounds. They won the title of Young Wine Merchant of the Year in a competition sponsored by Pol Roger Champagne and *Decanter* wine magazine – so it looks as though they are getting it just right.

They've certainly moved into fashionable areas, with a carefully organised listing of Australian wines. Although big wineries like Seppelts and Hill-Smith are in evidence, particularly interesting are the smaller and medium-sized boys – like Montrose in Mudgee, Peter Lehmann in the Barossa Valley, Geoff Merrill in McLaren Vale, South Australia and Taltarni in Victoria (Moonambel Red 1984 at £4.65 is very good value); Upper Crust also carry the full range of wines from Rosemount in the Upper Hunter Valley.

Similar care is shown with New Zealand wines – look for the Stoneleigh Vineyard range and the wines of Nobilo (the Nobilo Pinot Noir 1984 at £5.75 is not quite world class yet, in our opinion, but getting pretty close). Other countries or regions to fare well include Chile and Oregon, and the Lebanon, with an enormous range of Ch Musar going back to the superb 1964 vintage.

In Europe, particular strengths are in Spain, especially Rioja (Campo Viejo 1984 at £3.45 up to the oak-aged white Marqués de Murrieta 1976 at £12.25), while Portugal has wines from João Pires as well as the huge red Redondo from the Alentejo (1982 vintage at £3.45). There is plenty of interest in Germany (and the promise of more to come) but a curious blank spot in Italy.

Last comes France: Alsace wines from Schlumberger; claret back to 1961 with strong points in 1983, 1982 and 1981; plenty of domaine-bottled wines from Burgundy (St-Véran 1986, Pax at £5.35; Monthélie Premier Cru 1983, Michel Pont at £10), Beaujolais from Loron; and treats from the South-West, including the Jurançon wines of Clos Guirouilh. While the Rhône is perhaps less interesting at the moment, the Loire is expanding. A huge range of Champagne rounds this startling list off.

Best buys

Moonambel red and white, Taltarni, Victoria, £4.65; Cousiño Macul
Cabernet Sauvignon 1980, £4.50; Rioja Campo Viejo 1984, £3.45;
Sauvignon de Touraine 1987, Thierry et Dorothée Michaud, £3.85;
Côtes du Roussillon 1981, Ch St-Martin, £3.95; Chinon 1983, Domaine
du Morilly, £4.19

Valvona & Crolla

19 Elm Row, Edinburgh EH7 4AA   TEL 031-556 6066
OPEN Mon–Sat 8.30–6   CLOSED Sun, 1–7 January   CREDIT CARDS Access,
Visa; business accounts   DISCOUNTS 5% on 1 case   DELIVERY Free on UK
mainland (min £50 order); elsewhere at cost; mail order available
GLASS HIRE Free with £50 case order   TASTINGS AND TALKS Italian wine
tastings 3 times a year   CELLARAGE Not available until end 1989

The Italian Wine Centre, they call themselves, and it's certainly Italy,
Italy all the way at this delicatessen and wine merchants. As they have
expanded their list, so they have also broadened their wine-related
activities and hope to have in-store tasting facilities ready by the end of
1989.

The list reads a little like a *Who's who*. Divided into regions, it starts in
the far north with the Südtirol/Alto Adige, including wines from
Kettmeir, Tiefenbrunner and Pojer e Sandri. Friuli offers the top-flight
Jermann wines, Lombardy Inferno and Sassella from Nino Negri and
Oltrepò Pavese wines from the Fugazza sisters.

There are Piedmontese wines in depth – with a big range of Gaja
Barbarescos (at big prices), followed by a dazzling array of Barolos from
other producers. The Veneto provides wines from Bolla, Santi,
Allegrini and Montresor, while moving on south there are Chiantis
from Coltibuono, Brolio, Ruffino and Frescobaldi.

In other regions, we find wines from Mastroberardino, from Sella e
Mosca in Sardinia and from Regaleali and Donnafugata in Sicily.
There's a fine collection of dessert wines as well.

Best buys

Vin Santo 1980, Lungarotti, £4.99; Bonardo Oltrepò Pavese 1985,
Fugazza, £3.59; Trebbiano d'Abruzzo 1986, Illuminati, £3.32; Chianti
Classico 1981, Vigneto la Selvanella, Mellini, £4.69; Rosso Cònero 1982,
Mario Marchetti, £3.79

Special awards

🐷 is for bargain prices   ▱ is for a very good range of wines

❀ is for high quality wines   ▱ is for exceptional service

Helen Verdcourt Wines ▱ ☞

Spring Cottage, Kimbers Lane, Maidenhead, TEL (0628) 25577
Berkshire SL6 2QP

OPEN All hours (24-hour answerphone) CREDIT CARDS None accepted;
personal and business accounts DISCOUNTS 5% for order of more than 12
cases DELIVERY Free in central London and most of south-east England (min 1
case) GLASS HIRE Free with 1-case order TASTINGS AND TALKS Tastings at 2
local wine clubs monthly; to groups on request CELLARAGE Available (limited
space) ∎

'No staff, just me.' We continue to be amazed at the energy behind this
one-woman business, as Helen Verdcourt organises tastings, conducts
groups abroad, travels to buy wines and still manages to sell them.

She keeps a good, all-round list which is most at home in France.
Star areas are the Rhône, containing, for example, Ch de Beaucastel
Châteauneuf-du-Pape in a number of vintages and northern Rhône
wines from Jaboulet Aîné and Guigal. Or look for the three different
vintages of Mas de Daumas Gassac (none – even the 1984, sadly –
ready for drinking yet). Good value Alsace comes from the Turckheim
co-operative.

Other countries are not neglected: try the range of good Riojas
(Remelluri single estate 1983 at £5.90), the Diez Hermanos Sherries, the
Veneto wines of Guerrieri-Rizzardi in Italy. Helen Verdcourt has also
established a good link with Australia, with plenty of interest to be
found in Rosemount, Wynns, Hill-Smith and Cape Mentelle, as well as
the top Shiraz 1981 from Brands Laira (£5.95). Prices throughout are
very good.

Best buys

Taltarni Shiraz 1982, Victoria, £4.50; Terres Brunes 1987 Vin de Pays
d'Oc, £2.80; Côtes du Rhône Villages 1985, Rasteau, £3.65; Barco Reale
1982, Tenuta di Capezzana (Tuscany), £4.25

Victoria Wine Company

HEAD OFFICE Brook House, Chertsey Road, TEL (04862) 5066
Woking, Surrey GU21 5BE
Over 850 branches nationwide

OPEN Hours vary from branch to branch CREDIT CARDS All accepted;
personal and business accounts DISCOUNTS 3% on 6 mixed bottles, 5% on
12+ bottles (may be mixed) DISCOUNTS Not available; mail order available
GLASS HIRE Free with order TASTINGS AND TALKS Promotional tastings in
selected stores; to groups on request CELLARAGE Not available

The Victoria Wine Company has grown even bigger this year,
following the purchase of Haddows in 1987, and engulfing the Agnews
shops in March 1988.

But does bigger mean better? Last year, we expressed our

241

disappointment that Victoria Wine seemed to be buying wines down to the safest, lowest common denominator. Sadly, things don't seem to have improved. Readers have echoed this: 'Whatever has happened to Victoria Wine!' writes one. 'The big profit motive seems to have meant a move into sweets and stomach pills. I shall now take my custom elsewhere in the High Street.'

Although fine things can still be found on this list, they are generally in the Cellar Selection, most of which is on order rather than on the shelves. And it is the own-label wines that the Company seems to be getting particularly wrong. All too often in comparative blind tastings run by our sister magazine *Which? Wine Monthly*, a Victoria wine turns up near the bottom. There seems to be no good reason for this – after all, they use a formidable buying team. What a pity that the nation's most widespread wine retailer should be following a course of beer, tobacco and confectionery rather than one of wine.

Through this gloom we perceive a chink of light, the conversion of two branches into Gares du Vin, in South Kensington and Winchester. Although another venture, the opening of a shop called South of Bordeaux in Chelsea, described as a designer wine shop and aimed at the yuppie market, was deemed a failure, the Gare du Vin has prospered, and two more branches are poised to undergo similar conversion.

Gare du Vin follows a separate buying policy, and have put together a good collection of wines, bought in smaller quantities than Victoria Wine itself can ever do. The range constantly changes, and the two shops are certainly worth a visit.

Victoria Wine's other plans include a revitalised wine club which will include free mailings and special offers of wines not stocked in the shops.

Best buys (from Victoria Wine Company)

Mildara Sauvignon Blanc 1987, £3.89; Maison Royale Champagne, £8.29; Raimat Sparkling Chardonnay, £5.59; St-Chinian Cuvée Jules Gaston, £2.69

La Vigneronne

105 Old Brompton Road, London SW7 3LE   TEL 01-589 6113

OPEN Mon–Sat 10–9   Sun 12–2, 7–9   public holidays usually 11–8
CLOSED Chr Day   CREDIT CARDS All accepted   DISCOUNTS 5% on 1 case (may be mixed)   DELIVERY Free locally (min 1 case) and nationally (min 3 cases); otherwise £3.50 per delivery; mail order available   GLASS HIRE Free with suitable order   TASTINGS AND TALKS Regular series of tutored tastings; occasionally to groups   CELLARAGE £5 per case per year (inc insurance)

This mammoth list is one of the best in the country. Liz Berry and husband Mike have set themselves a hard reputation to live up to, but they seem to be maintaining standards both in wine buying and in the service they offer to customers. Liz Berry runs regular tastings which attract some top producers to come along to show their wines.

Although the Berrys now have more staff and are seen less often themselves, as far as the wines themselves are concerned, we feel that Liz Berry is still very much in charge. Very sensibly, she avoids competition with the local off-licences in which the Old Brompton Road abounds and goes instead for the rare and unusual as well as the best quality from more familiar areas.

In the league of the unusual, you will find vintage after vintage of Ch Grillet, the estate that makes up the whole of the tiny white wine appellation on the Rhône. Just further south, there is Ch Simone in Palette in Provence. Or, here you can choose between two vintages of Vega Sicilia from Spain, which is double what most merchants offer. Old vintages of Ch Musar from the Lebanon (1961 vintage at £12.85 for a half-bottle) are other desirable bottles, and one should not forget the superb range of old solera and vintage Madeiras (the oldest is Averys vintage Verdelho 1822 at £79 a bottle).

In more familiar areas, it's not hard to find wines you've heard of, but rarely if ever tasted. An example would be Chapoutier's Cuvée Numerotée 1966, a fine old red Hermitage (£18.95 a bottle). There are also old vintages of Bourgueil on the Loire, just to show how well this red wine can age, old vintages of German estate wines, and the unusual sweet Recioto di Soave from Italy to set against classic tastes such as the Pieropan Soave, Antinori wines and Barolos from Fontanafredda.

Enthusiasms shine through the list. A major one is Alsace – in fact the Berrys started a separate company called L'Alsacien which had by far the most Alsace wines in the country – now incorporated in La Vigneronne. Another passion is pudding wines, which adorn every section. Yet another seems to be a praiseworthy desire to sell wines that are actually mature rather than much too young to drink.
wines that are actually mature rather than much too young to drink.

It's not just fine wine all the way. Those after everyday drinking will be happy here, although inevitably prices are not the cheapest around. But there's good stuff from the French regions, Italy, Spain and, increasingly, from the New World, too.

Regular customers on a mailing list can now subscribe to a regular newsletter which contains the list, and can also attend a wide-ranging series of tastings.

Best buys

Alsace wines; old Madeiras; Ch de Jau Côtes de Roussillon 1983, £4.25; Ch Musar 1979, £5.50; Ch Septy 1979, Monbazillac, £5.95

Vinceremos Wines

Beechwood Centre, Elmete Lane, Leeds,	TEL (0532) 734056
West Yorkshire LS8 2LQ	

OPEN Mon–Fri 9–5.30 Sat 10–4 CLOSED Sun, public holidays
CREDIT CARDS Access; personal and business accounts
DISCOUNTS Available DELIVERY Free nationally (min 6 cases); otherwise
£5.75 per order; mail order available GLASS HIRE Free
TASTINGS AND TALKS Biannual tastings; monthly members' wine club; to
groups on request CELLARAGE Not available　　　　　　　　　　■

As last year, it is the organically produced wines and bottles from some unusual sources that put this firm in the Guide.

All the wines from conventional sources – France, Italy, Greece and England – are made organically, with no use of chemical weedkillers, fertilisers, sprays or additives (apart from a minimum use of sulphur dioxide). The range – quite short – includes a good selection of petit château Bordeaux, Alsace wines from Pierre Frick and Muscadet from Guy Bossard, along with English ciders and apple wine, the top quality Greek wines from John Calliga, and the Veneto wines of Guerrieri-Rizzardi.

The somewhat more unusual sources take in the Flame Lily range from Zimbabwe, Algerian and Crimean wines, and Indian sparkling Omar Khayyam. Also look for Australian examples from Peter Lehmann and Montrose.

Best buys

Algerian wines; Biovin Valdepeñas 1986, £2.95; Mauzac, Vin de Pays de l'Aude Blanc, £3.20; Greek wines from John Calliga

Vintage Roots

25 Manchester Road, Reading,	TEL (0734) 662569
Berkshire RG1 3QE	

OPEN Mon–Fri 9–6 Sat 9.30–6 Sun, public holidays if necessary; also 24-hour answerphone CREDIT CARDS None accepted; personal and business accounts DISCOUNTS 5% on orders of £250, 7.5% on orders of £400; £1.50 per case collected; charities 12% DELIVERY Free within 30-mile radius of Reading (min 1 case); elsewhere 1 case £3.50, 2 cases £3 each, 3 cases £2 each, 4 cases £1.50 each; mail order available GLASS HIRE Not available
TASTINGS AND TALKS In-store tastings on request; to groups on request
CELLARAGE Not available　　　　　　　　　　　　　　　■

This is, as its name might suggest, a firmly organic range of wines. While the majority of the contents are French, roots have also been put down in Italy, Germany and Australia.

France includes selections from Muscadet (Guy Bossard) and Alsace (Stentz), from the Rhône (Domaine St-Apollinaire) and Patrick Javillier in Meursault, and from Bordeaux (Ch Renaissance 1986 at £3.80; Ch de Prade 1985, Bordeaux Supérieur, £4.25).

Germany offers four estate wines, while in Italy we find the excellent Veneto wines of Guerrieri-Rizzardi. English wine comes from Sedlescombe. Australia's offering is a Shiraz from Botobolar in Mudgee, New South Wales (1984 vintage at £4.60), while California comes up with wines from Frey Vineyard in Mendocino.

Best buys

Bianco San Pietro 1986, Guerrieri-Rizzardi, £3.29; St-Gilbert Shiraz 1984, Botobolar, Mudgee, £4.60; Côtes du Rhône Cuvée d'Apollinaire 1985, £3.80

The Vintner/Viticulteur

See Arthur Rackhams.

A L Vose

Town House, Main Street,   TEL (05395) 33328
Grange-over-Sands, Cumbria LA11 7BB
(OFFICE) 92 Kentsford Road,
Grange-over-Sands, Cumbria LA11 7BB

OPEN Mon–Fri 9.30–6   Sat 9–5   public holidays 10–5   CLOSED Sun
CREDIT CARDS Access, Visa; personal and business accounts
DISCOUNTS 10% on 1 case   DELIVERY Free in Cumbria, North Lancashire and North Yorkshire; elsewhere at cost; mail order available   GLASS HIRE Free with case order   TASTINGS AND TALKS Wine always available in shop; to groups on request   CELLARAGE Not available

While many of the wines sold here are the same as at the Wine Schoppen (*qv*), A L Vose are one of the few merchants in the country to carry wines from Austria, and are one of very few sources of supply for Brazilian wines from Palomas.

Austrian bottles include some from the co-operative of Krems, which makes a full range of wines from Lower Austria, and others from the firm of Sepp Hold in the Burgenland. We would recommend the Kremser Neuberger Rhine Riesling 1983 at £5.05 (prices on the list do not include VAT – we have included it here) for a mature Riesling taste, or the typical Austrian tastes of the Kremser Schmidt 1986 Grüner Veltliner (£3.06). Look, too, for the sparkling wines.

The wines from the Palomas winery in Brazil form a complete contrast, with their emphasis on French varietal flavours: look for the Pinot Noir 1986 at £3.85 or the Chardonnay 1986 at the same price. A L Vose also stock a few Swiss wines at Swiss prices.

Best buys

Palomas Brazilian wines; Bouvier Beerenauslese 1983, Sepp Hold
£4.39, (half-bottle); German estate wines

Waitrose

HEAD OFFICE Doncastle Road, Southern   TEL (0344) 424680
Industrial Area, Bracknell, Berkshire RG12 4YA
85 licensed branches in London, Midlands and the Home Counties
OPEN Mon, Tue 9–6   Wed 9–8   Thur, Fri 8.30–8 (some branches 9)   Sat
8.30–5.30   CLOSED Sun, public holidays (open Good Friday)
CREDIT CARDS None accepted   DISCOUNTS 5% on £100 expenditure
DELIVERY Not available   GLASS HIRE Free (deposit required)
TASTINGS AND TALKS Occasional evening tastings for customers; occasionally
to groups on request   CELLARAGE Not available

A top-quality list that wouldn't disgrace many specialist wine
merchants. Unlike most other supermarket groups, Waitrose go in for
very few own-label wines and those that they do are the most basic.
Instead, a wide-ranging selection gives a good choice from most
countries and most areas.

From recent tastings of their wines, we have enjoyed the Fitou 1983
(£2.59), the Teroldego Rotaliano 1986 from Gaierhof in the Trentino
region of Italy (£2.75), two clarets (Ch Senailhac 1985 Bordeaux at £3.25
and Ch Haut Portets 1985, Graves at £4.65), the basic Bourgogne Rouge
1985 from the Buxy co-operative at £3.99, the Sauvignon du
Haut-Poitou 1987 (£2.99), the Mountain View California Chardonnay
1986 at £3.99 and the new range of Kabinett wines from Germany.

Other areas of interest are as varied as Portugal, Italy (especially for
red wines), Cook's wines from New Zealand, the deliciously fragrant
Moorlynch English wine from Somerset (£3.79) and good sparkling
Crémant de Bourgogne. The Waitrose Champagne and Vintage
Champagne 1984 are always good value.

Best buys

Bairrada 1984, Adega Cooperativa de Mealhada, £2.29; Pinot Noir de
Bourgogne 1985, Cave Co-opérative de Buxy, £3.99; Romero Superior
Dry Amontillado Sherry, £3.79; Mountain View California Pinot Noir
and Chardonnay, £3.99; Cava, Castellblanch Cristal Brut NV, £3.99

We have tried to make the *1989 Which? Wine Guide* as comprehensive as
possible, but we should love to hear from you with commonts on any other
wine merchants you feel deserve an entry, or on existing entries. Write to
us either by letter or using the report forms supplied at the back of the
book.

Peter Watts Wines

Wisdom's Barn, Colne Road, Coggeshall,   TEL (0376) 61130
Colchester, Essex CO6 1TD

OPEN Mon–Fri 9–1, 2–5.30 Sat 9–1 CLOSED Sun, public holidays
CREDIT CARDS Access, Visa; personal and business accounts
DISCOUNTS Quantity discounts DELIVERY Free in England and Wales (min 5
cases); otherwise 1–4 cases £6 per order; mail order available GLASS HIRE Free
with 1-case order TASTINGS AND TALKS Wines always available in-store;
larger tastings held in June and November at local venues CELLARAGE Not
available ■

Peter Watts Wines specialise in importing wines from small growers,
particularly in France, but to an increasing extent in Germany, Italy,
Portugal and Australia.

In France, they have unearthed a number of Bordeaux estates such
as Ch Fontbaude in Côtes de Castillon and Ch la Bécasse in Pauillac
(1983 vintage at £9.70). In Alsace, wines come from Louis Siffert, while
on the Rhône Roger et Patrick Jaume are the names (look for their
Châteauneuf). There are country wines, too – Vin de Pays de l'Hérault
from Domaine de Laval and Domaine de Mallemort (red 1985 at £3).

German estate wines come from Dr Josef Hofer in the Nahe and
Selbach on the Mosel. New to the Italian section are the wines of Santa
Sofia (Soave and Valpolicella), Livio Pavese (Gavi and Barolo) and
Contessa di Radda (Chianti). New also are Portuguese wines from
Quinta de Pancas in Alenquer in the Ribatejo. Ports are from the small
family firm of de Souza.

Best buys

Beaujolais Supérieur 1987, Ch de Bionnay, £3.55; Scarpantoni
Cabernet Sauvignon 1984, McLaren Vale, South Australia, £5.10; Vin
de Pays de l'Hérault, Domaine de Luch 1985, £2.55; Ch Fontbaude
1985, Côtes de Castillon, £3.95

Weatherbury Vintners

5 Trinity Street, Dorchester, Dorset DT1 1TU   TEL (0305) 65586

OPEN Mon–Sat 9.30–6 CLOSED Sun, public holidays CREDIT CARDS None
accepted; personal and business accounts DISCOUNTS 2.5% on 1 case
DELIVERY Free within 50-mile radius; elsewhere at cost; mail order available
GLASS HIRE Free TASTINGS AND TALKS Two major tastings a year; to groups
on request CELLARAGE 5p per week (inc VAT)

A new merchant in the Guide, who covers most areas of the world and
cultivates a number of areas of particular interest.

While bearing in mind the good range of Champagnes, and the
expansive selection of clarets (including some classed growths from the
1979 vintage), as well as the Moillard Burgundies, it would also be
worth looking at Ch de Beaulieu in Coteaux d'Aix-en-Provence for

good value (red, white and rosé at £3.55), not to mention Alsace wines from Jean-Preiss Zimmer, a range of German estate bottles, including some from Huesgen and Schloss Johannisberg, and Italian wines, which include some from Sella e Mosca in Sardinia and Sartori wines from the Veneto.

Spain, too, has interest with Riojas from Berberana, and an excellent set of Sherries (Duke of Wellington and Barbadillo), while Ports are mainly from Smith Woodhouse and Dow. Australia offers good ranges from Mildara, Krondorf in the Barossa Valley and Brown Brothers.

Best buys

Ch de Beaulieu Rouge 1986, Coteaux d'Aix-en-Provence, £3.55; Côtes du Marmandais 1985, Cave de Beaupuy, £3.17; Pinot Bianco di Aquileia 1986, Ca'Bolani, £3.74

Welbeck Wine

3 Montrose Road, Dukes Park, Springfield,   TEL (0245) 461210
Chelmsford, Essex CM2 6TE

OPEN Mon 9–5   Tue–Thur 9–6   Fri 9–7   Sat 9.30–6   CLOSED Sun, public holidays   CREDIT CARDS Access, Visa; personal and business accounts DISCOUNTS Negotiable   DELIVERY Free in Essex (min 2 cases) and UK mainland (min 5 cases); elsewhere by negotiation; mail order available GLASS HIRE Free with suitable wine order   TASTINGS AND TALKS Regular weekly tastings (Sat); large annual tasting; to groups on request CELLARAGE £3.45 per case per year   ■

Welbeck's is a short list with certain firm specialisations. One is the Côtes de Francs in Bordeaux, a small appellation to the north-east of St-Emilion on the edge of the Bordeaux region. Look for Lauriol, Ch Laclaverue and Ch Puyguéraud, as well as a small selection of other clarets.

Also appealing are a useful range of cru Beaujolais, the Burgundies of Jean-Marie Delaunay, and the Côtes du Rhône Villages Beaumes de Venise of Ch Redortier (the 1985 vintage is £3.99). On the Loire, there is Sancerre and Pouilly Fumé from Domaine Saget. House Champagne is Pannier at £8.19.

Welbeck Wine has also sought out a small selection of German wines, Barolos from Bruno Giacosa, Chianti from Berardenga Fattoria di Felsina, and a good value range of Bulgarian wines. In the New World we find Orlando and Rosemount wines from Australia and Joseph Phelps and Ridge from California.

Prices throughout are very competitive.

Best buys

Valdespino Martial Sherries; Spanna del Piemonte 1984, Agostino Brugo, £2.89; Bulgarian wines; Côtes du Rhône Villages Beaumes de

Venise 1985, Ch Redortier, £3.99; Lauriol 1985, Bordeaux Côtes de Francs, £3.94

Wessex Wines

197 St Andrews Road, Bridport,   TEL (0308) 23400
Dorset DT6 3BT

OPEN Mon–Sat 8.30–9 (including most public holidays)   CLOSED Sun
CREDIT CARDS None accepted; personal and business accounts
DISCOUNTS 5% on minimum of 6 bottles unmixed   DELIVERY Free within
20-mile radius of Bridport (min 1 case); elsewhere at cost; mail order available
GLASS HIRE Free with 1+ case order   TASTINGS AND TALKS Regular in-store
tastings in November; occasionally at other times of the year; to groups on
request   CELLARAGE Not available

In concentrating on wines under £5 a bottle, this merchant has come up with some very good value bottles from all over the world. It's a well-balanced, attractive list, with enthusiasm the keynote.

After house wines, the list moves into Bordeaux, with some good petit château wines, plus more serious things from Fronsac and in the realm of crus bourgeois. There's considerable interest in Bergerac as well – look for red and white from Domaine de Coutancie. Burgundy inevitably breaks the £5 barrier but not too gravely while still maintaining interest.

Domaine Beaujolais Villages and cru wines are followed by Côtes du Rhône from the Celliers des Dauphins, Alsace wines from Muré and Champagne from Maurice Delabaye at £8.95. In Spain, there are Riojas from CVNE while Bairrada Garrafeira of Caves Aliança 1985 in Portugal is terrific value at £5.22.

Worth trying, too, are the Pilton Manor English wines, Chiantis from Rocca delle Macie, a big range of Bulgarian wines (including the new Reserve wines), Ch Musar 1980 in the Lebanon (£5.26) and examples from Rosemount Estates in Australia. More of a curiosity are wines from Zimbabwe. Garvey and de Morales Sherries are classics of their kind, while Niepoort supplies the Ports.

Best buys

California wines from Jekel Vineyards; Bourgogne Rouge Les Varennes 1985, Emile Voarick, £4.84; Ockfener Bockstein Riesling Kabinett 1979, Nikolas Max Erben, £4.48; Franciacorta Rosso Colle San Stefano 1986, £4.37

West Heath Wine

West Heath, Pirbright, Surrey GU24 0QE   TEL (04867) 6464

OPEN Mon–Fri 9–6 Sat 10–4 CLOSED Sun CREDIT CARDS None accepted; personal and business accounts DISCOUNTS Not available DELIVERY At cost; 1 case £3.75, then on a sliding scale to 4+ cases £2 per case; mail order available GLASS HIRE Free with 2-case order TASTINGS AND TALKS Regular tastings in warehouse; to groups on request CELLARAGE Not available ∎

Another of the new breed of 'organic wine only' merchants. West Heath have put together a list which inevitably concentrates on France (because that is where the greatest numbers of organic wine producers are working), but also includes wines from Germany and Italy.

Look for Alsace wines from P Frick, an expanded range of clarets (Ch Haut Mallet 1986, Bordeaux Supérieur at £5.25), plus wines from C Courtois in the Provence VDQS area of Coteaux Varois (Cuvée St-Cyriaque 1985 at £4.46), Burgundy from J-C Rateau and Champagne André Beaufort (£11.37).

In Germany, look for the Rheingau wines of Graf von Kanitz in Lorch and Heyl zu Herrnsheim in Nierstein in Rheinhessen. Italy has Veneto wines from Guerrieri-Rizzardi and Chianti from Roberto Drighi (the 1986 vintage at £3.38).

Best buys

Alsace Klevner Pinot Blanc 1985, P Frick, £4.47; Ch le Rait 1986, Bordeaux Supérieur, £3.18; Ch Haut Mallet 1986, Bordeaux Supérieur, £5.25

Whighams of Ayr

8 Academy Street, Ayr, Ayrshire KA7 1HT   TEL (0292) 267000
Whighams, Young & Saunders,   TEL 031-220 0600
57 North Castle Street, Edinburgh EH2 3LF
(wholesale)
Whighams, Young & Saunders at Jenners,   TEL 031-225 2442
48 Princes Street, Edinburgh EH2 2YJ
(Retail)

OPEN Mon–Sat 9.30–5.30 CLOSED Sun, public holidays
CREDIT CARDS Amex, Visa; personal and business accounts DISCOUNTS 15% on 1 case DELIVERY Free in UK (min 1 case retail and 10 cases wholesale); mail order available GLASS HIRE Free with 1-case order
TASTINGS AND TALKS Biannual tastings; to groups on request CELLARAGE £3 per case per year

This merchant has expanded to Edinburgh from its original Ayr base, and now has an office (Whighams, Young and Saunders) and a shop in the food hall at Jenners.

They run a solid list with a bias towards France, which is evident in the good range of clarets (including petit château wines and a collection of mature classed growths back to 1970), and in Burgundies from Chanson (look for their Bourgogne Pinot Noir and Bourgogne Chardonnay as good value examples) as well as Albert Bichot. On the Loire there is good Chinon from Domaine de Narçay (the 1984 vintage is £4.60) as well as Muscadet sur lie from the Domaine du Landreau Village at £3.45. House Champagne is £9.99.

In Germany, wines are mostly from Michael Wilkomm, plus some Baden wines, while in Italy Chianti is from Castell'in Villa (1980 Riserva, £7.19). House wines – mainly from Bordeaux – are designed for golf enthusiasts with names like Le Putt and Le Birdie.

Best buys

Ch Puyfromage 1985, Bordeaux Supérieur, £5.55; Ch Malard 1985, Bordeaux Supérieur, £4.88; Bourgogne Pinot Noir NV, Chanson Père et Fils, £4.79

White Hart Vaults

See Wines Galore.

Whiteside's of Clitheroe

Shawbridge Street, Clitheroe,   TEL (0200) 22281
Lancashire BB7 1NA

OPEN Mon 9–5.30   Tue–Fri 9–8   Sat 9–6   CLOSED Sun, public holidays
CREDIT CARDS Access, Visa; personal and business accounts
DISCOUNTS 2.5% on 1 case unmixed table wine; quantity discounts negotiable
DELIVERY Free locally (min 1 case); elsewhere at cost; mail order available
GLASS HIRE Free with any case order   TASTINGS AND TALKS Weekly in-store
tastings; quarterly wine club tastings; to groups on request   CELLARAGE Free
on own premises; in bond at cost

Big changes have taken place over the past year – sufficient to bring this merchant back into the Guide after a year's absence. They've refurbished their shop, started a wine club and greatly expanded the range of wines they offer. All very encouraging.

There's plenty of interest in Bordeaux, with a good range of petit château wines from the 1985 vintage, many under £4. The same strength, at slightly higher prices, is evident with older vintages. In Burgundy, Whitesides keep négociant wines from Chandesais, Antonin Rodet and Labouré-Roi, while Beaujolais sports a big selection from Georges Duboeuf. The Rhône is less interesting, but look for the Muscadet of Donatien Bahuaud on the Loire, Alsace wines from Louis Sipp and the Côtes du Lubéron wines of Ch Val-Joanis in the South of France. A big range of Champagnes, too.

In Germany, the best bets are estate wines from Deinhard. In Italy, worth considering are a good range of Chiantis (Villa Cerna, Ruffino, Rocca delle Macìe) and varietal wines from Ca' Bolani in Aquileia.

Plenty of Riojas, including a number of Gran Reservas, while Portugal offers wines of J M da Fonseca.

There is now a considerable range of Australian wines – from Brown Brother's, Lindeman's, Hill-Smith, Penfold's, Rosemount, Wolf Blass, Yalumba, and many more. Try the Liqueur Muscats of Chambers and Baileys (Baileys Founders Award Liqueur Muscat, £8.59). New Zealand has wines from Nobilo and Babich. Ports are from Gould Campbell, Cockburn and Taylor, plus a good few Sherries, too.

Best buys

Quinta de Santo Amaro 1986, João Pires, £3.15; Côtes du Ventoux 1986/Côtes du Lubéron 1986, La Vieille Ferme, £2.99; Orlando Eden Valley Gewürztraminer 1986, £5.25; Côtes du Rhône 1985, Valvigneyre, £4.15

Whittalls Wines

Darlaston Road, Walsall,   TEL (0922) 36161
West Midlands WS2 9SQ

OPEN Mon–Fri 9–5.30   CLOSED Sat, Sun, public holidays
CREDIT CARDS None accepted; personal and business accounts
DISCOUNTS Not available   DELIVERY At cost; mail order available
GLASS HIRE Available   TASTINGS AND TALKS To groups on request
CELLARAGE £1.50 per case per year   ■

This merchant, also known as Château Pleck Fine Wines, used to be part of a Midlands chain but now operates only from this address, developing a fine wine list and other activities such as a newsletter.

The list is essentially French, although look for J M da Fonseca wines from Portugal and Brown Brothers wines from Australia.

On a recent list, a strong selection of fine clarets goes back to the mid-1970s, and other attractions include Burgundy from Antonin Rodet and Chandesais as well as some domaine wines, some good Rhône wines from Guigal and Jaboulet Aîné in the north, with Châteauneuf-du-Pape of Domaine de la Tour St-Michel in the south. There is some interest on the Loire, such as Quincy, Domaine de la Maison Blanche (£3.33 – prices on the list do not include VAT, but we have added it here). Alsace wines are from Louis Sipp, while there is a big selection of Champagnes from De Venoge.

Best buys

Ch Haut St-Lambert 1985, Pauillac, £4.45; Champagne from De Venoge; Côtes du Ventoux 1985, Jaboulet Aîné, £3.05

Willerby Wine Market

See J Townend & Sons.

Willoughbys

53 Cross Street, Manchester M2 4JP	TEL 061-834 6850/0641
98–100 Broadway, Chadderton, Oldham,	TEL 061-620 1374
Greater Manchester OL9 0AA	
1 Springfield House, Water Lane,	TEL (0625) 533068
Wilmslow, Cheshire SK9 5AE	

OPEN Mon–Fri 9–6 Sat 9–5 (Chadderton branch closed on Wed and Sat afternoons) CLOSED Sun, public holidays CREDIT CARDS Access, Visa; personal and business accounts DISCOUNTS By arrangement DELIVERY Free within locality of each outlet (min order by arrangement); mail order available GLASS HIRE Free with wine order TASTINGS AND TALKS In-store tastings and evening presentations 2–3 times per month; to groups on request CELLARAGE Usually £3.50 per case per year

Willoughbys also own George Dutton in Chester and Thomas Baty in Liverpool as well as their own shops in Greater Manchester and Wilmslow.

While they cover the three French classic areas of Bordeaux, Burgundy and – especially – Champagne in depth, they don't ignore other parts of the wine world.

There are unexpected pockets: for example, a good range of Corsican wines and wines from Haut-Poitou are both welcome, as are Hugel Alsace wines in profusion, and Loire wines from Donatien Bahuaud and a good range of bargains from the Midi. Beyond France, the German list specialises in wines from Louis Guntrum as well as the Baden co-operative, and the Italian section in the Venegazzù wines from Loredan Gasparini and Chiantis from Ruffino and Frescobaldi. Look in Spain for wines from Torres and Berberana and Muga Riojas. There's a good range of Bulgarian wines, Cook's and Montana wines from New Zealand and Brown Brothers wines from Australia.

Back to those classics. The huge range of Champagnes is one of the biggest in the country and comes from the majority of the great names. Clarets go back in vintages to 1976, with more great names to be found here. In Burgundy, look for wines from Chandesais, Labouré-Roi and Antonin Rodet as well as Domaine de la Romanée-Conti.

Best buys

Willoughbys Sunday Claret, Bordeaux Supérieur, £3.29; wines from Haut-Poitou; Brown Brothers Meadowcreek Cabernet Sauvignon/Shiraz 1985, Australia, £5.95; Bulgarian wines.

Winchester Wine Company

68 Fairfield Road, Winchester,   TEL (0962) 69518
Hampshire SO22 6SG
(mainly mail order)

OPEN By appointment only CREDIT CARDS None accepted DISCOUNTS Not available DELIVERY Free for 5+ cases; otherwise 1 case £6, 2 cases £9, 3–4 cases £12 GLASS HIRE Free with 2-case order TASTINGS AND TALKS To groups on request CELLARAGE Not available ■

This firm specialises in the Südtirol/Alto Adige in northern Italy, including wines from producers in the Eisack Valley north of Bolzano which are not otherwise available in this country. As we went to press, the stocks had been run down and the list was short, but we were told that more wines were due in the autumn. Then you should look for Eisacktaler Kellereigenossenschaft at Klausen, Weinkellerei Josef Brigl (especially his Goldmuskateller), Franz Gojer who makes wines at St Magdalener, and Hofstätter in Tramin, the home of the Traminer grape.

Windrush Wines

The Barracks, Cecily Hill, Cirencester,   TEL (0285) 67121
Gloucestershire GL7 2EF

OPEN Mon–Fri 9–5.30 Sat 10–2 CLOSED Sun, public holidays
CREDIT CARDS None accepted; personal and business accounts
DISCOUNTS 'In bond' and 'ex-cellar' terms available by arrangement
DELIVERY Free within 30-mile radius of Cirencester and mainland UK (min 5+ cases); otherwise 1–2 cases £5.75 per case, 3–4 cases £4.03 per case; mail order available GLASS HIRE Free with 1-case order
TASTINGS AND TALKS Approximately quarterly tastings for members; to groups on request CELLARAGE £3.45 per case per year ■

We hope that people get round to ordering wines from Windrush rather than just remaining absorbed by the opinionated notes written by owner Mark Savage, because those opinions underlie some very rewarding wines.

Mr Savage is perhaps best known for devoting himself to the north-west states of America. He offers as big a range of wines from this region as anybody, and has worked hard to promote their considerable qualities, especially in the case of Chardonnay and Pinot Noir wines. Look for Eyrie Vineyards and Tualatin in Oregon, Columbia and Salishan in Washington State, Rose Creek in Idaho. Prices are quite high, because quantities produced are small.

The Windrush list also features California – Stag's Leap Wine Cellars, Philip Togni, Diamond Creek, Conn Creek, Matanzas Creek, Sanford.

On the other side of the Atlantic, clarets get some similarly firm opinions, about prices and recent vintages, and thorough coverage from 1985 back to 1978. Ch Le Tertre Rôteboeuf in St-Emilion is a featured estate. In other areas of France, the emphasis is likewise on family estates: Domaine des Malandes in Chablis, Jean-Claude Fourrier in Gevrey-Chambertin, Pierre Boillot in Meursault (both in Burgundy), Domaine la Fourmone in Vacqueyras and Gigondas on the Rhône, Sylvain Fessy in Beaujolais.

Then to Italy, which, after the Pacific North-West, is the most obvious area of interest. Some great names abound here: Il Palazzino Chianti Classico, Avignonesi Montepulciano, Pertimali's Brunello di Montalcino, Luciano Sandrone's Barolo, Gaja's Barbaresco.

Finally, Windrush offers a good way to celebrate with its range of Billecart-Salmon Champagnes.

Best buys

Mâcon Villages 1986, Domaine de la Condamine, £5.48; Alsace Tokay Pinot Gris 1986, Hubert Krick, £3.97; Chianti Classico 1985, San Giusto, £4.77; Hawk Crest Cabernet Sauvignon 1985, Napa Valley, £4.94; Barolo 1984, Sandrone, £10.21

Wine and Ale House

See Direct Wine Shipments.

Winecellars 🐷 🏵 🖾

153/155 Wandsworth High Street,   TEL 01-871 2668
London SW18 4JB
HEAD OFFICE Bretzel Foods,   TEL 01-359 6238
213/215 Upper Street, London N1 1RL

OPEN Mon–Fri 10.30–8.30   Sat 10–8.30   Sun, public holidays 10.30–6
CLOSED Chr Day, Boxing Day   CREDIT CARDS Access, Visa; personal and business accounts   DISCOUNTS Approximately 10% on 1 case   DELIVERY Free in Barnes, Battersea, Fulham, Putney, Wandsworth, Wimbledon (min 1 case); otherwise £2.50 for under 3 cases in London, 3+ cases free in London; elsewhere at cost; mail order available   GLASS HIRE Free with 1-case order
TASTINGS AND TALKS Regular series of tutored tastings; to groups on request
CELLARAGE Negotiable

This wine warehouse also acts as the wine-buying and supply side for The Market and Le Provençal supermarkets (qv).

Their reputation as Italian specialists is so high that the rest of the list risks being forgotten. That would be a pity, because Winecellars also have a good range of French wines – plenty from the South-West, for instance, as well as Terres Blanches from Coteaux des Baux en Provence and Mas de Daumas Gassac in the Hérault. In Beaujolais, there are wines from Les Eventails (Juliénas 1987, Domaine René Monnet at £4.95), while the Loire has Guy Bossard's Muscadet and Alsace wines from the Turckheim co-operative. There's a useful range of clarets (Ch Haut Portets, 1985 Graves at £4.75) and Champagne from Alfred Gratien.

The shelves of other parts of the world are expanding, showing considerable interest in Australia and Portugal, and the good value Mountain View collection from California.

And so to Italy. Winecellars' listing is exemplary and anything they stock from this country is usually full of what the Italians call '*tipicita*' – wines that are absolutely typical, in the best sense, of the region from which they come. From such a large range, we would pick out as favourites those from Ronco in Piedmont, the Moscato d'Asti of Ascheri, the Oltrepò Pavese wines of the Fugazza sisters, wines from Masi and Pojer e Sandri in the Veneto and Lageder in the Südtirol.

Moving south, we find terrific value in Chianti Rufina from Grati, Brunello di Montalcino of Altesino, Frascati of Colli di Catone, Montepulciano d'Abruzzo of Valentini. And from right down in Sicily, look for the Marsalas (and other wines) of Marco de Bartoli and the Cellaro range of wines from Sambuca di Sicilia.

Best buys

Barbera d'Asti 1985, Ronco, £2.99; Chianti Rufina Banda Blue 1986, Grati, £2.95; Champagne Philippe Flaurent, £7.95; Vin de Pays des Coteaux du Quercy 1986, Domaine de Lafage, £2.99; Sherries from Valdespino

---

The Wine Emporium

7 Devon Place, Haymarket,   TEL 031-346 1113
Edinburgh EH12 5HJ
498 Crow Road, Glasgow G11 7DW   TEL 041-337 1816

OPEN Mon–Sat 10–8   Sun 11–5   CLOSED 25–26 Dec and 1–2 Jan
CREDIT CARDS Access, Visa; personal and business accounts
DISCOUNTS Available only for trade customers   DELIVERY Free in Edinburgh and Glasgow (min 1 case); mail order available   GLASS HIRE Free
TASTINGS AND TALKS Wines available for tasting most days in-store; to groups on request   CELLARAGE Available in local bond for duty purchases only

---

The Wine Emporium's list has improved and expanded over the past year, which means that we are delighted to welcome them to the Guide for the first time. In addition to the regular list they offer bin ends and small parcels of fine wines which change constantly. The empire has grown, too, with new premises in Glasgow.

The standard list spans the world. Plenty of good value is to be found in their petit château clarets (Ch les Douves de Francs 1986 from the Côtes de Francs, £3.99; or, at the Grand Cru level, Ch de Pressac 1982, St-Emilion, £6.29). Other good areas in France include the country wines (especially in the South-West), Châteauneuf-du-Pape from Ch de Beaucastel and Domaine de Mont-Redon, Sancerre from Guy Saget and Alsace wines from the Turckheim co-operative.

Italy is strong – look for the top quality Vernaccia di San
Gimignano of San Quirico (1987 vintage at £3.55), the red Morellino di
Scansano 1985 at £4.59 from south-west Tuscany or the Brunello di
Montalcino 1981 of Filippo (£8.70), as well as less expensive Veneto
wines. Portugal has wines from the Almerim co-operative and a rare
Colares red from Beira Mar (1979 vintage at £3.99). From neighbouring
Spain, there are Garvey Sherries, while from further afield, worth
considering are Australian wines from Wyndham Estate, Brown
Brothers and Tisdall, New Zealand wines from Cook's and Matua
Valley and California wines from Mondavi and Trefethen.

Best buys

Ch les Douves de Francs 1986, Côtes de Francs, £3.99; Alsace Riesling
1986, Cave Co-opérative de Turckheim, £3.79; Colares 1979, Beira Mar
Reserva, £3.99; Concha y Toro Chilean Cabernet/Merlot 1984, £2.99

Wine Growers Association

MAIL ORDER ONLY 430 High Road,   TEL 01-451 0981/1135
Willesden, London NW10 2HA *or*
Freepost, London NW10 1YA

CREDIT CARDS Access, Amex, Diners, Visa, THF Goldcard; business accounts
DISCOUNTS Available   DELIVERY Free on UK mainland (min 6 cases); 1 case
£3.75   GLASS HIRE, TASTINGS AND TALKS Not available   CELLARAGE £3 per
unmixed case per year for wines bought from premises only

Although much of the interest with this merchant centres on Italy,
Wine Growers Association have been building up plenty to admire in
France as well.

But we start this report in Italy. Many of the wines can be found on
the list of the associated importers, Italian Wine Agencies. It's quite a
galaxy of famous – and less well-known – names, and all are worth
investigating: Tedeschi and Boscaini in the Veneto, Brugo and
Borgogno in Piedmont, the main co-operative in the Südtirol, Zeni in
Trentino, Fugazza in Lombardy, Pagliarese Chiantis, Torre Ercolana of
Colacicchi, Bucci Verdicchio, the Aglianico del Vulture of Fratelli
d'Angelo and wines from Sella e Mosca in Sardinia.

In France, a recent list was making a special offer of 1985 clarets, and
there are certainly plenty of classed and bourgeois growths from this
vintage. There's a good section of Barsac from Ch Doisy-Védrines,
Burgundies from Jaboulet-Vercherre and Reine Pédauque, Alsace from
Jules Müller and Coteaux d'Aix-en-Provence from the largest estate in
the area, Ch de Beaulieu. Champagnes are from Ayala and Riojas from
Don Jacobo Bodegas Corral. Look, too, for Ports from Calem
(10-year-old tawny at £9.40).

WHERE TO BUY

Best buys

Claret 1986, Chevalier de Védrines, £3.65; Spanna del Piemonte 1985, Agostino Brugo, £3.25; Chianti Classico 1985, Pagliarese, £4.65; Chardonnay di Appiano 1987 (Südtirol/Alto Adige), Cantina Sociale di Appiano, £4.15

The Wine House

10 Stafford Road, Wallington, TEL 01-669 6661
Surrey SM6 9AD

OPEN Tue–Sat 10–6 Sun 12–2 public holidays variable CLOSED Mon
CREDIT CARDS Access, Visa; business accounts DISCOUNTS To members of
Wine Circle only (membership £3 annually) DELIVERY Free within 5-mile
radius (min 1 case); elsewhere £5 first case, £2.50 subsequent cases; mail order
available GLASS HIRE Free with 1-case order
TASTINGS AND TALKS Occasional tastings by invitation only; to groups on
request CELLARAGE Not available

This former branch of the Sherston Wine company (*qv*) is now run independently and has taken on board a completely new range of wines, although Spain – as with the original Sherston – is a treasure trove.

But Italy is far from unimpressive, as is Spain's Iberian neighbour. Come to that, so is Australia. France, by comparison (and probably by design), takes a secondary role, although even here there is plenty of interest.

Spain has Riojas galore from many of the famous bodegas, with the house Rioja coming from Señor Burgues (the second label of Faustino). There is a good choice of Reservas and Gran Reservas as well. In Navarra, Señorio de Sarria and Agramont are the names, joined by the prestigious Vega Sicilia in Ribera del Duero. There are Torres wines from Penedès and a range of Cavas featuring Freixenet.

Turning to Italy: worth considering are Barolos from Franco-Fiorina and Franciacorta of Ca' del Bosco, Tiefenbrunner Südtirol wines, Veneto wines of Guerrieri-Rizzardi, Chiantis of Frescobaldi and Ruffino and Rubesco from Lungarotti. In Portugal, there's plenty of interest, too: Quinta da Aveleda dry Vinho Verde, and wines from Hill-Smith, Hardy's, Mildara, Andrew Garrett and Renmano in South Garrafeira 1982 from the Alentejo (£5.49).

Moving across the oceans to Australia, we are greeted by another major line-up: Evans & Tate and Forest Hill in Western Australia; Hill-Smith, Hardys, Mildara, Andrew Garrett and Renmano in South Australia; Tisdall, Yarra Yering and Idyll in Victoria; and Rosemount, Montrose and Tamburlaine in New South Wales.

Cellarage is generally provided at the rates quoted only when the wines have been bought from the merchant concerned.

Best buys

Peter Lehmann Shiraz/Cabernet 1984, £3.96; Breganze Rosso 1983,
Brentino, Maculan, £5.90; Manzanilla, de Soto, £3.60; Rioja 1984,
Montecillo Viña Cumbrero, £3.56; Cava Parxet Brut Nature NV, £6.75

The Wine Schoppen

1 Abbeydale Road South,	TEL (0742) 365684/368617
Sheffield, South Yorkshire S7 2QL	

ASSOCIATED OUTLETS

Wine Schoppen (Kidderminster),	TEL (0562) 823060
121 Stourbridge Road, Broadwaters, Kidderminster,	
Hereford & Worcester DY10 2UH	
A L Vose & Co, 92 Kentsford Road,	TEL (04484) 3328
Grange-over-Sands, Cumbria LA11 7BB	
Wine Warehouse, Holme Leigh, East Lane,	TEL (0302) 841254
Stainforth, Nr Doncaster,	
South Yorkshire DN7 5DT	
Pennine Wines, 5/7 Station Street,	TEL (0484) 25747
Huddersfield, South Yorkshire HD1 1LS	
C C Enterprises, 157 Woodlands Avenue,	TEL 01-866 9745
Eastcote, Ruislip HA4 9QX	
(mail order only)	
Classic Wines, 12 Woodhouse Road,	TEL (0274) 691053
Shelf, Halifax, West Yorkshire HX3 7PB	

OPEN Mon–Fri 9.30–6 Sat 9–5 CLOSED Sun, public holidays
CREDIT CARDS Access, Visa; personal and business accounts
DISCOUNTS 2½% for 3–5 cases, 5% for 6–9 cases, 7½% for 10–15 cases, 10% for
16–25 cases DELIVERY Free within 15-mile radius of Sheffield, Kidderminster
and of all associated companies (min 1 case); elsewhere at cost; mail order
available GLASS HIRE Free with 1-case order TASTINGS AND TALKS In-store
tastings 4–6 times per year by invitation; weekly (Fri, Sat) for specific wines;
monthly tastings to Club; to groups on request CELLARAGE £1.95 per case per
year

This group of shops has been expanded by the opening of a branch in
Kidderminster (see also the separate entry for A L Vose). As the name
suggests, German wines have pride of place, but the Australian,
French, Chilean and Brazilian sections are all worth a look.

To Germany first. The Wine Schoppen is one of the few firms we
have found to stock the wines of the Ahr (the most northerly German
area, making light red wines) and Württemberg (another red wine
area). There's also a good range from Franconia (1983 Iphöfer Julius
Echterberg at £5.24) and plenty of top Prädikat wines from the
Rheinhessen, Mosel-Saar-Ruwer and Rheinpfalz. A major complaint is
that the list doesn't always contain an indication of producer – a vital
piece of information, especially for German wines.

France has some appealing vins de pays and Rhône wines (from

Laudun), which include the Gigondas Cuvée de Beauchamp at £7.14. Burgundy is from Mommessin, while Beaujolais sports some domaine wines. Elsewhere in Europe, there are the top quality Portuguese wines of J M da Fonseca (Periquita Reserva 1975 is £4.78) and Campo Viejo Rioja. And, much further afield, look for the Tisdall wines from Australia, Chilean wines from Cousiño Macul (Antiguas Reservas 1980 at £4.25 is a bargain for such quality), and the Palomas range of Brazilian varietal wines.

Best buys

Jumilla Condestable Tinto (Spain), £2.76; Calem Ports; Antiguas Reservas 1980, Cousiño Macul, £4.25; Dorn-Dürkheimer Hasensprung, Kabinett Riesling 1985, Arno Kreichgauer, £3.85

The Wine Shop

7 Sinclair Street, Thurso,   TEL (0847) 65657
Caithness KW14 7AJ

OPEN Tue–Sat 9.30–12.45, 2.30–5.30   CLOSED Sun, Mon, 2 days at Chr, 2 days at New Year   CREDIT CARDS Access, Visa; business accounts
DISCOUNTS Available   DELIVERY Free within 10-mile radius of Thurso; otherwise, within county of Caithness and Orkney, £1 per case
GLASS HIRE Free with ½-case order   TASTINGS AND TALKS Occasionally by invitation   CELLARAGE Not available

We continue to be impressed by the range of wines that Antony Collett has put together in this northernmost outpost of the Guide. His strengths are the regions of France and – especially – the whole of Italy. Inevitably, considering the location, prices are not the cheapest in the Guide.

In France, wines from Listel, the red Coteaux Varois Abbaye St-Hilaire at £3.55, the Côtes de Buzet 1985 at £4.96, or, in whites, the Roussillon Ch de Cap de Fouste at £4.11 would all be interesting choices.

The Bordeaux selection has a good fan of wines from the 1983, 1982 and 1981 vintages, especially the middle year, ranging from £5.53 for Ch du Castanet to £15.85 for Ch Brane-Cantenac. Burgundies take in some good estate names (Rion, Emile Voarick, Domaine Clerget) as well as co-operative wines from Buxy. Alsace wines from Muré, the Haut-Poitou varietal wines (Sauvignon 1986 at £4.24) and Lirac and Tavel from Maby are stars from other areas.

In the introduction to his list, Mr Collett has highlighted his German selection. We would agree but for the fact that we don't know who makes the wines, a strange omission on an otherwise carefully annotated list.

The producers return in the Italian section, which buzzes with Veneto wines from Tedeschi, Südtirol wines from Kupelwieser, Barolos from Borgogno and Livio Pavese, Chianti Classico from

Ripanera and Villa Cerna (look also for the Chianti Putto of Capezzana at £4.20). And on down south the names go: Frascati from Villa Catone, Lacryma Christi from Mastroberardino, d'Angelo's Aglianico del Vulture, Cirò from Calabria.

Highlights from the rest of the list are a good selection of Riojas and Sherries, Fonseca wines from Portugal, a number of Greek bottles, Concha y Toro from Chile, and Brown Brothers, Rosemount and Penfolds from Australia.

Best buys

Naoussa 1981, Tsantali (Greece), £4.05; Domaine de Torraccia 1981, Porto-Vecchio (Corsica), £3.20; Chianti Putto 1982, Uggiano, £3.50; Roussillon, Ch de Cap de Fouste red and white, £4.11

The Wine Society

REGISTERED OFFICE (mail order)	TEL (0438) 741177
Gunnels Wood Road, Stevenage,	(0438) 740222
Hertfordshire SG1 2BG	(24-hour answering service)
53 Bolsover Street, London W1P 7HL	TEL 01-387 4681

OPEN Mon–Fri 9–5 Sat 9–12 noon at Christmas for collections CREDIT CARDS Access, Visa DISCOUNTS £1.20 on 1 unmixed case DELIVERY Free in UK (min 1 case); otherwise £2.50 GLASS HIRE Free to members TASTINGS AND TALKS Tutored tastings held annually in Stevenage and all over the country; to groups on request CELLARAGE £3 per case per year (including insurance)

With every new issue of the list, members of The Wine Society (or the International Exhibition Cooperative Wine Society, to give it its full title) can always expect to find plenty of interest. The contents are helpfully arranged into red and white wines, with a central section of value-for-money, everyday drinking wines. The Society's own-label wines are often a good starting point in any area.

The list kicks off with fortified wines, and a very good range they are, too: dry amontillados from Valdespino and Rosario Benitez Girón, and old olorosos as well as some good manzanillas. Port-lovers will find plenty of ready-to-drink vintage Ports, and some superb 20-year-old tawnies. There's vintage Madeira, too – a pity the list doesn't tell us from whom.

In the red wines, we are immediately reminded of the Society's traditional strengths of claret and Burgundy. An enviable range of clarets goes back to 1978, and many good petit château wines can be had at attractive prices (Ch la Grange 1985, Blaye, £4.30; Ch Graves de Bitot 1982, Bourg, £4.40). Domaine Burgundies – both white as well as red – balance négociant bottlings (with Louis Latour and Remoissenet as featured négociants).

Other well-served French areas are the Rhône (with wines from Jaboulet Aîné), the Loire (look especially for sweet Quarts de Chaume and Bonnezeaux), Jura (Ch Chalon and Vin Jaune from Bourdy) and Alsace (wines from Hugel and Léon Beyer). The French regions also do well, with attractive vins de pays from the South and South-West.

Outside France, Italy and Germany score best. There are some very serious reds from Italy (Lungarotti, Antinori, Fontodi Chianti Classico), and some top-quality estate wines from Germany (Friedrich Wilhelm Gymnasium, Guntrum, Bürklin-Wolf). Spain presents some good Riojas from Remelluri and La Rioja Alta, while the New World selections are short, but of pretty high quality (Yarra Yering and Wirra Wirra in Australia; Saintsbury Pinot Noir and Trefethen in California).

If the choice proves too much, the Society has put together plenty of tasting cases; they also run a 'Wine without fuss' scheme through which members receive regular supplies of wine chosen for them by the Society.

Best buys

Mystic Park Red and White, Australia, £3.90 and £3.85; Concha y Toro Chilean Cabernet Sauvignon 1983, £3.65; Cabernet Vin de Pays de Thongue 1986, Domaine de la Condamine l'Evêque, £2.95; Marsanne, Vin de Pays de l'Hérault 1987, Domaine de la Gardie, £3.30

The Wine Spot 🐷

200 Stretford Road, Urmston,	TEL 061-748 2568
Manchester M31 1NA	
Wine Spot 2, 408A Manchester Road,	TEL 061-432 1646
Heaton Chapel, Stockport,	
Greater Manchester SK4 5BY	

OPEN Mon–Thur 10–10.30 pm   Fri–Sat 10–11 pm (Stockport 10.45 pm)   Sun, Chr Day, Good Friday 12–2, 7–10.30   CREDIT CARDS None accepted; personal and business accounts   DISCOUNTS 5% on unmixed cases   DELIVERY Free locally (min order negotiable); elsewhere at cost   GLASS HIRE Free with appropriate order   TASTINGS AND TALKS Occasional in-store tastings; occasionally to groups on request   CELLARAGE Not available

Plenty of good things are to be found in these two shops: for a start, a good range of petit château clarets at sensible prices (as are most of the prices from this merchant). In Burgundy, domaine wines from estates such as Pousse d'Or and Domaine Paquet mingle with bottles from Jacques Dépagneux and Ropiteau. Other French areas which do well are the South generally and the Midi in particular (look for Terres Blanches Coteaux des Baux en Provence and Ch de l'Ile Corbières). Champagnes come from a good number of grande marque houses.

The German listing of estate wines remains sound, as does the selection from Italy, which has a leaning towards Tuscany and Piedmont. In Spain, go for the Faustino Riojas if you want good value, although there are top flight wines from La Rioja Alta and CVNE as well (and also Torres wines). More Yugoslav wines can be found here then usual. In Australia, Peter Lehmann and Wolf Blass rub shoulders with Rouge Homme and Berri Estate/Renmano wines.

Best buys

Teroldego Rotaliano 1986, Ca' Donini, £3.15; Peter Lehmann Shiraz/Cabernet 1984, £3.99; Côtes du Rhône 1986, Cuvée du Maître du Chai, Vignerons de Rasteau, £3.29; Viña Santa Rita 1984, Chilean Cabernet Sauvignon, £8.29

Wine Warehouse (Stainforth)

See the Wine Schoppen.

Wines from Paris   🐷

The Vaults, 4 Giles Street, Leith,   TEL 031-554 2652
Edinburgh EH6 6DJ

OPEN Tue–Sat 10–6   Sun 11–6   CLOSED Mon (usually), Chr, New Year, Easter   CREDIT CARDS Access, Visa; personal and business accounts DISCOUNTS Available; £1 off per case collected   DELIVERY Free on mainland Scotland (min 1 case); otherwise £2 extra on mainland England and Wales; mail order available   GLASS HIRE Available   TASTINGS AND TALKS Tutored tastings approximately one a month; to groups on request   CELLARAGE Not available   ■

Forget the jokes about Paris in Scotland. This is a well-balanced range of wines, full of interest, which Judith Paris operates both by mail order and through her 12th-century warehouse vaults in Leith. (Plans are afoot for the development of part of the vaults, possibly as a wine bar.)

There's a good selection from most parts of France: from Bergerac the wines of Ch la Jaubertie, from the Rhône plenty from the Perrin family (La Vieille Ferme, Cru de Coudoulet Côtes du Rhône and Ch de Beaucastel Châteauneuf-du-Pape), from Alsace, the wines of André Ostertag. The Loire is weaker, but in Burgundy we find plenty of domaine wines (Monthélie-Douhairet, Domaine de la Pousse d'Or), while Beaujolais has wines from Pierre Ferraud. Champagne reflects a penchant for Pommery.

Other regions of particular interest include Italy, with good quality and value in most regions; Torres wines from Chile; Stratford wines from California; and a strong section of Australian wines, with some good boutique wineries represented (Yarra Yering, Forest Hill, Evans & Tate) as well as Taltarni and Orlando. There are a number of mixed case selections in case you can't make up your mind. Prices are good.

Best buys

Canterbury Sauvignon Blanc 1986, California, £2.99; Ch du Petit Thouars 1986, Touraine Cabernet Franc, £3.97; Pécharmant 1983,

Ch de Tiregand, £4.89; Quinta do Cotto 1982, Champalimaud, Douro, £4.39; Gutturnio del Colli Piacentini 1985, Fugazza, £3.99

Wines Galore

169 Greenwich High Road,	TEL 01-858 6014
London SE10 8JA	
White Hart Vaults, 64 South Street,	TEL (0392) 73894
Exeter, Devon EX1 1EE	

OPEN (Wines Galore) Mon–Fri 10–7   Sat 10–5; (White Hart Vaults) Mon 5–8
Tue–Thur 10–8   Fri, Sat 10–9   CLOSED Sun, public holidays
CREDIT CARDS All accepted; Davy's of London account card
DISCOUNTS Available on case lots   DELIVERY At cost   GLASS HIRE Free with
appropriate case order   TASTINGS AND TALKS Monthly/six-weekly tastings in
Greenwich; to groups on request   CELLARAGE Not available

Although this wine warehouse is part of the same group as Davys of London (*qv*), it operates from a different (though overlapping) list (Wines Galore bottles are often a few pennies cheaper).

While classic France is an important element of the list, there are more petit château wines than in the Davys version, Beaujolais from Loron, some estate Burgundies, Rhône wines from La Vieille Ferme, Sancerre from Masson-Blondelet. In other areas, look for Veneto wines of Guerrieri-Rizzardi and Barolo from Terre del Barolo, Riojas from Marqués de Murrieta, Brown Brothers Australian wines and Stoneleigh Vineyard wines from New Zealand. There are a few good Sherries (Manzanilla Pasada la Guita of Perez Marin at £5), and a fine wine list which includes Vintage Ports.

Best buys

Davy's Rioja 1984, £3.80; Champagne Veuve Clicquot NV, £12.95; Barbera del Monferrato 1986, Marchesi di Barolo, £3.60; Beaujolais Villages-Regnié 1986, Loron, £4.20

Wines of Argentina

See Pond Farm Wines.

Wines of Interest

46 Burlington Road, Ipswich,   TEL (0473) 215752
Suffolk IP1 2HS
ASSOCIATED OUTLET Burlington Wines,
at same address as above

OPEN Mon–Fri 9–5.45 Sat 9–1 CLOSED Sun, public holidays
CREDIT CARDS None accepted; business accounts DISCOUNTS 5% on
minimum of £200 order DELIVERY Free in City of London and central Ipswich
and elsewhere for 6+ cases; otherwise £1.50 per case in London postal districts,
elsewhere £1.95 per case with a minimum of £5 per delivery; mail order
available GLASS HIRE Free TASTINGS AND TALKS Wines always available
in-store; to groups on request CELLARAGE £1.50 per case per year

This merchant is the retail side of Burlington Wines (*qv*). The list may
be quite short, but there is enough of interest to keep them in the
Guide. In France, we find Alsace wines of Rolly-Gassmann, Pouilly
Fumé of J-C Dagueneau, a number of good value petit château clarets
and Champagne from Philippe Flaurent (NV Brut at £8.85).

From other countries, look for Campo Viejo Riojas, a number of
Bulgarian wines, Wyndham Estate from Australia and Cousiño Macul
Antiguas Reservas 1980 from Chile (£4.89). Fortified wines include
Messias, Ferreira and Santos and there are Sherries from Barbadillo

Best buys

Côtes de Gascogne Colombard 1987, £2.49; Ch Notton 1973, Margaux,
£5.95; Gran Colegiata 1985, Toro, £3.49; Ch Carras 1979, Côtes de
Méliton, Greece, £4.45

Wines of Westhorpe

Unit L-22, Park Avenue Estate,   TEL (0582) 598040
Sundon Park, Luton, Bedfordshire LU3 3AE

OPEN (Warehouse) Mon–Fri 8–5.45 CLOSED (Warehouse) Sat, Sun, public
holidays CREDIT CARDS None accepted; personal and business accounts (cash
with order) DISCOUNTS 10–24 cases £1.10 per case, 25–49 £1.30 per case, 50+
cases £1.70 per case DELIVERY Free on UK mainland (min 5 cases), Isle of Man
and Isle of Wight (min 10 cases) and Northern Ireland (min 6 cases); mail order
available GLASS HIRE Not available TASTINGS AND TALKS Occasionally
CELLARAGE Not available ■

This is the company to come to for Bulgarian and Hungarian wines:
Wines of Westhorpe single-mindedly concentrate on wines from these
two countries alone. They carry the full range of Bulgarian wines,
including the new country wines as well as the superior Reserve and
Controliran wines and the familiar Mehana brands.

In Hungary, we find a sensible range of the varietal offerings, many
from Vilány and Lake Balaton. Some of Hungary's greatest wine

offerings are here, the Tokays, from the basic Szamorodni Dry to the fabled Tokay Essencia at £36.68 a bottle.

Best buys

Plovdiv Bulgarian Cabernet Sauvignon 1983, £2.11; Asenovgrad Bulgarian Mavrud 1981, £2.69; Tokay Aszu 4 Puttonyos 1982, £4.10

Wizard Wine Warehouses 🐷

HEAD OFFICE 226 Purley Way, Croydon, Surrey CR0 4XG	TEL 01-686 5703
Unit 2, 226 Purley Way, Croydon, Surrey CR0 4XG	TEL 01-680 7826

8 other outlets in London, Surrey, Buckinghamshire, Dorset, Berkshire and Kent

OPEN Long hours, 7 days a week (may vary from branch to branch)
CREDIT CARDS Access, Visa, Wizard and Bejam Chargecard; business accounts   DISCOUNTS 5% for 10 unmixed cases   DELIVERY Free on UK mainland (min £100 order); otherwise at cost; mail order available
GLASS HIRE Free with reasonable order   TASTINGS AND TALKS Weekly tastings (Fri, Sat, Sun); to groups on request   CELLARAGE Not available

Having become part of the Bejam freezer foods group in the past year, this small group of wine warehouses has expanded from two branches in Croydon and Kingston to seven more in the south of England. A number of the branches are within Bejam stores.

Whether extra sophistication in the form of proper printing is a bad sign or not, there have been changes of emphasis in the range of wines, especially in the New World section, and prices have increased only slightly. Value is mostly good.

Coverage has shrunk in some of the classic French regions: fewer clarets and Burgundies are probably a reflection of the prices of many of these wines. Mind you, there are bargains to be had – Ch Thieuley red is £3.59 and white is £3.49, and in Burgundy, try the Bourgogne Pinot Noir 1983 of Cottin at £3.99.

Other parts of France fare better, with Beaujolais from Duboeuf, a range of Loire wines from Guy Saget and Rhône wines from La Vieille Ferme (Côtes du Ventoux 1985 at £2.79) and Guigal. House Champagne is Bauchet Père et Fils at £6.99, while Alsace wines are from Boeckel. Wizard have conjured up a good range of regional wines, especially Corbières and Minervois.

Italy also does well, with wines which include the Orvieto of Bigi (Vigneto Torricella at £3.99), the fresh Moscato d'Asti of Fontanafredda (£3.99) and, in reds, Chianti from Antinori, Rosso Cònero San Lorenzo, and the bargain Chianti of Rocca delle Macie (1986 vintage at £3.19). Prices here are very good.

While the rest of Europe is covered (including a full Bulgarian range), look to the New World for more interest. California weighs in with 40 bottles including the good-value Fetzer wines at £2.69 and a number of smaller wineries, also at good prices. Australia flaunts some big names – Hardy's, Tyrrell's, Orlando, Rosemount, Wynns – at the usual good-value Australian prices. Other bargains come from Chile and Argentina.

Best buys

Coteaux de Quercy, Vigouroux, £2.29; Chianti Classico 1986, Rocca delle Macie, £3.19; Lugana 1986, Santi, £3.29; Bulgarian wines; Periquita 1983, J M da Fonseca, £2.89; Fetzer Premium white and red California, £2.69

Woodleys Wine Stores

See Morris's Wine Stores.

W R Wines

See Morris's Wine Stores.

Peter Wylie Fine Wines

Plymtree Manor, Plymtree, Cullompton, Devon EX15 2LE   TEL (088 47) 555

OPEN Mon–Fri 9–6   CLOSED Sat, Sun, public holidays   CREDIT CARDS None accepted; business accounts   DISCOUNTS Available on unmixed cases DELIVERY Free in central London (min 3 cases); otherwise 1–2 cases £5.75 in London; on UK mainland 1 case £6.90, 2–4 cases £4.60; mail order available GLASS HIRE Not available   TASTINGS AND TALKS Monthly by invitation CELLARAGE £4 per case per year (insurance extra)

This is one of those lists that wine lovers can have a good drool over, because it contains a roll-call of some of the finest wines ever made. There are great clarets back to pre-phylloxera times, and in some depth from about 1900 onwards. Sauternes and Barsac start a little later – 1927 – while Burgundy begins after the War with a 1948 Grands-Echézeaux from Domaine de la Romanée-Conti, and estate and négociant wines from that point onwards. There's vintage Champagne (old vintages of Krug to the fore) and Vintage Ports, starting with the mysterious 'unknown shipper 1896' and taking us to modern times with the 1983 vintage. Obviously quantities of many of the wines on the list are small so it changes frequently.

Best buys

Rare and old wines

Most wine merchants will supply wine for parties on a sale or return basis.

Yapp Brothers

The Old Brewery, Water Street, Mere,   TEL (0747) 860423
Wiltshire BA12 6DY

OPEN Mon–Fri 9–5   Sat 9–1   CLOSED Sun, public holidays
CREDIT CARDS Access, Visa; personal and business accounts   DISCOUNTS On
orders of 5+ cases   DELIVERY Free on UK mainland (min 2 cases); mail order
available   GLASS HIRE Free with 1+ case order   TASTINGS AND TALKS Very
occasional in-store tastings; tastings/dinners organised around the country each
year; to groups on request   CELLARAGE £2.50 per case per year or part-year

'Loire, Rhône, Yapp', says the advertisement for this merchant. And
that sums it up pretty well – with three additions: Alsace (from Charles
Schléret), Champagne (from Jacquesson) and Provence.

Robin Yapp's translation from dentist to wine merchant
extraordinaire is described in his memoirs (*Drilling for wine* – see under
WINE BOOKSHELF for details): it chronicles the way he lighted upon
these French areas in what seems an almost haphazard fashion.
Having taken the plunge, though, he has been serious and thorough
about it, and come up with what were once unknown producers who
are now revered as among the best in their regions.

In the Rhône, for instance, Yapp imports wines from Chave in
Hermitage, Robert Jasmin in Côte Rôtie and Auguste Clape in Cornas,
and Ch Grillet. On the Loire, we find Paul Filliatreau in Saumur, Jean
Berger in Montlouis and Jean Vatan in Sancerre, while Provence offers
us Coteaux des Baux of Domaine de Trévallon, Ch Simone, and the
Bandol of Bunan. Heady stuff, all of it.

What is equally appealing about this list is that it's not just the top
(and most expensive) wines that get here. There are wines from
co-operatives and from small producers in out-of-the-way appellations
(Brézème, for instance, in an area of the Rhône valley that was not
supposed to have any vines at all). So on the same page as Jean-Louis
Grippat's St-Joseph, you will also find the varietal wines from the
Ardèche co-operative, and the Vignerons de Saumur can be found
alongside the Saumur Champigny of M Filliatreau.

Best buys

Sancerre, Clos les Perriers 1987, £6.25; Lirac Rouge 1985, La Fermade,
Armand Maby, £4.55; Vin de Thouarsais 1986, Blanc Sec, Michel
Gigon, £3.75; Coteaux des Baux en Provence 1986, Domaine de
Trévallon, £7.50

Prices were correct to the best of our knowledge as we went to press. They,
and ranges of wines stocked, are likely to change during the course of 1989,
and are intended only as a rough indication of an establishment's range
and prices.

Yorkshire Fine Wine Company

Sweethills, Nun Monkton, York,   TEL (0423) 330131
North Yorkshire YO5 8ET

OPEN Mon–Fri 8.30–5.30   Good Friday 8.30–5.30   CLOSED Sun, public
holidays   CREDIT CARDS All accepted; personal and business accounts
DISCOUNTS 4% for 7-day settlement   DELIVERY Free within area of Scottish
Borders to the north and Midlands to the south (min 1 case); elsewhere 1 case £8,
2 cases £6 per case, 3 cases £5 per case, 4 cases £4 per case, over 4 cases free; mail
order available   GLASS HIRE Free   TASTINGS AND TALKS Various tastings
held on request   CELLARAGE £5 per case per year   ■

While this serious range of wines, full of great names, is certainly
strongest in the French classic areas, a good hard look at the New
World has also been taken. Prices are by no means inexpensive, but
there is a free delivery service covering a large area in the north of
England by way of some compensation.

Champagne is there a-plenty, from many of the major grande marque
houses, and with a nice line in large bottles (this is one of the few wine
merchants with a Nebuchadnezzar – 20 bottles – if you are strong enough
to carry one off). Burgundy is extensively covered, with a good mix of
domaine and négociant wines (from Mommessin, Louis Latour and
Faiveley). There are some older reds, and a very good set of top whites.

In Bordeaux, the story is much the same. Here, the range goes from
some decent petit château wines such as Ch Bel Air Fonroque 1985 at
£4.40 (prices on the list do not include VAT, but we have added it here)
or Prince de la Rivière 1982, the second wine of Ch la Rivière in Fronsac
(£6.17). Ch Cissac features quite heavily, with vintages back to 1970.

While the rest of France is treated more briefly, look for the Sancerre
of Domaine Gueneau at £6.31 or the Hugel and Dopff au Moulin Alsace
wines. Moving across the Rhine from Alsace, some good German
estate wines, particularly on the Mosel, are worth perusing (look also
for the Baden wines).

The Italian listing is still rather short, although we have admired the
Montepulciano d'Abruzzo Invecchiato of Illuminati (£6.46). Spain
offers a few good Riojas, while Portugal has a star Vinho Verde, the
Alvarinho of Palacio da Brejoeira at £11.12 (yes, it's the most expensive
wine in Portugal as well). Vintage Ports also present a good
front.   Then we move to the New World, with Australia showing
best. There are wines from Moss Wood in the west, and other smaller
wineries such as Redgate, Wright's and Cape Mentelle. From New
Zealand, look for the Stoneleigh Vineyard wines as well as Cloudy
Bay and Matua Valley.

Best buys

Mâcon-Clessé 1985, Jean Thévenet, £7.43; Beaujolais Villages 1986,
Trenel, £4.57; Sancerre 1987 La Guiberte, Domaine Gueneau, £5.72;
Champagne Camuset Brut, £10.49

Wine at auction

World record-breaking prices are the only time wine auctions make the news. Not so long ago, an American paid £105,000 for a bottle of 1787 Ch Lafite which was promptly ruined when the bottle went on display under hot lights, the cork shrank and fell into the bottle – making the contents undrinkable. And, this year, headlines were again made by Ch Lafite when a double magnum of the 1832 vintage was sold for £24,000.

But those are rare examples. Most of the time, the lots sold in wine auctions cover a wide spectrum of styles and prices. The auction houses form a useful alternative way of buying fine wine to going to a specialist wine merchant. They are often the only places where mature wines regularly appear for sale. And since any wine merchant who lists older wines will probably have bought them at auction, you are likely to pay less at auction for a particular wine than you would at a merchant.

Britain is one of the world's principal centres for wine auctions. The two major houses – Christie's and Sotheby's – hold sales regularly in their main rooms in central London, which concentrate on the finest wines, with a strong emphasis on claret and Port. They also have separate auction rooms – Christie's at South Kensington in West London and now in the City, and Sotheby's at Billingshurst in Sussex, where wider ranges of less expensive wines are auctioned.

One other London-based firm, International Wine Auctions, holds quarterly sales, again mainly of top clarets. Auctions are also held by country auctioneers on a less regular basis.

Details of all these auction houses are given at the end of this section.

Sticking up your hand

Most people have been to a country auction – or even one in the West End of London – and have bid for something that took their fancy, even if it was only a brass bedhead or a small kitchen table. Bidding for wine is basically no different, except in one thing: you can't always inspect the lots beforehand. There are exceptions even to this: there may be a pre-sale tasting of many of the wines to be auctioned, but not every lot will be available for tasting. However, a knowledge of vintages, and some memory for names, is really all that's necessary to get by, which is where our WHAT TO BUY section can help.

What to buy in 1989

We go to press at the end of the 1987/88 auction season. Looking at the most recent auctions, it seems that prices for fine claret are almost stable compared to a year ago. The vintages which have produced the greatest increases in price have been those from the 1970s, while more recent vintages (1982 and 1983 especially) have shown a slow downward spiral. Neither of these two vintages has regained the prices it reached at auction when it first went under the hammer.

The advice from auctioneers is that the best bargains in claret (and these are the wines which are most often seen at auction) at the moment are from what are called 'off' vintages – and from the most recent vintages. 'Off' vintages are those, such as 1981 and 1979, which don't receive the continuing rave notices of vintages such as 1978. The 1982 and 1983 wines were simply too highly priced when they appeared in auctions for the first time, and are now fetching a more realistic price.

Of course, the top classed growths of Bordeaux are never cheap. Much better value is to be found in the realm of the crus bourgeois or the lower categories of classed growth. Forget about Pomerol wines, but look for St-Emilion. And if you want older wines, go for clarets that were not bottled at the château (English bottlings or Belgian bottlings, for example): they often taste just as good as the château-bottled wines, but are simply not fashionable.

Red Burgundy is a much rarer visitor to the sale rooms. The estate that seems to be providing the most interest is the Domaine de la Romanée Conti, but prices for these wines are normally stratospheric, and not worth it. If you see Burgundy from 1978 or 1983 vintages (and the possible appearance of a 1985), it would be worth pursuing (as long as the producer's name is reputable).

The other two French wine areas which provide auction lots are vintage Champagne (almost always from grande marque houses) and sweet white Bordeaux. With Champagne, avoid the magic circle of Krug, Dom Pérignon and Roederer Cristal, and you might find a bargain, especially from the early 1970s. With sweet white Bordeaux, avoid Ch d'Yquem, but other Sauternes and Barsac are often undervalued.

Vintage Port seems to be the bargain of the moment. Prices fell over the last year, and showed no sign of bottoming out. Look especially for vintages of the 1970s – 1975 (for drinking now), 1970 and 1977 (for keeping). 1980 vintage is a bargain, 1983 and 1985 are only just appearing in the auction catalogues. Port from Portuguese-named houses will be cheaper than wine from British-named houses (but will also be less long-lasting).

Preparing for the sale

Sale dates *Decanter* magazine gives dates and times of forthcoming sales, and both Christie's and Sotheby's advertise their sales in the national press. You can also put yourself on an auction house's mailing list, which, for a fee, will provide you with pre-sale catalogues, and possibly perks, such as access to the pre-sale tastings. Catalogues are normally sent out three weeks before a sale. If you are not a subscriber, you can buy catalogues individually, by post, or call in to collect one.

Bidding by post Postal bidding forms arrive with the catalogue: most auction houses provide a free postal bidding service. You merely need to indicate the maximum you are prepared to pay for a particular lot. The auctioneer will secure the lot for you at a lower price if possible. The estimates in the catalogue will be based on prices fetched for the same or a similar wine at recent auctions, and on the reserve price the vendor has placed on his wine, so it's rare to find a successful bid going below the minimum of the estimate.

Pre-sale tastings These are normally held the day before the auction (the catalogue will tell you when and where). Don't expect to taste 1905 Ch Mouton-Rothschild if it happens to be in the sale, but most wines tend to be available for tasting. If you have a particular wine in mind, telephone in advance to see if the wine will be available for tasting, or ask advice. Arrive early and remember that catalogue subscribers are allowed in first.

What's in the catalogue

The estimated price against a wine is only the beginning of what you will have to pay at auction. It pays to read the small print at the front of the catalogue carefully, but here are some pointers.

Duty paid Wines marked 'duty paid' (normally in the second section of the auction) will have been cleared by Customs and Excise, so the estimated price will include duty. Foreign buyers prefer to buy wines 'in bond' (see below) so you will more likely be bidding against British buyers in this section of the sale.

In bond No excise duty has yet been paid. When you have secured the lot, the auctioneers will sort out the Customs paperwork for a small fee. Whatever the price of the wine, you pay a flat rate per bottle.

Duty paid available in bond For British buyers, duty is already paid. For foreign buyers, duty will be subtracted after the auction.

VAT The estimates do not include VAT. VAT is charged only if the wine is being sold by a merchant registered for VAT. Wines being sold by private individuals do not attract VAT. Remember, VAT is payable as a percentage of the final price – and not, as with duty, as a flat rate: so higher-priced bottles attract more VAT than cheaper ones.

FOB Free on Board is the term used to describe wine that is being sold while still overseas. You will have to pay a proportion of the shipping costs, plus duty, VAT and customs clearance charges, which can be arranged by the auction house.

Ex cellar This means that the wine is still in the cellar of the estate where it was made. It's a guarantee that the wine will have been kept in the best possible conditions.

How to bid

You are bidding for a numbered lot. The lot can either consist of one wine (generally in one case or multiples of cases) or what is called a mixed lot – a ragbag of wines which have been lumped together because they are odd bottles. If you want only one particular wine in a mixed lot you will have to buy everything else as well. Occasionally special bottles will be auctioned separately.

Bid steps The catalogue sets out in the front the steps in which bidding is conducted. These vary according to the price reached – lower prices in the bidding will rise by small steps, higher prices by larger steps, for example, by single pounds up to £30, say, then by £2 a time up to £100, £5 a time up to £200 and so on.

Bidding Back to the country auction and the kitchen table. Just raise your hand when you want to make a bid, and preferably wave your catalogue. The auctioneers have eagle eyes, and once your first bid is noted, they'll keep an eye on you until that lot is sold. Once the hammer has fallen, the wine is legally yours. If you make a mistake, such as bidding for the wrong lot, tell the staff at once, before the end of the sale, and it will normally be re-auctioned.

Options The buyer of the first lot may be offered the option to buy the remaining lots of the same wine at the same price. This practice will be announced at the beginning of the sale, and is designed to help trade customers who need to buy large quantities of one particular wine. So if you really want a wine, make sure you bid for the first lot.

Paying for the wine

Once the hammer has fallen, the auction house staff will take your name and address. Invoices are posted after the sale, and you will then be told where the wine can be collected from. If it is actually on the sale room premises, you can pay for it and take it away – but that's less common because it is normal practice not to move the wine too much. Delivery can usually be arranged.

You may have to pay the buyer's premium (see the details for each auction house), normally 10 per cent of the sale price. You will also have to pay VAT on the premium. Vendors have to pay a commission to the auction house, at a percentage depending on the wine and the volume involved.

If the wine is faulty, tell the auction house. They are not responsible since they are acting as middlemen between you and the vendor, but they will normally help in negotiations.

London auction houses

Christie's

8 King Street, London SW1Y 6QT   TEL 01-839 9060
85 Old Brompton Road, London SW7 3LD   TEL 01-581 2231
50–60 Gresham Street, London EC2V 7BB   TEL 01-588 4424
164–166 Bath Street, Glasgow G2 4TB   TEL 041-332 8134

Christie's run the largest number of auctions. The King Street auctions are of finer wines; Old Brompton Road sells everyday wine as well as finer wines and bin-ends; and the City branch tends to deal in Port, Burgundy and claret. Catalogue subscriptions cost £24 per year (King Street) or £15 (the other two rooms). Pre-sale tastings take place between 11 am and noon the day before the sale at King Street and on the day of the sale at Old Brompton Road and in the City. Advice on the market in general and on whether to sell in particular is available. Delivery from the South Kensington branch to elsewhere in the UK is charged at £4 plus VAT per case or part case, and insurance is the responsibility of the purchaser. Insurance is included in the price and delivery is free from the other two addresses if the wine is paid for within 21 days. There is a 10 per cent buyer's premium. Two sales a year are held in Glasgow and Edinburgh.

Sotheby's

34–35 New Bond Street, London W1A 2AA   TEL 01-493 8080
Summers Place, Billingshurst, West Sussex RH14 9AD
TEL (040 381) 3933

Sotheby's hold fewer auctions than Christie's. The auctions in London correspond to the auctions at Christie's King Street rooms, with fine wines dominating. A wider range is sold in Sussex. Sotheby's have set up a computer-linked bidding service. Subscription to the catalogues is £31 (London) and £12 (Sussex). Delivery is free, including insurance, within the UK. There is a 10 per cent buyer's premium. (Wines are also very occasionally sold at the Glasgow and Chester auction rooms.)

International Wine Auctions
PO Box 760, London SE1 9BD   TEL 01-403 1140

This auction house attracts the top end of the wine market, and is aimed very much at the international wine-buying connoisseur. They hold six auctions a year. Catalogues are £5, and there is no buyer's premium. Delivery is free during working hours. Insurance is the responsibility of the purchaser after 5.30 pm on the day of the sale.

Country auctioneers

While all the country auctioneers deal principally in goods other than wine, those below do hold a few wine auctions a year. Since international buyers tend not to come to these auctions, you can often find amazing bargains, but prices can also go sky-high for no apparent reason.

Bigwood Auctioneers Ltd
The Old School, Tiddington, Stratford-upon-Avon, Warwickshire CV37 7AW   TEL (0789) 69415

Sales take place on Thursday evening, quarterly. There is a pre-sale tasting that afternoon. Subscription to the mailing list is £10. There is a buyer's premium of five per cent (plus VAT), and the vendor's commission is negotiable. Wines must generally be collected, although delivery can be arranged.

Lacy Scott
10 Risbygate Street, Bury St Edmunds, Suffolk IP33 3AA
TEL (0284) 763531

One sale a year. Subscription to the catalogue is free; wines must be collected. There is no buyer's premium, but vendors pay a 12½ per cent commission. Insurance is the responsibility of the buyer.

Lithgow, Sons & Partners
The Auction House, Station Road, Stokesley, Middlesbrough, Cleveland   TEL (0642) 710158

Two sales a year in December and June. Sales are advertised locally and sometimes in *Decanter* and the *Daily Telegraph*, but you can be put on their list to be sent catalogues (30p each). Wines must be collected. Vendors pay a commission, but there is no buyer's premium. Insurance is the responsibility of the buyer.

Phillips, Son & Neil
39 Park End Street, Oxford OX1 1JD   TEL (0865) 723524

The largest of the country auctioneers. There are four sales a year, held on Tuesdays, with a pre-sale tasting on the day of the sale. You can subscribe to the mailing list for £9 per year. There is a 10 per cent buyer's premium, and a vendor's commission. Wines must be collected from the saleroom within two weeks of the sale. Insurance is the responsibility of the buyer.

Buying wine en primeur

There has been one word of advice from most wine merchants this year to anyone considering buying wine en primeur: don't.

What has happened to a market that was booming earlier in the 1980s? There are two reasons: quality and price. But first some explanation about what buying a wine en primeur means.

The system worked like this. Every spring, wine merchants would go to Bordeaux to assess (as well as possible with wine that might still be going through its second, malolactic, fermentation and which anyway tasted of little more than tannin) the quality of the wine from the previous harvest. At the same time, the major châteaux announced the selling price on the first amount (or *tranche*) of wine they intended to release. Negotiations between the merchants (merchants from other countries besides Britain were there doing the same thing, of course), the châteaux and the middlemen (the Bordeaux négociants) followed to agree on how much wine the overseas merchant could have – and at what price.

Back in Britain, the wine merchants prepared reports on the quality of the wine they had tasted and sent out to their customers brochures offering wines from the châteaux they had selected. The offer was normally based on a first-come-first-served basis, because the amount of wine was limited. The price did not include VAT or duty: this was payable when the wine arrived in the country two – or even more – years later.

This year is different

But this year, everything has changed. No doubt wine merchants have gone to Bordeaux, but they've gone as much to see what wines from older vintages they can pick up as to buy the 1987 vintage.

This latest vintage suffered from a bad press from the moment the grapes were picked. It was written off as having produced pale, thin wines. In the end, it turned out to be a mixed bag: some parts of the Bordeaux vineyard did reasonably well, others did badly (see the section on Bordeaux in the WHAT TO BUY section for more information on the vintage). But everybody agrees that 1987 was not a great year.

There then followed the usual discussions about the price of the wines, with everybody expecting the Bordelais to be reluctant to drop their prices. It was the first growths of the Médoc who led the way with cuts of as much as 30 per cent. But still nobody came to buy.

The reason is that there is still plenty of wine from 1986, 1985 and even older vintages sloshing around in cellars. Those wines, it is felt, are of better quality than the 1987s, and their prices are getting better, too, especially with the lack of interest from the American market.

What this has shown is that buying en primeur is a risky business. Those who bought claret for investment may find that it hasn't brought the return they were hoping for. Of course, those who bought it to drink needn't worry so much: the wine is theirs and they can afford to wait to enjoy it. They can also buy a little more at good prices.

It is generally felt among wine merchants that it would be a good thing to let the wine that is already for sale in Bordeaux move out into the wider world before en primeur offers begin again. The concept of en primeur buying was right for the great vintages of the mid-1980s – and even made sense as late as 1986. There is no reason why those conditions can't recur. It may even happen with the 1988 vintage.

Outside Bordeaux

Beyond the heady confines of Bordeaux, the idea of en primeur buying has spread, although in a different form. In Burgundy, for instance, they prefer to wait for a couple of years before putting wine on the market, so early 1987 saw offers of reds from the 1985 vintage. In the Rhône, similar offers were made for the 1986 vintage at the same time. There is talk (but only talk) of selling top Italian reds en primeur.

The only other form of en primeur selling takes place with Port. 1987 saw the release of the 1985 vintage, and at the time of writing it looks unlikely that either the 1986 or 1987 vintages will be declared as a general vintage year. Port shippers tend to wait until they are ready to bottle their vintage Port before declaring a vintage.

Few merchants made an offer of 1987 Bordeaux: Corney & Barrow, Hungerford, Raeburn, Tanners and the Wine Society.

Part II

What to buy

Which? Wine Guide
Best Buys for 1989

White sparkling wines

Seaview Brut, Australia (*Majestic; Oddbins*)
Crémant d'Alsace, Dopff et Irion Cuvée Extra (*Eldridge Pope*)
St Michael Sparkling White Burgundy (*Marks & Spencer*)
Saumur, Gratien et Meyer (*Peter Dominic; Wine Society; Wizard Wine Warehouses*)
Blanc Foussy de Touraine (*Victoria Wine Company*)
Dominique Charnay Blanc de Blancs, Burgundy (*Bibendum*)
Sainsbury's Spanish Cava (*J Sainsbury*)
Raimat Chardonnay (*Victoria Wine Company; La Reserva Wines*)

Grapey sweet sparkling white wines

St Michael Asti Spumante (*Marks & Spencer*)
Asti Spumante Sandro (*Waitrose*)

Champagnes

De Telmont NV Champagne (*Majestic*)
Pierre Vaudon Blanc de Noirs NV Champagne (*Haynes, Hanson & Clark*)
Sainsbury's 1982 Vintage (*J Sainsbury*)
Heidsieck Dry Monopole 1982 (*Oddbins; Willoughby's*)

Pink sparkling wines

Crémant de Bourgogne Rosé, Caves de Bailly (*Majestic; Waitrose*)

Pink Champagne

Asda Champagne Rosé Brut (*Asda*)
Alfred Gratien Rosé Brut (*Arthur Rackhams*)

Bone dry white wines

Sauvignon de Haut-Poitou (*Richard Harvey Wines; Lay & Wheeler; Majestic; Morris & Verdin; Nobody Inn; Willoughby's*)
Sauvignon Blanc 1987, Erraruriz Panquehue, Chile (*Thresher*)
Ch Thieuley 1987, Bordeaux Blanc (*Rose Tree Wine Co*)
Sauvignon de Touraine 1987, Vignerons de Oisly-et-Thésée (*Anthony Byrne Fine Wines; Cachet Wines*)
Muscadet de Sèvre-et-Maine sur lie, Domaine de la Chauvinière 1986 (*Oddbins*)
Vinho Verde Solar das Boucas (*La Réserve*)

Fruity (but dry) white wines

Coromandel Rhine Riesling 1987, Australia (*Majestic*)
Tokay Pinot Gris d'Alsace 1986, Cave Co-opérative de Turckheim (*Barnes Wine Shop; Ilkley Wine Cellars*)
Sainsbury's Alsace Gewürztraminer 1985 (*J Sainsbury*)
Vin de Pays des Côtes de Gascogne 1987, Grassa (*Tesco; Waitrose and others*)

Full white wines

Chardonnay Khan Krum Reserve 1984, Bulgaria (*Direct Wine Shipments; Majestic; Oddbins; Victoria Wine Company; Wines of Westhorpe*)
St Michael Barossa Valley Semillon 1986 (*Marks & Spencer*)
Asda White Burgundy, Alain Combard (*Asda*)
Côtes du Lubéron, La Vieille Ferme (*widely available*)
Tesco Bianco di Custoza (*Tesco*)
Soave Zenato 1987 (*Davisons; Arthur Rackhams*)
Vernaccia di San Gimignano 1987, San Quirico (*J Sainsbury; Wine Emporium*)

White wines with some wood flavours

Cuvée Vincent Jeunes Vignes, Vin de Table de France (*Thos Peatling*)
Chardonnay di Miraduolo 1987, Lungarotti (*Great Northern Wine Company*)
Rioja Blanco 1981, Tondonia (*Bottle and Basket; Majestic*)
Torres Gran Viña Sol 1987 (*widely available*)
California Chardonnay 1986 Mountain View (*Waitrose*)
Montana New Zealand Chardonnay 1987 (*Master Cellar Wine Warehouse; Oddbins*)

Medium white wines with fragrant fruit

Moorlynch 1986 Medium, England (*Waitrose*)
Saarburger Antoniusbrunnen Riesling Kabinett 1985, R Müller (*Tanners Wines*)
Serriger Scharzberg Kabinett 1982, Bert Simon (*Mayor Sworder*)
Freinsheimer Goldberg Riesling Kabinett 1985, Lingenfelder (*Oddbins*)

Sweet white wines

Loupiac 1986, Domaine de Noble (*Bibendum*)
Premières Côtes de Bordeaux 1985, Ch de Berbec (*Waitrose*)
Jurançon Moelleux, Clos Guirouilh (*James Aitken & Son*)

Light dry red wines

Coteaux du Lyonnais Rouge, Sarrau (*Snipe Wine Cellars*)
Beaujolais Villages 1987, Jean-Charles Pivot (*Roger Harris*)
Bourgogne Passetoutgrains 1986, Henri Jayer (*Hampden Wine Company; Raeburn Fine Wines and Foods*)
Bourgogne Pinot Noir 1985, Cave Co-opérative de Buxy (*Waitrose*)
Coteaux du Giennois Pinot Noir 1986 (*Waitrose*)
Valpolicella Classico Superiore 1985, Guerrieri-Rizzardi (*widely available*)

Medium weight red wines

Plovdiv Cabernet Sauvignon, Bulgaria (*Majestic; Oddbins*)
Côtes de Provence, Domaine de St-Baillon 1985 (*Bibendum; Green's*)
Viña Linderos Cabernet Sauvignon 1983, Chile (*Richard Granger*)
Ch Méaume 1985, Bordeaux Supérieur (*Majestic*)
Ch Trinité Valrose 1985, Bordeaux Supérieur (*Anthony Byrne Fine Wines; Hadleigh Wine Cellars; Justerini & Brooks*)
Beau Rivage 1983, Borie-Manoux, Bordeaux (*Davisons*)
Ch de Bosquet 1986, Côtes de Bourg (*J Sainsbury*)
Minervois 1986, Domaine Ste-Eulalie (*Davisons*)
Vin de Pays des Sables du Golfe du Lion 1985, Domaine du Bosquet (*Chaplin & Sons; Hungerford Wine Co; Unwins*)
Vin de Pays des Coteaux du Quercy 1986, Domaine de Lafage (*The Market/Winecellars*)
Chianti Rufina Banda Blue 1986, Grati (*Green's; The Market/Winecellars*)
Chianti Classico 1986, Rocca delle Macie (*widely available*)

Full-bodied red wines

Orlando RF Shiraz, Australia 1983 (*Oddbins*)
St Michael South Australian Shiraz/Cabernet Sauvignon 1986 (*Marks & Spencer*)
Domaine des Baumelles, Ch Val Joanis (*Tesco*)
Côtes du Ventoux, La Vieille Ferme (*widely available*)
Syrah Vin de Pays des Coteaux de l'Ardèche, Vignerons Ardéchois (*Chesterford Vintners; Desborough & Brown*)

BEST BUYS FOR 1989

Crozes-Hermitage 1985, Tardy et Ange (*widely available*)
Spanna del Piemonte 1984, Agostino Brugo (*Seckford Wines; Welbeck Wines; Wine Growers' Association*)
Barbera d'Asti 1985, Ronco (*The Market/Winecellars*)
Bonarda Oltrepò Pavese 1985, Fugazza (*The Market/Winecellars; Valvona & Crolla*)
Torre Quarto Rosso 1981 (*Bin 89 Wine Warehouse*)
Tinto da Anfora, João Pires (*Queens Club Wines; Waitrose*)
Reguengos de Monsaraz 1985 (*Barrel Selection*)
Garrafeira 1974, Caves Velhas (*G E Bromley & Sons*)
Rioja Reserva 1983, Faustino V (*A&A Wines; Findlater Mackie Todd*)
Valdepeñas Gran Reserva 1978, Señorio de los Llanos (*widely available*)
Toro Gran Colegiata 1982, Bodegas Farina (*widely available*)
California Zinfandel 1983, Wente Brothers (*Moffat Wine shop*)

For **fortified wine best buys**, see the sections on Port, Madeira, Spanish fortifieds (Sherry, Málaga, Montilla) and Sicily (Marsala).

Argentina

There's still only one importer of Argentine wines to this country, but he was promising a big shipment of wine during the summer of 1988, with more to follow. So maybe we are about to renew our acquaintance with the wines from the fifth largest producer in the world.

Most of the wine produced in Argentina is of the immediately enjoyable, quaffing sort. Not much seems to be exported but there is an attractive range of wines from Peñaflor (see below).

The Italian influence is strong, with Nebbiolo, Barbera and Sangiovese grapes all adding sophistication to wines made generally from Malbec and Criolla (reds) and Palomino and Torrontes (whites). But noble French varieties – Chardonnay, Sylvaner (called Riesling), Chenin Blanc (called Pinot Blanc) and lesser varieties like Ugni Blanc – are now being added to the whites. Cabernet Sauvignon, Merlot, Syrah and Pinot Noir are also putting in an appearance.

Who's who in Argentina

Peñaflor The largest producer in Argentina. Wines are sold under the Andean brand name.
B H Wines; Continental Wine House; Grape Ideas; Wizard Wine Warehouses

Specialist stockists
Grape Ideas Wine Warehouse; Pond Farm Wines

285

Australia

On 26 January, 1988, while the Aussies were staging their 200th
birthday firework displays in Sydney Harbour, Lord's cricket ground
back in the mother country was the scene for the annual wine trade
tasting of what Australia had to offer.

It was quite a scene. Anybody who was anybody in the wine trade –
and many more besides – were crammed into the tasting room. There
were hundreds of Australian wines to taste – more than even the most
enthusiastic palate could cope with – and they were all good.

At one point, we overheard one wine trade veteran say to another:
'When was the last French tasting you went to where every wine was
worth recommending?' The answer was swift and simple: 'Never.' The
same could probably be said of any European country. And yet here is
this parvenu of a wine country – whose wine industry dates exactly
from the arrival of the First Fleet in 1788 – showing the Europeans how
to make wine of excellent quality and – equally important – very good
value.

Figures tell the tale. In March 1987, Australia sent us nearly two
million litres of wine. In March 1988, the figure was nearer five million
litres . . . and we're still crying out for more. Every time a retailer starts
selling a good value Aussie wine, the 'out of stock' signs go up pretty
quickly. It's not because they didn't buy enough – it's very often
because they bought all they could.

Running out of wine

Wine stocks are beginning to dry up down under. When the current export drive started, the locals, while manfully downing over 20 litres a head each year (compared with our wimpish 10 litres a head), were still leaving a lake of good-quality wine without a home. So, with a weak Australian dollar to help, exports were the thing.

But foreign customers became very enthusiastic – too enthusiastic. They drank more than anticipated. Not just us – the Swedes are the biggest export market for Australian wine and even the French are buying some. So the lake began to dry up, and then in 1987 and 1988 came two small harvests, which slowed down the supply even more.

The inevitable result has been some price increases. But the Australians have learned from what happened when the same thing occurred with California wines a few years ago – the exports just dried up. So they are being as careful as they can. The big companies can afford to peg their prices for a year in the hope that the 1989 harvest (don't forget the Australian harvest is at the beginning of the year) will bring in a bumper crop.

They are also busily planting new vineyards to cope with the increased demand. It takes time for a vineyard to become fully productive (three years before the first crop and five or six years before full production), so there will inevitably be a time lag. But, now they've got the export bug, the Australians aren't going to let the opportunity slip away.

The EEC spanner in the works

Mind you, the EEC is making it as difficult as possible for Australia . . .

The scene is an idyllic vineyard in the Barossa Valley, South Australia. By the lake, glasses of sparkling wine are being consumed. It is a Pinot Noir/Chardonnay blend (the classic Champagne blend) made in the same way as Champagne. In Australia, the label gives the method of production, and indicates the fact it is from a single year (1985). 'But we can't use that label for export to Europe', we are told. 'We have to drop any indication that the wine is bottle-fermented (the *méthode champenoise*) and we can't even put the vintage on.' 'Why not?' we exclaim, taking another cooling slurp of one of the top Australian sparklers. 'Because,' comes the answer, 'that would imply it's a quality product, and the EEC doesn't accept that any Australian sparkling wine can be a quality product.' Who are these bureaucrats in Brussels to tell us what is or is not a quality product? Our own tastebuds are, we think, the best judge of that.

The same goes for fortified wines. The EEC rules suggest that they should all be described as Vins de Liqueur, but, as we all know, a liqueur is something sticky that comes in small glasses at the end of a meal, not a passable copy of a Portuguese tawny Port, and certainly not some of the great Muscats and Muscadelles for which Australia is famous.

If the Australians get round these labelling problems – negotiations were underway in the middle of 1988 – no doubt Brussels, probably egged on by the French, will come up with some more objections.

Why are they so good?

What makes Australian wines so good? Technology is one answer. The Australian winery is probably the most advanced in the world. The winemakers have used technology to get round the problems caused by climate or simply to enhance qualities they want to bring out. Having conquered the techniques, they are now thinking about the different ways of treating the grapes, experimenting with different types of wood, fermenting some of a particular wine in wood and some in stainless steel; ageing parts of a blend for different periods in different containers. And then putting it all together to get the right results.

Now that wine technology is almost a plaything, winemakers are looking at the vineyards. At the moment, anybody can plant any vine wherever he or she likes. That's probably not going to change – there's much more freedom in Australia than in regulated Europe. But certain areas are now considered suitable for certain grapes – Clare and Eden Valley in South Australia for Rhine Riesling, Rutherglen for Muscat, Coonawarra for Cabernet Sauvignon, for example. In addition, the different clones of each grape are being examined to see which work best in which conditions.

There are also certain vineyard areas which are seen as quality producing areas (see below for a list) – these names appear on wine labels. So while it is still possible to blend grapes from anywhere in Australia, or from anywhere within a particular state, the top-quality wines are increasingly likely to come from a specific area.

Certification schemes have already been set up in one or two areas: Tasmania is one state with its own scheme, as is the Mudgee area of New South Wales. Basically, such schemes guarantee that the wine in the bottle comes from the specified area and is of the grape variety it says on the label; they also guarantee a basic quality.

What's what in Australia

Australian wines are named after the grape variety from which they are made. If there is only a single variety on the label, the wine must contain 85 per cent of that variety. Many wines are a blend of two or more grapes, and these will be indicated on the label.

Nearly a hundred grape varieties are planted in Australia. Most are used in branded blends for the domestic market while others are

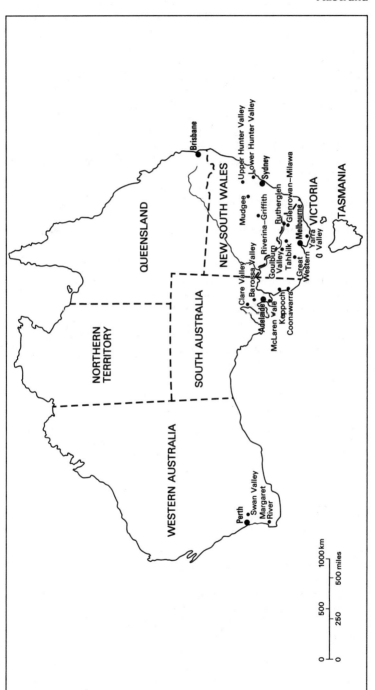

grown only in tiny quantities. Here we give the ones we come across in Britain.

White grapes

Chardonnay This was the grape which started the fashion for Australian wines. Larger than life, full of fruit and the taste of new wood, they were almost over the top. But they worked. When softened with a year or so in bottle, the balance of ripe tropical fruit and oak was a fine combination. Chardonnay produced the finest wines in cool years like 1981, 1984, 1985 and 1986.

There has been a change in style with the 1985 and 1986 vintages from some producers. They have been cutting down the oak, and letting the quality of the fruit come through more easily. It's a more sophisticated approach, but unlikely to take over from the older style completely.

Best areas: most Australian vineyard areas seem to produce good examples.

Semillon The grape that produces Sauternes in France makes some really fine dry wines in Australia, either with oak or without, and with some ageing potential. Australia has realised the possibilities of the Semillon to produce dry wines in a way that France never has, and good examples are well worth seeking out. The variety is also blended with Chardonnay and occasionally Chenin Blanc. (The Hunter Valley Riesling is Semillon by another name.)

Best areas: Hunter Valley (New South Wales), Southern Vales (South Australia), Barossa Valley (South Australia), but other areas make good examples as well.

Muscadelle The grape used in Australian liqueur Tokays. Like the Muscats (see below), these are intensely liquorous dessert wines, often of great age. There's nothing quite like them outside Australia.

Best areas: the best Muscadelle wines come from Rutherglen (Victoria) and nearby Milawa and Glenrowan.

Muscat This makes rich, sweet wines, especially in Victoria – deliciously luscious, with the taste of orange marmalade. Some Dry Muscat styles are also available.

Best areas: Rutherglen and Milawa/Glenrowan (Victoria).

Rhine Riesling This variety makes full, dry, medium-dry and sometimes sweet wines, and is another with a special Australian style, which we hope will gain wider acceptance. Don't confuse Australian Rhine Rieslings with German wines in any way, nor with so-called Hunter Valley Riesling, which is in fact Semillon.

Best areas: Barossa Valley, Clare and Eden Valleys (South Australia).

Sauvignon Blanc This cool-climate variety inevitably works best in cooler areas of the country. Some Australian wine producers bring in wine from New Zealand to give their Sauvignon Blanc wines the herbaceous character which their own warmer climate cannot provide.

Best areas: Margaret River (Western Australia), Pyrenees (Victoria), King Valley (Victoria).

Red grapes

Cabernet Sauvignon A major varietal style in red wines. Wood is an important element of the style, as with Chardonnay. The wines tend to develop fast – faster than they ever do in France, so that three- and four-year-old Australian Cabernets are very drinkable. Moreover, they don't necessarily fade – ten-year-old wines can still be very good.

Best areas: most areas produce good examples, but Coonawarra (South Australia), Tasmania, Margaret River (Western Australia), Geelong (Victoria), Langhorne Creek and McLaren Vale (South Australia) stand out.

Shiraz This is the other widely grown red variety, and is used to make a distinctively Australian style of wine. It has a direct relationship with the Syrah of the northern Rhône, but in Australia makes much more of a hot country wine than it does in France. It produces rich, soft, rounded, peppery wines, often more approachable than the more tannic Cabernet Sauvignons, with which it is often blended.

Best areas: Hunter Valley (New South Wales), Barossa Valley (South Australia), Southern Vales (South Australia), Coonawarra (South Australia).

Pinot Noir The hardest red vine of all to grow outside Europe. At last it seems that the Australians are getting it right, with some soft, mellow wines with good colour, and a typically vegetal taste.

Best areas: areas to watch are Yarra Valley (Victoria), King Valley (Victoria), Upper Hunter Valley (New South Wales), Tasmania, Margaret River (Western Australia).

Cabernet Franc, Merlot and **Malbec** are also planted in many areas, but are rarely seen unblended.

Australian wine regions

SOUTH AUSTRALIA

The biggest wine-producing state, producing 60 per cent of the country's total. Much of this comes from the high-yielding **Riverlands** area (where South Australia, New South Wales and Victoria meet), source of most of the boxed wines. A similar area in New South Wales is **Riverina**, based on the Murrumbidgee Irrigation Area.

Higher quality areas are:

Barossa Valley Originally best known for its Rhine Riesling wines, but increasingly for its Chardonnay and Cabernet Sauvignon as well as Shiraz. Home of the biggest Australian wine producers.

Clare Smaller area, generally considered to be making very high quality wines. Good for Rhine Riesling, but also Cabernet Sauvignon, Malbec and Shiraz, with smaller amounts of Semillon.

Coonawarra Generally agreed to be one of the best quality producing areas in Australia. Its finest wines are red, especially Cabernet Sauvignon, but increasingly whites – Sauvignon Blanc, Chardonnay and Gewürztraminer – are being planted.

Southern Vales Small wineries abound in this area just outside Adelaide. McLaren Vale and Reynella are here, and the Adelaide Hills, a new vineyard area, is close by. Cabernet Sauvignon, Chardonnay, Shiraz all do well.

NEW SOUTH WALES

The original home of vines in Australia. The vineyards now consist of two areas in the Hunter River Valley, close to the coast, and two inland areas.

Hunter Valley First planted as early as 1828, this is now a small area, the furthest north (and therefore one of the hottest) of the quality wine-producing areas. The heat is tempered by summer rains and the ocean. The classic grapes grown here are Shiraz (once called Hermitage) and Semillon, but Chardonnay is also cultivated.

Upper Hunter Valley A new area, on higher and cooler land than the Hunter Valley proper. Chardonnay is the success story here, as well as Semillon and Cabernet Sauvignon.

Mudgee A small area on the west of the Great Dividing Range, which produces high-quality Chardonnay as well as Cabernet Sauvignon.

Riverina A huge area of vineyard in the Murrumbidgee Irrigation Area.

VICTORIA

The vineyard area in this state was once much larger, but the phylloxera louse sniffed it out (it never even discovered South Australia). The vineyards never fully recovered in size: growers seem to have re-planted where it suited them, so the areas are now scattered.

Geelong An area to the south west of Melbourne, suited to cool-climate whites and Cabernet Sauvignon.

Goulburn Dominated by three estates, Ch Tahbilk, Mitchelton and Tisdall. Cabernet Sauvignon and Marsanne are the specialities.

Milawa/Glenrowan An amorphous area which includes the cool-climate King Valley vineyards, plus the hotter Ovens River Valley.

Pyrenees A cooler area, north of Ballarat, which produces some good Cabernet Sauvignon.

Rutherglen Best known for its Liqueur Muscats and Liqueur Tokays (Muscadelles), sweet dessert wines that wine expert Hugh Johnson suggests may be the descendants of the Cape Constantia wines of the beginning of the 19th century. Also some fine Tawny Port-style wines, made from the Shiraz, Grenache and (to a lesser but increasing extent) Portuguese grape varieties.

Yarra Virtually every grape variety – including the notoriously difficult Pinot Noir – seems to work in this small area just outside Melbourne. High prices are charged for top wines from the boutique wineries here.

WESTERN AUSTRALIA

The newest wine State, but one of the most interesting: the best vineyards are clustered in the cool south-western corner of the State, where the Southern Ocean meets the Indian.

Margaret River Cool-climate area which produces wines full of flavour. Estates include the Leeuwin Estates, backed by Californian Robert Mondavi. Most grapes seem to work here.

Mount Barker/Frankland River Whites seem to work best here, especially Rieslings.

Swan River The original vineyard area of Western Australia, just outside Perth. Its hot summers make it more suitable for fortified and dessert wines than table wines.

TASMANIA

The southernmost Australian state reproduces northern European growing conditions. White wines and cool climate reds, like Pinot Noir, work best here, although in good years Cabernet Sauvignon can be very fine too.

Australian vintages – they do matter

Despite its seemingly permanent sunny climate, there are differences in Australian weather from year to year.

1988 A good quality vintage in many regions, but quantities were down, especially in South Australia which was badly hit by frost and hail.

1987 A mixed bag of a vintage, with low yields and poor weather affecting South Australia and Victoria. Western Australia and New South Wales were better off.

1986 Average crop but exceptional quality. Whites benefited from cooler weather.

1985 Another cool year, giving flavoursome wines with high natural acidity.

1984 A cloudy period during the harvest made high-class whites and elegant reds.

1983 A much warmer year producing some great red wines and rather fuller whites.

1982 Some of the best red wines for many years, with quality good to very good.

1981 Variable harvest. South Australia was the best, New South Wales the least successful.

Who's who in Australia

Tim Adams (Clare, South Australia). Small operation, with extremely careful winemaking. Wines: Rhine Riesling, Cabernet Franc, Shiraz, Tawny.
Barnes Wine Shop; Bibendum; Tanners Wines; Henry Townsend; Malcolm Bruce Wines (Pottery Road, Bovey Tracey, Devon)

All Saints (Rutherglen, Victoria). Old family wine company making fine Liqueur Muscats.
Barnes Wine Shop; Thomas Baty; D Byrne & Co; Claridge Fine Wines; George Dutton; Nobody Inn; Ostlers; Selfridges; Supergrape; Willoughbys; Wine Emporium

Allandale (Hunter Valley, New South Wales). Makes single vineyard wines from grapes bought in from individual farmers. Wines: Semillon, Chardonnay, Shiraz, Cabernet Sauvignon.
Nobody Inn

Balgownie (Bendigo, Victoria). Well-balanced wines from one of the coolest areas of Victoria. Wines: Chardonnay, Cabernet Sauvignon, Pinot Noir.
D Byrne & Co; Alex Findlater; Pavilion Wine Company; Raeburn Fine Wines and Foods; La Vigneronne

Bannockburn (Geelong, Victoria). Good reds, including a Pinot Noir, from cool southern vineyards. Wines: Chardonnay, Pinot Noir, Shiraz, Cabernet Sauvignon.
Christopher & Co

Jim Barry (Clare, South Australia). One of the best producers of Rhine Riesling. Wines: Chardonnay, Cabernet Sauvignon, Rhine Riesling.
Cumbrian Cellar; Ostlers; Tanners Wines; Henry Townsend; Wine Emporium

De Bortoli (Bilbul, New South Wales). Specialises in sweet dessert whites from botrytised grapes. Wines: Traminer, Riesling, Fumé Blanc, Chardonnay, Cabernet Sauvignon, Botrytised Semillon, Merlot.
Averys; Barnes Wine Shop; D Byrne & Co; Peter Green; J E Hogg; Master Cellar Wine Warehouse; Nobody Inn; Ostlers; La Vigneronne

Beresford (McLaren Vales, South Australia). Small winery making a good Sauvignon Blanc. Wines: Sauvignon Blanc, Chardonnay.
David Baillie Vintners; Ostlers

Berri Estates/Renmano (Riverland, South Australia). Major co-operative selling wine in boxes and finer wines in bottle, some very good value. Wines: Chardonnay, Fumé Blanc, Rhine Riesling, Traminer Riesling, Cabernet Sauvignon, Merlot, Cabernet/Shiraz.
Widely available, including Peter Dominic, Sainsbury's, Unwins, Waitrose

Brand's Laira (Coonawarra, South Australia). Small premium winery. Wines: Cabernet Sauvignon, Shiraz, Cabernet Sauvignon/Malbec, Malbec.
Alex Findlater; Ostlers

Brown Brothers (Milawa, Victoria). High-quality family winery, with a full range of whites and reds and excellent late-harvest Liqueur Muscat. Wines: Dry Muscat, Late Picked Muscat, Estate Chardonnay, Estate Shiraz, Cabernet Sauvignon (from cool vineyards at Koombahla).
Adnams; David Baillie Vintners; Barnes Wine Shop; Berry Bros & Rudd; D Byrne & Co; Rodney Densem Wines; Peter Dominic; Alex Findlater; Peter Green; Lay & Wheeler; Majestic; Nobody Inn; Ostlers; Unwins

Campbells of Rutherglen (Rutherglen, Victoria). One of the oldest Rutherglen producers. Wines: Liqueur Muscat, Old Rutherglen Liqueur Muscat.
Ostlers

W H Chambers (Rutherglen, Victoria). One of the top two Rutherglen Muscat producers. Wines: Liqueur Muscat, Special Liqueur Muscat, Old Liqueur Muscat.
Averys; Barnes Wine Shop; Thomas Baty; George Dutton; Nobody Inn; Ostlers; Raeburn Fine Wines and Foods; Supergrape; La Vigneronne; Willoughbys; Yorkshire Fine Wines

Conti–Forest Hill (Mount Barker, Western Australia). First vineyard in this cool climate area. Best known for Rhine Riesling and Cabernet Sauvignon. Wines: Rhine Riesling, Cabernet Sauvignon, Traminer, Chardonnay.
Alex Findlater; Ostlers

Coriole (McLaren Vale, South Australia). Attractive wines, with good Chenin Blanc. Wines: Chenen Blanc, Sangiovese, Cabernet Sauvignon.
Ostlers; Henry Townsend

Delatite (Mansfield, Victoria). Small family winery producing some very good Pinot Noir. Wines: Rhine Riesling, Pinot Noir, Cabernet Sauvignon/Merlot.
Anthony Byrne Fine Wines; Ostlers; Brasserie Wine Cellars (6 Angel Lane, Bury St Edmunds, Suffolk)

Evans and Tate (Swan Valley, Western Australia). High reputation for good, flavoured reds, well made. Wines: Semillon, Gnangara Shiraz, Redbrook Cabernet Sauvignon, Redbrook Hermitage.
Alex Findlater; Peter Green

Jeffrey Grosset (Clare, South Australia). Small, high quality boutique winery. Wines: Chardonnay, Rhine Riesling, Cabernet Sauvignon.
Master Cellar Wine Warehouse; Ostlers

Hardy's (based in Adelaide, South Australia). Large company making big wines and a range of lighter, more European-style wines. Wines: Bird series, Cabernet Sauvignon, Chenin Blanc, Fumé Blanc, Chardonnay, Rhine Riesling, Keppoch Cabernet Sauvignon, Keppoch Cabernet/Shiraz, McLaren Vale Shiraz, Ch Reynella Cabernet Sauvignon and Chardonnay.
H Allen Smith; D Byrne & Co; Alex Findlater; Nobody Inn; Ostlers; Queens Club Wines; Ubiquitous Chip; Wizard Wine Warehouses

Hill Smith Estate (Barossa Valley, South Australia). Family firm making premium varietal wines largely from their own vineyards. Wines: Old Triangle Vineyard Rhine Riesling, Estate Semillon, Estate Chardonnay, Old Triangle Shiraz/Malbec, Estate Shiraz, Estate Cabernet Sauvignon, Botrytised Semillon, own Barossa Valley Estates brand and Yalumba (*q.v.*).
David Baillie Vintners; Berry Bros & Rudd; D Byrne & Co; Peter Dominic; Alex Findlater; Grape Ideas; Peter Green; Nobody Inn; Ostlers; Queens Club Wines; Yorkshire Fine Wines

Houghton (Swan River, Western Australia). One of the first commercial vineyards of Western Australia, now part of Hardy's (see above). Wines: Chardonnay, Cabernet Sauvignon, Blue Stripe Supreme (blend of Chenin Blanc and Verdelho), Rhine Riesling, Frankland River Cabernet Sauvignon.
H Allen Smith; Alex Findlater; Ostlers; Waitrose

Idyll Vineyard (Geelong, Victoria). Cool climate vineyards making elegant wines. Wines: Gewürztraminer, Shiraz Rosé, Cabernet/Shiraz.
Alex Findlater; J E Hogg; Mayor Sworder; Nobody Inn; Ostlers; La Vigneronne

Lake's Folly (Hunter Valley, New South Wales). Only two wines are made here, but they are among the best. Wines: Chardonnay, Cabernet Sauvignon.
Averys; D Byrne & Co; Lay & Wheeler; Ostlers; Raeburn Fine Wines and Foods

Lindeman's (Hunter Valley, New South Wales). A large firm, one of the top three in Australia, with vineyards in most regions and a number of estate wines. Wines: Padthaway Chardonnay, Rouge Homme Chardonnay, Rouge Homme Coonawarra Cabernet Sauvignon, St George Cabernet Sauvignon, Rouge Homme Pinot Noir, Rhine Riesling.
Averys; Barnes Wine Shop; D Byrne & Co; Cumbrian Cellar; Davisons; Rodney Densem Wines; Peter Dominic; Alex Findlater; Fortnum & Mason; Lay & Wheeler; Master Cellar Wine Warehouse; Nobody Inn; Ostlers; Tesco; La Vigneronne

McWilliams (Hunter Valley, New South Wales). Estate wines are a welcome addition to a rather dull range of old-style wines. Wines: Hanwood Estate Chardonnay, Fumé Blanc, Rhine Riesling, Cabernet Sauvignon, Shiraz, Beelbangera Semillon, Traminer Riesling, Yenda Cabernet Sauvignon, Hermitage, Pinot Noir, Mount Pleasant Estate.
Berry Bros & Rudd; Davisons; Peter Dominic; Alex Findlater; Peter Green; Master Cellar Wine Warehouse; Ostlers; Ubiquitous Chip

Geoff Merrill (McLaren Vale, South Australia). The winemaker at Hardy's (see above) also makes two very fine wines from his own vineyards. Wines: Cabernet Sauvignon, Semillon.
H Allen Smith; D Byrne & Co; Alex Findlater; Nobody Inn; Ostlers; Wizard Wine Warehouses

Mildara (Coonawarra, South Australia and Mildura, Victoria). Best wines, improving all the time, come from Coonawarra vineyards rather than the firm's original Mildura vineyards. Wines: Coonawarra Chardonnay, Sauvignon, Cabernet Sauvignon, Fumé Blanc, Traminer Riesling, Shiraz, Cabernet/Merlot, Church Hill Chardonnay, sparkling wines.
Cumbrian Cellar; Alex Findlater; Fortnum & Mason; Peter Green; Nobody Inn; Ostlers

Mitchelton (Goulburn, Victoria). Commercial vineyard making straightforward wines. Wines: Mitchelton Rhine Riesling, Marsanne (white), Cabernet Sauvignon.
D Byrne & Co; Alex Findlater

Montrose (Mudgee, New South Wales). Award-winning wines, including a top Chardonnay. Wines: Chardonnay, Show Reserve Chardonnay, Fumé Blanc, Pinot Noir, Cabernet Sauvignon, Special Reserve Shiraz.
D Byrne & Co; Alex Findlater; Fortnum & Mason; Ostlers

Moorilla Estate (Tasmania). Fine claret-style wines from cool climate vineyards. Wines: Cabernet Sauvignon.
D Byrne & Co

Morris (Rutherglen, Victoria). Morris of Rutherglen makes some of the top Liqueur Muscats in an area renowned for that style. Wines: Liqueur Muscat, Liqueur Tokay, Durif (red table wine). Part of Orlando (see below).
Oddbins; Ubiquitous Chip

Moss Wood Estate (Margaret River, Western Australia). Its high-quality Cabernet Sauvignon gave the winery its reputation. Wines: Semillon, Chardonnay, Pinot Noir, Cabernet Sauvignon.
Adnams; D Byrne & Co; Alex Findlater; Nobody Inn; Ostlers; Raeburn Fine Wines and Foods; La Vigneronne; Yorkshire Fine Wines

Orlando (Barossa Valley, South Australia). Commercial wines, made on a large scale, but with good quality. Wines: Jacob's Creek brand, RF brand, Rhine Riesling, Chardonnay, Shiraz/Cabernet, St Hilary Chardonnay, St Hugo Cabernet Sauvignon.
David Baillie Vintners; D Byrne & Co; Cumbrian Cellar; Davisons; Alex Findlater; Richard Granger; Peter Green; J E Hogg; Master Cellar Wine Warehouse; Oddbins; Queens Club Wines; Ubiquitous Chip; Wizard Wine Warehouses

Peel Estate (Mandurah, Western Australia). Single estate wines from south of Perth. Wines: Shiraz, Chenin Blanc, Cabernet Sauvignon.
Alex Findlater

Penfold's (Barossa, Coonawarra, Clare, Morgan in South Australia). Largest wine producer in Australia, but with very high quality in both whites and reds. Wines: Chardonnay, Traminer Riesling, Grange Hermitage, St Henri Cabernet/Shiraz, Dalwood Shiraz/Cabernet, Kalimna Bin, selected Bin wines, Koonunga Hill, Magill Estate, Seaview, Kaiserstuhl, Grandfather Tawny.
Adnams; Berry Bros & Rudd; D Byrne & Co; Chaplin & Son; Davisons; Alex Findlater; Fortnum & Mason; J E Hogg; Majestic; Master Cellar Wine Warehouse; Nobody Inn; Oddbins; Ostlers; David Scatchard; La Vigneronne; Yorkshire Fine Wines

Petaluma (Adelaide Hills, South Australia). Some of Australia's most prestigious wines, made by Brian Croser; a driving force in this sphere. Wines: Rhine Riesling, Chardonnay, Coonawarra Cabernet Sauvignon.
Les Amis du Vin; D Byrne & Co; Alex Findlater; Fortnum & Mason; J E Hogg; Majestic; Nobody Inn; Ostlers; La Vigneronne

Quelltaler (Clare Valley, South Australia). Best known for its white wines. Part of the Wolf Blass (see below) empire. Wines: Rhine Riesling, Semillon, Chardonnay.
Fortnum & Mason; Ostlers

Rosemount Estate (Hunter Valley, New South Wales). The firm that was in at the beginning of the current enthusiasm for Australia. Recent

vintages of the standard Diamond Label range seem less exciting than before, but look out for the Show Reserve and Roxburgh range. Wines: Traminer, Sauvignon Blanc, Fumé Blanc, Chardonnay, Shiraz, Cabernet/Malbec, Cabernet Sauvignon, Show Reserve Chardonnay, Cabernet Sauvignon, sparkling wine.
Widely available

Rothbury Estate (Hunter Valley, New South Wales). Top-quality wines made by Len Evans, one of the gurus of Australian wine-making. Wines: Chardonnay, Shiraz, Pinot Noir, Semillon.
H Allen Smith; Les Amis du Vin; David Baillie Vintners; D Byrne & Co; Alex Findlater; Fortnum & Mason; J E Hogg; Lay & Wheeler; Majestic; Nobody Inn; Ostlers; La Vigneronne

Saint Huberts (Yarra Valley, Victoria). The largest winery in this top-quality region. Wines: Rhine Riesling, Pinot Noir, Chardonnay, Shiraz, Cabernet Sauvignon, dessert wines.

Saltram (Barossa Valley, South Australia). Large producer of good-quality wines. Part of Seagrams. Wines: Mamre Brook Chardonnay, Metala Shiraz.
Oddbins

Seppelt (Barossa Valley, South Australia). Large-scale commercial producer whose fortified wines are the best. Wines: Rhine Riesling, Chardonnay, Shiraz, Cabernet Sauvignon, Mount Rufus Finest Tawny, Rutherglen Liqueur Muscat.
D Byrne & Co; Alex Findlater; Nobody Inn; Ostlers; La Vigneronne

Stanley (Clare, South Australia). The Leasingham range is the best of this firm's wines. Wines: Leasingham Rhine Riesling, Bin 56 Cabernet/Malbec, Cabernet Sauvignon, Coonawarra Shiraz/Cabernet.
Richard Granger; Grape Ideas; J E Hogg; Nobody Inn

Stanton and Killeen (Rutherglen, Victoria). Another of the high-quality Muscat producers of Rutherglen. Wines: Liqueur Muscat.
H Allen Smith; Averys; Thomas Baty; Rodney Densem Wines; Peter Dominic (some branches); George Dutton; Nobody Inn; Ostlers; Raeburn Fine Wines and Foods; Selfridges; Supergrape; Willoughbys

Chateau Tahbilk (Goulburn, Victoria). Very traditional producer, making stupendous, long-lived wines. Wines: Marsanne, Cabernet Sauvignon, Shiraz.
Buckingham Wines; Peter Green; Ostlers; Premier Wine Warehouse; Wapping Wine Warehouse; Winecellars

---

Stockists given in italic type after wines in this section will be found in the WHERE TO BUY section earlier in the book.

Taltarni (Moonambel, Victoria). Cool-climate vineyard, mainly planted with red varieties. Wines: Cabernet Sauvignon, Shiraz.
David Baillie Vintners; D Byrne & Co; Alex Findlater; Nobody Inn; Oddbins; Ostlers; Reid Wines; Wizard Wine Warehouses

Tisdall (Goulburn Valley, Victoria). Pricey but good Chardonnay is the star from this winery. Wines: Traminer Riesling, Mount Helen Chardonnay, Pinot Noir, Cabernet Sauvignon.
G E Bromley & Sons; Cumbrian Cellar; Alex Findlater; Peter Green; Master Cellar Wine Warehouse; Nobody Inn; Ostlers; Henry Townsend; The Wine Schoppen

Tollana (Barossa Valley, South Australia). Sound commercial wines, but nothing exciting. Part of Penfold's (see above). Wines: Langhorne Creek Chenin Blanc, Barossa Valley Shiraz.
Oddbins

Tyrrell's (Hunter Valley, New South Wales). Strange names hide some interesting blends. Reds are better than whites. Good fortified wines as well. Wines: Long Flat White, Vat 1 Semillon, Vat 47 Chardonnay, Long Flat Red, Pinot Noir, Shiraz.
Adnams; H Allen Smith; Averys; Alex Findlater; Lay & Wheeler; Ostlers; La Vigneronne; Wizard Wine Warehouses; Yorkshire Fine Wines

Vasse Felix (Margaret River, Western Australia). Small winery producing very fine complex wines. Wines: Riesling, Cabernet Sauvignon, Hermitage.
Alex Findlater; La Vigneronne

Wirra Wirra (McLaren Vale, South Australia). Top-quality, small-scale winery. Wines: Rhine Riesling, Sauvignon Blanc, Pinot Noir, Church Block Cabernet/Shiraz/Merlot.
Alex Findlater; Thos Peatling; Seckford Wines

Wolf Blass (Barossa Valley, South Australia). One of the showmen of Australian wine, Wolf Blass specialises in top-quality blended wines, but owns few vineyards. Wines: Classic Dry White, Cabernet/Shiraz, Yellow Label Cabernet Sauvignon, Presidents Selection Cabernet Sauvignon.
Averys; D Byrne & Co; Davisons; Alex Findlater; Peter Green; Nobody Inn; Oddbins; Ostlers; Reid Wines

Wyndham Estate (Hunter Valley, New South Wales). The oldest continuously operating winery in Australia, started in 1828. The wines are good, middle-of-the-road quality, with the white dry Verdelho a speciality. Wines: Oak Cask Chardonnay, Bin TR2 Gewürztraminer Riesling, Bin 444 Cabernet Sauvignon, Bin 555 Shiraz, Verdelho, Pinot Noir.
Alex Findlater; Grape Ideas; Majestic; Ostlers; Sainsbury's; David Scatchard

Wynns (Coonawarra, South Australia). Large firm making sound reds and excellent whites. Part of Penfold's (see above). Wines: Coonawarra Chardonnay, Rhine Riesling, Shiraz, Cabernet Sauvignon, Ovens Valley Shiraz.
D Byrne & Co; Alex Findlater; Nobody Inn; Arthur Rackhams; Victoria Wine Company; Wizard Wine Warehouses

Yalumba (Barossa Valley, South Australia). Owned by the Hill-Smith family, this winery makes a wide range of good-quality wines. Wines: Semillon, Sauvignon Blanc, Signature Series Chardonnay and Cabernet Shiraz, Galway Pipe Tawny.
Adnams; Les Amis du Vin; Berry Bros & Rudd; D Byrne; Peter Dominic; Fortnum & Mason; Nobody Inn; Ostlers; Yorkshire Fine Wines

Yarra Burn (Yarra Valley, South Australia). Small boutique winery in a beautiful setting at the head of the Yarra Valley. Wines: Cabernet, Pinot Noir, Chardonnay.
Adnams; Barnes Wine Shop

Yarra Yering (Yarra Valley, Victoria). Leading winery in a small, exciting area. Wines: Pinot Noir, Chardonnay, Dry Red No 1, Dry Red No 2.
Adnams; Barnes Wine Shop; Alex Findlater; Fortnum & Mason; Ostlers; La Vigneronne

Best buys from Australia

WHITES

Coromandel Rhine Riesling 1987 (*Majestic*)
St Michael Barossa Valley Semillon 1986 (*Marks & Spencer*)
Seaview Semillon/Chardonnay 1985 (*Oddbins*)
Killawarra Selection Yenda Chardonnay 1987 (*Oddbins*)
Penfold's Semillon/Chardonnay 1985 (*Drunken Mouse; Thresher*)

REDS

St Michael South Australian Shiraz/Cabernet Sauvignon 1986 (*Marks & Spencer*)
South Australian Dalwood Shiraz/Cabernet 1984, Penfold's (*Sainsbury Brothers*)
Morris Durif 1984 (*Oddbins*)
Orlando RF Shiraz 1983 (*Oddbins*)
Australian Red Shiraz (*Christopher & Co*)
Yalumba Signature Reserve Shiraz/Cabernet 1985 (*Christopher & Co; Drunken Mouse*)
Botobolar St Gilbert 1984, Mudgee (*Vintage Roots*)
Wynns Coonawarra Estate Shiraz 1985 (*Arthur Rackhams; Thresher; Wizard Wine Warehouses*)
Mildara Cabernet Sauvignon/Merlot 1984 (*Charles Hennings*)
Tyrrell's Long Flat Red 1984 (*Averys; G E Bromley & Sons*)

Langhorne Creek Malbec 1984, Bleasdale (*Henry Townsend*)
Water Wheel Shiraz 1985 (*Seckford Wines*)

Specialist stockists

Averys of Bristol; Barnes Wine Shop; Bibendum; D Byrne & Co; Chaplin & Son; Christopher & Co; Claridge Fine Wines; Cumbrian Cellar; Drunken Mouse; Alex Findlater; Great Northern Wine Company; Gerard Harris; Master Cellar Wine Warehouse; Oddbins; Ostlers; Raeburn Fine Wines and Foods; Seckford Wines; Selfridges; Tanners Wines; Henry Townsend; Upper Crust; Whitesides of Clitheroe; La Vigneronne; The Wine House

Austria

Still on a trickle

Austria's wine exports fell from 478,000 hectolitres in 1984 down to a mere 42,000 hectolitres in 1986, and with no great increase since. Not encouraged by attitudes in Britain, only a trickle gets on to the shelves and into our glssses.

The dedicated band of Austrian importers are busy saying that this is about to change. They've stuck by Austria since the diethylene glycol scandal, and insist that a new generation of Austrian wines are emerging, made under new draconian wine laws which should prevent another scandal. These show that Austria is a serious wine-producing country that doesn't deserve to be lumped together with Germany in the bland, medium-sweet sugar-water stakes.

Austrian wines are indeed quite different from German. Although some of the grapes used are the same – Rhine Riesling, for example, and Gewürztraminer – the main Austrian grape, the Grüner Veltliner, is unique to that country. Moreover, Austria, unlike Germany, has the ability to produce regular quantities of lusciously sweet, botrytis-affected wines, as a counterbalance to the essentially dry character of most of its white wines.

One other change that has come about since the wine scandal affects the price of Austrian wines. Previously they were attempting to compete with German branded wines, but all that has changed. Austria is not a huge wine-producing country, production costs are high, the Austrian schilling is a strong currency – consequently, there are no bargains to be had from Austria today.

Higher prices have also been forced upon growers by a series of small harvests in Austria. This run culminated in a harvest in 1987 which was down by as much as 60 or 70 per cent in some areas after a cold spell earlier in the year.

Wine law bureaucracy

The situation is not helped by the new Wine Law, heralded when it was passed as the toughest in Europe. That may be so, but it was rushed through in such a hurry that many of its provisions are widely recognised as unworkable, stupid, or both.

A classic case is the renaming of the vineyards. The idea was to reclassify vineyard areas so that grapes in wines came from much more tightly defined regions. Thus in Gumpoldskirchen, one of the most famous Austrian wine villages south of Vienna, four villages previously had the right to use this name. Now its use is restricted to Gumpoldskirchen itself: the result is likely to be that very little wine will see the markets at all, since the thirsty inhabitants will drink all the tiny production from a mere 480 hectares.

Again, familiar names like Falkenstein in Lower Austria have officially disappeared, to be replaced by Wienviertel. The area of Klosterneuberg, another well-known name, is now Donauland-Carnuntum (there's a name for the marketing men to conjure with).

And having conformed to all the new rules for testing and won official approval (all Austrian wine now needs to get a seal, or Banderol, before it can be sold), the producer decides to export. He is then faced with almost insurmountable bureaucratic hurdles: he has to get approval for wine from every vineyard he owns, even if he may be blending the wines later. He has to pay nearly four times what he paid before the new law was passed to get the official export paperwork. The wine has to be tested yet again before the container is sealed at the frontier by customs officials.

Now while we may applaud the intention to prevent further scandals, all this strikes us as rather like the proverbial shutting of the stable door after the horse has bolted. The vast majority of honest producers in the country are being penalised for the misdemeanours of a few. Small wonder that producers seem reluctant to export at the moment.

The taste of Austria

Austria is a white wine country. Only about 20 per cent of her wines are red, and while refreshingly light and fruity, they are quite expensive for what they are. Most of the whites are dry (apart from the luscious sweet ones from the Burgenland), but because the best grape varieties are the very floral, fruit-flavoured ones such as Rheinriesling and Grüner Veltliner, they tend to have much more attractive perfumed fruit flavours than French dry white wines. Austria also produces wines based on the Pinot Blanc (or Weissburgunder), but these are less exciting.

To get the true flavour of Austria, go for the Grüner Veltliner. It has quite high acidity, a slightly peppery taste, but is crisply refreshing. It's not a wine style for ageing: look now for 1986 or 1987 wines.

The other taste of Austria is its sweet wines. Despite price rises, any of the sweet dessert wines from the Burgenland are still bargains compared to their German equivalents. They are rather more obviously sweet than the German wines, and lack some of that stunning acidity which balances the cloyingness of the sweetness, but at maybe a third of the price it's difficult to complain.

Some of the reds, soft and not quite dry with a vanilla touch, are light and easy to drink, fuller than Germany's pale efforts, but in the same style. Blauer Portugieser and Blaufränkisch (similar to Gamay) are the popular grape varieties here. Reds up to two or three years old are good now, but tend to dry out if left for much longer.

Austrian grapes

Most Austrian wines now carry the name of the grape variety on their labels.

White grapes

Gewürztraminer Typically spicy grape variety, used in Austria also to make sweet wines.

Grüner Veltliner Austria's own white grape variety, producing slightly spicy, dry wines, with a hint of steeliness. Best drunk young, except for some better Prädikat wines.

Muskat Ottonel An aromatic grape variety, producing slightly honeyed wines. Used in many sweet wines.

Rheinriesling The familiar German grape variety, here making dry white wines, especially in the Wachau.

Spätrot-Rotgipfler Blend of two grape varieties from which much Gumpoldskirchener wine is made.

Weissburgunder The Pinot Blanc of Alsace and the Pinot Bianco of Italy. Makes fresh, dry white wines.

Welschriesling Also the Italian or Laski or Olasz Riesling (depending on which part of central or eastern Europe you're in). Its acidity in Austria makes it a good base for sparkling wines. Also used for some sweet wines in Burgenland.

Red grapes

Blauer Portugieser Popular grape variety making wines for early drinking.

Blaufrankisch Similar to the Gamay but not related.

St Laurent Produces deep, plum-covered wines with a distinctive flavour.

What's what in Austria

Apetlon Village on the eastern shore of the Neusiedlersee, near the Hungarian border. Famous for sweet wines.

Burgenland Austria's easternmost wine district which includes the shallow Neusiedlersee. Sandy soils and a warm, humid climate encourage a regular production of sweet wines made from botrytis-affected grapes.

Donnerskirchen Town in Burgenland famous for its Trockenbeerenauslese wines.

Dürnstein Town on the Wachau (see below), home of the Wachau co-operative and the castle in which Richard Lionheart was imprisoned.

Falkenstein Village of Lower Austria, north-west of Vienna, producing easy-drinking wines from the Grüner Veltliner grape.

Gumpoldskirchen Village south of Vienna source of modern-style fresh white wines (especially those made at the local co-operative).

Heurigen Jug wines drawn from the barrel, associated especially with the suburbs of Vienna, where they are sold in bars also called Heurigen.

Klosterneuberg Government testing station, viticultural school and wine producer all share this green-domed abbey complex just outside Vienna. The wines are straightforward, the red very acceptable.

Krems/Langenlois Quality districts just east of the Wachau.

Niederösterreich This province of Lower Austria is the largest wine region and is divided into sub-districts (eg Wachau).

Ried Single vineyard (similar to German 'Lage').

Rust Lakeside village in Burgenland famous for its sweet white wines. The surrounding area is called Rust-Neusiedlersee.

Voslau Red wine district just south of Gumpoldskirchen.

Wachau Top quality dry and medium-dry white wine area based on vineyards lining the Danube gorge west of Vienna. Some wines are made from the Rhine Riesling and some have keeping qualities rare for Austrian wines.

The Austrian wine law

The basis for the Austrian wine law is similar to Germany's and is based upon the degree of ripeness of the grapes as much as the geographical origin. All the categories are the same as in Germany but are based on different (usually higher) levels of natural sugar in the grape (because Austria is further south, the grapes have a chance to get riper than in Germany).

There is only one extra category of which examples are hardly ever seen in this country. This is Ausbruch, midway in sweetness between Beerenauslese and Trockenbeerenauslese.

Who's who in Austria

H Augustin Good quality wines, many based on the Grüner Veltliner grape.
H Augustin (271/273 King Street, London W9; mainly supply restaurants and wine bars)

Sepp Hold Burgenland producer of sweet wines.
Premier Wines (Ayr); A L Vose; Boisdale Wines (65 Ebury Street, London SW1); Papanicholas (13/15 Plough Way, London SE16)

Johann Kattus Lower Austria producer of some sparkling wines.
Contact Caxton Tower (239 Munster Road, London SW6, who supply restaurants)

Klosterneuberg A range of sound wines made at Klosterneuberg monastery, including the branded Klosterdawn and Klostergarten.
Safeway

Metternich Weinguter Princely family firm in Lower Austria who make very drinkable Grüner Veltliner.
Bordeaux Direct

Lenz Moser The top quality producer of Austria, producing branded Blue Danube and Schluck as well as some fine estate wines.
Victoria Wine Company

Fritz Saloman Small firm near Krems, producing some of the best and most long-lasting dry whites.
Contact Caxton Tower (239 Munster Road, London SW6)

Winzergenossenschaft (means co-operative). The best are at Wachau (*William Morrison*) and Krems (*A L Vose*).

Best buys from Austria

Kremser Neuberger Rhine Riesling 1983 (*A L Vose*)
Kremser Schmidt Grüner Veltliner 1986 (*A L Vose*)
Bouvier Beerenauslese 1983, Sepp Hold (*A L Vose*)

Specialist stockists

Premier Wines (Ayr); A L Vose

Brazil

Yes, there's more than coffee in Brazil. Most of the wine comes from the south of the country, around São Paulo, where it's not so hot as in Rio de Janeiro. It has become a serious industry, because the American (now British-owned) firm of Heublein set up shop there a few years ago. The Sherry firm of Domecq followed, as well as Cinzano and Moët et Chandon, so there must be something to these vineyards.

Now we have the chance to find out, thanks to one enterprising shipper who is importing wines produced in the 1200-hectare estate of Palomas Wines in the Rio Grande do Sul. They are making varietal wines – Pinot Noir, Cabernet Sauvignon, Chardonnay, Merlot and Chenin Blanc – which are probably not going to set the wine world on fire, but should make an interesting talking point.

Best buys from Brazil

Palomas Cabernet Sauvignon
Palomas Chardonnay
A L Vose

Bulgaria

We can't stop drinking it

The clever Bulgarians continue to get it right. Every year we drink over 12 million bottle of their wines – and the quantity seems to be growing. Their red Suhindol Cabernet Sauvignon is the biggest-selling red wine in Britain. How have they managed it?

Bulgaria is a country without a long wine tradition. Centuries of Muslim occupation saw to that. So when, after the Second World War, some bright spark spotted that a good way to obtain much-needed foreign currency was through exporting wine, the wine industry was modelled on that of western Europe without any resistance from traditionalists.

Bulgaria went straight down the varietal path. Although the cheapest brand, Mehana, is a blended wine of a number of local Bulgarian varieties, the bulk of the wines are Cabernet Sauvignon, Rhine Riesling, Chardonnay, Merlot – names we know and understand already, so there's absolutely no recognition problem.

Then there's the price. For wine of such good quality, Bulgarian wine is absurdly cheap. At least until the beginning of 1988, the Cabernet Sauvignon was selling for just under £2 in some shops – and it probably will not have gone up much since then. Even the next range of quality costs less than £3 – and for that you are getting some sophisticated, quite complex wines. Nowhere else in the world is this price/quality ratio so favourable to the consumer.

The role of a heavy state subsidy is irrelevant – the fact is that the wines are here, and they're good and inexpensive.

New emphasis

There has been a shift of emphasis in the range of Bulgarian wines available in the UK. While the Mehana red and white along with the basic varietals are the big sellers, we are now also seeing more wines from the Controliran regions (see the list below) and from the Reserve range. In addition to the western European varietal wines, top-quality varietal wines made from Bulgarian grapes such as the red Damianitza and Mavrud are making an appearance.

The first step towards this new range of quality was with the launch some years ago of a wine known here as Sakar Mountain Cabernet – the 1976 wine was a superbly classic Cabernet Sauvignon, with a touch of wood and a taste of violets. After an initial hiccough, the 1978 proved equally good, but the 1980 is much more disappointing.

The Bulgarians decided to go further along the up-market road. They created the Controliran system – specially designated regions like super appellation contrôlée areas. A number of wines made under Controliran rules have now reached our shops – from Svichtov (Cabernet Sauvignon), Oryahovica (Cabernet/Merlot) and Novi Pazar (Chardonnay).

Now the plan has been moved one stage further with the introduction of Reserve wines. These come from larger areas than Controliran wines, but yields are strictly controlled, and the wines are aged in smaller oak barrels than the standard Bulgarian wines, and are bottled earlier but allowed to rest in bottle for some time. The Bulgarians reckon that all this attention to detail will add a layer of complexity to the simple varietal character of their ordinary wines. The Damianitza Melnik and the Khan Krum Chardonnay are examples of these Reserve wines.

And still they're cheap. The Reserve wines made from Cabernet Sauvignon and Chardonnay sell for well under £3 a bottle. And during 1988, a new middle range of wines arrived, called Country Wines (see below).

What's what in Bulgaria

The Bulgarian system of labelling is deliberately simple: most wines are simply sold under their varietal name. There is also a basic range of wines which are blends of local grapes, sold either under the Mehana brand name or under a shop's own label.

The middle range consists of the varietal wines which first made Bulgaria famous. The most usual varietals to be seen here are Riesling and Chardonnay in whites, Cabernet Sauvignon and Merlot in reds. Above this come the Reserve wines, and at the top the Controliran wines.

A new category of wines has arrived in the the UK during 1988. These are called Country Wines and fall somewhere near the varietal range in quality and price. At present there are four examples:

Russe (white), a blend of Riesling and Misket
Bourgas (white), a blend of Muscat and Ugni Blanc
Pavlikeni (red), a blend of Cabernet Sauvignon and Merlot
Suhindol (red), a blend of Merlot and Gamza

The new Controliran wine areas are:

Asenovgrad: makes Cabernet Sauvignon, Merlot and Mavrud
Harsovo (Melnik): makes wine from local grapes
Juzhnyabryag: makes rosé styles
Kralevo and Preslav: make Riesling
Lozica: makes Cabernet Sauvignon
Novi Pazar: makes Chardonnay
Novo Selo: makes Gamza

Oryahovica: makes Cabernet Sauvignon and Merlot
Preslav: makes Chardonnay
Rozova Dolina: makes Misket – mainly white
Sakak: makes Merlot
Sakar: makes Cabernet Sauvignon
Stambolovo: makes Merlot
Svichtov: makes Cabernet Sauvignon
Varna: makes Chardonnay
  More regons are expected to follow.
  Ultimately, Reserve Controliran wines will appear – but, with tiny
quantities of production, they could sell for as much as £20 a bottle.
A change indeed from £1.99.

Best buys from Bulgaria

WHITES

Bulgarian Chardonnay (*widely available*)
Bulgarian Riesling (*widely available*)
Reserve Khan Krum Chardonnay 1984 (*Direct Wine Shipments; Majestic;
Oddbins; Victoria Wine Company; Wines of Westhorpe*)

REDS

Bulgarian Suhindol Cabernet Sauvignon (*widely available*)
Plovdiv Cabernet Sauvignon (*Majestic; Oddbins*)
Damianitza Melnik Reserve 1978 (*Majestic; Wines of Westhorpe*)
Asenovgrad Mavrud 1980 (*Majestic*)

Specialist stockists

*Ad Hoc Wine Warehouse; Direct Wine Shipments; Majestic; Oddbins; Thos
Peatling; Wessex Wines; Wines of Westhorpe*

Canada

Life after hybrids

Canada's wine industry is based mainly on the hybrid *Vitis labrusca* wines (banned in Europe in favour of the better quality *Vitis vinifera*) and Baby Duck, Canada's answer to alcoholic Coca-Cola. Most are well avoided and few are available in Britain.

However, there is a small pocket of *Vitis vinifera* wine production in Ontario where some decent if rather expensive wines are made. The best-known producer is Inniskillin (best-known because theirs are the only Canadian wines available here). They make a Chardonnay and a Riesling, both of which have varietal character, and also some of the better wines from the hybrids – a sweet white Vidal and a red Maréchal Foch, as well as a Gamay Noir.

Best buys from Canada

Inniskillin Chardonnay 1986 (white) and Inniskillin Maréchal Foch 1985 (red) (*both available from Averys and La Vigneronne*)

Specialist stockist

Averys of Bristol

Chile

Is their time nigh?

Last year, we predicted that Chile's turn as most fashionable winemaking country was about to come. This year, we *think* it has, but we're not quite sure.

There was certainly plenty of talk about Chilean wines at the main London wine trade fair, which generally means that the wine trade is interested and tasting the wines. Our uncertainty about Chile's arrival on the wine fashion scene is because we're not quite sure about the quality of the wines.

Chile starts out with all the advantages, viticulturally speaking. The

Chilean vineyards are just across the Andes from the main Argentine vineyard areas. But the climb up to 17,000 feet and down again does wonders for the climate. Where Argentine vineyards are in almost desert land, in Chile the rainfall is twice as high and the cool, moist winds from the Pacific Ocean make for a climate not unlike that of Bordeaux.

There's another link with Bordeaux in the well-drained soil sitting on a high water table which keeps the vines well watered but not sodden. Add to that the fact that Chile's vineyards are phylloxera-free (so the vines don't have to be grafted on to American root stock as they do in Europe and California), plus a low incidence of all the dreadful diseases that can strike vines – and it's not surprising that Chile has the potential to be one of the most exciting vineyard areas in the world.

One man's influence

There was a time – not so long ago – when many of Chile's white wines were oxidised and many of her reds tasted more of dirty barrels than of fruit, because they had been kept in wood for too long. Even other Chilean producers would acknowledge that the situation has changed because of one man's influence.

Miguel Torres Jnr, the energetic wine producer from the Penedès in Spain, has bought estates in some of the cooler wine-growing areas of Chile and already his first releases have burst upon the wine world, provoking a mixture of suspicion ('is this really Chilean white? It's much too clean and fresh') and reluctant admiration ('that man has done it again').

Torres has applied the techniques he was already using in the Penedès region of Spain. Stainless steel, cold fermentation, only a short ageing time in wood for reds – all these contribute to some very exciting wines. His vineyard is in the Maule Valley, well to the south of the existing vineyard area around the capital of Chile, Santiago. That means that the climate is cooler and the ripening period of the grapes is longer – all aids to making good wine.

Playing the numbers game

So what we are now seeing are some very good wines coming from Chile. Some are made by traditional firms who have stayed firmly traditional, but have nevertheless taken advantage of new techniques to make their wines more acceptable on the international stage. Others are made by companies who have embraced wholeheartedly the modern school of winemaking: often their wines taste as though they come from Australia or California (other influences on Chile's wine producers).

All those wines are good in their different ways. But what we are also seeing is a number of producers who are making cheap wine and selling it at a low price, often under an own label: not only is it cheap, it tastes cheap.

Chile can't afford to start devaluing its reputation before it is even established. Much better for producers to concentrate on quality at what are often very reasonable prices rather than trying to beat the Germans and French at a game they can play only too well.

What's what in Chile

There are two main growing regions in Chile. Both are in the central valley zone, around the capital of Santiago. The furthest north (and therefore warmest) is the Maipo Valley, on a level with Santiago. This has long been the traditional area for premium wine production. Further south, cooler climate areas have been planted more recently in the Lontué and Maule Valleys. Here, the grapes – especially those for white wines – can take advantage of a longer ripening season to attain excellent fruit flavours.

Many Chilean wines are labelled varietally, in the manner of New World wines. The main grape varieties likely to appear on UK wine shelves are:

Whites – Muscat, Semillon, Sauvignon, Riesling;
Reds – Cabernet Sauvignon, Merlot, Pinot Noir, Cot.

Other wines have fancy names as well as grape varieties. If a grape is specified on the label, the wine must contain 85 per cent of that grape. With two varieties, the more important will be mentioned first.

Categories of quality are also indicated on the label. The standard quality will have no qualification, but a wine called **Special** will have been bottled after two years in tank or wood; **Reserve** after four years; **Gran Vino** after six years.

Who's who in Chile

There are now ten producers whose wines are available in Britain:

Concha y Toro, Maipo Valley. Chile's largest wine producer who turns out reliable wines at good prices. The top wines are getting better all the time. Wines: Cabernet Casillero del Diablo, Cabernet/Merlot blends, Cabernet Marquès de Casa Concha (worth keeping for six or seven years), white Sauvignon/Semillon blend (drink young); also good sparkling Brut and rosé.
David Alexander; Buckingham Wines; Hicks & Don; Christopher Piper Wines; Queens Club Wines; La Reserva Wines; Stapylton Fletcher; Tanners Wines; Unwins; Waitrose

---

Please write to tell us about any ideas for features you would like to see in next year's edition or in *Which? Wine Monthly*.

Cousiño Macul, Maipo Valley. Source of Chile's best red wines – some of the Cabernet Sauvignons last for years. Also make Chardonnay wines. Wines: Cousiño Macul Antiguas Reserva (will last 10 or 15 years) and Chardonnay (drink it at two years).
David Alexander; Peter Dominic; Alex Findlater; Nobody Inn; Queens Club Wines; La Reserva Wines; Stapylton Fletcher; Tanners Wines; A L Vose

Erraruriz Panquehue Producer of two good value wines: Sauvignon, Cabernet Sauvignon.
Thresher

Los Vascos, Colchagua. Make superb Cabernet Sauvignon wines, full of fruit. Wines: Cabernet Sauvignon (drink now, but worth keeping for a couple of years).
Bordeaux Direct

Linderos, Maipo Valley. Top quality Cabernet Sauvignon with good ageing potential. Wines: Viña Linderos Cabernet Sauvignon.
Asda; D Byrne & Co; Continental Wine House; Davisons; Peter Dominic; Grape Ideas; Lay & Wheeler; Nobody Inn; Wizard Wine Warehouses

Santa Carolina, Maipo Valley. Dull, commercial range. Wines: Chardonnay, Sauvignon Blanc, Cabernet Sauvignon, Merlot.
For more information, contact Caxton Tower (239 Munster Road, London SW6)

Santa Marta, Maipo Valley. Modern-style wines, of good quality, which could come from any New World country, but none the worse for that. And their prices are good as well. A name to watch. Wines: Sauvignon Blanc, Chardonnay, Cabernet/Merlot, Cabernet Sauvignon.
Eldorobo Wines (105 Uxbridge Road, London W12)

Santa Rita, Maipo Valley. One of the oldest wineries in Chile, started in the 1700s. Now makes an excellent, if pricy, range of varietal wines. Wines: Chardonnay, Sauvignon Blanc, Cabernet Sauvignon.
Moreno Wines; La Reserva Wines

Torres, Maule Valley. The great innovator in Chile, as in Spain. Whites and reds are in the modern style but have considerable character. Wines: Wines appear under the Santa Digna and Bellaterra names; also Cabernet Sauvignon, Sauvignon Blanc, Rosé (made from Cabernet Sauvignon), Don Miguel (Riesling and Gewürztraminer).
B H Wines; D Byrne & Co; Lay & Wheeler; La Reserva Wines; Tesco

Viña San Pedro, Lontué Valley. A mixed bag of wines. The best are called Llave de Oro and Castillo de Moline. Avoid the Gato de Oro wines. Wines: Sauvignon Blanc, Chardonnay, Cabernet Sauvignon, Merlot.
Buckingham Wines; Majestic

Best buys from Chile

WHITES

Santa Rita Sauvignon Blanc 1986 (*Moreno Wines; La Reserva Wines*)
Chardonnay 1987, Cousiño Macul (*Desborough & Brown*)
Sauvignon Blanc 1987, Torres (*Broad Street Wine Co, The Holloway, Market Place, Warwick, Warwicks*)
Sauvignon Blanc 1987, Erraruriz Panquehue (*Thresher*)

REDS

Marqués de Casa Concha 1979, Concha y Toro (*Rex Norris*)
Los Vascos Cabernet Sauvignon (*Bordeaux Direct; Taste Shops*)
Viña Linderos Cabernet Sauvignon 1983 (*Richard Granger*)

Specialist stockists
Peter Green; Pond Farm Wines; La Reserva Wines

Cyprus

Modernising – slowly

At last, slowly perhaps, but at last, Cyprus wines seem to be getting their act together. While Cyprus 'Sherry' is still the main bottled export (the very biggest exports are of wine sold in bulk to the Soviet Union to wean the Russians off vodka), there are signs that the well-made, modern-style table wines which have been promised for what seems like years are at last reaching our shops in quantity.

In last year's Guide, we reported on one new wine, Thisbe, which had been produced by Keo, perhaps the most go-ahead firm in Cyprus. It has now been joined by a dry white and a light red from another of the Big Four Cypriot wine producers, Loel. They are all attractive wines, reasonably inexpensive, but are unlikely to set the world alight.

But at least they show what Cyprus is capable of after Cyprus Sherry. Mind you, sales of that are still considerable, helped by large promotional budgets in the UK for the leading brands – Emva, Mosaic, Lysander. And, while we may argue that they shouldn't use the term Sherry, at least the products are genuine, with the dry Cyprus Sherry made with flor just as they do it in Jerez – all very unlike the ersatz British Sherries.

One reason why Cyprus has been slow to move with the times is its fear of the phylloxera louse. This scourge of European vineyards never reached the island of Cyprus, and the authorities want to keep it that way. So any new varieties of vine that come in for experimental purposes have to be tested for years to make sure they are not infested.

This tends to leave the Cypriot wine producers relying mainly on rather dull local varieties, but with recourse to a strange collection of lesser southern European vines such as Carignan and the Jerez Palomino (for making table wines, not Sherry). Probably if they could get round their fears of phylloxera and import some more interesting varieties, things would look up even more.

Meanwhile, the biggest-selling Cyprus table wine is the sweet style in the Hirondelle range, and the best-selling red is the one served by every Greek and Cypriot restaurant – Otello.

But for a unique style, the Cyprus wine to look out for is the overpoweringly sweet Commandaria of St John. This is made from grapes laid out in the sun to dry and dates at least from the Middle Ages when the island was governed by the Knights Templar, although its origins are much older. Although much Commandaria is simply straightforward dessert wine used widely in churches, some examples of the true style are available as well – dark and sweet but still with the taste of grapes.

Best buys from Cyprus

Bellapais Medium-sweet, slightly fizzy white wine, a good example of a modern-style white.
G E Bromley & Sons; Cumbrian Cellar; Victoria Wine Company; Wine Spot

Commandaria of St John (See above.) The best two that are widely available are made by Keo and Etko.
Continental Wine House; Cumbrian Cellar; Peter Green; Wine Spot

Domaine d'Ahera A light style of smooth red wine made from Carignan grapes.

Thisbe A medium-dry white wine launched to compete with German-style wines.
Cumbrian Cellar; Whitesides of Clitheroe; Wine Spot; many North London Cypriot stores and off-licences

Palomino Another new dry white.
Valvona & Crolla; many North London Cypriot stores and off-licences

Amathus The dry red partner to the Palomino, a blend of Carignan, Oellade and Mataro grapes.
Valvona & Crolla; many North London Cypriot stores and off-licences

England and Wales

The Wine and Spirit Benevolent Banquet is, for many people in the wine trade, the highspot of the year. Well over a thousand people sit down to dinner in one of London's big hotels, and, being in the wine trade, they expect to enjoy their wine.

At the 1988 Banquet, while the guest of honour was French, the best wine of the evening was without doubt English. And it wasn't a young one, either: it was a 1983 vintage wine – four and a half years old – and still tasted fresh, fruity, dry, but deliciously perfumed. By comparison, the French and Italian wines which followed were very dull and boring.

So England and Wales don't just produce wines which must be drunk in a couple of years. Those same wines can also age surprisingly well. Occasional bottles of even older wines do surface, and they, too, show how well these delicate northern wines (after all the French don't reckon we can make wine at all this far north) can survive and mature.

Putting down new roots

There's expansion afoot in the English vineyards. Existing vineyards are growing, new ones are being created. It's a sign of confidence, certainly, but also a realisation that time for planting may be running out.

The reason is that England and Wales are still regarded as 'experimental' vineyard areas, and as such don't come under the rules of the EEC which currently prohibit any new vineyards anywhere in Europe, and pay farmers vast sums of money to grub up existing vines. It's all to do with the wine lake, of course, but the rules apply equally – in theory at least – to first-growth Bordeaux vineyards and to vineyards in the south of Italy.

The feeling among English and Welsh vineyard owners is that the day will come soon when their vineyards are no longer experimental, and the rules about no new vineyards will apply to them as well. So they are keeping their heads down and putting in the vines as quietly – and as fast – as possible.

Not much around

The new vineyards actually come not a moment too soon, because from 1988/89, there's going to be a temporary shortage of English wines. The appalling weather in 1987 meant that many vineyards in

East Anglia and Kent produced no wine at all, while even those further west found their production cut.

Shortages shouldn't mean price rises, though. Because around half of English and Welsh wine is sold at the vineyard gate, notices will simply go up saying 'sorry, sold out'. It's all part of the gently amateurish image much English winemaking still has. Only a handful of the bigger, more professional vineyards sell to supermarkets or wine shops, and an even tinier number sell their wine abroad (some even sell to France – unthinkable!).

But once you do get your hands on a bottle of English wine, you will find that the quality is good – and the standards are getting higher. There is good technology around now, and about 30 top-notch winemakers making the bulk of the wine that is for sale. It's rare to find a bad bottle. All bodes well for the future.

The taste of England and Wales

Most vineyards make two styles of wine: a dry and a less dry version. In good years (that 1983 at the Benevolent Banquet was a good example), the dry style is superb, making a crisp, clean-tasting wine that some have likened to the smell of an English country garden and which has piercing fruit and acidity. In poor years, the producers are allowed to add some unfermented grape juice or sugar to raise the alcohol level and keep the acidity from overwhelming the unripe fruit. So – with exceptions – 1985 and 1986 wines are slightly better in a medium dry or off dry style. The same is certainly true of 1987. Even then, though they may be made with German varieties, they don't taste the same – their acidity is keener and their steely quality sets them apart.

A few intrepid souls also make red wines, and some achieve surprisingly good results considering the way nature is stacked against them. But such wines should be approached with caution, and shouldn't be bought before tasting, simply because they are so unlike the red wines we are used to in their lightness and considerable acidity.

A word of warning

There are many wines around that describe themselves as British. For those who have never tasted them, we would point out that British 'wines' are not the same as English and Welsh wines which are the subject of this section. British 'wines' are made from concentrated grape must imported into this country, to which is added British water. The resulting combination is best undescribed.

Another category is made in this country, which derives from a long and honourable tradition. Called Country Wines, they are the commercial equivalent of home-made wines – damson, elderflower and the like. Some achieve high quality and shouldn't be dismissed as the source of instant headaches. Again, though, they should not be confused with wines made in this country from grapes grown here.

English and Welsh vintages

1987 The flowering, which takes place in early July, was completely rained off in East Anglia and Kent. Many vineyards produced hardly any grapes, let alone wine, and in any case the hurricane forced many growers to pick at a less than ideal time. Further west, while wine has been made, it is quite acid stuff, and needed the addition of some sugar. Stick to the medium dry styles.

1986 After a wet, cold summer, sunshine in September and October did much to improve the final quality of wines, although quantity is down on 1985. The wines are attractive to drink now, but should last into the spring of 1989.

1985 Could almost have been a disaster with a cold, wet summer. But the harvest was again saved by a dry September and October. Although the quantity was down by a third on 1984, the wines from the good vineyards are excellent, crisp and full of summery acidity, as English wine should be. They should be drunk now.

1984 A very good harvest of 1.5 million bottles with every vineyard making some of the best wines they've ever made. Some bottles will be very attractive in a mature way, but they should be drunk soon.

1983 Another good vintage, with some fine dry wines being made. The best should still be drinkable.

Not all English and Welsh wines carry a vintage indication, and may be a blend of two years – rarely more. They will probably be dominated by the most recent vintage, and so should be drunk accordingly.

What's what in England and Wales

The Certification Trade Mark system is run by the English Vineyards Association. Wines which bear the Seal are those which have been submitted for testing in the early part of the summer following the vintage. It's a voluntary system and lack of the Seal doesn't necessarily reflect on the quality of the wine.

The grapes

Nearly all English and Welsh vineyards are planted with strains of vine developed in Germany for northerly vineyards. Many actually produce better wine in Britain because the ripening season is long and slow and this brings out their flavours without a loss of acidity.

WHITE GRAPES

Bacchus Can be very flowery and fragrant, but also rather sharp.

Ehrenfelser Adaptable, disease-resistant variety. Very useful for making wines that can mature.

Gutenborner Neutral-tasting grape giving comparatively fat wines.

Huxelrebe Can be honeyed and muscat-like in good years, with firm acidity.

Madeleine Angevine A hybrid grape, which has table grapes somewhere in its ancestry and which has adapted to producing slightly honeyed wines.

Müller-Thurgau The German workhorse grape has been galloping around England as well. It's the most widely planted vine and makes medium-bodied wines of good acidity with a taste reminiscent of blackcurrants.

Ortega An early-ripening variety with a very perfumed flavour, often quite full, and quite successful in blends.

Reichensteiner A neutral grape variety, widely planted, with a hint of honey and ripe fruit.

Schönburger One of the most successful grapes produced in England. Gives a honeyed, fruity wine with good balancing acidity. Hints of Muscat and Gewürztraminer in the taste.

Seyval Blanc A hybrid vine well suited to northern vineyards because it is resistant to frost. Produces wines with quite acid fruit.

Siegerrebe Highly aromatic variety. A little goes a long way in a blend.

RED GRAPES

Triomphe d'Alsace A hybrid variety which originates – as its name suggests – in Alsace, but is now little seen there.

Wrotham Pinot A variation of Pinot Meunier which was developed in England.

Many English and Welsh wines will be blends of one of more of these grapes and will simply go under a brand name and a description of 'dry' or 'medium'. There is a trend towards blends, and away from single varietal wines: this helps to bring out the best characteristics of two or more grapes, and is producing successful wines.

Who's who in England and Wales

Here we give a selection of vineyards with a reliable record and whose wines are distributed beyond the vineyard gate.

A list of English and Welsh vineyards open to the public appears on page 608. For further information, write with a stamped addressed envelope to the English Vineyards Association, 38 West Park, London SE9 (telephone 01-857 0452).

Adgestone Wines on the dry side from Müller-Thurgau, Reichensteiner and Seyval Blanc grapes.
Cantina Augusto; Gerard Harris; Harrods; La Reserva Wines; Tanners Wines; Victoria Wine Company; Wine Growers Association; Yorkshire Fine Wines

Barton Manor Medium dry and dry wines, usually blended.
Harrods; John Harvey & Sons

Biddenden Müller-Thurgau, Reichensteiner and Ortega, plus a rosé from Pinot Noir grapes.
Berry Bros & Rudd; English Wine Centre; Fortnum & Mason; Victoria Wine Company; Winecellars

Bruisyard St Peter Medium dry wines from Müller-Thurgau. Widely distributed.
Berry Bros & Rudd; D Byrne & Co; English Wine Centre; Hicks & Don; Majestic; Victoria Wine Company; Willoughbys

Carr-Taylor The vineyard that's sold in Fauchon in Paris. Gutenborner, Huxelrebe, Kerner and Reichensteiner grapes all go to produce a blended wine. Making a successful Champagne method sparkling wine.
Curzon Wine Company; Ellis Son & Vidler; English Wine Centre; English Wine Shop; Fortnum & Mason; Waitrose; Wine Growers Association

Cavendish Manor Dry wines from the Müller-Thurgau.
Bentalls of Kingston, Surrey

Chilford Hundred Müller-Thurgau, Huxelrebe, Schönburger, Ortega, making a dry wine.
Curzon Wine Company

Chilsdown Müller-Thurgau, Reichensteiner, Seyval Blanc. Full wines in a dry style.
Chaplin & Son

Ditchling A Sussex vineyard making a pleasant Müller-Thurgau.
English Wine Centre

Elmham Park Dry blended wines which need a little time to lose their acidity.
Hicks & Don

Hambledon The first modern vineyard to be planted. Chardonnay, Pinot Noir and Seyval Blanc.
English Wine Centre; English Wine Shop

Ightham Reichensteiner, Huxelrebe, Schönburger and good Müller-Thurgau wine.
Partridges (133 Lower Sloane Street, London SW1)

Joyous Garde Make blended wines on the dry side.
W H Brakspeare (Hart Street, Henley, Oxon); Wine Warehouse (16 Market Street, Bracknell, Berks)

Lamberhurst The biggest vineyard and most widely distributed wines. Always high quality. Now making a sparkling Champagne method wine.
Berry Bros & Rudd; Curzon Wine Co; Davisons; English Wine Centre; Gerard Harris; Harrods; Hilbre Wine Company; Russell & McIver; Upper Crust; Victoria Wine Company; Wine Growers Association

Michaelmas House Highly perfumed blended dry wine.
English Wine Shop

Pilton Manor Müller-Thurgau and Seyval Blanc.
Averys; English Wine Shop

Pulham Magdalen Müller-Thurgau (or Rivaner as they call it). Make rich, tropical fruit wines.
Yorkshire Fine Wines

Saint Edmund Make a blended medium dry blend of Huxelrebe and Müller-Thurgau.
Tesco

St George's Wine sold in Japan and the House of Commons. Müller-Thurgau and Gewürztraminer.
Ellis Son & Vidler; Wine Growers Association

Spots Farm Müller-Thurgau, Gutenborner. Make a good dry wine.
English Wine Centre

Staple St James Medium dry wines from Müller-Thurgau grapes.
English Wine Centre; Fortnum & Mason

Staplecombe Madeleine Angevine, making a dry style of wine.
A & A Wines

Three Choirs Large vineyard with Müller-Thurgau and Reichensteiner.
D Byrne & Co; English Wine Centre; English Wine Shop; Grape Ideas; Hicks & Don; Majestic; Christopher Piper Wines; Tanners Wines; Victoria Wine Company; Wine Growers Association

Wootton Schönburger, Müller-Thurgau and Seyval Blanc. Good quality and long established (by English standards).
David Baillie Vintners; Curzon Wine Company; English Wine Centre; English Wine Shop; Gerard Harris; Hilbre Wine Company; Reid Wines; Victoria Wine Company; Wine Society; Yorkshire Fine Wines

Best buys from England and Wales

Moorlynch 1986 Medium (*Waitrose*)
Heywood Medium Dry 1983 (*Hicks & Don; Whighams of Ayr*)
Wootton Müller-Thurgau 1983 (*English Wine Centre*)

Specialist stockists

The English Wine Centre; English Wine Shop; Hicks & Don

France

ALSACE

Confusion returns

'A glass of Alsace before dinner?' was the polite suggestion from the (very French) waiter in the smart London restaurant. 'No thanks,' was the reply, 'I don't like sweet wines.' Collapse in Gallic bewilderment of waiter, and the introduction of some Muscadet to the table.

It's instructive to be reminded how many drinkers still think of Alsace wines as sweet, even after all the years that wine writers have gone on about the fact that Alsace uses German grapes, yes, but in a very French dry white sort of way.

There are perhaps two confusions here. One is that Alsace certainly does use Germanic grapes. The other is that although Alsace wine is dry, the sheer fruitiness of most of her wines gives the impression of sweetness. The net result is that anyone looking for a dry white wine will walk away from the Alsace shelf in favour of wines from the Loire, say, or something safely labelled Chardonnay.

Sales down again

This perhaps explains why, after a massive surge in 1985/86, when Alsace wines outperformed the wine market in a way nobody could

ALSACE

CHAMPAGNE

CHABLIS

BURGUNDY

LOIRE
Touraine
Pouilly-
sur-Loire
Côte de Nuits

JURA

Sancerre
Reuilly
Quincy
Côte de
Beaune

Muscadet
Anjou et
Saumur
Haut-
Poitou
Mâconnais

BEAUJOLAIS

St-Pourçain

Bugey

SAVOIE

BORDEAUX

NORTHERN
RHÔNE

Hermitage
Côte Rôtie

Monbazillac
Bergerac

Clairette
de Die

Duras

Lot

Tricastin

SOUTHERN
RHÔNE

SOUTH-
WEST
FRANCE

Buzet
Cahors
Marcillac
Gaillac

Beaumes
de Venise

Ventoux
Lubéron

Costières du Gard

Madiran

Languedoc

Côtes de Provence

PROVENCE

Irouléguy

Minervois

THE MIDI

Cassis

Jurançon
Corbières
Fitou
Roussillon

Bandol

Seine

Loire

Saône

Rhône

Geronne

0   100   200 km

0   50   100 miles

explain, sales have fallen back, and the phrase 'the wine the wine trade drinks' can be heard again lamenting the fact that Alsace wine doesn't sell as well as its quality suggests it should.

Mind you, back in 1986, we were enjoying the glorious 1983 vintage. Maybe when the 1984 vintage came along, people thought it wasn't quite so good: but in some cases (certainly with Gewürztraminer and Tokay Pinot Gris wines), the extra acidity imparted by a less sunny year was no bad thing. Then along came another super year in 1985, followed by a better-than-average 1986, and what the Alsaciens themselves optimistically (after all, they have to sell the wine) describe as a 'most attractive vintage' in 1987.

Wider range

Despite the steadying of sales after the dizzy rises in 1985/86, we now have a much wider range of Alsace wines to choose from. While much of what we buy is the simple, clean fruit of the Pinot Blanc wines, which have become staple wine bar and aperitif fare, we can also buy more of the top estate wines from small growers who wouldn't have thought about sending their wines to Britain a few years ago, because there was no demand.

Now there is, and people can discover a fascinating range of quality, not only from village to village, but also from producer to producer. Style – some make drier, lighter wines, others make richer wines – is as relevant to Alsace as it is to, say, the vineyards of Sancerre on the Loire. But, like Sancerre, there is also an overall style in Alsace that makes its wines some of the most easily recognisable (and none the worse for that).

That style, as we have suggested, is fruitiness. The flavours are vigorous and don't require some wood-ageing to bring them out. They are 'up front' (as the Californians might say), which, of course, is what makes them so attractive. There is no question of an Alsace Gewürztraminer being coy about its taste or bouquet. The same is true of the spicy, tropical fruit tastes of the Tokay Pinot Gris. Even the aristocratic Riesling shows a surprising forwardness in Alsace.

Good value – but not cheap

Alsace wines will never be cheap and cheerful. For one thing, the French themselves drink nearly half of what is made, the Germans take an awful lot more, so the growers don't need to discount their prices to get regular sales.

But the wines – across the full range of quality – are nevertheless value for money. At the cheaper end, the supermarkets have come up with some jolly good wines at around £3.50 a bottle, while at the top end, the vendange tardive and Grand Cru wines (see below) are showing that Alsace doesn't just produce middle of the road wines, but some great wines as well.

Maturity and reliability

It's these greater wines that reveal a hitherto unrealised aspect of Alsace wines: they age. That's true especially of wines made from the Riesling, the Gewürztraminer and the Tokay Pinot Gris. Wines made from Riesling, for example, in the superb 1976 vintage, are now perfectly mature, smelling and tasting petrolly (that's a good characteristic in Alsace), still retaining much of their fresh fruit but in a grown-up way.

What is more, you will almost never find a bad bottle of Alsace wine. Controls are probably some of the tightest in France: all the bottling has to be done in Alsace where the local officials can keep an eye on what's going on, so the reliability is good.

The Alsace label

Alsace is the only region of France where the wine is labelled varietally – that is, it is called after the name of the grape from which it is made.

There are two appellations for still wines, and one for sparkling, which cover the whole or parts of the region, from the German border in the north to the Swiss border in the south.

Alsace AC This is the basic appellation which covers 85 per cent of the vineyard area. All the grape varieties (see below), either singly or in blends, can be used in an Alsace AC wine.

Alsace Grand Cru A superior AC covering specific vineyards. At the moment, there are 25 Grand Cru vineyards, with another 22 up and coming. If the wine comes from just one Grand Cru vineyard, this will be specified on the label. If it's a blend of Grand Cru wines, the label will simply say Alsace Grand Cru without any vineyard name. Only the three noble grape varieties – Tokay Pinot Gris, Gewürztraminer and Riesling – can go to make Alsace Grand Cru. All other grape varieties – even if grown on Grand Cru sites – are straight Alsace AC.

Crémant d'Alsace This is the name for all sparkling wine in Alsace. It is made by the Champagne method and much of it is very good. For recommendations, see the chapter on sparkling wines (page 568).

Three more specific terms can appear on the label:

Edelzwicker A relatively cheap blend of two or more of the permitted grape varieties (see below). More widely seen in Alsace than outside.

Sélection de grains nobles An official category since 1983, describing wine made using grapes infected with noble rot.

Vendange tardive Late-picked grapes with a higher, more concentrated sugar content. The resultant wines can be sweet or dry. Quality is good – and the price high.

The terms **Réserve spéciale**, **Sélection spéciale** and **Cuvée spéciale** are fancy names which may mean a top cuvée from a producer – or just fancy prices.

The grapes of Alsace

Chardonnay This is grown specifically for Crémant d'Alsace and cannot be used in any Alsace still wines.

Gewürztraminer Heavily spicy, perfumed grape variety that made its name in Alsace before spreading elsewhere in the world. Can be a little cloying and unsubtle, but is the easiest wine to spot with your eyes shut.

Muscat Muscat à Petits Grains makes full-bodied, honey-smelling wines while Muscat Ottonel makes lighter wines; both are dry. A blend of the two grape varieties is often the best. The label on the bottle will not specify which is used.

Pinot blanc Simple, fruity wines, with just a hint of Chardonnay; to be drunk young. The vineyard area has increased, owing to greater demand.

Pinot noir Some rosé or pale red wines are made in Alsace. They don't leave the region (and most shouldn't), although a couple of producers (Hugel among them) are trying some wood-ageing with success.

Riesling The finest wines in Alsace are made from this grape – full but elegant, often steely dry but always giving off perfumed fruit. Quality varies from not bad to very good indeed – prices indicate the range.

Sylvaner Rather neutral wines, but in cool years have pleasant, straightforward acidity. Often attractive with a slight prickle.

Tokay Pinot Gris Used to be called Tokay d'Alsace (and still is unofficially) until the EEC did a deal with Hungary (home of the sweet Tokay wines) and banned its use. The grape produces rich, dry, peppery wines, sometimes lacking in acidity, but making up for that in the full body. An underrated grape variety.

The Alsace vintages

1987 A good average vintage, with reasonable quantity. Not a great year, but certainly one that will be ready to drink quite early.

1986 A lighter vintage than either 1983 or 1985, producing easy-to-drink wines which are now ready to drink. Good quantity, too.

1985 Widely acclaimed as an exceptional vintage. The wines are fine, excellently balanced, with richness but also elegance. The most successful varieties have been Gewürztraminer and Tokay Pinot Gris. Large quantities of vendange tardive and sélection de grains nobles were made. Apart from high quality, the crop was down by 20 per cent of a normal year.

1984 Turned out to be more of a success than originally predicted. It was a cool year, producing wines that were quite high in acidity. The more luscious varieties (Gewürztraminer and Tokay Pinot Gris) benefited from this. Most of the wines, though, should be drunk soon.

1983 Another great vintage, with very full wines, possibly lacking acidity but certainly not alcohol. Rieslings are delicious now but will keep for many years, while the Gewürztraminer is highly spiced, and the Pinot Gris also rich and delicious. Apart from Riesling, drink now.

1982 Rieslings and vendange tardive wines are still worth drinking now, as are better Gewürztraminers and Tokay Pinot Gris. Other wines will be tired.

1978 Top Rieslings are still good, as are some Gewürztraminers. Other wines should have been consumed, although exceptional wines will last for a few years yet.

1976 Still a few miraculous vendange tardive Rieslings, which will keep even longer. A few good Rieslings, Tokay Pinot Gris and Gewürztraminers to be drunk now.

Who's who in Alsace

The Alsace wine trade is divided into growers, some of whom also bottle and export – but using only wines from their own vineyards; and the merchants who, as in Burgundy, may own vineyards but also buy in wines. Much of the production also goes through co-operatives, some of a good standard, such as those at Eguisheim and Turckheim, who are supplying much of the wine bought for supermarket brands.

Caves Jean-Baptiste Adam, Ammerschwihr Large négociant house with some vineyards, dating from 1614. Wines are of acceptable quality: Grand Cru Sommerberg, Riesling, Gewürztraminer Cuvée Jean-Baptiste.
La Vigneronne; Waitrose; Cockburn & Co (1 Melville Place, Edinburgh); Sutton at Hone Wine Cellars (210 Main Street, Sutton at Hone, Dartford, Kent)

Which? Wine Guide does not accept payment for inclusion, and there is no sponsorship or advertising.

Caves J Becker, Zellenberg Long-established firm, now run by a young brother and sister. One-third of production comes from their own land. Wines: Pinot Blanc, Riesling Hagenschlaff, Tokay Pinot Gris Sonnenglanz.
Berkmann Wine Cellars/Le Nez Rouge; Mayor Sworder

Léon Beyer, Eguisheim Merchant who owns vineyards, selling full-bodied, very dry wines, which can last for years. Specialises in Gewürztraminer. Wines: Riesling Cuvée des Ecaillers, Gewürztraminer Cuvée des Comtes.
Curzon Wine Company; Fortnum & Mason; T & W Wines; La Vigneronne; Wine Society

Blanck, Kientzheim High quality grower making wines with good ageing potential.
Adnams; Lay & Wheeler; Tanners Wines

E Boeckel, Mittelbergheim Long-established grower and merchant making wines in a traditional style. Wines: Zotzenberg Sylvaner, Riesling and Gewürztraminer, Brandluft and Wibelsberg Rieslings, Ch d'Issembourg Gewürztraminer.
Tanners Wines

Dopff au Moulin, Riquewihr Merchant who also has a large vineyard holding in the best wine-growing area, central Alsace. Wines from Schoenenburg (Riesling) and Turckheim (Gewürztraminer) vineyards; Fruits de Mer blend; Crémant d'Alsace sparkling.
D Byrne & Co; Fortnum & Mason; Harrods; Lay & Wheeler; La Réserve; La Vigneronne; Yorkshire Fine Wines

Dopff et Irion, Riquewihr Growers and merchants who have been in business for three centuries. Wines: Riesling les Murailles, Gewürztraminer les Sorcières, Muscat les Amandiers, Pinot Gris les Maquisards, branded Crustaces and Crystal, Crémant d'Alsace.
D Byrne & Co; Eldridge Pope/Reynier Wine Libraries; Fortnum & Mason

Théo Faller, Kaysersberg One of the top growers, making superb wines from the Clos de Capucins vineyard. Small production, high prices. Wines: Cuvée Théo (Riesling and Gewürztraminer), vendange tardive, Domaine Weinbach.
D Byrne & Co; Fine Vintage Wines/Grape Ideas; O W Loeb; La Réserve; La Vigneronne

Rolly Gassmann, Rorschwihr Small estate making high quality wines which are only now becoming well known as they win at tastings time and again. Wines: Gewürztraminer, Tokay Pinot Gris, Muscat, Riesling, Pinot Noir.
Bibendum; Green's; Lockes; Raeburn Fine Wines and Foods; Tanners Wines; Ubiquitous Chip

Louis Gisselbrecht, Dambach-la-Ville Small vineyard holding and
négociant business making some reliable wines. Best are the Rieslings;
also Gewürztraminer, Pinot Blanc.
Alston Wines; D Byrne & Co; Hicks & Don; Hungerford Wine Company;
Lockes; Christopher Piper Wines; La Réserve; David Scatchard

Willy Gisselbrecht, Dambach-la-Ville Négociant and grower with a
large vineyard holding in Dambach-la-Ville.
Martinez Fine Wine

Hugel et Fils, Riquewihr Most famous (partly because of high quality,
partly good publicity) grower and négociant in Alsace. Their wines
tend to be rounder, less dry than others in Alsace. They developed the
idea of vendange tardive wines. Wines: those from the Schoenenburg
and Sporen vineyards; Cuvée Personnelle and Vendange Tardive are
top wines; house brands are Flambeau d'Alsace, Fleur d'Alsace.
Berry Bros & Rudd; D Byrne & Co; Christopher & Co; Rodney Densem Wines;
Peter Dominic; Fine Vintage Wines/Grape Ideas; Fortnum & Mason; Harrods;
Hicks & Don; Hungerford Wine Company; Lay & Wheeler; T & W Wines;
Tanners Wines; Yorkshire Fine Wines

Kientzler, Ribeauvillé Grower with land in Grand Cru vineyards
around Ribeauvillé. Wines: Grand Cru Geisberg, Grand Cru Kirchberg
de Ribeauvillé.
La Vigneronne

Domaine Klipfel, Barr One of the best domaines in the Bas-Rhin (in
the north of the region). Wines: Clos Zisser Gewürztraminer,
Kirchberg Riesling, Pinot Gris Freiberg.
Cadwgan Wines; Paul Sanderson Wines; Ubiquitous Chip Wine Shop;
Yorkshire Fine Wines; Satchels (North Street, Burnham Market, Norfolk);
Simkin & Jones (5 Cank Street, Leicester, Leics); Tollhouse Wines (47 Horse
Street, Chipping Sodbury, Avon)

Marc Kreydenweiss, Andlau High-quality grower and négociant
(married to Catherine Lacoste – see below) in the northern Alsace
vineyards, including the Domaine Fernand Gresser. Wines: Riesling,
Grand Cru Moenchberg, Gewürztraminer, Muscat, Pinot Noir.
La Vigneronne

Kuentz-Bas, Husseren-les-Châteaux Small family house making
excellent wines. Wines: Riesling, Gewürztraminer, Muscat, Pinot
Blanc, Pinot Gris.
Berry Bros & Rudd; Alex Findlater; Fortnum & Mason; Harrods; Oddbins;
Wine Society

Catherine Lacoste, Andlau Grower (married to Marc Kreydenweiss –
see above) in northern Alsace, producing very good Tokay Pinot Gris.
Wines: Pinot Gris, Grand Crus Kastelberg.
La Vigneronne

Michel Laugel, Marlenheim Négociant and grower in the northernmost Alsace wine village. Wines: Riesling de Wolxheim, Pinot Rosé de Marlenheim, Gewürztraminer de Wangen.
France Vin (20 Perivale Industrial Park, Horsenden Lane South, Perivale, Middx)

Gustave Lorentz, Bergheim Large firm of growers and négociants, producing good Gewürztraminer. Wines: Altenberg, Kanzlerberg vineyards are top crus.
D Byrne & Co; Threshers

Jos Meyer, Wintzenheim Grower and négociant making Grand Cru and good Gewürztraminer and Riesling wines from local vineyards. Wines: Gewürztraminer les Archenets, Riesling, Pinot Blanc, vendange tardive wines.
Augustus Barnett

A & O Muré, Rouffach Three-centuries-old firm, making intense, smooth wines from a single vineyard. They are wines to keep: Clos St-Landelin.
Alex Findlater; La Réserve; La Vigneronne

Jean Preiss-Zimmer, Riquewihr Top Rieslings and Gewürztraminers.
Fortnum & Mason; Harrods; Victoria Wine Company

Domaine Ostertag, Epfig Grower making Riesling and Gewürztraminer. Since his name means 'Easter' his labels carry a picture of a paschal lamb. Wines: Tokay Pinot Gris, Riesling, Gewürztraminer.
H Allen Smith; Morris & Verdin; La Vigneronne

Schlumberger, Guebwiller The biggest domaine in Alsace, based in the southern end of Alsace. Firm, concentrated wines of high quality. Wines: Kitterlé vineyard; Gewürztraminer Cuvée Christine Schlumberger.
Curzon Wine Company; Alex Findlater; Harrods; Lay & Wheeler; Yorkshire Fine Wines

Sick-Dreyer, Ammerschwihr Clean, straightforward domaine wines for early drinking. Wines: Riesling and Gewürztraminer from Kaefferkopf vineyard.
Alston Wines; La Vigneronne

Pierre Sparr, Sigolsheim A large négociant house, which also manages to produce some good wines from its own vineyards in Sigolsheim, Kaysersberg and Turckheim. Wines: Grand Crus Mambourg and Brand, Edelzwicker, Pinot Blanc, plus some vendange tardive wines.
Barwell & Jones

F E Trimbach, Ribeauvillé Family domaine and négociant founded in the 17th century. Fine, lighter style of wine which nevertheless lasts. Wines; Riesling Clos-Ste-Hune, Réserve and Réserve Personnelle wines, Riesling and Gewürztraminer.

Berry Bros & Rudd; D Byrne & Co; Curzon Wine Company; Alex Findlater; Fortnum & Mason; Harrods; Oddbins; La Reserve; T & W Wines

Alsace Willm, Barr Best known for Gewürztraminer, but also make good Riesling and Sylvaner. Wines: Grand Cru Gaensbroennel, Riesling Kirchberg de Barr.

Christopher & Co

Zind-Humbrecht Single vineyard wines made with painstaking care from Turckheim, Wintzenheim, Thann. Wines: Thann Clos St-Urbain (Riesling), Turckheim Brand (Riesling), Turckheim Herrenweg (Gewürztraminer).

Berkmann Wine Cellars/Le Nez Rouge; Laytons; Windrush Wines

Best buys from Alsace

Riesling 1986, Caves de Bennwihr (*Thos Peatling*)
Riesling 1986, Caves Vinicole de Turckheim (*Eaton Elliot Winebrokers; Wine Emporium*)
Tokay d'Alsace 1986, Cave Co-opérative de Turckheim (*Barnes Wine Shop; Ilkley Wine Cellars*)
Riesling 1986, Rolly Gassmann (*Bibendum*)
Tokay Pinot Gris Réserve 1986, Wiederhirn (*High Breck Vintners*)
Tokay Pinot Gris 1985, Dopff et Irion (*Eldridge Pope; J E Hogg*)
Sainsbury's Alsace Gewürztraminer 1985 (*J Sainsbury*)

Specialist stockists

Bibendum; D Byrne & Co; Croque-en-Bouche; Eldridge Pope; Farthinghoe Fine Wine and Food; Alex Findlater; Peter Green; High Breck Vintners; J E Hogg; Justerini & Brooks; O W Loeb; Raeburn Fine Wines and Foods; Henry Townsend; La Vigneronne

BEAUJOLAIS

Catching up with Nouveau

We were out of the country on Wednesday, 18 November, 1987, so we missed Beaujolais Nouveau Day. We almost missed Beaujolais Nouveau as well – by the Saturday, it seemed, Beaujolais Nouveau was dead, forgotten, almost unobtainable.

An exaggeration, perhaps, but only just. There's no doubt that our annual infatuation with the young, gushy, purple, fruity Beaujolais is becoming shorter and shorter. Once it extended almost to Christmas, now it's only a week, and even that may dwindle in a year or two.

Apart from Beaujolais Nouveau, how often do we drink Beaujolais the rest of the year? Certainly not as regularly as the Beaujolais producers would like. They invented the wine marketing man's dream, a wine that sells within weeks of the harvest so that the producers can have their money in time to buy their Christmas presents, but they forgot that Beaujolais Nouveau still accounts for only 30 per cent of Beaujolais production. The result is that we seem to have forgotten about the other 70 per cent.

The other Beaujolais

While Beaujolais Nouveau is a wine which demands the minimum of thought – and should give the maximum instant pleasure – some of the other wines made in the Beaujolais region are of quite a different calibre. In the northern part of the region, where the vineyards of Beaujolais Gamay run into those of the Mâconnais Chardonnay of Burgundy, the nine cru villages (listed below) make some very fine wines indeed. And in the area surrounding these special villages, the Beaujolais-Villages vineyards make something that is much more a thinking man's Beaujolais than ever Beaujolais Nouveau can – or is intended to – be.

Strange to think of the Gamay grape – the grape that was banned from Burgundy because it was inferior – making great wines in the Beaujolais. What is even stranger is to taste old Beaujolais cru wines, and to notice how much like old red Burgundy they become. Both lose the different types of fruitiness of the Gamay or the Pinot Noir and develop earthy aromas, perfumed, vegetal, attractively old but not too dry. Tasted together, there's not much difference between them.

So here is a style of Beaujolais that we tend to overlook. While we should not forget about the few days of Beaujolais Nouveau frenzy – after all, November can be a very gloomy month – let's make a resolution to taste some of the classier offerings from Beaujolais as well.

Certainly more Beaujolais cru wines are around in the shops, or at least at specialist merchants. Prices have remained stable, so they represent good value at the moment (compared with red Burgundy). A new and interesting trend is for single vineyard domaine-bottled Beaujolais, an obvious emulation of the success of domaine-bottled Burgundy, so while the Beaujolais from the well-known merchant houses (see below) is the most commonly available, it would be worth looking out for some of the estate wines as well.

Where's where in Beaujolais

Beaujolais classification is divided into three groupings. The basic wine is simply called **Beaujolais** and comes from the southern half of the region. This wine forms the basis of most Beaujolais Nouveau and as such is drunk fairly fast, but try it slightly chilled in the summer of the following year for a deliciously fruity drink.

Beaujolais-Villages Forty villages in the northern half of the region are entitled to this appellation. The wine is stronger, has greater depths than ordinary Beaujolais and keeps better. Some is sold as Beaujolais Nouveau, which is a bit of a waste.

Beaujolais crus
Nine villages are entitled to their own individual appellations. Their styles vary from quite light to serious wines with some ageing potential. All the villages regard themselves as having individual character.
Brouilly – the lightest and fruitiest style among the crus. Needs to be drunk fairly young.
Chénas – less often seen than some of the crus, but full of flavour and worth keeping.
Chiroubles – another light style, which should be drunk within a year of the harvest. Full of fruit.
Côtes de Brouilly – smallest of the crus making strong wines with some keeping power. They tend to age gracefully.
Fleurie – the most expensive of the cru wines (probably because the name is so attractive). They need to be drunk young. Not worth the money at the moment.
Juliénas – long-lasting wines (for Beaujolais), with a more serious style than other crus.
Morgon – another long-lasting cru. These are the wines which as they age really take on some of the characteristics of Burgundian Pinot Noir.
Moulin-à-Vent – the finest of the crus, the wine of this village will last well and is worth laying down.
St-Amour – soft, easy-drinking wines – as the name might suggest.
Regnié-Durette – an aspiring cru which wants to join the ranks of the other nine. It still hasn't quite made it, perhaps because the wines aren't quite up to it?

White Beaujolais
Made from the Chardonnay grape, this normally appears under the Burgundy appellation of St-Véran.

The vintages of Beaujolais

1987 A very good year for the more serious Beaujolais wines – the crus and Beaujolais Villages. Beaujolais Nouveau had less immediate fruit so was not so attractive.

1986 A lean year at first, with some hard, tannic acidity, so the Nouveau was less successful than the 1985. However, the wines have improved and are becoming more attractive. Lighter cru wines can be drunk now, but some of the weightier wines will last. Villages wines should have been drunk by the autumn of 1988.

1985 A very fine year, compared to 1976, with wines of considerable fruit. The best crus are Fleurie, Juliénas and Côtes de Brouilly. Morgon is disappointing. The best cru wines are still improving. Finish up the other cru wines and Villages wines.

1984 Wines with high acidity, most of which should have been drunk by now. Even the crus – Morgon, Moulin-à-Vent – should be drunk.

1983 Longer-lasting cru wines will still be worth keeping. Other crus and Beaujolais-Villages should be drunk by now.

Older vintages 1981, 1978 and 1976 Moulin-à-Vent, Morgon, Juliénas, Côtes de Brouilly are still interesting.

Who's who in Beaujolais

The growers

Merchants still tend to be more important than growers in Beaujolais. However, there is an increasing tendency for the better estates in the crus to bottle their own wine (see above). In this list, some of the names below will be from individual growers, and some from merchants who bottle individual estate wines with special labels (indicated here with the name of the merchant or group of growers, such as Duboeuf or Les Eventails).

Brouilly
Ch de Bluizard, Duboeuf (*D Byrne & Co*); Ch de la Chaize (*Stapylton Fletcher*).

Chénas
Jean Benon (*Lay & Wheeler*); Domaine Louis Champagnon (*Morris & Verdin*); Ch de Chénas, Les Eventails (*High Breck Vintners; Stapylton Fletcher*); Manoir des Journets, Duboeuf (*Anthony Byrne Fine Wines*).

Chiroubles
Domaine Desmeures Père et Fils, Duboeuf (*Davisons; Alexander Hadleigh, Herald Road, Hedge End, Southampton – by the case*); Ch de Javernand, Duboeuf (*Berkmann Wine Cellars/Le Nez Rouge; D Byrne & Co; Lockes; Noble Grape*); Domaine de la Grosse Pierre (*Gerard Harris; Haynes, Hanson & Clark*); Ch de Chénas, Les Eventails (*Eldridge Pope; Winecellars*); Ch de Raousset, Duboeuf (*Christopher Piper Wines*).

Côtes de Brouilly
Domaine André Large, Les Eventails (*High Breck Vintners*); Ch Thivin (*Waitrose*); Domaine Verger, Les Eventails (*Welbeck Wine*); Ch du Grand Vernay (*Roger Harris; Lay & Wheeler*).

Fleurie

Cave Co-opérative de Fleurie (*Roger Harris*); Ch de Fleurie, Loron (*Averys; Peter Green; Lay & Wheeler; Ubiquitous Chip*); Domaine de Montgenas, Les Eventails (*High Breck Vintners; Stapylton Fletcher*); Ch des Déduits, Duboeuf (*Anthony Byrne Fine Wines; Christopher Piper Wines; Wizard Wine Warehouses*); Domaine des Quatres Vents, Duboeuf (*Berkmann Wine Cellars/Les Nez Rouge; Anthony Byrne Fine Wines; Noble Grape; Pennyloaf Wines*); Michel Chignard (*Roger Harris; Morris & Verdin*).

Juliénas

Ch des Capitans, Sarrau (*Yorkshire Fine Wines*); Domaine Monnet, Les Eventails (*High Breck Vintners; Winecellars*); François Condemine (*Roger Harris*); Domaine André Pelletier, Les Eventails (*Gerard Harris; Haynes, Hanson & Clark; La Vigneronne*); Domaine de la Seigneurie de Juliénas, Duboeuf (*J Townend & Sons*).

Morgon

Domaine Georges Brun, Les Eventails (*Gerard Harris; Seckford Wines; Stapylton Fletcher*); Domaine le Clochet, Les Eventails (*Eldridge Pope; Gerard Harris*); Domaine Jean Descombes, Duboeuf (*Berkmann Wine Cellars/Le Nez Rouge; Anthony Byrne Fine Wines; D Byrne & Co; Pennyloaf Wines; Christopher Piper Wines*); Domaine Lieven, Duboeuf (*Anthony Byrne Fine Wines*); Domaine des Vieux Cèdres, Loron (*Direct Wine Shipments; Lay & Wheeler; Sebastopol Wines; Tanners Wines*).

Moulin-à-Vent

Ch des Jacques, Thorin (*Findlater Mackie Todd*); Domaine Jacky Janodet (*Morris & Verdin; Tanners Wines*); Ch du Moulin-à-Vent (*Adnams; Roger Harris*).

St-Amour

Domaine des Ducs (*Roger Harris; Lay & Wheeler*); Domaine du Paradis, Duboeuf (*Anthony Byrne Fine Wines; Pennyloaf Wines*); Domaine Guy Pâtissier, Les Eventails (*Seckford Wines*); Domaine de Breuil, Sarrau (*Tanners Wines; David Burns Vintners, Old Barn Farm Road, Three Legged Cross, Wimborne, Dorset; Rosetree Wine Company*).

Beaujolais-Villages

Ch la Tour Bourdon, Duboeuf (*Noble Grape; Christopher Piper Wines*); Ch du Grand Vernay (*Roger Harris*); Geny de Flammacourt (*Roger Harris*); André Depardon, Les Eventails (*Haynes, Hanson & Clark; Henry Townsend*); Ch Vierres, Duboeuf (*Davisons; George Hill of Loughborough*); Domaine de la Chapelle de Vatre, Sarrau (*David Burns Vintners – see above under St-Amour; Curzon Wine Co*).

Send us your views on the report forms at the back of the book.

The merchants

Chanut Good quality range of Beaujolais and Beaujolais Villages.
David Alexander; Hedley Wright; Hicks & Don; Irvine Robertson; Wizard Wine Warehouses

Joseph Drouhin One of the Beaune merchants to take Beaujolais seriously. His wines are quite heavy, almost Burgundian, but well made.
Gerard Harris; Michael Menzel

Georges Duboeuf Top quality range, often from individual growers. One of the most reliable – and best – names. Also use the Paul Bocuse label.
Widely available

Les Eventails de Vignerons Producteurs A grouping of nearly 50 growers who have joined together for central bottling and marketing, although still making their own wine. A range of very good wines.
High Breck Vintners; Stapylton Fletcher

Pierre Ferraud High quality reputation, making good Nouveau and Villages.
Eldridge Pope; Market Vintners; Seckford Wines; Wines from Paris

Sylvain Fessy
A good range of wines at most quality levels.
Ian G Howe; Windrush Wines

Loron Sound, fruity wines at all quality levels. Occasional estate cru wines aim higher.
Averys; D Byrne & Co; Champagne de Villages; Chaplin & Son; Direct Wine Shipments; Eldridge Pope; Ellis Son & Vidler; Peter Green; Lay & Wheeler; Oddbins; Sebastopol Wines; Tanners Wines; Ubiquitous Chip

Mommessin A Burgundy merchant with an interest in Beaujolais, especially of the basic type.
Averys; G E Bromley & Sons; Direct Wine Shipments; A L Vose; Yorkshire Fine Wines

Pasquier-Desvignes Light style of wines, but of good commercial quality. The St-Amour is the best cru.
Victor Hugo Wines

Piat Their best claim to fame is the attractive bottle. They are better at Beaujolais cru wines than basic Beaujolais. They also make the branded Piat d'Or which everybody thinks is a Beaujolais but is in fact a vin de table.
Peter Dominic; Oddbins; Tesco; Victoria Wine Company

Les Producteurs Réunis Excellent co-operative with good basic Beaujolais as well as the crus.
Roger Harris Wines

Sarrau Good quality crus and Villages. A go-ahead young firm.
G E Bromley & Sons; Gerard Harris; Tanners Wines; Yorkshire Fine Wines

Louis Tête Serious basic Beaujolais, as well as cru wines.
Peter Green; F & E May, Carlton House, 66/69 Great Queen Street, London WC2

Thorin Good wine from Moulin-à-Vent, Ch des Jacques and also a rare Beaujolais Blanc.
Berry Bros & Rudd; Findlater Mackie Todd

Trenel Small firm making good Morgon.
Barwell & Jones; Tanners Wines; Yorkshire Fine Wines

Best buys from Beaujolais

Beaujolais Villages 1986, Domaine de la Croix Jacques (*Summerlee Wines*)
Coteaux du Lyonnais Rouge, Sarrau (*Snipe Wine Cellars*)
Juliénas 1987, Domaine René Monnet, Les Eventails (*The Market/ Winecellars*)
Beaujolais Villages 1987, Jean-Charles Pivot (*Roger Harris*)
Beaujolais Villages-Regnié 1986, Loron (*Blayney's*)

Specialist stockists

Anthony Byrne Fine Wines; Roger Harris; High Breck Vintners; Hicks & Don; Le Nez Rouge/Berkmann Wine Cellars; Thos Peatling; Christopher Piper Wines; J Townend & Sons

BORDEAUX

The public relations circus

This has been a very good year for public relations consultants in Bordeaux. They have been inundated with château owners and négociants wanting publicity for their wines in particular and the region in general. Spectacular beanfeasts have been organised for journalists (one involved a special train from Paris and what seemed like miles of red carpet), old vintages of great wines have been poured, egos have been massaged.

The reason for all this hype is that the great châteaux have an awful lot of wine to sell – and not enough buyers. Huge vintage has followed huge vintage, and the quality has, on the whole, remained remarkably high. The problem has been the price, which rose inexorably from the great 1982, the pretty great 1983, the indifferent 1984 but then the great 1985. It levelled off in 1986, but not until the 1987 vintage was about to be placed on the market did the château owners suddenly take the plunge and cut prices.

When they did, some of them did it on a grand scale. Ch Margaux went down by 38 per cent, Ch Mouton-Rothschild by 39 per cent. But still the selling was difficult. People were much too busy looking at older – and therefore more mature – vintages to worry about buying any more claret en primeur. The Bordeaux merchants took some, but their inventories are now bulging with unsold (or, worse still, sold and returned) wines.

Hence the media hype. Journalists were expected to go away and write about how superb great Bordeaux is (we all know that) and how everybody ought to rush out and buy.

Well, of course, in the UK we buy huge quantities of red Bordeaux anyway (and white, come to that – but that's a different set of problems); indeed, we're the largest export market (2.8 million cases in 1986/87). But most of that wine is basic Bordeaux or Bordeaux Supérieur, and at that level the stock problems, the huge prices and the heavy publicity machine are quite irrelevant – worlds away, in fact.

The haves and the have nots

The sad truth for many of the petit château producers (the term used to describe small farmers whose few hectares of vines are at the end of a dirt track in the wrong area of the Bordeaux region) is that their wine is now cheaper than basic Côtes du Rhône. It does seem rather unfair that the rich château owners can rake in their millions only a few miles away from somebody who can just about afford a new tractor.

However, for the consumer, the situation is much more satisfactory. Never has there been a time with more good value Bordeaux on the market than now. A glance at the list of any of our Bordeaux specialist stockists (and many other merchants in the WHERE TO BUY section) will reveal a wealth of well-priced wines, many – if not most – with unknown names.

Obviously, the very anonymity of many of the petit château wines means that we have to rely on wine merchants to make good selections. Again, we have indicated by inclusion in the specialist stockists at the end of this section which merchants have cultivated close links with Bordeaux and are therefore able to buy with knowledge and care.

We also suggest some names of our own – these will be found towards the end of this section. But with over 4,000 properties in the Bordeaux wine area – which, incidentally, is the largest concentration of vineyards in the world – we're bound to miss more than a few.

Bordeaux

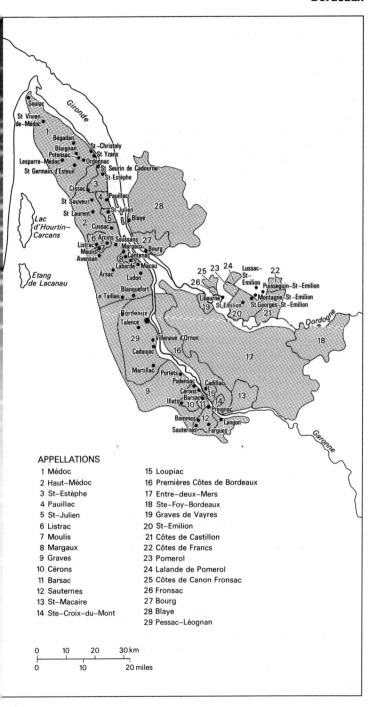

Gironde

Soulac
St Vivien-
de-Médoc
Bégadan
Blaignan
Potensac
Lesparre-Médoc
St Germain d'Esteuil
St -Christoly
St Yzans
Ordonnac
St Seurin de Cadourne
St-Estèphe
Cissac
Pauillac
St Sauveur
St Laurent
St-Julien
Blaye
Cussac
Arcins
Listrac
Moulis
Avensan
Soussans
Margaux
Cantenac
Labarde
Macau
Arsac
Ludon
Blanquefort
Le Taillan
Bordeaux
Talence
Villenave d'Ornon
Cadaujac
Martillac
Portets
Podensac
Cérons
Illats
Barsac
Preignac
Bommes
Langon
Sauternes
Fargues

Lac d'Hourtin-Carcans

Etang de Lacanau

Lussac-St-Emilion
Puisseguin-St-Emilion
Montagne-St-Emilion
St Georges-St-Emilion
Libourne
St-Emilion

Dordogne

Cadillac

Garonne

APPELLATIONS

1 Médoc	15 Loupiac
2 Haut-Médoc	16 Premières Côtes de Bordeaux
3 St-Estèphe	17 Entre-deux-Mers
4 Pauillac	18 Ste-Foy-Bordeaux
5 St-Julien	19 Graves de Vayres
6 Listrac	20 St-Emilion
7 Moulis	21 Côtes de Castillon
8 Margaux	22 Côtes de Francs
9 Graves	23 Pomerol
10 Cérons	24 Lalande de Pomerol
11 Barsac	25 Côtes de Canon Fronsac
12 Sauternes	26 Fronsac
13 St-Macaire	27 Bourg
14 Ste-Croix-du-Mont	28 Blaye
	29 Pessac-Léognan

0   10   20   30 km
0   10   20 miles

The whites – sweets yes, dries only maybe

Although for many people Bordeaux means claret, we shouldn't forget the whites. The sweet whites, of course, are in a class of their own, and we are delighted to report that the world is beginning to wake up to the great pleasures of drinking sweet white wines with puddings. If there are any readers who haven't tried this delicious combination recently, they should read our featured articles on dessert wines and food and wine combinations at the beginning of the Guide, then act.

Of course, increased interest in sweet whites means that their prices have shot up. The bargains of a few years ago are no longer to be had, and it is to the lesser areas of Bordeaux (Ste-Croix-du-Mont, Loupiac or Premières Côtes de Bordeaux) that we need to look for bargains.

While the sweet whites have been making a deserved comeback, the dry whites have been struggling. A few top estates – particularly in the northern Graves – are creating classic, top-quality dry white wines, using wood for ageing. Most, though, are turning out white wines to be drunk young. The Sémillon, the traditional white grape of Bordeaux, may be great for sweet wines, but it hasn't succeeded so well with dry wines (something the Australians, who have created a great tradition of dry wines from the grape, cannot understand). So the Sauvignon Blanc has been used increasingly – either in a blend or on its own – to give some zing and freshness to these wines.

The success has been partial. Dry white Bordeaux is still really only worth buying on price (apart from those few top estates). The talk now is of bringing back the Sémillon and trying again with new vinification methods – the French have obviously been watching the Australians with some jealousy.

What happens next?

As we go to press, the Bordelais are busy praying for a lousy 1988 vintage. They are already putting out noises about a small vintage – and predicting that heavy rains at flowering time may mean a poor harvest as well.

The last thing they want is a good vintage. They need to have a poor year to – as the stock market likes to say – firm up prices of previous vintages, cut down the stocks a bit and generally get things in order.

As far as we are concerned, the more good wine that's made in our favourite red wine vineyard, the better. For the moment, we echo the advice of most of the wine merchants in our WHERE TO BUY section: there's no need to buy the youngest vintages of claret unless you want to lay some down for your children or grandchildren. If you are buying for your own pleasure, look at older vintages. And don't forget that for everyday drinking, this is a great time to be buying.

The taste of Bordeaux

THE REDS

Claret (red Bordeaux) is a blended wine, containing varying proportions of Cabernet Sauvignon, Cabernet Franc and Merlot. Two lesser varieties (in quantity but not in quality) that are planted increasingly rarely are Petit Verdot and Malbec.

Cabernet Sauvignon This is the major grape in the Left Bank properties of the Médoc and Graves. It is also the most important red grape variety of quality in the world. In Bordeaux, it makes long-lasting wines, full of blackcurrant or cassis fruit when young, but always heavily structured with tannin. With maturity, it mellows and a complex of tastes and flavours – spice, cedar, cigar-box – come in as the tannin softens. In Bordeaux, there is no such thing as a 100 per cent Cabernet Sauvignon wine, although some estates (especially in Pauillac) get quite close.

Cabernet Franc Lower tannin than the Cabernet Sauvignon gives a fresh, faster-maturing wine which, when blended, takes the hard edges off the Cabernet Sauvignon.

Merlot The grape variety that comes into its own on the Right Bank, in St-Emilion and Pomerol. It makes wines with quite high initial acidity, but which soften and mellow faster than Cabernet Sauvignon. Jammy fruit is often the characteristic of these wines – plump, opulent and easier to appreciate than the more austere Cabernet Sauvignon wines of the Médoc.

THE WHITES

Sémillon Used for sweet wines, this grape produces the luscious, honeyed style of Sauternes and Barsac, with great ageing ability derived from the noble rot. In dry whites, great care needs to be taken over its vinification, although the great dry whites of Bordeaux also rely on its ageing qualities.

Sauvignon The great white grape of the Loire. In Bordeaux, it makes wines which have crispness and freshness when young, but which do not age well. A little Sauvignon in some of the sweet whites adds firmness.

The Bordeaux vineyard

The Bordeaux vineyard is huge, spreading out in all directions from the city of Bordeaux. It is unique in French terms in that all the wine produced in the region is AC (appellation contrôlée).

There are various levels of appellation. The most basic wines are labelled either Bordeaux or Bordeaux Supérieur (Bordeaux Supérieur has half a degree more alcohol than Bordeaux and is generally slightly better wine). These wines can come from anywhere in Bordeaux not covered by one of the more localised appellations, or ones produced from young vines or vines which have given a higher yield than is allowed for a village or local AC.

Bordeaux and Bordeaux Supérieur represent bargain country – provided you can find the right wine.

REGIONAL APPELLATIONS

Above the basic appellation, there are a number of regional appellations.

Côtes de Bourg This is the large area facing the Médoc on the north bank of the Gironde. Its vineyards stretch well back from the river, the best being on the river front itself, but red wines from the smaller châteaux in the hinterland make good bargains.

Côtes de Castillon and Côtes de Francs Two small areas to the east of St-Emilion which make some delicious, easy-drinking wines mainly from Merlot and Cabernet Franc. Try them if you come across them.

Entre-Deux-Mers This appellation covers the spit of land between the Rivers Dordogne and Garonne. Traditionally it is the home of rather over-sulphured white wines, some of them medium sweet, but recent improvements have brought a spate of good dry whites and some quaffable reds.

Graves The huge stretch of vineyard south of Bordeaux. This was the original vineyard of the region before the Médoc was opened up. Whites and reds are both produced here. The finest wines come from the northern end in the suburbs of Bordeaux itself, some of which are in a new appellation of Pessac-Léognan (see below).

Graves Supérieur A stronger version of a white Graves. Sometimes medium dry, so beware if you want a dry wine.

Médoc This normally refers to wines produced at the northernmost end of the strip of land which juts out into the Atlantic on the left bank of the Gironde. Here the top-quality gravelly soil of the Haut-Médoc (see below) has been replaced by clay. Formerly almost completely ignored by wine buyers in this country, this is now the home of many up and coming petits châteaux – an area to watch.

Haut-Médoc The term geographically refers to the rest of the Médoc as far as the northern edge of the city of Bordeaux. In wine terms, châteaux using this appellation for their red wines will generally be further away from the river than the principal Médoc vineyards. In practice, most of this area is covered by one of the village appellations (see below). Villages without their own appellations include: St-Seurin-de Cadourne, Cissac, St-Saveur, St-Laurent, Ludon.

Premières Côtes de Blaye A small area attached to Côtes de Bourg. Somewhat more refined than the average Bourg wine, the red wines are also somewhat more expensive, but still acceptable value.

Premières Côtes de Bordeaux A narrow strip of vineyards on the north bank of the Garonne facing the Graves. Produces some good red wines as well as sweet whites.

VILLAGE OR COMMUNE APPELLATIONS

Fronsac A couple of miles west of Pomerol, this area is producing some really exciting wines. Prices are rising, but they are still comparatively good value for money. They have something of the smoothness of St-Emilion and the intensity of Pomerol. There is also a smaller, slightly superior appellation of **Canon-Fronsac**. Both are worth looking for.

Margaux (Haut-Médoc) The perfumed bouquet of a good Margaux is the thing. Less concentrated than, for example, a Pauillac, the wines have immense charm, finesse and breeding.

Moulis and **Listrac** Two smaller appellations in the hinterland of the Haut-Médoc. Less well known and therefore less expensive, making more austere wines but also some wines with class.

Pauillac (Haut-Médoc) The most famous village appellation because it contains three of the five first growths (Lafite, Latour, Mouton-Rothschild – see below under Crus classés). The wines are intense, full, firm and tannic with the greatest ageing potential. Words like 'blackcurrant' are used to describe the young wines; matured, they can offer some of the greatest wine experiences anywhere – if you can afford them.

Pessac-Léognan New appellation at the northern end of the Graves which takes in the best vineyard areas of the area. The châteaux include Haut-Brion, La Mission-Haut-Brion, Pape-Clément, La Louvière, Malartic-Lagravière and Domaine de Chevalier.

Pomerol Next door to St-Emilion on the northern bank of the River Dordogne, but making wines with much greater intensity and strength. A tiny production from a small vineyard area ensures that even the least wines from this appellation are expensive, while Ch Pétrus, at the top, is the most expensive wine in the world. A satellite appellation of **Lalande de Pomerol** is less expensive (but also not so top class).

St-Emilion The vineyards surround the most attractive town in the Bordeaux region, built on a hill on the north bank of the River Dordogne. There is a complex system of classification – at the top is Premier Grand Cru Classé, then Grand Cru Classé, then Grand Cru, then the basic level. A number of villages use the St-Emilion name as well, but their wines are not so good.

St-Estèphe The northernmost of the great Haut-Médoc villages. The wines tend to be sturdier, darker in colour, more tannic than other Haut-Médoc wines.

St-Julien Haut-Médoc village making round, soft, elegant wines, which – for the Médoc – mature early. The (predominantly male) wine trade sometimes describes them as 'feminine'.

THE SWEET WHITE WINE AREAS

Sauternes and **Barsac** The two great dessert wine areas, carved out of the forests of the Landes, relying on the noble rot – 'pourriture noble' which grows on the grapes in the humid autumn weather – to make intense, luscious, honeyed sweet wines. Under-valued for many years, their prices are beginning to rise, but the experience of drinking them makes it worth paying the prices (especially if you can find half-bottles).

Cadillac, Premières Côtes de Bordeaux, St-Macaire and **Cérons** Lesser sweet wines for drinking young and well chilled as aperitifs.

Loupiac and **Ste-Croix-du-Mont** Somewhere between the two groups in intensity and with some noble rot in good years. Generally best drunk young, but will keep in better years.

THE DRY WHITES OF BORDEAUX

The range in dry whites is as great as in the reds. Some of the top châteaux in the Graves produce a white wine that matures well to deep, rich flavours (Haut-Brion Blanc, Laville-Haut-Brion, Domaine de Chevalier, Malartic-Lagravière, Rahoul, Carbonnieux).

At the bottom end of the scale, dry white is downright dull, relieved only by flashes of the grassy acidity of Sauvignon. If the name of one of these wines includes 'Cépage Sauvignon' or an equivalent phrase, the latest vintage will be fresh, crisp and fruity, but the wines fade fast. While much basic white Bordeaux is under the Bordeaux AC, look also for the small appellation of **Graves de Vayres**, which is a small area of Entre-Deux-Mers, and for wines from **Bourg** and **Blaye**.

What's on the Bordeaux label

Château The name signifies only that the wine in the bottle comes from a specified vineyard in an estate. The vineyard doesn't have to be in one piece of land, provided it is all in the same appellation area.

Crus bourgeois A local classification of wines which are just under the formal crus classés. Often good-value wines at this level.

Crus classés Most of the major Bordeaux areas are classified in one way or another. In the Médoc, the most famous classification of all (which took place in 1855 and, with one adjustment, still stands) places the top estates in classes one (first growth, the top) to five (fifth growth). While many of the estates still justify their placing, others have disappeared or live on the reputation of their classification rather than on their wine.

In the Graves there has also been a classification system, but this seems to have been swallowed up by the creation of the new appellation of Pessac-Léognan (see above). In St-Emilion, a complex system has three tiers of quality – from Premier Grand Cru Classé, through Grand Cru Classé to Grand Cru. Sauternes and Barsac have 22 classed growths which were classified in 1855 at the same time as those in the Médoc.

Grand Vin Can be used for any wine from Bordeaux Supérieur upwards. It has no legal significance, but it helps sales.

Mis/Mise en bouteille au château/à la propriété Loose terms: propriété can mean a huge warehouse in Bordeaux owned by the owner of the vineyard or the négociant or a co-operative or it can mean a cellar on the estate. Bottled at the château may mean bottled on a bottling line hired for the occasion.

Négociant Bordeaux merchant who buys wine to blend, as well as holding stocks of fine wines.

SECOND WINES

Many of the top châteaux do not put all their wine from a vintage into the blend for their best wine. Some wine – good, but not the absolute best (often from more youthful vines) – is put aside and sold separately as a second wine. By any other standards, it is still very good. It's not cheap, but it's cheaper than the first wine and gives some idea of what all the fuss is about.

Nearly every estate puts out a second wine (fashion is very important in Bordeaux); we give a list in the section of Bordeaux names to watch (see below) of those we reckon are the best value. Other names you might come across are (with the main château in brackets):

de Marbuzet (Cos d'Estournel), La Parde de Haut-Bailly (Ch Haut-Bailly), Les Forts de Latour (Ch Latour), de l'Amiral (Ch Labégorce-Zédé), de Clairefont (Ch Prieuré-Lichine), la Dame de Montrose (Ch Montrose), Moulin-Riche (Ch Léoville-Poyferré), Amiral de Beychevelle (Ch Beychevelle), Ch Abiet (Ch Cissac), Ch Cantebeau and Ch Clos du Roi (Ch Louvière), Ch Gallais-Bellevue (Ch Potensac), Ch La Tour d'Aspic (Ch Haut-Batailley), Moulin des Carruades (Ch Lafite-Rothschild), Marquis de Ségur (Ch Calon-Ségur), Pavillon Rouge (Ch Margaux).

Many other classified growth and cru bourgeois châteaux sell a second wine; it would be worth asking merchants what they stock.

Bordeaux vintages

It's not true to say – as some commentators have suggested – that it is impossible to have a bad vintage in Bordeaux any more. It is just much more difficult. The last really bad vintage for reds was 1977, and since then better winemaking and vineyard husbandry have kept up standards even in years with bad weather. The great sweet white wines need the right climatic conditions much more than the reds, so there are fewer fine vintages – but even in lesser years, the wines are still better than they used to be.

1987 *Reds:* a year of mixed fortunes, depending on whether the crop was picked before or after the rain. It was also the year which saw helicopters being used for the first time to dry off the grapes before picking. The vintage will never be a great one, but some producers – especially in St-Emilion and Pomerol – will have made average quality wines, which will probably mature quickly. It's also likely to be a year when the best producers will declassify much of their wine down to their second wines – so there may be some bargains in this area. *Sweet whites:* a small crop of wines which will mature quickly.

1986 *Reds:* a large vintage. The Merlot regions on the right bank of St-Emilion and Pomerol suffered from high yields, and those producers who removed bunches during the summer to cut the final yield will have made the best wines. In the Médoc and Graves, the wines are big and tannic after a long, hot September. They should last for a long time. *Sweet whites:* it looks as though this has been a very great vintage, with good botrytis (causing noble rot) and plenty of fruit. Medium levels of acidity mean medium-term development.

1985 *Reds:* the largest vintage ever. Generally regarded as a very good year, although not hitting the heights of 1982. The finest wines have immense richness, depth of colour and concentration which presage a long, slow maturation. Wines from the Graves are developing fast, while those from the Médoc need a long time to soften up. St-Emilion and Pomerol wines are rich and concentrated. *Sweet whites:* a middle quality vintage, with only the top estates producing really good wines. They will be ready to drink by 1990.

1984 *Reds:* generally lack fruit and also the roundness given by the Merlot, which failed to flower in the cold, damp spring. The wines will have a short life (three to ten years) but when made by a reputable château should give some austere pleasure. Prices were initially too high for the quality, but look likely to fall. *Sweet whites:* soft, early-maturing wines. Drink now.

1983 *Reds:* elegant, structured wines which have been going through a lean patch during 1988, but which will go on to mature slowly. The

Médoc wines are better than those of St-Emilion and Pomerol, but prices for all areas have remained good. *Sweet whites:* a very great year indeed in Sauternes, with honeyed fruit but quite high levels of acidity which will give the wines a long life. Don't even touch them before the mid-1990s.

1982 *Reds:* the big ones – in price as well as quality. At the petit château level, some very fine wines were made, and there are some bargains to be had. At the higher levels, prices are high. The wines of St-Emilion and Pomerol will be drinkable by the mid 1990s, but most wines may not really mature until the turn of the century. *Sweet whites:* a quick-maturing vintage which can be drunk now.

1981 *Reds:* a bargain vintage. Lean, austere wines, often well structured. The best – from the Médoc in particular – will mature for another two or three years, but many are ready to drink now. St-Emilion, too, is ready to drink, but keep Pomerols. *Sweet whites:* variable vintage in which only the top estates made wines with any lasting power. These can survive till the 1990s, but drink the others now.

1980 *Reds:* wines to drink now. Soft, without staying power, but enjoyable and at good prices. Most have already been drunk – check on any you have that they are not drying out, and taste before you buy. *Sweet whites:* medium quality vintage, which is ready to drink. Plenty of bargains here.

1979 *Reds:* suddenly, everybody expects these wines to go on developing. The petits châteaux and St-Emilions are tasting good now, but will last. The best Médoc wines will go on for another eight or nine years before reaching their peak. *Sweet whites:* another rather light vintage, but there is some pleasure in the top wines.

1978 *Reds:* slow-maturing wines. Most petit château wines are for drinking now and over the next few years, but the top wines will go on and on. The Médoc and Graves wines will last the longest.

1977 *Reds:* a few good wines in a generally poor year. Only the very best are worth keeping – and then only those chosen with discrimination. Don't buy from this vintage unless the price is good and you've tasted.

1976 *Reds:* ripe wines that can be slightly watery as well, but good examples are packed with slightly sweet fruit which tastes good now. Keep top Médocs, drink the rest. *Sweet whites:* This is a great vintage to drink now – the wines are rich and oily. The best will keep, but are enjoyable now.

1975 *Reds:* a problem year. After great initial enthusiasm, because the power and tannin suggested a long life, nothing has happened. The wines are still very dry and tannic and don't have much underlying fruit. Only the best will open out, the rest will probably just get drier. *Sweet whites:* lighter than 1976, with excellent balance of fruit and acidity. They are developing an attractive, mature taste, so start drinking them now.

1971 *Reds:* going past their best, these wines confounded the pundits who expected great things of them. Stylish, balanced and rather delicate, they won't keep. *Sweet whites:* rather too sweet, lacking acidity initially. They need drinking now.

1970 *Reds:* this is a year with a great future still ahead of it. Although petits châteaux should be drunk (if they haven't been already), top wines will go on for a long time into the next century. *Sweet whites:* big, rich, almost over-the-top wines that may mature even longer. Drink most of them, but keep the top classed growths.

DRY WHITES

There are two levels of drinkability for dry whites. Most – especially if they have a high amount of Sauvignon – need to be consumed within one or two years of the harvest, so drink 1986 and 1987 this year. Wines aged in wood from some top estates (especially in the Graves) will go on for much longer – decades even. Consult the vintage guide for reds for these wines.

Drink now – or keep?

As a general rule, the higher up the classification scale, the longer a red Bordeaux will keep. So ordinary Bordeaux appellation wine needs drinking first, basic St-Emilion next – and so on up the scale: the top classed growths of the Médoc seem to last decades. The same rule goes for sweet white Sauternes.

Bordeaux names to watch

It is not possible to indicate stockists against Bordeaux châteaux since British merchants do not buy every vintage. In the WHERE TO BUY section, and under *Specialist stockists* at the end of this section, we indicate those merchants who keep large stocks of Bordeaux and specialise in buying direct from the area. Get hold of their lists and ask their advice as well as looking for some of the names below.

The reds

For the first time, we are including in this section a list of branded and own-label wines which we can recommend. Some are non-vintage wines (indicated here by the letters NV) – not necessarily a bad thing when consistency of style is important. If they are vintage wines, look for the vintage and buy according to the vintage notes above. Wines from the 1985 and 1986 vintages will generally be better than those from 1987.

BRANDED AND OWN-LABEL CLARETS

Sandeman Claret (*Oddbins*)
Tanners Claret NV (*Tanners Wines*)
Maître d'Estournel (*Laytons; André Simon*)
Ch Chauffepied (*Wizard Wine Warehouses*)
Chevalier de Védrines (*Wine Growers Association*)
Beunier Claret NV (*Buckingham Wines*)
Tesco Claret NV (*Tesco*)
Ch de Brondeau (*Balls Brothers*)
Ch Haut-Genestat (*The Market/Le Provençal; Winecellars*)
Willoughbys Sunday Claret (*Thomas Baty; George Dutton; Willoughbys*)
Beau Rivage, Borie Manou (*Davisons*)
Claret, Yvon Mau (*Unwins*)
St-Emilion, Sélection Jean-Pierre Moueix (*Adnams; Corney & Barrow*)

THE CHÂTEAUX

Châteaux listed here are enjoying a high reputation at the moment. Additionally, their wines are good value for money.

Bordeaux and **Bordeaux Supérieur** Ch Méaume, Ch Timberlay, Ch de Belcier, Ch Tour de Mirabeau, Ch la Combe des Dames, Ch Sables-Peytraud, Ch Le Gardéra, Ch La Pierrière, Ch du Juge, Mouton Cadet, Ch la Dominique Siegla.

Médoc Ch du Castéra, Ch La Cardonne, Ch Haut-Canteloup, Ch Patache d'Aux, Ch Potensac, Ch La Tour de By, Ch La Tour St-Bonnet, Ch Greysac, Ch Hanteillan, Ch Terre Rouge, Ch le Boscq, Ch Liversan, Ch les Ormes-Sorbet.

Haut-Médoc Ch de Camensac, Ch Cantemerle, Ch La Lagune, Ch Bel-Orme-Tronquoy-de-Lalande, Ch Caronne-Ste-Gemme, Ch Cissac, Ch Citran, Ch Coufran, Ch Lamarque, Ch Malescasse, Ch Reysson, Ch Larose-Trintaudon, Ch Sociando-Mallet, Ch La Tour-Carnet, Ch Villegeorge, Ch Fonpiqueyre, Ch Barreyres, Ch Lanessan, Ch Pichon, Ch Soudars, Ch Beaumont.

St-Estèphe Ch Calon-Ségur, Ch Beau-Site, Ch Haut-Marbuzet, Ch Tronquoy-Lalande, Ch Cos Labory, Ch Commanderie, Ch Montrose, Ch de Pez, Ch Lafon-Rochet, Ch Meyney, Ch Chambert-Marbuzet, Ch Les Ormes-de-Pez.

Pauillac Ch Clerc-Milon, Ch Haut-Bages-Avérous, Grand-Puy-Lacoste, Ch Haut-Bages-Libéral, Ch Haut-Batailley, Ch Pontet-Canet, Ch Fonbadet, Ch Pédesclaux.

St-Julien Ch Lagrange, Ch Léoville-Barton, Ch Talbot, Ch Terrey-Gros-Caillou, Ch St-Pierre-Sevaistre, Ch Gloria, Ch Hortevie, Ch Branaire-Ducru.

Margaux Ch d'Angludet, Ch d'Issan, Ch Monbrison, Ch Pouget, Ch du Tertre, Ch La Gurgue, Ch Siran, Ch Dauzac, Ch La Mouline-de-Labégorce, Ch Kirwan, Ch Rauzan-Gassies, Ch Desmirail, Ch Tayac.

Moulis and **Listrac** Ch Chasse-Spleen, Ch Fourcas-Dupré, Ch Maucaillou, Ch Moulin-à-Vent, Ch Dutruch-Grand-Poujeaux, Ch Fonréaud, Ch Fourcas-Hosten, Ch Clarke, Ch Lestage.

Graves Ch Roquetillade La Grange, Ch Rahoul, Ch de Fieuzal, Ch Haut-Bailly, Ch La Louvière, Ch La Tour du Haut Moulin, Ch Les Lauriers, Ch Pouyanne, Ch Coucheroy, Ch Carbonnieux, Ch Chicane, Domaine de Gaillat, Ch Picque-Caillou, Ch Bouscaut, Ch Olivier, Ch Bahans-Haut-Brion.

St-Emilion Ch L'Arrosée, Ch Fombrauge, Ch Fonroque, Ch La Fleur, Ch Monbousquet, Ch Larmande, Ch Cadet-Piola, Ch La Dominique, Ch Destieux, Ch Ripeau, Ch Croque-Michotte, Ch Fonplégade, Ch Corbin-Michotte, Ch Haut Bardoulet, Ch Le Tertre Rôteboeuf, Ch Balestard-La-Tonnelle, Clos des Jacobins, Ch Cap-de-Mourlin, Ch Haut-Sarpe, Ch La Tour-de-Pin-Figeac.

In the sub-appellations (Puisseguin-St-Emilion, Lussac-St-Emilion, Montagne-St-Emilion, St-Georges-St-Emilion, Parsac-St-Emilion), look for: Ch Belair-Montaiguillon (St-Georges), Ch des Laurets (Puisseguin), Ch Maison Blanche (Montagne), Ch Roudier (Montagne), Ch St-Georges (St-Georges), Ch Vieux-Bonneau (Montagne), Ch Haut Bernon (Puisseguin), Vieux-Château Guibeau (Puisseguin).

Pomerol (and **Lalande de Pomerol**) Clos du Clocher, Ch Le Gay, Clos René, des Annereaux (Lalande de Pomerol), Ch le Bon Pasteur, Ch Lafleur Gazin, Ch L'Eglise-Clinet, Ch Belles-Graves (Lalande de Pomerol), Ch La Grave (formerly La Grave Trignant de Boisset), Ch Petit-Village.

Fronsac and **Canon-Fronsac** Ch Coustolle, Ch Pichelèbre, Ch La Rivière, Ch Mayne-Vieil, Ch Canon de Brem, Ch Mazeris, Ch Rouet, Ch La Dauphine.

Côtes de Bourg Ch La Croix de Millerit, Ch Lalibarde, Ch Mille-Secousses, Ch de Barbe, Ch Eyquem, Ch Tour-Séguy, Ch du Bousquet, Ch Mendoce, Ch Falfas.

Côtes de Blaye Ch Charron, Ch L'Escadre, Ch Segonzac, Ch Peyraud, Ch Les Moines, Ch Petits Arnauds, Ch Fontblanche, Ch Haut-Sociondo, Ch Perenne, Ch Cap-Martin.

Premières Côtes de Bordeaux Ch Gardéra, Ch Reynon, Ch Peyrat, Ch Lafitte, Ch Bel Air Montaigne, Ch Laroche, Ch le Clyde.

Côtes de Castillon, Côtes de Francs Ch Montbadon, Ch de Clotte, Ch Moulin Rouge, Ch Pitray, Ch Laclaverie, Ch Puyguéraud, Ch de Belcier, Ch Les Douves de Francs, Ch du Palanquey, Ch Bois des Naud.

SECOND WINES

Here we give a selection of second wines from major estates that are good value. The main estate name is given in brackets.
Connétable Talbot, St-Julien (Ch Talbot)
Prieur de Meyney, St-Estèphe (Ch Meyney)
Sarget de Gruaud-Larose, St-Julien (Ch Gruaud-Larose)
Baron Villeneuve de Cantemerle, Haut-Médoc (Ch Cantemerle)
Ch Artigues Arnaud, Pauillac (Ch Grand-Puy-Ducasse)
Ch Ségonnes, Margaux (Ch Lascombes)
Les Fiefs de Lagrange, St-Julien (Ch Lagrange)
Ch Abiet, Haut-Médoc (Ch Cissac)
Ch La Salle Poujeaux, Haut-Médoc (Ch Poujeaux)
Clos du Marquis, St-Julien (Ch Léoville Las Cases)
Ch Lamouroux, Margaux (Ch Rausan-Ségla)

The sweet wines

Sauternes and **Barsac** Ch Sigalas-Rabaud, Ch Broustet, Ch Doisy-Dubroca, Ch Doisy-Védrines, Ch Bastor-Lamontagne, Ch du Mayne, Ch Roumieu-Lacoste, Ch Coutet, Ch Cantegril (second wine of Ch Doisy-Daëne), Ch de Fargues, Ch Suduiraut, Ch Lafaurie-Peyraguey, Ch Raymond-Lafon.

Other sweet whites Ch Loubens, Ch des Coulinats, Ch de Tastes (both St-Croix-du-Mont), Ch Loupiac-Gaudiet (Loupiac), Ch de Berbec (Premières Côtes de Bordeaux)

Dry whites

Graves Ch Malartic-Lagravière, Ch La Tour-Martillac, Ch Montalivet, Ch Olivier, Ch Rahoul.

Premières Côtes de Blaye Ch Charron.

Bordeaux Le Bordeaux Prestige de Peter Allan Sichel, Maître d'Estournel, Ch Loudenne.

Best buys from Bordeaux

DRY WHITES

Bordeaux Blanc, Ch d'Auros 1987 (*Bibendum*)
Ch Coucheroy 1986, Graves (*Oddbins*)
Ch Thieuley 1987, Bordeaux (*Rosetree Wine Company*)

SWEET WHITES

Loupiac 1986, Domaine de Noble (*Bibendum*)
Ste-Croix du Mont 1985, Ch des Tours (*Hicks & Don*)

Ch Filhot 1980, Sauternes (*Davisons*)

Premières Côtes de Bordeaux 1985, Ch de Berbec (*Waitrose*)

REDS

Ch Puyfromage 1985, Bordeaux Supérieur (*Whighams of Ayr*)

Ch Lalène 1985, Bordeaux Supérieur (*Clink Street Wine Vaults*)

Nathaniel Johnston Reserve Claret (*Irvine Robertson*)

Ch Trinité Valrose 1985, Bordeaux Supérieur (*Anthony Byrne Fine Wines; Hadleigh Wine Cellars; Justerini & Brooks*)

Ch Méaume 1985, Bordeaux Supérieur (*Majestic*)

Ch de Bousquet 1986, Côtes de Bourg (*J Sainsbury*)

Ch Haut Sociondo 1985, Premières Côtes de Blaye (*Edward Sheldon*)

Ch de Brondeau 1985, Bordeaux Supérieur (*Balls Brothers*)

Ch Bel Air 1986, Bordeaux Supérieur (*Corney & Barrow; Davids of Ashby*)

Ch la Tour St-Bonnet 1983, Médoc (*Davisons*)

Ch Lavergne 1983, Côtes de Castillon (*Hopton Wines*)

Specialist stockists

Adnams; Averys of Bristol; David Baillie Vintners; Nigel Baring; Berry Bros & Rudd; Bibendum; Buckingham Wines; D Byrne & Co; Christchurch Fine Wines; Classic Wines; College Cellar; Corney & Barrow; Curzon Wine Company; Davisons; Eldridge Pope; Ben Ellis & Associates; Farr Vintners; Alex Findlater; Fine Vintage Wines; Fortnum and Mason; Friarwood; Andrew Gordon Wines; Greens; Gerard Harris; John Harvey & Sons; Haynes, Hanson & Clark; Victor Hugo Wines; Hungerford Wine Company; S H Jones; Justerini & Brooks; Richard Kihl; Kurtz & Chan; Laytons; O W Loeb; Master Cellar Wine Warehouse; Nickolls & Perks; Nobody Inn; Thos Peatling; Arthur Rackhams; Raeburn Fine Wines and Foods; Edward Sheldon; Stones of Belgravia; T & W Wines; Tanners Wines; Philip Tite Fine Wines; Henry Townsend; Willoughbys; The Wine Society; Peter Wylie Fine Wines; Yorkshire Fine Wines

BURGUNDY

Still to see sense

The Burgundy scene moves fast. Last year, we were saying that the 1986 Hospices de Beaune auction – often regarded as a barometer for Burgundy prices – had seen sense and brought prices down by as much as 40 per cent for red wines and 27 per cent for whites.

Well, forget all that. The 1987 auction showed rises of 10 per cent in reds and 3.5 per cent in whites. And that was at a time when exports were falling (we in Britain bought 41 per cent less Burgundy between 1984 and 1986) because the prices were too high, and when the 1987 wine wasn't particularly spectacular anyway.

Why is it that Burgundy thinks it can get away with hiking the price of its wines and never reap the consequences? Why is it, indeed, that the section on Burgundy in the Guide always has to start with prices before even considering the wines? The answer is simply that the wines of Burgundy are, on the whole, grossly over-priced. The Burgundians rely on their great name to sell wine which might only be worth having at half the price.

Of course, at its finest, there is little to compare with a top red Burgundy. But there's plenty to compare with great white Burgundy. The taste of Chardonnay long ago stopped being the exclusive property of Burgundy. A number of tastings of Chardonnays round the world have been covered in the wine press over the past year: in one (reported in *Decanter* in June 1988), the best French wine – a Chablis – came in at number 16, and was over twice the price of any of the top 15. The top white wine from Burgundy itself was number 18.

Lovers of Burgundy will argue that such tastings, where the 'up-front' flavours of New World wines always shine, are no gauge of the taste of true Burgundy. We would reply that if experienced tasters – who will make allowances for the differences – can still come up with this result, there must be something wrong.

What has gone wrong?

Burgundy often seems to be governed by a mixture of greed and distrust: greed because her wines have been in such demand that there's the easy temptation (all too often succumbed to) to produce more and more from the same number of vines, with the result that the wines taste dilute; and distrust between growers and négociants because the growers always suspect that the négociants will buy wine or grapes from them at a low price and then sell it on at a very high price.

Some growers – an increasing band – have tried to avoid the blandishments of the négociants and have taken to bottling their own wine and selling it under their own name. It is generally agreed – even in Burgundy, when the speaker is being honest with himself – that the very best Burgundy is domaine-bottled by a grower. But move down a notch in quality, and the négociant begins to come into his own. If he does his job properly, he is able to search out the best wines from the confusion of villages and vineyards of Burgundy and put together a reliable wine that is really rather good.

In the last few years of boom – when Burgundy was the taste that everybody, especially the Americans, wanted – the growers seemed to have it all their own way. Now that life has become tougher, there are discreet phone calls from growers (who last year wouldn't have been seen dead talking business to a négociant) asking whether Monsieur le négociant would be interested in a few barrels of a very interesting little wine they just happen to have in their cellar. The négociants are back on top – as everybody predicted they would be.

Burgundy's problems are compounded by the fact that it is a small area. The whole of Burgundy produces only twice the volume of one village – St-Emilion – in Bordeaux. When demand is high – as it has been in the early 1980s – there just isn't enough wine to go round. And, unlike Bordeaux, where perfectly good petit château wines come at ridiculously low prices, there is no such thing as cheap Burgundy. Basic Bourgogne Blanc (see below for the appellation system in Burgundy) still costs the same as a medium-quality château in Bordeaux, or, to compare like grape with like, the same as a very good Australian Chardonnay.

Until very recently, we would have said that while Burgundy had lost its exclusive hold on Chardonnay, it had managed to retain that of Pinot Noir. The Pinot taste was proving very difficult to reproduce successfully elsewhere in the world: the rich, soft, truffly flavour of good red Burgundy took on a harshness and a bitterness outside the region.

Not any more. Now areas such as the north-west United States, Carneros in California, Western Australia, the Yarra Valley in Victoria, and – potentially – New Zealand, are all coming up with Pinot Noir reds that have terrific style and quality. It looks as though Burgundy's stranglehold on the Pinot Noir is about to be broken.

There we go, the French will say, making comparisons again. Well, the reason we make these comparisons is because we love the taste of Burgundy, but can't afford it – and are not sure why we should pay so much anyway. So we search the rest of the world for wines that will satisfy our taste at lower prices. If we can find those wines, then it's the Burgundians who are the losers, not us.

And yet, and yet . . . after all these strictures, there is still something incomparable about the really finest Burgundy. The rich tastes of the reds, the delicacy of the whites, still overawe in a way not even fine claret can quite manage. But those bottles are few and rare, and certainly not for more than once or twice a year. For the rest of the time, we will look elsewhere for our Chardonnay and Pinot Noir, and hope the Burgundians may learn that the world doesn't owe them a living.

Names are the thing

Buying Burgundy is a question of detective work. Layers of names have to be peeled away before we may get some indication of the quality of the wine. We need to understand something of the appellation system in Burgundy. We also need to know the name of the village it comes from, but in Burgundy, that's less important than the name of the grower or négociant who made it (or, as the French would say, did the élevage). And – probably the most important of all – we need to know the name of good Burgundy wine merchants in this country who have carefully built up a reputation for buying wine from the right people in France.

Where's where in Burgundy

The appellation system is the most complex in France, with five different levels, from the region-wide appellation to one that refers to a single vineyard.

General appellations A wine bearing an appellation such as Bourgogne or (even lower in quality) Bourgogne Grand Ordinaire can come from anywhere within the whole Burgundy region. The wine can be white or red: Bourgogne Rouge has to be made from Pinot Noir, while Bourgogne Grand Ordinaire can be made from Gamay. Other general appellations include Bourgogne Passetoutgrain (a blend of Pinot Noir and Gamay) and Bourgogne Aligoté (a white made from the Aligoté grape).

The success of the basic Burgundy wines depends on the grower or négociant. Some Bourgogne Rouge is very good at comparatively modest prices, but some can be a bit of a disaster, so shop around at this level with care.

Regional appellations Terms like Côte de Nuits Villages, Côte de Beaune Villages, Hautes Côtes de Nuits fall into this category. Each covers more than one village and the wine will probably be a négociant's blend.

Village appellations Most Burgundian communes or villages are entitled to their own appellation and the vineyards covered by the appellation will be strictly defined. Any vineyards that fall outside the defined area go under one of the more general categories. Typical appellations would be Vosne-Romanée or Savigny-lès-Beaune, Pommard or Nuits St-Georges (see also below).

While these are supposedly not so good as single vineyard wines, it is often the case that village wines are every bit as good and much cheaper. Like the Burgundy-wide appellation wines, but to a lesser degree, they can rely on judicious buying from a reasonable variety of vineyards. The smaller the area from which grapes can come, the greater the risks (from localised hail storms, for instance), but the greater the rewards as well.

Premier Cru appellations Confusingly, this is only the second rank of greatness. Certain single vineyards are designated Premier Cru and are entitled to their own appellation which is normally put on the label in conjunction with the village name, eg Meursault (the village)-Charmes (the vineyard). A wine that is a blend of wines from different Premier Cru vineyards in one appellation can be called simply Beaune Premier Cru, for example.

Grand Cru appellations These are the very top vineyards, and can appear on the label as appellations in their own right with no reference to the village, eg Le Montrachet, La Tâche. At their best, they are the stars of Burgundy but, inevitably, their prices reflect their star quality.

The Burgundy villages

Burgundy's main vineyards face east across the valley of the Saône from low slopes that mark the eastern edge of the Massif Central. The northern end is a low ridge, broken up by small side valleys. This is the Côte d'Or. Moving south from Dijon, the first section of the Côte d'Or is known as the Côte de Nuits, but as it nears Beaune, it becomes the Côte de Beaune. In the hilly country behind this main slope, there is the lesser area of the Hautes Côtes – again divided into the Hautes Côtes de Nuits and the Hautes Côtes de Beaune.

South of Beaune, the slope breaks up and the Côte Chalonnaise starts. This leads into the Mâconnais, which in turn runs into the northern end of the Beaujolais hills (see earlier in the French section).

Côte de Nuits From north to south, the main villages are: Marsannay, Fixin, Gevrey-Chambertin, Morey St-Denis, Chambolle-Musigny, Vougeot, Vosne-Romanée, Nuits St-Georges.

The villages in the Côte de Nuits to watch as offering better value for money than others are Fixin and Marsannay (red wines).

Côte de Beaune Continuing south, the villages are: Aloxe-Corton, Pernand-Vergelesses, Chorey-lès-Beaune, Savigny-lès-Beaune, Beaune, Pommard, Volnay, Monthélie, Auxey-Duresses, Meursault, Puligny-Montrachet, Chassagne-Montrachet, St-Aubin, St-Romain, Santenay.

Villages in the Côte de Beaune to watch as offering better value for money than others are: (*for reds*) Auxey-Duresses, Chorey-lès-Beaune, Savigny-lès-Beaune, Monthélie and Santenay; (*for reds and whites*) St-Aubin; (*for whites*) St-Romain.

The Côte Chalonnaise The villages here are: Bouzeron, Rully, Mercurey, Givry, Montagny. Look for Bouzeron whites and Mercurey reds.

The Mâconnais The region is best for whites – and we don't mean the over-priced Pouilly-Fuissé. Go instead for St-Véran, Pouilly-Vinzelles, Mâcon-Prissé, Mâcon-Viré, Mâcon-Clessé, Mâcon-Lugny.

Vintages in Burgundy

Of all the great wine-producing areas in France, Burgundy seems to suffer most from extreme climatic conditions. It can have harsh winters, and the quality of a summer cannot be guaranteed: it may be short and too hot, or wet and too cold. Probably in only three years each decade will the weather be absolutely right.

The weather that is right for red wines may not be right for white, and vice versa, a comment that is more appropriate to Burgundy than any other wine-producing area. Add to that the fact that Burgundian weather seems to operate in tiny areas – a terrible hailstorm may devastate one vineyard, while a couple of hundred yards down the road, the sun is shining brilliantly – and it becomes obvious that great store cannot be put by generalised comments about Burgundian vintages.

1987 A year of small crops, following a wet spring. *Reds:* these are probably better than the whites, with every sign of a useful medium-term vintage of soft, fruity wines. Nothing exciting, though. *Whites:* early tastings of these wines suggested that high acidity may be a problem, although after the second malolactic fermentation, they may have softened. They will need to be drunk relatively quickly – watch out for the hint of rot on some wines from lesser producers.

1986 A classic hit-and-miss vintage. *Reds* are better than whites, especially in the Côte de Beaune, but only producers can guarantee the quality. The wines will have a medium-term life, although Côte d'Or wines may last a little longer. *Whites* are immediately attractive, but tend to lack the acidity which would give a long life.

1985 It was considered impossible to make bad wine with the quality of the grapes at harvest time, provided the grower could control his fermentation in the intense heat prevailing then. The *reds* are quite firm with good, rounded tannin and decent acidity, but definitely need to be kept for some time. This could be a great vintage. The *whites* are delicious now, somewhat like the 1983s in character but with lower alcohol, more fruit and more acidity. Again, they will age well.

1984 *Reds:* light in colour and alcohol, many of these wines can be drunk now. Premier Cru and Grand Cru will go on until the 1990s. *Whites* should also be drunk young. They are light and a touch on the acid side (although that aspect has softened in the past couple of years). Except for Grand Cru and Premier Cru, drink now.

1983 *Reds:* a fine year, with many of the wines expected to have a long life, but avoid the wines that taste of rot. The vintage has been compared to 1964. *Whites:* full, rich wines that are not typical of Burgundy and seem to have something of the New World in them. The top wines have good keeping potential.

1982 *Reds:* a difficult year. More than ever the quality of a wine depends on its producer. Much is thin and watery, although better producers made some delicious wines. Drink them before 1990. Drink any *whites* you have now and taste carefully before buying any more.

1981 *Reds:* a few fine wines are around in an otherwise mediocre vintage. *Whites:* Very varied, but more successful than the reds. Taste before buying.

1980 *Reds:* this vintage is turning out to be better than originally billed, and although most reds need drinking now, the occasional bottle – especially in the Côte de Nuits – will survive for a year or two. *Whites:* most are either too old or too acid.

1979 *Reds:* while some of these easy-to-drink wines will survive for a while yet, others should be drunk. Taste what you have in order to assess them. *Whites:* while these wines are now fully mature, the top growths should still provide plenty of enjoyment.

1978 *Reds:* great wines with plenty of life in them yet. Wines from the Côte de Nuits will last longer than those from the Côte de Beaune – but that is generally the case anyway. *Whites:* lesser village wines should be drunk now. The top crus will last another three or four years.

Older vintages Approach older vintages of Burgundy with caution – in general the wines are not tremendously long-lived. On the other hand, the right bottle from the right wine merchant (see our list of specialist stockists at the end of this section) will provide a treasured experience.

Who's who in Burgundy

We have compiled a listing of the firms and estates which we consider to be producing good Burgundy at the moment. Our advice in Burgundy is always to look for the producer's name. Where the wine was actually grown is often less important. We look at growers first and then merchants. Stockists are indicated in italic type, but the list is not exhaustive.

Burgundy growers

The strange and complex structure of the vineyard holdings in Burgundy means that a grower may have a couple of rows of vines in a number of different villages. He will produce small quantities of many wines. If he is any good, all his wines will achieve a certain standard. So look for the name of the grower first, then the name of the wine.

Robert & Michel Ampeau *David Baillie Vintners; Lay & Wheeler*
Marquis d'Angerville *Corney & Barrow; O W Loeb; Ubiquitous Chip*
Domaine Arnoux *Anthony Byrne Fine Wines; Fine Vintage Wines*
Bernard Bachelet *Anthony Byrne Fine Wines*
Jean-Claude Bachelet *Bibendum; Henry Townsend*
Barthod-Noëllat *Adnams*
Bitouzet-Prieur *La Vigneronne*
Simon Bize *Adnams; Haynes, Hanson & Clark; S H Jones; La Vigneronne; The Wine Society*
Jean Boillot *Russell & McIver*
Bonneau de Martray *O W Loeb; La Réserve; Yorkshire Fine Wines*

Bourée *The Wine Society*
Roland Brintet *Russell & McIver*
Henri Buisson *Bibendum; S H Jones*
Luc Camus-Bruchon *Bibendum; Raeburn Fine Wines and Foods*
Carillon *Lay & Wheeler*
Domaine Chantal-Lescure *Justerini & Brooks; Christopher Piper Wines*
Jean Chauvenet *Bibendum; John Harvey & Sons; La Vigneronne*
Jean Chofflet *S H Jones*
Lupé Cholet *Findlater Mackie Todd*
Daniel Chouet-Clivet *La Vigneronne*
Bruno Clair *David Baillie Vintners*
Henri Clerc *Averys; David Baillie Vintners; Eldridge Pope; Lay & Wheeler; The Wine Society*
Georges Clerget *Bibendum; Anthony Byrne Fine Wines; Justerini & Brooks*
Michel Clerget *Haynes, Hanson & Clark*
Raoul Clerget *The Wine Society; Yorkshire Fine Wines*
Yvon Clerget *Lay & Wheeler*
P Cogny *Adnams; Tanners Wines*
Domaine Colin *Ingletons Wines; S H Jones; Christopher Piper Wines; The Wine Society*
Domaines des Comtes Lafon *Adnams; Domaine Direct; Tanners Wines; Wines from Paris*
J-J Confuron *Laytons*
Domaine Corsin *Adnams; Domaine Direct*
Marc Dudet *Corney & Barrow*
Guy Dufouleur *Davisons*
Domaine Dujac *Adnams; Anthony Byrne Fine Wines; Corney & Barrow; Lay & Wheeler; O W Loeb; The Wine Society*
Domaine Gagnard-Delagrange *Anthony Byrne Fine Wines; Haynes, Hanson & Clark; Laytons; La Réserve; The Wine Society*
Abel Garnier Fils Aîné *David Baillie Vintners; O W Loeb*
Michel Gaunoux *Domaine Direct*
H Germain *Adnams; S H Jones; Tanners Wines*
Jacques Germain *David Baillie Vintners*
Jean Germain *S H Jones; Yorkshire Fine Wines*
Vincent Girardin *Helen Verdcourt Wines*
Domaine Girard-Vollot *Market Vintners*
Henri Gouges *S H Jones; O W Loeb; Henry Townsend*
Jean Grivot *David Baillie Vintners; Anthony Byrne Fine Wines; Haynes, Hanson & Clark; Lay & Wheeler*
Jean Gros *Anthony Byrne Fine Wines*
Michel Gros *Anthony Byrne Fine Wines*
Guillemard-Pothier *Lay & Wheeler*
Domaine Antonin Guyon *J E Hogg*
Patrick Javillier *Anthony Byrne Fine Wines; Russell & McIver*
Henri Jayer *Justerini & Brooks; Raeburn Fine Wines and Foods*
Jacqueline Jayer *Haynes, Hanson & Clark; Lay & Wheeler*

Jayer-Gilles *Adnams; The Wine Society; Yorkshire Fine Wines*
Domaine Michel Juillot *Domaine Direct*
Michel Lafarge *Bibendum; Haynes, Hanson & Clark; Christopher Piper Wines*
Henri Lamarche *Lay & Wheeler; O W Loeb*
Hubert Lamy *S H Jones; Lay & Wheeler; Tanners Wines*
Domaine Laroche *Christopher Piper Wines*
Domaine Leflaive *Adnams; Corney & Barrow; Ferrers le Mesurier; Haynes, Hanson & Clark; Ingletons Wines; S H Jones; Lay & Wheeler; Tanners Wines*
Lequin-Roussot *Bibendum; Anthony Byrne Fine Wines*
Georges Lignier *Bibendum; Justerini & Brooks; Henry Townsend*
Domaine Machard de Gramont *Adnams; Fine Vintage Wines; S H Jones; Justerini & Brooks; Yorkshire Fine Wines*
Duc de Magenta *Fine Vintage Wines*
Henri Magnien *Haynes, Hanson & Clark*
Jean Maréchal *Haynes, Hanson & Clark*
Jean Mathias *Christopher Piper Wines*
Domaine Matrot *Corney & Barrow*
Mazilly Père et Fils *Matthew Gloag & Son; Master Cellar Wine Warehouse; Ubiquitous Chip*
Domaine Méo-Camuzet *Haynes, Hanson & Clark*
Jean-Pierre Meulien *Haynes, Hanson & Clark*
Bernard Michel *Domaine Direct*
Alain Michelot *Domaine Direct*
Millot-Battault *Eldridge Pope*
Mongeard-Mugneret *Adnams; Ingletons Wines*
Jean-Claude Monnier *David Baillie Vintners*
René Monnier *Ingletons Wines*
Domaine Monthélie-Douhairet *Wines from Paris*
Domaine de Montille *Adnams; Domaine Direct; Haynes, Hanson & Clark*
Albert Morey *Christopher Piper Wines*
Bernard Morey *Anthony Byrne Fine Wines; J E Hogg; Henry Townsend*
Georges Mugneret *Anthony Byrne Fine Wines; Lay & Wheeler*
Bernard Naune *Bibendum*
Domaine Newman *Corney & Barrow*
Michel Niellon *O W Loeb; Market Vintners*
André Nudant *Matthew Gloag & Son; Ingletons Wines*
Domaine Parent *Ferrers le Mesurier; Fine Vintage Wines; Christopher Piper Wines; The Wine Society*
Perrières *Fine Vintage Wines*
Jean-Marie Ponsot *Lay & Wheeler; Wines from Paris*
Domaine de la Pousse d'Or *Anthony Byrne Fine Wines; Domaine Direct; Tanners Wines; La Vigneronne; The Wine Society; Wines from Paris; Yorkshire Fine Wines*
J Prieur *Fine Vintage Wines; Matthew Gloag & Sons*
Henri Prudhon *Bibendum*
Pascal Prunier *Haynes, Hanson & Clark*

Jean-Marie Raveneau *Haynes, Hanson & Clark*
Domaine Daniel Rion *Buckingham Wines; Raeburn Fine Wines and Foods*
Rollin Père et Fils *Bibendum; Justerini & Brooks*
Domaine de la Romanée-Conti *Adnams; Hungerford Wine Company; Lay & Wheeler; La Réserve; Henry Townsend; La Vigneronne; Yorkshire Fine Wines*
Philippe Rossignol *Haynes, Hanson & Clark; Christopher Piper Wines*
Marc Rougeot *Market Vintners; La Réserve*
Domaine Guy Roulot *Ferrers le Mesurier; Lay & Wheeler*
Georges Roumier *Tanners Wines*
Domaine Armand Rousseau *Adnams; Anthony Byrne Fine Wines; Eldridge Pope; Lay & Wheeler; O W Loeb; Henry Townsend; The Wine Society*
Roux Père et Fils *Eldridge Pope; The Wine Society*
Etienne Sauzet *Adnams; Ingletons Wines; Lay & Wheeler; O W Loeb; Tanners Wines; Ubiquitous Chip*
Daniel Senard *Corney & Barrow; Ingletons Wines*
Luc Sorin *Haynes, Hanson & Clark; Ingletons Wines*
M Sorin *Barnes Wine Shop*
Domaine Baron Thénard *Adnams*
Jacques Thévenet *Adnams*
Thévenot Le Brun *Ingletons Wines*
Domaine Tollot-Beaut *David Baillie Vintners; Anthony Byrne Fine Wines; Lay & Wheeler; O W Loeb; Christopher Piper Wines; Henry Townsend*
Domaine Louis Trapet *David Baillie Vintners; Anthony Byrne Fine Wines; Corney & Barrow, Ingletons Wines; Christopher Piper Wines*
Léonice de Valleroy *John Harvey & Sons*
Domaine des Varoilles *Fine Vintage Wines; Haynes, Hanson & Clark; S H Jones; Justerini & Brooks*
Aubert de Villaine *Adnams; The Wine Society*
Domaine Vincent *Adnams; S H Jones; Tanners Wines; Henry Townsend; The Wine Society*
Michel Voarick *Fine Vintage Wines; Lay & Wheeler*
Domaine Comte de Vogüé *Fine Vintage Wines; Christopher Piper Wines*
Joseph Voillot *Market Vintners*
Girard Vollot *Morris & Verdin*

Burgundy co-operatives

Despite the growth of domaine-bottling, much of Burgundy in the lesser-known appellations is still handled through the co-operatives. The biggest concentration is in the Mâconnais and Côte Chalonnaise, while there are relatively few in the Côte d'Or.

Les Producteurs de Prissé Wines: St-Véran, Mâcon-Prissé.
Haynes, Hanson & Clark

Cave des Vignerons de Buxy Wines: Montagny, Bourgogne Rouge and Blanc.
Adnams; O W Loeb; Henry Townsend; Waitrose

Cave Co-opérative des Hautes-Côtes Wines: Hautes Côtes de Beaune, Hautes Côtes de Nuits.
Eldridge Pope

Cave Co-opérative de Viré Wines: Mâcon-Viré.
Alex Findlater

Groupement de Producteurs Lugny-St-Genoux-de-Scisse
Wines: Mâcon-Lugny, Mâcon-Villages.
Bibendum

Burgundy merchants

Bouchard Aîné Wines: Pinot Chardonnay, Bourgogne Chardonnay, Puligny Montrachet, Meursault.
Bottle & Basket; Hopton Wines

Bouchard Père et Fils Wines: Beaune, Le Montrachet, Corton, Volnay.
Fine Vintage Wines; Haynes, Hanson & Clark; J E Hogg; The Wine Society

Chandesais Wines: Beaune, Hospices de Beaune.
Eldridge Pope

Chanson Père et Fils Wines: Beaune, Pernand-Vergelesses, Côte de Beaune, Chambertin, Vosne-Romanée.
Direct Wine Shipments; S H Jones; Tanners Wines; Whighams of Ayr

Chartron et Trébuchet Wines: Hospices de Nuits, Mercurey, Meursault, Le Montrachet, Puligny Montrachet.
Laytons

B et J-M Delaunay Wines: Savigny-lès-Beaune, Gevrey-Chambertin.
Matthew Gloag & Sons; Henry Townsend

Doudet-Naudin Wines: Savigny, Beaune, Aloxe-Corton.
Berry Bros & Rudd

Joseph Drouhin Wines: Beaune, Puligny, Corton-Charlemagne, Corton-Bressandes, Volnay, Chambertin, Chambolle-Musigny, Echézeaux, Musigny.
Adnams; Findlater Mackie Todd

Georges Duboeuf Principally in Beaujolais but also in Mâcon and St-Véran.
Berkmann Wine Cellars/Le Nez Rouge; Henry Townsend

Joseph Faiveley Wines: Nuits St-Georges, Mercurey, Rully, Corton, Clos de Bèze, Echézeaux, Gevrey-Chambertin, Chambolle-Musigny.
Adnams; Fine Vintage Wines; J E Hogg; Yorkshire Fine Wines

Geisweiler The négociant firm which opened up the Hautes Côtes de Nuits. Wines: Hautes Côtes de Nuits, Hautes Côtes de Beaune.
S H Jones

Louis Jadot Wines: Corton, Beaune, Pernand-Vergelesses. Now own Domaine Clair-Daü.
John Harvey & Sons; La Réserve; Henry Townsend; Victoria Wine Company

Jaffelin Wines: Gevrey-Chambertin, Hospices de Beaune, Pommard.
Averys; Martinez Fine Wine

Labouré-Roi Wines: Meursault, Auxey-Duresses, Beaune, Pommard, Chassagne Montrachet.
Christopher Piper Wines

Louis Latour Wines: Corton, Romanée St-Vivant, Chambertin, Pommard, Beaune, Montagny.
Buckingham Wines; Direct Wine Shipments; Fine Vintage Wines; S H Jones; Russell & McIver; Tanners Wines; Henry Townsend; Ubiquitous Chip; The Wine Society; Yorkshire Fine Wines

Olivier Leflaive Frères Part of the Leflaive family at Puligny, but acting as négociant. Wines: Rully, Puligny Montrachet, Meursault Porusots, St-Aubin.
Corney & Barrow

Loron et Fils Wines: Mâconnais wines (plus Beaujolais – see under that section).
Direct Wine Shipments; John Harvey & Sons

P de Marcilly Wines: Bourgogne Rouge, Bourgogne Réserve.
Matthew Gloag & Sons; Ubiquitous Chip

Prosper Maufoux Wines: best are the Santenay wines.
Berry Bros & Rudd; J E Hogg; Mitchell & Son

Moillard Wines: Large vineyard holdings on Côte de Nuits and Côte de Beaune. Wines of 1983 and later are better.
Berry Bros & Rudd; Eldridge Pope

Mommessin Owners of Clos du Tart. Wines: Chassagne Montrachet, Clos du Tart.
Buckingham Wines; Direct Wine Shipments; Mitchell & Son; Yorkshire Fine Wines

Remoissenet Wines: Le Montrachet, Beaune.
Averys; The Wine Society

Antonin Rodet Wines: Gevrey-Chambertin (plus Beaujolais).
Eldridge Pope

Charles Viénot Wines: Givry, Côte de Nuits, Morey-St-Denis.
John Harvey & Sons

Stockists given in italic type after wines in this section will be found in the WHERE TO BUY section earlier in the book.

Best buys in Burgundy

WHITES

Bourgogne Chardonnay 1986, Roux Père et Fils (*T & W Wines*)
Asda White Burgundy, Alain Combard (*Asda*)
Mâcon Villages 1987, Jean Berger (*Bibendum*)
Mâcon-Prissé 1986, Cave Co-opérative de Prissé (*Goedhuis & Co*)
Cuvée Vincent Jeunes Vigniers, Vin de Table (*Thos Peatling*)
Sauvignon de St-Bris, Sorin (*widely available*)

REDS

Bourgogne Rouge 1986, Sorin-Defrance (*Summerlee Wines*)
Bourgogne Rouge 1985, Cave Co-opérative de Buxy (*Waitrose*)
Bourgogne Rouge 1985, Emile Voarick (*Wessex Wines*)
Bourgogne Passetoutgrains 1986, Henri Jayer (*Hampden Wine Company; Raeburn Fine Wines and Foods*)
Bourgogne Pinot Noir 1986, Domaine Talmard (*Russell & McIver*)
Mâcon Rouge 1985, Chauvenet (*William Rush*)
Côtes de Beaune Villages 1985, Les Fusières, René Monnier (*Ingletons Wines*)

Specialist stockists

Adnams; Averys of Bristol; Bibendum; Anthony Byrne Fine Wines; Christchurch Fine Wines; College Cellar; Corney & Barrow; Curzon Wine Company; Domaine Direct; Eldridge Pope; Alex Findlater; Goedhuis & Co; Greens; Gerard Harris; Farr Vintners; Friarwood; Haynes, Hanson & Clark; Ingletons Wines; S H Jones; Justerini & Brooks; Richard Kihl; Kurtz & Chan; Laytons; O W Loeb; Market Vintners; Morris & Verdin; Le Nez Rouge/Berkmann Wine Cellars; Nickolls & Perks; Pavilion Wine Company; Thos Peatling; Christopher Piper Wines; Raeburn Fine Wines and Foods; La Réserve; Edward Sheldon; T & W Wines; Tanners Wines; Henry Townsend; La Vigneronne; Willoughbys; The Wine Society; Peter Wylie Fine Wines; Yorkshire Fine Wines

Burgundy

CHABLIS

Supply and demand

Where did all the Chablis come from in the days when it was the automatic accompaniment to sole in 100 disguises in London's fish restaurants? We'd like to know, because there wasn't that much of it then – only 500 hectares were planted in the 1950s. Now the vineyard area is five times that – and still Chablis seems in short supply.

What is it about this small area between Paris and Burgundy? At their best, the wines have clean acidity and fresh, green, grassy, flinty flavours, sometimes tinged with oak. This is cool climate Chardonnay, gulpable as well as elegant. Somehow this taste caught the imagination of the fish-eating world. Perhaps there was also something about the easy-to-pronounce name . . .

But supply and demand have always, it seems, been a major problem in Chablis. It is partly to do with the fact that the growers – typically disunited – can't agree on a price above which they will not go. Somebody gets greedy, demands a higher price – and the rest follow suit. That happened with the 1985 vintage, and then suddenly Chablis growers found that nobody wanted (or could afford) their wines. So down came the price for the 1986 vintage, and prices seem to have stabilised for the 1987 – so far.

The price hike in the 1985 vintage was triggered by the bad frosts that year. (Of course, the reason that Chablis can produce such delicate, clean wine, is precisely because it is in a cool place – and cool places

368

mean winter and spring frosts.) In fact, the frosts were more of an excuse than a reason – the 1986 vintage, in a year when there were no frosts, saw a total production only marginally higher than the 1985.

The frosts were certainly an excuse for the rise in prices of basic Chablis. Those vineyards were not affected, but still the growers thought it too good an opportunity to miss to get together the deposit on the second Mercedes and the boat. In short, while Chablis is a lovely wine, nobody needs to be sorry for the growers when the prices come down to more sensible levels.

More vineyards

To try and cope with the demand for their wines, the Chablisiens have increased the area under vine dramatically – as we have already seen. These new vineyards are fine for basic Chablis (see below for *The styles of Chablis*) – the soil and the lie of the land are perfectly good, but it is not the classic Kimmeridgian clay soil of the Premier and Grand Cru vineyards. While the Grand Cru vineyards have stayed the same, the Premier Cru vineyards have spread enormously on to the ordinary soil. We would like to know what is Premier about a Cru that's grown on the same soil as standard Chablis? It certainly means that the standard of Premier Cru wines is not what it was.

We would also like a proper answer to how all the Petit Chablis vineyards (those that didn't even make the basic Chablis standard) were suddenly upgraded and are now called plain Chablis. We're told that's because the growers of Petit Chablis thought it made their wine sound inferior to Chablis. But that was the whole point, wasn't it?

The styles of Chablis

We've already said something about the taste of Chablis, but what you won't always find is wood. There's considerable argument in Chablis about whether it's preferable to use wood to add a layer of complexity, or whether to call on the latest stainless steel technology to bring out the best in the Chardonnay fruit. Both schools of thought are equally valid – the choice is up to you. Where possible, we've indicated under the *Who's who* section which producer follows which style.

Where's where in Chablis

Chablis' appellation system is much simpler than that of the rest of Burgundy. For a start, only white wine can be Chablis: any red wines made in the area go under the appellation of Bourgogne or of one of the small village names (see below under *The other wines of the Chablis region*). All Chablis is made from Chardonnay grapes.

The Chablis vineyards are graded on a quality basis. At the bottom, there is the basic Petit Chablis vineyard. There's not much of this around now, because most of it has been upgraded to the next quality level, Chablis, which covers the vast bulk of the Chablis vineyard.

Above Chablis AC are the Premier Cru vineyards. These are divided into 12 different groupings which consist of more than one vineyard. They are: Beauroy, Côte de Léchet, Fourchaume, Les Fourneaux, Mélinots, Montée de Tonnerre, Montmains, Monts de Milieu, Vaillons, Vaucoupin, Vaudevey, Vosgros.

If a wine is a blend of more than one Premier Cru, it will simply be called Chablis Premier Cru without a vineyard name.

At the top of the Chablis tree are the seven Grands Crus, making fabulous classic wines, at top prices. These are: Blanchots, Bougros, Les Clos, Grenouilles, Les Preuses, Valmur, Vaudésir.

Vintages in Chablis

Expect the wines made with some wood-ageing to last a little longer than those made entirely in stainless steel. Drink basic Chablis in three years – depending on the vintage. Premier Cru wines will last anything from three to five or eight years. Grand Cru wines are not really ready for six years after the vintage.

1987 Not prolific, with still smaller than average production of Premier and Grand Cru due to the 1985 frosts. But the quality is good, even if acidity is low. More like white Burgundy than classic Chablis.

1986 A small crop – not much bigger than 1985. It produced wines with some attractive acidity, which are therefore more typically Chablis.

1985 A small crop of high quality – if quite full – wine, 35 per cent lower than in 1984 because of frost in January and February. The main problems with quantity were in the Grand Cru and Premier Cru vineyards. Quantities of Chablis and Petit Chablis were nearer normal. Drink the Chablis, but keep the top wines.

1984 Rot was the problem in the vineyards after a wet September and warm October. The wine has more acidity than vintages immediately preceding and has not lasted that long.

1983 Soft, full-bodied wines which lack the edge that is the hallmark of a good Chablis vintage. If you can find them, they should be reasonable value, but drink up fast. Premiers Crus are ready to drink, but keep Grands Crus.

1982 Even the top wines have suffered from a very soft vintage. Don't keep and don't buy.

1981 Some really good Chablis with intense flavours and a lovely tangy bite were made, but only the Grands Crus wines are worth keeping.

Few vintages before 1981 (apart from some Grands Crus 1978) are worth keeping now, and it's unlikely that there will be any to buy. Any bottles of 1975 Grand Cru are still worth considering.

Who's who in Chablis

Much standard Chablis AC has lost the steely nervosity and green acidity that made it such a special wine – and that has a lot to do with the way vineyards have been upgraded, even though they were not planted in the right soil conditions. It also has to do with the use of stainless steel (see above). To taste the Chablis of yore, you will have to go for Premier Cru at the very least (and pay a lot of money) or make sure you are buying wines made by the right producer. This makes names of producers as important in Chablis as they are in Burgundy.

THE GROWERS

J Brocard Makes big, mellow wines, often quite rich, using wood. Wines: Domaine Ste-Claire.
Adnams; Balls Brothers; Berkmann Wine Cellars/Le Nez Rouge; D Byrne & Co; Victor Hugo Wines; Justerini & Brooks; Oddbins

René Dauvissat One of the well-established names of Chablis, with some complexity to his wines, which spend some time in oak. Wines: Grands Crus – Les Clos, Les Preuses; plus Premier Cru.
Domaine Direct; Sainsbury's; Tanners Wines; Waitrose

Bernard Defaix Modern winemaking without the use of wood; the wines tend to be fat and Burgundian in taste. Wines: Premiers Crus – Côte de Léchet, Vaillons.
Berry Bros & Rudd; Andrew Mead Wines; Thos Peatling

Jean-Paul Droin Very fine Chablis made using judicious amounts of oak-ageing. Wines: Grands Crus – Vaudésir, Les Clos, Grenouilles, Valmur; Premiers Crus – mainly Vaillons.
Bibendum; Davisons; Domaine Direct; Christopher Piper Wines; Tanners Wines

Jean Durup Large holding of 140 acres makes him a major force in Chablis. Uses modern stainless steel in his winemaking, and achieves high standards. Wines: Durup, Domaine de l'Eglantière, Ch de Maligny, Domaine de la Paulière, Domaine de Valéry, Les Folles Pensées.
H Allen Smith; Anthony Byrne Fine Wines; Domaine Direct; Hedley Wright; Victor Hugo Wines; Hungerford Wine Company; Lockes; Wizard Wine Warehouses

William Fèvre A proponent of the use of new oak barrels for Chablis, making rich, rounded wines. Wines: Grands Crus – Les Clos, Bougros, Les Preuses, Grenouilles, Vaudésir, Valmur; Premier Cru, Chablis.
Bedford Fine Wines; Findlater Mackie Todd; Irvine Robertson Wines; Oddbins

Alain Geoffroy Elegant, light wines, made in stainless steel.
Victor Hugo Wines; Irvine Robertson Wines

J-P Grossot Young grower, owning land in Chablis as well as having
Premier Cru vineyards. Uses some wood. Wines: Premiers Crus –
Vaucoupin, Monts de Milieu.
Lay & Wheeler

Louis Michel Modern, fruity wines that are ready to drink young. No
wood is involved. Wines: Grands Crus – Vaudésir, Grenouilles, Les
Clos; Premiers Crus – Montée de Tonnerre, Montmains. Domaine de la
Tour Vaubourg is a second label.
*Anthony Byrne Fine Wines; Gerard Harris; Lay & Wheeler; O W Loeb; Morris
& Verdin; Oddbins; Sebastopol Wines; Wine Society; Yorkshire Fine Wines*

Louis Pinson Traditional wines, aged in wood, and needing at least
three years before drinking. Wines: Grand Crus – Les Clos; Premiers
Crus – Montmains, La Forêt, Montée de Tonnere.
Bibendum; Morris & Verdin

François Raveneau Very traditional wines, intended for long ageing.
Plenty of wood here. Wines: Grands Crus – Valmur, Les Clos,
Blanchots; Premier Cru.
Haynes, Hanson & Clark

Philippe Testut The remains of an old estate, most of which was sold
by the family. The wines are classic Chablis, with both wood and tank
maturation. Wines: Grand Cru – Les Grenouilles; Premier Cru,
Chablis.
Majestic

Robert Vocoret Ferments his wine in barrels, but ages them in
stainless steel to keep some of the freshness. Wines: Grands Crus –
Les Clos, Blanchots, Valmur; Premier Cru, Chablis.
Laytons; The Market/Le Provençal; Reid Wines; Winecellars

Cave Co-opérative La Chablisienne Controls a quarter of all Chablis
production, producing straightforward wines which may lack some of
the depths of smaller producers. Also puts the name of some of its star
growers on wines – watch for this, as the wine doesn't necessarily
come from the grower's own land. Wines: About 50 different labels,
including La Chablisienne and co-op members' own labels (such as
Domaine Jean Bourcey, Suzanne Tremblay, Rémy Lefort, Fèvre Frères,
Jean-Claude Dauvissat, Michaut Frères).
*The most widely available Chablis: look for the co-op's name as bottler
on the label*

Stockists given in italic type after wines in this section will be found in the
WHERE TO BUY section earlier in the book.

THE MERCHANTS

Bacheroy-Josselin Successful and expanding Chablis merchant with vineyards divided between Domaine Laroche and Domaine de la Jouchère. The holding company is called Henri Laroche.

Albert Bichot Burgundy négociant with interests in Chablis. Also owns Domaine A Long-Depaquit in La Moutonne, whose wines are a better bet than their standard Chablis.
Unwins

Joseph Drouhin Another Burgundy merchant who now owns vineyards in Chablis, and uses lots of wood in his wines.
Rodney Densem Wines; Findlater Mackie Todd; Michael Menzel Wines; Selfridges

Labouré-Roi Famous Burgundy négociant now taking an interest in Chablis. Wines: Premiers Crus – Montmains, Montée de Tonnerre.
Majestic; Christopher Piper Wines; Willoughbys

Moreau The largest landowner and, after the co-operative, the largest producer. The wines are good and reliable if without great excitement, and are best drunk young. Moreau Blanc, the firm's branded wine, is not Chablis but Vin de Table. Wines: Domaine de Bieville Chablis; Premier Cru – Les Vaillons; Grand Cru – Les Clos.
Berry Bros & Rudd; Blayney Wines; Corney & Barrow; Davisons; Findlater Mackie Todd; Wine Society

Guy Mothe et ses Fils Small firm, also owning vineyards, including Domaine du Colombier.
Thos Peatling

A Regnard et Fils Firm of négociants owning no vineyards but buying in grapes from a wide range of properties. Now owned by de Ladoucette of Pouilly Fumé. Wines: Albert Pic, Michel Rémon, Premier Cru – Fourchaume; Grands Crus – Valmur, Vaudésir.
Berry Bros & Rudd; John Harvey & Sons; Hungerford Wine Company; Lay & Wheeler; Victoria Wine Company

Simmonet-Febvre Small vineyard holding backed up by large négociant business. Good source of wines from the smaller appellations around Chablis as well as Chablis itself. Wines: Grand Cru – Les Preuses; Premiers Crus – Monts de Milieu, Montée de Tonnerre, Fourchaume, Vaillons.
Christopher & Co

The other wines of the Chablis region

While Chablis itself covers a fairly small vineyard area, in the surrounding country of the Yonne are a handful of tiny appellations which were once mightier. Some have almost disappeared, others are coming back to life. All provide some interest.

Coulanges-la-Vineuse Strictly speaking not an appellation; the red wine from this village is actually called Bourgogne (with the name of the village appearing as a second thought). The grape is the Pinot Noir, the style light and elegant.
Peter Dominic

Irancy Another red wine village, this time with its own appellation. Pinot Noir is again the grape, with a little César to give body. The wines sometimes have surprising depth.
Bibendum; Domaine Direct; Haynes, Hanson & Clark

St-Bris-le-Vineux and Chitry-le-Fort These two villages combine to produce Sauvignon de St-Bris, now enjoying something of a cult following. The wines are not dissimilar to some Sancerre, which is not that far away.
Domaine Direct; Peter Dominic; Lay & Wheeler; Majestic; Market Vintners; Reid Wines; La Vigneronne

Best buys from Chablis and the environs

Jeunes Vignes, Vin de Table, La Chablisienne (*Marks & Spencer*)
Chablis 1986, Jean-Pierre Grossot (*Lay & Wheeler*)
Chablis 1986, G A E C Les Réunis (*Waitrose*)
Chablis Vallée Mignotte 1986 (*Haynes, Hanson & Clark*)
Chablis Domaine des Manants 1986, Jean-Marc Brocard (*Balls Brothers*)

Specialist stockists

David Baillie Vintners; Bibendum; D Byrne & Co; Domaine Direct; Haynes, Hanson & Clark; Ingletons Wines; O W Loeb; Raeburn Fine Wines and Foods; Tanners Wines; Philip Tite Fine Wines; Henry Townsend

CHAMPAGNE

Well done, all you British Champagne drinkers! You've kept us ahead in the Champagne league yet again. We still drink more of the stuff – 16.1 million bottles every year, to be precise – than any other country (except the French, who go really overboard with 60 million bottles).

We at *Which? Wine Guide* modestly admit that we did our little bit to keep the total high. Try as we might to find other, less expensive sparkling wines, we always come back to the Real Thing in the end. The Guide's sister publication, *Which? Wine Monthly*, organised a tasting of other top French sparkling wines from Saumur, Burgundy and Alsace. The general conclusion from our panel of tasters was that their different qualities just couldn't measure up to Champagne itself, and that it was worth paying the extra. At the moment, the extra is not all that much. In *WWM*'s tasting, the top non-Champagne sparklers were only about £1 less than many supermarket Champagnes.

Keeping the name to themselves

The Champenois (the folk who actually make the stuff) are understandably keen that the name Champagne should not be taken in vain. Not only have they launched law suits round the world to protect it (and generally won), they have now persuaded the EEC to prohibit the term 'méthode champenoise' (from 1993). So even if the Champagne method is being used by a producer, say, in Saumur, the label on the bottle won't be able to say so.

Such legislation is going to remove a useful shorthand term to describe the process of secondary fermentation in the same bottle from which the wine will eventually be poured. That slightly pedantic phrasing is important: there are other methods of making sparkling wine in which the wine is certainly fermented in a bottle rather than a big tank (another, even cheaper system), but is then transferred to a big vat before being bottled. This 'transfer method' cuts out the awkward process of disgorging the yeast sediment that remains after the fermentation. But it also cuts down on the elegance and fine mousse that characterises real Champagne method wines – and Champagne above all else.

Quality first

The Champenois are out to protect their name because they regard it as an extremely valuable property. But they are also concerned to protect the quality image which they have built up over generations: Champagne is the best, they say; accept no substitutes.

We agree with both those sentiments in principle, often in practice, too, but along with others we have started to notice an awful lot of rather immature Champagnes on the market at the moment, tasting green, sharp and acid, and just too young. These green Champagnes aren't necessarily the cheaper supermarket brands. Some of the most famous names have been guilty at times of releasing young Champagnes on to an unsuspecting public.

Our advice with virtually any Champagne is to keep it for a while after buying it: six months would be a good idea. Of course, that is ideal advice: most Champagne is bought for a spur-of-the-moment celebration, or in a restaurant, where you have to take what's on offer, but that is precisely why we are complaining now about the immaturity of many of the bottles we have been offered in the past year. If the Champenois are concerned about quality, that's an area they should tackle.

To give them their due, they have in fact done something about it, by changing the earliest permitted date that the wine may be bottled to 1 January after the vintage – the date may even be moved to 1 April. Previously, some devious producers were bottling as soon as they could in order to get round the rule which says that no Champagne can be released before it has had 12 months in bottle – and therefore could get their Champagne on to the market before the Christmas of the year after the harvest. Now at least that temptation will be removed.

We would still expect some less expensive Champagnes to taste a little green, and would be prepared to lay the bottle aside for a few months accordingly. But for the big names to do it as well – and still charge high prices – is less than fair to the consumer.

Down in the vineyard

In Champagne itself, the annual argument between the growers and the producers over the price of the grapes seems at last to have swung back to the producers. Champagne is the most closely regulated of all the French vineyard areas, and each year the two groups sit round a table (with a French government official to stop fisticuffs breaking out) to thrash out the price that the producing houses will pay for grapes they buy from the growers.

Big crops in the harvests of 1986 and 1987 have meant that the price of grapes has actually fallen for the first time for a very long time. It was only a 5.3 per cent fall over two years, and it still leaves the cost of the grapes in a bottle of Champagne at £2.30, but it does show that the growers aren't getting it all their own way.

Another development has been in the realms of big business. Although all the Champagne houses like to present themselves in a traditional, elegant, countrified way, the reality is a highly industrialised process, with enormous stocks of bottles and expensive techniques for getting the bubbles to stay in them.

Big business moved into Champagne in a big way in 1987, in the shape of a merger between two of the most famous houses – Veuve Clicquot and Moët et Chandon. This new firm controls two-fifths of all Champagne sales: besides Clicquot and Moët, they also own Ruinart, Mercier, Canard Duchêne and Joseph Henriot.

Other conglomerates also control much of Champagne. The Canadian firm of Seagram, for example, owns Heidsieck Monopole, Mumm and Perrier-Jouët. The family firms which remain – Taittinger, Bollinger, Piper Heidsieck, Roederer – are tiny by comparison with the giants.

Doing their own thing

At the other end of the scale are the growers who thought they would like to see their own name on a bottle, rather than just sell grapes to a producing house or a co-operative. They started making Champagne and bottling it and selling it themselves. The trend took off, and by the early 1980s around half of the Champagne sold came from growers or co-ops.

The growth of this trend seems to have stopped now. For a while, it left the houses with a problem of where to buy grapes. Sometimes they ran short (especially after small harvests) and had to resort to buying wine rather than grapes (which meant they lost some control over the way their Champagne was made). This is called buying 'sur lattes' (literally, wine that is in the process of being worked on), and while the houses that bought in this way claimed that their Champagne was no different, others reckon that the taste is affected. Big harvests in 1986 and 1987 may have put a stop to this practice for the time being.

White wine from black grapes

Champagne is made from three grape varieties – one white and two black. Because the juice of the black grapes is white (only the skins are black), it is possible with careful pressing of the grapes to extract the white juice completely uncoloured by the skins.

Chardonnay is the white grape, which may appear by itself in Blanc de Blancs. Pinot Meunier and Pinot Noir are the black grapes. Pinot Noir makes the better quality wine, but the less prestigious Pinot Meunier is an important constituent even of top blends.

What's what in Champagne

Most Champagne is sold under a brand name, whether it's from one of the great houses (Bollinger, Veuve Clicquot, Moët et Chandon, etc), or a smaller house or co-operative, or under a buyer's own label (Sainsbury's or Tesco's Champagne).

But it is also possible to find out from the label something about the type of producer and his status. At the bottom of the label are two letters followed by a series of numbers. The numbers can be traced in Champagne to tell you the name of maker, and the letters indicate what sort of company it is:

NM (négociant manipulant) means that the Champagne was made by a merchant or négociant who buys grapes and wine from anywhere in the region and then makes his own blend. All the major houses are merchants like this and those two letters are a good guarantee of quality.

RM (récoltant manipulant) indicates that the producer is a grower who makes the wine only from grapes grown in his own vineyard. Often this wine can be very good indeed, but because the grower cannot buy in grapes from elsewhere, he is at the whim of weather and general crop failures – always a risk in vineyards so far north as Champagne. Look for growers who describe their wines as grand or premier cru – the terms have a definite quality status in the highly regulated world of Champagne.

MA (manipulant acheteur) means that the brand is a buyer's own brand – a merchant or retail chain has put its own name on the label of Champagne which it has bought from a producer. The best guide to the quality of this Champagne is the quality of the merchant or shop.

CM (co-opérative manipulant). This indicates that the wine has been made by a co-operative. The reputation of the brand name is the best guide to quality here.

What else is on the label?

There are many other terms used to describe Champagne on the label. Here are those most commonly found:

Blanc de Blancs Champagne made only from the Chardonnay grape. Generally light, flowery, delicate.

Blanc de Noirs Champagne made only from black grapes (Pinot Noir and Pinot Meunier). Full, quite heavy and not often seen.

Bouzy Rouge Still red wine made from Pinot Noir grapes. Expensive and very light in style: an acquired taste.

Brut Very dry, the standard term used to describe most of the Champagne we drink. A few firms make extremely dry Champagne as well as their standard brut: this will be described as something like Ultra Brut (Laurent Perrier) or Brut Sauvage (Piper Heidsieck).

Coteaux Champenois Red, white or rosé still wines made from Champagne grapes grown in Champagne.

Crémant Fermented in the bottle to a lower pressure than Champagne so that the bubbles are creamier and less fizzy.

Crus All the Champagne vineyards are graded on a quality scale. The best are graded at 100 per cent and are called grands crus; the next level – at 90 to 99 per cent – are premiers crus. Deuxième crus run from 80 to 90 per cent. Some Champagnes will be made only from grand cru vineyards and can then describe themselves as such. But many of the finest Champagnes use lesser vineyards for their grapes in order to achieve the consistent blend: it's not necessarily a way of cutting corners.

De luxe or prestige cuvées On the theory that Champagne is like perfume (the more you charge for it, the more people want to buy it), Champagne houses are falling over themselves to launch top-price blends which can be either vintage or non-vintage. They are often distinguished more by the flamboyance of the bottle than the quality of the wine, although some de luxe cuvées are very fine. Better quality and value is to be found in straightforward vintage Champagne or the RD brands (see below).

Demi-sec A medium sweet Champagne, best drunk at the end of a meal.

Doux Sweet Champagne. Not much in demand in the UK, but very popular in South America.

Extra dry Not as dry as brut but drier than sec.

Non-vintage The vast bulk of Champagne is a blend, using wines from different years to give continuity of style. These Champagnes reflect their house styles, and the master blenders (who may be putting 40 or 50 different wines in the blend) are highly regarded.

RD (Récemment dégorgé). A few houses (Bollinger, Gratien and Joseph Perrier) don't remove the yeasts from the wine as soon as the second fermentation in the bottle has finished, but leave the sediment in the wine for some time afterwards to give added richness to the Champagne. It's done for only a small proportion of the production which will be labelled accordingly and for which large sums of money will be charged. But for special occasions these wines are very memorable – and certainly better value than many de luxe blends.

Riche The sweetest category of Champagne. The term is no longer permitted on its own – it must also say 'doux'.

Rosé Champagne Normally made by adding red wine to white wine to give consistency of colour. The old method was to leave the red grape juice in contact with the skins after pressing to get its colour and then ferment the wine as a rosé.

Sec Medium dry, less dry than extra brut or brut.

Vintage Champagne A Champagne in which all the wine will be from one year. Vintage Champagne is made only in exceptional years which are 'declared', but not every producer will make a vintage each declared year. This was the way Champagne always used to be made until the Second World War. Vintage Champagne can represent very good value for money for a top-rate wine, but needs some time in bottle before drinking – at least six or seven years. There's no point in drinking vintage Champagne too young – you might as well buy the less expensive non-vintage.

Bottle sizes
Apart from the standard 75cl Champagne bottle, Champagne comes in a whole range of other sizes. The larger the bottle size, the more slowly the wine will mature.

Halves and quarters Champagne matures very quickly in these small bottles – especially the quarter-bottles sometimes seen on aeroplanes. Be cautious with quarters – the quality of the wine tends to suffer.

Magnums Two ordinary bottles.

Jeroboam Four ordinary bottles.

Rehoboam Six ordinary bottles.

Methuselah Eight ordinary bottles.

Salmanazar Twelve ordinary bottles.

Balthazar Sixteen ordinary bottles.

Nebuchadnezzar Twenty ordinary bottles.

Champagne vintages

1987 A big vintage, of fairly average quality, but at least it has kept the price of grapes down, which means the price of wine to consumers should remain stable. Unlikely, though, to produce vintage wines.

1986 The first big crop since 1983, producing good rather than great quality. The general opinion is that Blanc de Blancs style wines will be the best.

1985 Small crop because heavy frosts at the beginning of the year did immense damage to the vineyards. The quality, though, was high after a warm summer and autumn, and some vintage wines have been announced. Wine held back from the bumper 1982 and 1983 vintages has been used to augment the quantity.

1984 A pretty awful vintage, small in quantity and with rather thin, acid wines. No vintage wines have been made, and the wines themselves will need considerable additions of older wines to maintain quality for non-vintage blends.

1983 and **1982** Bumper years in Champagne – both for quality and quantity. Most producers declared vintages, and these are now available – but are too young to drink yet.

1981 The current crop of vintage Champagne that is ready to drink. The crop was small and the wines tend to be a little acid, so buy vintage bottles with care.

1979 An excellent vintage. Stocks are still around of this year's wines and are showing very well at the moment.

1978 A thin vintage, with concentrated acidity. But some vintage wines are developing very well in an austere sort of way, and will last for some time.

1976 Many of the lesser vintage wines from this year are past their best. Some of the top houses' wines, though, are still delicious.

1975 One of the great vintages of the past 15 years. If you see a bottle, buy it, just to see what mature Champagne can really taste like.

Older vintages: 1973, 1971, 1966, 1964, 1961 Generally only the top cuvées from the best producers are worth considering – although there can be surprises.

Who's who in Champagne

Here is a list of producers whose Champagnes are available in UK shops. We have not included own-label Champagnes, but since most wine merchants as well as supermarkets and wine warehouses have an own-label brand, we would recommend trying them for value for money.

Ayala Fair, reasonably enjoyable wines with consistent quality and some bottle age. Non-vintage, vintage and rosé are available.
Majestic; Selfridges; Willoughbys; Wine Growers Association

Besserat de Bellefon Lightish style, better at Crémant than straight Champagne. Non-vintage, vintage, Crémant, Crémant Rosé, de luxe Cuvée B de B.
Peter Green; La Réserve; Willoughbys; Cliff & Co (Symons Street, London SW3)

Billecart-Salmon Serious Champagne in a dry, austere style. Non-vintage, Blanc de Blancs, rosé, de luxe Cuvée Nicolas-François Billecart.
Bibendum; Alex Findlater; Windrush Wines

Boizel Good value Champagne, without excitement but reliable. Non-vintage, vintage, rosé.
D Byrne & Co; George Hill of Loughborough

Bollinger Full, rich Champagnes in a traditional style with a faithful following. Non-vintage, vintage, rosé, RD, Vieilles Vignes Françaises.
Widely available

Bonnaire A small producer in the top quality village of Cramant. Makes a non-vintage, and Blanc de Blancs Cuvée Anniversaire.
Willoughbys

Canard-Duchêne Easy-drinking, good value Champagne. Non-vintage, rosé, de luxe Charles VII.
Fortnum & Mason; Stones of Belgravia; Waitrose; Willoughbys

de Castellane Soft wines with a hint of wood to give them character. Non-vintage and vintage.
Hedley Wright

Cattier Light Champagnes, producing straightforward, non-vintage and vintage wines, and a stylish Clos du Moulin non-vintage prestige brand.
Mail order only from Patrick Grubb (Orchard Lee House, Steeple Aston, Oxfordshire)

Charbaut Light, perfumed wine of good quality. Non-vintage, vintage, rosé, de luxe Certificat Blanc de Blancs.
Reid Wines (rosé only); Seckford Wines

Deutz Well-aged wines, full and soft. Non-vintage, vintage, rosé, de luxe Cuvée William Deutz.
Curzon Wine Company; Laytons; André Simon Wines

Nicolas Feuillatte Light style of wines. Makes a rosé and a non-vintage.
Eaton Elliot Winebrokers; Cockburn & Campbell (Buckhold Road, London SW18)

Roland Fliniaux Small producer with four hectares under vine. Non-vintage, vintage, rosé.
The Champagne House

Michel Gonet Good value Blanc de Blancs.
Noble Grape (26 The Highway, London E1)

Gosset Quite rich wines with Pinot predominating. Non-vintage, vintage, rosé, de luxe Grand Millésime, Cuvée Quatrième Centenaire.
The Champagne House; Fortnum & Mason

George Goulet Mature wines on the lighter side. Non-vintage, vintage, rosé de luxe Cuvée de Centenaire.
H Allen Smith; Les Amis du Vin; Lockes; Nobody Inn; Willoughbys

Granier Well-matured wines with a high proportion of Pinot. Non-vintage, vintage, rosé, de luxe Cuvée Réserve.
Willoughbys; Wines from Paris

Heidsieck Light, commercial wines, but good value. Non-vintage, vintage, de luxe H de Heidsieck.
Highgate Wines (9a Swains Lane, London NW6)

Charles Heidsieck Full-bodied wines which sometimes suffer from being too young. From a poor period a few years ago, quality is looking up. Non-vintage, vintage, rosé, de luxe Champagne Charlie.
Widely available

Heidsieck Monopole Attractive, biscuity-yeasty wines, very dry. Non-vintage, vintage, rosé, de luxe Diamant Bleu.
Fortnum & Mason; Oddbins; Willoughbys

Henriot One of the brands in the Moët/Clicquot conglomerate, making wines under the Baron Philippe de Rothschild name as well as a non-vintage called Henriot.
Alex Findlater; Stones of Belgravia; Willoughbys

Jacquart High quality wines from one of the Champagne co-operatives. Good bottle age. Vintage, non-vintage, rosé.
Blayneys; L'Esprit du Vin (51a Upper Berkeley Street, London W1); Paten Wines (The Maltings, Alderman's Drive, Peterborough, Cambs); Vinnicombe Wines (104 Teignmouth Road, Torquay, Devon)

Jacquesson Drinkable, soft, high quality. Non-vintage, vintage, rosé, de luxe Signature.
Yapp Brothers

Louis Kremer Full, fruity, quite heavy wines. Non-vintage, vintage, rosé.
D Byrne & Co; George Hill of Loughborough; Willoughbys

Krug Great Champagnes that are (almost) worth the price. Vintages last for years and the rosé is a great experience. Vintage, rosé, de luxe Grande Cuvée.
Adnams; H Allen Smith; Bibendum; Eldridge Pope; Alex Findlater; Fortnum & Mason; Peter Green; Lay & Wheeler; Majestic; Oddbins; André Simon Wines; Stones of Belgravia; Willoughbys

Lanson Light, fresh wines with a predominance of Chardonnay. Non-vintage, vintage, rosé, de luxe Noble Cuvée.
Widely available

Abel Lepitre Very high class Champagnes with good bottle age and maturity in the taste. Non-vintage, vintage, de luxe Prince A de Bourbon.
O W Loeb

Laurent Perrier Lovely, traditional wines, very clean-tasting. Non-vintage, vintage, rosé (one of the few made traditionally), de luxe Cuvée Grande Siècle.
Widely available

Mercier The second company in the Moët et Chandon group makes good, reliable Champagne which is also generally good value. Non-vintage, vintage, rosé.
Davisons; Peter Green; Lay & Wheeler; Market Vintners; Waitrose; Willoughbys

Moët et Chandon The biggest seller, often maligned, but actually of good, reliable quality. Quite full-bodied. Non-vintage, vintage, rosé, de luxe Dom Pérignon.
Very widely available

Mumm Slightly sweeter than most bruts, which gives a full, creamy taste. Non-vintage, vintage, rosé, de luxe René Lalou, Mumm de Mumm.
Curzon Wine Company; Fortnum & Mason; Oddbins; Stones of Belgravia; Willoughbys

Oudinot Light, undemanding wines. The top cuvée is called Gold Label.
Contact Giles de la Mare (The Old Dower House, Maiden Bradley, Warminster, Wilts)

Bruno Paillard Delightful Champagne – light, elegant, fruity. Vintage, non-vintage, rosé.
Berkmann Wine Cellars/Le Nez Rouge; Henry Townsend

Joseph Perrier Ripe, rich, firm Champagne, which matures well. Non-vintage, vintage, rosé, de luxe Cuvée de Cent-Cinquantenaire.
H Allen Smith; Lay & Wheeler; Seckford Wines; Willoughbys

Perrier-Jouët Light, predominantly Chardonnay wines, with hints of lemon. Non-vintage, vintage, rosé Belle Epoque, de luxe Belle Epoque, Blason de France.
Curzon Wine Company; Alex Findlater; Fortnum & Mason; Peter Green; Oddbins; Stones of Belgravia; La Vigneronne; Waitrose; Willoughbys

Philipponnat Good value, very approachable Champagne. Non-vintage, vintage.
Oddbins; Ostlers

Piper Heidsieck Light, flinty, well-structured wines. Non-vintage, vintage, rosé, de luxe Champagne Rare (very dry).
Fortnum & Mason; André Simon Wines; Stones of Belgravia; Willoughbys

Pol Roger Light, elegant, firm wines. Non-vintage, vintage, rosé, de luxe Cuvée Sir Winston Churchill.
H Allen Smith; Curzon Wine Company; Eldridge Pope; Alex Findlater; Fortnum & Mason; Peter Green; Majestic; Reid Wines; Willoughbys

Pommery et Greno Just known as Pommery. Dry, light, balanced wines. Non-vintage, vintage, rosé, de luxe Cuvée Louis Pommery.
Fortnum & Mason; Peter Green; Arthur Rackhams; Stones of Belgravia; Willoughbys; Wines from Paris

Louis Roederer Fruity, rich, firm wines with a lot of character. Non-vintage, vintage, rosé, de luxe Cristal.
Adnams; Bibendum; Curzon Wine Company; Alex Findlater; Fortnum & Mason; Peter Green; Lay & Wheeler; Majestic; André Simon Wines; Stones of Belgravia; La Vigneronne; Willoughbys

Ruinart Another Moët et Chandon company, making soft, gentle wine of good quality. Vintage Blanc de Blancs, de luxe Dom Ruinart.
Curzon Wine Company; Fortnum & Mason; Willoughbys; Wine Growers Association

Salon Tiny production of superb 100 per cent Chardonnay wines made only in the best years. Vintage Salon le Mesnil, de luxe Cuvée S.
Les Amis du Vin; Fortnum & Mason; Harrods; The Market/Le Provençal; Oddbins; Raeburn Fine Wines and Foods; Willoughbys

Jacques Selosse Wines of character and depth which age well. Non-vintage, vintage, de luxe Club Spécial.
Oldacre-Field (Hazel Road, Altrincham, Cheshire)

Taittinger Attractive, lively, dry, gentle. Non-vintage, vintage, rosé Comtes de Champagne, de luxe Comtes de Champagne, Taittinger Collection.
Widely available

de Venoge Well-balanced with elegance and some finesse. Non-vintage, vintage, rosé, de luxe Champagne des Princes.
Thomas Baty; Willoughbys

Veuve Clicquot Great quality and consistent style make this one of the most popular Champagnes. Non-vintage, vintage, rosé, de luxe La Grande Dame.
Widely available

Best buys in Champagne

LESS EXPENSIVE NON-VINTAGE

Tesco Non-Vintage
Waitrose Non-Vintage
Ellner Extra Brut (*Davisons*)
De Telmont Non-Vintage (*Majestic*)
Pierre Vaudon (*Haynes, Hanson & Clark*)
André Jacquart Carte Blanche (*Morris & Verdin*)
Roland Fliniaux (*The Champagne House*)

MORE EXPENSIVE NON-VINTAGE

Mumm Crémant de Cramant (*Curzon Wine Company; Oddbins*)
Bruno Paillard Crémant Brut (*Market Vintners*)
The Chairman's Elegantly Dry (*Eldridge Pope/Reynier Wine Libraries*)
Alfred Gratien non-vintage (*Curzon Wine Company; The Market/Le Provençal*)
Lanson Black Label (*Eldridge Pope; Stones of Belgravia; Waitrose*)
Louis Roederer Brut Premier (*Curzon Wine Company; Majestic*)

VINTAGE

Sainsbury's 1982
Waitrose Extra Dry 1984

Louis Roederer 1982 (*Bibendum; Fortnum & Mason; Lay & Wheeler; Reid Wines; La Vigneronne; Willoughbys*)

Perrier-Jouët 1979 (*Curzon Wine Company; Fortnum & Mason; Willoughbys*)

Heidsieck Dry Monopole 1982 (*Oddbins; Willoughbys*)

DE LUXE AND SPECIAL CUVÉES

Jacquesson Signature 1979 (*Yapp Brothers*)

Jacques Selosse Grand Cru Brut 1979 Cuvée Club Spécial (*Oldacre-Field, Hazel Road, Altrincham, Cheshire*)

Deutz Cuvée William Deutz (*The Champagne House; Fortnum & Mason; Laytons; André Simon Wines*)

Laurent Perrier Cuvée Grande Siècle (*Curzon Wine Company; Stones of Belgravia; Henry Townsend; Willoughbys*)

Heidsieck Monopole Diamant Bleu (*Fortnum & Mason; Oddbins; Willoughbys*)

De Courcy Cuvée de Prestige (*contact de Courcy Père et Fils, PO Box 50, Ashford, Kent*)

ROSÉ CHAMPAGNE

Charbaut Rosé non-vintage (*Reid Wines*)

Asda Champagne Rosé Brut

Alfred Gratien Rosé Brut (*Arthur Rackhams*)

Sainsbury's Rosé Champagne Brut

De Telmont Rosé (*Majestic*)

Laurent Perrier Rosé (*Châteaux Wines*)

Specialist stockists

Barnes Wine Shop; Bibendum; Buckingham Wines; Cadwgan Wines; Champagne and Caviar Shop; The Champagne House; Champagne de Villages; Curzon Wine Company; Fortnum and Mason; Peter Green; Harrods; Hungerford Wine Company; Nickolls & Perks; Oddbins; Quintet Wines; Arthur Rackhams; La Réserve; T & W Wines; Selfridges; Unwins; Upper Crust; Willoughbys; Peter Wylie Fine Wines; Yorkshire Fine Wines

CORSICA

Corsican wine producers are divided into two camps. There are those who believe in the local grapes and make their wines under a number of appellation names; and there are those who have imported the international grape varieties to the island, but are allowed to call their wines only vins de pays.

On the whole, the international grapes make the better wines. While the typical Corsican wine tends to be a heavy red, some very refreshing tastes are coming out in the guise of Vin de Pays de l'Île de Beauté, at good value prices.

Such wines wouldn't be possible without new technology. The producers of the AC wines are also benefiting from this, so if you want to see what the local red Nielluccio and Sciacarello and the white Vermentino taste like, there are now some well-made wines to try.

Where's where in Corsica

The two main AC regions are Patrimonio and Ajaccio. In Patrimonio, reds are made from the Nielluccio while whites come from the Malvoisie. In Ajaccio, Sciacarello provides the reds and Vermentino the whites. Other AC areas are Coteaux du Cap Corse, Porto-Vecchio, Sartène and Calvi.

The Vin de Pays de l'Île de Beauté comes from grapes grown all over the island. Reds can be made from Syrah and Cabernet Sauvignon, whites from Chardonnay.

Best buys from Corsica

Domaine de Fontanella, Vin de Pays (*Waitrose*)
Domaine Comte Peraldi, Vin de Corse Ajaccio (*Bordeaux Direct*)
Vin de Pays de l'Île de Beauté Chardonnay (*Cadwgan Wines; Stones of Belgravia*)

Specialist stockist

Willoughbys

HAUT-POITOU

This region has virtually come back from the dead as the result of the efforts of the local co-operative of Haut-Poitou. The vineyard area near Poitiers produces a range of varietally labelled wines: an excellent aromatic Sauvignon similar to that made in Touraine, a light, fruity Gamay, and a soft Chardonnay. Drink the wines young. (See also *Other French sparkling wines* on page 568.)

Best buys from Haut-Poitou

Sauvignon de Haut-Poitou (*Richard Harvey Wines; Lay & Wheeler; Majestic; Morris & Verdin; Nobody Inn; Stapylton Fletcher; Willoughbys*)
Chardonnay de Haut-Poitou (*Richard Harvey Wines; Lay & Wheeler; Majestic; Morris & Verdin; Stapylton Fletcher; Willoughbys*)
Gamay de Haut-Poitou (*Stapylton Fletcher; Lay & Wheeler; Willoughbys*)

Specialist stockists

G Hush; Willoughbys

JURA

Strange tastes emanate from the beautiful Jura mountains in the east of France. While reds, whites and rosés are made (and the rosés are, on the whole, the most successful), it is the vin jaune which most people know in connection with the Jura.

But it's unlikely to be the most familiar taste. A strong, Sherry-like wine which grows a natural flor – the only other place in Europe outside Jerez to do so – and which needs considerable ageing before it's drinkable, vin jaune is an acquired taste. But it is one of the more unusual wine tastes of France and worth trying.

The reds are made from the local Trousseau grape and a little Pinot Noir. They're rather heavy and coarse in style and best appreciated on the spot. The whites also use a local grape variety, the Savagnin, plus a little Chardonnay (which is used also for some sparkling wines).

The rosés, from the Pulsard grape, are also known as vins gris. They're full, dry and quite dark in colour, and have a high reputation.

The appellations of the Jura are: Arbois, Côtes de Jura, l'Etoile. Village names to look for are Ch Chalon, Poligny and Pupillin.

Who's who in the Jura

By far the biggest shipper of note from the Jura is Henri Maire who makes the full range of styles (*Willoughbys carry many of these, and Nobody Inn also offers a selection*). Jean Bourdy makes Ch Chalon and Vin Jaune (*O W Loeb; La Vigneronne; Wine Society*), while a third name to look for is the single vineyard Ch d'Arlay which produces red and white wines as well as Vin Jaune (*Eaton Elliot Winebrokers; Harrods; O W Loeb; Sainsbury's*).

Best buy from the Jura
Ch d'Arlay Blanc 1985 (*Eaton Elliot Winebrokers*)

Specialist stockists
O W Loeb; Wine Society

THE LOIRE

Discovering new areas

Among the Loire wines we've tasted in the last year, two have stood out, not because they were the greatest wines in the world, far from it, but because they came from areas we'd hardly heard of and moreover were so enjoyable and such good value.

These two wines were a Coteaux du Giennois 1986, a VDQS wine from vineyards just down the Loire from Sancerre (*Waitrose*), and a Côtes du Forez, from another VDQS right up river, just across the mountains from the Beaujolais (*Bordeaux Direct*). They were both enjoyable, quaffable wines, ideal for summer days.

And they were both red. They made us rethink our conventional view that the Loire produces only white wines and some sugar-watery rosés, and it made us look again at some of the unknown Loire vineyards. Our views on the quality of Loire reds were influenced by a tasting organised by our sister publication, *Which? Wine Monthly*, in the summer of 1987, at which some of the tastes from areas such as Chinon and Bourgueil were a revelation in quality and individuality.

Forgotten corners

The Loire, with its wide variety of wine styles, does seem to collect these forgotten vinous corners. There are the superb sweet wines from Quarts de Chaume and Bonnezeaux in Anjou. There are the crisp red Gamays of the Fiefs Vendéens at the mouth of the river. There are the white wines of Ménétou-Salon, Reuilly and Quincy, producing Sancerre look-alikes often at a fraction of the price. There are long-lived, honeyed wines from Vouvray and Montlouis. And more: the Loire has a complete repertoire of vinous tastes.

So many different tastes from the vineyards on this 600-mile long river abound that it is not possible to categorise them under one heading. But they do have one thing in common: they are northern wines. Champagne and Alsace are further north, so is Chablis; but the cool, wet winds from the Atlantic flow up the Loire valley, keeping summertime temperatures down, dragging out the ripening season dangerously into November, and giving poor years even when the wine producers further south are complaining of the heat. Even in wines from the vineyards far up-river, like Côtes du Forez, there is an extra sharpness and acidity that seems to characterise the Loire.

The result for many Loire wines is an intensity of fruit that is unequalled elsewhere. There is also a certain directness of taste, a lack perhaps of layers of complexity, that makes Loire wines (when they're any good) instantly recognisable and, above all, drinkable. It's no coincidence that the Loire is the second largest producer of sparkling wine in France (outside Champagne): good sparkling wine needs a sound, simple-tasting, quite acidic base wine to show at its best. It's no coincidence, either, that Muscadet should have become so popular with wine bar habitués – its easy quaffability defies convoluted tasting notes or too serious discussion.

High quality, good prices

At the moment – with one or two exceptions (of which more in a moment) – Loire wines have that happy combination, rare in France, of good quality and good value. There have been some good vintages recently – 1985 and 1986 were star years for different styles of wines. Although 1987 seems to have broken that happy state of affairs (too much rain right through the year – much like Britain), average rather than poor wines have been the result (the exception being Muscadet, which had a long, hot summer).

Statistics show that we are lapping up Loire wines at a rapidly increasing rate: in the first nine months of 1987, 21 million litres reached Britain, an increase of 9.3 per cent over 1986. And there's plenty more where those wines came from: the average annual harvest in the Loire valley is 230 million litres.

The bulk of our intake is of white wines: the easy tastes of Muscadet, of Anjou (the white wines of Anjou are getting much better), of sparkling Saumur, and, increasingly of Touraine wines, while Sancerre and Pouilly Fumé, though expensive, still seem to prop up many a restaurant wine list.

But for 1989, we suggest that you look at some of those vinous forgotten corners and at the red wines. Give them some thought over the next glass of Muscadet . . .

We've divided the sections on Loire wines by styles: dry whites, sweet whites, and reds and rosés.

Dry white wines – what the Loire's all about

If any tastes epitomise the Loire, they are the crispness of Sauvignon Blanc and the clean acidity of Muscadet. These are produced at the eastern and western extremities of the main Loire vineyard areas: the Sauvignon of Sancerre and Pouilly Fumé, far to the east, almost in Chablis; the Muscadet, the wine of Brittany, from the mouth of the river near Nantes.

In between, there are the excellent value Sauvignon Blanc wines of Touraine, and the varied quality of the Chenin Blanc wines of Anjou. We say 'varied quality' because the Chenin Blanc, a notoriously fickle grape variety, can produce some wonderfully long-lived dry whites in small pockets such as Savennières, or in Vouvray and Montlouis in Touraine, while in large swathes of vineyard south of Angers, it comes up with agonisingly acidic mouthfuls, softened by sweetness and sulphur, that compare equally unfavourably with European Tafelwein. Quite why the Chenin Blanc is so widely planted in the Val de Loire is a mystery of history, bearing in mind that it performs so much more reliably in the south of France.

Besides the appellation contrôlée wines of the Loire, there are a number of excellent vins de pays – from the basic regional Vin de Pays du Jardin de la France (only the French could have the cheek to think up such an evocative name, which also happens to be very apt) to smaller areas which have hardly left the vineyard, let alone reached our shops. There are also the VDQS areas, of which the most interesting (for dry whites, that is) is away from the main river: St-Pourçain on the Allier.

Where's where in dry white Loire wines

Sancerre and Pouilly Fumé

These two vineyards face each other across the north-flowing Loire just before it turns west. The whites are the most important wines in terms of quality. Made from the Sauvignon grape they have hints of blackcurrants and gooseberries and a slightly smoky flavour (hence the Fumé in Pouilly Fumé) and at their best are some of the most flavourful wines around. Pouilly Fumé tends to be more full-bodied than Sancerre, and needs just a little more time before it is ready to drink.

Certain villages in each area are reckoned to make exceptional wines: in Sancerre – Bué, Chavignol, Verdigny, St-Satur; in Pouilly – Les Loges, Les Berthiers, Tracy, Maltaverne. Look for the grower's address on the label.

Other appellation areas producing white wines of similar style but at lower prices than the fashionable Sancerre and Pouilly Fumé are Reuilly, Quincy and Ménétou-Salon. The appellation of Pouilly-sur-Loire uses the Chasselas grape to make unmemorable whites.

Although it is true that most of these wines don't improve with keeping – so you should be drinking 1986 and 1987 wines now (with the 1986 a better vintage) – the special character of a mature Sancerre or Pouilly Fumé makes older wines worth seeking out. They certainly don't fade away but develop a mellow acidity that is often less penetrating and more subtle than the taste of the younger wines.

Vouvray and Montlouis

The best vineyards of Touraine in the central Loire are just to the west of the city of Tours. Another pair of towns – Vouvray and Montlouis – face each other across the river. Both Vouvray and Montlouis are made from the Chenin Blanc grape.

We've neglected these wines – unfairly. The trouble is that many wines are bottled by négociants elsewhere on the Loire, and are not very good. It would be much better to spend a little more and buy wines bottled in Vouvray or Montlouis ('mise en bouteilles au château/domaine' or a Vouvray or Montlouis address will give a clue).

Vouvray wines range from bone dry to sweet and also include sparkling versions (see under *Sparkling wines* at the end of the WHAT TO

BUY section). It's important to check the style and sweetness or dryness of the Vouvray you're buying. Good, still, dry Vouvray can have considerable depth and richness, but the sweeter wines tend to aim higher. Montlouis is softer and more likely to be sweet.

Jasnières

This tiny area of dry white production is away to the north of the Loire on the River Loir (confusingly, the Loire is La Loire, the Loir is Le Loir). The wine made in Jasnières is from the Chenin Blanc which here achieves some quality in a dry, under-ripe sort of way.

Sauvignon de Touraine

A wide appellation which covers any wine made in Touraine from the Sauvignon grape. The value for money of these wines is good and the quality reliable, so they make a good cheaper substitute for the Sancerre/Pouilly wines.

Saumur

This small town west of Angers is the first important white wine quality area in Anjou. It's best known in this country for its sparkling wines, made by the Champagne method and using the often under-ripe wines made of Chenin Blanc (see more under *Sparkling wines* at the end of the WHAT TO BUY section).

Still dry white wines are made here under the Saumur appellation, but few achieve greatness or even leave the area. More important still dry whites are made in Coteaux de Saumur but, again, few leave France.

Savennières

A minuscule appellation with a deservedly growing reputation. The wines are some of the best dry wines made in the Loire from the Chenin Blanc grape, with all the overtones of sweetness in the honey and lemon bouquet but crisp, deep fruit on the palate. They need some ageing – around five or six years – to be at their best. Sadly, their reputation has forced the price up of the small amount of wine made. Superior Savennières is made in the single vineyard appellations of Coulée de Serrant and La Roche aux Moines.

Anjou Blanc

Hitherto, few attractive dry wines have appeared under this appellation. Many of the sweeter wines (apart from the legendary Moulin Touchais) suffered from too much sulphur and too little attention, while the dry wines were just sharp and acidic. There does, though, seem to be a general improvement in quality, so it might be worth reconsidering this appellation.

Muscadet

What started life as the base wine made from the Muscadet grape for distillation by the Dutch into brandy has become the wine everybody drinks by the glass in the wine bar, with fish or shellfish, or at any time. It's the second most popular French wine in this country – after red Bordeaux.

After a sudden price rise in 1986/87, the price of Muscadet seems to have levelled off again. So, although it is more expensive than it was two years ago, it is still decent value. However, don't be attracted by really cheap Muscadet (say under £2.50/£2.75 a bottle). Unless it's on special offer, it could be a really unpleasant, sulphurous beverage.

The new development in Muscadet is the growth of domaine bottling. This has big advantages for the best style of Muscadet – 'sur lie'. It has been known for a while that keeping the wine on its lees until it is bottled (rather than fining and filtering as soon as the fermentation is over) improves the depth and quality of the wine. But then moving the wine for bottling away from the grower's cellar to the merchant's disturbs the lees and spoils the flavour. The less disturbance the wine suffers the better: hence bottling the wine where it's made. The term 'mise en bouteille au château/domaine' should give a clue.

However, price will also be a determining factor: cheap Muscadet sur lie may be bottled in a 'château' which is in fact a large négociant's bottling hall, in which case the full benefit of bottling 'sur lie' will be lost. Be prepared to pay a little more (say around £4).

Another trend in an effort to improve the image of Muscadet has been the growth in single vineyard wines, of which the best can be surprisingly full-flavoured and individual.

A number of useful words on a Muscadet label will give you a strong indication of quality – important in an area where a lot of very dull wine is still being made.

Sèvre et Maine This is the name of the region at the heart of Muscadet production. The quality is higher than ordinary Muscadet and it's worth paying the premium for a wine of greater intensity and depth.

Sur lie See above. This indicates that the wine has been kept on its lees until it was bottled.

Mis/mise en bouteille au château (or au domaine) In theory, the wine should not have been moved from the cellar before bottling, thus preserving all the advantages of keeping it 'sur lie' (although see the caveat above).

Other styles of wine made in the Muscadet region are generally less worth buying. They are:

Muscadet AC The basic stuff – and it tends to taste like it.

Gros Plant A VDQS appellation for wine made using the Gros Plant grape. Very tart, acid stuff, possible as a thirst-quencher on a very hot day and not much cheaper than Muscadet.

Drink all these wines from the Muscadet area as young as possible. The 1988 vintage will be in the shops by the late spring and by then it will be the only one to buy. Muscadet Primeur (a white copy of Beaujolais Nouveau) should arrive here by Christmas and will be a good quaffing wine over the Christmas period and into January.

Sweet white wines – finding their value

For quite a while now this Guide has been praising the qualities of the sweet white wines, made with the Chenin Blanc grape in corners of Anjou and Touraine. We may at last have had an effect: the price of these superb wines has, sad to say, begun to rise to meet those of Sauternes and Barsac. They haven't reached those levels yet, but they're on the way, so stock up before it's too late (if you can find them, that is: hardly any were made in 1987 or 1986, because the weather wasn't right).

These sweet wines are an excellent example of what a microclimate can achieve. While Anjou can be the source of some pretty unpleasant sweet wines, in the valleys of the Layon and Aubance, south of Angers, the Chenin Blanc grape suddenly becomes the source of some very fine noble rot sweet wines. The autumn mists here act in the same way as they do in Sauternes – causing a benign fungus on the grapes to shrivel them up, removing the water and leaving just the sweet essence of grape juice.

Four main appellations produce sweet wines. Two – Coteaux du Layon and Coteaux de l'Aubance – produce simple, sweet fruity wines but without the added extra of the noble rot. But Quarts de Chaume and Bonnezeaux are two tiny pockets of vineyard where the noble rot creates rich, intense, peach-and-apricot wines of great stature and immensely long life. These wines don't really come into their own for as much as 10 or 15 years, but the wait is worthwhile in great vintages (see below). Bonnezeaux is better value than Quarts de Chaume.

Back on the main Loire valley, Vouvray and Montlouis, source of dry whites and sparkling wines, also make some intense sweet wines with a honey-like consistency, again capable of long ageing but rarely with noble rot. They are less intense than Quarts de Chaume or Bonnezeaux, and seem more attractive when young, but age seemingly indefinitely, going through sweetness and out to dryness again in maturity.

SWEET WHITE WINES – VINTAGES

1987 Not a particularly good year, with virtually no true noble rot wines made. Vouvray and Montlouis fared better than Bonnezeaux and Quarts de Chaume.

1986 On the whole soft, quick-maturing wines, but with plenty of attractive fruit. No classic sweet wines, though.

1985 An exceptionally fine year with a good deal of noble rot. The wines will need some years before they are ready to drink.

1984 Charming, agreeable wines of comparative lightness. Most will be drinkable within five years.

1983 Great depth and richness mean that most of the sweet wines will last for anything from 15 to 25 years. Don't drink any before the 1990s.

1981 Just coming through a period of dumbness, these wines are beginning to be drinkable in a light sort of way.

1978 Slow developing vintage that is just beginning to show its potential as one for great richness. Worth keeping for some time yet.

1976 Very ripe fruit, full of flavours and complexity. This is a year where the lesser wines are ready to drink now but the greater wines need another five to ten years before they begin to mature.

Older vintages 1969, 1964, 1961 and 1959 are the great long-term vintages of recent years. They're not cheap and are hard to find, but worth buying for the future drinking experience (but not for the investment).

Red and rosé Loire wines – uncharted territory

We've long been familiar with Anjou Rosé, a much-maligned sweetish pink wine that was the French equivalent to Mateus Rosé. It seems that we don't like it quite so much nowadays, but prefer dry rosé (if we prefer rosé at all), which leaves Loire rosé producers with a problem: what to do with all those red grapes?

One solution has been to call rosé Blush, and then it sells – up to a point. But that ploy is an easy one to see through. A much better answer is to increase the production of red wine. There's much more to Loire reds than could be expected from such a northern growing area.

Pinot Noir and Cabernet Franc are the two principal grape varieties used to make both Loire reds and rosés, with Gamay coming up fast. If you are in Côtes du Forez on the Upper Loire, you will find wines from Gamay gulpable, but with rather too much acidity in poor years and not quite the fruit flavours of Beaujolais. Further down river, in Sancerre or Coteaux du Giennois, it will be Pinot Noir (highly fashionable at the moment); in Touraine, Cabernet Franc or Gamay; and in Chinon, Bourgueil or Anjou, Cabernet Franc.

Most Loire reds are to be drunk young and chilled, if you like. They have a northern taste, with high acidity and not too much colour, but in Chinon and Bourgueil, the wines become smooth, velvety, intense with age, smelling of violets and vanilla and tasting herbaceous and surprisingly complex. Prices are still good.

The dry rosés are more of a mixed bag. The best are those from Sancerre and Reuilly, but prices are high (see below).

Where's where in Loire reds

Sancerre

The light reds and rosés of Sancerre, made from the Pinot Noir grape, have in recent years been very fashionable in smart restaurants in Paris and London. Consequently, the prices have shot up. At the moment they don't represent good value at all, even though the 1985 and 1986 wines have turned out to be very good indeed. A few reds mature for a surprisingly long time.

Chinon and Bourgueil

The most serious Loire reds are made from the Cabernet Franc (with a little Cabernet Sauvignon) in these two towns near Saumur, west of Tours. Chinon produces a lighter wine but with some ageing potential in good years, while Bourgueil makes more austere wine that is not particularly attractive when young, and does need three or four years. St-Nicolas-de-Bourgueil makes a lighter version of Bourgueil.

Touraine

The Gamay grape is used to produce very enjoyable light wine which goes under the Gamay de Touraine varietal name. The wines have much of the strawberry fruit of Beaujolais but tend to be a little more attenuated. The wines made from Cabernet Franc are more serious, but still don't need much ageing.

Saumur-Champigny

Light, fruity reds from the Cabernet make this tiny area around the town of Saumur a good source of wines. Prices, though, for the better wines, are not particularly cheap.

Anjou

The rosés of Anjou are the wines that have long been the staple production of the area. Slightly sweet wines made from the Gamay grape are now being supplemented by somewhat better (and drier) rosés made from the Cabernet. Since the appellations here are complex, here we give the major styles which appear in the shops:

Cabernet d'Anjou Good quality rosés, generally slightly sweet but with some depth.

Rosé d'Anjou The principal appellation of sweet rosés made from the Gamay and other grapes. On the whole, a dull lot.

Rosé de la Loire An appellation for dry reds using the Cabernet grape. Not widely found but worth looking out for.

Anjou also produces good, standard reds from the Cabernet, under the Anjou Rouge appellation.

Other reds of the Loire

Small outposts of red production are dotted in and around the Loire valley. In the south, look for Côtes Roannaises and Côtes du Forez, which are Gamay wines made not far from Beaujolais. Coteaux Giennois produces some good light wines from the Pinot Noir and Gamay, just north of Pouilly-sur-Loire. Near Saumur, apart from Saumur Rouge, small amounts of fresh Gamay wines are made under the VDQS of Thouarsais.

Red and rosé vintages

1987 Rather a wet, cool year with consequent high acidity in some of the wines.

1986 A middle-weight vintage, with some acidity in the wines. Drink the rosés now, but the reds from Chinon and Bourgueil have good staying power.

1985 A fine vintage producing some ripe wines from all areas. The Chinon and Bourgueil wines will keep for a while, as will other reds, including Sancerre. Drink the rosés.

1984 Avoid all reds and rosés.

1983 A good vintage with reds at their best. The top wines from all areas will last a while yet.

1982 Bourgueil and Chinon reds are still worth drinking, but others are beginning to fade.

1981 Keep going on Chinon and Bourgueil, but forget the rest.

Older vintages 1978 and 1976 are the two vintages of Bourgueil and Chinon still worth drinking.

Who's who on the Loire

Dry whites

SANCERRE

Vacheron (*Adnams; Averys; Eaton Elliot Winebrokers; Grape Ideas; Lockes; Reid Wines; Wine Society*) – also for reds; Jean and André Vatan (*Yapp Brothers*); Lucien Crochet, Clos du Chêne Marchand (*Peter Dominic; Michael Menzel Wines*); Ch de Thauvenay (*Tanners Wines*); Clos Beaujeu Vincent Delaporte (*David Baillie Vintners; Laytons*); Paul Millérioux, Clos du Roy (*Corney & Barrow; John Buccleugh, 20 Beatrice Street, Warrington, Cheshire; Clifton Cellars, 22 The Mall, Clifton, Bristol, Avon;* Le Grand Chemarin, Jean-Max Roger (*Davisons*); Les Monts Damnés, Bourgeois (*Irvine Robertson Wines*); Les Monts Damnés, Paul Prieur (*Pennyloaf Wines; Stapylton Fletcher*); Clos de la Crêle, Lucien Thomas (*Eldridge Pope; Peter Green*); Reverdy (*Ad Hoc Wine Warehouse; Barwell & Jones*); Comte Lafond, Ch de Nozet (*Tanners Wines*).

POUILLY FUMÉ

Jean-Claude Guyot (*Yapp Brothers*); Ch de Tracy (*Adnams; Fine Vintage Wines; Laytons; Lorne House Vintners; Frank E Stainton*); Didier Dagueneau (*Lay & Wheeler; Reid Wines; La Vigneronne*); de Ladoucette, Ch de Nozet (*Buckingham Wines; D Byrne & Co; Michael Menzel Wines; Tanners Wines; Ubiquitous Chip*); Domaine Saget (*Buckingham Wines; Grape Ideas; Tanners Wines*); Michel Bailly, Les Griottes (*Berkmann Wine Cellars/Le Nez Rouge; Eaton Elliot Winebrokers; Richard Harvey Wines; Hungerford Wine Company; Tesco*); Les Bascoins Domaine Masson-Blondelet (*Pennyloaf Wines; Christopher Piper Wines; Wines Galore*); Les Champs de Cri, Didier Pabot (*Majestic*); Les Chantalouettes, Gitton (*Sainsbury's*).

QUINCY, MÉNÉTOU-SALON, REUILLY, ST-POURÇAIN

Quincy Raymond Pipet (*Yapp Brothers*); Quincy Pierre Mardon (*Adnams; Champagne de Villages; Laytons*); Quincy, Domaine de la Maison Blanche (*Majestic; Stapylton Fletcher; Winecellars*); Ménétou-Salon, Henri Pellé (*Goedhuis & Co; Irvine Robertson Wines; Morris & Verdin; Wine Society*); Ménétou-Salon, Domaine Clément (*Anthony Byrne Fine Wines*); Ménétou-Salon Jean Teiller (*Yapp Brothers*); Reuilly Claude Lafond (*Haynes, Hanson & Clark*); St-Pourçain Cuvée Printanière, Union des Vignerons (*Averys; Nobody Inn; Pennyloaf Wines; Christopher Piper Wines*).

VOUVRAY/MONTLOUIS

Most producers here make both sweet and dry wines. See under *Sweet wines* below for list.

JASNIÈRES

Joël Gigou (*Adnams*).

SAUVIGNON DE TOURAINE

Confrérie des Vignerons de Oisly-et-Thésée (*Anthony Byrne Fine Wines; Ellis Son & Vidler; Ian G Howe; O W Loeb; Oddbins; Windrush Wines*); Domaine Guenault, Bougrier (*Willoughbys*); Domaine Octavie (*Majestic; Yorkshire Fine Wines*).

SAUMUR (STILL WHITE)

Ch de St-Florent Langlois Château (*Alex Findlater*); Albert Besombes Moc-Baril (*Frank E Stainton*); Domaine de Val Brun, Charrau (*Hedley Wright*).

SAVENNIÈRES

Domaine des Baumard (*Eldridge Pope/Reynier Wine Libraries; Reid Wines*); Mme Joly Coulée de Serrant and Roche aux Moines (*Victor Hugo Wines; Nobody Inn; Reid Wines; Tanners Wines; Ubiquitous Chip*); Yves Soulez Domaine de la Bizolière (*Sebastopol Wines; Wine Society; Yapp Brothers*); Ch de Chamboureau (*Adnams; Hicks & Don; Lay & Wheeler; Sebastopol Wines; Yapp Brothers*).

MUSCADET

Guy Bossard (*Bibendum; Eaton Elliot Winebrokers; Richard Harvey Wines; Lockes; Andrew Mead Wines*); Ch de l'Oiselinière Chéreau Carré (*Majestic; Reid Wines; Wine Society*); Ch de Chasseloir, Chéreau Carré (*Hungerford Wine Company; Lay & Wheeler; Lorne House Vintners; Market Vintners*); Domaine des Dorices Léon Boullault (*Peter Green; Sebastopol Wines*); Ch du Cléray Jean Sauvion (*Berkmann Wine Cellars/Le Nez Rouge; Nobody Inn; Christopher Piper Wines*); Marquis de Goulaine (*Averys; D Byrne & Co; Rodney Densem Wines*); Ch de la Berrière (*Ben Ellis and Associates; A L Vose; Wine Schoppen*); Donatien Bahuaud (*Thomas Baty & Sons; George Dutton & Sons; Peter Dominic; Irvine Robertson Wines; Arthur Rackhams; Willoughbys*); Clos de la Sablette, Martin (*Plato Harrison, 2 Mill Brow, Kirkby Lonsdale, Lancs; John Stephenson, Bradley Hall Road, Nelson, Lancs*); Ch la Noë (*Buckingham Wines; D Byrne & Co*); Ch de la Ragotière (*Hedley Wright; Vintage Wines, 116 Derby Road, Nottingham*).

VIN DE THOUARSAIS (VDQS)

Michel Gigon, Cépage Chenin (*Yapp Brothers*).

Sweet whites

VOUVRAY

Ch de Moncontour (*Eaton Elliot Winebrokers; The Market/Le Provençal; Waitrose; Winecellars*); Gaston Huet (*Adnams; Averys; Bibendum; Thos Peatling; Pennyloaf Wines; Wine Society*); Prince Poniatowski Clos Baudoin (*Hungerford Wine Company; La Vigneronne*); Marc Brédif (*Sebastopol Wines*); Foreau Clos Naudin (*Adnams; D Byrne & Co; Lay & Wheeler; O W Loeb; Market Vintners; Ubiquitous Chip*).

MONTLOUIS

G Delétang Montlouis (*Adnams; Wine Society*); Berger Domaine des Liards (*Lay & Wheeler; Pennyloaf Wines*).

QUARTS DE CHAUME, BONNEZEAUX, COTEAUX DU LAYON

Domaine des Baumard Coteaux du Layon/Quarts de Chaume (*Peter Green; Eldridge Pope/Reynier Wine Libraries*); Quarts de Chaume Lalanne Ch de Belle-Rive (*Oddbins; Wine Society*); Quarts de Chaume Ch de Fesles (*Buckingham Wines*); Bonnezeaux René Renou (*Ian G Howe; Ubiquitous Chip*); Ch de Gauliers Mme Fourlinnie (*La Vigneronne; Yapp Brothers*); Coteaux de l'Aubance, Domaine des Richou, G Chauvin (*Prestige Vintners*); Coteaux du Layon, Ch de Plaisance (*Victor Hugo Wines*).

ANJOU BLANC

Les Vins Touchais renowned recently for a rare collection of old vintages of sweet Anjou Blanc (*Adnams; Averys; Tanners Wines; Castang Wine Shippers; 8 Cardwen Estate, Pelynt, Cornwall*); Maison Prunier (*La Réserve*).

Reds and rosés

SANCERRE

Sancerre Rosé and Rouge Vacheron (*Averys; Eaton Elliot Winebrokers; Grape Ideas; Reid Wines; Wine Society*); Sancerre Rosé Paul Thomas Chavignol (*Bow Wine Vaults, 10 Bow Churchyard, London EC4*); Sancerre Rouge Domaine Daulny (*Haynes, Hanson & Clark*); Bernard Michel Bailly (*Eaton Elliot Winebrokers*).

BOURGUEIL, ST-NICOLAS DE BOURGUEIL AND CHINON

Chinon Raymond Desbourdes (*Yapp Brothers*); Chinon Domaine de la Chapellerie (*Bibendum*); Chinon Olga Raffault (*Alex Findlater; Lay & Wheeler*); Chinon Charles Joguet (*Adnams; Haynes, Hanson & Clark; O W Loeb*); Bourgueil Maître et Viemont (*O W Loeb*); St-Nicolas de Bourgueil J-C Mabilot (*Pennyloaf Wines*); Bourgueil Caslot-Galbrun La Hurolaie (*Eaton Elliot Winebrokers; Winecellars*); Chinon Couly-Dutheil (*Lay & Wheeler; Stapylton Fletcher*); Chinon Domaine du Colombier Yves Loisseau (*Sainsbury's*); St-Nicolas de Bourgueil, P Jamet, Domaine du Fondis (*Averys; Tanners Wines*); St-Nicolas-de-Bourgueil, Anselme et Marc Jamet (*Richard Harvey Wines*).

TOURAINE

Confrérie de Oisly et Thésée (*Haynes, Hanson & Clark; Ian G Howe; Oddbins*); Ch du Petit Thouars (*Tanners Wines*); Domaine Octavie (*Majestic*).

SAUMUR-CHAMPIGNY

Paul Buisse (*Berkmann Wine Cellars/Le Nez Rouge*); Domaine Filliatreau (*Ian G Howe; Nobody Inn; Yapp Brothers*); Domaine Vinicole de St-Cyr (*Bordeaux Direct; Upper Crust*); Pisani-Ferry, Ch de Targe (*Alex Findlater; Haynes, Hanson & Clark; Ian G Howe; Lay & Wheeler*).

CÔTES DU FOREZ

Les Vignerons Foréziens Gamay (*Bordeaux Direct*).

VINS DE PAYS

Vin de Pays de Loire-Atlantique, Domaine de la Mecredière (*Oddbins*); de Loire-Atlantique, Domaine du Cléray (*Le Nez Rouge*); du Jardin de la France, Caves de Vignerons de Saumur (*H Allen Smith*).

Best buys from the Loire

DRY WHITES

Muscadet de Sèvre-et-Maine sur lie 1987, Pommeraye (*Snipe Wine Cellars*)
Sauvignon de Touraine 1987, Domaine Guenault (*Lorne House Vintners*)
Vin de Pays du Jardin de la Loire, Le Chardonnay, Paul Boutinot (*Ostlers*)
Ménétou-Salon, Jacky Rat (*Oxford and Cambridge Fine Wine*)
Sauvignon de Touraine Vieilles Vignes 1987, Preys et Sinson (*Prestige Vintners*)
Sauvignon de Touraine, Domaine du Grand Moulin (*Balls Brothers*)
St-Pourçain-sur-Sioule 1986, Domaine Ray (*Bibendum*)
Sauvignon de Touraine 1987, Vignerons de Oisly-et-Thésée (*Anthony Byrne Fine Wines; Cachet Wines*)
Savennières Clos du Papillon 1986, Baumard (*Cadwgan Wines; Eldridge Pope*)
Reuilly 1987, Lafond (*Ferrers le Mesurier*)
Muscadet de Sèvre-et-Maine sur lie, Domaine de la Chauvinière 1986 (*Oddbins*)
St Michael Chardonnay, Vin de Pays du Jardin de la France (*Marks & Spencer*)

SWEET WHITES

Coteaux du Layon Chaume 1983, J-P Tijou (*High Breck Vintners*)
Anjou Moulin Touchais 1976 (*Eldridge Pope*)

REDS

Touraine Cabernet 1986, Vignerons de Oisly-et-Thésée (*Oddbins*)
Chinon 1984, Domaine de Narçay (*Whighams of Ayr*)
Côtes Roannaises 1986, Domaine du Picatier (*Pavilion Wine Company*)
Ch du Petit Thouars 1986, Touraine (*Wines from Paris*)
Bourgueil 1987, Domaine Audemont (*Peter Green*)
Coteaux du Giennois Pinot Noir 1986 (*Waitrose*)

Specialist stockists

*Adnams; Anthony Byrne Fine Wines; Chesterford Vintners; Desborough &
Brown; Eldridge Pope; Alex Findlater; Peter Green; Ian G Howe; Ilkley Wine
Cellars; O W Loeb; Nobody Inn; Old Street Wine Company; Pennyloaf Wines;
Prestige Vintners; Sapsford Wines; Madeleine Trehearne Partners; Yapp
Brothers*

THE MIDI

Changes to the workman's tipple

This is the area which, less than ten years ago, was the source of 80 per
cent of 'le gros rouge', the blue-overalled French workman's coarse red
wine. While there's still quite a bit of that stuff around, France's deep
south has seen some dramatic changes with the advent of good value,
drinkable wines.

These are the vins de pays. Despite a fairly rural, traditional-
sounding name, the vin de pays is a new creation, dating only from
1979. They are officially super vins de table, basic wines in other
words, but coming from specially delimited areas, having to achieve
certain standards in the vineyard and the cellar, and having to pass a
tasting test.

You find vins de pays all over the south and south-east of France.
Those in Languedoc and Roussillon are covered here and those in
Provence in the next section. The vins de pays range from the huge,
region-wide Vin de Pays d'Oc, through departmental designations
(such as Vin de Pays de l'Hérault), to those from small zones, such as
communes or carefully defined areas (such as Vin de Pays des Bouches
du Rhône in Provence, or Vin de Pays des Sables du Golfe du Lion).
On the whole – and there are plenty of exceptions – the more defined
the area covered by a vin de pays, the better the wine will be, simply
because it will be covered by tighter regulations, such as lower yields
and the use of specific grape varieties which are suitable to a small area
of land.

A foreign feel

Because they are not controlled by AC rules which set down that only
local grape varieties may be used, some vin de pays producers are
experimenting with grape varieties that are 'foreign' to this part of the
south of France, sometimes with spectacular results. Cabernet
Sauvignon, Merlot and Chardonnay are inevitably present, but so, too,
are Sauvignon Blanc, and the Rhône varieties of Syrah and Mourvèdre
(a much-underrated grape which had, until recently, almost
disappeared).

These noble grape varieties (as the French like to describe them) are used either by themselves or in blends with local, traditional grapes such as Grenache, Carignan, Cinsault in reds, Ugni Blanc or Clairette in whites.

Blended, they beef up the quality of what can be innocuous, if sound, wines. Used varietally, the grape's name is stuck on the label, the latest fad in the south of France (obviously somebody has been to California or Australia). France may sometimes be chauvinist, but when it comes to marketing, she's willing to learn from anybody.

Don't forget tradition

The growth of vins de pays as good value wines from the south of France shouldn't let us forget the older-established AC and VDQS wines. While the great mass of plonk was produced on the plains of Languedoc near the sea, inland – on the hills – were smaller areas of historic vineyards that were producing much better quality. Areas such as Minervois, Corbières, Fitou (see under *Where's where* for more details) are now combining tradition with modern, hygienic winemaking practice to provide some highly enjoyable and not too expensive drinking.

Where's where in the Midi

The French have a neat system for promoting wine areas. So yesterday's vin de pays may well be today's VDQS (vin délimité de qualité supérieur) and tomorrow's AC (appellation contrôlée) wine. New areas get promoted all the time, as local politicians apply pressure in the right places: sometimes the wines get better as well.

This survey of the Midi moves from east to south, in the huge arc of the Gulf of Lyons, from the mouth of the Rhône near Marseilles right down to the Spanish border south of Perpignan.

LANGUEDOC (GARD)

Most of the AC and VDQS wines in this *département* are only just beginning to be other than dull. The vins de pays are better.

Clairette de Bellegarde White wines of an uninspired nature.

Costières du Gard VDQS area near Nîmes which is best for full-bodied reds of a reliable quality. Whites here are dull.

Vins de pays Vin de Pays du Gard, Côtes du Salavès and Uzège: all cheap and reasonably cheerful, especially the Gard wines. The very best vins de pays are from the Sables du Golfe du Lion (the home of the largest single vineyard in France, owned by Listel and planted on the sands by the sea).

LANGUEDOC (HÉRAULT)

The heartland of the wine lake vineyards, but in the sea of vines, there are some traditional areas, and also vin de pays producers who are working hard to show that this area is not just a source of cheap, bad plonk. All the best wines seem to come from the slopes away from the flat coastal plain – as might be expected.

Coteaux du Languedoc is the main AC appellation and its best wines are sturdy, simple reds. La Clape, one of 12 Coteaux du Languedoc villages, makes good red, rosé and white on chalky soil. St-Saturnin, another sub-division, makes solid reds. Quatourze produces some heady reds and lighter whites.

Faugères Soft and full-bodied red AC wines that have suddenly become popular in France. In theory they can be good, but too many we have tasted recently are rather coarse.

St-Chinian Tough, spicy, tannic wines which are worth keeping a year or two. The 1983 or 1985 would be ideal now.

Vins de pays

There are some 28 vin de pays zones in the Hérault *département*. The largest production area is Vin de Pays de l'Hérault, which ranges in quality from the pretty ordinary to the superb Cabernet Sauvignon wines of Mas de Daumas Gassac. Other vins de pays in the Hérault represented in our shops include Côtes de Thongue and Coteaux du Salagou.

LANGUEDOC (AUDE)

Languedoc is perhaps the area of the Midi where the greatest strides have been made – helped by the strong traditions of the hill wines which are now the main AC and VDQS areas.

Blanquette de Limoux Sparkling wine from near Carcassonne (see under *Sparkling wines* at the end of the WHAT TO BUY section).

Cabardes Red wines from just north of Carcassonne, which are best drunk young and fresh.

Corbières AC area that makes a large amount of reds by carbonic maceration (which brings out plenty of fruit and colour but requires the wine to be drunk young). Occasional pockets of better quality.

Côtes de la Malapère An area which includes Cabernet Sauvignon and Cabernet Franc in its blend, with consequent high quality.

Fitou Carignan grapes make some well-aged wines in this AC area which will last for three to five years from vintage and are characterised by good ruby-coloured fruit.

Minervois A huge AC area using Carignan and Cinsault in its big, beefy reds. The wines are good value and one or two producers make something that much better (see under *Who's who* section). An area that represents good value.

Vins de pays
Vin de pays regions in the Aude include the Vin de Pays de l'Aude, Coteaux de la Cité de Carcassonne, Val d'Orbieu and the romantically named Vallée du Paradis. The two big French wine merchants, Nicolas and Chantovent, have made much of vins de pays from the Aude, and have certainly helped keep standards up.

ROUSSILLON (PYRÉNÉES-ORIENTALES)

There's an interesting cross-fertilisation with Spain in some of the grapes used in Roussillon, with the white Macabeo and Malvoisie in evidence. This is home, too, of the unusual red, sweet, Grenache-based Banyuls.

Côtes du Roussillon and Côtes du Roussillon Villages The main area, Côtes du Roussillon, makes good, soft, colourful reds from Carignan and Grenache grapes. Interspersed are wines from the better sites of the Villages with slightly higher alcohol but also greater finesse. Collioure is a smaller area for some very good reds.

Vins de pays
Best in Roussillon are Catalan and Pyrénées-Orientales, making large quantities of reds and whites. The majority of the wines for the Vin de Pays d'Oc, which covers the whole of the Midi, come from the Pyrénées-Orientales.

VINS DOUX NATURELS

Sweet fortified wines from the Muscat grape are made at Sète (Muscat de Frontignan) and in Roussillon (Muscat de Rivesaltes). Banyuls, right on the Spanish border, specialises in a sweet wine made from the Grenache grape.

Vintages in the Midi

It's rare for vintages to be much affected by the weather in this part of France. A general rule is that, except where indicated under the *Where's where* section above, most white wines are ready to drink when they reach the shops, while two or three years should be enough for reds.

Who's who in the Midi

LANGUEDOC (GARD)

Costières du Gard Ch Roubaud (*Findlater Mackie Todd*); Domaine St-Louis (*Wine Society*); Domaine de St-Louis la Perdrix (*Corney & Barrow; Wine Society*).

Vin de Pays des Sables du Golfe du Lion, Listel Domaine du
Bosquet-Canet (*Chaplin & Son; Ellis Son & Vidler; Alex Findlater*);
Domaine de Villeroy Blanc de Blancs (*Chaplin & Son; George Hill of
Loughborough*); Gris de Gris (*D Byrne & Co; Chaplin & Son; Curzon Wine
Company; Alex Findlater; George Hill of Loughborough; Willoughbys*).

Vin de Pays du Gard Domaine de Valescure (*Bibendum*).

LANGUEDOC (HÉRAULT)

Coteaux du Languedoc Domaine de Lavabre (*Morris & Verdin; Tanners
Wines*); Château de St-Series (*Grape Ideas*); Ch de la Condamine
Bertrand (*Stapylton Fletcher*); Domaine de l'Abbaye Valfernière
(*Bordeaux Direct*).

St-Chinian Rouanet (*Waitrose*).

Faugères Domaines Fontainilles (*Wine Society*); Cuvée Jules Gaston
(*D Byrne & Co; Victor Hugo Wines; Winecellars*).

La Clape Ch de Pech Redon (*Bordeaux Direct/Taste Shops*).

Vin de Pays de l'Hérault Domaine de Mas de Daumas Gassac
(*Adnams; Berkmann Wine Cellars/Le Nez Rouge; Bibendum;
D Byrne & Co; Nobody Inn; Christopher Piper Wines; Raeburn Fine Wines
and Foods; Tanners Wines; La Vigneronne; Wines from Paris*); Domaine de
St-Macaire (*Waitrose*); Cante-Cigale Syrah (*Waitrose*); Domaine des
Lenthéric (*Majestic*).

Vin de Pays des Collines de la Moure Abbaye de Valmagne (*Eldridge
Pope*).

LANGUEDOC (AUDE)

Corbières Ch les Palais (*Victoria Wine Company*); Ch de Montrabech
(*B H Wines; Lay & Wheeler; Tanners Wines*); Ch de l'Isle (*Wine Spot*).

Fitou Domaine Mme Parmentier (*widely available*); Chantovent
(*Wapping Wine Warehouse*); Caves de Mont-Tauch (*Berry Bros & Rudd;
Chesterford Vintners; Laytons*); Le Carla (*Sainsbury's*).

Minervois Ch de Gourgazaud (*Sainsbury's*); Domaine de Ste-Eulalie
(*Adnams; Davisons; Lay & Wheeler; Tanners Wines*); Ch de Rivière (*David
Baillie Vintners*); Domaine du Pech d'André (*Majestic*); Domaine Maris
(*Majestic*).

Vins de pays
Vin de Pays de la Vallée du Paradis (*Majestic; Sainsbury's*); Vin de Pays
du Val d'Orbieu (*Adnams; Bibendum; Tanners Wines*); Vin de Pays de
l'Aude, Foncalieu Cabernet Sauvignon (*Waitrose*); Tesco Vin de Pays de
l'Aude (*Tesco*).

ROUSSILLON (PYRÉNÉES-ORIENTALES)

Côtes du Roussillon and Côtes du Roussillon Villages Caramany (*Ian G Howe*); Coteaux Catalans (*Peter Dominic; Tesco*); Ch de Corneilla (*Richmond Wine Warehouse*); Bouffet (*Majestic*); Full French Red Côtes du Roussillon (*Marks & Spencer*); Côtes du Roussillon (*Sainsbury's*).

DESSERT WINES IN LANGUEDOC AND ROUSSILLON (VINS DOUX NATURELS)

Muscat de Frontignan Aphrodis (*Barnes Wine Shop*); Muscat de Rivesaltes (*Nobody Inn; Oddbins; Tanners Wines; La Vigneronne*); Banyuls, R Dutres (*Oddbins*).

Vin de Pays d'Oc
Listel Cabernet Sauvignon and Chardonnay (*David Alexander; D Byrne & Co; Alex Findlater; Morrisons – Cabernet Sauvignon only*); Listel Syrah (*Oddbins*); Vin de Pays d'Oc, Domaine d'Ormesson (*Buckingham Wines; D Byrne & Co; Christopher Piper Wines*).

Best buys from the Midi

WHITES

Vin de Pays de l'Hérault, Marsanne, Domaine du Bosc (*Adnams*)
Chardonnay Vin de Pays de l'Hérault 1987, Domaine de la Source (*Hedley Wright*)

REDS

Vin de Pays de Vaucluse (*Asda*)
Cabernet Sauvignon Vin de Pays des Pyrénées Orientales (*Asda*)
Corbières, Domaine St-Julien-de-Septime (*David Baillie Vintners*)
Minervois, Domaine Ste-Eulalie (*Balls Brothers; G E Bromley & Sons*)
Minervois 1986, Ch de Pouzols (*Bedford Fine Wine*)
Minervois 1986, Domaine Ste-Eulalie (*Davisons*)
Cabardes 1986, Ch la Seigne (*Matthew Gloag*)
Cabernet Sauvignon Vin de Pays de l'Aude, Les Vignerons de Val d'Orbieu (*Bibendum; Greens*)
Vin de Pays de Sables du Golfe du Lion 1985, Domaine du Bosquet (*Chaplin & Sons; Hungerford Wine Company; Unwins*)
Fitou Mont Tauch 1983 (*Moffat Wine Shop*)

Specialist stockists
Eldridge Pope; Andrew Gordon Wines; Peter Green; Hicks & Don; Majestic; Thos Peatling; Tanners Wines

---

If you disagree with us, please tell us why. You will find report forms at the back of the book.

PROVENCE

Rosé and skittles

Provence, rosé wines in skittle-shaped bottles, easy drinking by the
sea. Nothing too serious there, you might think. And you would, we
are delighted to say, be wrong – some very fine wines are emerging
from this region, especially reds.

But Provence is also the classic example of a French AC meaning no
more than that a wine comes from a delimited area: it doesn't
necessarily mean that the wine is any good. While some of the smaller
appellation areas in Provence are producing some superb wines (see
under the *Where's where* section below), the main Côtes de Provence AC
is a wildly mixed bag of good, indifferent and downright ugly. It covers
too big an area, with too many different production zones – and too
much, still, of the rosé and skittles mentality.

Because they are in Provence, where money speaks volumes, many
producers think they can charge quite a lot for not much, so although
the top wines are worth paying for, there's not much that's cheap and
good, and quite a lot that's expensive and not good value.

Back to nature

Provence, with its reliably dry climate, is the principal source of
organic wines in France. In some AC areas (Coteaux des Baux in
particular), most of the producers use organic methods. This approach,
which means low yields and almost hand-crafted wines, also leads to
high prices – but here for those who want top quality and no artificial
fertilisers or chemicals, it's worth paying the extra. (For more about
organic wines, see the chapter at the end of the WHAT TO BUY section.)

The organic generation of wine producers is comparatively new; and
although 'foreign' grape varieties like Cabernet Sauvignon have been
grown in the region for many years, their increasingly widespread use
is also new. They – and other quality varieties like Mourvédre and
Syrah – are being used to bolster up the lesser quality of the Grenache
and Cinsault. In whites, it is the new technology of stainless steel
which is improving the quality of wines made from Ugni Blanc, Rolle
and Clairette, aided also by the introduction of the Sémillon grape.

Which brings us back to the rosés. Some good examples are being
made, courtesy of the new technology. But they account for 40 per cent
of production, while in Britain, they make up only five per cent of our
consumption (and that includes Mateus Rosé). So obviously we feel
they are best left for the sun and sea and the smart, pricey beaches of
the Riviera.

Where's where in Provence .

Bellet A tiny area of white wine production in the mountains north of Nice. Most of the wine is consumed in the area, although one or two examples are available in Britain.

Côtes de Provence Catch-all appellation that takes in most of southern Provence. Whites, reds and rosés are made. The whites are getting better and cleaner, and the same can be said for the rosés (by far the bulk of production), which have tended to be dry and on the full side: some of the better wines now have fruit as well – quite an innovation. Reds, too, are much better, due to the use of imported grape varieties like Syrah and Mourvèdre.

Bandol Traditionally, *the* appellation of Provence, making fine reds and dry whites and rosés. The reds made from the Mourvèdre grape are the most impressive. While the wines are not cheap, they have some unusual, spicy, peppery flavours worth experiencing.

Cassis A dry white wine, with a delicious buttery taste, made from Clairette, Ugni Blanc, Marsanne and Sauvignon grapes. Small production means high prices. (Nothing to do with the blackcurrant liqueur.)

Coteaux d'Aix-en-Provence This, with Coteaux des Baux en Provence (see below) is the most interesting area of Provence. Mainly reds and rosés, with a few whites – the reds are the best. While the usual southern grape varieties predominate, some enterprising producers are using Cabernet Sauvignon as well.

Coteaux des Baux en Provence An AC area producing reds that are more expensive than Aix-en-Provence, but also achieve greater things. The best producers, many of whom operate using organic farming methods, use Cabernet Sauvignon and Syrah grapes.

Palette Small appellation making long-lasting whites and reds covering an impressive range of tastes, but which perhaps lack immediate drinkability.

Coteaux Varois A VDQS zone with large-scale production (30 million bottles) and variable quality, making individual producers important.

Vin de Pays regions These include the reds and rosés of the Bouches du Rhône. Mont Caume encompasses the lesser offerings from Bandol plus some Cabernet Sauvignon wines. The Vin de Pays d'Oc region covers Provence and the rest of the Midi.

Send us your views on the report forms at the back of the book.

When to drink Provence wines

The quality in vintages varies little in the sunny south of France. Most whites and rosés – except those from top producers or from specialist areas like Bandol and Palette – can be drunk in the year after the vintage. Reds from Côtes de Provence need two or three years, while those from Bandol, Coteaux d'Aix and Coteaux des Baux need at least five or six years, and will go on maturing for ten or more years.

Who's who in Provence

Bellet Ch de Crémat (*La Vigneronne; Yapp Brothers*).

Côtes de Provence L'Estandon (*Yapp Brothers*); Domaine des Hauts de St-Jean (*Yapp Brothers*); Domaines Ott (*Harrods; Majestic; Michael Menzel Wines; La Vigneronne*); Domaine des Féraud (*Yapp Brothers*); Les Maîtres Vignerons de la Presqu'île de St-Tropez (*Berkmann Wine Cellar/Le Nez Rouge; Hedley Wright; Nobody Inn; Christopher Piper Wines*); St-André de Figuière (*Morris & Verdin*); Domaine de St-Baillon (*Bibendum; Greens*); Ch Grand'Boise (*Leeds Wine Co, Units 5 & 6, 39–41 Barrack Road, Leeds*); Domaine Castel Roubine (*Eldridge Pope; Fortnum & Mason*).

Bandol Domaine Tempier (*Windrush Wines*); Ch Vannières (*Buckingham Wines; Eldridge Pope; Nobody Inn; Reid Wines; La Vigneronne*); Mas de la Rouvière (*La Réserve; Yapp Brothers*); Domaine de la Bastide Blanche (*Christpher Piper Wines; The Wine Society*); Domaines Ott (*D Byrne & Co; Harrods; Michael Menzel Wines*).

Cassis Clos Ste Magdelaine (*Sebastopol Wines; Yapp Brothers*); Domaine du Paternel (*Wine Society*).

Coteaux d'Aix-en-Provence Commanderie de la Bargemone (*Barwell & Jones*), Domaine du Paradis, Fonscolombe (*Adnams; Direct Wine Shipments; Sherborne Vintners; Tanners Wines*); Domaine de la Crémade (*Peter Dominic*), Ch Vignelaure (*D Byrne & Co; Curzon Wine Company; Reid Wines; Rosetree Wine Company; La Vigneronne*); Ch de Beaulieu (*Wine Growers Association*); Ch la Coste (*D Byrne & Co; Winecellars*); Ch Bas (*Welbeck Wines*); Ch la Gaude, Baron de Vitrolles (*Yapp Brothers*), Ch la Gordonne (*Rosetree Wine Company; Wizard Wine Warehouses; Pimlico Dozen, 46 Tachbrook Street, London SW1*); Domaine les Bastides Jean Salen (*Berkmann Wine Cellars/Le Nez Rouge; D Byrne & Co*).

Coteaux des Baux en Provence Domaine de Trévallon (*Sebastopol Wines; La Vigneronne; Yapp Brothers*); Mas de Gourgonnier (*Les Bons Vins Occitans, 19A Wetherby Gardens, London SW5; Haughton Fine Wines, The Coach House, Haughton, Tarporley, Cheshire*); Mas de la Dame (*Chesterford Vintners; Davids of Ashby*); Domaine des Terres Blanches (*Anthony Byrne*

Fine Wines; D Byrne & Co; George Hill of Loughborough; The Market/Le Provençal; La Vigneronne; The Wine Spot).

Palette Ch Simone (*La Vigneronne; Yapp Brothers*).

Coteaux Varois Domaine de St-Jean (*Ellis Son & Vidler*); Domaine des Chaberts (*Adnams; High Breck Vintners*); Domaine St-Estève Gassier (*Balls Brothers; G E Bromley & Sons*).

PROVENCE VIN DE PAYS

Bouches du Rhône Domaine de Boullery (*Wine Growers Association*); Domaine de Temps Perdu (*Berry Bros & Rudd*).

Mont Caume Bunan (*Yapp Brothers*).

Best buys from Provence

WHITES

Domaine du Paradis 1986, Coteaux d'Aix-en-Provence (*Thresher*)
Coteaux d'Aix-en-Provence, Ch de Fonscolombes (*Adnams; Lay & Wheeler; Tanners Wines*)
Côtes de Provence 1985, Ch du Berne Blanc (*Arthur Rackhams*)

ROSÉS

Coteaux d'Aix-en-Provence, Ch de Beaulieu (*Weatherbury Vintners*)

REDS

Côtes de Provence, Domaine de St-Baillon 1985 (*Bibendum; Greens*)
Coteaux d'Aix-en-Provence, Ch Bas 1986 (*Welbeck Wines*)
Coteaux d'Aix-en-Provence, Ch de la Gaude Cuvée Spéciale 1986 (*Yapp Brothers*)
Côtes de Provence 1984, Ch la Gordonne (*Wine Spot; Wizard Wine Warehouses*).
Coteaux des Baux en Provence, Mas de Gourgonnier Réserve du Mas 1984 (*Les Bons Vins Occitans, 19A Wetherby Gardens, London SW5*).

Specialist stockists

Ian G Howe; Le Nez Rouge/Berkmann Wine Cellars; La Vigneronne; Windrush Wines; Yapp Brothers

THE RHÔNE

American discovery

What a pity. The guru of American wine writing, Robert Parker, has discovered the Rhône. He has written a book about it (a very good one), praising the high quality of the wines which he regards as undervalued.

Quite right, you might say. Just what this Guide has been saying for some years. The only problem is that now that Mr Parker has discovered the Rhône, the wines won't remain undervalued for very long. We reported last year that the prices of the northern Rhône wines were now the equivalent of the better châteaux of Bordeaux, and rapidly creeping up on Burgundy. Sad to say, all of us who missed out on buying the early 1980s vintages from the northern Rhône – or even the miraculous 1978 – had better start consulting our bank managers if we want to lay in a stock of these wines.

Not much land – not much wine

The problem in the northern Rhône vineyards is one of quantity. The areas are tiny – Hermitage has only 122 hectares, with no room for expansion; Côte Rôtie's decent vineyards occupy only about 80 hectares. Just one of the first growth châteaux in Bordeaux is larger than that. So there's not much wine, and not much more can be made – just like Burgundy.

However, so far, the growers (on the whole) have resisted following the Burgundian route of increasing yields from each of the precious hectares, thereby diluting the quality. That may be because the growers have tried and failed – the vineyards are mainly on precipitous slopes and the Syrah, the red grape variety, doesn't come up with high yields on rather poor soil.

But actually we doubt that as a reason: there aren't many growers, and most seem more concerned about their reputation than do many of their Burgundian counterparts. So even if the price of Rhône wines continues to rise, maybe the quality will remain constant.

Different in the south

The situation is different in the southern Rhône vineyards. Here the vast plains north of Orange and Avignon and the stretches of the Côtes du Lubéron allow plenty of room for plenty of wine. There's no shortage of Côtes du Rhône, and although much of it is pretty awful, much is very good, too. The same goes for Châteauneuf-du-Pape (although perhaps here the differences between the good and the bad are even more marked simply because the good are really great).

But, even so, we still fear the Parker effect. Certainly we fear it on the estates he picks out, partly through selfishness at wanting to go on buying these longtime favourites of ours at under-valued prices, partly because we ought to give the growers a chance to earn the money to which they are property entitled. But still it is a pity.

Which? Wine Guide does not accept payment for inclusion, and there is no sponsorship or advertising.

The north–south divide

Traditionally, the Rhône valley vineyards have been divided into two. The northern section, from just south of Vienne to Valence, has vineyards on steep hillsides, mainly in the narrow confines of the Rhône Valley as it flows between the eastern outcrops of the Massif Central. The area is dominated by two grape varieties – one widely planted, the other a rare breed indeed.

The Syrah, the only variety that produces the red wines of the northern Rhône, is the driving force behind the great wines of Hermitage, of Côte Rôtie, of Cornas, and provides the backbone of the more immediately accessible – and affordable – wines of St-Joseph and Crozes-Hermitage.

While the principal white grape varieties used in Hermitage, Crozes-Hermitage Blanc and St-Péray are the Marsanne and Roussanne, it is to the rare Viognier that experts turn for a unique taste. This is the grape variety that makes the whites of Condrieu and Ch Grillet dry but full of ripe, southern, peachy flavours – they are immensely expensive because so little is produced. The Viognier is also used in red wines to soften the Syrah in Côte Rôtie.

Compared with the northern Rhône, the grape varieties of the southern Rhône are legion. Thirteen different permitted grape varieties can be used to produce a Châteauneuf-du-Pape. The same varieties, in differing combinations, turn up all round the flat, sprawling, southern Rhône vineyards. They're the varieties of the south of France – the Grenache, Cinsault, Carignan, Mourvèdre are the predominant grapes for the reds, Clairette, Picpoul, Marsanne, Roussanne and Bourboulenc for the whites.

But the southern Rhône red wines are being dosed with increasing amounts of Syrah, which acts just as Cabernet Sauvignon does elsewhere in France, as a *cépage améliorateur* – a noble grape variety used to lift the quality of the local wine. And it is the Syrah which is behind much of the fine wine production in the area.

NORTHERN RHÔNE

What's on the label in the Northern Rhône

Clairette de Die See *Sparkling wines* at the end of the WHAT TO BUY section

Condrieu A tiny appellation of 35 acres which produces small quantities of intensely lush white wines from the Viognier grape. Although the wines are dry, they have such ripe, peach-and-apricot tastes that they almost seem sweet. An experience, even if an expensive one.

Cornas Huge, robust red wines made from 100 per cent Syrah in a small vineyard area on steep hillsides south of Hermitage. The small vineyard area means that the prices are on the increase, but they probably anyway deserve their recognition.

Côte Rôtie The 'roasted slope' is the most northerly Rhône appellation, called 'Côte Rôtie' because of its exposure to the sun. The old vineyards that make superb reds from the Syrah grape, with a little white Viognier, are on the steep hillside tumbling down to the River Rhône. The terms Brune and Blonde are used to describe the principal slopes, from which the best wines come. Sadly, new plantings on the top of the hill threaten to dilute the quality.

Crozes-Hermitage These vineyards currently represent the best value for money in the northern Rhône. They lie on the lower slopes and flatter land around the hill of Hermitage (see below). Less intense or punch-packing than Hermitage, they are nevertheless often of good quality, displaying the dry fruit and spicy flavours of Syrah. Whites, made from Marsanne and Roussanne, are improving all the time.

Ch Grillet The smallest French appellation (a mere 7.5 acres) producing a more intense version of Condrieu (see above). Very expensive, difficult to find, and not as good as its owner likes to make it. You would be better off buying Condrieu instead.

Hermitage The hill of Hermitage (so called because a knight, returning from the Crusades, built a hermit's cell on top of the hill), dominates the towns of Tain l'Hermitage and Tournon. The wines traditionally had the reputation of being the finest in France long before Bordeaux became top dog. When young, they are the epitome of the almost inaccessible fruit of the Syrah, softened here with up to 15 per cent of white grapes, but they develop into a rich, powerful, smooth maturity. White wines are also made in small quantities, mainly traditional in style and with considerable ageing ability.

St-Péray Sparkling wines from the Marsanne and Roussanne grapes, made by the Champagne method. Not very exciting and not often seen in Britain.

St-Joseph A lighter, more delicate version of Hermitage which is approachable younger and doesn't last as long. New vineyards, as with Côte Rôtie, may lower the general quality. Like Crozes-Hermitage, they are still reasonable value for money.

Northern Rhône vintages

1987 Rain during the harvest meant that the red wines will be quite light and will mature quickly. Whites, picked before the rain, will be much more powerful and high in alcohol.

1986 A medium term vintage, classic rather than great, with wines that will mature between five and ten years old.

1985 Although not one of the very greatest Rhône vintages, the wines are not far off the quality of the 1983s (see below). The best areas are Côte Rôtie, Cornas and St-Joseph. Hermitage made some great wines, but also some that were less good. Whites are powerful and lack acidity.

1984 Elegance and early maturity are the hallmarks of this vintage. Côte Rôtie has lower alcohol and tannin and less concentration than usual, while Hermitage is a middle-range wine. The whites have high acidity – especially those made from the Viognier grape. Drink whites and Crozes-Hermitage now, the top appellations in a couple of years.

1983 A very great year, especially for reds, concentrated, rich wines which will last for 20 years or more without any difficulty. Hermitage and Côte-Rôtie will last very well; Crozes-Hermitage and Cornas will mature in eight to ten years' time. The whites, too, are rich and will last.

1982 Too many grapes and too hot temperatures during fermentation have dogged this vintage. While some wines are fine and will last for 10 to 15 years, others lack structure and their fruit is too 'hot' and jammy. Drink the white wines now.

1981 Careful selection is necessary in the reds for this lean year. Good growers, though, made decent wine which is good value. The whites should be drunk up.

1980 Well-balanced wines, much better than those of northern France, which are now mature. Crozes-Hermitage and St-Joseph should be drunk now, but keep other reds a bit longer. Most whites have faded.

1979 Much better vintage than generally thought, overshadowed by 1978. Most reds are now mature (although keep Hermitage and Cornas a while yet). A good value vintage.

1978 Magnificent wines that are still almost infants. Hermitage and Côte Rôtie won't really be mature until the turn of the century, if then. Other reds will mature sooner, but don't touch them yet. Whites are in fine fettle at the moment.

Earlier vintages 1976 and 1971 are still at their peak, as are the 1969s. Other vintages of the early 1970s need to be bought with care.

Northern Rhône – growers and négociants

Firms below are listed under the area in which their main production is located. Négociants, of course, make wines from a number of different appellations.

RED WINES

Cornas

G de Barjac Very concentrated wines, highly tannic and never quite softening out. Give them years to mature.
Adnams; Bibendum; Claridge Fine Wines; Justerini & Brooks; Lay & Wheeler; Nobody Inn; La Réserve; La Vigneronne

Clape One of the finest producers in the Rhône. Deep, long-lasting wines of impenetrable blackness when young. Also makes some sparkling St-Péray.
Adnams; Nobody Inn; Yapp Brothers

Michel Old-fashioned family holding whose wines need plenty of time.
Lay & Wheeler; Nobody Inn; Christopher Piper Wines; La Vigneronne

Côte Rôtie

Roger Burgaud A young grower who is making a name for himself in rich wines.
College Cellar

Albert Dervieux-Thaize Very traditional wines from the President of the local growers. Look for his La Vallière single vineyard wine.
Berkmann Wine Cellars/Le Nez Rouge; D Byrne & Co; Lay & Wheeler; Lockes; Christopher Piper Wines; La Réserve

Marius Gentaz-Dervieux Long-lasting wines that should go for ten or twelve years before being broached. Look for La Garde, Côte Brune and Viaillère.
Richard Harvey Wines; Lockes; Windrush Wines

Guigal A specialist in wood ageing of wines, Guigal keeps his wines in barrel for three years. Look for La Landonne and La Moulieu, also Côte Rôtie Brune et Blonde and white Hermitage. Makes top quality Hermitage and also owns Vidal-Fleury (see below).
Adnams; Corney & Barrow; Gerard Harris; Richard Harvey Wines; Haynes, Hanson & Clark; Justerini & Brooks; Lay & Wheeler; Market Vintners; Nobody Inn; Oddbins; Thos Peatling; Seckford Wines; Windrush Wines; Wine Society

Jasmin The greatest individual vineyard producer making classic but not heavy wines. Look for La Chevalière d'Ampuis.
Adnams; Lay & Wheeler; La Vigneronne; Yapp Brothers

Rostaing Another young producer whose deep-flavoured wines receive at least two years in cask. Look for La Landonne Côte Brune. Also makes St-Joseph.
Justerini & Brooks; Reid Wines

Vidal-Fleury Now owned by Guigal, this is the largest firm in Côte Rôtie. Long-lasting wines which need at least ten years. Their top wine is La Chatillonne, but they also make Hermitage.
Berkmann Wine Cellars/Le Nez Rouge; Sebastopol Wines; La Vigneronne

Hermitage

Chapoutier One of the two big négociants in the region. Makes very traditional wines in Hermitage, Crozes-Hermitage, St-Joseph and Châteauneuf. The white Hermitage Chante Alouette is remarkable.
Adnams; Berry Bros & Rudd; G E Bromley & Sons; D Byrne & Co; Corney & Barrow; Direct Wine Shipments; Gerard Harris; Ian G Howe; Lay & Wheeler; Nobody Inn

Chave The greatest of the single vineyard growers. Long-lived reds and whites.
Adnams; Lay & Wheeler; Nobody Inn; La Vigneronne; Wine Society; Yapp Brothers

Delas Frères Growers and négociants with vineyards in Hermitage, Cornas, Côte Rôtie and Condrieu. The top Hermitage is Cuvée de la Tourette.
David Alexander; D Byrne & Co; Laytons

Jaboulet Aîné The other big négociant house that's setting the pace for the area. In Hermitage they own La Chapelle for red and Chevalier de Sterimbourg for white. Also make Crozes-Hermitage, St-Joseph (La Grande Pompée), Côte Rôtie (Les Jumelles), Tavel, Châteauneuf and the famous Côtes du Rhône (Parallèle 45).
Adnams; Gerard Harris; Richard Harvey Wines; Ian G Howe; Hungerford Wine Company; Lay & Wheeler; Laytons; Majestic; Oddbins; Tanners Wines; La Vigneronne

H Sorrel Owners of a small parcel of land on the Le Méal vineyard on the Hermitage hill. Look for wines after 1983 or before 1978.
Bibendum; College Cellar; La Réserve; Upper Crust

St-Joseph

E Florentin Quite light wines, made in a traditional style, although more recent vintages (1983 on) seem to have gained some weight. Their vineyard is Clos de l'Arbalestrier.
Adnams; Bibendum; Raeburn Fine Wines and Foods

Jean-Louis Grippat Makes a light, early-maturing (five years) wine.
Adnams; Yapp Brothers

Crozes-Hermitage

Names to look for are Jaboulet Aîné, Domaine des Clairmonts, Desmeure, Fayolle, Albert Bégot (who makes wine organically), Tardy & Ange, plus the wines of Jaboulet Aîné and Chapoutier.

WHITE WINES

Condrieu and Ch Grillet

Ch Grillet The single-estate appellation which makes famous, if over-priced wines.
Nobody Inn; La Vigneronne; Yapp Brothers

Guigal The Côte Rôtie négociant makes deliciously fresh Condrieu wines.
Adnams; Lay & Wheeler; Tanners Wines; Whitesides of Clitheroe

Ch du Rozay Paul Multier's young-style wines made mainly in stainless steel with a little wood, absolutely catch the flavour of the Viognier grape. A little traditional wine is also made from old vines.
Hungerford Wine Company; Michael Menzel Wines; Wine Society; Yapp Brothers

Georges Vernay Largest producer of Condrieu, making wines for a quick sale and a fresh drink.
D Byrne & Co; Corney & Barrow; Eldridge Pope; Gerard Harris; Ian G Howe; Lay & Wheeler; Reid Wines; La Réserve

White Hermitage and Crozes Hermitage

Good producers include: Chapoutier (*Adnams; D Byrne & Co; Curzon Wine Company; Fine Vintage Wines; Gerard Harris; Ian G Howe; Michael Menzel Wines*); J L Chave (*Lay & Wheeler; La Vigneronne; Yapp Brothers*); Ferraton (*Justerini & Brooks*); Guigal (*D Byrne & Co; Nobody Inn*); Jaboulet Aîné, Le Chevalier de Sterimbourg and La Mule Blanche (*G E Bromley; Corney & Barrow; Gerard Harris; Hungerford Wine Company; Lay & Wheeler; Majestic; Tanners Wines*).

Vins de Pays

Vin de Pays les Sables (*Lorne House Vintners*); Vin de Pays de l'Ardèche Syrah (*Ian G Howe; Yapp Brothers*); Vin de Pays des Coteaux de l'Ardèche (*Yapp Brothers*); Vin de Pays des Coteaux de l'Ardèche Gamay, Cave Co-opérative de St-Désirat (*Bibendum; Yapp Brothers*).

Best buys from the northern Rhône

Côte Rôtie 1982, Domaine Michel Bernard (*Tesco*)
Hermitage, H Sorrel (*Bibendum; La Réserve; Upper Crust*)
Côte Rôtie, E Guigal 1980 (*Adnams; D Byrne & Co*)
Côte Rôtie 1984, Joseph Jamet (*Bibendum*)
Hermitage 1985, L de Vallouit (*Lay & Wheeler*)
St-Joseph Clos de l'Arbalestrier, Emile Florentin 1985 (*Bibendum*)
Crozes-Hermitage 1985, Tardy et Ange (*widely available*)

SOUTHERN RHÔNE

What's on the label in the southern Rhône

Châteauneuf-du-Pape It may be a much abused name but there is nevertheless a top level of very high quality, at attractive prices. The reds are big and chewy with lots of ripe fruit, mature quite fast and then go downhill slowly. The whites are getting much better with modern vinification techniques.

Côtes du Lubéron A newly-established VDQS area in the south of the southern Rhône vineyards. One or two producers are using new technology to make some robust reds and fresh whites and rosés. Very good value.

Côtes du Rhône The basic appellation of the region. Large vineyard areas produce plenty of basic quaffing red wine, some of it terrific value, but even more is best avoided. Producers are important here because some growers (and co-operatives) are outstanding (see below).

Côtes du Rhône Villages A more closely controlled wine than simple Côtes du Rhône, this comes from specific villages which have better sited vineyards. More flavour and concentration make some of these Villages wines very good. Names to look for: Cairanne, Vacqueyras, Beaumes-de-Venise (yes, they don't just grow Muscat there), St Pantaléon-les-Vignes, Rasteau (also sweet Muscat), Sablet, St-Gervais, Séguret, Valréas, Visan, Laudun (also makes white) and Chusclan (also makes rosé).

Coteaux du Tricastin Fast-maturing reds which should be drunk within two or three years of the harvest. Excellent value, smooth wines which are worth seeking out.

Côtes du Ventoux A relatively new appellation which makes light, fresh reds with a hint of pétillance and is delicious drunk slightly chilled.

Côtes du Vivarais Lighter than straight Côtes du Rhône, the reds from this VDQS area are made using the same grapes with additional Syrah and Gamay.

Gigondas A less refined version of Châteauneuf, from a village that was until 1971 just another part of the Côtes du Rhône Villages. Southern-tasting wine, ideal for barbecues and rich foods, quite long-lasting, but not terribly subtle. So what's wrong with that?

Lirac Excellent value wines from south of Châteauneuf. Full but really fruity reds are generally well made. Rosés are dry and quite powerful.

Rasteau Strange, fortified sweet red wines which some people find very attractive with a lump of ice as an aperitif. There's also a white version. The village also makes Côtes du Rhône Villages (see above).

Tavel Famed rosé, the delightful colour belying the fact that this is strong stuff. Dry but with good fruit, these can be some of the best French rosés.

Southern Rhône vintages

Apart from Châteauneuf and Gigondas, with occasional Côtes du Rhône Villages, southern Rhône wines are not for laying down. Wines earlier than 1978 should certainly have been drunk by now.

1987 A light vintage, with even the top areas producing wines which will be ready to drink soon.

1986 A big vintage, with some rot at harvest time. Drink the fresher reds now, but leave top areas such as Châteauneuf for some time.

1985 A fine harvest both for quality and quantity was aided by just the right amount of rain in June and July and fine sunny weather thereafter. Châteauneuf is full of fruit and looks set to mature well. Whites are quite heavy, but full of fruit if well made.

1984 Light, mid-range wines in both Châteauneuf and Gigondas. They will be drinking well in four or five years' time. Lighter Côtes du Rhône Villages are for drinking now. The whites, with some acidity, are now very mature. Rosés are fading.

1983 Light reds in Côtes du Rhône, but elsewhere in Châteauneuf and Lirac the wines will take plenty of time to mature fully. Gigondas is heavier and slower to develop. Drink Tavel rosé fast.

1982 Many rather flabby, overweight wines were made by careless producers burdened with extraordinary quantities of fruit. Stick to reds from very good producers, and probably stay with Châteauneuf. Forget about whites and rosés.

1981 Châteauneuf is beginning to be very drinkable with firm, structured wines. Some Gigondas are a little acid and watery, but some good ones are to be found as well. A few Côtes du Rhône Villages – those made with Syrah – are still drinkable.

1980 What were initially severe, tough wines have begun to mature in Châteauneuf, but they will last well. The same goes for Gigondas. Drink up Côtes du Rhône and Côtes du Rhône Villages. Red Lirac is very good.

1978 Long-lasting Châteauneuf is still maturing and will keep – lots of fruit and tannin need time to soften together. The same goes for Gigondas. A great year.

Other vintages Try 1972 and 1970 in Châteauneuf.

Who's who in the southern Rhône

Red Châteauneuf-du-Pape

There are two styles of red Châteauneuf – the lighter style, ready for comparatively early drinking, and the heavier, richer style which needs longer maturation. Different producers specialise in one or other.

LIGHTER STYLE

Clos de l'Oratoire des Papes (*D Byrne & Co; Irvine Robertson*); Domaine de Nalys (*Ian G Howe; Irvine Robertson; Windrush Wines*); Domaine de Beaurenard (*Ian G Howe; Seckford Wines; Victoria Wine Company*); Domaine du Vieux Télégraphe (*Adnams; G E Bromley; Gerard Harris; Ian G Howe; Lay & Wheeler; Laytons; Lockes; Nobody Inn; Tanners Wines*); Château des Fines Roches (*Unwins*); Domaine de Mont-Redon (*D Byrne & Co; Chaplin & Son; Eldridge Pope; Laytons; Lorne House Vintners; Majestic*); Vieux Lazaret (*Wine Society*).

RICHER STYLE

Château de Beaucastel (*Adnams; G E Bromley; Curzon Wine Company; Lay & Wheeler; Lockes; Morris & Verdin; Oddbins; Seckford Wines; Windrush Wines*); Bosquet des Papes (*Hopton Wines*); Brunel les Cailloux (*Hicks & Don*); Domaine Chante-Cigale (*Corney & Barrow; Nobody Inn; La Vigneronne; Yapp Brothers*); Domaine Chante Perdrix (*D Byrne & Co*); Clos des Papes (*Bibendum; Richard Harvey Wines; Lay & Wheeler*); Château Fortia (*G E Bromley & Sons; La Réserve; Oddbins*); Jaboulet Aîné, les Cèdres (*Fine Vintage Wines; Gerard Harris; Hungerford Wine Company; O W Loeb; Majestic; Tanners Wines; La Vigneronne; Wine Society*); Château de la Nerthe (*Mayor Sworder; Nobody Inn*); Château Rayas (*Adnams; O W Loeb; Nobody Inn; La Réserve*).

White Châteauneuf-du-Pape

Although only a small amount of white Châteauneuf is made, the modern style of vinification does produce some attractive, early-drinking wines. Don't keep them for more than a couple of years. Château de Beaucastel (*Adnams; La Réserve; Seckford Wines*); Domaine de Nalys (*Rodney Densem Wines; Windrush Wines*); Domaine de Mont-Redon (*Eldridge Pope; Wine Society*); Domaine du Vieux Télégraphe (*Adnams; D Byrne & Co; Haynes, Hanson & Clark*); Château de la Nerthe (*Mayor Sworder*).

Gigondas

Guigal (*Anthony Byrne Fine Wines*); Domaine de la Fourmone (*Windrush Wines*); Gabriel Meffre (*Gerard Harris; George Hill of Loughborough; Wine Society*); Domaine de St-Gayan (*Oddbins; Yapp Brothers*); L'Oustau Fauquet (*Adnams; Lay & Wheeler; Majestic; Tanners; La Vigneronne; Windrush Wines*); Domaine du Grand Montmirail (*Chaplin & Son; Davisons; Ellis Son & Vidler; Ian G Howe; Windrush Wines; Yapp Brothers*); Les Gouberts (*Sebastopol Wines; Seckford Wines*); Domaine de la Longue-Toque (*Barwell & Jones*); Les Pallières (*Bibendum; Hedley Wright; Ian G Howe; Christopher Piper Wines*); Domaine Raspail-Ay (*Hicks & Don; Lay & Wheeler*).

Lirac (red, rosé and white)

Domaine de Ch St-Roch (*Lay & Wheeler*); Domaine de Castel-Oualou (*D Byrne & Co; Ian G Howe; Michael Menzel Wines; Ubiquitous Chip*); Domaine Maby (*Berry Bros & Rudd; D Byrne & Co; Findlater Mackie Todd; Gerard Harris; Lorne House Vintners; Wine Society; Yapp Brothers*).

Côtes du Lubéron

Domaine Val Joanis New vineyards are producing some good whites, reds and rosés at very good prices.
Berry Bros & Rudd; Claridge Fine Wines; Findlater Mackie Todd; Windrush Wines

Cellier de Marrenon Good reds capable of ageing up to four years.
Peter Dominic; Safeway; Stapylton Fletcher

Côtes du Rhône

La Serre du Prieur (*Waitrose*); Ch du Grand Moulas (*Adnams; Lay & Wheeler; Tanners Wines*); Jaboulet Aîné Parellèle 45 (*Lay & Wheeler; O W Loeb; Majestic*); Cave des Vignerons de Vacqueyras (*Tanners Wines*); Cru du Coudoulet (*Morris & Verdin; Noble Grape; Seckford Wines*); Domaine Rabasse-Charavin (*Berkmann Wine Cellars/Le Nez Rouge; Windrush Wines*); Fonsalette (*O W Loeb*); Domaine Goubert, Jean-Pierre Cartier (*Ian G Howe*); Domaine Ste-Anne, Notre Dame des Cellettes (*Bedford Fine Wines; Justerini & Brooks; Tanners Wines*); Vidal-Fleury (*Berkmann Wine Cellars/Le Nez Rouge*); La Vieille Ferme (*Hedley Wright; La Réserve; Wines from Paris*); Domaine Bel-Air (*Haynes, Hanson & Clark; Richard Harvey Wines*); Domaine St-Estève (*Direct Wine Shipments*); Brézème, Jean-Marie Lombard (*Yapp Brothers*).

Côtes du Rhône Villages

In this list, we give the name of the village first, followed by the producer's name or estate. Villages wines without the name of a particular village are a blend of wines from two or more villages.

Côtes du Rhône Villages, Jaboulet Aîné (*Haynes, Hanson & Clark; Majestic*); Sainsbury's Côtes du Rhône Villages (*Sainsbury's*).

Beaumes de Venise Domaine de Coyeux (*Prestige Vintners*); Beaumes de Venise, Goubert (*Ian G Howe; Sebastopol Wines*); Beaumes-de-Venise, Ch Redortier (*Champagne de Villages; Gerard Harris; Windrush Wines*).

Cairanne, Brusset (*Upper Crust*); Cairanne, Rabasse-Charavin (*Berkmann Wine Cellars/Le Nez Rouge; Windrush Wines*).

Rasteau Cave des Vignerons de Rasteau (*H Allen Smith; The Market/ Le Provençal; Winecellars*).

Séguret La Fiole du Chevalier d'Elbène Gabriel Meffre (*Ubiquitous Chip*).

Vacqueyras Domaine de la Couroulu Ricard Pierre (*Berry Bros & Rudd; Buckingham Wines; Hedley Wright; Ian G Howe*); Vacqueyras Jaboulet Aîné (*Averys; Corney & Barrow; Hungerford Wine Company; Lay & Wheeler; O W Loeb; La Vigneronne*); Vacqueyras La Fourmone Réserve du Paradis (*La Vigneronne*).

Vinsobres Domaine du Moulin (*Majestic*).

Visan Domaine de la Cantharide Cuvée de l'Hermite (*Alex Findlater*).

Tavel

La Forcadière (*Wine Society; Yapp Brothers*); Caves des Vignerons (*La Vigneronne*); Domaine Maby (*Richard Harvey Wines; Irvine Robertson; Lorne House Vintners*); Ch d'Aqueria (*Alex Findlater*).

Coteaux du Tricastin

Pierre Labaye (*Helen Verdcourt Wines*); Waitrose Coteaux du Tricastin (*Waitrose*).

Côtes du Ventoux

La Vieille Ferme (*Berkmann Wine Cellars/Le Nez Rouge; Bibendum; Cachet Wines; Morris & Verdin; Sebastopol Wines; Seckford Wines; Helen Verdcourt Wines; Wines from Paris; Yorkshire Fine Wines*); Domaine des Anges (*Adnams; Bibendum; D Byrne & Co; Haynes, Hanson & Clark*); Sainsbury's Côtes du Ventoux (*Sainsbury's*); Jaboulet Aîné (*Majestic*).

Côtes du Vivavais

Producteurs Réunis Ardéchois (*Yapp Brothers*).

Muscat de Beaumes-de-Venise

Domaine de Durban (*Eldridge Pope; Gerard Harris; Christopher Piper Wines; Windrush Wines; Yapp Brothers*); Sélection Paul Jaboulet Aîné (*Corney & Barrow; Curzon Wine Company; O W Loeb; Majestic; Wine Society*); Domaine de Coyeux (*Adnams; Corney & Barrow; Richard Harvey Wines; Lay & Wheeler*); Cave Co-opérative de Beaumes de Venise (*Buckingham Wines; Sainsbury's*); La Vieille Ferme (*Berkmann Wine Cellars/Le Nez Rouge; Berry Bros & Rudd; Bibendum; Thos Peatling; Sebastopol Wines; Seckford Wines*).

Vins de Pays

White: Coteaux de l'Ardèche, Chardonnay, Louis Latour (*Hicks & Don*).
Red: Vin de Pays des Bouches du Rhône, Domaine de la Forêt (*Eldridge Pope*); St Michael Vin de Pays des Bouches du Rhône (*Marks & Spencer*).
Vin de Pays des Collines Rhodaniennes, de Vallouit (*Gerard Harris; Lorne House Vintners; Wessex Wines*).
Vin de Pays de la Principauté d'Orange (*Buckingham Wines*).
Vin de Pays du Vaucluse (*Hicks & Don; Tesco*).

Best buys from the southern Rhône

WHITES

Côtes du Lubéron, La Vieille Ferme (*widely available*)
Côtes du Rhône Blanc 1986, Domaine Pelaquie (*Bibendum*)

REDS

Domaine des Baumelles, Ch Val Joanis (*Tesco*)
Côtes du Ventoux, La Vieille Ferme (*widely available*)
Côtes du Rhône, Ch du Grand Moulas 1987 (*Lay & Wheeler; Marlow Wine Shop; Morris's Wine Stores; Tanners Wines*)
Côtes du Rhône 1985, Domaine du Mont Redon (*Majestic*)
Lirac Rouge 1985, La Fermade (*Yapp Brothers*)
Syrah Vin de Pays des Coteaux de l'Ardèche, Vignerons Ardéchois (*Chesterford Vintners; Desborough & Brown*)
Côtes du Ventoux 1986, Jaboulet Aîné (*Fullers*)
Côtes du Rhône Villages 1986, Rasteau (*Ilkley Wine Cellars*)
Côtes du Rhône 1985, Domaine St-Apollinaire (*J Sainsbury*)
Côtes du Vivarais 1986, Domaine du Belvezet (*Lay & Wheeler*)
Crozes-Hermitage 1985, Tardy et Ange (*Nigel Baring*)
Coteaux Varois, Ch St-Estève (*Direct Wine Shipments*)

Specialist stockists of Rhône wines

David Baillie Vintners; Bibendum; Nigel Baring; Christchurch Fine Wines; College Cellar; Croque-en-Bouche; Peter Green; J E Hogg; Ian G Howe; S H Jones; Justerini & Brooks; Kurtz & Chan; O W Loeb; Majestic; Raeburn Fine Wines and Foods; La Réserve; Tanners Wines; Philip Tite Fine Wines; Henry Townsend; Helen Verdcourt Wines; La Vigneronne; Yapp Brothers

SAVOIE

We've tasted more Savoie wine this year than ever before, not because we've been skiing, but because more has reached UK shops. It could be that skiers want to recreate something of their holiday on a suburban dry ski slope, but whatever the reason we're not complaining, because the fresh, crisp tastes of these mountain wines is very refreshing and invigorating.

Red, white and sparkling wines are all made in Savoie. The grapes used are a mix of local and more widely grown: Chardonnay, Chasselas (the Swiss Fendant), Jacquère, Altesse (or Roussette), Bergeron (the southern Rhône Roussanne) and Molette for the whites, Mondeuse and Gamay for the reds.

The appellation system is complex for such a small vineyard region, with nine appellations:

Crépy: dry sparkling wines made from Chasselas grapes.

Roussette de Savoie: dry white wines made from Roussette and Chardonnay.

Roussette de Savoie Cru: wines from four communes which can add their name to ordinary Roussette.

Seyssel: dry white wines from Altesse grapes.

Seyssel Mousseux: sparkling wines made from Altesse and Chasselas.

Vin de Savoie: appellation covering the whole region, producing reds, dry whites and rosés.

Vin de Savoie Cru: wines from 15 communes which can add their name to Vin de Savoie.

Vin de Savoie Ayze Mousseux: sparkling wine made in the commune of Ayze.

Vin de Savoie Mousseux: white and rosé sparkling wines made anywhere in the region.

Most wine we see is Vin de Savoie, but some cru wines from Apremont are also available. The most widely known sparkling wine is a Seyssel Mousseux from Varichon et Clerc.

Best buys from Savoie

Vin de Savoie Apremont (*Eaton Elliot Winebrokers; Majestic; Tanners Wines; Tesco*)

Seyssel Mousseux Varichon et Clerc (*Waitrose; Windrush Wines*)

THE SOUTH-WEST OF FRANCE

Hugh Johnson has a good phrase for the South-West of France in his *Wine Companion*: 'it exists in calm self-sufficiency'. He's right: there is something remote and untouched by time about this corner of vinous France, tucked between the huge mass of Bordeaux and the Pyrenees.

One reason may be because some of the local grape varieties just don't exist anywhere else. The litany is formidable: for reds, Manseng Noir, Tannat, Fer, Auxerrois, Jurançon Noir, Negrette; for whites, Meslier, Picpoul, Mauzac, Courbu, Baroque. And that's just for starters: one of the smallest vDQs areas has nine permitted grape varieties for its reds, with probably only one producer making the wines.

Of course, being so close to Bordeaux, the Cabernets and the Merlot, Sauvignon Blanc and Sémillon also put in a strong appearance. Indeed, some of the vineyard areas (Bergerac, Duras, Côtes du Marmandais) were once regarded as being part of the Bordeaux vineyard. Unluckily for them, they were on the wrong side of the departmental boundaries when the extent of Bordeaux was set as the *département* of Gironde.

So while Bordeaux prospered and recovered from phylloxera at the turn of this century, these other vineyard regions of the South-West slipped further into decline. It's only in the last couple of decades that first Bergerac, then Cahors, and now the other areas, have come back – almost literally, in some cases, from the dead.

Although all the appellations and most of the vin de pays wines of the South-West can be found in UK shops, many come in small quantities, simply because production is tiny. Bergerac is the most widely available, and is probably a good starting point for getting to know the region's wines, being like claret in style. But once started, this is a voyage of discovery, of strange, sometimes exotic tastes, of wines that are never lacking in character.

BERGERAC

This is an eastward extension of the St-Emilion vineyards of Bordeaux, at the beginning of the Dordogne valley. There are nine different appellations, ranging from dry red through dry white to sweet white. The wines most likely to be found in the UK are Bergerac (red, rosé and dry white), Côtes de Bergerac (red and medium sweet white), Monbazillac (sweet white) and Pécharmant (very fine red).

Vintages in Bergerac

Our advice is to drink the youngest dry whites and rosés – 1986 or 1987 vintages. Ordinary red Bergerac should also be drunk within three years. Côtes de Bergerac red and Pécharmant last longer – vintages to look for are 1983, 1985 and, for keeping, 1986. Sweet Monbazillac is best in warm, ripe years – try the 1983s and keep the 1985s for a year or two.

Who's who in Bergerac

DRY WHITES

Ch la Jaubertie (*Majestic, and others*); Ch Court-les-Mûts (*Bibendum; Sookias & Bertaut*); Ch du Treuil de Nailhac (*Sookias & Bertaut*); Ch de Belingard (*Barwell & Jones*); Ch de Fayolle (*Old Street Wine Company*).

SWEET WHITES

Clos Fontindoule Monbazillac (*La Vigneronne*); Ch de Treuil de Nailhac (*Sookias & Bertaut; Ubiquitous Chip*); Ch de Belingard (*Barwell & Jones*); Cave Co-opérative de Monbazillac (*Waitrose*).

REDS

Ch la Jaubertie (*Lay & Wheeler; Majestic; Wines from Paris*); Ch de Tiregand (*Sookias & Bertaut*); Domaine de Plaisance (*Grape Ideas*); Ch Jaquet Montcharme (*Peter Dominic*); Ch la Borderie (*Sookias & Bertaut*), Ch Court les Mûts (*Bibendum; Sookias & Bertaut*); Persigny de Bergerac, Mähler-Besse (*Averys*).

CÔTES DE BUZET

This is another of the areas which were once part of the Bordeaux vineyard. Whites and rosés are made, but virtually only the reds reach the UK. They have some ageing potential, with jammy fruit and some tannin. Bordeaux grape varieties are used.

Who's who in Buzet

Ch de Gueyze (*Thos Peatling; Sebastopol Wines; Tanners Wines*); Domaine Roc de Cailloux (*Prestige Vintners*); Les Vignerons Réunis, Cuvée Napoléon (*Pennyloaf Wines; Sebastopol Wines*); Sainsbury's Buzet (*Sainsbury's*); Côtes de Buzet (*Peter Dominic*); Ch Sauvagnères (*Sookias & Bertaut*).

CÔTES DE DURAS

The Côtes de Duras reds made from the Merlot grape are light and made for drinking early: they're delicious chilled. The dry whites from the Sauvignon (look for the grape name on the label) are typically fresh.

Who's who in Duras

WHITE

Le Seigneuret (*Waitrose*); Domaine de Ferrant (*Duras Direct*).

RED

Le Seigneuret (*Waitrose*); Domaine Mau Michau (*Duras Direct*); Ch la Pilar (*The Market/Le Provençal; Winecellars*); Clos du Moulin (*Desborough & Brown*); Poulet Père et Fils (*Grape Ideas*); Domaine de Laulan (*Hungerford Wine Company*).

CÔTES DU MARMANDAIS

Soft, easy reds for early drinking at good prices. Most wine comes from one or other of the two co-operatives (only one seems to be available in the UK).

Who's who in Marmandais

Côtes du Marmandais Cave de Cocumont (*widely available*).

CAHORS

This is one of the wines about which much used to be written and much less drunk. One of the legends told of 'the black wines of Cahors', dark, tannic wines with great longevity. In fact, they resulted from boiled up juice concentrate being added to wine for stability – which doesn't sound like a recipe for fine wine.

Nothing like that seems to happen today. Modern red Cahors ranges from fresh wines which have been made for early drinking to those which are fairly tough and tannic, ideal for undergoing some bottle ageing – for as much as 15 to 20 years in some cases – before accompanying rich, spicy foods.

The grape varieties used here are the Malbec or Auxerrois (to provide the concentration), the Merlot (to soften the Auxerrois and give extra alcohol) and the Tannat (to provide tannin). The co-operative, Côtes d'Olt, makes much of the wine here but there are also 80 individual growers.

Who's who in Cahors

Clos la Coutale (*George Hill of Loughborough; Windrush Wines*); Ch de Haute-Serre (*Victor Hugo Wines*); Les Côtes d'Olt (*widely available*); Domaine de la Pineraie (*Sookias & Bertaut*); Domaine de Gaudou (*Adnams; The Market/Le Provençal; Sookias & Bertaut; Winecellars*); Ch Didier-Parnac, Rigal et Fils (*H Allen Smith; Bibendum; Richard Harvey Wines; Lay & Wheeler; Oddbins*); Clos Triguedina (*Sookias & Bertaut*); Ch de Chambert (*Gerard Harris*); Domaine Eugénie (*Touchstone Wines*); Domaine de Meaux (*Majestic*); Ch les Bouysses (*Sainsbury's*); Ch Cayrou d'Albas (*Pennyloaf Wines; Tanners Wines; Unwins*); Domaine des Savarines (*Sookias & Bertaut*).

FRONTONNAIS

Red and rosé wines are made in this small area to the north of
Toulouse. They're excellent value for everyday drinking, although
quantities available in this country tend to be small. Drink them young
as quaffing wines.

Who's who in Côtes du Frontonnais

Ch Flotis (*Sookias & Bertaut*); Ch Bellevue la Forêt (*Berkmann Wine
Cellar/Le Nez Rouge; Market Vintners; Christopher Piper Wines*);
Ch Montauriol (*Barwell & Jones*); Co-opérative of Côtes du Frontonnais
(*Age of Wine – tel 09277 60166*).

GAILLAC

The slightly sparkling, rather dull Gaillac Perlé is the most common
wine seen here. But there are also more interesting and traditional reds
which combine a rustic character with reasonably fast maturation. The
still dry white – the majority of the production – is also rather dull. One
sparkling wine made by the 'méthode gaillaçoise' (a method which
results in fewer bubbles than Champagne), is well worth seeking out.

Who's who in Gaillac

Jean Cros – for high quality, traditional wines, including the méthode
gaillaçoise sparkler (*Adnams; Richard Harvey Wines; Lay & Wheeler;
Moffat Wine Shop; Pennyloaf Wines; Sookias & Bertaut; Stapylton Fletcher;
Tanners Wines*); Cave Co-opérative de Labastide de Lévis (*Richard
Harvey Wines; Hicks & Don*); Domaine de la Gravette (*Majestic*);
Domaine de Labarthe (*Sookias & Bertaut*).

JURANÇON

While much Jurançon is dry and most is drunk along the nearby
Atlantic coast at Biarritz, there are still small pockets of the
old-fashioned sweet wines, called Jurançon Moelleux, on which this
area's reputation used to rest. The corollary is that their rarity value
makes them expensive.

Who's who in Jurançon

Clos Concaillau sweet (*Sookias & Bertaut*); Cru Lamouroux sweet and medium dry (*Richard Harvey Wines*); Jurançon Brut Caves Vinicoles de Gan (*Anthony Byrne Fine Wines*); Clos Guirouilh (*D Byrne & Co; Chaplin & Son; Curzon Wine Company; Moffat Wine Shop*); Domaine Cauhape (*Eaton Elliot Winebrokers; Sookias & Bertaut*).

MADIRAN AND PACHERENC DU VIC-BILH

Heady stuff, these two names. In reality, though, while Madiran is a fine red wine, often dark in colour and very tannic when young (although there are lighter wines around as well), Pacherenc du Vic-Bilh is a straightforward, rather pricy white, most of which is drunk locally. Both come from the Armagnac country of Gascony.

Who's who in Madiran and Pacherenc

Madiran

Ch d'Arricau-Bordes (*Sookias & Bertaut*); Ch de Peyros (*Eaton Elliot Winebrokers*); Domaine Bouscassé (*Bibendum*); Alain Brumont Ch Montus (*Pennyloaf Wines; Sookias & Bertaut*); Domaine Pichard (*Old Street Wine Company; Tanners Wines*); Domaine de Margalide (*Martinez Fine Wine*).

Pacherenc du Vic-Bilh

Domaine du Crampilh (*George Hill of Loughborough; Sookias & Bertaut*).

LESSER REGIONS OF THE SOUTH-WEST

While there are many more small demarcated wine areas in the South-West, not many of their products reach our shops. Here is a selection of the better ones which do:

Côtes de St-Mont

Good, simple, rough red wines from the edge of the Armagnac region. The local co-op, Producteurs Plaimont, have a good value example (*Adnams; Lay & Wheeler*).

Entraygues et du Fel

A vdqs area on the southern slopes of the Massif Central in the Lot Valley. Try Jean-Marc Viguier's wines (*Sookias & Bertaut*).

Irouléguy

Right on the Spanish border at the western end of the Pyrenees, this makes red, white and rosé.

Marcillac

Deep-coloured reds from a small VDQS area also in the Lot valley. Look out for: Laurens Teulier (*Sookias & Bertaut*); Cave de Valady (*Taste Shops*).

Tursan

Perfumed dry whites and soft reds from the heart of Gascony. Worth trying: Domaine de Perchade-Pourruchot, Dulucq et Fils (*Sookias & Bertaut*).

VINS DE PAYS OF THE SOUTH-WEST

The most important vins de pays, as far as we are concerned, are: Côtes de Gascogne, Côtes du Tarn, de la Dordogne, des Pyrénées Atlantiques. All make good, everyday drinking wines. The whites (made using modern high tech equipment) are generally on a higher plain than the reds.

Who's who in the vins de pays of the South-West

Vin de Pays des Pyrénées Atlantiques (*Eldridge Pope; Richard Harvey Wines; Tanners Wines*); Vin de Pays des Côtes de Gascogne (*Chaplin & Son; Eaton Elliot Winebrokers; Richard Harvey Wines; Majestic; Oddbins; Sainsbury's; Waitrose*); Vin de Pays des Côtes de Thongue (*Claridge Fine Wines; Stapylton Fletcher*).

Best buys in the South-West

WHITES

Bergerac Blanc 1986, Ch Theulet (*Marlow Wine Shop*)
Vin de Pays des Côtes de Gascogne 1987, Domaine d'Escoubes (*Tesco*)
Bergerac Blanc 1986, Ch le Fage (*Lamb Wine Company*)
Ch la Jaubertie Sauvignon 1986 (*Majestic*)
Jurançon Moelleux, Clos Guirouilh (*James Aitken & Son*)
Bergerac Blanc 1987, Ch Court-les-Mûts (*Bibendum*)
Vin de Pays des Côtes de Gascogne 1987, Domaine du Tariquet (*widely available*)
Ch Septy 1979 (*La Vigneronne*)

REDS

Vin de Pays des Coteaux de Quercy 1986, Domaine de Lafage (*The Market/Winecellars*)

Cahors 1982, Clos Camp d'Auriol (*Morrisons*)
Gaillac Domaine Jean Cros (*Old Maltings Wine Company*)
Bergerac Rouge 1985, Ch de Fayolle (*Old Street Wine Company*)
Pécharmant 1986, Domaine des Bertranoux (*Pennyloaf Wines*)
Vin de Pays du Comte Tolosan, Domaine de Callory (*Raeburn Fine Wines and Foods*)
Vin de Pays du Comte Tolosan, Domaine de Callory (*Hampton Wine Company*)
Côtes du Frontonnais, Ch Bellevue la Forêt 1985 (*Four Vintners*)
Marcillac 1986, Laurens-Teulier (*Sookias & Bertaut*)
Cahors 1985, Métairie Grande du Théron (*Berry Bros & Rudd*)
Cahors 1983, St-Didier Parnac (*Great Northern Wine Company*)

Specialist stockists

Desborough & Brown; Duras Direct; Ian G Howe; Pennyloaf Wines; Prestige Vintners; Sookias & Bertaut; Upper Crust; Winecellars

Germany

Catching a cold

A cold chill ought to be running down the spines of German wine producers as they see their livelihood slip away in the shape of cellars full of unwanted wines. For Germany's biggest export market – Britain – has taken against German wines in a big way.

In 1986, we drank less German wine for the first time since the beginning of the Liebfraumilch boom in the late 1970s. That pattern was repeated in 1987. We just don't want more sugar-water bottles of Liebfraumilch and Piesporter, Niersteiner and Zeller Schwarze Katz. We have, it seems, become more sophisticated, which means we want something dry.

Certainly Germany does make dry wines (of which more below), but that hasn't been spelt out clearly enough: the German Wine Information Service, based in London, has a derisory budget compared with the amount of money lavished on promoting French or Spanish wines. Even if we did know more about the wines, there is a strong suspicion that we wouldn't care: German wines are so poorly served by their current image, that only a dedicated few will consider experimenting with some of the great things the country has to offer.

Considerable correspondence about German wine has appeared in the wine press during the past year. It stemmed from an article by a consumer journalist complaining about the poor quality of much of the German wine available in British shops. He wasn't writing about the rock-bottom £1.99 Liebfraumilch either, but about various middle-range wines, some of them from the Prädikat categories (see below for definitions), and which certainly ought to have been better than he found them.

Inevitably – considering how personally people take an attack on their pet subject – those who enjoy German wines rose to their defence by questioning the tasting ability, the objectivity and the sincerity of the journalist. But somewhere in the welter of personal abuse, a number of grains of truth about the sorry state of German wines did surface. Also there, buried deep, were a few signs that at last the German producers may be doing something.

What a pretty mess

Germany has no monopoly on greedy wine producers, or on bad winemaking. But many of the problems facing the German wine industry are very much of its own making. They arise partly out of German winemaking philosophy. To a German, there is nothing wrong in wringing as many grapes off a vine as possible. While French legislation works on the theory that the better the vineyard, the lower the permitted yield, concentrating the potential of a vine in a limited quantity of high quality grapes, in Germany it is the ripeness of the grape that determines the quality, and the yield is irrelevant.

The absurd result is that yields of twice that of French vineyards are considered the norm. These are from the vineyards from which Liebfraumilch comes: the flat countryside of the Rheinhessen south of the city of Mainz, where more grapes mean more Deutschmarks in the pocket of the small-time farmer. And the result of this over-production of grapes, of course, is the tasteless sugar-water that fills our shops' shelves.

When those high-yield tasteless grapes reach the winery, they are treated to high technology that only the Germans could devise. Winemaking, certainly in the hands of the big co-operatives and producers who supply most of our Liebfraumilch, consists of churning out industrial, mass-produced wines, easy to make and drink and very easy to forget.

But there is another side to German wine, and it's the side we must remember and encourage before it's too late. The great estates, many in private hands or run by the Church or religious charities, have been making wine on the same land for centuries. It is very common to meet a courtly German producer whose family has been growing grapes since the Middle Ages. There is a marvellous continuity about the way they work and what they are doing, which we should be discovering before we completely forget that Germany can produce quality as well as quantity.

A good German wine is all about balance – between sweetness, fruit and acidity. The German vineyards are at the northernmost boundary

Germany

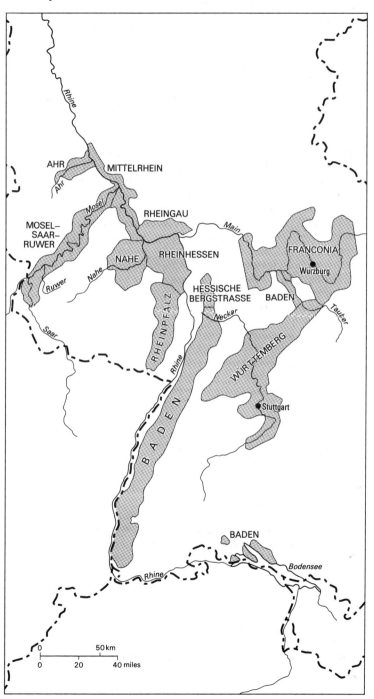

AHR

MITTELRHEIN

Rhine

Ahr

Mosel

RHEINGAU

Main

MOSEL–
SAAR–
RUWER

NAHE

RHEINHESSEN

FRANCONIA

● Würzburg

Ruwer

Nahe

HESSISCHE
BERGSTRASSE

BADEN

Saar

RHEINPFALZ

Neckar

Tauber

Rhine

WÜRTTEMBERG

B A D E N

● Stuttgart

BADEN

Rhine

Bodensee

0

50 km

0   20   40 miles

of winemaking – in some years it is a struggle to get the grapes to ripen at all. And that tension should be reflected in the delicate, almost nervous poise of top quality German wines.

On the dry side

It is generally assumed that German wine has always been on the sweet side. But that's not quite true. Before the last War, most German wine drunk here was dry and accompanied food, generally the first course. This is still the case at many royal functions, where the Queen continues to serve German wines at many banquets.

There is a move back to making drier German wines. Anybody who tasted some of the tart offerings around in the 1970s, which simply served to remind you to go to the dentist, will probably wince at the thought of dry German wines. But the new generation of Trocken (dry) and Halbtrocken (semi-dry) wines are quite different – fuller, rounder and with enough ripe fruit to make them very enjoyable with even rich meats.

They are food wines, as German wine producers are very keen to get across. Because the German Wine Information Service can't do the job, the top producers have decided they must do their own promotion. An organisation called itself Charta (pronounced 'karta') has been set up by some of the best Rheingau producers to make dry wines specifically for drinking with food. They've developed a special bottle with an arched window symbol on it. The wines from the 1985 vintage are in our shops now, and are worth seeking out.

Estates are forming themselves into other groupings: one of the more recent, Vintners' Pride, comprises one famous estate from each of six growing regions. Their plan is to demonstrate through tastings the range of quality that the major German wine areas can produce.

It's not cheap – and it needs time

Commentators on German wines are keen to wean us away from viewing all German wine as Liebfraumilch and its ilk.

One essential misconception that we must rid ourselves of is that good German wine is cheap. Liebfraumilch may be cheap, but estate wines can never be. Since Germany is at the furthest limits of vineyard cultivation, making top quality wines is always a risky business. German producers see large sums of money being paid for white Burgundy which is produced in less risky conditions, and wonder why no one seems prepared to reward their risk-taking more generously.

So, be prepared to spend £5 or £6 at least for German wine – and then you are beginning to get into quality levels. Moreover, be prepared to age them. Again, Liebfraumilch has conditioned us into drinking German wine as young as possible – as soon as we get it home from the shop. But finer German wines need time in bottle: for instance, 1985 Kabinett wines were beginning to come on nicely by the spring of 1988 – before that they hadn't really come into balance.

If that's true of the Kabinett level of quality (see below for definitions), how much more true is it of the richer, sweeter wines – the fabled Auslesen, Beerenauslesen and Trockenbeerenauslesen. They seem to be able to go on for decades, losing some of their initial obvious sweetness, but developing complexities and depths that make them vinous wonders of the world.

Improving the image

Last year, we commented that the Germans had realised that they should put their house in order. There is talk about restricting yields, about improving the labelling, and about restricting the number of labels for quality wines – so that only the amount which passes the official test can actually get bottled (amazingly, at the moment, there is no control over this).

But it's still talk. The Germans say that the 1989 vintage may see the changes take effect. We'll believe that, etc. . . . Until then, it's back to the good producers (many of whom are listed below) to keep our faith in the belief that quality can come out of Germany.

A few definitions

Germany is nothing if not thorough in giving information on the label about the wine inside the bottle, which will be tall and green if it comes from Mosel–Saar–Ruwer and brown from elsewhere, except Franconia which has dumpy green bottles. Some wines from the Rheingau are now bottled in blue bottles.

1 The label will indicate which category of wine it falls into: Tafelwein, the most basic; Landwein, a sort of German vin de pays; *Qualitätswein bestimmter Anbaugebiete* (QbA), the lowest quality wine level; or, at the top level, *Qualitätswein mit Prädikat* (QmP, which has six sub-divisions). As an indication of what Germans mean by quality wine, 90 per cent of all German wine falls into a quality category. To get real quality, you need to go to the level of QmP wines.

QmP wines are divided by sweetness: Kabinett (the driest), Spätlese, Auslese, Beerenauslese and Trockenbeerenauslese (the sweetest). Eiswein, made from frozen grapes, can be either Beerenauslese or Trockenbeerenauslese quality.

2 Next, the wine region. **Tafelwein** can come from four big districts: Rhein–Mosel, Bayern (Bavaria), Neckar, Oberrhein (basically Baden). **Landwein** districts number 15, but little is sold in Britain. **Quality wine** areas (for QbA and QmP wines) are (from north to south): Ahr, Mittelrhein, Mosel–Saar–Ruwer, Nahe, Rheingau, Rheinhessen, Hessische Bergstrasse, Franken, Württemberg,

Rheinpfalz, Baden. In the UK we see wines from all areas (although in small quantities from Ahr, Mittelrhein, Hessische Bergstrasse and Württemberg).

3 The label will tell you which sub-region (*Bereich*) the wine comes from, which district (*Grosslage*), which village in that district (*Gemeinde*) and which single vineyard (*Einzellagen*).

   Which of these categories is indicated will depend on the quality of the wine. The best wines will have single vineyard names, the most straightforward simply a Bereich name.

4 Other information will include:

The AP number given to the wine after it has been tested by a central testing station (useful to know only if something's wrong with the wine).

The degree of dryness (relates to QbA wines only): Trocken (dry), Halbtrocken (less dry), Diabetikerwein (for diabetics) or nothing (for standard styles).

The grape variety: not compulsory, but always included if the *Riesling* (the finest German variety) is predominant. Other grapes you might see are *Müller-Thurgau* (the most widely planted, although the Riesling is coming back into favour), *Silvaner* (in Franconia especially), *Scheurebe* (which produces a highly scented wine), *Kerner* (a stylish grape with some similarity to Riesling), *Spätburgunder* or *Blauer Portugieser* (if you are looking for a red wine – not often seen in Britain).

The vintage: see below for details of recent vintages.

The producer: if the wine has been estate-bottled the label will bear the term Erzeugerabfüllung.

The bottler: if the wine is not estate-bottled it will carry the name of the merchant or shipper who bottled it.

German sparklers

Before 1986, Deutscher Sekt on a label simply meant that the wine had German bubbles in it – in other words, inserted into the wine on German territory. Now the wine itself has to be German. The best check for quality is to look for Riesling on the label – that *will* be German. Other Sekts are simply sparkling wines from anywhere – generally Italy – sold under a German producer's name.

   Some of the biggest German merchants – Deinhard, Kupferberg, Sichel (of Blue Nun fame) – make sparkling wines. The Deinhard brands are very good, as are some which go under estate names: Schloss Rheingarten, Schloss Böchingen, Fürst von Metternich. For more details see the *Sparkling wines* section on page 572.

Harvests – getting bigger all the time

German harvests can vary considerably in quantity as well as quality. The early 1980s produced the biggest harvests on record, and on the whole, harvests are now much bigger than they used to be – the most obvious result of high yields. Most ordinary QbA wines need to be drunk within 1–2 years or they will lose their freshness, but QmP wines start to mature only after 2–3 years (for Kabinett wines).

Recent harvests all made some decent wines in the lower categories, but only rarely are there many wines in the top very sweet ones. As a comparison, before 1983, the most recent star vintages for these great sweet wines were 1976, 1959, 1945 and 1921.

1987 After a poor start to the growing season, a fine September and October saved the harvest, giving an average crop, with 75 per cent standard QbA wines, and 21 per cent QmP wines, most of which are of Kabinett level. The vintage is characterised by clean, fresh wines.

1986 A mixed bag of a vintage, with bad weather during the harvest and only small quantities of the wine likely to be at the higher QmP levels, but good acidity has resulted in plenty of easy-drinking wines.

1985 Good quality, especially for the Riesling. As much as 60 per cent reached Prädikat levels (mainly Kabinett). But quantity was cut by as much as half because of frost in the early part of the year. Start to drink the Kabinett wines now, but keep higher QmP wines.

1984 Little but QbA wines were made in a poor year. These should be drunk by now.

1983 A very fine year, with some good wines up to Auslese quality, but little above. A very large crop, especially in the Mosel–Saar–Ruwer. Keep the top qualities for at least four or five years, enjoy the rest now and for a while yet.

1982 A year of huge quantities, caused by high rainfall during the harvest, so only QbA wines were produced – they should be drunk now.

1981 Some of the Spätlese wines are still definitely worth drinking, and a few will keep.

1979 Only top Riesling wines are still enjoyable, but they will last at least until 1990.

1976 The top quality wines from this vintage are German classics. If you find a bottle of Spätlese or above in the QmP wines, buy it and save it for drinking with some appreciative friends.

Who's who in Germany

This selection of German producers includes some of the best estates and also some of the merchants whose wines are regularly seen in Britain.

Anheuser, Weingut Ökonomierat August E Large estate of 60 hectares in the Nahe, making racy wines mainly from the Riesling grape.
Alex Findlater

Aschrott'sche Erben, Geheimrat High quality estate in Hochheim in the Rheingau. Almost entirely Riesling wines.
Berry Bros & Rudd; O W Loeb

Badischer Winzergenossenschaft, Zentralkellerei A long name for the main co-operative of Baden, making 400 to 500 different wines. High standards for a co-operative.
Oddbins; Waitrose

Balbach Erben, Bürgermeister Anton, Weingut One of the great estates in Nierstein in Rheinhessen, with a modern outlook to winemaking.
Lay & Wheeler

Bassermann-Jordan, Weingut Geheimer Rat Dr von Rheinpfalz estate, founded in the 13th century, with vineyards in many of the best sites of Deidesheim and Forst.
Lay & Wheeler

Bergweiler-Prüm Erben, Zach Small Mosel–Saar–Ruwer estate with vineyards in Graach, Bernkastel, Wehlen and Zeltingen–Rachtig. One of the Vintners' Pride estates (see *On the dry side* above).
Alex Findlater

Bischöflichen Weinguter, Verwaltung der Four estates (105 hectares) of ecclesiastical origin in Mosel–Saar–Ruwer, based in the city of Trier. Other ecclesiastical names you will see are Bischöfliche Priesterseminar and Bischöfliche Konvikt.
Lay & Wheeler; Wine Society

Brentano'sche Gutsverwaltung, Baron von Good Rheingau estate, whose holdings of ten hectares include part of Winkeler Hasensprung.
Lay & Wheeler

Breuer, Weingut G Small estate, part of the merchant company of Scholl and Hillebrand (see below). Main holdings are in Rüdesheim on the Rheingau.
Alex Findlater

Buhl, Weingut Reichsrat von Great Rheinpfalz estate, now one of the Vintners' Pride group, and with a dynamic young American in charge, making wines from vineyards in Forst, Deidesheim and Ruppertsberg.
H Allen Smith; Berry Bros & Rudd; Eldridge Pope; O W Loeb

Burgerspital zum Heiligen Geist Despite the name (Holy Ghost) of this ancient charity hospital, the wines are true, down-to-earth examples of Franconian production.
German Food Centre (Knightsbridge, London SW1); Grange Wines (3 Tower Road, Tadworth, Surrey)

Bürklin-Wolf, Weingut Dr Large estate based at Wachenheim in the Rheinpfalz, making very fine wines.
Adnams; Eldridge Pope; Lay & Wheeler; O W Loeb; Wine Society

Castell'sches Domänenamt, Fürstlich Estate owned by the former rulers of the tiny state of Castell in Franconia, now one of the Vintners' Pride estates. Wines made of the Rieslaner grape are a great speciality.
Curzon Wine Company

Crusius, Weingut Hans Very high standards at this family-run estate in the Nahe, which has holdings in the Traiser Bastei and Rotenfels.
George Hill of Loughborough; Lockes

Deinhard & Co Wine merchant and vineyard owner based in Koblenz. Vineyards in Mosel–Saar–Ruwer (where they own most of the Bernkasteler Doktor vineyard), Rheingau and Rheinpfalz. Apart from estate wines, Deinhard make good branded wines (Green Label) and sparkling wine (Lila Imperial).
Adnams; Berry Bros & Rudd; Alex Findlater; Haynes, Hanson & Clark; Lockes

Diefenhardt'sches Weingut Estate of 12.2 hectares on the Rheingau, with vineyards in Eltville, Martinsthal and Rauenthal.
Gerard Harris; Ian G Howe; Thos Peatling

Drathen KG, Ewald Theodor Large-scale exporters of cheap EEC table wine.
Oddbins; Waitrose

Eltville, Verwaltung der Staatsweingüter The German state's holdings on the Rheingau and Hessische Bergstrasse, comprising 160 hectares in many of the best sites, including all of the walled Steinberg vineyard.
Adnams; Eldridge Pope; Lay & Wheeler

Fischer, Weinguter Dr Saar estate with holdings in Ockfen, Saarburg and Herrenberg.
John Harvey & Sons

Friedrich-Wilhelm-Gymnasium, Stiftung Staatliches Estate founded by the Jesuits with 45 hectares of vineyard in the Mosel–Saar–Ruwer, based in Trier.
Adnams; Bibendum; Alex Findlater; Lay & Wheeler; Henry Townsend

Geltz Zilliken, Weingut Forstmeister A Saar estate with holdings in Ockfen and Saarburg, and the deepest cellar in the region.
Lay & Wheeler

Guntrum-Weinkellerei GmbH, Louis Wine merchant and vineyard owner based in the Rheinhessen (one of the Vintners' Pride estates). Many wines from top vineyards as well as more straightforward ones.
Berry Bros & Rudd; E H Booth; Rodney Densem Wines; Harrods; George Hill of Loughborough; Martinez Fine Wine; Arthur Rackhams; Selfridges; Unwins; Willoughbys

Hallgarten GmbH, Arthur Firm of wine exporters selling estate-bottled wines as well as brands and standard wines. Linked with the Pieroth group (see below).
Selfridges; Unwins; Victoria Wine Company

Henkell & Co, Sektkellerein Producer of sparkling wine, including Henkell Trocken.
Asda; Eldridge Pope; Thresher; Victoria Wine Company

Hovel, Weingut von One of the principal estates in the Saar, making classically delicate wines in rare good years.
O W Loeb; Wine Society

Huesgen GmbH, A Firm of wine merchants based in Traben–Trarbach in the Mosel–Saar–Ruwer, specialising in inexpensive wines.
Les Amis du Vin; Haynes, Hanson & Clark; Hilbre Wine Company

Juliusspital-Weingut Charitable hospital in Würzburg, Franconia, dating from the 16th century. Makes excellent examples of Franconian wines.
O W Loeb

Kesselstatt, Weingut Reichsgraf von Four estates at Graach, Piesport, Kasel and Oberemmel in Mosel–Saar–Ruwer.
Eldridge Pope; O W Loeb; Henry Townsend

Kupferberg & Cie, Christian Adalbert Large producer of sparkling wines, based in Mainz.
Reihill McKeown (38 Annesborough Industrial Area, Craigavon, Co Armagh)

Lang, Weingut Hans Small estate in the Rheingau, with holdings in Kiedrich and Hattenheim. Lists old vintages.
Green's; George Hill of Loughborough; Laytons; The Market/Le Provençal; Mayor Sworder; Christopher Piper Wines; Stapylton Fletcher

Langenbach Large-scale producers whose wines include Black Tower Liebfraumilch. Now owned by a joint Allied-Lyons and Whitbread company.
Widely available

Liegenfelder, Weingut K & H Estate at the northern end of the Rheinpfalz.
Adnams; Fortnum & Mason; Newman & Gilbey; Ostlers; La Vigneronne

Loeb GmbH, Sigmund Exporter owned by O W Loeb in London (see WHERE TO BUY section), dealing in high quality estate-bottled wines.
O W Loeb

Loosen-Erben, Weingut A Mosel estate with vineyards at Erden and Ürzig.
Adnams; Berry Bros & Rudd; Fortnum & Mason; Gerard Harris; John Harvey & Sons; Oddbins; Selfridges; Windrush Wines

Metternich Sektkellerei GmbH, Fürst von Sparkling wine producer who uses the Metternich name but is not part of the family.
Arthur Rackhams; Garland Wines (3 Garlands Road, Leatherhead, Surrey)

Müller GmbH, Rudolf Wine merchant and estate owner based in Mosel–Saar–Ruwer. Sells branded wines by the name of the Bishop of Riesling.
Adnams; Haynes, Hanson & Clark; Hungerford Wine Company; Lay & Wheeler

Müller-Scharzhof, Weingut Egon Old Saar estate making fabulous wines in good years.
O W Loeb

Nägler, Weingut Dr Heinrich A small Rüdesheim (Rheingau) estate, still using casks for maturing the wine.
O W Loeb

Niederhausen-Schlossböckelheim, Verwaltung der Staatlichen Weinbaudomänen German state holdings in the Nahe producing some of the best wines of the region.
Lay & Wheeler; Henry Townsend

Pauly KG, Weingut Otto Mosel–Saar–Ruwer estate, with holdings in Graach and Bernkastel, making wines of good quality.
Averys

Pieroth, Weingut Weinkellerei, Ferdinand One of the largest wine merchants in Germany, specialising in doorstep-selling QmP wines to consumers by the 16-bottle case. Despite being sold direct, wines are generally expensive for what they are. Pieroth own a large number of subsidiary companies.

Plettenberg'sche Verwaltung, Reichsgräflich von A large Nahe estate
producing a wide range.
O W Loeb

Prüm, Weingut J J One of the finest Mosel–Saar–Ruwer estates, with
holdings all the way along the Middle Mosel.
Bibendum; Wine Society

Reh & Sohn, Franz Large wine merchant with some vineyard
holdings in the Mosel–Saar–Ruwer, mainly exporting standard wines.
*Edward Crisp (13 Cumber Gate, Peterborough, Cambs); Tates of Grimsby
(8 Cleethorpe Road, Grimsby, Humberside); Leicester Co-Op; Yorkshire Co-Op*

Ress KG, Balthasar Family firm owning vineyards in the central
Rheingau, including leaseholding of Schloss Reichhartshausen. Classic
Rheingau wines, with labels specially commissioned from artists.
Richard Harvey Wines; Windrush Wines

Richter, Weingut Max Ferd Old-established family business with top
quality wines from a 15-hectare estate.
Green's; Summerlee Wines

St Ursula Weingut and Weinkellerei Firm of wine merchants based in
Bingen which make Goldener Oktober branded wines.
Rodney Densem Wines; Oddbins; C A Rookes

**Schloss Groenesteyn, Weingut des Reichsfreiherrn von Ritter zu
Groenesteyn** Estate founded in the 14th century concentrated around
Rüdesheim on the Rheingau.
Berry Bros & Rudd; Lay & Wheeler

Schloss Johannisberg Most famous name on the Rheingau, making
wine from its 35-hectare estate in Johannisberg. Not to be confused
with Bereich Johannisberg wines, which can come from anywhere in
the Rheingau.
Alex Findlater; Hilbre Wine Company

Schloss Reinhartshausen Large estate of 67 hectares on the Rheingau,
owned by descendants of the German Emperors. Holdings at Erbach,
Hattenheim, Kiedrich, Rauenthal and Rüdesheim.
Berry Bros & Rudd; Eldridge Pope; Henry Townsend

Schloss Schönborn, Domänenweingut Rheingau estate with
vineyards in Oestrich, Winkel, Rüdesheim, Geisenheim, Hochheim,
Hattenheim, Johannisberg and Erbach.
D Byrne & Co

**Schloss Vollrads, Graf Matuschka-Greiffenclau'sche
Gutserverwaltung** Estate dating from the 12th century, still owned by
the same family which has been very active in promoting dry wines for

food. A member of the Vintners' Pride grouping, making very fine wines.
Eldridge Pope; Alex Findlater; Reynier Wine Libraries

Scholl & Hillebrand One of the firms in at the founding of the Rheingau Charta group (see the beginning of the section). Their brand is called Riesling Dry, but they produce a range of fine estate wines.
Berry Bros & Rudd; Thos Peatling; Unwins; Victoria Wine Company; La Vigneronne

Schubert'sche Gutsverwaltung, C von Thousand-year-old estate on the Ruwer, near Trier, which produces great wines in good years.
Lay & Wheeler; Henry Townsend; La Vigneronne

Sichel Söhne GmbH Producers of Blue Nun, but also selling estate wines.
Widely available

Simmern'sches Rentamt, Freiherrlich Langwerth von A large Rheingau estate owned by the same family since 1464. Its vineyards are at Erbach, Hattenheim, Rauenthal and Eltville.
Lay & Wheeler

Simon, Bert A recently (1968) established estate with land at Serrig, Eitelsbach, Mertesdorf and Kasel, all in the Mosel–Saar–Ruwer.
Mayor Sworder & Co

Strub, Weingut J & H A 17-hectare estate in Rheinhessen, with land at Dienheim and Nierstein, including land on the famous Rheinterrasse (the slope facing the river) at Nierstein.
Mounts Bay Wine Co (Bread Street, Penzance, Cornwall)

Vila Eden Fine wine arm of St Ursula Weingut (see above). Its vineyards are at Bingen on the Rhine.
Berry Bros & Rudd

Weil, Weingut Dr R Estate with holdings in Kiedrich on the Rheingau.
H Allen Smith; Eldridge Pope; Alex Findlater

Best buys from Germany

Saarburger Antoniusbrunnen Riesling Kabinett 1985, R Müller (*Tanners Wines*)
Ockfener Bockstein Riesling Kabinett 1981, Nikolas Max Erben (*Wessex Wines*)
Serriger Scharzberg Kabinett 1982, Bert Simon (*Mayor Sworder*)
Durkheimer Abstfronhof Riesling Spätlese 1983, Ritter (*James Aitken & Son*)
Schlossböckelheimer Burgweg Riesling Auslese 1976, Berthold Pleitz (*Douglas Henn-Macrae*)

Waldracher Romerlay Riesling Spätlese 1983, Peter Scherf (*Hicks & Don*)

Freinsheimer Goldberg Riesling Kabinett 1985, Lingenfelder (*Oddbins*)

Ockfener Bockstein Riesling Kabinett 1983, Rudolf Müller (*Charles Hennings*)

Reiler vom Heissen Stein Riesling und Müller-Thurgau Kabinett 1985, Rudolf Müller (*G E Bromley & Sons*)

Bernkasteler Badstube Riesling 1984, Friedrich Wilhelm Gymnasium (*Classic Wine Warehouse*)

Specialist stockists

H Allen Smith; Berry Bros & Rudd; D Byrne & Co; Christchurch Fine Wines; Corney & Barrow; Eldridge Pope; Alex Findlater; Peter Green; Greens; Gerard Harris; Douglas Henn-Macrae; J E Hogg; S H Jones; Justerini & Brooks; O W Loeb; Mitchell's Wine Bin; Thos Peatling; Pennine Wines; Henry Townsend; A L Vose; Wine Schoppen; Wine Society; Wine Spot

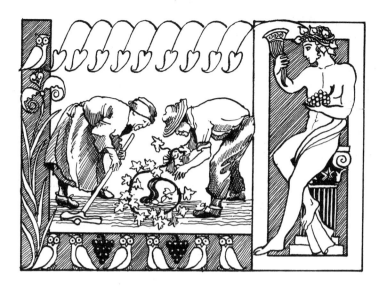

Greece

Back to normal

Nothing much seems to have changed in our perception of Greek wines. While there are a handful of excellent wines around in our shops, the majority of Greek wines would have been much better left in the tavernas back home.

The Greeks themselves don't seem too bothered about it, either. There have been some fainthearted attempts to persuade us that they make a good range of quality wines, but they all seem to have petered out. Perhaps they don't need to export, perhaps we all drink enough when we get to Greece. Who knows?

Now a series of controls has been applied to what was seemingly uncontrollable. Since entering the European Community in 1981, Greece has designated regional wines along the lines of the French AC and VDQS rules. There are 28 of these, and a strange collection some of them make: all of the eight AC wine areas, for instance, produce only sweet wines. With two exceptions, the Greeks have simply delimited existing areas, but have added regulations about yields, grape varieties and sugar content.

What all this will add up to is hard to say. For now, Greece remains best known for her one unique contribution to viticulture: retsina, produced mainly around Athens. You either love it or hate it. If you love it, some good versions are available here and they certainly cut through oily food.

Elsewhere, it is the islands that produce some of the sweet dessert wines, made from the Malvasia and Muscat grapes. Samos makes the best-known Muscats, while Crete has a luscious Malvasia. Sweet red wines are a speciality of the Peloponnese, of which the Mavrodaphne of Patras is the most widely known.

And then there are a few estate wines. Much attention has recently been focused on the efforts of Greek tycoon John Carras who has flown in the famous Professor Peynaud from Bordeaux to advise on making a French-style wine in one of the Khalkidhiki peninsulas in northern Greece. Château Carras is the result, made from Bordeaux grapes, and a very well-made wine it is. The white Domaine Porto Carras, made from Sauvignon grapes, is less successful.

More recent arrivals are two wines from the island of Cephalonia, and both prove that native Greek grape varieties can produce some decent wines if only somebody tries. John Calliga's two red wines (Monte Nero, made from Agioritiko grapes, and, especially, the Calliga Ruby – don't be put off by the asymmetrical bottle) are wines that should begin to make us take Greece more seriously.

What's what in Greece

Brand, rather than company, names rule in Greece.

John Calliga Try his red Monte Nero and Calliga Ruby. The white Robola is less interesting.
Peter Green; Hicks & Don; Noble Grape; Oddbins; Ostlers; Tanners Wines

Château Carras This is the top wine produced by the Domaine de Porto Carras. Others, going under the name Côtes de Méliton, are a dry white Blanc de Blancs, Sauvignon, Grand Vin Blanc, Grand Vin Rouge.
Hicks & Don; Nobody Inn; Reid Wines; Sainsbury's; Selfridges; Tanners Wines; Victoria Wine Company; La Vigneronne; Willoughbys

Mavrodaphne of Patras Sweet red wine, akin to the Reciotos of Italy, but not as good.
G E Bromley & Sons; La Reserva Wines; Tanners Wines

Muscat of Samos Sweet dessert wines made from the Muscat grape on the island of Samos. The most widely available comes from the island's co-operative.
G E Bromley & Sons; Peter Green; Majestic; Tanners Wines

Retsina Metaxas Produced by the firm best known for its brandies. A good example of this style of wine.
Adnams; Cantina Augusto

Retsina Attiki Another good example from Attica.
Morrisons; Sainsbury's (own-label); Thresher; Victoria Wine Company

Tsantali Lousy labels hide some tasty wines – there are fresh grapes there. Try Red Superb, Golden Delicious sweet Samos (no apples), Mavrodaphne, Naoussa. .
Wine Shop (Thurso)

Best buys from Greece

WHITE WINES

Retsina Metaxas (*widely available*)
Mavrodaphne of Patras, Tsantali (*Wine Shop, Thurso*)

RED WINES

Ch Carras 1979 (*Hicks & Don; Sainsbury's; Tanners Wines; Victoria Wine Company; La Vigneronne*)
Monte Nero 1981 (*Peter Green; Ostlers*)
Calliga Ruby 1981 (*Hicks & Don; Oddbins; Tanners Wines*)
Demestica, Achaia Clauss (*Peter Dominic*)

Specialist stockists

James Aitken & Sons; Cumbrian Cellar; Peter Green

Hungary

Those were the days

Older readers will remember the days when Bull's Blood almost tasted like its name: big, beefy, full of rich peppery fruit – wine with horns on.

Not any more. Buy a bottle of Hungary's most famous wine for the first time, and you will be surprised at how harsh and tannic it is, closed in and rather dull. Buy another bottle, and it may taste just plain oxidised. Those two bottles sum up the problems that Hungarian wines have been encountering in this country over the past few years.

Hungary has a long and proud tradition of winemaking, and it still has a world-class wine in Tokay, but we now seem to be getting wines that are not as good as they used to be. As an alternative, the wines seem to have been made to a marketing man's formula: the British like medium sweet wines, so that's what we will make for them. These turn out to be vaguely sweet white wines made from the Welsch Riesling grape (absolutely no relation of the great Rhine Riesling of Germany), or slightly sweet – because soft and spineless – red wines made out of local grapes with memorable names and forgettable tastes.

The comparison must inevitably be with neighbouring Bulgaria,

which has chosen the route of quality and value, bringing rich
rewards.

The taste of Hungary

As so often, a country's wines go with its food. Even Hungary's whites
can cut through the spiciness that is a common theme of much
Hungarian cooking, and the reds, full and smooth, sometimes slightly
sweet and mellow, complement the rich paprika sauces and strong
tastes of the meat dishes.

One wine keeps Hungary firmly on the world's wine map – Tokay. It
is one of the world's great dessert wines, and is still extremely good
value for money as well as being a memorable wine: look for the top
qualities of sweetness (Tokay Aszu 5 Puttonyos) or, justifiably more
expensive, Tokay Aszu Essencia, which is made only from the free-run
juice of grapes carrying noble rot. All Tokays are sold in 50 cl bottles.

What's what in Hungary

The Hungarian language is like no other (apart, it seems, from
Finnish). Our advice is not to try to pronounce the words on the bottle
but just point. Place names tend to come first, with the suffix 'i',
followed by the grape name. This is only a general rule but may be
helpful.

Badacsony Quality wine district, producing mainly white wines, on
the northern shore of Lake Balaton.

Balaton Wines from Lake Balaton, the Hungarian 'inland sea' which
enjoys a favourable micro-climate. Larger area than Badacsony.

Egri Wine from the district of Eger in the north of the country. Source
of the red Bull's Blood brand.

Furmint Hungarian white grape variety, making crisp, clean, slightly
peppery wines. Can be fresh, but too often dull.

Kadarka Red grape, making a full-bodied, gutsy wine that goes well
with meaty stews.

Kisburgundi A light, slightly peppery red, made from the Pinot Noir.

Somló Small wine-growing district to the west of Lake Balaton.

Sopron Wine-growing district on the border with Austria. Much of the
wine is red, made either from the Kékfrankos grape or from a
Hungarian version of the Gamay.

Tokay The great dessert wine area in the east of Hungary (see above).
The top wines will keep for years, the others can be drunk straight
from the shop. *Adnams* and *La Vigneronne* have some older vintage

Tokay. Some dry whites – Tokay Furmint and Tokay Szamorodni – are also made, but are rather flabby and dull.

Vilány Red-wine-growing district south of Lake Balaton. Some wines made with Pinot Noir (here called Kisburgundi – see above) can be good.

Best buys from Hungary

WHITE WINES

Tokay 5 Puttonyos (*Adnams; Berry Bros & Rudd; Lay & Wheeler; Oddbins; Tanners Wines; Ubiquitous Chip; La Vigneronne; Willoughbys; Wines of Westhorpe*)
Somló Furmint (*Peter Dominic*)

RED WINES

Vilány Kisburgundi (*Peter Dominic; Wines of Westhorpe*)
Hungarian Merlot (*Oddbins; Wines of Westhorpe*)
Szekszárd Nemes Kadarka (*Peter Dominic*)

Specialist stockists

Adnams; Wines of Westhorpe

India

New wine country

Despite its vast production of table grapes, and the questionable delights of Golconda Ruby (made in Hyderabad from some of those black table grapes), only one Indian wine reaches the UK – and it's surprisingly good.

But it has French technology behind it. Omar Khayyam sparkling wine is the result of a venture by Indian entrepreneur Shyam Chougule with expertise imported from Champagne.

The wine, a more than adequate brut sparkling wine, made using Champagne technology, is not cheap, but it's definitely a wine to start a conversation.

Adnams; Nobody Inn; Selfridges; Tanners Wines; Vinceremos; Wine Save Cash and Carry, 7/8 Whitchurch Lane, Edgware

Israel

At last something vinous has emerged from Israel that's more than pious words and over-oxidised baked wines. While the bulk of Israeli wine production – much of it from the huge Carmel winery – continues to be the unhappy yardstick by which most Israeli production is measured, one winery, just starting out, has proved that the country can produce decent wine – if the vineyard site is right and care is taken in production.

That winery is on the Golan Heights, in a 400-acre vineyard growing on the site of a major battleground of the Yom Kippur war of 1973 – and from which 250 tank carcases had to be removed before planting could take place. They produce wines under the Yarden and Gamla brand names: those available in this country include the white Yarden Mount Hermon White, cold-fermented and fruity in the modern tradition; Gamla White, a medium dry wine, also in a modern and fruity style; and varietal wines (by far the most interesting) – Gamla Cabernet Sauvignon and Yarden Sauvignon Blanc. A rosé is also now being made.

While these wines are not cheap, at least they're good, and orthodox Jews will be pleased to learn that they're Kosher.

For the rest, though, the prices are high and the quality uninteresting.

Best buys from Israel
Yarden Sauvignon Blanc 1986 (*Selfridges*)
Gamla Cabernet Sauvignon 1985 (*Grape Ideas; Nobody Inn; Selfridges*)

Specialist stockists
Amazing Grapes; Grape Ideas Wine Warehouse; Selfridges; Tesco

Italy

All directions at once

It must have been a fascinating scene at the annual 1988 Vinitaly fair in Verona: a group of British wine importers were showing the Italians what they were up against on the British market. They were letting them taste Australian wines, Spanish wines, plenty of French wines, even some Liebfraumilch. It was a well-chosen range.

What the Italians made of it is difficult to gauge. There was certainly nothing to show that Italy is unable to compete strongly in the British market – her wines are every bit as good as those of any other country. But . . . with Italy there are always buts.

There is the but of the continuing stream of cheap plonk that still pours in from Italy bearing the quality authentication of a Denominazione di Origine Controllata (DOC). There is the but that an awful lot of that wine goes to Italian restaurants, most of which couldn't care less about the quality of the wine they sell, only how much it costs. There is the but that all too many wine drinkers first taste Italian wine in those restaurants. There is the but that any awareness of Italian quality comes not from the national promotional agency (as it does with the French or Spanish) but from a handful of dedicated (some would say determined and probably a bit crazy) importers of the best that Italy can produce.

And, of course, there is the big but, Italian wine itself. Like the people, Italian wine consists of a range of complete individualists all trying to go in different directions at once, and all much more loyal to their region, their village even, than to any concept of Italy. It's great fun, it makes for a huge diversity of styles and character, but it's so, so confusing to most wine drinkers.

The tendency to move off in different directions seems to be getting more and more prevalent. When the DOC regulations were introduced in 1973, it was thought that all the best wines from a particular area would bear that area's DOC – after all, that is what happens in France with AC areas.

Breaking the rules

But this was Italy. No sooner had the DOCs been established than it was realised that many of them simply enshrined old traditions and bad practices, and that they just weren't flexible enough for innovation. So instead of changing the rules, the best producers went off and did their own thing. They made the wines they wanted to make, and if they didn't fit the DOC rules, they simply called them 'vini da tavola', charged high prices and created what every Italian wine enthusiast now calls the 'super vini da tavola'.

Experimentation was all. Of all the wine-producing countries in Europe, Italy is the busiest at experimentation. There is almost the air of 'we'll try anything once' in some of the wines that are being made. But there are also some superb, top-quality wines that richly deserve the high prices charged for them.

Experimentation has been going on in a number of areas. For a start, Italy was late coming to the 'international' grape varieties like Chardonnay, Cabernet Sauvignon, Merlot, Rhine Riesling. Fair enough: after all, she has a rich range of her own grape varieties. But – taking a long-term historical view – it is a fair bet that most of the French varieties came from Italy in the first place at the time of the Romans, so maybe it is simply a case of the prodigals returning home. Certainly Italy is as much justified in working with these grape varieties as any New World country. And some of the wines she is making with them are world-class, although others (especially the whites) suffer from the Italian tendency to make wines for instant drinking rather than ageing, and to produce too many grapes from each vine.

Status symbols and enthusiasms

Another area of experimentation is with barrels. The small French oak barrels, called 'barriques', which are the standard barrels in Bordeaux, are now to be found everywhere in Italy. They have become a status symbol – 'my barrels are newer than yours, and I have more of them' – and every wine producer who aims higher than basic plonk has seen

Italy – White Wines

Chardonnay
Gewürztraminer
Pinot Bianco
Sylvaner
Goldmuskateller
Rhine Riesling
Müller-Thurgau

Pinot-based
sparkling wines
Lugana

Asti Spumante
Moscato d'Asti
Gavi
Arneis

Picolit
Pinot Grigio
Tocai di Lison
Tocai del Piave

VAL
D'AOSTA

SOUTH TYROL
(ALTO
ADIGE/
TRENTINO)

FRIULI-
VENEZIA-
GIULIA

LOMBARDY

PIEDMONT   Po

VENETO

Bianco di Custoza
Soave
Chardonnay
Prosecco

EMILIA-
ROMAGNA

LIGURIA

Albana di Romagna

Arno

Galestro
Trebbiano
Vernaccia di San Gimignano
Chardonnay

TUSCANY

Verdicchio

MARCHES

Orvieto

UMBRIA

Tiber

LATIUM

ABRUZZI

Est! Est!! Est!!!
Frascati

MOLISE

CAMPANIA

Fiano di Avellino
Greco di Tufo
Lacryma Christi

APULIA

BASILICATA

SARDINIA

CALABRIA

SICILY

Bianco di Alcamo
Moscato di Pantelleria

0		100	200 km

0	50	100 miles

Try Which? Wine Monthly FREE for 3 months, and see for yourself how it gives you the facts.

The publishers of Which? Wine Guide 1989 present a highly informative companion newsletter, designed to give you the most up-to-date advice on buying wine – including news of special bargains, prices and availability – the results of blind tastings and the latest news and views from the wine world.

Accept this remarkable offer and you'll receive the next 3 issues ABSOLUTELY FREE and WITHOUT COMMITMENT. **See overleaf for further details.**

▲ DETACH ALONG PERFORATION ▲

HOW TO CLAIM YOUR **FREE** ISSUES

To receive Which? Wine Monthly FREE for 3 months, just complete and return the direct debiting mandate on the coupon below. We will send you the next three issues of Which? Wine Monthly as they appear. If you do not wish to continue receiving Which? Wine Monthly, you can cancel your subscription by writing to us – and your direct debiting mandate by writing to your bank – before payment is due on 1st March 1989. You can keep everything you have received, and it won't have cost you a penny.

If you want to go on receiving Which? Wine Monthly, you don't need to do anything more. Your subscription will bring you Which? Wine Monthly each month for £4.75 a quarter, until you cancel your mandate or we advise you of a change in the price of your subscription. If there should be any change in the price of your subscription at any time we would advise you at least six weeks in advance. This gives you time to tell us if you do not wish to continue your subscription, and to cancel your direct debiting mandate. You are, of course, free to do this at anytime. To accept this offer, just complete the coupon and post it – you don't even need a stamp. So why not post it off now?

Consumers' Association,
Castlemead, Gascoyne Way,
Hertford SG14 1LH.

WHICH? WINE MONTHLY

I would like to accept this free offer. Please send me the next 3 months' issues of Which? Wine Monthly as they appear. I understand that I am under no obligation – if I do not wish to continue with Which? Wine Monthly after the free trial, I can cancel my order before payment is due on 1st March 1989. But if I decide to continue, I need do nothing – my subscription will bring me Which? Wine Monthly each month for the current price of £4.75 a quarter, payable by Direct Debit.

FREE TRIAL ACCEPTANCE

Direct Debiting Mandate.

I/We authorise you until further notice in writing to charge to my/our account with you on or immediately after 1st March 1989 and quarterly thereafter unspecified amounts which may be debited thereto at the instance of Consumers' Association by Direct Debit.

Date of first payment, on or within the calendar month from 1st March 1989.   WX89A

Signed	Date
Bank Account in the name of	Bank Account Number (if known)
Name and address of your bank in BLOCK LETTERS PLEASE	Your name and address in BLOCK LETTERS PLEASE
TO	Mr/Mrs/Miss

Banks may decline to accept instructions to charge direct debits to certain types of account other than current accounts.

Italy – Red Wines

Barbaresco
Barbera
Barolo
Carema
Dolcetto
Grignolino
Nebbiolo
Spanna

Sorni
Casteller
Lago di Caldaro
Lagrein
Santa Maddalena
Teroldego

Franciacorta
Oltrepò Pavese
Valtellina

Cabernet/Merlot di Friuli
Cabernet/Merlot di Pramaggiore

VAL
D'AOSTA

SOUTH TYROL
(ALTO
ADIGE/
TRENTINO)

FRIULI-
VENEZIA-
GIULIA

PIEDMONT

Po

LOMBARDY

VENETO

Breganze
Bardolino
Raboso
Valpolicella/Recioto di Valpolicella

EMILIA–
ROMAGNA

LIGURIA

Arno

Lambrusco
Gutturnio dei Colli Piancentini
Sangiovese di Romagna

TUSCANY

Rosso Cònero

Brunello di Montalcino
Carmignano
Chianti
Rosso di Montalcino
Vino Nobile di Montepulciano

MARCHES

UMBRIA

Colli del Trasimeno
Torgiano

Tiber

LATIUM

Montepulciano d'Abruzzo

ABRUZZI

MOLISE

Castel del Monte
Salice Salentino

CAMPANIA

SARDINIA

Cannonau

Taurasi

APULIA

BASILICATA

Aglianico del Vulture

CALABRIA

Cirò

SICILY

0   100   200 km

0   50   100 miles

the need to make at least an experimental wine in new wood 'barrica'.

Italians go by enthusiasms. The first flush of enthusiasm for the small barricas may be about to wear off, although it won't go away: too much has been learnt from their use. But the return of the typical Italian large barrels, the 'botti', is a sign that equilibrium is being restored. The same is true of the international grape varieties: they are just as likely now to be used in blends with Italian varieties as used individually.

Which brings us back to the super vini da tavola. Everybody who was somebody used to have to make such a wine, even if only to cock a snook at the DOC bureaucrats. But a sign of the times comes when the progenitor of all the super vini da tavola, Antinori of Tuscany, the creators of Tignanello, launch their latest prize wine as a proper Chianti Classico (for more details see under the Tuscan section). Maybe the old ways have something in them after all.

White wine revolution

While the return to tradition mainly concerns red wines, it is in white wines that a modern approach remains essential. There has been a terrific change in the quality of Italian white wine over the past five years. Gone are the days of oxidised wines which were badly made, badly bottled and badly stored, and which probably came in two-litre screw-top bottles.

What we have today is a range of clean, well-made, fruity white wines. There are, as we have seen, some very fine whites, some made with Chardonnay and aged in small barrels in a New World style. But even more encouraging is the return of traditional white grape varieties being treated with care in modern conditions: Malvasia in Orvieto and Frascati is one example, Arneis in Piedmont is another, Grechetto in Tuscany and Umbria a third.

There has been the consequent dramatic improvement in some rather too familiar names: Soave, Frascati, Verdicchio, Orvieto. While too many bad examples are still around, the good producers (including the ones we mention here) are getting the best of both worlds in white winemaking: clean-tasting wines made in stainless steel, but also wines that retain local character, unlike so many of the well-made, cheap but bland whites that reach our shops from some other countries. At the upper end, there are now single vineyard white wines, just as there are single vineyard reds, showing that a patch of land is always of vital importance in winemaking.

Too much juice

Of course, with all this constant change and improvement in the quality of Italian wines, there are also minuses. The major one is a familiar theme in Germany: over-cropping. The vines are being expected to produce too many grapes, with a consequent thinning of the flavour of each grape and a watery end-product. The north-east of Italy (the Veneto, Friuli and Trentino/Alto Adige) is the worst offender, churning out many thin, weedy wines without much tannin or flavour.

This happened because while Italy was developing the technology to a high degree, the vineyards were being neglected. It's only recently that the picturesque system of promiscuous cultivation – growing a second crop underneath vines trained high on pergolas – began to disappear from Italian vineyards. Now most serious vineyards are single crop. And, gradually, the realisation that yields must be restricted is percolating around Italy: the top producers are already cutting back on yields; others will surely follow.

While yields are being cut back, so the grape varieties are being improved. One way is to cut down on the high-yielding neutral varieties, like the white Trebbiano, which only rarely goes higher than dull in quality (it's the grape variety which produces the base wine for Cognac in France, where a neutral wine is just what's needed). They're being replaced by the traditional, low-yielding varieties which have much more character and quality.

The other way grape varieties are being improved is by clonal selection. For instance, in the 1970s many of the new Sangiovese vines planted in Tuscany to make Chianti were of the prolific, low-quality Sangiovese di Romagna grape. Now those vines are being replaced by the superior local clone, the Sangiovese Grosso or Sangioveto, making smaller quantities of higher-quality wine. Clonal selection is now spreading to other Italian grape varieties.

A resolution for 1989

What these trends, overall, mean is that Italian wine producers reckon that the best way they can survive in their country, where wine consumption generally is falling, but where demand for better wines is on the increase, is to aim higher, to raise their quality, and generally to make less, but better, wine.

Good news for us, certainly. Our resolution for 1989 should be to be prepared to experiment with unknown Italian wines. And to be prepared to pay a little more for the familiar names. That way we will get a taste of traditional wines in a modern context, and some insight into the huge variety of tastes that Italy has to offer.

The Italian wine label

There are three quality designations in Italy:

Vino da tavola This, as we have already seen, can refer to the rock-bottom local wines or to the finest designer wines from a top producer which do not conform to the DOC or DOCG regulations.

Denominazione di Origine Controllata (DOC) This indicates that the wine comes from a specified zone and has been made in accordance with the rules of that zone. It is like the French AC in that it is a guarantee of origin only, not of quality.

The name of the DOC may appear in a number of ways: as a geographical name for a region (Frascati); as the name of a village (Barolo); or it may appear as a grape variety attached to a geographical name (Barbera d'Asti – wines made from the Barbera grape in the town of Asti). It may appear as a combination of a geographical name and a fantasy name (Oltrepò Pavese Buttafuoco – Oltrepò Pavese the geographical name, Buttafuoco the fantasy name). Occasionally, the name may be sheer fantasy (Lacryma Christi).

Denominazione di Origine Controllata e Garantita, DOCG This is the top Italian controlled quality level. The 'garantita' part of the title means that the wine has been tested by government-appointed officials and conforms to the rules they have set out. Until 1988, it applied to only five areas: Barolo, Barbaresco, Brunello di Montalcino, Vino Nobile di Montepulciano and Chianti.

In these areas, the scheme has worked, more or less, and the quality and selection of wine being given the DOCG has raised the quality of wines. Even in the enormous area of Chianti, the quality levels have risen.

But, typically Italian, the whole system has been demeaned by the introduction of a DOCG zone in an area of pretty average wine-making. Albana di Romagna has received a DOCG – and there are few duller white wines than these. Others are threatened. Politics, of course, are at the bottom of it, with wine quality a minor consideration.

Apart from that aberration, the DOCG does mean something, and wines going out under the DOCG seal (normally placed over the cork) do guarantee that a reasonably high standard has been reached.

Other terms on the label

Abboccato Medium sweet.
Amabile A little sweeter than Abboccato.
Amaro Bitter.
Annata Year or vintage.
Azienda agricola, azienda vitivinicola Farm or wine estate.
Bianco White wine.
Bottigilia Bottle.
Cantina Winery.
Cantina sociale Co-operative.
Casa vinicola A wine house, usually one which buys in grapes to make wine.
Chiaretto Rosé.
Classico The heartland of a particular region, not necessarily – but generally – where the best wines of a particular type come from.

Consorzio A voluntary grouping of producers to control standards of production.
Dolce Sweet.
Etichetta Label.
Fattoria Central Italian term for farm or estate.
Fermentazione Fermentation.
Frizzante Lightly sparkling.
Imbottigiato da Bottled by.
Invecchiato Aged.
Metodo Champenois/metodo classico The Champagne method.
Passito Strong, generally sweet wines made from semi-dried grapes.
Produttore Producer.
Riserva Applied to DOC or DOCG wines that have undergone specific ageing, generally in barrel. Riserva Speciale means even longer ageing.
Rosato Rosé wine.
Rosso Red wine.
Secco Dry.
Spumante Sparkling wine, usually, but not always, sweet.
Superiore A DOC wine that meets higher standards (alcohol, ageing, area of production) than the norm.
Tenuta Another word for farm or estate.
Vecchio Old.
Vendemmia The year of the harvest.
Vigna, vigneto Vineyard.
Vino novello New wine (as in Beaujolais Nouveau).

Vintage chart for Italian wines

	Barolo/ Barbaresco	Amarone/Recioto della Valpolicella	Chianti Classico Riserva (plus Riservas of Rufina & other sub-zones)	Brunello di Montalcino (plus Vino Nobile)
1987	Excellent	Good	Good	Very good
1986	Very good	Excellent	Excellent	Very good
1985	Excellent	Excellent	Excellent	Excellent
1984	Fair to good	Very good	Poor	Fair
1983	Very good	Excellent	Very good	Fair to good
1982	Excellent	Poor	Excellent	Excellent
1981	Mediocre	Fair	Fair to good	Fair to good
1980	Good	Good	Fair	Good
1979	Very good	Very good	Very good	Excellent
1978	Excellent	Excellent	Good	Good

PIEDMONT

Family rows

There's a good, old-fashioned row going on in Piedmont. It's between the traditionalists and the modernists (most rows are), and it has even led one family to build a wall in the middle of their vineyard to divide modernist son from traditionalist father. Another traditionalist father left his vineyards to his daughter rather than to his modernist son. It's not just a question of generations, though. Some of the younger generation are just as traditionalist as their parents.

What they are rowing about is fruit and how much fruit a Nebbiolo wine should have. The Nebbiolo is the grape used to make Barolo and Barbaresco – often seen as Italy's greatest red wines – and a number of lesser wines. It is the most important grape in Piedmont (although the lesser quality Barbera is more widely planted). Traditionally it has made a dark, tannic, impenetrably dry red wine that some (the modernists) would say spends too much time on the thick, tannin-filled skins during fermentation, and too much time in wood afterwards.

The modernists are cutting down the time on skins and keeping barrel-ageing to a minimum (or alternatively, heresy of heresies, using French oak barriques instead of good old Slovenian oak botti). They are making fresher, more immediately approachable wines that taste of fruit. Traditionalists would argue that what they gain on fruit they lose on the truffles and violets flavours of old Nebbiolo. For us, it makes an interesting set of contrasts; for those in Piedmont it is the most serious matter in the world.

Other wines in Piedmont are less serious – and less expensive – than Barolo and Barbaresco. The other Nebbiolo wines like Ghemme, Gattinara or Nebbiolo d'Alba are less expensive and still give some hint of what this great grape variety can achieve.

The most enjoyable Piedmontese red wine is based on the Dolcetto grape, which produces a really jammy, fruity wine akin to Beaujolais. Like Beaujolais, it's lovely drunk chilled and young.

The workhorse red grape is Barbera, whose name is generally associated with a town – as in Barbera d'Alba or Barbera d'Asti (the same is true of the Nebbiolo and Dolcetto grapes). It makes a heavy, rich, fruited wine with a strong edge of acidity, which tends to need some ageing. Another grape to look out for is Freisa.

Whites – getting better known

The Piedmontese whites have tended to be overshadowed by the reds. But everyone must be familiar with the most famous whites, Asti Spumante and its associate Moscato d'Asti. At their best – and very freshest – they are absolutely delicious and one of the most refreshing drinks imaginable on a warm day.

Other whites are less exciting, but are now benefiting from the white wine revolution to reveal some exciting flavours. They are pricy, though, probably because they are drunk on the Italian Riviera and are anyway produced in small quantities. Best known are Cortese di Gavi and Gavi dei Gavi which are heavily overpriced. Less common is Erbaluce di Caluso, while the unusual bone dry Arneis is a case of a grape variety returning almost from the grave, since its plantations almost disappeared but are now being revived.

Who's who in Piedmont

(For details of Asti Spumante and Moscato Spumante producers not also making still wines, see the sparkling wine section on page 572.)

Altare Make non-DOC wines in the Barolo region, using small French barriques for ageing. Wines: Nebbiolo Vigna Arborina, Barbera Vigna Larigi.
For stockist information, contact R Trestini Ltd (114a Vallance Road, London E1)

Ascheri Rich, powerful Barbaresco which still manages to preserve the fruit.
Winecellars; Wines from Paris

Duca d'Asti Wide-ranging company with a large portfolio of wines. Wines: Barbaresco, Barbera d'Asti, Barbera del Monferrato, Cortese di Gavi, Dolcetto d'Ovada, Nebbiolo d'Alba. Granduca Brut sparkling.
Berry Bros & Rudd; Eaton Elliot Winebrokers; Oddbins; Wine Society

Giacomo Borgogno e Figli Renowned producers of Barolo, specialising in old vintages. Wines: Barbera d'Alba, Barolo, Dolcetto d'Alba.
A & A Wines; David Alexander; Averys; Eldridge Pope; Lay & Wheeler; Millevini; Nobody Inn; Tanners Wines; Valvona & Crolla; Wine Growers Association

La Brenta d'Oro Old-style production of Barbarescos which need 20 years before they can be drunk. Wine: Barbaresco Riserva.
A & A Wines; Peter Green; Wine Growers Association

Agostino Brugo Good examples of the Nebbiolo in their Ghemme and Gattinara wines. Wines: Ghemme, Gattinara, Spanna.
David Alexander; Cantina Augusto; Eldridge Pope; Lay & Wheeler; Millevini; Oddbins; Seckford Wines; Valvona & Crolla; Wine Growers Association; Wine Society

Castello di Neive Produce small amounts of fine Barbaresco, also very good white wines. Wines: Barbaresco, Barbera d'Alba, Dolcetto d'Alba, Moscato d'Asti, Arneis.
Curzon Wine Company; Alex Findlater; Millevini; Ostlers; Valvona & Crolla; La Vigneronne; Winecellars; Wines from Paris

Fratelli Cavallotto Own the renowned Bricco Boschis vineyard in Barolo. Wines: Barbera d'Alba, Barolo, Dolcetto d'Alba, Favorita, Grignolino, Nebbiolo.
Market Vintners; Ostlers; Valvona & Crolla; Winecellars; Wines from Paris

Ceretto A producer of ripe, fruity, plummy Barolos in a fresher, less traditional style. Top quality, especially for single vineyard (called bricco) wines. Wines: Barbaresco, Barbera d'Alba, Barolo, Dolcetto d'Alba, Nebbiolo d'Alba. Try Barolo Bricco Roche or Barbaresco Asiy.
Berry Bros & Rudd

Pio Cesare Traditional producer making very fine wines. Wines: Barbaresco, Barbera d'Alba, Barolo, Dolcetto d'Alba, Nebbiolo d'Alba, Grignolino, Gavi, Cortese di Gavi.
D Byrne & Co; Cantina Augusto; Alex Findlater; La Reserva Wines; Ubiquitous Chip; Valvona & Crolla; Willoughbys

Aldo Conterno Makes Monforte d'Alba and Barolo Bussia Soprana and Colonello di Bricco Bussia. Look out especially for his Dolcetto. Wines: Barbera d'Alba, Barolo, Dolcetto d'Alba.
Adnams; H Allen Smith; Berkmann Wine Cellars/Le Nez Rouge; Christopher Piper Wines; Tanners Wines; Winecellars

Giacomo Conterno Makes a single vineyard Barolo Monfortino. Very traditional, heavy wines. Wines: Barbera d'Alba, Barolo, Dolcetto d'Alba.
Bibendum; Millevini; Ostlers; Winecellars

Guiseppe Contratto Specialises in spumante (sparkling wines). Wines: Asti Spumante, Contratto Brut, Riserva Bacco d'Oro, Gavi.
H Allen Smith; David Baillie Vintners; D Byrne & Co; Alex Findlater; Stapylton Fletcher; Wine Society

Carlo Deltetto Makes some attractive white wines. Wines: Favorita, Gavi, Arneis.
Winecellars; Wines from Paris

Luigi Ferrando e Figli Producers of pricy Carema Black Label, of marvellous quality.
D Byrne & Co; Curzon Wine Company; Millevini; Ostlers; Valvona & Crolla; Winecellars

Fontanafredda An estate founded by the son of King Victor Emmanuel II. Make fine spumante as well as accessible Barolo. Some of their single vineyard Barolos are excellent, if pricy. Wines: Asti Spumante, Barbaresco, Barbera d'Alba, Barolo, Dolcetto d'Alba, Brut Spumante Contessa Rosa.
H Allen Smith; D Byrne & Co; Majestic; Upper Crust; Valvona & Crolla; La Vigneronne; Wizard Wine Warehouse

Franco-Fiorina Believers in stainless steel rather than oaks who buy in grapes. Wines: Barbaresco, Barbera d'Alba, Barolo, Dolcetto d'Alba, Nebbiolo d'Alba.
Alivini (120 Vallance Road, London E1 – case only); Luigi Delicatessen (349 Fulham Road, London SW10)

Gaja The guru of Piedmont who makes the most expensive and some of the finest Barbarescos. Wines: Barbaresco, Barbera d'Alba, Dolcetto d'Alba, Nebbiolo d'Alba, Vinot, Chardonnay, Cabernet Sauvignon.
Adnams; D Byrne & Co; Valvona & Crolla; La Vigneronne; Willoughbys; Windrush Wines

Bruno Giacosa Very fine aged reds, including single vineyard wines. Wines: Barbaresco, Barbera d'Alba, Barolo, Dolcetto d'Alba, Grignolino d'Alba, Nebbiolo d'Alba, Arneis, Moscato d'Asti.
Adnams; Winecellars

Marchese di Barolo A long-established firm, recently sold by its founding family. Wines: Asti Spumante, Barbaresco, Barbera d'Alba, Barolo, Cortese di Gavi, Dolcetto d'Alba, Freisa d'Alba, Nebbiolo d'Alba.
Demijohn Wines; Peter Green

Luigi Nervi e Italo Make reasonably quick-maturing Gattinara.
David Baillie Vintners; Lay & Wheeler

Produttori del Barbaresco A small co-operative specialising in top-quality single vineyard Barbaresco. Wines: Barbaresco, Nebbiolo.
Tesco; Victoria Wine Company

Alfredo Prunotto Traditional style of wine and single vineyard Barolo. Wines: Barbaresco, Barbera d'Alba, Barolo, Dolcetto d'Alba, Nebbiolo d'Alba.
Hicks & Don; Wine Society

Renato Ratti Rich but also elegant wines. Minimum ageing in cask ensures good fruit. Wines: Barolo Marcenasco, Dolcetto.
Adnams; Tanners Wines; Wine Society

Terre di Barolo A large co-operative which makes a lighter style of wine. Wines: Barbera d'Alba, Barolo, Dolcetto d'Alba, Dolcetto di Diano d'Alba, Nebbiolo d'Alba.
D Byrne & Co; Davisons; Marks & Spencer; Ubiquitous Chip; Victoria Wine Company

Best buys from Piedmont

Spanna del Piemonte 1984, Agostino Brugo (*Seckford Wines; Welbeck Wines; Wine Growers Association*)
Barbera d'Asti 1985, Ronco (*The Market/Winecellars*)
Barolo 1981, Ferruccio Nicolello (*Lay & Wheeler*)
Gavi Fontanafredda 1987 (*Chiswick Wine Cellars*)

LOMBARDY

Until recently, Lombardy was a neglected wine area as far as most of our wine merchants are concerned. Luckily, some more enterprising souls have gone to the Oltrepò Pavese (south of the River Po) to find some excellent red wines made of the local Bonarda or the Piedmontese Barbera. Other red wines of renown include Franciacorta, (made from Cabernet Franc, Merlot, Barbera and Nebbiolo) and wines from Valtellina which rejoice in names like Grumello, Inferno and Sassella.

In the whites, there is a very fine sparkling wine from Ca' del Bosco, and spumantes based on Pinot Nero and Pinot Grigio from Oltrepò Pavese. From around Lake Garda in the north of the region, the white Lugana is similar in style to – and often better than – Soave, while an attractive pink Chiaretto comes from Riviera del Garda.

Who's who in Lombardy

Ca' del Bosco Producer of very fine Chardonnay-based spumante. Also Franciacorta. Wines: Franciacorta Pinot, Franciacorta Rosso, Rosa Ca' del Bosco sparkling.
D Byrne & Co; Ostlers; Valvona & Crolla

Ca' del Frati Top-class white Lugana producer.
Winecellars

Enologica Valtellinese Very fine Valtellina wines. Wines: Grumello, Sassella, Inferno, Sforzato.
Winecellars; Wine Growers Association

Fugazza, Castello di Luzzano The Fugazza sisters make excellent Oltrepò Pavese wines on their organically-run vineyard. Part of the vineyard is just inside Emilia-Romagna and so makes Gutturnio.

Wines: Oltrepò Pavese Bonarda, Oltrepò Pavese Barbera, Colli
Piacentini (Emilia-Romagna).
*Millevini; Oddbins; Valvona & Crolla; Wine Growers Association; Wines from
Paris*

Longhi-de Carli A Franciacorta producer using Cabernet, Merlot,
Nebbiolo and Barbera. Wines: Franciacorta.
Millevini; Wine Growers Association

Nino Nera Makes wine in Valtellina. Wines: Sassella, Inferno,
Grumello.
D Byrne & Co; Ostlers

Santi Soave producer who also makes Lugana.
*D Byrne & Co; Tanners Wines; Upper Crust; Valvona & Crolla; Wizard Wine
Warehouses*

Zenato Producer of Lugana and Riviera del Garda as well as Soave.
H Allen Smith; Tanners Wines; Winecellars; Wine Growers Association

Best buys from Lombardy

For sparkling wine best buys from Lombardy, see page 573.
Bonarda Oltrepò Pavese 1985, Fugazza (*Valvona & Crolla; Winecellars*)
Franciacorta Rosso 1987, Contessa Camilla Martinoni (*Alastair's
Grapevine*)
Lugana Ca' dei Frati 1986 (*The Market/Winecellars*)

TRENTINO

Coming out of the shadow

In the past few years, this region has seemed to be in the shadow of the
more go-ahead Alto Adige (Südtirol). But it makes an interesting range
of wines in its own right, with standards as high as those of its
neighbour just up the Adige Valley. Judging by the efforts its local
wine trade is making, we may see more of its wines in our shops quite
soon.

Trentino is the northern outpost of Italy. Travellers coming south
over the Brenner Pass go through the essentially German Südtirol
before bursting through a narrow gorge and into the wider plain of the
Trentino, where Italy takes over.

While most wines in the Trentino are named after grape varieties,
there are a number of DOC zones. There is the region-wide Trentino
DOC, which produces red, white and rosé wines. Then there are a
number of smaller DOC zones: Sorni (for whites), Teroldego Rotaliano
(red and rosé), Valdadige (red, white and rosé) and Casteller (red).

The main grape varieties found in the Trentino include:

467

Whites: Chardonnay, Pinot Bianco, Pinot Grigio, Müller-Thurgau, Riesling Renano, Riesling Italico, Moscato Gaillo, and the local grape, Nosiola.

Reds and rosés: Lagrein, Pinot Nero, Merlot, Cabernet Franc, Cabernet Sauvignon, Schiava, and the local specialities, Teroldego and Marzemino.

Trentino is also famed for its sparkling wines, most made by the Champagne method, and some of world-class quality. For more details of these, see under sparkling wines (page 573).

Who's who in Trentino

Càvit The main Trentino co-operative, making 70 to 77 million litres of wine a year. Quality tends to vary widely; the Chardonnay and Teroldego Rotaliano wines are best. Wines: Casteller, Teroldego Rotaliano, Vicariati (a premium red made from Cabernet Franc and Merlot), Valdadige, Chardonnay, Pinot Grigio.
Victoria Wine Company; Wine Society

Fedrigotti A 75-acre family-owned vineyard south of Trentino. Their top wines are both vini da tavola. Wines: Cabernet and Merlot Trentino; Foianeghe Bianco and Rosso Vini da Tavola.
Millevini; Valvona & Crolla

Gaierhof A small estate at the northern end of the region. Wines: Riesling Italico, Pinot Bianco, Pinot Grigio, Müller-Thurgau, Teroldego Rotaliano, Caldero, Schiava.
Waitrose

Pojer & Sandri Top producer in Trentino specialising in white wines. Wines: Chardonnay, Müller-Thurgau.
Valvona & Crolla; Winecellars

Santa Margarita Large producer who also makes wine in other regions. Good, commercial standards. Wines: Valdadige Bianco and Rosso.
Valvona & Crolla

Simoncelli Producer of a good red Marzemino as well as a number of other Trentino wines.
Richard Harvey Wines

Roberto Zeni Trento wine maker specialising in Teroldego Rotaliano. Wines: Chardonnay, Teroldego Rotaliano.
Millevini; Tanners Wines; Valvona & Crolla; Wine Growers Association

Best buys from Trentino
Vinatteri Bianco (*Bibendum*)
Chardonnay Trentino, Roberto Zeni (*Wine Growers Association*)

Marzemino Trentino, Armando Simoncelli (*Richard Harvey Wines*)
Teroldego Rotaliano, Gaierhof 1986 (*Waitrose*)

ALTO ADIGE

More reds than whites

Despite what we see in our shops, nearly 70 per cent of the produce of this region is red wine. While we have come to know the Alto Adige (or Südtirol as many of the locals call it) for its zesty, fresh whites, the region still sends much of its red wine in tankers to Austria and Switzerland.

This is a relic of former days when the Südtirol was the southernmost part of the Austro-Hungarian Empire, and the one most suited to red wine production. But now the top producers of the region have realised that the future lies in white wines. They have the right climate: cold winters, hot summers (but always with cool nights), and many of the vineyards are planted high up in the spectacular mountains of the region – some as much as 3,000 feet up.

For white wine production, a mix of German, Italian and French varieties are used. The most famous may have become the Chardonnays, but the Traminer (Gewürztraminer) has its home in the region (there is a village called Tramin to this day). Other white grape varieties include the Pinot Bianco, Pinot Grigio, Goldmuskateller, Müller-Thurgau (highly successful here), Riesling Renano, Sauvignon Blanc and Sylvaner.

The reds don't travel as well as the whites – except to those familiar with the light, fruity wines of St Magdalener made from the local Vernatsch (Schiava) grape, or the richer Lagrein. There are international varieties too: Merlot and Pinot Nero, Cabernet Sauvignon and Cabernet Franc.

Increasingly, producers are ageing some of their wines in small new barrels – white Chardonnay as well as red Cabernets and Pinot Nero – and producing some top-class wines of an international model and standard.

Some concern has been expressed about the yields from some vineyards – which are extraordinarily high by Italian standards, and nearer to German levels. It has been suggested that the high yields decrease the concentration and fruit flavours of the wines. But better producers are cutting down on the yields and are producing piercingly fragrant white wines, still at very good prices.

Although Alto Adige wines are all labelled varietally, the labels can be confusing because they are mainly in German rather than Italian. They may describe themselves as Qualitätswein rather than DOC. Only the small print, Produce of Italy, will show they are not from Austria or Germany.

Who's who in the Alto Adige (Südtirol)

Arunda Make brut spumante, one of the finest Italian sparklers, high up in the Alps of the Alto Adige. Wines: Arunda Brut.
H Allen Smith

Josef Brigl Very traditional firm making good whites. Wines: Weissburgunder (Pinot Bianco), Goldmuskateller (dessert wine).
Winchester Wine Company

Eisacktaler Kellereigenossenschaft (Co-operative of the Isarco Valley) Make wines from vineyards nearest the Austrian border. Wines: Sylvaner, Gewürztraminer, Grüner Veltliner.
Winchester Wine Company

J Hofstätter Some of his wide range of wines – especially reds – age remarkably well. Wines: Pinot Grigio, Rhine Riesling, Gewürztraminer, Schiava, Cabernet Sauvignon.
Wine Society

Kettmeir Make the full range of varietal Alto Adige wines. Now part of the Santa Margherita company (see below).
Valvona & Crolla

Alois Lageder Family-owned company making a wide variety of wines in the Alto Adige. One of the top two producers of the region. Wines: Chardonnay, Moscato (sweet), Pinot Grigio, Sauvignon, Gewürztraminer (from the village of Tramin, claimed to be the home of this grape), Schiava, Cabernet Franc.
Berry Bros & Rudd; Eldridge Pope; Hedley Wright; Lockes; Market Vintners; Nobody Inn; Oddbins; Christopher Piper Wines; Winecellars; Wines from Paris

Santa Margherita Firm based in the Veneto which has considerable interests in the Alto Adige, including the Kettmeir company (see above). Make a top-quality white vino da tavola called Luna dei Feldi.
La Reserva Wines; Tanners Wines; Valvona & Crolla

Schloss Schwanburg Based in one of the Alto Adige's many old castles, making good quality wines. Wines: full range of varietals.
Alston Wines

J Tiefenbrunner One of the top two Alto Adige producers, Tiefenbrunner is the proud owner of the highest vineyard in Europe, called Feldmarschal, planted with Müller-Thurgau. Look for his barrique-aged wines. Wines: makes every varietal in Alto Adige, all of very high quality.
Adnams; H Allen Smith; Alston Wines; David Baillie Vintners; D Byrne &

Co; Curzon Wine Company; Majestic; Market Vintners; Millevini;
Sainsbury's; Seckford Wines; Tanners Wines; Tesco; Valvona & Crolla;
Willoughbys; Winecellars

Viticoltori Alto Adige The main co-operative of the Alto Adige, with
very high standards. There are associated co-operatives at St Michael
in Eppan and Terlan. Wines: Sauvignon, Gewürztraminer, Rhine
Riesling, Chardonnay, Pinot Bianco, Lagrein Dunkel, Cabernet Franc,
Schiava.
A & A Wines; Lay & Wheeler; Seckford Wines; Tanners Wines; Ubiquitous
Chip; Valvona & Crolla; Wine Growers Association

Best buys from Alto Adige

Chardonnay di Appiano 1987, Cantina Sociale di Appiano (*Wine*
Growers Association)
Weissburgunder 1986, Niedermayer (*Cantina Augusto*)
Südtiroler Cabernet Sauvignon 1985, Hofstatter (*Wine Society*)

VENETO

The Veneto is the largest producer of DOC wines in Italy. It also
possesses the most industrialised wineries, and has made the greatest
investment in technology. Those two facts are strongly connected, in
that this is the home of the terrible two – Valpolicella and Soave – both
household names, not for quality but for cheapness.

The Veneto has embraced the industrialisation of wine
wholeheartedly. It has allowed its classic vineyard areas on hillsides to
expand dramatically down to the plains to satisfy the thirst of Europe,
relying on technology in the winery to make up for the deficiencies
inherent in grapes that come from high-yielding vines on flat vineyards
better suited to corn. The result has been a debasement of famous
names.

Only in the last year or so have we become aware that some
producers are still making quality wines – some of them world-class.
We have seen a growth of interest in single vineyard wines, here as in
the rest of Italy. We have seen the development of super vini da tavola.
And we have seen the arrival of international grape varieties.

We have also learned about the great Veneto contribution to
winemaking – the Reciotos, which come from both Valpolicella and
Soave. The Valpolicella Reciotos are huge red wines made from partly
dried grapes. Deep, rich, bitter-tasting when dry – called Amarone – or
smooth and creamy in their sweet version, Amabile, they are some of
the finest red wines of Italy. Rarer, but equally exciting, are the sweet
white Recioto Soaves, made in the same way.

The Veneto does not just produce Soave, Valpolicella and its near neighbour the light red Bardolino (a much underrated wine, and one which we are seeing more of). It is the home of the wines from Bianco di Custoza, a neighbour of Soave, making wines that are often more reliable than run-of-the-mill Soave at only slightly higher prices. Further to the east, there are several DOCs new to us – Colli Berici, south of Vicenza, making a range of varietal wines (Pinot Bianco, Tocai Italiano, Merlot, Pinot Noir), and Breganze to the north of Vicenza, and the Colli Euganaei near Padua, both making a similar range. Further east, in the Valdobbiadene, the white Prosecco produces sparkling wines and the red Raboso makes sturdy wines.

Who's who in the Veneto

Allegrini Old-fashioned family firm. Excellent Valpolicella and Amarone. Wines: Valpolicella Classico Superiore, Recioto Amarone.
Alex Findlater; Market Vintners; Millevini; Oddbins; Valvona & Crolla; Winecellars

Anselmi One of the top two Soave producers (the other is Pieropan – see below). Wines: Soave, Soave Capitel Foscarino, Recioto di Soave.
Valvona & Crolla; Winecellars; Wines from Paris

Bertani Traditional family company specialising in old Valpolicella Amarone. Wines: Bardolino, Soave, Valpolicella, Valpolicella Recioto.
David Baillie Vintners; Berry Bros & Rudd; Lay & Wheeler; Stapylton Fletcher; Valvona & Crolla; Wine Society

Bolla Well-established company whose wines are widely available in Britain. Look for single vineyard Soave (Castellaro) and Valpolicella (Jago Bolla). Wines: Soave, Valpolicella, Bardolino, Amarone.
Haynes, Hanson & Clark; Russell & McIver; Valvona & Crolla

Boscaini A family firm with sound wines, now also specialising in single vineyard wines. Wines: Soave, Valpolicella, Bardolino, single vineyard Soave (Cantina di Monteleone), single vineyard Valpolicella (Vigneti di Marano) and single vineyard Bardolino (Tenuta Le Cane). Red super vino da tavola, Le Cane.
A & A Wines; Berry Bros & Rudd; Seckford Wines; Ubiquitous Chip; Winecellars; Wine Growers Association; Wines from Paris

Maculan High quality wines from Breganze. Look for sweet white Tercolato, and a new Chardonnay. Wines: Breganze Cabernet, Rosato Tercolato.
Adnams; Anthony Byrne Fine Wines; D Byrne & Co; Alex Findlater; Tanners Wines; Winecellars

Masi One of the best Valpolicella and Soave producers. Also associated with Boscaini. Wines: Bardolino, Soave, Valpolicella, Amarone. Also single vineyard wines (Serego Alighieri is a fine

Valpolicella), red super vino da tavola (Campo Fiorín) and white (Masianco).
Adnams; David Alexander; D Byrne & Co; Direct Wine Shipments; Alex Findlater; Lockes; Nobody Inn; Christopher Piper Wines; Tanners Wines; Valvona & Crolla; Winecellars; Wines from Paris

Pieropan Often reckoned to be the finest Soave producer. He makes a number of single vineyard Soaves as well as a wider blend. Taste his wines, and Soave will never be the same again. Wines: Soave and Recioto Soave.
Adnams; Alex Findlater; Millevini; Oddbins; Valvona & Crolla; La Vigneronne; Winecellars; Wines from Paris

Portalupi Producer of Bardolino and rosé Chiaretto.
Adnams; Bibendum; Alex Findlater; Market Vintners; Millevini; Valvona & Crolla; Winecellars

Giuseppe Quintarelli Traditional firm making small amounts of high-quality wines. Their Reciotos are sensational. Wines: Valpolicella Recioto Amabile and Amarone.
Adnams; Raeburn Fine Wines and Foods; Ubiquitous Chip

Santa Margherita This large merchant house is based in the Lison area and makes a number of wines under this DOC, as well as Piave and Prosecco.
Peter Dominic

Santa Sofia Sound quality wines from around Lake Garda. Wines: Bianco di Custoza, Soave, Valpolicella, Bardolino.
Eaton Elliot Winebrokers; Ubiquitous Chip

Santi A medium-sized producer of Soave.
D Byrne & Co; Upper Crust

Tedeschi A specialist in Recioto-style wines, and some top-quality vini da tavola. Wines: Bianco di Custoza, Soave, Valpolicella, Bardolino, Recioto, Capitel San Rocco super vini da tavola white and red.
A & A Wines; Adnams; David Alexander; Lay & Wheeler; Millevini; Oddbins; Seckford Wines; Valvona & Crolla; Winecellars; Wine Growers Association

Venegazzù-Conte Loredan-Gasparini The Loredan family are descendants of Doges of Venice and the wines still sport the Doge's cap of office on their label, although the firm is now owned by a businessman. Produce some top vini da tavola. Wines: Venegazzù della Casa, Venegazzù Etichetta Nera (Cabernet Sauvignon), Venegazzù Rosso, sparkling Venegazzù Prosecco Brut.
D Byrne & Co; Alex Findlater; Laytons; Majestic; Millevini; Tanners Wines; Ubiquitous Chip; Upper Crust; Valvona & Crolla; La Vigneronne; Winecellars

Zenato Make very good value whites around Lake Garda, plus
Valpolicella. Wines: Soave, Valpolicella, Bianco di Custoza.
*Davisons; Arthur Rackhams; Tanners Wines; Waitrose; Winecellars; Wines
from Paris*

Best buys from the Veneto

WHITES

Tesco Bianco di Custoza (*Tesco*)
Bianco San Pietro 1986, Guerrieri-Rizzardi (*Vintage Roots*)
Soave 1987, Zenato (*Davisons; Arthur Rackhams*)
Bianco di Custoza 1987, Portalupi (*Cadwgan Wines*)
Soave Costeggiola Classico 1987, Guerrieri-Rizzardi (*Barwell & Jones*)

REDS

Valpolicella Classico Superiore 1985, Guerrieri-Rizzardi (*widely
available*)
Valpolicella Classico 1983, Vigneti di Marana, Boscaini (*Great Northern
Wine Company*)
Capitel San Rocco Rosso 1984 (*Wine Growers Association*)

FRIULI-VENEZIA-GIULIA

Suddenly, we're beginning to take notice of what's going on in this far
north-eastern outpost of Italy. We're discovering producers whose
wines far outshine what we already knew, and we're realising that
here is a new area waiting to be discovered.

Or rediscovered. We knew their wines some years ago, and those
from one or two producers have always been around, but they seemed
to fade a little – the quality wasn't as good, perhaps, or, more likely, we
found out about the Alto Adige and forgot about Friuli.

There are certain similarities between the two regions. They are both
frontier territories, once part of the Hapsburg Empire and before that
of the Venetian Empire. Their wine traditions are different from the
rest of Italy. Their insistence on varietal labelling is the same – this
certainly helps us to find our way around. As with the Alto Adige,
Friuli uses German and French grapes as well as Italian varieties, and
even has one all of its own.

But the Friuli producers are also following trends in other parts of
Italy: the single vineyard wines are an example, as is the use of
barriques for maturing some white wines.

There are two levels of DOC: the wide regional one (Grave del Friuli),
and smaller ones for more specific areas. The five DOC areas to look out
for are Collio Goriziano, Colli Orientali del Friuli, Collio, Grave del
Friuli and Aquileia. They all have a range of grape varieties which can
carry the DOC name.

The whites that can do this are Tocai, Traminer, Pinot Bianco, Pinot Grigio, Riesling Italico, Verduzzo and the new imports of Sauvignon and Riesling Renano (Rhine Riesling). The rare Picolit, making a sweet wine, is less often seen than talked about.

In the reds, Cabernet Franc and Merlot make reliable, good value wines. Also look out for some examples of Pinot Nero (Pinot Noir) and the local Refosco which often makes the most interesting wines.

Who's who in Friuli-Venezia-Giulia

Collavini Wines from the Collio and Grave del Friuli. Look out for their unusual white Ribolla and red Schioppettino, both local grape varieties. Wines: Varietals from Grave del Friuli and Collio. Also a good cheap sparkler, Il Grigio.
A & A Wines; Lay & Wheeler; Millevini; Sainsbury's; Seckford Wines; Valvona & Crolla

Livio Felluga Wines from both Collio and Collio Orientale del Friuli. Look for some of their single vineyard wines.
Valvona & Crolla; Yorkshire Fine Wines

Silvio Jermann Internationally recognised wines from the Collio DOC. Also make some top-class vini da tavola. Look for the Moscato Rosa and Vintage Tunina.
Millevini; Valvona & Crolla; Winecellars

Fratelli Pighin New firm which has already established a reliable reputation. Wines: Varietals from Collio Goriziano and Grave del Friuli. One of the best Picolits.
Valvona & Crolla

Tenuta Ca' Bolani Estate in Aquileia owned by the Zonin family. Look for their Tocai Friuliano.
Marks & Spencer; Willoughbys; Winecellars

Best buys from Friuli-Venezia-Giulia
Pinot Bianco di Aquileia 1986, Ca' Bolani (*Weatherbury Vintners; Whitesides of Clitheroe*)
Refosco dal Peduncolo, Grave del Friuli (red) 1986, Collavini (*Wine Growers Association*)

TUSCANY

Back to basics?

In Italian wine, it often seems that where Tuscany leads, others follow. The Tuscan producers were the first to launch into the super vini da tavola, into barrique ageing, and into the use of Cabernet Sauvignon to make premium wines. In the process, they almost forgot Chianti. Chianti became such a denigrated wine, on a par with Soave and Valpolicella in public esteem, that the top winemakers wanted to distance themselves from it.

That seems to have changed. A sign of the times is when one of the top experimenters in Tuscany – Count Antinori – decides that his latest release isn't going to be another Tignanello or Solaia, but a very good Chianti Classico, which he has called Peppoli. It is a single estate wine (an Italian fashion which has impinged less in Tuscany than elsewhere, simply because so many Chiantis are already single estate wines), and it is rich and tarry, with just the right amount of acidity and bitterness. It's a return to first principles.

But it's a return to first principles with the addition of all the knowledge gained during those years of experimentation. That's what makes the new Antinori wine so good, and so essentially different from the cheap Chianti we still see around (although much less than we used to). Undoubtedly other wines in the same mould will follow from all those talented winemakers who are working in Tuscany at the moment.

Another change has occurred in Tuscany with the advent of the DOCG for Chianti. It has really worked here, upgrading the quality, and has meant that we do see much less of the nasty stuff. The tasting tests do actually weed out some inferior wines, necessary when there is such a wide range of quality and styles in Chianti, suggesting that there is an urgent need for a DOC quality level below Chianti DOCG to take in all the wines that are good but not so good as to justify a DOCG seal.

For the time being, the best way to decide on which style of Chianti to buy is first by producer, and second by the level of quality as indicated on the label. No indication means it is a 'normale', a straightforward, relatively fresh wine to be drunk young – the descendant of the Chianti in wicker bottles. The next level up is the Riserva, a wine made for ageing. Above that, the name of the wine changes, and you are in the realm of the Chianti producer's super vino da tavola, often made with a similar recipe to Chianti grapes, but breaking the rigid DOCG rules in some way.

But innovation isn't just going on in the creation of new wines or the rediscovery of old techniques. The Tuscans have looked to the vineyard as well. They've discovered that Sangiovese, the standard grape for Chianti, comes in a whole variety of different clones. Much of the Tuscan vineyard was planted with an inferior clone in the 1950s and 1960s, and it's only more recently that producers have gone back to the true Tuscan clone, the Sangiovese Grosso. The latest fashion is for the Sangioveto, which is used in many of the super vini da tavola as well as in top estate Chiantis.

The Chianti area is enormous. Basic Chianti DOCG can come from a huge area starting at Pisa on the coast and finishing at Cortona almost into Umbria in the south-east of the region. Within that large zone are smaller areas. Some – like Chianti Classico, Chianti Rufina and Chianti Colli Fiorentini – produce some top wines; others – like Chianti Colline Pisane, Chianti Colli Aretini, Chianti Colli Senesi and Chianti Montalbano – are the source of the basic flask wine that's consumed locally. With the change to DOCG you won't see the name of the zone on the label unless it's Chianti Classico, Chianti Rufina or Chianti Colli Fiorentini.

Under the new DOCG rules, the traditional recipe of Chianti has been modified to cut down the white grapes and increase the use of noble grape varieties like Cabernet Sauvignon to blend with the principal constituent, Sangiovese. The surplus of white Trebbiano grapes has been put to good use: Galestro is the new Tuscan white DOC, making beautifully clean, fresh wines using the most modern technology.

Two DOC zones west of Florence – one red, one white – are worth looking out for. Carmignano makes super Chianti, using a certain amount of Cabernet Sauvignon. The white is the long-established Vernaccia di San Gimignano, making wine with a hint of almonds on the palate.

In the south of Tuscany, Brunello di Montalcino continues to command high prices and it sometimes suffers from too much wood. But things may change, and the lesser Rosso di Montalcino DOC is making some very approachable wines. Neighbouring Vino Nobile di Montepulciano has shown considerable improvements in the quality of its reds.

To the west, in the hills around Grossetto is a new red DOC zone, Morellino di Scansano, producing long-lasting wines entirely from Sangiovese.

Then there is the clutch of super vini da tavola. Every self-respecting estate, especially in Chianti Classico, makes one, such as Antinori's Tignanello and Solaia and Incisa della Rocchetta's extremely expensive Cabernet Sauvignon Sassacaia or Vinattieri, another 100 per cent Cabernet Sauvignon wine. Others in this group include Prima Vigna from Castello Vicchiomaggio, Sangioveto di Coltibuono, Palazzo Altesi of Altesino, Ser Niccolò of Serristori, Ghiaie della Furba of Capezzana, Coltassala of Castello di Volpaia – and many others. And while many of the producers have used varying quantities of Cabernet Sauvignon in these wines, they are increasingly returning to the virtues of the Sangiovese to produce truly Tuscan wines.

Now there's a new grouping of super vini da tavola from some estates, under the name Predicato. These producers make their vini da tavola following certain rules. These include low yields from vineyards at least 150 metres above sea level, earliest release dates for the wines, and tastings by fellow members of the group before the wines can be described as Predicato. Members of the group include top houses such as Antinori, Frescobaldi and Ruffino. The name Predicato is followed by a village name, such as Predicato di Cardisco or Predicato di Biturica. Red and white wines are being made using Cabernet Sauvignon, Chardonnay, Pinot Bianco and Sauvignon as well as Italian grape varieties.

Tuscany also makes the incomparable Vin Santo, a sweet Sherry-style but unfortified wine of great character and interest. A few examples are available: Villa di Vetrice (*Winecellars*); Frescobaldi (*S H Jones; Valvona & Crolla*); Capelli (*Wine Society*); Antinori (*Cantina Augusto; Selfridges; Valvona & Crolla*).

Who's who in Tuscany

Altesino Make some fine Brunello di Montalcino. Wines: Brunello; super vini da tavola: Palazzo Altesi, Alte d'Altesi.
H Allen Smith; Peter Dominic; Valvona & Crolla; Winecellars

Antinori One of the great names of Chianti. Makes Chianti and fine vini da tavola like Tignanello. A new Chianti Classico is Peppoli. Also makes some of the best Orvieto (see under Umbria). Wines: Chianti Classico, sparkling Brut, Tignanello, Solaia, Galestro.
Adnams; David Baillie Vintners; Berry Bros & Rudd; D Byrne & Co; Cantina Augusto; Corney & Barrow; Direct Wine Shipments; Alex Findlater; Hicks & Don; Lay & Wheeler; Majestic; Market Vintners; Oddbins; Sainsbury's; André Simon Wines; Valvona & Crolla; La Vigneronne; Winecellars; Wine Society; Wizard Wine Warehouses

Argiano Brunello di Montalcino producer whose cellars are in a spectacular crumbling castle. Wines: Brunello di Montalcino, Rosso di Montalcino.
Peter Dominic

Avignonesi Producer of some of the best and longest-lived Vino Nobile di Montepulciano; super vini da tavola: Il Marzocco, Grifi.
Windrush Wines

Badia a Coltibuono Top-quality Chianti Classico producer. Not cheap. Wines: Great Chianti Classico Riserva, Chianti Classico; super vino da tavola: Sangioveto di Coltibuono.
D Byrne & Co; Alex Findlater; Market Vintners; Valvona & Crolla; Winecellars

Biondi-Santi (Il Greppo) The godfathers of Brunello di Montalcino – they invented it. Their wines command enormous prices, not always justified by the quality.
Valvona & Crolla

Tenuta Caparzo One of the currently top two or three Brunello di Montalcino producers: Wines: Rosso di Montalcino, Brunello di Montalcino.
Valvona & Crolla; Wine Growers Association; Wines from Paris

Tenuta di Capezzana One of the largest producers in Carmignano DOC, of which this estate was the creator. Wines: Carmignano, Barco Reale; super vino da tavola: Ghiaie della Furba.
Ellis Son & Vidler; Alex Findlater

Castelgiocondo Large producer of Brunello di Montalcino. A more modern style – with more modest prices – than Biondi-Santi (see above). Wines: Brunello di Montalcino, Rosso di Montalcino.
Valvona & Crolla

Castellare A producer of high-quality Chianti Classico; super vino da tavola: I Sodi di San Niccolò.
Christopher & Co; Valvona & Crolla

Castello Vicchiomaggio Fine winemaking, bringing together modern and traditional methods. Wines: Chianti Classico; super vino da tavola: Prima Vigna; also modern-style white wine.
David Baillie Vintners; Hedley Wright; Lorne House Vintners; Marks & Spencer; Valvona & Crolla; La Vigneronne

Castello di Volpaia Top estate based around a hilltop village. Wines: Chianti Classico; super vini da tavola: Coltassala (Sangiovese), Mammolo (aged in small barrels).
Adnams; Eaton Elliot Winebrokers

Col d'Orcia Brunello producer now owned by Cinzano. Wines: Brunello di Montalcino.
Barwell & Jones

Fontodi Chianti Classico estate in the heart of the region. Wines: Chianti Classico; super vino da tavola: Flaccianello.
Wine Society

Frescobaldi Long-established firm (since the 13th century), producing all their wines from their own estates. Wines: Chianti Rufina (Nipozzano, Montesodi), Chianti Classico, Pomino Chardonnay, sparkling brut, rosé, Galestro, Vin Santo.
Adnams; D Byrne & Co; Alex Findlater; Lay & Wheeler; Nobody Inn; Christopher Piper Wines; Valvona & Crolla; Wines from Paris

Grati Producers in Chianti Rufina, making some good value wines. Wines: Chianti Rufina Poggio Galiga, Villa di Monte.
Bibendum; D Byrne & Co; Grape Ideas; Lay & Wheeler; Winecellars; Wines from Paris

Isole e Olena Small, high-quality Chianti Classico producer. Wines: Chianti Classico; super vino da tavola: Borro Cepparello.
Winecellars; Wines from Paris

Marchesi Incisa della Rocchetta Produce 100 per cent Cabernet Sauvignon Sassicaia. Very expensive.
David Baillie Vintners

Mellini Large producer in Chianti Classico making some single vineyard wines. Wines: Vernaccia di San Gimignano, Chianti Classico, Brunello di Montalcino, single vineyard Chianti (La Selvanella and Granaio); super vino da tavola: I Coltri (Sangiovese and Cabernet Sauvignon).
Selfridges

Pagliarese Make good commercial quality Chianti Classico, and very fine Riservas.
David Alexander; Oddbins

Poggio Antico Modern-style Brunello di Montalcino. Wines: Brunello di Montalcino, Rosso di Montalcino.
Master Cellar Wine Warehouse; Morleys (5 Station Approach, Purley Oaks, South Croydon, Surrey)

Poliziano Producer of Vino Nobile di Montepulciano. Wines: Vino Nobile Chianti; super vino da tavola: Elegia.
David Alexander; Oddbins; Valvona & Crolla

Le Pupille Producer of Morellino di Scansano, the new high-quality DOC from south-west Tuscany.
Curzon Wine Company; Alex Findlater; Millevini; Oddbins; Winecellars

Fattoria La Querce Top estate producing small quantities of high-quality Chianti.
David Alexander; La Reserva Wines

Ricasoli The Baron Ricasoli was the inventor of modern Chianti in the 19th century. While the estate has had its ups and downs (more downs recently), it is getting better. Wine: Chianti Classico.
D Byrne & Co; Millevini

Rocca della Macie Superb fruity Chianti Classico, designed to be drunk in two or three years at good value prices. Wines: Chianti Classico, Chianti Classico Riserva; white Numero Uno.
Widely available

I L Ruffino Large-scale producer with a very fine Chianti Classico Riserva. Wines: Chianti Classico, Riserva Ducale, Torgaio, Galestro.
D Byrne & Co; Cantina Augusto; La Reserva Wines; Valvona & Crolla

Castello di San Polo in Rosso Chianti Classico made by one of the best winemakers in Tuscany. Ought to be great, but sometimes disappoints. Wines: Chianti Classico; super vino da tavola: Centinaia.
H Allen Smith; D Byrne & Co

San Quirico Producer of classic Vernaccia di San Gimignano.
Averys; J Sainsbury; Wine Growers Association

Selvapiana Chianti Rufina producer, employing the services of one of the top winemakers in Tuscany. Wine: Chianti Rufina.
Winecellars

Conti Serristori The property includes the house where Machiavelli lived in exile. Wines: Chianti Classico, Riserva Machiavelli; super vino da tavola: Ser Niccolò; white wine, I Pianacci.
D Byrne & Co; Alistair Cameron

La Torre Good-quality Vernaccia di San Gimignano.
Peter Green; Valvona & Crolla

Val di Sugo Brunello di Montalcino which is approachable reasonably early. Wines: Brunello, Rosso di Montalcino.
Lorne House Vintners; Marks & Spencer

Villa Banfi Highly successful firm of Riunite (producers of Lambrusco) have branched into Montalcino with a huge estate mainly designed for sparkling Moscato wines, but also a little red. Wines: Brunello di Montalcino, Rosso di Montalcino, Chianti Classico.
Anthony Byrne Fine Wines; D Byrne & Co; Alex Findlater; Oddbins; Valvona & Crolla; Willoughbys

Villa Cafaggio Chianti Classico producer with a 28-hectare estate.
Europa Foods (77 Old Brompton Road, London SW7)

Best buys from Tuscany

WHITES

Vernaccia di San Gimignano 1987, San Quirico (*J Sainsbury; Wine Emporium*)
Numero Uno 1986, Rocca delle Macie (*Gare du Vin; The Market/ Winecellars; Valvona & Crolla*)
Vino a Tavola Bianco, Antinori (*Ad Hoc Wine Warehouse*)
Coltibuono Bianco 1987 (*Demijohn Wines*)

REDS

Chianti Rufina Banda Blue 1986, Grati (*Greens; The Market/Winecellars*)
Chianti Classico 1985, Isole e Olena (*Andrew Gordon Wines*)

Chianti Rufina, Villa Vetrice (*Morris's Wine Stores*)
Chianti Classico 1986, Rocca delle Macie (*widely available*)
Chianti Classico Santa Cristina 1986, Antinori (*Corney & Barrow*)
Chianti Putto 1986, Fattoria del'Ugo (*G Hush; Paul Sanderson Wines*)

EMILIA-ROMAGNA

Italian Coca-Cola

Emilia-Romagna, to the north-east of Tuscany, is the home of
Lambrusco. Most of it is sweet and fizzy – and fun. A few examples are
dry and delicious with pasta or rich foods (see *Who's who* below).
Lambrusco with a DOC is better than without.

Some serious reds are also produced in the Colli Piacentini
(Piacenza), particularly the Gutturnio. The Sangiovese di Romagna
makes standard quality reds. Albana di Romagna makes whites which
can be attractive, but whose quality varies wildly – and this is the new
DOCG!

Who's who in Emilia-Romagna

Cavacchioli Make top-quality dry Lambrusco (various DOCs); also
white Lambrusco.
D Byrne & Co; Oddbins

Fattoria Paradiso Good-quality red Sangiovese wines, and the best
white Albana di Romagna. Wines: Sangiovese di Romagna, (red)
Barbarossa, (white) Albana di Romagna.
Millevini; Winecellars

Pasolini Fruity, good-value Sangiovese. Wines: Sangiovese di
Romagna, (white) Trebbiano di Romagna.
Gerard Harris; The Market/Le Provençal

Cantine Romagnoli Good-quality Gutturnio. Wines: Gutturnio dei
Colli Piacentini.
Valvona & Crolla

Zerioli Producer of Gutturnio. Wines: Gutturnio dei Colli Piacentini.
Haslemere Wine Co (Caxton House, Lower Street, Haslemere, Surrey)

Best buys from Emilia-Romagna

Lambrusco di Sorbara 1985, Gavioli (*Valvona & Crolla*)
Sangiovese di Romagna 1982, Riserva Vigna delle Lepri, Fattoria
Paradiso (*Millevini*)

THE MARCHES

Into the Burgundy bottle

Verdicchio has always been the wine in the peculiar amphora-shaped bottle. Cynics said that was the only noticeable attribute this often dull wine had. Now a few growers have started putting the wine in Burgundy bottles.

Somehow this change of bottling seems to have changed the quality of Verdicchio at the same time. Producers of this popular white wine are forging ahead in the same way as the producers in Tuscany just across the hills.

Verdicchio dei Castelli di Jesi is the standard white DOC of the region (Jesi is a town up in the hills above Ancona). Many claim Verdicchio di Matelica DOC is better, but none seems to find its way out of Italy.

The red of the region, Rosso Cònero, has suddenly stopped being just another red made from Montepulciano grapes – of which there are so many on Italy's east coast. Again, just as with Verdicchio, producers are suddenly coming out with really exciting wines, some from single vineyards (here they're called Vigneti). They shouldn't be left around too long, though – three to five years is ideal.

Who's who in the Marches

Bianchi Make a delicious Rosso Cònero. Wines: Rosso Cònero, Verdicchio. Brand name is CaSal di Serra.
D Byrne & Co; Majestic; Upper Crust; La Vigneronne

Bucci One of the Verdicchio producers who uses a Burgundy bottle for his wine. The weight and quality seems to have improved with the change in bottle shape. Wine: Verdicchio dei Castelli di Jesi.
Lay & Wheeler; Wine Growers Association

Colle del Sole The brand name of the main Verdicchio co-operative. Wines: Colle del Sole, Coste del Molino, Monte Schiavo – all Verdicchio.
Christopher Piper Wines

Fazi-Battaglia The inventors of the amphora bottle. Wines: Titulus Verdicchio dei Castelli di Jesi, Rosso Cònero.
David Baillie Vintners; Berry Bros & Rudd; Alex Findlater; Haynes, Hanson & Clark; Hedley Wright; Tanners Wines; Wine Society

Marchetti Weighty, comparatively long-lasting Rosso Cònero. Wines: Rosso Cònero, Verdicchio.
H Allen Smith; Valvona & Crolla

Mecvini Well-balanced Verdicchio from a private producer. Wines:
Verdicchio dei Castelli di Jesi.
Barwell & Jones; Majestic

Umani Ronchi Good-quality wines made to a commercial standard;
also a single vineyard Verdicchio. Wines: Verdicchio dei Castelli di Jesi,
Rosso Cònero.
Peter Dominic; Millevini; Valvona & Crolla

Best buys from the Marches

Verdicchio dei Castelli di Jesi Classico 1986, Bucci (*Wine Emporium;
Wine Growers Association*)
Rosso Cònero 1983, San Lorenzo, Umani Ronchi (*Majestic; Wizard Wine
Warehouses*)

UMBRIA

The forgotten grape variety

Umbria is the attractive backwater of central Italy. Few big cities, miles
of rolling green hills and a magical light that derives from lack of
pollution. There are patches of wine production right round the
region, isolated from each other, all going their own way.

It's hardly surprising, therefore, to find two grape varieties in
Umbria which have often been ignored, but which are now being used
to transform two DOC areas into something rather interesting.

The most familiar wine of Umbria is the white Orvieto. Dominated
by the ubiquitous and boring Trebbiano grape, it used to be neutral
and flabby, and is – even now – too often just dull and clean. But in the
permitted blend there is one grape variety – the Grechetto – which is
now being used in super vini da tavola and shows just how good
Orvieto can be if the Grechetto is given its head. The Cervaro della Sala
of Antinori is a blend of 25 per cent Grechetto and 75 per cent
Chardonnay, a heady mixture, fermented in barrels – a new star wine.
The same is true of Marrano from Bigi, which is 100 per cent Grechetto.

The other change which has shown up the promise of Orvieto is the
development of single vineyard wines, and both Bigi and Antinori
have released some top-notch wines from their own estates.

Across the hills in the centre of Umbria, south of Assisi, can be found
the other unappreciated grape of the region. This is a red wine grape,
the Sagrantino, rich, tannic, intense. It is used in the DOC of
Montefalco Rosso, and also in the sweet red Sagrantino Passito, made
from dried grapes.

Another great entrepreneur in Umbria has been Lungarotti who
dominates the Torgiano red DOC near Assisi. He seems to have

overcome the problems with varying quality between bottles, and now his standard Rubesco di Torgiano is a well-crafted wine. Look also for his single vineyard white and red and his Riserva wines which set very high standards.

Elsewhere in Umbria, the Colli del Trasimeno red and white and the Colli Altotiberini red (made using Merlot) and white are good, standard wines: the reds are generally better than the whites.

Who's who in Umbria

Adanti Make white Bianco d'Arquata and red Montefalco.
Valvona & Crolla; Winecellars

Antinori The great Tuscan firm also has vineyards in Orvieto. Their Orvieto is reliable, but their star wines are a single vineyard Castello della Sala and the Grechetto/Chardonnay Cervaro della Sala.
H Allen Smith; David Baillie Vintners; Corney & Barrow; Lay & Wheeler; Tanners Wines; Valvona & Crolla; Winecellars

Barberani Producer of some top-quality Orvieto.
Wine Growers Association

Luigi Bigi Commercial, reliable wines on the one hand and some exciting single vineyard Orvieto on the other. Wines: Orvieto, Vigneto Torricella, Vigneto Orzalume, Colli de Trasimeno (also makes Est! Est!! Est!!! from Latium and Chianti).
Adnams; D Byrne & Co; Cantina Augusto; Majestic; Market Vintners; Millevini; Oddbins; Upper Crust; Valvona & Crolla; La Vigneronne; Winecellars

Lungarotti The creator of the Torgiano DOC and generally regarded as one of Italy's finest winemakers. Wines: Rubesco di Torgiano, Cabernet Sauvignon di Miralduolo, Chardonnay, Solleone (a Sherry-like wine).
Adnams; H Allen Smith; David Baillie Vintners; Berry Bros & Rudd; Corney & Barrow; Alex Findlater; Hedley Wright; Hicks & Don; Lay & Wheeler; Sainsbury's; Tanners Wines; Valvona & Crolla; La Vigneronne; Winecellars; Wine Society

Best buys from Umbria

Vin Santo 1980, Lungarotti (*Valvona & Crolla*)
Chardonnay di Miraduolo 1987, Lungarotti (*Great Northern Wine Company*)
Orvieto Classico 1986, Vigneto Toricella, Bigi (*The Market/Winecellars; Oddbins; Wessex Wines*)
Rubesco di Torgiano 1983, Lungarotti (*Smedley Vintners*)

LATIUM

Frascati – another of those much abused Italian wines – is at last beginning to show why it was so popular in the first place. While there is still too much thin, badly made stuff around, selling too cheaply, we now have access to a regular supply of the real thing as well.

Frascati is a surprisingly delicate wine. Its flavours don't come out and hit you, but steal up on you. A good Frascati will taste slightly honeyed, aromatic, perfumed. It should also taste fresh. And one of the problems has always been that the grape that lends Frascati its character, the Malvasia, oxidises quickly without the aid of modern technology. In the past, most producers cut out the Malvasia and just used boring old Trebbiano, which produces large amounts of watery grapes – hence the dullness of most Frascati. Now, with cold fermentation and stainless steel, producers can concentrate on the Malvasia. So not only are we getting a few really characterful Frascatis, but also some single vineyard wines of surprising quality.

As for the other major DOC of Latium, the notorious Est! Est!! Est!!!, nothing seems to have improved here, and our advice is still to avoid it.

Who's who in Latium

Bruno Colacicchi Maker of the legendary Torre Ercolana, a blend of Cabernet Franc, Merlot and the local Cesanese. Only about 200 cases made a year, so count your buys in bottles. Wines: Torre Ercolana vino da tavola.
Millevini; Valvona & Crolla; Wine Growers Association

Colli di Catone The best Frascati available in our shops is made by Antonio Pulcini. Look for his single vineyard Villa Catone, and the white bottle Bottiglia Satinata.
A & A Wines; Alex Findlater; Lockes; Nobody Inn; Oddbins; Christopher Piper Wines; La Reserva Wines; Tanners Wines; Valvona & Crolla; Winecellars; Wine Growers Association; Wines from Paris

Fontana Candida A large-scale Frascati producer, whose best wine is the single vineyard Vigneto Santa Teresa.
Majestic; Upper Crust; Valvona & Crolla; La Vigneronne; Winecellars

Best buys from Latium
Frascati Superiore 1986, Villa Catone (*Ilkley Wine Cellars*)
Frascati Superiore 1987, Vigneto Santa Teresa, Fontana Candida (*Michael Menzel Wines; Valvona & Crolla*)

ABRUZZO AND MOLISE

The land of the Montepulciano

There's only one grape that matters in these two mountainous regions on the east coast level with Rome: the Montepulciano. In the Abruzzo, the DOC is Montepulciano d'Abruzzo, and the wines, at their best, can be rich and elegant; at their least they are full of good, peppery fruit. In Molise, look for the Biferno DOC for good bargain reds.

There's also some charming rosato – rosé – wine made with the Montepulciano grape. It's called Cerasuolo because of its cherry colour.

The whites – made of the Trebbiano grape – are normally as dull as only that grape can make them. One producer, Valentini, does something better – but he knows he does, and his prices have shot up accordingly.

Who's who in the Abruzzo and Molise

Barone Cornacchia Makes red and very good rosé. Wines: Montepulciano d'Abruzzo, rosé.
Millevini; Winecellars; Wines from Paris

Tenuta del Priore Specialising in Riserva wines, plus a delicious fruity Cerasuolo. Wines: Montepulciano d'Abruzzo, Cerasuolo.
Wine Growers Association

Ramitello Luigi de Majo's organically produced red Biferno is the only wine from this Molise DOC to reach the UK. Wine: Di Majo Norante Biferno.
Bordeaux Direct

Cantina Sociale di Tollo Make widely available vino da tavola. Wines: Montepulciano d'Abruzzo, (red) Colle Secco.
H Allen Smith; Bibendum; Winecellars

Edoardo Valentini Makes one of the few decent Trebbiano d'Abruzzo wines, as well as Montepulciano.
Millevini; Winecellars

Vini Citra A large co-operative in the Abruzzo making robust, peppery reds. Wines: Montepulciano d'Abruzzo, vino da tavola Castel Citra.
Wine Growers Association

Best buys from the Abruzzo and Molise

Trebbiano d'Abruzzo Illuminati 1986 (*Valvona & Crolla*)

Montepulciano d'Abruzzo 1985, Barone Cornacchia (*Millevini*)
Montepulciano d'Abruzzo, Cantina Tollo (*H Allen Smith*)
Cerasuolo d'Abruzzo 1986, Barone Cornacchia (*Demijohn Wines*)

CAMPANIA

Vesuvio erupts

It has been a sad reflection on the quality of the most famous wine of
Naples – Lacryma Christi – that until five years ago there was no DOC.
Those few producers who made good wine were being pulled down by
the many who weren't. We wouldn't say things have improved much
yet – although they have dropped the melodramatic name and now call
the wines Vesuvio – but we're more hopeful.

For those who want a white from this region, the Greco di Tufo is a
much better bet, and, to an even greater degree, Fiano di Avellino.

There's really only one red that has more than local renown and
that's Taurasi. Made from the Aglianico grape (see also Basilicata
below), in the hands of Antonio Mastroberardino, the wine has a
plummy, almost sweet richness that leaves awe and puzzlement in
equal proportions on the faces of those who taste it for the first time.

Who's who in Campania

Mastroberardino A great producer of both white and red wines – at a
price. Wines: Fiano di Avellino, Greco di Tufo, (red) Taurasi.
*David Baillie Vintners; D Byrne & Co; Lay & Wheeler; Tanners Wines;
Valvona & Crolla; Wine Growers Association*

PUGLIA (APULIA)

This is the home of the wine lake. And to look at the vast acres of
vineyards on the flat plains stretching for two hundred miles down the
heel of Italy, it's hardly surprising that few really good wines emerge.
But some producers are making very fine wines and a few – too few –
are available here. There's a whole range of DOCs, but, as often, the
vini da tavola are just as good.

Who's who in Puglia

Taurino The wines from this family firm come from deep inside the
heel of Italy in the Salentino peninsula. They make heavy, full-bodied

wines which need time to soften. Wines: Salice Salentino, Rosso di Salentino, Rosso Brindisi.
Millevini

Torre Quarto Run by Belgians, making their best wines from French grapes. Wines: Torre Quarto Rosso (made from Malbec), DOC Rosso di Cerignola; vini da tavola.
Millevini; Winecellars

Best buys from Puglia
Torre Quarto Rosso 1981 (*Bin 89 Wine Warehouse*)
Salice Salentino Riserva 1981, Taurino (*Wine Growers Association*)

BASILICATA

The forgotten region

A wider variety of wines are made in Basilicata than this small, neglected region's one DOC would suggest. But only one wine is available in Britain – Aglianico del Vulture, a serious, somewhat austere red, sometimes seen as the best red from southern Italy.

Who's who in Basilicata

Fratelli d'Angelo Small family company, by far the best producer of Aglianico del Vulture.
Lay & Wheeler; The Market; Millevini; Valvona & Crolla; Winecellars; Wine Growers Association

CALABRIA

The Greek vineyard

The Greeks called this Enotria, the land of wine. Things may have slipped since then (although that the Greeks watered their wine may say something for its quality), but there are a few characterful wines to be found in the toe of Italy.

Who's who in Calabria

Librandi The only producer of more than local renown, using the Cirò brand name. The red is better than the white, and there is a good Riserva.
Millevini; Valvona & Crolla; Wine Growers Association

Best buys from Calabria

Cirò Rosso Classico (*Continental Wine House*)
Cirò Librandi Bianco 1987 (*Valvona & Crolla*)

SICILY

There's as much innovation going on in Sicily as anywhere in vinous Italy. Most of it is being done outside the DOC system, which has simply hampered innovation while clinging on to tradition.

So most of Sicily's interesting wines are vini da tavola. They're not of the super vino da tavola type found in Tuscany, which are the top of a range which includes DOC wines. Here they tend to be made instead of DOC wines, and are the main production of the go-ahead companies – brand names are therefore important (see below under *Who's who*).

Of the DOC wines, Alcamo is one of the more interesting, while Etna tends to be drunk by the holidaymakers on the beaches of Taormina.

Marsala – the cooking wine

Virtually all the Marsala, the fortified wine from the town of the same name in western Sicily, which is sold in this country, is intended for cooking. It's used in zabaglione, of course, and in a host of other dishes, often produced in Italian restaurants with much flamboyance.

We can be thankful that the appalling flavoured Marsalas seem to be disappearing. If you value your tastebuds, we suggest you steer clear of any remaining examples.

True Marsala can be a delicious aperitif wine or equally successful as a digestif. It shouldn't be ridiculously sweet but have a touch of dryness to stimulate the appetite. There's a range of styles (as in Sherry) from the lightest to the darkest in colour – and the darker styles go well after a meal. The standard style is called Marsala Fine, the next grade up is Marsala Superiore, and the best is Marsala Vergine. The producers mentioned below make good examples of the traditional styles.

Who's who in Sicily

Corvo, Duca di Salaparuta Modern winery making modern-tasting, straightforward wines of good quality. Wines: Corvo Bianco and Rosso, Corvo Bianco Colombina Platino.
David Alexander; David Baillie Vintners; D Byrne & Co; Cantina Augusto; Millevini; La Reserva Wines; Tanners Wines; Upper Crust; Valvona & Crolla; Willoughbys

Donnafugata Red and white vini da tavola from an estate owned by

the Rallo (Marsala producer) family. Rising stars for quality and character. Wines: Donnafugata Bianco and Rosso.
Valvona & Crolla

Pellegrino Old-established Marsala producer. Look for the examples of their Madeira-like Vergine. Wines: Marsala Vergine, Marsala Garibaldi Superiore.
Fullers; Safeway; Sainsbury's; Unwins

Rallo Apart from table wines, also produce a good Vergine (light style) Marsala. Wines: Marsala, DOC Alcamo.
Morrisons

Rapitalà Make better whites than their DOC would suggest. Wines: Rapitalà Bianco di Alcamo DOC, Rapitalà Rosso.
Hicks & Don; Valvona & Crolla

Regaleali The star among Sicilian table wines. Both red and white are top class and good value. Wines: Regaleali Rosso, Regaleali Bianco, Rosso del Conte.
Tanners Wines; Valvona & Crolla

Sambuca di Sicilia A co-operative in south-west Sicily making a good value red, rosé and white vino da tavola. Wines: Cellaro Rosso, Rosato, Bianco.
Berry Bros & Rudd; Valvona & Crolla; Winecellars

Samperi Producer of the finest Marsala-style wines. Wines: Vecchio Samperi, Bukkuram (an old moscato wine from the island of Pantelleria near the North African coast).
Adnams; Winecellars

Settesoli Co-operative making light, fruity wines on the southern coast. Wines: Settesoli Bianco, Rosso, Rosato.
Chiswick Wine Cellar; Valvona & Crolla

Best buys from Sicily

Donnafugata Rosso 1984 (*Selfridges*)
Settesoli Bianco and Rosso (*William Addison; Demijohn Wines*)
Cellaro Bianco 1986, Sambuca di Sicilia (*Corney & Barrow; The Market/ Winecellars*)

SARDINIA

Craftsmanship

One would have thought that Sardinia should, by all the rules, make highly traditional wines with absolutely no saleable value outside the island. Instead, from one ultra-modern winery comes a stream of beautifully crafted wines which would do credit to any part of Italy. And while this firm is exceptional, some good value reds from one of the island's co-operatives are also starting to be exported.

Who's who in Sardinia

Cantine Sociale di Dolianova Three good-value DOC wines: (red) Monica di Sardegna and Cannonau di Sardegna; (white) Vermentino di Sardegna.
H Allen Smith; Winecellars; Wines from Paris

Sella & Mosca The innovator in Sardinia, whose total production equals that of the whole Côte d'Or of Burgundy, yet makes distinctive wines. Virtually all their wines are vini da tavola rather than DOC. *Whites*: Riviera del Corallo, Vermentino di Alghero, Torbato di Alghero, Terre Bianche; *reds*: Cannonau di Alghero, Tanca Farra; dessert wine: Anghelu Ruju.
Averys; David Baillie Vintners; Millevini; Winecellars; Wine Growers Association

Best buys from Sardinia

Torbato di Alghero 1987, Bianco, Sella e Mosca (*Hedley Wright; Wine Growers Association*)
Cannonau 1981, Sella e Mosca (*Great Northern Wine Company*)

Specialist stockists of Italian wines

Adnams; Ad Hoc Wine Warehouse; H Allen Smith; David Baillie Vintners; Barwell & Jones; Bibendum; D Byrne & Co; Cantina Augusto; Chiswick Cellar; Christophers; Continental Wine House; Demijohn Wines; Alex Findlater; Peter Green; J E Hogg; The Market; Martinez Fine Wine; Marske Mill House; Millevini; Oddbins; Ostlers; Raeburn Fine Wines and Foods; Selfridges; Tanners Wines; Philip Tite Fine Wines; Valvona & Crolla; La Vigneronne; Windrush Wines; Winecellars; Wine Growers Association; The Wine House; The Wine Shop (Caithness); The Wine Society; The Wine Spot

Lebanon

Wine has been made in the Lebanon since grapes were first fermented. And – if there were no war – there would probably be a flourishing export industry. But our knowledge of Lebanese wine has developed because of one remarkable man.

Serge Hochar, the owner of Château Musar, was in London while this Guide was being prepared. He was here to show his latest two vintages, the 1979 and 1980, and gave radio interviews and received coverage in the press. Inevitably, most people were concerned to ask him about how he managed to make such fine wines in such a chaotic country.

In the years of civil war, with Château Musar's vineyards in the Bekaa Valley and the winery across at least two front lines in the Christian area north of Beirut, only one vintage (1984) was completely missed, although 1985 only just made it.

Mr Hochar, on the other hand, was much more interested in talking about how his wines were received in the United States. He wants, as he says, to put the war on one side and concentrate on wine – at least he can have an influence on that.

He was trained in Bordeaux and uses French grapes – Cabernet Sauvignon, Syrah and Cinsault – to make a world-class wine. He produces two reds – Château Musar and a second wine, Cuvée Musar – plus a white, but we see only the red Château Musar. It is powerful, rich, elegant and long-lasting: 20-year-old wines are still full of fruit. Old vintages are occasionally available.

Specialist stockists

A & A Wines; Adnams; D Byrne & Co; Peter Dominic; Ellis Son & Vidler; Alex Findlater; Grape Ideas; Gerard Harris; Lay & Wheeler; Majestic; Christopher Piper Wines; Sainsbury's; Tanners Wines; Upper Crust; Victoria Wine Company; La Vigneronne (old vintages); Waitrose; Willoughbys; Winecellars; Wizard Wine Warehouses

Luxembourg

Vineyards grow on either side of the Moselle River as it flows through
the Grand Duchy of Luxembourg. They produce very light,
German-style wines which need to be drunk young but can be quite
refreshing. A small amount reaches our shops.

A greater quantity of Luxembourg sparkling wine is also available.
While some of this is made from Luxembourg grapes, much of it is
based on cheap Italian wine to which is added some Luxembourg air
(a habit the Luxembourgeois have picked up from their German
neighbours). So read the small print carefully on a label – it should
indicate where the wine has come from. If it is simply described as
'bottled in Luxembourg' that means the wine has come from
elsewhere.

The best wines are all white. They are officially classified, in
ascending order of quality, as: marque nationale, vin classé, premier
cru and grand premier cru. The only regular producer of Luxembourg
wines to reach our shops is the co-operative of Wormeldange.

Grapes on the label

Auxerrois Fairly neutral but pleasant wine which can be quite full and
almondy in good years from good sites.

Elbling Light, fresh, crisp wines.

Gewürztraminer Very little is grown, but it makes good, fresh, only
slightly spicy wines.

Pinot Gris Little is grown, but it makes full, soft wines.

Riesling Makes flowery wines, with good varietal character, thin in
poor years but clean and delicate in better ones.

Rivaner The Müller-Thurgau under another name. Makes soft, fruity,
sometimes medium dry but often dry wines.

Best buys in Luxembourg

Pinot Blanc 1986, Cave Co-opérative de Wormeldange (*Luxembourg
Wine Company*)

Specialist stockists

A & A Wines; Eldridge Pope; The Luxembourg Wine Company

New Zealand

On everybody's lips

Suddenly, at last, everybody is raving about New Zealand's wines. She was the featured nation at the 1988 London Wine Trade Fair in May, and her stand – packed with producers as well as wines – was mobbed from start to finish. Go to her Big Brother neighbour, Australia, and they will tell you that they are buying their Sauvignon Blanc wine from New Zealand, because New Zealand does it so much better than Australia.

The New Zealanders have coined a slogan which sums up their wines very well: 'the home of cool climate wines'. That is indeed the secret of their success. Although the country lies across the equivalent latitudes to Rioja and much of Spain in the northern hemisphere, her island situation with nothing further south before you reach Antarctica means a comparatively long, cool growing season for many of the vineyard areas. That's what produces the intensely fruity nature of the New Zealand white wines.

So far, white wines have been the stars. Chardonnay and Sauvignon Blanc are the two in greatest demand, regularly selling out as soon as they are made available. In fact, 'sold out' signs seem to be all too familiar when dealing with New Zealand wines. There are only 4,500 hectares of vineyard, and that has been cut down by 25 per cent in the past three years because of a controversial 'vine pull' scheme, which was designed to root out the poor quality vineyards but managed to destroy some 25 hectares of precious Chardonnay as well.

So now, with the sudden upsurge in demand, New Zealand wine is in short supply. We are lucky in Britain, because the New Zealanders are keen to sell to us: it's often easier to get a top NZ wine in London than in Auckland. Even here, it's only the two or three largest producers whose wines we can confidently expect to find. What a change from a couple of years ago, when *Which? Wine Guide* was praising the virtues of NZ wines, but the British wine trade just weren't buying.

While extravagant praise has been showered on the white wines, the reds have been catching up fast. They have always had very direct varietal flavours, but have tended to be rather one-dimensional. Now they are gaining extra complexity, because, some experts say, the vines are getting older and yielding better fruit. So while NZ reds haven't entered the world-beating class of the whites yet, they are highly enjoyable even now.

Whether white or red, all NZ wines are well made. We just don't see any bad bottles or bad winemaking – more than can be said for wine from some European countries. Plenty of investment has gone into the new technology in NZ wineries, and the new generation of winemakers are trained oenologists (many have been to the Australian wine colleges). So technology has arrived to boost the already high potential of the wines.

While the biggest selling wines come from the two giant companies – Cooks and Montana – a good range of smaller wineries is now represented in the UK as well. The big two have also decided to go for a 'small is beautiful' philosophy, with the advent of single vineyard wines and up-market ranges of wines. But at all levels NZ wines are still terrific value. Compare Chardonnay and Sauvignon Blanc – as they should be compared – with top white Burgundy and Sancerre, and the point is made very quickly.

The taste of New Zealand

White wines

The principal grape variety in terms of acreage is still the Müller-Thurgau. Occasionally it is used unblended, but normally it provides the basis of the slightly sweet blends which still form the staple part of New Zealand wine production.

More important, in terms of quality, are the Chardonnay and the Sauvignon Blanc, and coming up fast on the outside are the Gewürztraminer and the Rhine Riesling. All four produce wines with intense fruit, good acidity and a very pure varietal taste, a result of long, comparatively cool summers and slow ripening. Most of the whites are best drunk young – 1985 is probably the oldest vintage worth considering in 1989.

Red wines

Cabernet Sauvignon is the most frequently found red variety, but some Pinot Noir wines – especially in the cooler South Island – are beginning to show delicious strawberry fruit.

New Zealand vintages

1988 A late harvest with reduced quantities. Quality is good for most varieties except Gewürztraminer which suffered from heavy spring rains. Red wines will be particularly good.

1987 A year with a late harvest. Mixed quality for whites, with Müller-Thurgau, Sauvignon and Chardonnay the most successful. Reds should be good.

1986 Low yield but high quality. The whites are excellent, the reds beginning to mature well.

1985 Again a good year. Start drinking reds, and drink up the whites.

1982 Reds are the only wines worth drinking now. It was a fine year, and the pricier Cabernet Sauvignons should still be good.

Where's where in New Zealand

New Zealand's vineyards have shifted their gravity as growers realised where their strength lay. The hot, humid and lush area around Auckland was where the original Yugoslav growers planted their vineyards, but now the best vineyards are at Gisborne and Hawkes Bay on the east coast of North Island, at Marlborough on the northern coast of South Island, and even as far south as Christchurch.

Who's who in New Zealand

Babich Wines (Henderson, Auckland). Descendants of Dalmatian settlers. Their Cabernet Sauvignon, Pinot Noir and Gewürztraminer are regular prize-winners. Wines: Chardonnay, Irongate Chardonnay, Gewürztraminer, Müller-Thurgau, Pinot Noir, Pinotage, Cabernet Sauvignon.
Davisons; Alex Findlater; Richard Harvey Wines; Nobody Inn; Ostlers; La Reserva Wines; Upper Crust; Wines from Paris

Cloudy Bay (Marlborough, South Island). Western Australian producer, Cape Mentelle, who makes superb, but pricy, Sauvignon Blanc in New Zealand, and has now launched a Chardonnay of equal quality. Wines: Sauvignon Blanc, Chardonnay.
Adnams; Averys; Corney & Barrow; Alex Findlater; Majestic; Ostlers; Raeburn Fine Wines and Foods; La Reserva Wines; Tanners Wines; Ubiquitous Chip; La Vigneronne

Cooks/Corbans (Te Kauwhata, North Island). One of the biggest producers, and the best distributed in British shops. Luckily, quality is good as well. They have just launched the premium Stoneleigh range from their Marlborough vineyards. Wines: Cooks New Zealand Medium White and Dry White, Chardonnay, Gewürztraminer, Dry Red, Hawkes Bay Cabernet Sauvignon; Stoneleigh Marlborough Rhine Riesling, Chardonnay, Sauvignon Blanc, Cabernet Sauvignon.
David Baillie Vintners; D Byrne & Co; Davisons; Rodney Densem Wines; Alex Findlater; Haynes, Hanson & Clark (Stoneleigh Vineyards); Majestic; Ostlers; La Reserva Wines; Tanners Wines; Ubiquitous Chip; Wine Society; Wizard Wine Warehouses

---

Find the best new wine bargains all year round with our newsletter, *Which? Wine Monthly*, available for £15 a year from: Dept WG89, Consumers' Association, FREEPOST, Hertford SG14 1YB – no stamp is needed if posted within the UK. •

Delegats Vineyard (Henderson and Hawkes Bay, North Island). Family winery producing award-winning whites, including fine dessert wines. Wines: Chardonnay, Fumé Blanc, Réserve Semillon, Müller-Thurgau Auslese.
Corney & Barrow; Alex Findlater; Hungerford Wine Company; Kiwi Fruits; Nobody Inn; Ostlers; La Vigneronne

Matua Valley Wines (Auckland and Hawkes Bay). Modern winery in Auckland making some exciting white wines. Wines: Sauvignon Blanc, Cabernet Sauvignon.
Adnams; H Allen Smith; Corney & Barrow; Alex Findlater; Hedley Wright; Hungerford Wine Company; Kiwi Fruits; Nobody Inn; Ostlers; Stapylton Fletcher; La Vigneronne; Wines from Paris

Mission Vineyards (Hawkes Bay). As its name suggests, a vineyard run by a religious order. Wines: Semillon/Sauvignon Blanc.
Alex Findlater; Hedley Wright; Kiwi Fruits; Ostlers; Stapylton Fletcher

Montana Wines (Gisborne, North Island and Marlborough, South Island). The pioneer of vineyards in the South Island. The experiment has paid off with some good, crisp whites, widely available in British shops. Wines; Gisborne Chardonnay, Sauvignon Blanc, Fumé Blanc, Pinotage, Cabernet Sauvignon.
Christopher & Co; Corney & Barrow; Davisons; Alex Findlater; Oddbins; Ostlers; Christopher Piper Wines; Tanners Wines; Unwins; Wine Growers Association

Morton Estate (Hawkes Bay, North Island). Talented young winemaker specialising in white wines. Wines: Sauvignon Blanc, Chardonnay, Chardonnay Reserve.
Berkmann Wine Cellars/Le Nez Rouge; Alex Findlater; Lay & Wheeler; Ostlers; Christopher Piper Wines; La Reserva Wines; Wines from Paris; Wizard Wine Warehouses

Nobilo (Auckland, North Island). Red wine specialists who make one of the best Pinot Noirs. Wines: Riesling/Sylvaner, Chardonnay, Pinotage, Cabernet Sauvignon, Pinot Noir.
Averys; Christopher & Co; Alex Findlater; Majestic; Nobody Inn; La Reserva Wines; Stapylton Fletcher; Upper Crust; La Vigneronne

Selaks Wines (Auckland, North Island). One of the longest established New Zealand producers. Wines: Chardonnay, Sauvignon Blanc/Semillon, Rhine Riesling.
Adnams; Alex Findlater; Ostlers; Reid Wines; Willoughbys; Wizard Wine Warehouses

St Nesbit (South Auckland, North Island). New winery making an exciting Cabernet Sauvignon.
Kiwi Fruits

Te Mata (Hawkes Bay). High-class small winery, with one of the best NZ red wines. Wines: Castle Hill Sauvignon Blanc, Elston Chardonnay, Coleraine Cabernet/Merlot.
Alex Findlater; Lay & Wheeler; Ostlers; Upper Crust; La Vigneronne

Best buys from New Zealand

WHITES

Stoneleigh Vineyard Chardonnay (*Haynes, Hanson & Clark; Martinez Fine Wine; Rattlers Wine Warehouse*)
Montana New Zealand Chardonnay 1987 (*Master Cellar Wine Warehouse; Oddbins*)
Delegats Sauvignon Blanc 1987 (*Addison Avenue Wine Shop*)
Cook's Hawkes Bay Chenin Blanc 1985 (*Davisons; Peter Dominic*)

REDS

Nobilo Pinot Noir 1984 (*Averys; Alex Findlater*)
Cook's Hawkes Bay Cabernet Sauvignon 1985 (*Waitrose*)

Specialist stockists

Alex Findlater; Peter Green; J C Karn; Kiwifruits; Ostlers; Stapylton Fletcher; Upper Crust; La Vigneronne

North Africa

Once over half the world's wine trade was in wine from French North Africa – Algeria and Tunisia. While the French ran the vineyards, the Muslim locals didn't touch the stuff, and it all went abroad. Some of it was sold in its own right, but an awful lot of it went into blending vats in France, quite possibly in Burgundy, certainly at points further south. After independence, because of official indifference, the quality of the wines – mainly red – tended to decline; and when the European Community started banning foreign blending, the bulk trade of North African wines dried up.

But there are now a few signs of improvement: one or two decent ranges of good, robust, quaffing wines have turned up in UK shops – at competitive prices.

Morocco, which was never involved in the bulk export market to the same extent as Algeria and Tunisia, is the country which has managed to retain a place on world markets most successfully. However, in the past year, it has been Algeria which has come up with new wines, based on grape varieties from the Rhône and Bordeaux. One Algerian wine even beat all-comers in a national newspaper tasting. And rumblings from Tunisia suggest that we will be seeing some of their wines soon.

Who's who in North Africa

Morocco

Tarik – a red blend of Cinsault, Carignan and Grenache
Agent: Ricketts Export, 3 Daleside Road, Epsom, Surrey; also available at Evesham Hotel, Coopers Lane, Evesham, Heref & Worcs

Algeria

Sidi Brahim – straight Cinsault and better quality.
William Pitters International, Lowgate House, Backbarrow, Ulverston, Cumbria
Coteaux de Tiemcen Red Infuriator – A good basic powerful red wine.
Peter Dominic
Wines produced by the state monopoly under a variety of names:
Medea Rouge, Coteaux de Zaccar, Dahra, Coteaux de Mascara and Cuvée du President (regarded as the top wine).
Alston Wines; Vinceremos; for other stockists contact Masons of Holbrook, Reed Hall, Holbrook, Ipswich, Suffolk

Portugal

In the smartest restaurant in Oporto, high up in a modern tower block overlooking the city, the wine list is long and impressive. There's a range of quality, both white and red, and it's available at some surprisingly attractive prices considering the surroundings.

The clientele is cosmopolitan, obviously much travelled. They must be used to drinking French, Spanish, probably California wines. But what they are being offered here is only Portuguese, and they seem perfectly happy with it. It's a situation which sums up the Portuguese attitude to wine: 'We like what we make, so don't bother us with any foreign stuff.' With the exception of Spanish sparkling Cava, it is virtually impossible to find any imported wine in Portugal, either in posh restaurants or in the top wine shops.

We know what we like

The Portuguese make their wines the way they like to drink them: heavy, very dry, tannic reds, oxidised whites. The only exceptions are the hugely acidic dry red and white Vinhos Verdes. Until recently, we had to accept those wines as they came, or, very politely, we were told that there was nothing else, Senhor.

But there are changes afoot. Some wines coming out of Portugal – especially the reds – are full of fruit as well as tannin. They may be big and beefy, but they have quality as well as sinew. Now that Portugal has joined the European Community, we're finding a much greater interest in what is going on in the wider wine world.

But still – and we are delighted to report this – the Portuguese reckon their own grape varieties are best. There is no doubt that the much-travelled Cabernet Sauvignon and Chardonnay do very well here – a few examples prove it. But, on the whole, even the new generation of red wines is based on the bewildering array of unknown grape varieties that Portugal has developed over the centuries.

A terrific conservatism still reigns in much Portuguese winemaking. It is the one European wine-producing country without much of a wine lake, simply because the locals drink so much of it – they have the highest consumption of wine per capita in the world. Much of the wine is still made on small farms for family consumption – and much of what is sold goes to the co-operatives who supply the local area first, the big cities second and the export market not at all.

It does mean that standards of winemaking are not always very high, and that some rather unpleasant wines do get into the local shops. But Portugal is also a land of contrasts: slap against the small farmer's cellar with its dirty old barrels, you will find a stainless steel space-age winery, pumping out Portugal's answer to Coca Cola – sparkling pink wine. It's a sign of Portugal's wine-drinking conservatism that the only Portuguese rosé that is actually drunk in Portugal is sold to tourists in the restaurants of the Algarve.

An eye to exports

Increasingly, though, those modern wineries are turning out good, clean wines, partly because of a growing demand from the young set of Lisbon for a more international style of drink, but mainly because the Portuguese producers are realising that there is a potential export market out there.

Most of the successful exporters are merchant houses, the equivalent of French négociants. While they may have some vineyards, they buy in the bulk of their grapes to make their wines, which are, more often than not, branded wines. They may either be wines from undemarcated areas (see below for the Portuguese production areas) or blends of wines from different areas. They are table wines, made up to a quality set out by the producer rather than the state.

Of course, the demarcated regions are increasing their exports of wine as well. Two, Bairrada and Douro, are making some impact on the British scene. The Dão we have been familiar with for some time, and the Minho, the production area of Vinho Verde, is a major quencher of our thirst, but of those areas only in the Minho do merchant houses make demarcated wines in any quantity.

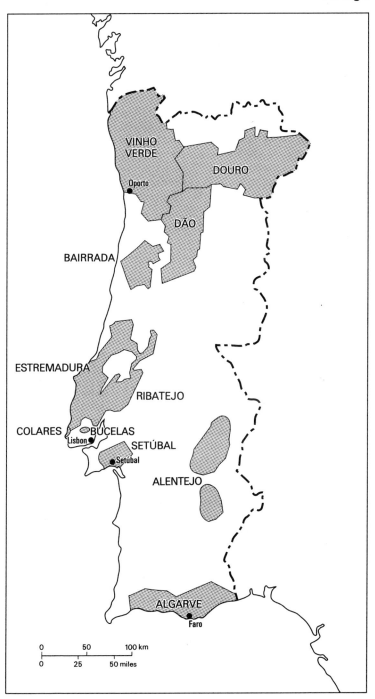

VINHO
VERDE

DOURO

Oporto

DÃO

BAIRRADA

ESTREMADURA

RIBATEJO

COLARES · BUCELAS
Lisbon ·

SETÚBAL

· Setúbal

ALENTEJO

ALGARVE
· Faro

| 0 | 50 | 100 km |
| 0 | 25 | 50 miles |

Estate wines

It is also in the Minho that a newer aspect of Portuguese wine production has appeared: the wine estates. While obviously all wine comes from grapes grown on farms, most of the grapes, as we have seen, go either to co-operatives or to the merchant houses. It is the same situation as in the south of France until recently. But, just like the south of France, a few larger or more quality conscious estates are now making their own wine and bottling and selling it as well. In Vinho Verde country, the estate wines are the best wines around; the same is true in Dão, where the one estate wine is consistently the best. Even in the newly demarcated area of the Alentejo, one estate is doing great things. In many cases, these are the producers to watch to find out the highest quality in Portuguese wines.

The great divide

Portuguese wine is conveniently divided into two categories – Vinhos Verdes and Vinhos Maduros. The first category is of wines which are made to be drunk young – the name refers to the youth of the wine rather than its colour. The second category covers all other wines, both red as well as white: these are the wines which are designed for some ageing, both in the winery and in bottle.

Vinhos Verdes

The best-known wines in this category are Vinhos Verdes from the Minho, the northern province of Portugal. In Britain we see only white Vinhos Verdes, but about half the production is red: very acid and astringent, but fabulous with a plate of sardines or oily food.

The Minho is the most verdant part of Portugal, constantly washed by rains from the Atlantic. The vines, grown in opulent, lush countryside, twirl themselves around trees, posts, pergolas, anything; other crops often grow beneath them because land is so short.

The initial success of Vinho Verde in Britain was as slightly sweet, pétillant, branded white wine – an alternative to Liebfraumilch, in fact. But gradually the truth dawned that true Vinho Verde as drunk in Portugal is bone-dry, with a cooking-apple acidity. A few wines of this style are available in UK shops (see *Best buys*), and they are definitely worth snapping up for cool summer drinking.

There are also now some superior estate-bottled Vinhos Verdes: Quinta da Aveleda, Alvarinho (also a grape name), Palacio de Brejoeira.

Drink Vinho Verde as soon as possible: it doesn't keep. It is unlikely to have a vintage on the label, because it is meant to be consumed as soon as it is bottled, so buy from a merchant with a good turnover of wine.

One other style of wine should also be classed as Vinho Verde. Portuguese rosé, slightly sweet and slightly pétillant, has enjoyed a revival after a couple of years in the doldrums. Some of the brands of Portuguese rosé have been joined by white stablemates, which have something (but not very much) of the quality of sweetened Vinho Verde.

Vinhos Maduros

Where else but from Portugal could you buy red wines – decent, interesting red wines, carrying vintages over ten years old and more – for under £4? The range of older vintages still available in our shops continues to delight. These are the second category of Portuguese wines – the Vinhos Maduros.

Of course, in many cases, if we were presented with young versions of some of these reds, they would be quite undrinkable, but some of them last remarkable lengths of time. They start off inky black and shot through with tannin. Gradually, the tannin wears off, and slight fruit comes through, until eventually a soft, rich, complex wine emerges after, maybe, 15 years.

Sometimes, of course, the fruit never gets a chance, and the dryness remains, simply changing from the dryness of tannic fruit to the dryness of a wine that's too old. This is true of many examples of Dão wines around. But as well as the branded wines we've already mentioned, some wines from demarcated areas are now much more approachable (see below for a full list).

Many of the best of these red wines comes from Bairrada. This is a newly-demarcated region lying west of Coimbra in central Portugal. The red grape, the Baga, makes rich, soft wines, with plenty of fruit and not excessive tannin. An area with great potential, whose wines are now in many shops (see *Best buys*).

The Douro is the second region with potentially good reds. About 40 per cent of its wine is made into Port (see below), the rest being turned into rather fat and oily white or much better red. Indeed, what is often regarded as Portugal's finest wine – Barca Velha, made by Ferreira – is produced here, but only in very good years, and in limited quantities. Another Port producer, Champalimaud, makes a red that's Californian in its intensity, although it's made with Portuguese grape varieties. Other, cheaper, Douro wines are much more disappointing.

In the past Dão has been the major area for red wines from Portugal, but a strange system whereby only farmers are allowed to make wine, which they then sell to the merchants and négociants (rather than letting the big companies buy in grapes and use sophisticated equipment to make the wine), has meant that the vast majority of the wine from the area is disappointing. Two Dãos which get round this problem are Grão Vasco from the producers of Mateus Rosé, who control and buy the production of one co-operative, and the estate wine, Conde de Santar.

One small demarcated area on the Atlantic coast is also worth looking for. Colares wines are made from vines grown in sand dunes (so they don't have to be grafted, because the phylloxera louse can't cope with sand). Only a few firms make this wine now: it suffers from the true Portuguese red astringency and toughness in youth, but matures into an amazingly perfumed wine given many years.

South of the Dão and Bairrada regions are huge areas of flat plains which make up the Alentejo, which stretch right down to the Algarve. To the west are the Tagus Valley vineyards of the Ribatejo. While much of the wine from these areas goes into the merchants' blending vats, emerging as some of the most immediately attractive Portuguese reds around, there are now pockets of more than local interest where the idea of estate wines is gaining ground. Best known of these is the Alentejo town of Reguengos de Monsaraz, whose wines we are now seeing in this country.

South of Lisbon, in the Setúbal peninsula, the firm of J M da Fonseca make a range of branded wines, some of which are generally regarded as Portugal's finest (see below under *Who's who*).

Few white excitements

Few really exciting Portuguese whites come from south of the Minho with its Vinhos Verdes. Some are made in the Dão and in Bairrada, but there are better wines to be had from other countries.

You have to look again to branded wine producers for some unusual and interesting white wines. João Pires, as associate company of J M da Fonseca, make a 100 per cent dry Muscat wine called after the company name, and a Chardonnay wine, called Caterina. Fonseca also make a long-lived fortified dessert wine from Muscat grapes, called Moscatel de Setúbal, full of grapy richness.

What's what in Portugal

Some names that appear on Portuguese labels:
Colheita Vintage
Engarrafedo Bottled (by)
Garrafeira A wine merchant's best wines, generally selected after some years in cask and bottle. This will normally be a branded wine, and can be a blend of vintages
Região Demarcada Demarcated region, similar to AC or Italian DOC (see below for list)
Reserva Another term for an older wine, but, unlike Garrafeira, one from a demarcated region
Velho (or Velha) Old.

Vintages in Portugal

These notes apply to red wines only.

1987 Heavy rains during the harvest meant either a ruined crop or a crop of swollen grapes. Most areas have made light wines, not for keeping. Only in the Alentejo are there better things.

1986 Small quantities were made after spring frosts. Only in the south, in Ribatejo and Alentejo, are quality and quantity good.

1985 A great year all round. Everybody did well, although in the Alentejo, quantity was down because of the dry summer.

1984 A light vintage which will be ready to drink soon. Better for white wines.

1983 A classic vintage in the north. Average quality and small quantities in Ribatejo and Alentejo.

1982 Another classic vintage, this time right across the country. These wines are for keeping.

1980 A good start to the decade with long-lived wines being made right round the country.

Older vintages: 1978, 1975, 1974, 1971 and 1970 are drinking well now.

Where's where in Portugal

There are twelve demarcated regions in Portugal, some of very minor significance.

Alentejo High area of production east of Lisbon. Reds are best.

Algarve Reds and whites, both high in alcohol, seen only in the holiday resorts of the Algarve

Bairrada Good quality reds from the centre of the country. Some whites, mostly made into sparkling wine

Bucelas Dry white wines from near Lisbon, sometimes with a slight prickle. They have a tendency to oxidise

Carcavelhos Almost impossible to find this slightly sweet fortified wine, made near Lisbon (buildings cover almost all the vineyards)

Colares Huge red wines from the sand dunes (see above)

Dão Big tough reds and dull dry whites

Douro Some very good reds, less interesting whites

Estremadura Red and white wines from just north of Lisbon

Moscatel de Setúbal Fortified dessert wines (see above)

Ribatejo Area north of Lisbon. Source of many of the branded wines.

Vinho Verde Largest demarcated region, producing a quarter of all Portugal's wine. Slightly pétillant, crisp, dry whites and acid reds.

Who's who in Portugal

Names of some producers to look for:

Adega Cooperativa de Cantanhede Producer of some excellent Bairrada reds.
Berry Bros & Rudd

Adega Cooperativa de Chamusca An enterprising co-operative in the Ribatejo, making good, tarry reds.
Oddbins

Adega Cooperativa de Mealhada Another reliable quality co-op in Bairrada.
Asda; Waitrose; Winecellars

Caves Aliança A whole range of good quality wines, from Vinho Verde, Dão, Bairrada and Douro.
Majestic; Wessex Wines

Quinta da Aveleda Producer of a straightforward Vinho Verde (Aveleda) and a superior estate-bottled wine (Quinta da Aveleda).
D Byrne & Co; Davisons; Nobody Inn

Julio Bastos Alentejo producer of an elegant red, under the name of his estate, Quinta do Carmo.
For stockist information, contact Wineforce, New House, 67–8 Hatton Garden, London EC1

Borges e Irmão Make the best-selling Vinho Verde, Gatão, but also a drier style and Dão wines.
Marks & Spencer; Victoria Wine Company

Carvalho, Ribeiro e Ferreira A major table wine producer, specialising in branded and Garrafeira wines of high quality, mainly from the Ribatejo. Brands include Serradayres.
Peter Dominic

Champalimaud Single vineyard Port producer (see under Ports) who also makes some top quality Douro table wines. Names are Cotto Grande Escolha, Quinta do Cotto.
Adnams; Bibendum; Alex Findlater; Hicks & Don; Lockes; Oddbins; Ubiquitous Chip; La Vigneronne; Winecellars; Wines from Paris

Caves Dom Teodosio Garrafeiras under the brand name Casaleiro are huge, peppery and long-lasting.
D Byrne & Co

Conde de Santar The only single vineyard Dão; its quality shines out against other Dãos.

Ferreira Port producers who also make Douro table wines. Their finest wine, Barca Velha, is made only in exceptional years. The less expensive brand, Esteva, is now widely available.
Oddbins; Thresher; A L Vose

J M da Fonseca One of the best wine firms in Portugal. A whole range of branded wines include Camarate, Periquita, Pasmasdos and Garrafeiras. Also the major producer of Moscatel de Setúbal. Now making a good wine from Reguengos de Monsaraz in the Alentejo.
Adnams; D Byrne & Co; Alex Findlater; Hicks & Don; Hungerford Wine Company; Lockes; Majestic; Nobody Inn; Christopher Piper Wines; La Reserva Wines; Tanners Wines; Ubiquitous Chip; La Vigneronne; Waitrose; Winecellars; Wine Society; Wizard Wine Warehouses

João Pires Source of some fine branded red and white wines made in a brand-new, space-age winery. Reds include Tinto da Anfora, whites João Pires and Quinta da Palmela. Also make the claret-like Quinta da Bacalhoa, one of the few Cabernet Sauvignon-based wines in Portugal.
(For Bacalhoa) Sainsbury's; (for other wines) H Allen Smith; Curzon Wine Company; Davisons; Alex Findlater; Hungerford Wine Company; Lockes; Majestic; Oddbins; Christopher Piper Wines; La Reserva Wines; Tanners Wines; Ubiquitous Chip; A L Vose; Waitrose; Winecellars; Wizard Wine Warehouses

Caves São João Good red wines under the Frei São João name.
D Byrne & Co; Lay & Wheeler

Sogrape Producers of Mateus Rosé and Mateus White. They also make Grão Vasco Dão wines.
Mateus Rosé and Mateus White widely available. Other wines available from: Curzon Wine Company; Davisons; Majestic; Oddbins

Caves Velhas Sole remaining producer of the Bucelas wines. Also make Dãos and some good Garrafeiras under the Romeira name.
(For Bucelas) D Byrne & Co; Lay & Wheeler; Tanners Wines; (for Garrafeiras) Peter Dominic; Tesco; Winecellars

Best buys from Portugal

WHITES
Palmela Branco, João Pires (*Ubiquitous Chip*)
Vinho Verde, Paco de Texeiro, Champalimaud (*Bibendum*)
Vinho Verde Solar das Boucas (*La Réserve*)

REDS

Bairrada 1984, Adega Cooperativa de Mealhada (*Waitrose*)
Quinta de Abrigada 1984 (*Del Monico's Wine Emporium; Oddbins*)
Tinto da Anfora, João Pires (*Queens Club Wines; Waitrose*)
Sainsbury's Arruda (*J Sainsbury*)
Quinta de Santa Amaro, João Pires (*Sherborne Vintners*)
Colares 1979, Beira Mar (*Wine Emporium*)
Quinta da Camarate 1982, J M da Fonseca (*H Allen Smith*)
Reguengos de Monsaraz 1985 (*Barrel Selection*)
Garrafeira 1974, Caves Velhas (*G E Bromley & Sons*)

Specialist stockists

H Allen Smith; Bibendum; Alex Findlater; Peter Green; Oddbins; Wine House

PORT

Quietly, subtly, changes are taking place in the Port wine trade. Quite where they're going is still anybody's guess. But that they will at least lead to greater quality and a more sophisticated image for Port is not in doubt.

Port took a while to recover from the loss of a lucrative part of its sales – the Port and lemon trade. The people who drank this popular combination were going for cheap rubies, or tawnies made by blending young ruby with white Port (instead of ageing the wine in cask to let it acquire the light tawny colour naturally). When they stopped drinking Port and lemon, the market for these cheap Ports slumped in Britain (in France, they quite happily carry on drinking ruby Port on the rocks as an aperitif).

The question was how to replace a large part of the trade? The answer was Late Bottled Vintage. But it didn't actually replace the bottom end of the Port market – what it did was to move on people's appreciation of Port to greater things – classic Vintage Port was not the only style of Port which could be sophisticated.

That solution worked well – nearly every Port shipper has a Late Bottled Vintage (or Vintage Character) Port whose sales are climbing very nicely indeed. And now some Port houses are introducing a further level of sophistication – aged tawnies. These are high quality wines which have been aged in wood for a period of several years. They are lighter than vintage or LBV Ports, more elegant perhaps – certainly the preferred tipple of the Port producers themselves.

Focus on the vines

Alongside this change of emphasis, the Port producers are hard at work improving the quality of the wine itself.

Everybody agrees that the Douro Valley, in which the Port wine is produced, is one of the most beautiful vineyard areas in the world, but only those who have actual experience of the vineyards there know how difficult it is to cultivate vines when the slopes down to the river are almost vertical. Terracing used to be standard practice, but now there is great controversy as producers argue whether modern techniques of hillside contouring will allow them to plant the vines up and down the hills in long rows, or whether wide terraces without the traditional stone walls will allow mechanical harvesting to take place. Still others are moving away from the river to find flatter land where they can plant in a more conventional manner following the contours of the land.

The other, more important change, as far as Port drinkers are concerned, is in the approach to the grape varieties. Forty-eight varieties are planted in the Douro vineyards. Until recently nobody knew – or cared much – which variety got into the wine: the vineyards were planted haphazardly and everything was thrown in together at harvest time.

Now a new breed of trained oenologists is taking an interest in the quality of the vines. The local authorities have suggested that six varieties have the highest quality, and will, in varying proportions, contribute everything that is needed in a blend (Port is always a blended wine). Portuguese grape varieties are far from the international world of Cabernet Sauvignon and Chardonnay, and these six varieties are no exception: Touriga Nacional, Touriga Francesca, Barroca, Roriz, Tinto Cao and Mourisco. Hardly names to trip off the tongue, but they are going to form the new generation of Ports.

The grapes will be handled differently, as well. Instead of planting the vines in a muddle, and subsequently fermenting everything together, the new approach is to plant the varieties separately in the land which best suits their character, then to vinify them separately. Treating the raw material in this way means that careful blending is then possible. That might seem obvious to a Bordelais (they've been treating their grape varieties separately for years) but it's news in Portugal – and good news for quality.

Two nationalities

Port has often been regarded as the British fortified wine. British names have been, and still are, associated with the Port trade, and most of the Port we see in Britain comes with a British name on its label. Although some of those 'British' houses are now owned by multi-national conglomerates, the nature of the Port they make hasn't radically changed.

In all this, we forget that most of the Port isn't made by 'British' houses at all, but by Portuguese firms, with Portuguese names. On the whole, they have a different approach to Port – they prefer to make lighter tawnies, for example. They make vintage wines every year (unlike the traditional three or four declarations made by the British firms each decade), and then they leave them in wood to become vintage tawnies, called colheitas. The approach is different, but every bit as valid. Although these Portuguese Ports are less widely available in our shops, they are worth seeking out as an alternative style.

Styles of Port

White Port Usually put last in a listing of styles because it has never taken off. We suggest it should, because it makes a marvellous aperitif, served chilled. It's made from white rather than red grapes, but is fortified in the same way.

Ruby The most basic quality. Youthful, simple wine. Widely available.

Tawny This term has two completely different meanings. One is an alternative to ruby, of basic quality. But there are also aged tawnies – 10-year-old, 20-year-old, etc – which are some of the finest Ports available. This second type of tawny has a lighter style than a ruby, and is delicious slightly chilled, drunk as an aperitif or after a meal.

Colheita A tawny style of which the base is wine from one particular year. The wine is kept in wood and then bottled ready for drinking. However, the casks are topped up in the interim with wine that can come from any year, and so a Colheita wine really becomes more of a solera-type wine, like Sherry.

Crusted A blend of qualities either from different years or from a single vintage, bottled after three or four years in wood. It matures reasonably quickly in bottle – generally five or six years from bottling (this date should be on the label). It tends to throw a sediment – hence the name – and therefore needs decanting. There is still argument over the legal definition for crusted, but for the time being, we can certainly recommend it as a good value alternative to expensive Vintage Port.

Late Bottled Vintage The poorer man's Vintage Port, kept in wood for four to six years and then bottled. This means that it is virtually ready to drink when bottled. The vintage will be on the label, but not the bottling date.

Late Bottled or Vintage Character Similar to Late Bottled Vintage in style, but not necessarily from one year.

Single Quinta Port Up until now, single quinta Port has been wine from one estate made in a year which the shipper doesn't consider quite good enough for a general vintage declaration (see Vintage Port below and vintage information). It is bottled after two years, and needs some years to mature in bottle. Now single quinta Ports also come from smaller producers who produce wine from only one vineyard.

Vintage The finest of Ports – and the most serious. In style, it is like a very superior ruby. A vintage will be 'declared' only in the best years and bottled after two years in wood. It needs many years to mature, because glass ages wine more slowly than wood. Decant Vintage Port before serving it. Some of the Portuguese houses leave their Vintage Ports in cask longer, and they tend to be ready to drink sooner.

The great vintages

1985 Looks like being a great vintage year since the weather was boiling hot right through the summer. The wines were bottled in early 1987, and are rather expensive.

1983 Well-coloured, aromatic wines. The majority of shippers have declared this vintage. The wines are quite forward and should be ready in the mid-1990s.

1982 Declared by a minority of shippers. The wines are maturing quite fast, and are full of fruit. Ready by the 1990s.

1980 A longer-lasting vintage. Good quality wines from many of the oldest-established shippers. Ready in the late 1990s. Excellent value for money.

1977 The classic vintage since 1963, much admired. Keep it until the turn of the century.

1975 A light vintage. Drink in the next few years.

1970 Much better than originally considered, this vintage is still underpriced.

1966 Wines from this year started off by being underrated, but the world has caught on to their quality and now, though good, they are over-priced.

1963 Great post-war vintage, the best since 1945. Keep those you have and grab any you can. Will keep for years.

In addition to these general vintage years, single quinta Ports (see above) were declared by shippers in 1980, 1972, 1968 and 1967.

Who's who in the Port trade

Cálem A Portuguese house which surprised the world by making one of the best 1985 vintage Ports, in a true 'British' style. The quality of all their wines has improved enormously in the past few years, and prices are still relatively inexpensive. Single quinta: Quinta da Foz.
La Vigneronne; A L Vose; Wine Growers Association; Wine Society

Churchill Graham Small independent family firm making extremely good wines. Descendants of the Graham family (see below). Single quinta: Quinta do Agua Alta.
Corney & Barrow; Alex Findlater; Lay & Wheeler; Laytons; Lockes; Seckford Wines; T & W Wines; Wine Society

Cockburn Biggest firm on the British market with Special Reserve. Some good tawnies.
Adnams; Berry Bros & Rudd; Cantina Augusto; Corney & Barrow; Davisons; Eldridge Pope; Lay & Wheeler; Oddbins; Tanners Wines; Tesco; T & W Wines; Waitrose

Croft Specialise in LBV and Distinction brands, also Gilbey's Crown Triple Port. Single quinta: Quinta da Roêda.
Adnams; Berry Bros & Rudd; Corney & Barrow; Davisons; Peter Dominic; Hungerford Wine Company; Lay & Wheeler; Oddbins; Tanners Wines; La Vigneronne

Delaforce Owned jointly with Croft, but still managed by the family. His Eminence Choice and Vintage Character as well as lighter vintage styles. Single quinta: Quinta da Corte.
Berry Bros & Rudd; Peter Dominic; Alex Findlater; Upper Crust; La Vigneronne

Dow One of the leading vintage houses. Wines have a dry and nutty style. High quality. Single quinta: Quinta do Bonfim.
Widely available, including Adnams; Averys; Curzon Wine Company; Davisons; Grape Ideas; Gerard Harris; O W Loeb; Oddbins; Willoughbys

Ferreira The leading Portuguese Port house (as opposed to those owned by British families). Some good tawnies. Also produce table wines, of which the best is called Barca Velha (see under table wine section). Duque de Braganca 20-year-old Tawny Port is famous. Single quinta Tawny: Quinta do Porto.
Thresher

Fonseca Best-known brand is Bin 27, but also make long-lasting Vintage Ports. Very high reputation. Their Late Bottled Vintage Port is one of of the best.
Adnams; Berry Bros & Rudd; Corney & Barrow; Curzon Wine Company; Alex Findlater; Grape Ideas; Gerard Harris; Hicks & Don; Lockes; O W Loeb; Christopher Piper Wines; Prestige Vintners; Reid Wines; Waitrose

Graham Big, luscious vintage Ports. Other styles emulate these qualities. Single quinta: Quinta do Malvedos.
Berkmann Wine Cellars/Le Nez Rouge; Berry Bros & Rudd; Bibendum; Corney & Barrow; Curzon Wine Company; Davisons; Eldridge Pope; Gerard Harris; Haynes, Hanson & Clark; Lay & Wheeler; Oddbins; Reid Wines; T & W Wines; Willoughbys

Martinez Associated with Cockburn. Produce some really very attractive Ports at good prices.
Adnams; Averys; Curzon Wine Company; Majestic; Oddbins; Tanners Wines; La Vigneronne; Wine Society

Niepoort Firm with Dutch origins, specialising in Colheita Ports.
Contact Celtic Vintner for stockist information: 73 Derwen Fawr Road, Sketty, Swansea, W Glamorgan

Noval High quality Ports made in one of the finest Douro vineyards. Late Bottled is their best known brand. Also make the rare (and very expensive) Nacional Port, from ungrafted vines.
Adnams: Davisons; Ellis Son & Vidler; Gerard Harris; High Breck Vintners; Ian G Howe; Upper Crust; Waitrose; Wine Society

Offley Forrester One of the most famous names in Port through the activities of Baron Forrester in the 19th century. Now owned by the Italian vermouth house of Martini.
Tanners Wines

Quarles Harris Another small Port house, part of the Symington group, which also owns Dow, Graham and Warre.
Adnams; Berry Bros & Rudd; Ellis Son & Vidler; Grape Ideas; Haynes, Hanson and Clark; Seckford Wines; Tanners Wines; Upper Crust; La Vigneronne; Wine Society

Ramos Pinto Small Portuguese house making a range of light style wines of good quality. Single quinta tawny Ports: Quinta da Bom Retiro: Quinta da Ervamoira.
Berkmann Wine Cellars/Le Nez Rouge; Andrew Mead Wines

Rebello Valente Brand name of Robertson Brothers, a small Port house, now owned by Sandeman.
Berry Bros & Rudd; Ellis Son & Vidler; Laytons; Upper Crust; Winecellars

Royal Oporto The largest Port producer, controlling 20 per cent of the trade. They make light-style wines, including Vintage Ports every year. Many of their wines are sold under own-label brands.
Alex Findlater; Hungerford Wine Company; Andrew Mead Wines; Tesco; T & W Wines

Please write to tell us about any ideas for features you would like to see in next year's edition or in *Which? Wine Monthly*.

Sandeman A range of Ports in all styles from this firm which is linked to the Sandeman Sherry firm.
Adnams; Berry Bros & Rudd; Eldridge Pope; Oddbins; Tanners Wines; Willoughbys; Wine Society

Taylor Expensive, top quality Ports. Late Bottled Vintage is widely available. Lighter tawnies of high standard. Single quinta: Quinta de Vargellas.
Berry Bros & Rudd; Curzon Wine Company; Davisons; Eldridge Pope; Alex Findlater; Grape Ideas; Gerard Harris; Haynes, Hanson & Clark; Lay & Wheeler; Lockes; Andrew Mead Wines; Tesco; La Vigneronne; Waitrose; Willoughbys

Warre Oldest Port house, now jointly owned with Graham and Dow. Single quinta: Quinta da Cavadinha.
Adnams; Berkmann Wine Cellars/Le Nez Rouge; Berry Bros & Rudd; Corney & Barrow; Curzon Wine Company; Davisons; Eldridge Pope; Alex Findlater; Grape Ideas; Haynes, Hanson & Clark; Andrew Mead Wines; Waitrose; Winecellars

Best buys in Port

Ferreira Quinta do Porto 10-year-old tawny (*Thresher*)
De Souza Wood Port 1978 (*Richmond Wine Warehouse, 138C Lower Mortlake Road, London SW9*)
Ramos Pinto 10-year-old tawny, Quinta da Ervamoira (*Russell & McIver; Le Nez Rouge/Berkmann Wine Cellars*)
Martinez Crusted Port (bottled 1986) (*Prestige Vintners*)
10-year-old tawny (*Corney & Barrow*)
Gould Campbell Crusted (bottled 1980) (*Eldridge Pope*)
Cockburn Light White (*Tesco*)

MADEIRA

There's more money in bananas

Consider that the island of Madeira has only 400 square miles of land – most of it mountainous – to support a population of 250,000. Consider also that there are only 200 hectares of vineyard on the island, and that bananas are a much better cash crop . . . that the bulk of the wine produced on the island is a rather unpleasant table wine made entirely for local consumption. It is a minor miracle that any Madeira wine is made at all.

But it is – and we must be very thankful. Madeira is a unique taste. It is a fortified wine – which means that brandy is added to stop it fermenting – but it is also a cooked wine, giving it its special taste. After the brandy has been added, the wine is heated up to 40°C in an estufa or stove, and then cooled. The whole process can last up to a year. Such a strange way of treating a wine derives from the 18th and 19th centuries when it was discovered that the heat in the holds of ships transporting the wine to hot countries improved it no end.

The resulting wine has three characteristics – a burnt, caramel taste, oxidation (hence the word for a wine that has been oxidised – maderised) and considerable acidity because of high volatility. An unlikely range of tastes to make a great wine, but with the essentially rich base they all work together.

Because the island of Madeira is part of Portugal, Madeira wine is often equated with Port, but a better comparison would be with Sherry: there is a range of styles, from comparatively dry to very sweet. Moreover, Madeira can be drunk in the same circumstances as Sherry.

The driest style is Sercial, which makes an excellent aperitif, just like Fino Sherry. Verdelho is also an aperitif wine, but being slightly fuller, will also go well with food like soups, rather like Amontillado. Both Bual and Malmsey make magnificent after-dinner drinks, like the richest Oloroso Sherries.

Those wine names are also the names of the best quality grapes grown on the island. There are two other quality varieties – Terrantez and Malvasia – both of which are grown in tiny quantities, but which make superb and fascinating wines.

However, these 'noble' varieties account for only a small proportion of the island's vines. A much larger area of vineyard is occupied by a variety called Tinta Negra Mole. Another large area of vineyard is planted with American vines which rejoice in names like Black Spanish and Barrete de Padre. Until recently, all these varieties used to be chucked into Madeira, which was still sold as Sercial or Malmsey regardless of the fact that those grape varieties might have made up only 10 per cent of the whole.

With the arrival of Portugal in the EEC, that had to stop (the wine laws of the European Community do have some uses). The new rules specify that 85 per cent of the wine in a bottle of Sercial must be made from Sercial. If it isn't, it must be called Dry. The same, of course, applies to other grape varieties. The farmers are also being encouraged to plant more of the noble varieties in place of the lesser types.

That means that the quality of Madeira now available in British shops is improving all the time. Apart from standard ranges, which cost around £5 a bottle, there are older wines and – in small quantities – Madeiras based on soleras which date from the beginning of the 19th century.

Categories have been developed, and these will be indicated on the label:

Reserve: over five years old.
Reserve Velho: over ten years old.
Special Reserve: over 15 years old.

Fresqueira (vintage): wine from a specified year that has been in cask for over 20 years.

Wine that lasts for ever

We've already indicated something of the taste of Madeira. What is also so special about the cooking process (known as the estufagem) is that it has the effect of allowing the best wines to last seemingly for ever without really ageing. It is possible (but very expensive) to drink vintages of Madeira that date back well into the last century – there are still some 1795 wines on the island that have plenty of fruit. While that's a characteristic of the top wines, ordinary Madeiras are wines which are at their best when they are bottled and are not designed to improve in bottle.

If you plan to open a bottle of Madeira, don't be worried that it may fade if it isn't finished at one sitting. Unlike any other wine, a bottle of Madeira once opened will survive unchanged for months.

Good, basic Madeira is available at most specialist off-licences priced at just above ruby or Vintage Character Port – remarkable when the very high costs of production are taken into account. But there are shortages of some of the finer Madeiras while producers build up stocks of wines based on the noble grape varieties (which is all they are now allowed to export from Madeira). Recent harvests have been small: 1984 was appalling, while 1985 was high quality but tiny in quantity. But luck changed with a good, bumper crop in 1986; 1987 was good as well.

It's certainly worth the effort to search out fine old Madeira. Its complexities, its distinctive nutty, slightly 'cooked' taste and classic balance between sweetness and dried fruit are well worth savouring.

Who's who in Madeira

Barbeito Family-owned firm which has a superb collection of vintage wines. Sadly, all we see is the basic range. Wines: Rainwater Dry, Island Dry, Island Rich, Crown Malmsey.
Christopher & Co; Beeswing, Morpeth, Northumberland

Blandy Brothers One of the most famous Madeira companies, which also owns Reid's Hotel, one of the island's top hotels. Wines: Duke of Sussex Sercial, Duke of Cambridge Verdelho, Duke of Cumberland Bual, Duke of Clarence Malmsey, 5-year-old and 10-year-old wines.
Augustus Barnett; Peter Dominic; Oddbins; Tanners Wines; Thresher; La Vigneronne

---

Stockists given in italic type after wines in this section will be found in the WHERE TO BUY section earlier in the book.

Cossart Gordon Producer of classic Madeira, often in a light style. Top quality wines. Wines: Good Company Sercial, Cossart Rainwater, Good Company Bual and Malmsey, 5-year-old Reserve, 10-year-old Special Reserve.
Adnams; Berry Bros & Rudd; Richard Harvey Wines; Hedley Wright; Hicks & Don; Lay & Wheeler; Oddbins; Christopher Piper Wines; Tanners Wines; La Vigneronne; Winecellars; Wine Society

Harveys Part of the famous Sherry firm, whose Madeiras are produced for them by Henriques & Henriques. Wines: Very Superior Old Dry Sercial, Royal Solera Verdelho, Old Bual, Old Rich Malmsey.
Cantina Augusto; John Harvey & Sons; Tesco; Victoria Wine Company

Henriques & Henriques Large producer who makes wines under a number of different labels. Wines: Henriques & Henriques, Belem, Casa dos Vinhos de Madeira.
Claridge Fine Wines; Alex Findlater; Laytons; T & W Wines; La Vigneronne

Leacock Rich, deep Madeiras which are balanced by clean fruit. Wines: Leacock St John Reserve Sercial, Verdelho and Bual, Special Reserve Malmsey.
Adnams; Nobody Inn; La Vigneronne

Lomelino The oldest Portuguese Madeira house. Wines: Imperial Sercial, Verdelho, Reserve 5-years, Special Reserve.
Nobody Inn; Russell & McIver; La Vigneronne

Rutherford & Miles Very stylish wines in quite a light style. Wines: Old Custom House Sercial, La Reina Verdelho, Old Trinity House Bual, Reserve, Special Reserve.
Curzon Wine Company; Eldridge Pope; Hicks & Don; High Breck Vintners; Nobody Inn; Tanners Wines; Windrush Wines; Wizard Wine Warehouses

Veiga Franca The largest exporter of Madeira, much of which goes to France. They supply a number of wines to our shops under own labels.
Majestic

Best buys from Madeira

Most houses stock small quantities of vintage solera wines which make for memorable drinking. Of the more widely available Madeiras, here are our best buys:
Cossarts Finest Old Sercial (*Ellis Son & Vidler; Lay & Wheeler*)
Rutherford and Miles Reserve Bual (*J E Hogg*)
Blandy's Malmsey 10-years (*Buckingham Wines; Peter Green*)

Specialist stockists of Port and Madeira

Adnams; Alastair's Grapevine; Berry Bros & Rudd; Bibendum; Bin Ends; Cairns & Hickey; Classic Wines; College Cellar; Corney & Barrow; Davisons; Eldridge Pope; Ellis Son & Vidler; Farr Vintners; Fine Vintage Wines;

Andrew Gordon Wines; Peter Green; Greens; Justerini & Brooks; Richard Kihl; Master Cellar Wine Warehouse; Nickolls & Perks; La Réserve; Russell & McIver; T & W Wines; Selfridges; Edward Sheldon; Stones of Belgravia; Tanners Wines; La Vigneronne; Peter Wylie Fine Wines

Rumania

We have had the chance to taste one Rumanian wine this year – a 100 per cent increase on last year. That was a sweet Muscat Ottonel from Transylvania. We didn't think much of it: 'dull and oxidised' were the tasting notes.

And after that, nothing. They make wine in Rumania – quite a lot of it – but we hardly hear anything about it. Perhaps the Rumanians are thirsty, perhaps they are sending it to the USSR to stop the Russians drinking vodka.

The potential for good winemaking is certainly there. There is a long tradition, never interrupted (as it was in Bulgaria) by Moslem prohibitions on alcohol. The most familiar wines are from Transylvania and are white: Pinot Gris, Furmint (the Hungarian grape) or Traminer. But the best wines come from further east – from Murfatlar near the Black Sea which makes a sweet Muscat wine.

The one wine for which Rumania should be famous is Cotnari, a white dessert wine from Moldavia and the equivalent of the Hungarian Tokay. It used to be all the rage in Paris at the turn of the century but is difficult to find now.

A few other wines have made their way here. Of the reds, there is a good fruity Merlot from the Dealul Mare region of the Carpathians and the Minis brand of Cabernet Sauvignon. Of the whites, look for the medium dry Tirnave made in the Dracula country of Transylvania, a reasonable Laski Riesling, and a wine made from the local grape variety, the Fetească (also called by the German name of Mädchentraube), which makes an aromatic, grapy wine.

Specialist stockists

Averys; Irvine Robertson; Oddbins; Touchstone Wines; Waitrose; City Wines, Kingsway Trading Estate, Norwich

Spain

The revolution is beginning

The French are rather worried by Spain. Ask which country they see as the greatest threat to their wine hegemony, and they will not give the automatic answer of California, or Australia – or even Italy – but Spain.

They fear two things. One is the vast amount of wine Spain produces – she has the largest area under vine in the world. The second is that most of that land is not realising its full potential. Spain's wine revolution is still only just beginning.

Spain's arrival in the European Community in 1987 saw an upsurge in her exports of wine. Just the thing the French are worried by, maybe, but from our point of view it showed that at last Spain is being taken seriously as a producer of good wines, and not just plonk.

It has taken years to get rid of the plonk image. People still remember Spanish Chablis and Spanish Sauternes: for many they were the days of wine-drinking innocence when Spanish wine was the cheapest thing in the shop, great for parties and don't worry about the hangover. And, of course, plenty of wine still has much the same effect. The difference is that most of that wine is staying in Spain and what we are seeing is something much better.

The great – and the cheerful

Nowadays Spain's wines, as far as we are concerned, fall into two categories. There are the fine wines, almost invariably red, which come from the top bodegas (wineries). They are hand crafted, aged in wood, made to last, and are, on the whole, excellent value considering their quality. The second category is the modern equivalent of the cheap'n'cheerfuls of yesteryear: they are still cheap, they are – most of them – pretty cheerful, but now they are well made, tasting of fruit and very drinkable.

The change from the bad old days of hangover juice has come about – like so much in the wine world – through the advent of new technology. Every wine country has benefited from the arrival of stainless steel and cool fermentation, but probably none more so than Spain. Her vineyards are the most arid in the world, because they are naturally dry and because (unlike the dry New World vineyards) irrigation is forbidden in Europe. So having burnt and shrivelled in the searing heat, the grapes were then traditionally stuck into huge earthenware jars, Moorish in design, called tinajas, in which they fermented at any temperature that happened to be going on outside. It was a recipe for entirely predictable disaster.

Today, the grapes are picked at their carefully measured optimum ripeness (and for whites they are often picked under-ripe), and the whole fermentation process is carefully controlled. Even with the great Spanish wines, new technology has been called upon at the fermentation stage to improve on what was already high quality.

Reds still better than whites

Most of the success of Spanish wines in Britain has focused on her red wines. The first area to show that Spain could make great wines was Rioja, and it was her red Reservas and Gran Reservas that did it. Other areas which have been important in widening our knowledge of Spanish wines have been Penedès and Navarra. Penedès seems to be the only Spanish region to produce whites which are as good as the reds – and that's as much to do with the fact that the best of those whites are made from that familiar grape variety, the Chardonnay, as for any other reason.

Spain does not seem to have many white grape varieties capable of making interesting table wines. Perhaps the Viura of Rioja is an exception – one bodega in Rioja has proved this by making a 100 per cent Viura wine which is streets ahead of anything else in the freshness and taste leagues. The only other (and splendid) exceptions are the two or three Rioja bodegas which still age their whites in oak.

Otherwise, Spanish white wines are uninspired. Those that benefit from the new technology are at least fruity and fresh, but even those

Spain

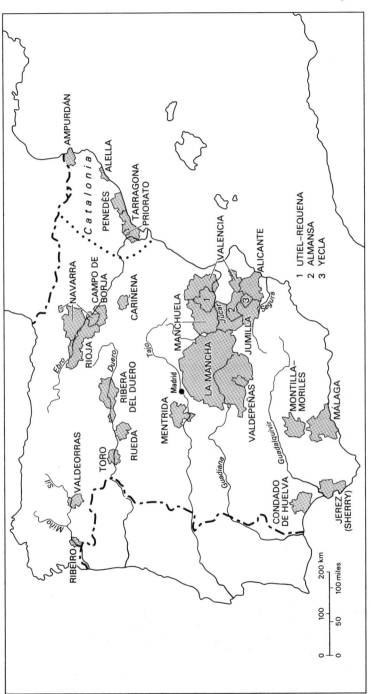

qualities are short-lived: anything apart from the most recent vintage is fading fast.

DOs don't help

If Spain is still a country of potential as much as achievement in quality wines, that is because her system of quality wine regions – the Denominación de Origen (DO) – doesn't help. It is much more a statement of geographical fact than a reflection of the wine produced. The DOS cover too much of the country (62 per cent of the vineyards as against 10 per cent in Italy) to be of real use to the consumer.

The big DO areas – such as Rioja and, even worse, La Mancha – are much too loosely defined. Inevitably, too many different styles of wine are being produced in these large areas for a DO to mean anything much.

The DO idea is much more relevant to some of the smaller areas, largely unexplored except by the specialist importers. Places like Galicia, Ribera del Duero, León and Rueda still have a long way to go before they reach anything like the familiarity of similar small areas in France or even Italy. But at least one of them – Ribera del Duero (see below) – is making wines that can really cause the French to get worried.

What's on a Spanish label

Like every country, Spain has its own set of terms to describe the wine inside the bottle. Here are a few of the most common.

Abocado Medium sweet.
Anejado por Aged by.
Año In the past Spain has used terms like 2 año and 3 año which indicate that the wine was bottled in the second (or third) year after the vintage – *not* that it is two or three years old. This term is banned by the Common Market so only older wines will now carry it.
Blanco White.
Bodega Winery.
Brut Dry – generally used for sparkling wines.
Cava A generic term for sparkling wine made by the Champagne method (the word means cellar).
Con crianza Means that the wine has been aged in wood. Each region has different regulations concerning wood-ageing.
Cosecha Harvest; vintage.
Criado por Blended and/or matured by.
Dulce Sweet.
Elaborado por Made/blended/matured by.
Embotellado por Bottled by.
Espumoso Sparkling wine made by any method.

Generoso Fortified or dessert wine.

Gran Reserva Top-quality wine aged in the winery for a specified period – the highest quality grading for the finest wines. Normally, it means two years in wood and three in bottle, or the other way round (ie a minimum of five years in total). Generally used for reds, but can apply to whites or rosés, in which case the rules specify at least six months in wood and four in bottle.

Reserva Good quality wine, aged (in Rioja) for one year in wood, two in bottle – or the other way round (a minimum of three years). Whites and rosés need at least six months in wood and 18 months in bottle.

Rosado Rosé.

Seco Dry.

Semi-seco Medium dry.

Sin crianza Without wood-ageing. A wine that is made to be drunk young.

Tinto Red wine.

Vendimia Vintage; the gathering of the grapes.

Viña Literally means vineyard, but is often used to refer to a wine as part of a brand name.

Vino de mesa Table wine.

Vintages in Spain

1987 Low quantity but good quality was the norm for this harvest. A hot, dry summer meant that yields were low, and that red wines will be much better than whites. Only in Ribera del Duero are quantities approaching normal.

1986 Good reds in the north of Spain – Rioja, Navarra, Penedès – but less satisfactory for whites. Further south, a good all-round harvest.

1985 Good generally. Very good, with good quantity as well, in Rioja and Navarra.

1984 Average to good quality, much better for whites than reds. Quantities badly down in Rioja.

1983 Good, but not great. Whites fared better than reds again – especially in Penedès. The reds are unlikely to last long.

1982 A great year, with some very fine reds on the way, especially in Rioja, Penedès and Ribera del Duero.

1981 Light reds, but very high quality. Some ageing potential in the Reservas. Best wines from Navarra for a decade.

1980 Variable generally. Very good in La Mancha, good in Rioja and Penedès, average in Navarra.

1979 Good to average vintage. Rioja and La Mancha good, Navarra average.

1978 Good vintage everywhere, very good in Navarra and La Mancha.

RIOJA

Rioja has been giving itself airs and graces. The producers are now used to being told that they are Spain's premier wine region, that they make the country's finest wines. The result is that prices have gone up – and quality has begun to come down.

One of the most ominous signs is the growth in the production of young wines 'sin crianza' – that is, without any wood-ageing. One of the hallmarks of Rioja has been the taste of vanilla imparted by the wood in which it was matured. Without that taste, Rioja is not actually a very interesting wine. At least four of the largest bodegas in Rioja are planning to turn their whole production over to sin crianza wines. We must hope that others don't follow suit.

Another sign that Rioja is getting a little bit above itself is a growing reluctance to export. Red tape in the export markets means that it is much easier to sell their wine in Spain – and the demand is there. Some of the smaller bodegas, previously delighted to be asked to export their wine, are backing off and sticking to the home market.

The problem of exports has been exacerbated by the poor crop of 1984 and the only average quantities of grapes in subsequent vintages. We have seen quite rapid price rises of Rioja in our shops, made worse by Spanish inflation. Those rises have affected the basic Riojas more than the Reservas and Gran Reservas which are in short supply and deserve the relatively high price tags they can now command.

Despite all this, though, Rioja still provides the best range of Spanish quality wines. It still has some of Spain's finest producers, and we can still find plenty of good wine to choose from. Nor should we forget that the quality of Rioja was founded on ageing its white wines as well as its reds in wood. That way we could taste the typical vanilla flavours of the reds and the properly oxidised scents of the whites, which set Rioja apart from other wine regions.

Luckily, we can still taste wines like that. A handful of firms – many still run by the founding families, all of them in private hands – have maintained the traditions and allow us to see a style of wine that is fast disappearing in the world of modern winemaking.

Who's who in Rioja

Bodegas Alavesas Soft, light but concentrated reds made from grapes grown in the Rioja Alavesa. Also a young, deliciously fruity red. Brand name: Solar de Samaniego.
Arriba Kettle; D Byrne & Co; Laymont & Shaw; Moreno Wines; La Reserva Wines; Tanners Wines

Bodegas Berberana Use of new barrels in maturation gives these

wines a strongly woody dimension, but early bottling prevents them losing their fruit. Brand name: Berberana.
Arriba Kettle; Ellis Son & Vidler; Gerard Harris; Martinez Fine Wine; Mi Casa; Reid Wines; La Reserva Wines; Sherborne Vintners; Willoughbys

Bodegas Beronia Good, soft, oaky reds and fresh whites. Brand name: Beronia.
D Byrne & Co; Alex Findlater; Laymont & Shaw; Oddbins; Sherborne Vintners; Upper Crust

Bodegas Bilbainas An old-fashioned family firm making wines in the old style. Brand names: Viña Pomal, Viña Zaco.
Arriba Kettle; Moreno Wines; La Reserva Wines; Sherborne Vintners

Bodegas Campo Viejo One of the largest bodegas, making reds in a plummy, fruity style. The top wine, Marqués de Villamagna, is very good. Brand name: Marqués de Villamagna, Campo Viejo.
David Alexander; Bibendum; D Byrne & Co; Grape Ideas; Hedley Wright; Mi Casa; La Reserva Wines; Sherborne Vintners; Ubiquitous Chip; Upper Crust

Bodegas El Coto Medium-sized bodega making light, soft, fragrant wines. Brand name: El Coto.
Laymont & Shaw; La Reserva Wines; Sherborne Vintners

CVNE (Compañia Vinícola del Norte de España) Produce an excellent range of old-style Riojas, including a white called Monopole. The Reservas and Gran Reservas are outstanding. Brand names: Imperial, Monopole.
Widely available

Domecq The famous Sherry and brandy producer has established a reputation for good quality Rioja from their own vineyards. Brand name: Domecq Domain.
D Byrne & Co; Sherborne Vintners

Bodegas Faustino Despite the terrible fake dust on the bottles, these are good wines, at all quality levels. The white, including the Viura-based Faustino V, is fresh in the modern style; red Reservas are very good. Brand name: Faustino.
David Alexander; Arriba Kettle; D Byrne & Co; Peter Dominic; Peter Green; Martinez Fine Wine; Mi Casa; La Reserva Wines; Sherborne Vintners; Ubiquitous Chip

Bodegas Franco-Españolas Old-style bodega, now producing fine wines after a poor period in the late 1970s. Brand names: Bordon, Royal.
Peter Green

Bodegas Lagunilla Reliable reds, but a rather dull white. Brand name: Lagunilla.
Peter Dominic; La Reserva Wines; Upper Crust

Bodegas Lan Modern producers of good young wines. The white is fresh, the red is fragrant. Brand name: Lan.
For stockist information contact Ehrmanns Wine Shippers Ltd (24–25 Scala Street, W1)

Sociedad Vinícola Laserna Single estate wine, one of the few in Rioja. Brand name: Contino.
Cadwgan Wines; Mayor Sworder

Bodegas Lopez de Heredia Old-fashioned bodega (in the best sense). Virtually everything, including fermentation, is done in wood. The results are glorious whites, more delicate reds. Brand name: Tondonia.
Hedley Wright; Laymont and Shaw; Majestic; Martinez Fine Wine; Moreno Wines; Nobody Inn; La Reserva Wines; Tanners Wines; La Vigneronne

Bodegas Marqués de Cáceres Pioneer of the new-style whites and softer, modern reds. Still some of the best of their type around. The Reservas age remarkably well for such modernity. Brand name: Marqués de Cáceres.
Widely available

Bodegas Marqués de Murrieta The finest white Riojas, made in the old style and superbly long-lasting, the nearest Spain gets to white Burgundy. The reds, less interesting, are still very good and age well. Brand name: Marqués de Murrieta, Castillo de Ygay.
Widely available

Marqués de Riscal A bodega that tends to disappoint despite its fine reputation. Its white is not from Rioja but from Rueda (none the worse for that), the red tends to be on the thin side and with harsh edges. Brand name: Marqués de Riscal.
David Baillie Vintners; D Byrne & Co; Mi Casa; Moreno Wines; Nobody Inn; La Reserva Wines; Tanners Wines; Willoughbys

Bodegas Montecillo Ultra-modern bodega that makes very good commercial wines. Brand names: Viña Monty, Viña Cumbrero.
Laymont & Shaw; La Reserva Wines; Ubiquitous Chip

Bodegas Muga Much better for reds, which are delicate and elegant, than for whites. Traditional methods still in operation. Brand name: Muga.
Arriba Kettle; D Byrne & Co; Hungerford Wine Company; Laymont & Shaw; Mi Casa; La Reserva Wines; Sherborne Vintners; Upper Crust; Willoughbys; Windrush Wines

Bodegas Olarra Brand new bodega making some excellent reds, including a very good Gran Reserva at a knock-down price. Brand name: Cerro Anon, Olarra.
D Byrne & Co; Mi Casa; Oddbins; La Reserva Wines

Bodegas Federico Paternina Vast, modern bodega but a long-established firm. Make sound, commercial wines, with the red better than the white. Brand names: Banda Azul (red), Banda Dorada (white).
D Byrne & Co; Peter Dominic; La Reserva Wines; Sherborne Vintners; Victoria Wine Company

Remelluri One of the few Rioja bodegas to estate-bottle their wines from their own vineyards. Make perfumed, rich, soft wines. Brand name: La Bastida de Alava.
Arriba Kettle; Lay & Wheeler; Laymont & Shaw; La Reserva Wines; Sherborne Vintners; Tanners Wines; Willoughbys; Wine Society

Bodegas La Rioja Alta A traditionalist producing one of the most reliable ranges in Rioja. Great heights can be reached in the Reservas and Gran Reservas. Brand names: Metropol (white), Viña Alberdi, Viña Arana, Viña Ardanza, Reserva 904.
Widely available

Bodegas Riojanas The influence of the French founders of this bodega can still be felt in the elegance of the wines. Quite a lot of old-fashioned reds. Brand names: Viña Albina, Monte Real.
Peter Green; Majestic; Mi Casa

Bodegas Santiago Lightweight wines which can be drunk young. Brand name: Gran Condal.
Ellis Son & Vidler; La Reserva Wines

Bodegas Unidas Large firm under American ownership making reliable wines. The Siglo is sold in a distinctive sacking cover. Brand names: Marqués de Romeral, Siglo, Fuenmayor.
D Byrne & Co; Reid Wines; Sherborne Vintners

Best buys from Rioja

WHITES

Tondonia 1981 (*Bottle and Basket; Majestic*)
Marqués de Cáceres 1987 (*widely available*)
Monte Real Blanco Seco 1984 (*Majestic*)

REDS

Campo Viejo 1982 (*Bibendum; David Scatchard*)
CVNE Tinto 1985 (*Arthur Rackhams*)
Montecillo Viña Cumbrero 1984 (*Barwell & Jones; The Wine House*)
Faustino V Reserva 1983, Faustino Martinez (*A & A Wines; Findlater Mackie Todd; Unwins*)

CATALONIA AND PENEDÈS

Behind the Costa Brava

Both still wines and sparkling wines are produced here, including some of Spain's best. Penedès, the region inland from the Costa Brava, is the most important Denominación de Origen in Catalonia, but there are others: Ampurdán-Costa Brava, Tarragona, Alella and Priorato. The last two are the source of some good value whites and rather heavy reds.

The sparkling wine industry here is the biggest in Spain and one of the biggest in Europe. The wines go under the generic name of cava, indicating that the wines have their secondary fermentation in the bottle as they do in Champagne. Some of the best producers make good, crisp wines, but there are also quite a few flabby sparklers around made from over-ripe grapes (see Sparkling wines at the end of the WHAT TO BUY section).

The quality of the still table wines of Penedès varies wildly. There are some pretty heavy, chunky reds and oxidised whites, but this area's proud boast are the wines of Miguel Torres, Spain's most famous winemaker, and at least two other firms are producing world-class wines. This is the region where the great international grape varieties are being used most effectively – notably Cabernet Sauvignon and Chardonnay, but also Pinot Noir, Gewürztraminer, Muscat and Sauvignon Blanc.

White wines from Penedès should generally be drunk young. Look for the 1987 vintage now. The only exceptions to this are some of the wines produced by Torres and Jean León (see below).

Reds also should be drunk younger than they would be from Rioja. Three-year-old wines are at their best, but some wines repay keeping for five or six years – again those from Torres and Jean León being the best keepers.

Who's who in Catalonia

Alta Alella Company producing the best whites from the Alella DO. Wines: Marqués de Alella.
Mi Casa; Moreno Wines

René Barbier Under the same ownership as the sparkling Conde de Caralt, this estate makes a fresh white and some reliable reds. Wines: Kraliner (dry white), red, Canals & Nubiola.
Mi Casa; La Reserva Wines; Sherborne Vintners

Ferret i Mateu Good-value Penedès wines. Wines: Viña Laranda.
Sherborne Vintners

Jean León Run by a Spaniard based in California. The influence shows in both his wines, which are both 100 per cent varietals. His Chardonnay is especially interesting. Wines: Chardonnay, Cabernet Sauvignon.
Widely available

Marqués de Monistrol Make a range of sound table wines. Part of the Martini e Rossi Italian company. Wines: Blanc de Blancs, Reserva.
David Alexander; Sherborne Vintners

Masía Bach Best known for its sweet wine which some regard highly, others dislike. Also make a good red wine, less good dry white. Wines: Masía Bach red, Extrísimo Bach sweet white.
Arriba Kettle; Alex Findlater; Moreno Wines; Sherborne Vintners; La Vigneronne; Wine Society

Raimat Large showplace estate in Lerida in western Catalonia, owned by sparkling wine producers Codorníu, making Cabernet Sauvignon and Chardonnay wines and an excellent blended red, called Abadía. They have just launched a Chardonnay sparkler (see under Sparkling wines at the end of the WHAT TO BUY section). Wines: Raimat Abadía, Chardonnay, Cabernet Sauvignon.
D Byrne & Co; Laymont & Shaw; La Reserva Wines; Tesco; Victoria Wine Company; Wine Society

Manuel Sancho Best known for both modern and old-style white wines. Wines: red Mont Marçal Añada and oaky, aged but well-balanced Mont Marçal Blanco Reserva.
Arriba Kettle

Jaume Serra Make a top Muscat wine.
Andrew Mead Wines; Sherborne Vintners; Stapylton Fletcher

Torres The most famous firm in Penedès and probably in Spain. Their reputation is based on the skills of Miguel Torres Jr in blending European grape varieties – Chardonnay, Sauvignon, Gewürztraminer, Muscat, Pinot Noir, Cabernet Sauvignon and Cabernet Franc – with local Spanish varieties to create innovative wines. Wines: Viña Sol (Parellada grapes), Tres Torres (Garnacha and Cariñena), Coronas (Tempranillo and Monastrell), Gran Sangredetoro (Garnacha and Cariñena). The French/Spanish blends are: Gran Viña Sol (Chardonnay and Parellada), Gran Viña Sol Green Label (Parellada and Sauvignon), Viña Esmeralda (Gewürztraminer and Muscat), Viña Magdala (Pinot Noir and Cariñena), Gran Coronas (Cabernet Sauvignon and Tempranillo) and Gran Coronas Black Label (Cabernet Sauvignon and Cabernet Franc). A new 100 per cent Chardonnay wine, Milmanda, has just been released.
Widely available

Best buys from Catalonia and Penedès

WHITES

Torres Gran Viña Sol 1987 (*widely available*)
Mont-Marçal 1977, Reserva (*H Allen Smith*)
Tesco Spanish Dry white wine (*Tesco*)

REDS

Torres Coronas 1984 (*widely available*)
Raimat Abadía Reserva 1983 (*Michael Menzel Wines; Victoria Wine Company*)
Penedès Tinto, Jaume Serra (*Eldridge Pope*)

NAVARRA

Navarra has suffered from being right across the river from Rioja – and from not producing such fine wines. Much of her production has been in rosado (rosé) made from the Garnacha grape and frankly only fit for local consumption. Only in the past few years have the producers here recognised that they needed to progress in reds and whites to get anywhere in foreign markets.

They've certainly made great progress in the reds – about the whites we are less sure. The planting of the Tempranillo grape (the quality grape of Rioja) has brought much more style and elegance to the reds, some of which are designed for drinking young, others for ageing in the style of Reserva wines from Rioja.

Terms in Navarra

Vinos de Crianza Red wines which have spent at least one year in barrel.

Reserva Aged for at least three years, one year at least of which must have been in barrel.

Gran Reserva Aged for two years in wood, then three in bottle.

Who's who in Navarra

Bodegas Bardon Owned by Olarra, the Rioja bodega, they produce two young reds and one Reserva style. Wines: Togal, Larums, Don Luis.
Contact D & D Wines (Brook House, Brook Street, Knutsford, Cheshire)

Cenalsa Marketing consortium producing good modern-style whites, rosés and reds. Wines: Agramont brand.
Tanners Wines

Julián Chivite Fresh, clean well-made wines. Wines: Gran Feudo range, Gran Vino Aniversario 125.
Laymont & Shaw; La Reserva Wines; Sherborne Vintners; La Vigneronne; Yorkshire Fine Wines

Bodegas Irache Make a good aged Reserva. Wines: Gran Reserva, Reserva.
Sherborne Vintners

Nuestro Padre Jesus del Perdón Nothing like invoking a top name to protect this co-operative. Their reds are much better than their whites. Wines: Nuevo Vino (red), Casa la Teja (white).
Laymont & Shaw; Majestic; La Reserva Wines

Bodegas Ochoa Lighter style reds and whites.
La Vigneronne

Señorio de Sarria One of the best producers in the region. A spectacular new-style red, plus oak-aged wines of some class. Wines: Viña Ecoyen, Viña del Perdón, Gran Viña.
Arriba Kettle; Laymont & Shaw; Majestic; La Reserva Wines; Sherborne Vintners; Upper Crust; La Vigneronne; Wine Society

Bodegas Villafranca Good nouveau-style red, among others. Wines: Monte Ory brand.
Adnams; H Allen Smith; Sherborne Vintners

Best buys from Navarra

Monte Ory Gran Reserva 1978 (*Andrew Gordon Wines*)
Señorio de Sarria Gran Reserva 1981 (*Rattlers Wine Warehouse*)

RIBERA DEL DUERO

One bodega from Ribera del Duero, Vega Sicilia, has always commanded high prices because its wines are so good and in such short supply. But now Robert Parker, the American wine guru, has discovered the area, so prices of wines from some other producers are now also at sky-high levels. Of course, Robert Parker is right in praising these wines from the Duero Valley just east of Valladolid (the Duero, by the way, crosses the frontier from Spain into Portugal where soon after it becomes the Douro of Port fame). In this small area, very hot in summer, freezing cold in winter, the Tempranillo of Rioja (called here the Tinto Fino) makes red wines which are some of Spain's finest. They are rich, almost sweet in their intensity, heavy with perfumed, peppery but elegant fruit. It is an expanding area, too, as more bodegas – and the local co-operative – realise that they are in a region where fine wine can be made. If any area could threaten the supremacy of Rioja in Spanish wine terms, this is it.

Who's who in Ribera del Duero

Bodegas Alejandro Fernández Founded in 1970, this estate makes red wines which are aged in small Bordeaux barriques for up to two and a half years. Described rather too enthusiastically by Robert Parker as the Château Pétrus of Spain – but they are good. Wines: Pesquera.
Adnams; Laymont & Shaw; Nobody Inn; Sherborne Vintners

Bodegas Mauro Small bodega making a rich, heavy wine with considerable ageing ability. Wines: Mauro.
Davisons

Bodegas Peñalba López A privately owned bodega, whose wines are some of the most immediately approachable in Ribera del Duero. Wines: Torremilanos.
Tanners Wines; Willoughbys

Ribera del Duero Co-operative Old-established but with a newly enhanced reputation. At the moment the younger wines are the best, but increased winemaking quality should improve the Protos Gran Reserva. Wines: Protos Gran Reserva red, Ribera Duero red.
H Allen Smith; Arriba Kettle; D Byrne & Co; Direct Wine Shipments; Laymont & Shaw; Moreno Wines; Oddbins; La Reserva; Sherborne Vintners

Bodegas Vega Sicilia They say that the wine here needs 30 years to reach its peak. Mainly a blend of Cabernet Sauvignon, Merlot and Malbec, it has enormous reserves of fruit which are intensely tannic and chewy when young, and still full of tobacco-rich flavours which emerge after ageing in bottle. It is made only in the best years and is then available only in small quantities at a high price. A second wine, Valbuena, made every year, is more approachable but is still expensive. Production is being expanded under new ownership. Wines: Vega Sicilia, Valbuena.
Adnams; Direct Wine Shipments; Alex Findlater; Laymont & Shaw; Majestic; Nobody Inn; La Reserva Wines; Sherborne Vintners; Tanners Wines; La Vigneronne

OTHER REGIONS OF SPAIN

JUMILLA

Ungrafted vines

Because of the high organic content of the soil in this region inland from Valencia, phylloxera never struck, so the vines are ungrafted. The results are some very rich reds, which, when the alcohol is lowered by early picking, are good drunk young. An area with potential. Wines available in the UK include **Condestable** (*Laymont & Shaw*) and **Castillo Jumilla** (*Euroscot Wines, Leet Street, Coldstream, Borders*).

RUEDA

New whites, classic red

Marqués de Riscal This white is the best known wine from the area. It's a modern-style wine, made for the Rioja bodega by Vinos Blancos de Castilla.
David Baillie Vintners; Laymont & Shaw; Moreno Wines; La Reserva

Bodegas de Crianza de Castilla la Vieja Wines from here are more of a find. The bodega has used the talents of the Bordeaux-based Professor Peynaud to make a top-class modern white and an outstanding oak-aged red (made near Toledo using Cabernet Sauvignon). Wines: Marqués de Griñon red and dry white.
Adnams; H Allen Smith; Gerard Harris; Laymont & Shaw; La Reserva Wines; Sherborne Vintners; Tanners Wines

VALDEPEÑAS

Island in a sea of vines

This region lies within the larger denominación of La Mancha. Valdepeñas produces some very good reds and less interesting whites at very good prices. Two bodegas are making above-average wines.

Cosecheros Abastecedores Produce good reds, especially at Reserva and Gran Reserva levels, at amazingly good prices. Wines: Señorio de los Llanos.
Peter Dominic; Alex Findlater; Richard Harvey Wines; Laymont & Shaw; Majestic; Sherborne Vintners

Bodegas Felix Solis Make a good red called Viña Albali.
H Allen Smith; Sherborne Vintners; Upper Crust

VALENCIA

Where the oranges come from

The fertile coastal plain of Valencia, besides being the source of most of Spain's oranges, is also one of the largest wine-producing areas in the country. Not that we would know, because most of the wine is exported in bulk and blended for selling as rock-bottom cheap red. But some bottled wine is now finding its way to our shops, most of it in the form of good value sweet Moscatel-based wines, such as Moscatel de Valencia (*Marks & Spencer*). There's also a smooth, very inexpensive red, Casa lo Alto red (*Safeway*).

GALICIA

The rain in Spain

Galicia is the north-west corner of Spain, above Portugal. And being right in the line of the Atlantic low fronts that also hit Britain, it is very wet. It is green, mountainous and makes piercingly crisp white wines, which have a close affinity with the Vinhos Verdes of Portugal – indeed are called Vinos Verdes. Galicia produces some equally tart red wines.

The best Galician white wines are made from the Albarino grape (the top quality Alvarinho of Portuguese Vinho Verde), but a number of other grape varieties (of which the most important are the Treixadura and the Torontes) are also used. Denominated areas are Valdeorras (which specialises in red wines) and, right on the coast, Ribeiro. Producers include: Bodegas Campante (*La Reserva Wines*) and Bodegas Chaves (*Laymont & Shaw; La Reserva Wines*).

Best buys from Spain's other regions

WHITES

Castillo de Alhambra (*Martinez Fine Wine; Oddbins*)
Valdepeñas 1987, Valdoro, Felix Solis (*Hampden Wine Company*)
Valdepeñas Armonioso, Bodegas los Llanos (*Tanners Wines*)

REDS

Valdepeñas Gran Reserva 1978, Señorio de los Llanos (*Laymont & Shaw; Sherborne Vintners; and many others*)
Toro Gran Colegiata 1982, Bodegas Farina (*Lorne House Vintners; Touchstone Wines; and many others*)
León Reserva Don Suero Tinto (*La Reserva Wines*)
Ribera Duero 1983, Bodegas Ribera del Duero (*Moreno Wines; Rose Tree Wine Company; Paul Sanderson Wines*)
Las Lomas Tinto, Utiel Requeña (*Buckingham Wines*)

Specialist stockists of Spanish table wines

A & A Wines; Ad Hoc Wine Warehouse; H Allen Smith; Arriba Kettle; Bottle and Basket; Cumbrian Cellar; Peter Green; Laymont & Shaw; Martinez Fine Wine; Mi Casa Wines; Moreno Wines; Premier Wine Warehouse; La Reserva Wines; Paul Sanderson Wines; David Scatchard; Sherborne Vintners; Sherston Wine Company; The Wine House

SHERRY

The Jerezanos – the people who live in Jerez in southern Spain where they make Sherry – have launched two campaigns this last year. One – a continuing one – is to persuade us in Britain (their main export market) to drink more of the stuff. The other – much more unusual – is to make sure we don't drink any poor imitations.

In an era of strict controls of wine names – think of the fuss if somebody takes the name of Champagne in vain – it seems incredible that anybody other than the Jerezanos should be able to use the name Sherry. But that's what's happening. If you make a fortified wine in Britain or Cyprus, you can call it British Sherry or Cyprus Sherry – and there is nothing the Spaniards can do about it.

What, of course, makes it worse, is that British Sherry is not wine in the true sense of the term at all, but unappealing reconstituted grape must. Cyprus Sherry is different: it is made in Cyprus from grapes grown on the island, and considerable care is taken in its production. But it is not Sherry, because it does not come from Spain.

Equally bad, in the eyes of the Jerezanos, is that these British and Cyprus 'Sherries' get charged a lower rate of duty in Britain than real Sherry. That's because they are made to weigh in at just under the 15 per cent alcohol level and can therefore be charged as table wines, whereas real Sherry cannot leave Spain until it is at least 15.5 per cent alcohol, so it attracts higher duty.

These things are important in Jerez, apart from the question of pride, because Sherry is still in the doldrums as far as Britain is concerned. There's too much indifferent Sherry around – some of it from the biggest producers – and too many shops are selling Sherry that is out of condition.

Sherry – especially the driest style, fino – is a delicate wine which deteriorates quickly once it is bottled. A careful shipper will ensure that his fino is sent to this country regularly and in small quantities to ensure freshness. A meticulous one will also give the date when the fino was bottled, and make sure that the shops in which his wine is sold store it properly and not in bright sunlight – we have seen that more than once in the past year.

The more chance we get to taste fresh fino and better quality Sherry in the other styles, the more we are likely to return to drinking what one Sherry producer modestly calls 'the only serious business aperitif in the world – Champagne without the bubbles'.

There have been encouraging signs that the better Sherry shippers want us to see how good Sherry can be. One firm – Sandeman – launched a spectacular range of old Sherries, ranging from a fino to the richest old Oloroso. They are not cheap, but they are not over-priced either, and the quality is exemplary.

Another move in recent years has been the advent of Almacenista Sherries shipped by the firm of Lustau. These are individual wines from small producers, and are available only in small quantities. Again, they prove that Sherry is as infinitely variable as any fine wine. Lustau have also, this year, introduced a range of Landed Age Sherries – Sherries which are exported from Spain in wooden butts and given some time in cellars in London before bottling. The only firm to do this in recent years has been Harveys with some butts of their Bristol Cream Sherry, but Lustau is giving landing age to a complete range of quality Sherries.

So the best Sherry producers are learning – like Port producers – that to survive in a world that doesn't automatically turn to fortified wines, they have to go up-market in quality. They have to show us that Sherry is not just a drink for 'those who don't drink', but a connoisseur's wine as well.

And to do that, the sort of associations provided by British and Cyprus 'Sherries' are just what Spanish Sherry shippers could do without.

The Sherry label

Six styles of Sherry are available in the UK:

Manzanilla The driest, lightest style of all, applied only to wines made in Sanlúcar de Barrameda by the Atlantic coast. Tasters detect a whiff of sea-salt on the nose and flavour. The wines certainly have a lighter, more pungent flavour than those from Jerez itself. Serve chilled.

Fino The classic dry Sherry. The flor yeast which protects the wine from oxidation in the barrel gives the yeasty flavour to this wine. The palate is dry and full of tangy flavour. Serve chilled.

Amontillado True amontillados are aged finos which have taken on an amber colour and nutty taste. They are dry, but much amontillado we see in Britain is sweet and not a patch on the real thing. Real amontillado will probably be labelled dry amontillado or 'amontillado secco', and will be more expensive than commercial sweetened stuff. Worth paying more for it.

Palo Cortado A rare intermediate style between amontillado and oloroso (see below). They are amber-coloured wines which started out growing a flor, but suddenly changed course in mid-life and veered towards oloroso. They should be dry.

Oloroso Wines which never grew flor. They should not be too sweet, but full of richness and flavour. Most are sweetened, but there are some Old Dry Olorosos around which make good winter aperitifs.

Cream and Pale Cream Marketing man's Sherry. Pale Cream (a British invention) is sweetened fino. Cream is oloroso with extra sweetening.

OTHER TERMS ON THE LABEL

Amoroso A sweetened oloroso style.

Brown A rich dessert Sherry.

Fina A manzanilla fino.

Fino Amontillado A fino which has been left to age in cask under its layer of flor until the flor dies. It is darker in colour than a fino, nuttier and more pungent to taste.

Manzanilla Pasada The manzanilla equivalent of fino amontillado.

Solera The system by which Sherry is matured and prepared for bottling. An individual solera is a series of sherry butts (barrels) containing wine of similar maturity. A series of criaderas (nursery wines) feeds a solera from which wine is drawn for bottling. The barrels are never emptied, but topped up with younger wines which quickly take on the character of the older wine already in the barrel. Thus the continuity of style is preserved.

Viejo and Muy Viejo Old and very old. A term used at the discretion of a producer.

Who's who in Sherry

Being a heavily branded product, most major retailers sell an own-label Sherry range. Some are good – it all depends on the quality of the retailer. Our recommendations are indicated in the WHERE TO BUY section under each merchant's entry. Here, we list those producers who sell under their own name. Many of these producers also supply the merchant's own-label Sherries.

Tomas Abad A small bodega in Puerto de Santa Maria selling its own good quality brands and some Sherries from other small producers. Wines: Tomas Abad, Don Tomas.
Bordeaux Direct/Taste Shops

Barbadillo, Antonio Based in Sanlúcar and recognised as manzanilla specialists, although they handle other styles of Sherry as well. Wines: Manzanilla, Fino de Balbaina, Principe (manzanilla pasada); also a table wine called Castillo de San Diego, made from the same Palomino grapes that are used in Sherry.
Bibendum; Ellis Son & Vidler; Alex Findlater; Richard Harvey Wines; Hicks & Don; Laymont & Shaw; Nobody Inn; Christopher Piper Wines; Stapylton Fletcher; Wine Society

Bobadilla Large company with good value, inexpensive fino.
Peter Green; Moreno Wines; La Reserva Wines

Burdon A range of good value Sherries of commercial character,

which have recently been improved. Wines: Superior Fino, Heavenly Cream, Don Luis Amontillado.
D Byrne & Co; La Reserva Wines

Croft British-owned firm whose main product is a Pale Cream Sherry – they were the inventors of this style – plus a range of other styles. Wines: Delicado Fino, Palo Cortado, Original Pale Cream.
Peter Dominic; Eldridge Pope; Peter Green; Justerini & Brooks; Oddbins; Willoughbys; Yorkshire Fine Wines

Díez-Merito Firm which makes one of the best older finos. Wine: Don Zoilo Very Old Fino.
La Reserva Wines

Díez Hermanos Very fine range of old Sherries. Wines: Manzanilla, Palma Fino, Figaro Amontillado, Realengo Oloroso, Favorito Cream, Victoria Regina Old Oloroso.
Gerard Harris; Laymont & Shaw; La Reserva Wines; Henry Townsend

Domecq One of the largest Sherry bodegas, producing a range of top quality wines. Wines: La Ina (fino), Botaina (dry amontillado), Rio Viejo (dry oloroso), plus the less classy Double Century Sherries.
H Allen Smith; D Byrne & Co; Haynes, Hanson & Clark; Oddbins; Sherborne Vintners; Wine Growers Association

Duff Gordon Old-established bodega, founded by a Scot in 1768. Wines: Fino Feria, Club Dry, El Cid Amontillado, Santa Maria Cream.
Decanter Wines, Godalming, Surrey

Duke of Wellington A very good light fino from Bodegas Internacionales, one of the most spectacular of the modern Jerez bodegas. Other Sherries in the range are less exciting but of a good standard.
Peter Green; Whighams of Ayr

Findlater Despite being the name of a British wine merchant, this has become a more widely available brand than just an own-label. Wines: Dry Fly, May Fly, River Fly, La Luna, Amontillado Fino Viejo.
Findlater, Mackie & Todd; Nobody Inn; La Reserva Wines

Garvey Make superb fino and an extremely good range of other styles. They have recently introduced a lower-priced 'popular' range. Wines: San Patricio Fino, Tio Guillermo Amontillado, Ochavico Dry Oloroso, Extra Dry, Amontillado Medium Dry, Pale Cream, Cream.
Arriba Kettle; David Baillie Vintners; D Byrne & Co; Peter Green; Gerard Harris; Laymont & Shaw; Majestic; Oddbins; La Reserva Wines; Sherborne Vintners; La Vigneronne; Wine Society

González Byass Large firm with some of the best-known brand names, which always do well in tastings. Wines: Tio Pepe (fino),

Elegante (fino – less expensive), La Concha (medium amontillado), San Domingo pale cream, Apostoles dry Oloroso, Amontillado del Duque Seco (dry).
Widely available; older Sherries from Oddbins

Harveys The biggest selling Sherry range in Britain. The top brand is a cream sherry. The newly launched premium range, 1796, is much more interesting than their standard range. Wines: Luncheon Dry (fino), Bristol Cream, Bristol Milk, Tico (mixer sherry), 1796 Manzanilla, Fino, Amontillado, Palo Cortado, Oloroso. Harvey's also have a rare range of late-bottled Sherries which are available in small quantities and worth looking out for.
Widely available; older Sherries from John Harvey

Hidalgo Small firm specialising in good quality manzanilla. They supply many of the own-label Sherries to wine merchants. Wines: La Gitana Manzanilla, Jerez Cortado Hidalgo, El Cuadrado Fino.
Adnams; Lay & Wheeler; O W Loeb; Tanners (under their own label); Windrush Wines; Wine Society

Lustau, Emilio A leading independent company known for its range of almacenista Sherries. Highly recommended. They have also just introduced a limited availability range of Landed Age Sherries (see above). Wines: main brand is Dry Lustau (fino). The almacenista Sherries are known by numbers as well as names and vary according to availability.
Arriba Kettle; David Baillie Vintners; D Byrne & Co; Davisons; Eldridge Pope; Peter Green; Hungerford Wine Company; Laymont & Shaw; Majestic; La Reserva Wines; La Vigneronne; Willoughbys

Osborne A large independent company based in Puerto de Santa Maria. Make a top-class fino and a full range of other styles. Famous in Spain for the use of their bull symbol on hoardings. Wines: Fino Quinta, Coquinero (amontillado), Bailen (dry oloroso), Osborne Cream.
D Byrne & Co; Grape Ideas

Palomino y Vergara Small bodega, now part of Harveys, but making its own high quality fino. Wines: Tio Mateo (fino).
Victoria Wine Company

Sánchez Romate A small, privately owned Bodega, mainly concerned with brandy, but also producing a good manzanilla and fino. Wines: Petenara Manzanilla, Marismeno Fino, Don Jose Oloroso, Iberia Cream.
H Allen Smith; Andrew Mead Wines; La Reserva Wines

Sandeman The same firm as the Port producers with the famous symbol of the cloaked Don. They have a fine range of old Sherries. Wines: Character Amoroso (a medium style), Don Fino, Bone Dry

Amontillado, Dry Old Palo Cortado, Royal Esmeralda, Royal
Ambrosante, Old Amoroso, Royal Corregidor, Imperial Corregidor,
Pale Cream.
*Adnams; Alex Findlater; Oddbins; Reid Wines; La Reserva Wines;
La Vigneronne*

De Soto A privately owned company which unusually makes wines
only from its own vineyards. Wines: Fino Soto, Manzanilla,
Amontillado Maravilla, Dry Oloroso, Amontillado Viejo.
Sherston Wine Company

Valdespino Family company producing some fine Sherries which
show well in tastings. Their fino is especially good, and they also have
a range of old Sherries. Wines: Inocente Fino, Tio Diego Amontillado,
Don Tomas Amontillado, Don Gonzalo Old Dry Oloroso, Manzanilla
Deliciosa.
*Adnams; H Allen Smith; Alex Findlater; Hilbre Wine Co; Oddbins; Prestige
Vintners; Sherborne Vintners; La Vigneronne; Wine Society; Wizard Wine
Warehouses*

Williams & Humbert One of the more spectacular bodegas, which
suffered under the ownership of Rumasa and was the subject of a court
case over its most famous brand. Wines: Pando Fino-Amontillado, Dry
Sack Amontillado, Canasta Cream, A Winter's Tale, Dos Cortados Palo
Cortado.
Alex Findlater; Oddbins; La Reserva Wines

Wisdom & Warter One of the Sherry firms with British origins, who
make a wide range of Sherries. Wines: Fino Oliva, Manzanilla la
Guapa, Amontillado Royal Palace, Wisdom's Choice Cream.
J Townend & Sons

Best buys in Sherry

FINOS AND MANZANILLAS

Sainsbury's Manzanilla (*J Sainsbury*)
Manzanilla de Soto (*Wine House*)
Osborne Fino Quinta (*Grape Ideas Wine Warehouse*)
James Bell Pale Dry Fino, Lustau (*Blayney's*)
Tio Mateo Fino, Palomino y Vergara (*Oddbins; Victoria Wine Company*)
Finest Pale Dry Fino, Bertola (*Peter Green*)
Peatlings Manzanilla, Barbadillo (*Thos Peatling*)
Manzanilla La Gitana, Hidalgo (*Gerard Harris; Henry Townsend*)
Fino Bandera, Gil Luque (*Askham Wines*)

AMONTILLADOS

Very Fine Old Sanlucar Amontillado (*Tanners Wines*)
Romero Superior Dry Amontillado (*Waitrose*)
Delgado Zuleta Amontillado (*Ashley Scott*)
Amontillado Tio Diego, Valdespino (*Wine Society*)

OLOROSOS
Alfonso Dry Old Oloroso, Gonzalez Byass (*Oddbins*)
Solera 1842, Oloroso Viejo Dulce, Valdespino (*Oddbins*)

MONTILLA AND MORILES

Heat and alcohol

Despite their similarity to the middle range and cheaper Sherries, these are not in fact fortified wines – they just taste like it. The heat from the sun in the vineyards right in the centre of southern Spain near Córdoba has the effect of pushing up the sugar content of the grapes to such an extent that an effortless 15 or 16 degrees of alcohol is achieved without any aid from brandy.

The word 'Montilla' was borrowed by the Jerez Sherry producers and used in the description 'amontillado'. Rather unfairly, the law now forbids Montilla to use its own name in describing its wines, so they are simply labelled 'dry', 'medium' or 'cream'.

Although they don't have the sophistication of top Sherries, the Montilla wines are probably better value at the lower price and quality levels. Most of the Montilla available in the shops is own-label, so the quality varies according to the quality of the stockist.

Moriles produces slightly lighter wines than Montilla, but the style is very similar. Try the two that *Tesco* stock.

Who's who in Montilla and Moriles

Apart from the readily available own-label wines, a classier example of Montilla is available in the UK.

Bodegas Valenzuela Top quality wines. Wines: De Luxe Dry Montilla. *For further information contact D & D Wines, Brook House, Brook Street, Knutsford, Cheshire*

Best buys from Montilla and Moriles

Moriles Solera Fina (*Tesco*)
Dos Reinos range (*Oddbins*)

MÁLAGA

Liquid sweetness

Málaga is sweet, fortified wine from the middle of the south coast to the east of Jerez. It is made from a blend of Moscatel and Pedro Ximenez grapes. At its best, it can be complex, either a sort of cross between old tawny Port and fino Sherry or darker, very nutty and intense. It's best drunk as a dessert wine.

The top quality Málaga is known as Lagrima, simply made from the free-run juice of uncrushed grapes (as in Tokay in Hungary). Other styles are Pajarete (more of an aperitif style), a pale semi-dulce and a darker Moscatel.

Who's who in Málaga

Scholtz Hermanos The great name in Málaga, making a whole range of styles. Wines: Solera Scholtz (light brown dessert wine), Seco Añejo (dry), Lagrima.
Alex Findlater; Laymont & Shaw; Nobody Inn; Sherborne Vintners; Tanners Wines; La Vigneronne; Wine Society

Bodegas Barcelo Family firm making less expensive wines. Wines: Bacarles Solera Vieja, Gran Málaga (very sweet), Lagrima, Gran Vino Sanson (lighter version of Lagrima).
Peter Green; Moreno Wines

Best buys in Málaga

Scholtz Hermanos 10-year-old (*Laymont & Shaw*)

Specialist stockists of Spanish fortified wines

Bin Ends; Alex Findlater; Great Northern Wine Company; Peter Green; John Harvey & Sons; Hicks & Don; Laymont & Shaw; Martinez Fine Wine; Moreno Wines; Morris's Wine Stores; La Reserva Wines; Paul Sanderson Wines; Selfridges; Tanners Wines; Wine House; Wine Society

Switzerland

Swiss wine is expensive. There are plenty of reasons for that: the high cost of land, the impossibly steep slopes which are hugely labour-intensive to work and, of course, the famously stable Swiss Franc.

So it is hardly surprising that we don't often see Swiss wine in this country. Anyway, the Swiss themselves are extremely fond of their own wines, as well as importing considerable quantities from other countries. A recent succession of large harvests, though, has meant that more wine has been available for export, and at least one firm is now working actively to encourage us to try Swiss wine.

Wine is made all over the country. The German speakers make German-style wines in the north-east of the country. In the south, the Italian speakers in the Ticino make red wines based on the Merlot grape. And in the west, it is the French speakers who produce wines in the Vaud around Lake Geneva, in the Valais and in Neuchâtel.

The most important areas as far as we are concerned are the French-speaking areas, since these are where most wine is made, and from which most is exported. The smallest of the three is Neuchâtel, which specialises in light rosé wines called Oeil de Perdrix (partridge's eye) made from the Pinot Noir. White Neuchâtel is made from the Chasselas grape.

In the Vaud, production is much larger, and it is here that the white Chasselas grape, almost the national grape of Switzerland, comes into its own. The large expanse of Lake Geneva keeps the temperature in the summer warmer than the surrounding areas, and vines are planted on the hillsides leading down to the lake. The wine-growing area is divided into three sub-zones: Chablais, Lavaux and La Côte. Inevitably production costs on these valuable areas of real estate are high.

The Valais to the east and near the source of the Rhône river is the largest production area. Chasselas (here called Fendant) and Sylvaner (called Johannisberg) produce the white wines, Pinot Noir and Gamay the reds. A blended red, made from the two grapes, is called Dôle.

Swiss wines are not complex, being quite delicate in flavour. The whites from the Chasselas tend to lack acidity but can age well. The reds are light and are attractive when slightly chilled.

Who's who in Switzerland

We list below only those producers whose wines are available in the UK.

Valais

Alphonse Orsat (*Eldridge Pope/Reynier Wine Libraries*); **Provins Valais** (*Swiss Centre – see below for address*).

Vaud

Bernard Bovy makes a very expensive St-Saphorin La Roche aux Vignes (*Swiss Centre*).

Hammel Large négociant and estate owner. Wines come from individual estates in the La Côte region of the Vaud: Ch de la Trêvelin, Domaine de la Bolliattaz, Ch de Pictet-Lullin (*Tanners Wines; for other stockist information contact Rolaz & Co Ltd, 3 Berkeley Square, London W1*)

Testuz Try the top estate white, Arbalète Dézaley Premier Cru (*Eldridge Pope/Reynier Wine Libraries*).

Neuchâtel

Samuel Chatenay (*Eldridge Pope/Reynier Wine Libraries*). Also try the attractive rosé Oeil de Perdrix from the **Caves des Coteaux Cortaillod** (*Swiss Centre*).

Other areas

Ticino, the Italian area, whose Merlot is the best style (Merlot del Ticino, Cantina Sociale Mendrisio, *available from the Swiss Centre*); **Schaffhausen** in eastern Switzerland (Steiner Beerliwein Faleberg, a red from Pinot Noir, *available from the Swiss Centre*).

For other wines, there is always a selection at the Swiss Centre, Leicester Square, London WC2.

Specialist stockists

Eldridge Pope/Reynier Wine Libraries

Turkey

Turkey has the fifth largest area under vine in the world, but under five per cent of the grapes are made into wine – the rest are table grapes. And it is in the areas with the strongest European links – in the small area of Thrace which is Turkey in Europe and on the Aegean coast – that the wine industry flourishes. The only other area to produce wine is around the capital, Ankara.

The best Turkish wines are red, big, not particularly complicated, but good with heavy stews or kebabs. New technology has not made a big enough impact to make decent white wines possible. Branded names are the thing, even though the wine may come from a specific area, and most exports go through the state monopoly.

What's what in Turkey

Buzbag Branded wine made on the Anatolian plateau near Ankara.

Cankaya Medium dry white wine from Anatolia.

Trakya A light red wine, made in Thrace.

Villa Doluca Regarded as the most interesting Turkish wine. Produced in Thrace from Gamay grapes.

To try these wines, your best bet would be to visit a Turkish restaurant in London, such as Efes Kebab House, 80 Great Titchfield Street W1 or Topkapi, 25 Marylebone High Street W1, or one of the many Turkish food shops/off-licences in London N1 and N16.

The United States

CALIFORNIA

Californian winemakers have been known to produce some good quotes. For instance, Monticello Cellars winemaker, Alan Phillips, interviewed in *Wine* magazine in June 1988, said: 'We let the vineyard decide the style.'

To a European that's so obvious, it is hardly worth saying. The vineyard inevitably decides the style of a wine, because grapes come from a vineyard and wine is a natural product. Only some areas are suitable for vines. But for a Californian, the approach has been very different: grapes can be grown anywhere, and what's important is the technology that's applied to them in the winery.

So Alan Phillips's remark indicates a change of emphasis in the California wine world. People are beginning to think about where grapes are grown, which particular varieties do best in which areas, which clones of which varieties are the most suitable. Being American, of course, they are going into this in considerable detail: microclimates are being mapped out, even small patches of land in the same vineyard are turning out to be more suitable for one variety than another.

Gauging the conditions

Such interest stems from a few basic discoveries. One of the most important ones concerns the Pinot Noir grape. California wine producers desperately want to make good wines from the Pinot Noir – it's known as the heart attack grape by some because it is so unpredictable, or as the Holy Grail because success seems so unattainable.

But it has now dawned on perceptive wine producers that certain areas of California have the right climate for Pinot Noir, which likes cool climates, long ripening and not too much sun. Carneros at the southern end of the Napa Valley fills the requirements because it is near the fogs and cool weather of San Francisco Bay. Another area is Monterey, cooled by winds straight off the Pacific Ocean, and a third the equally cool Santa Ynez Valley, 100 miles north of Los Angeles.

Now if Pinot Noir works best in certain areas, because conditions are right, so probably do other grape varieties. The logical extension of this process of discovery is that we are likely to come across more wines which bear names of specific areas (ie Carneros Pinot Noir) or even carry the name of a single vineyard. It's very much back to a European model.

Parallels with Europe

California is also turning to Europe over the question of blending. It is well known that the craze for varietally labelled wines started on the west coast, but what is less well known is that Californian labelling regulations gave varietal wines a lot of leeway – until the late 1970s, only 51 per cent of a wine had to be from one grape for it to be called after that grape. Now the figure is 75 per cent – but that still leaves plenty of scope for another grape variety or two.

Blending may not be new, but producers who previously were proud to go one better than the law and proclaim on their label that theirs was a 100 per cent varietal wine are now equally proud of ignoring the 75 per cent ruling and making a blended wine that has grapes in the proportions that suit the wine rather than the law. Under the regulations they have to call it simply red or white table wine if it contains less than 75 per cent of one grape – the term used for the most basic jug wine – but they will charge a top price for it. The situation has obvious parallels to the one in Italy with its super vini da tavola.

Fruits of the wine lake

A third way in which California looked like imitating Europe was in having its very own wine lake. The lake started swelling after the big 1982 harvest, and went on filling until even premium wines such as

Cabernet Sauvignon and Chardonnay were being poured into it. Prices of grapes tumbled, and two new wine styles were born using cheap wine from the wine lake. They were the Coolers – fruit-flavoured, low-alcohol wines, which were introduced into Britain two years ago but never really took off; and Blush wines – rosé wines made from Zinfandel grapes, which have had enough success for the French on the Loire to see it as a solution for the problem of what to do with unwanted Rosé d'Anjou.

Gradually the lake dwindled as California producers found new outlets for their products, and the small 1987 harvest finally dried it up. Now, to cope with a shortage of wine and higher prices for grapes, there has been a considerable increase in new vine plantings, especially of Chardonnay.

Apart from Coolers and Blush wines, a third new style of wine to emerge from the wine lake has been the medium-priced quality wine. California's producers previously seemed to go in for extremes: basic jug wines made in the huge vineyard area of the Central Valley, and high-priced premium varietal wines made in areas like the Napa Valley and Sonoma. Now that good quality wine is available, enterprising producers – led, as far as the British market is concerned, by Robert Mondavi – have started coming up with medium-priced wines that can fill the gap. The result is that California can become more competitive on price – and quality – with Australia.

An eye on Australia

Californians have watched with some amazement the success of Australia on the British market. They have been particularly surprised at the quality of wine the Australians are producing at such good prices. It has become more and more important to them that they do well in exports, because there is currently a decline in wine consumption in the United States, brought about by what California wine producers call 'neo-prohibitionism' and what others might consider an over-zealous scare about the effects of alcohol on health (see Jancis Robinson's feature on page 15 for a balanced view of this).

To keep in with the export markets at a time when the dollar is heavily weighted against exporting anything, the Californians have kept their prices down as much as possible. Some wines are cheaper now than they were in 1984. Even the price rises after the small 1987 harvest will affect those producers who rely on buying grapes from other growers rather than those who have their own vineyards – so the top-priced wines are likely to stay at the same level.

So this is one of the best times to buy California wines. Producers have found a new confidence to make wines in a more restrained style than the wood-laden blockbusters of yesteryear: in the search for slogans, Californians call them 'food wines', but to us, it means that they are not so over the top that one glass is enough.

The Californian label

Considering the American desire for information and facts, it's not surprising that Californian labels can generally reveal a great deal about the wine in the bottle: when the grapes were picked, how they were fermented, when the wine was bottled.

There is also considerable detail on the front label, such as the name of the vendor of the wine: so and so's vineyard. Whether the vendor actually made the wine or just bottled it from wine made elsewhere will be identifiable from the information at the bottom.

The phrases, 'estate grown' or 'grown, produced and bottled by' mean that the wine has been made by the vendor from his own grapes; if 'produced and bottled by' appears, he will have bought in the grapes – no bad sign, as many winemakers prefer to leave grape-growing to grape-growers as well as wanting to take advantage of the best grapes, wherever they may be grown. If the phrases are simply 'bottled by' or 'cellared and bottled by', the vendor will have bought in the wine and just matured and bottled it.

You will also see the phrase 'contains sulfites' (or sulphites as they are known in the UK). This is the result of new legislation which requires American wine producers to state if sulphur was used in their wine during its vinification. Since virtually all wine uses sulphur at some point, all wines have to have the phrase on their labels. There is nothing special about American wines in this respect – the vast majority of European wines also contain sulphur (and when exported to the United States likewise have to state 'contains sulfites' on their labels).

The varietal taste

Despite the growing interest in blended wines (see above), most top wines in California are still labelled varietally. By law, at least 75 per cent of such a varietal wine must consist of that grape. Below that percentage the wine will be regarded as a blend and will have a brand name (and a description saying which grapes go into the wine).

White grape varieties

Chardonnay The grape variety on which much of California's reputation has been built. This used to make wines that tasted more of new wood than ripe, creamy fruit. Now they're more delicate, but still have the characteristic overtones of tropical fruits.

Sauvignon Blanc (or Fumé Blanc) The currently fashionable flavour from California. A grape variety that lends itself well to the current trend for lighter, more acidic wines. Can be full of zing and freshness.

Chenin Blanc Lighter wines are beginning to bring out flavours from this often dull grape. Good, appley acidity is a characteristic.

Johannisberg Riesling Makes wines that are fuller than their German models, so don't have the same delicate balance of acidity and sweetness. But it also produces some marvellous sweet dessert wines from grapes affected by noble rot. New categories have been devised to describe the degree of sweetness of these wines: *Early Harvest* equals the German Kabinett with a slight sweetness but no noble rot; *Late Harvest* equals the German Auslese; *Select Late Harvest* equals Beerenauslese; *Special Select Late Harvest* equals Trockenbeerenauslese.

Red grape varieties

Cabernet Sauvignon As much of a success story as Chardonnay in the whites. The fruit can be over-ripe and a touch sweet, but more recent wines have become drier and less heavy. They're tannic when young, but tend to mature more quickly than Cabernet Sauvignon in Bordeaux.

Pinot Noir There are signs at last that California is coming to grips with this elusive Burgundian grape variety (see the introduction). It needs lighter treatment and less continuous sunshine than much of California provides, but areas like Carneros (a sub-district of the Napa Valley) with its climate more affected by the fogs of San Francisco Bay, are well suited to this grape variety.

Merlot Sometimes seen as a straight varietal – when it can be dull or stunning. Best used as a part of a blended wine.

Petit Syrah Makes rather coarse wines which rely on strength rather than character.

Zinfandel California's own grape variety, producing wines that range from the early-maturing (rather like Beaujolais) to the rich, ripe and peppery. Now also used as the basis for Blush or White Zinfandel wines. An exciting grape that we should learn to appreciate more.

California vintages

1987 A small harvest of high quality. Amounts of Cabernet Sauvignon were particularly small – down by 20 per cent on average.

1986 California became very excited about this vintage, and although enthusiasm has tempered a little, it still looks very good. A cool summer gave a very long ripening period which was good for white grapes and even suited the reds. Some whites have now arrived, but we will have to wait for the reds.

1985 An outstanding vintage, with very concentrated grapes after low rainfall. White wines are rich but with enough acidity, but the reds are the real stars – powerful Cabernet Sauvignon and Merlot and high quality Pinot Noir.

1984 Whites suffered from the heat in this vintage, and most are rather blowsy. Reds are uneven, but most seem ready to drink now. Cabernet Sauvignon did best, Pinot Noir worst.

1983 Medium-bodied whites are now fading. Pinot Noir reds are available and at the time were some of the best yet from that grape variety. Other reds will keep for a few years.

1982 The whites are now mostly past their best, but the occasional Chardonnay will still keep. The Cabernet Sauvignons are now mature, Pinot Noir and Zinfandels are fading a little.

1981 All the whites should be drunk now, except Chardonnays, which are still very good. Reds, too, are going into decline.

1980 Whites should have been drunk, except for top Chardonnays, but reds will continue to mature, especially Cabernet Sauvignons.

1978 and before Only top Cabernet Sauvignons from 1978, 1976, 1974, 1973 and 1970 are likely to last. Other wines should be approached with caution – if you find any, that is.

Where's where in California

As vineyards in California mature, so different areas develop different wine styles. Certain areas produce outstanding fine wines, others are better at jug wines. California is slowly getting round to organising a geographical appellation system. For the time being, here are some areas whose wines seem to have consistency and quality.

Livermore Area to the east of San Francisco Bay.

Mendocino County The northernmost wine-growing region. Sub-regions are Anderson Valley, Ukiah Valley, Potter and Redwood Valleys.

Monterey County A cool area inland from Monterey Bay. Sub-regions are Arroyo Secco, Carmel Valley, Greenfield, the Pinnacles, Salinas Valley.

Napa Valley The biggest quality wine area. Sub-regions include Calistoga, Carneros, Chiles Valley, Stag's Leap, Silverado Trail, Pope Valley, Mount Veeder, Yountville, Oakville, St Helena and Spring Mountain.

San Joaquin The Central Valley, which produces large quantities of jug wines from the biggest vineyard area in California.

San Luis Obispo Up-and-coming area. Sub-regions include Paso Robles, Edna Valley, Shandon.

Santa Barbara To the north of Los Angeles. Sub-regions are Santa Maria and Santa Ynez.

Santa Clara Vineyard area south of San Francisco. Sub-regions are Hecker Pass and Santa Cruz.

Sonoma County between Napa and the Ocean north of San Francisco, and approaching Napa in fame and quality. Sub-regions are: Sonoma Valley, Kenwood, Russian River Valley, Dry Creek, Alexander Valley, Knight's Valley.

Who's who in California

Acacia In Carneros, Napa Valley. Have been making wine for only ten years, but already the quality is high. Wines: Chardonnay, Pinot Noir.
H Allen Smith; Barnes Wine Shop; Bibendum; Christopher & Co; Alex Findlater; Peter Green; Haynes, Hanson & Clark; Ostlers; La Vigneronne

Alexander Valley Sonoma valley winery, famous for its Chardonnay, but also making good Cabernet Sauvignon. Wines: Chardonnay, Gewürztraminer, Cabernet Sauvignon.
Averys

Almadén Range of standard varietals from one of the largest California producers. Based in San Jose south of San Francisco Bay. Wines: Chardonnay, Chenin Blanc, Cabernet Sauvignon, Zinfandel.
David Alexander; Chaplin & Son; Upper Crust

Beaulieu One of the pioneering wineries of the Napa Valley. Still make very fine wines. Wines: Chardonnay, Pinot Noir, Cabernet Sauvignon (top wine is called Georges de Latour Private Reserve Cabernet – pricey but outstanding).
Nobody Inn; La Reserva Wines

Beringer Vineyards Medium-sized Napa Valley producer of sound varietals but no excitement. Wines: Chardonnay, Cabernet Sauvignon, Fumé Blanc and Riesling.
D Byrne & Co; Victoria Wine Company

Buena Vista Sonoma winery under German ownership. Straightforward commercial wines. Wines: Fumé Blanc, Zinfandel, Spiceling (an atrociously named blend of Riesling and Gewürztraminer).
David Alexander; Barnes Wine Shop; D Byrne & Co; Christopher & Co; Peter Green; Willoughbys

Calera Small winery at San Benito, inland from the Salinas Valley. Produces some of California's best Pinot Noir. Wines: Jensen Vineyard Pinot Noir, Zinfandel.
Adnams; Bibendum; Christopher & Co; Hungerford Wine Company; La Vigneronne

Carmenet New Sonoma winery making top quality blends, the red including Cabernet Sauvignon, Cabernet Franc and Merlot. Wines: Sauvignon Blanc, Carmenet Sonoma Red Table Wine.
H Allen Smith; Christopher & Co; Majestic; La Vigneronne

Chalone Vineyards Another winery, based in Monterey County, that has made top-class Pinot Noir and Chardonnay; also Pinot Blanc.
Christopher & Co; Majestic; La Vigneronne

Ch St Jean White wine producer in Sonoma specialising in noble rot Rieslings. Wines: Frank Johnson Chardonnay, Robert Young Vineyard Chardonnay, Riesling.
D Byrne & Co; Christopher & Co; Eldridge Pope

Clos du Bois Northern Sonoma producer with vineyards in Alexander Valley and Dry Creek, making very good Merlot and Chardonnay. Top Chardonnays are named after vineyards: Calcaire, Flintwood. There is also a top quality red blend, Marlstone. Wines: Sauvignon Blanc, Chardonnay, Pinot Noir, Cabernet Sauvignon, Merlot.
Widely available

Clos du Val Wines made by a Frenchman whose father was manager of Ch Lafite in Bordeaux, and whose brother makes wine at the Taltarni winery in Australia. Wines: Merlot, Chardonnay, Zinfandel, Pinot Noir, Cabernet Sauvignon.
David Alexander; David Baillie Vintners; Barnes Wine Shop; Alex Findlater; Nobody Inn; Ostlers; Reid Wines; Ubiquitous Chip; Upper Crust; Wizard Wine Warehouses

Conn Creek Elegant Cabernet Sauvignons from this St Helena, Napa winery. Wines: Chardonnay, Zinfandel, Cabernet Sauvignon.
Lay & Wheeler; Nobody Inn; Windrush Wines

Cuvaison Top-quality producer in the Napa Valley. Wines: Cabernet Sauvignon, Chardonnay, Zinfandel.
Barnes Wine Shop; Anthony Byrne Fine Wines; La Vigneronne

Diamond Creek Minute quantities of top-class single vineyard Cabernet Sauvignons in the Napa valley. Wines: Gravelly Meadow Cabernet Sauvignon, Red Rock Terrace Cabernet Sauvignon, Volcanic Hill Cabernet Sauvignon.
Windrush Wines

Dominus A new winery partly owned by the Moueix family who run Ch Pétrus in Pomerol. Their new red wine is called Dominus – and it's very expensive.
Adnams

Dry Creek Vineyards Good whites, especially the Fumé Blanc. Wines: Cabernet Sauvignon, Fumé Blanc, Chenin Blanc.
Barnes Wine Shop; D Byrne & Co; Christopher & Co; Nobody Inn; La Vigneronne

Edna Valley Vineyards Producer of rich, full-flavoured Chardonnay. Wines: Pinot Noir, Chardonnay.
David Alexander; Christopher & Co; Hungerford Wine Company; Majestic; La Vigneronne

Far Niente Highly-priced wines from the Napa Valley in superb packaging. Wines: Chardonnay, Cabernet Sauvignon.
T & W Wines

Fetzer Vineyards Good, middle-range wines, especially blended wines, from Mendocino – good value as well. The second label is Bel Arbres. Wines: Premium red and white, Cabernet Sauvignon, Chardonnay.
Alex Findlater; Great American Wine Company; Ostlers; Wizard Wine Warehouses

Firestone Vineyard Famous for its big, rich wines from the Santa Ynez Valley. Wines: Chardonnay, Cabernet Sauvignon, Pinot Noir, Merlot.
David Alexander; D Byrne & Co; Christopher & Co; Curzon Wine Company; Ellis Son & Vidler; Peter Green; Hicks & Don; Lay & Wheeler; Majestic; Oddbins; Reid Wines; Ubiquitous Chip; Victoria Wine Company; La Vigneronne

Freemark Abbey Well-established producer of expensive, high-quality Cabernet Sauvignon and Chardonnay. Also produce Edelwein Gold (dessert wine).
Averys; La Vigneronne

E & J Gallo The world's largest winery, in Central Valley, turning out a quarter of a million cases a day. Quality is, not surprisingly, reliable rather than inspired.
David Alexander; Peter Green

Grgich Hills Cellar Big wines from Rutherford, Napa. Wines: Cabernet Sauvignon, Chardonnay, Fumé Blanc, Zinfandel.
Eldridge Pope; La Vigneronne

Hanzell Vineyards Old-established winery in Sonoma which has now a high reputation for its Pinot Noir. Wines: Chardonnay, Pinot Noir.
Windrush Wines

Heitz Wine Cellars Famous small producer in Napa of top-quality single vineyard wines. Wines: Martha's Vineyard Cabernet, Bella Oaks Cabernet, Chardonnay.
Adnams; Bibendum; Christopher & Co; Alex Findlater; Peter Green; Lay & Wheeler; Nobody Inn

Inglenook Vineyards A Napa winery that has had some bad times recently but is on the rebound again. Wines: Cabernet Sauvignon, Cabernet Sauvignon Reserve Cask, Chardonnay, Merlot.
Peter Dominic; Hilbre Wine Co

Iron Horse Light, often austere wines from Sonoma; also good sparkling wines. Wines: Cabernet Sauvignon, Chardonnay.
D Byrne & Co; Christopher & Co; La Vigneronne

Jekel Vineyard Monterey County winery with vineyards in Arroyo Seco, making particularly good Johannisberg Rieslings. Wines: Chardonnay, Cabernet Sauvignon, Riesling.
Oddbins; Wessex Wines

Jordan Winery Expensive Sonoma winery making expensive Cabernet Sauvignon (blended with Merlot) and Chardonnay.
David Alexander; Curzon Wine Company; Peter Green; Lay & Wheeler

Paul Masson Mass producer in Santa Clara of the carafe wines whose containers now house more cut flowers than any other wine bottle. Wines: Varietal wines under the Pinnacle name, as well as red, white and rosé carafes.
G E Bromley & Sons; Rodney Densem Wines; Tanners Wines; Victoria Wine Company

Matanzas Creek Small Sonoma winery making some very good Chardonnays. Wines: Chardonnay, Merlot, Sauvignon Blanc.
Haynes, Hanson & Clark; Windrush Wines

Mayacamas Vineyards Tiny producer in the Napa of top-quality Chardonnay and Cabernet Sauvignon, which need ageing for a long time.
Christopher & Co

Robert Mondavi Winery Often described as the guru of California wine-making, Robert Mondavi and his family make some of the best, most reliable wines in the State. Co-producer of the expensive Opus One with Philippe de Rothschild of Bordeaux. What Mondavi does this year, others follow next. He has just launched two medium-priced wines of good quality. Wines: Opus One, Fumé Blanc, Chardonnay, Cabernet Sauvignon, Riesling, Robert Mondavi California red and white.
Widely available

The Monterey Vineyard Part of the group which also owns Paul Masson. Make a range of inexpensive blended wines under the Classic label.
Rodney Densem Wines; Alex Findlater

Monticello Cellars Southern Napa producer of distinguished Chardonnay. The winery house is modelled on Jefferson's house in Virginia. Wines: Cabernet Sauvignon, Chardonnay.
David Alexander; Barnes Wine Shop; Christopher & Co; Curzon Wine Company; Oddbins; Wine Growers Association

Joseph Phelps Vineyard One of the great producers of California, Phelps makes a huge range of wines, all good quality, some very fine. Wines: Riesling, Gewürztraminer, Chardonnay, Cabernet Sauvignon, Zinfandel.
Adnams; H Allen Smith; D Byrne & Co; Christopher & Co; Eldridge Pope; Alex Findlater; Peter Green; Majestic; Raeburn Fine Wines and Foods; Nobody Inn; Tanners Wines; La Vigneronne

Ridge Vineyards Single vineyard wines from Santa Cruz, with a reputation for longevity. Wines: Zinfandel, York Creek Cabernet Sauvignon, Monte Bello Cabernet Sauvignon (high reputation, but scarce).
Adnams; Barnes Wine Shop; Bibendum; D Byrne & Co; Christopher & Co; Peter Green; Nobody Inn; La Vigneronne; Wine Society

Rutherford Hill Winery A Napa winery that has leapt back to success with a new wine-maker. Wines: Chardonnay, Merlot, Cabernet Sauvignon.
Averys

Saintsbury Winery Carneros producer of fine Pinot Noir; also Chardonnay.
Adnams; Haynes, Hanson & Clark; Wine Society

Schramsberg Vineyards Napa Valley producer of top-quality (and expensive) sparkling wines made by the Champagne method. Wines: Blanc de Blancs, Blanc de Noirs.
Christopher & Co

Simi Winery Small winery in Sonoma making some superb Chardonnay. Wines: Sauvignon, Alexander Valley Chardonnay.
Corney & Barrow

Sonoma-Cutrer Small northern Sonoma winery, which has built its reputation on Chardonnays. Wines: Chardonnay Cutrer Vineyard, Chardonnay Les Pierres, Chardonnay Russian River Ranches.
Great American Wine Company

Stag's Leap Wine Cellars Small producer of top-quality Chardonnay and Cabernet Sauvignon, both worth the high price. Make a second wine (in the style of Bordeaux châteaux) called Hawk Crest. Wines: Chardonnay, Cabernet Sauvignon, Merlot.
Bibendum; Corney & Barrow; Lay & Wheeler; Majestic; Nobody Inn; Reid Wines; La Vigneronne; Windrush Wines

Stelzner Napa Valley producer of complex Cabernet Sauvignon.
Great American Wine Company; Ostlers; Wizard Wine Warehouses

Sterling Vineyard A spectacular winery in the northern Napa Valley.
Wines: Diamond Mountain Ranch wines; Cabernet Sauvignon.
La Vigneronne

Tjisseling Dutch-owned winery in Mendocino making wines in a full,
open style. Wines: Chardonnay, Cabernet Sauvignon.
Alex Findlater; Great American Wine Company; Wizard Wine Warehouses

Trefethen Vineyards Good value wines of high quality. The
Chardonnays are very good, and the blended wines very reliable.
Wines: Chardonnay, Pinot Noir, Cabernet Sauvignon, Eshcol branded
wine (red and white).
*Adnams; D Byrne & Co; Christopher & Co; Alex Findlater; Peter Green; Lay
& Wheeler; Majestic; Oddbins; Tanners Wines; Wine Society*

Wente Brothers Large-scale producer of middle-range wines. Good,
reliable quality, with some good aged Zinfandels. Wines: Sauvignon
Blanc, Chardonnay, Riesling, Cabernet Sauvignon, Zinfandel.
David Alexander; Davisons; Peter Green; La Reserva

Mark West Vineyards Light, elegant wines from the Russian River
valley. Wines: Chardonnay, Late Harvest Riesling.
*David Alexander; H Allen Smith; D Byrne & Co; Christopher & Co; Peter
Green; Hicks & Don; Nobody Inn; Christopher Piper Wines; La Vigneronne*

ZD Wines Lush, rich wines made from grapes bought in from other
vineyards. Wines: Cabernet Sauvignon, Chardonnay, Pinot Noir.
*Barnes Wine Shop; Great American Wine Company; Ostlers; Wizard Wine
Warehouses*

Best buys from California

WHITES

Chardonnay 1983, Concannon Vineyard (*Ubiquitous Chip*)
California Chardonnay 1983, Robert Mondavi (*Unwins*)
Chardonnay 1986, Mountain View (*Waitrose*)
Glen Oaks Classic White (*T & W Wines*)
Canterbury Sauvignon Blanc 1986 (*Wines from Paris*)
Monterey Classic Caiifornia white (*Alex Findlater; Grape Ideas Wine
Warehouse*)

REDS

Carneros Pinot Noir 1986, Mountain View (*Market Vintners*)
Fetzer Vineyards Red 1986 (*Great American Wine Company; Waitrose*)
Trefethen Eshcol Red (*Christopher & Co; Smedley Vintners*)
Zinfandel 1983, Wente Brothers (*Moffat Wine Shop*)
Hawk Crest Cabernet Sauvignon 1985 (*Windrush Wines*)

Specialist stockists

Adnams; Averys of Bristol; Barnes Wine Shop; Bibendum; D Byrne & Co; Christopher & Co; Croque-en-Bouche; Great American Wine Company; Peter Green; Hicks & Don; Irvine Robertson; Majestic; Nobody Inn; Ostlers; T & W Wines; Selfridges; La Vigneronne; Windrush Wines; Wizard Wine Warehouses

NEW YORK STATE

Still only a few wines from New York State are available in the UK. Well-made, flavoursome and with higher acidity than most West Coast whites, the Chardonnay is particularly good. The sparkling wine is more interesting than outstanding.

Best buys from New York State

Gold Seal Chardonnay 1982
Gold Seal Blanc de Blancs nv (sparkling)
Both available from: Great American Wine Company; Ostlers

NORTH-WEST USA

This is the area – covering the states of Oregon, Washington and Idaho – which everybody agrees can produce the cool climate wines that are much more difficult to make in California further south. The cooling influence of the Pacific Ocean and a more northerly latitude combine to produce conditions which are ideal for Pinot Noir and Chardonnay, as well as for light, elegant Cabernet Sauvignon.

However, there are two caveats to this scene of promise: the scarcity of the wines, and their high prices. Most of the wineries are still new, often almost experimental, and the amount of wine they make is tiny. But every year, new developments allow more and more exciting wines to come out of the Pacific North-West states of Oregon and Washington, and now some interesting examples are beginning to arrive from Idaho.

Where's where in the North-West

Oregon Most of the vineyards are south of the state capital of Portland in the Willamette River valley, in the lee of the small Coast Range of hills. In the summer of 1987, Oregon hosted an international Pinot Noir celebration, at which a number of top Burgundy producers were present. One, Robert Drouhin, has even bought some land.

California and North-West U.S.A.

WASHINGTON

Seattle

Columbia

YAKIMA
VALLEY

Portland

WILLAMETTE
VALLEY

OREGON

MONTANA

IDAHO

Snake

MENDOCINO

Sacramento

SIERRA
FOOTHILLS

Russian

EL DORADO

SONOMA
NAPA
VALLEY
SOLANO
San Francisco

AMADOR

ALAMEDA

SANTA CLARA

SANTA CRUZ

SAN
BENITO

MONTEREY

San Joaquin

NEVADA

UTAH

Owens

CENTRAL VALLEY

SAN LUIS
OBISPO

Salinas

CALIFORNIA

ARIZONA

SANTA
BARBARA

LOS ANGELES

Los Angeles

RIVERSIDE

SAN
DIEGO

San Diego

| 0 | 100 | 200 | 300 km |
| 0 | | 100 | 200 miles |

MEXICO

Washington State Most of the vineyards in this northernmost Pacific State are in the warmer areas to the east of the Cascade Mountains. A few growers are on the wet, cool western side, where they produce German-style wines.

Idaho A very new wine state, with vineyards high up in the Snake River valley in the Rocky Mountains.

The taste of the North-West

As with California, varietal wines are the principal quality wines. But here the wine must contain 90 per cent of that variety (although Cabernet Sauvignon needs only 75 per cent, to encourage a 'Bordeaux' blend with Merlot and Cabernet Franc).

Pinot Noir This is the flagship grape of the North-West. Pale in colour, the wines have a complexity of flavours and a perfumed aroma combined with relatively low alcohol.

Chardonnay Low alcohol and quite high acidity can again make for very sophisticated wines at their best, but quality can be variable. Oregon makes the best Chardonnays.

Riesling Some sweet late-harvest wines are produced in Washington State.

Cabernet Sauvignon and **Merlot** Some fine wines are arriving from Washington and Idaho. The combination of grapes is not always so successful in the cooler coastal climate of the Oregon vineyards.

Who's who in the North-West

Oregon

Adelsheim, Willamette Valley Best known for Pinot Noir and Chardonnay. More unusual are Pinot Gris and Merlot.
Douglas Henn-Macrae

Alpine Vineyards Family-owned vineyard in Willamette Valley, making small quantities of wine. Wines: Chardonnay, Pinot Noir, Cabernet Sauvignon.
Curzon Wine Company; Windrush Wines

The Eyrie Vineyards Pioneer Oregon vineyard that has won medals in France for its Pinot Noir. Wines: Pinot Gris, Pinot Noir, Chardonnay.
Curzon Wine Company; Haynes, Hanson & Clark; Windrush Wines

Elk Cove Small-scale family business making delicious Pinot Noir. Wines: Chardonnay, Riesling, Pinot Noir.
Nobody Inn; Windrush Wines

Knudsen Erath One of Oregon's largest producers who also makes sparkling wine. Wines: Pinot Noir.
Great American Wine Company

Sokol Blosser Specialists in Pinot Noir. Wines: Red Hills Pinot Noir, Hyland Pinot Noir, Chardonnay
Great American Wine Company

Tualatin Top-quality Chardonnay and consistent Pinot Noir. Wines: Chardonnay, Pinot Noir, Sauvignon Blanc.
Corney & Barrow; Nobody Inn; Windrush Wines

Tyee Wine Cellars Tiny, brand new winery making excellent Chardonnay.
Windrush Wines

Yamhill Valley Vineyards Wines: Pinot Noir, Chardonnay.
Great American Wine Company

Washington State

Arbor Crest Specialist in late harvest wines. Wines: Riesling Select Late Harvest.
Windrush Wines

Chinook Another small winery, already making white wines and gearing up to some reds. Wines: Sauvignon Blanc, Chardonnay, Merlot.
Windrush Wines

Columbia Formerly known as Associated Vintners, this has a high reputation for its white wines. Wines: Chardonnay, Cabernet Sauvignon.
David Baillie Vintners; Curzon Wine Company; Nobody Inn; Windrush Wines

The Hogue Cellars Specialists in white wines. Wines: Sauvignon Blanc, Chardonnay, late-harvest Riesling.
Great American Wine Company

Snoqualmie Unpronounceable winery making good whites, especially Semillon.
Windrush Wines

Staton Hill Nine varietal wines from a vineyard on the same latitude as Burgundy.
Stapylton Fletcher

Stewart Vineyards, Yakima Valley Very fine late-harvest as well as other Riesling-based wines. Wines: Chardonnay, Gewürztraminer, Riesling, Muscat, Cabernet Sauvignon.
Douglas Henn-Macrae

Idaho

Covey Rise Tiny vineyard whose owner is also a fishmonger. Wines: Chardonnay.
Bibendum; Curzon Wine Company; Windrush Wines

Rose Creek Snake River vineyard which also buys in grapes from Washington State. Wines: Chardonnay, Cabernet Sauvignon.
Douglas Henn-Macrae

Best buys from the North-West

WHITES

Salishan Dry Chenin Blanc, Washington State (*Windrush Wines*)
Rose Creek Chardonnay, Idaho (*Windrush Wines*)

REDS

Rose Creek Mercer Ranch Cabernet Sauvignon, Washington State (*Windrush Wines*)
Elk Cove Pinot Noir, Oregon (*Windrush Wines*)

Specialist stockists

Great American Wine Company; Douglas Henn-Macrae; Stapylton Fletcher; Upper Crust; Windrush Wines

TEXAS

Yes, Texas makes wine, too, and in the summer of 1988, quite a lot of it arrived in the UK. We had no chance to taste the wines before going to press, and much of it went into London restaurants owned by a Texas firm. They use the familiar varietal approach, with some additional varieties to the usual Cabernet Sauvignon and Chardonnay: Chenin Blanc, Riesling, Gewürztraminer, French Colombard.

Texas wineries whose wines are available here are: Fall Creek, Llano Estacado, Pheasant Ridge, Sanchez Creek (*all from Douglas Henn-Macrae and Nobody Inn*).

Best buy from Texas

Llano Fumé Blanc 1985 (*Douglas Henn-Macrae; G Hush*)

USSR

We still see very little from the third largest wine producer in the world. One reason is that the Soviet authorities are keen to encourage their citizens to drink wine instead of vodka. Another is that most of what is made in the Soviet Union is sweet – much of it sparkling – and of little appeal to us in the West.

The major areas of production are in the south of the European Soviet Union, in the Crimea and in Georgia, where there are long traditions of wine-making – going back in some cases to the Ancient Greeks. But the only wines to reach us are a couple of indifferent sparklers and a Crimean red.

Continental Wine House; Vinceremos; The Russian Shop, 278 High Holborn, London WC1

Yugoslavia

In the past year, we have been delighted to record that the Yugoslav wine we have tasted most often is not the Laski Riesling, but a red wine, made from the Merlot grape. It is chunky, enjoyable, and comes across as slightly sweet because it is so soft.

It shows that Yugoslavia can produce more than just the dull, often over-sulphured white Laski Riesling wines with which we are most familiar. As an alternative to Liebfraumilch, these don't have much going for them except the price. And they account for 95 per cent of all Yugoslav wines to reach the UK.

As elsewhere in Eastern Europe, French grape varieties have made inroads in Yugoslav vineyards: Cabernet Sauvignon, Merlot, Pinot Noir, Sauvignon, Gewürztraminer. The Cabernet Sauvignon is less successful than it is in Bulgaria, but the Merlot can be a winner.

White wines made in Slovenia from the Sauvignon, the Gewürztraminer and the Rhine Riesling (as distinct from the Laski) are lively with good, fresh acidity, reminiscent in a somewhat coarser way of the Italian Alto Adige. They tend to be softened and sweetened for the UK market (as in Grants of St James's varietals) – which is a pity.

Of native Yugoslav varieties, the most famous and interesting are the red wines made from the Vranac (the word means 'black stallion') in Montenegro – rich, robust and dark in colour (this wine will improve with some ageing). The white Zilavka from Herzegovina is a steely dry wine.

What's what in Yugoslavia

The Yugoslav label has some terms which may be unfamiliar, as well as the names of French grape varieties.

Beli Burgundec The Pinot Blanc grape.

Fruška Gora Quality white wine area of Serbia.

Faros A red wine from Hvar, with high acidity but a soft, slightly sweet finish.

Gamé The Gamay grape.

Modri Burgundec The Pinot Noir grape.

Strem (Stremski Karlovci) Formerly called Carlowitz, this area once famous for reds now makes some good whites as well. Traminer and Sauvignon are worth looking out for.

Best buys from Yugoslavia

WHITE WINE

Lutomer Sauvignon (*D Byrne & Co*).

RED WINES

Milion Merlot (*A & A Wines; David Alexander; Alex Findlater; Oddbins; Waitrose; Wine Spot*)
Montenegro Vranac (*Alex Findlater; Wine Spot; Del Monico, 64 Old Compton Street, London W1; Harrison Wines, 321 High Street, Berkhamsted; Intercounty Wines, Unit 9, Sandleheath Industrial Estate, Old Brick Yard Road, Fordingbridge, Hants; Waterloo Wine Co, 59 Lant Street, London SE1*)
Modri Cabernet Sauvignon (*D Byrne & Co*)

Specialist stockists
Wine Spot

Zimbabwe

Old Southern Rhodesia hands will know that there has been a small wine industry in what is now Zimbabwe for many years. Now a small selection of the wines has arrived in Britain. They are possibly more of a curiosity than something to rush out to buy, but the quality is acceptable, and likely to get better – and you could certainly put the wines in blind tastings with devastating effect.

Who's who in Zimbabwe

Flame Lily Brand name for wines from Philips Central Cellars of Harare. Wines: Dry White, Medium white, Premium white and red.
Vinceremos

Specialist stockists
Vinceremos; Wessex Wines

Sparkling wines

Here we give our recommended selection of the main styles of sparkling wines available in Britain. The vast majority of these wines are made in the same way as Champagne with the second fermentation in the bottle in which the wine is eventually sold; the exceptions are sweeter wines such as the Italian spumantes and some from southern France. However, the term 'méthode champenoise' is no longer permitted.

AUSTRALIA

Australian sparkling wines – made by the Champagne method – are now showing considerable style. Most tend to be fuller than their European equivalents, but some have attractive fruit and refreshing crispness.

Who's who in Australian sparkling wines

Angas Brut, from Hill-Smith in the Barossa Valley (*Christopher & Co; Oddbins*)
Yalumba D – one of the top Australian sparklers (*Christopher & Co*)
Great Western Chardonnay Brut, Seppelts (*Nobody Inn; Upper Crust; La Vigneronne*)
Yellowglen Brut, from Victoria (*Ostlers*)
Rosemount Chardonnay Brut, from New South Wales (*Yorkshire Fine Wines*)
Seaview Brut and Grande Cuvée, from South Australia (*Majestic; Oddbins; Yorkshire Fine Wines*)

ENGLAND

There is one enterprising – and attractive – Champagne method English sparkler on the market. More are promised.
Carr Taylor Sparkling (*Curzon Wine Company; English Wine Shop; Tanners Wines; Willoughbys*)

FRANCE

Details of **Champagne** will be found separately on page 374.

ALSACE

Alsace's sparkling wines are called Crémants d'Alsace. Unlike Champagne, where the term Crémant means a lower pressure and hence fewer bubbles, in Alsace it simply means a straightforward Champagne method sparkling wine. The wines can be made from the local grape varieties – Sylvaner or Riesling – or from Chardonnay. They are some of the best sparklers in France outside Champagne, but are not cheap.

Who's who in Alsace sparkling wines

Crémant d'Alsace, Dopff et Irion Cuvée Extra (*Eldridge Pope*)
Crémant d'Alsace, Dopff au Moulin (*Lay & Wheeler; La Vigneronne*)
Crémant d'Alsace, Louis Gisselbrecht (*Christopher Piper Wines*)
Crémant d'Alsace, Baron de Hoehn (*David Baillie Vintners*)
Crémant d'Alsace, Willy Gisselbrecht (*Martinez Fine Wine*)
Crémant d'Alsace, Marc Kreydenweiss (*La Vigneronne*)

BLANQUETTE DE LIMOUX

With a claim to have been sparkling even before Champagne, at their best these are attractively appley green wines. They come from the South-West near Carcassonne and are made from a blend of the local Mauzac grapes with some Clairette and Chardonnay to give body. All the available brands are dry.

Who's who in Blanquette de Limoux

Blanquette de Limoux, Cuvée Alderic (*Ellis Son & Vidler; Matthew Gloag & Son; Hicks & Don*)
Blanquette de Limoux, Fleur de Lys (*Christopher & Co; Waitrose*)
Blanquette de Limoux, Ets Salasar (*Hungerford Wine Company*)
Blanquette de Limoux, Cuvée la Centenaire Brut (*Sookias & Bertaut*)

BURGUNDY

Burgundy's sparkling wine production was organised relatively recently, in 1975. The appellation is called Crémant de Bourgogne and the grapes used are Pinot Noir (for reds – not often seen in our shops), and Pinot Blanc, Aligoté and Chardonnay (for the whites). There is also a lower category of sparklers, vins mousseux, and some examples are good value.

Who's who in Burgundy sparkling wines
White
Crémant de Bourgogne, Caves de Bailly (*Upper Crust; Waitrose*)
Crémant de Bourgogne, Cave de Viré (*Davisons; Majestic*)
Paul Robin Blanc de Blancs, Vin Mousseux (*Tanners Wines*)
Crémant de Bourgogne, Cave de Lugny (*Haynes, Hanson & Clark; Marks & Spencer; Oddbins*)
Asda Crémant de Bourgogne (*Asda*)
Crémant de Bourgogne Blanc de Blancs, Caves des Vignerons de Mancey (*La Vigneronne*)
Blanc de Blancs, Dominique Charnay, Vin Mousseux (*Bibendum*)
St Michael Sparkling White Burgundy (*Marks & Spencer*)

Red and rosé
Crémant de Bourgogne Rosé, Bailly (*Majestic; Waitrose*)
Chanson Père et Fils, Red (*Tanners Wines*)
Prosper Maufoux, Red (*Harrods*)

SAUMUR

The major source of sparkling wine on the Loire is the town of Saumur, whose cellars, carved out of chalk cliffs, are reminiscent of Champagne – so reminiscent, in fact, that many Champagne houses have bought up companies in Saumur. Quality is reliable and flavours are clean and refreshing, but the wines tend to lack individuality. Rosés are made as well as Blanc de Blancs.

Who's who in Saumur

La Grande Marque (*Adnams*)
Bouvet Ladubay (*Davisons; Ian G Howe; Nobody Inn; Wines from Paris*)
Gratien et Meyer (*Peter Dominic; Richard Harvey Wines; Wine Society; Wizard Wine Warehouses*)

Langlois Château (*Averys; Rodney Densem Wines; Alex Findlater; Oddbins; Tanners Wines; Winecellars; Yorkshire Fine Wines*)
De Neuville (*Grape Ideas; Ubiquitous Chip; Victoria Wine Company*)
Veuve Amiot (*Thresher*)
Sainsbury's Sparkling Saumur (*J Sainsbury*)
Tesco's Sparkling Saumur (*Tesco*)
Ackerman, Saumur 1811 (*Davisons; Alex Findlater; Fullers*)
Saumur de Neuville (*Victoria Wine Company*)

There is also a much wider appellation, Crémant de la Loire, whose production is more strictly controlled than that of Saumur, but the grapes for which can come from anywhere along the Loire.

Crémant de Loire, Marcel Neau (*Majestic*)
Blanc Foussy de Touraine (*Victoria Wine Company*)
Crémant de Loire, Gratien & Meyer (*Richard Harvey Wines*)

VOUVRAY AND MONTLOUIS

Upstream from Saumur, in Touraine, the twin wine towns of Vouvray and Montlouis both produce sparkling wines. They tend to be fuller than Saumur, and some producers also make a sweet style. Little difference is detectable between Vouvray and Montlouis – perhaps the wines of Vouvray are more intense, those of Montlouis softer.

Who's who in Vouvray

Aigle d'Or, Prince Poniatowski (*La Vigneronne*)
Marc Brédif (*Sebastopol Wines*)
Foreau Clos Naudin (*O W Loeb*)
Huet Brut (*Oddbins*)
Daniel Jarry (*Yapp Brothers*)
Prince Poniatowski (*La Vigneronne*)

Who's who in Montlouis

Montlouis Brut and Demi-Sec, Berger (*Yapp Brothers*)
Montlouis Brut, Gilles Verley (*Vinceremos*)

OTHER FRENCH SPARKLING WINES

Clairette de Die Tradition: a sweet Muscat-based sparkler from the Alps (*Lay & Wheeler; Waitrose*)
Clairette de Die Tradition Demi-Sec, Archard-Vincent (*Yapp Brothers*)
Brut de Listel: simple straightforward wine from the South of France (*Ellis Son & Vidler*)

Varichon et Clerc Blanc de Blancs: produced in Seyssel in Savoie
(*Hicks & Don; Hungerford Wine Company; Lay & Wheeler; Tanners Wines; Waitrose*)

Vin de Bugey Blanc de Blancs, made east of Lyons (*Wine Society*)

Vin Sauvage Brut: made in Gascony in the Armagnac country
(*Richard Kihl*)

Diane de Poitiers, Chardonnay Brut: made in Haut-Poitou (*Adnams; Ian G Howe*)

Diane de Poitiers, Chardonnay Blanc de Blancs (*Lay & Wheeler; Stapylton Fletcher; Willoughbys*)

Ryman Brut, made at Ch la Jaubertie in Bergerac (*Wines from Paris*)

GERMANY

The best German sparklers are made from the Riesling grape.
Regulations which came into force in early 1986 stipulate that all
sparkling wine labelled Deutscher Sekt will consist of German wine as
well as German bubbles (only the bubbles needed to be German before
then). Any wine labelled simply Sekt will consist of Italian or French
wine, or a blend, plus German air.

Who's who in German sparkling wines

Deinhard Lila Riesling Imperial (*Alex Findlater; Ian G Howe; Winecellars*)

Deinhard Sparkling Mosel (*Tanners Wines*)

Schloss Vollrads Sekt (*Eldridge Pope*)

Burgeff Rheingau Riesling (*Oddbins*)

Wehlener Hofberg Riesling Brut Sekt (*Hilbre Wine Co; Willoughbys*)

INDIA

Some surprisingly good sparkling wine – if expensive – is made in
Maharashtra state, near Bombay.

Omar Khayyam (*Adnams; Nobody Inn; Selfridges; Tanners Wines; Vinceremos; Wine Save Cash & Carry, 7/8 Whitchurch Lane, Edgware*)

ITALY

The most familiar sparkling wine from Italy is sweet and based on the
Moscato grape. It appears under the name Asti Spumante or the

slightly cheaper but often better quality Moscato d'Asti or Moscato Spumante. It needs to be very fresh and young to show off its delicious honeyed fruit taste.

Italy is also making more serious dry sparkling wines, some of very high quality. Some use the classic Champagne blend of Pinot Noir and Chardonnay, others turn to local grapes like Prosecco from the Veneto.

For details of **Lambrusco**, see page 482.

Who's who in Italian sparkling wines

Asti Spumante and Moscato

St Michael Asti Spumante (*Marks & Spencer*)
Asti Spumante Fontanafredda (*Adnams; Alex Findlater; Majestic; Ubiquitous Chip; La Vigneronne*)
Moscato d'Asti, Moscatel Vej, La Spinetta (*Adnams*)
Asti Spumante Sandro (*Waitrose*)
Asti Spumante, Tosti (*Findlater Mackie & Todd*)
Asti Spumante Calamandrina (*Wine Growers Association*)
Asti Spumante, Cinzano (*Peter Dominic; Hilbre Wine Co*)
Asti Spumante Martini (*Peter Dominic; Sainsbury's*)
Gallo d'Oro, Duca d'Asti (*Eaton Elliot Winebrokers; Wine Society*)
St Michael Moscato Frizzante (fewer bubbles than standard Spumante) (*Marks & Spencer*)

Dry sparkling wines

Arunda Extra Brut (*H Allen Smith*)
Brut Pinot Oltrepò Pavese, Villa Banfi (*George Hill of Loughborough*)
Ca' del Bosco, Franciacorta (*Adnams*)
Contessa Rosa Fontanafredda (*The Chocolate Box, 3 New Road, Leighton Buzzard, Beds; Italian Continental Stores, 40 Vicarage Road, Maidenhead, Berks*)
Cuvée Imperiale Brut, Berlucchi (*Majestic; Winecellars*)
Gancia di Gancia Chardonnay (*Linfood Cash & Carry, Cornwall Street, Gorton, Manchester*)
Marchese Antinori Nature, Cuvée Royale (*Corney & Barrow*)
Ferrari Gran Spumante Brut (also rosé) (*Wine Growers Association*)
Frescobaldi Brut (*Christopher & Co*)
Prosecco di Valdobbiadene, IEI (*Ostlers*)
Loredan Gasparini Brut di Venegazzù (*Majestic*)

LUXEMBOURG

Luxembourg's small wine industry produces some good, Champagne method sparklers.
Bernard Massard (*Eldridge Pope; Ubiquitous Chip*)

SPAIN

The generic name for Champagne method sparkling wines in Spain is cava (meaning cellar). The main centre of production is in Catalonia in the Penedès area west of Barcelona, although cava wines can come from anywhere in the country. The taste of Penedès cava is peppery and quite full, and the wines need to be drunk young or the fruit tends to fade. They work better with food than without. Other wines vary widely in style: one of the best uses the Chardonnay grape.

Who's who in Spanish cava

Castellblanch Brut Zero (*Sherborne Vintners; Waitrose*)
Codorníu Premier Cuvée (*Adnams; La Reserva Wines; Sherborne Vintners; Victoria Wine Company*)
Freixenet Cordon Negro (*Davisons; Laymont & Shaw; Majestic; Mi Casa; La Reserva Wines; Russell & McIver; Tanners Wines*)
Sainsbury's Spanish Cava (*J Sainsbury*)
Cavas Manuel Sancho, Mont Marçal (*Arriba Kettle*)
Raimat Chardonnay (*La Reserva Wines; Victoria Wine Company*)
Segura Viudas Blanc de Blancs (*Peter Green; Oddbins*)
Juve y Camps Brut Reserva de la Familia (*Harrods; Laymont & Shaw; Mi Casa; Nobody Inn*)

USA

Of the many American sparkling wines, only a few are available in the UK. Their standard is high – but so are their prices.

Who's who in American sparkling wines

Schramsberg Blanc de Blancs and Blanc de Noirs (*Adnams; Majestic; La Vigneronne*)
Iron Horse (*Majestic*)
Gold Seal, New York State (*Great American Wine Company*)

Organic wines

Most of today's wine producers use a bewildering array of chemical treatments in the vineyard and the winery. Each year, in the cause of agriculture, 1lb of pure chemical substance is deliberately applied to the surface of the planet for each human being on it – most of it in the western nations. During each growing season, a vine can receive as many as 12–14 applications of herbicides, fungicides and pesticides, depending on the position of the vineyard and the climatic conditions.

In the winery, another 20 additives are permitted to improve the taste, colour and clarity. The continued absence of any information about these chemicals and additives on the labels of bottles (except those from California which now indicate if they contain sulphur) means that consumers have no idea what – apart from grapes – was used in making the wine inside. The scandals in Austria, Germany and Italy have shown what can happen when chemicals finally take over from the produce of the vine.

Against this background, some producers in France, Germany, Italy and England have gone back to basics. They are producing what in the UK are called organic wines. What this means is that the soil is enriched through crop rotation and the use of natural fertilisers. Spraying of the vines is kept to a minimum (although Bordeaux mixture – copper sulphate and slaked lime – may be used against mildew). The grapes are carefully selected at the picking stage to cut down on the need for sulphur in the winery.

Methods of vinification are as traditional as possible. That means that fining is done using egg whites, filtering uses only natural substances and there is no pasteurisation. Sulphur is still used in many cases, but the levels are kept as low as possible – certainly below those set down by the European Commission. Some producers may take advantage of modern equipment to centrifuge their wine to clean it instead of using filtration or sulphur. Others may use a form of heating of the must to clean it early in the vinification processes.

Beyond these fairly vague guidelines, an organic wine is very much what its producer says it is. There are no strict legal definitions, although there should be an EC directive soon. There are, however, a number of organisations who either test wines to see if they fulfil their standards or lay down standards for organic wine producers to follow.

The International Federation of Organic Agricultural Movements (IFOAM) has members in over 40 countries, evaluates international standards and provides information and documentation as the basis for national standards.

The Farm Verified Organic Programme (FVO) operates in Europe and the United States. It awards a seal of quality to producers whose wines (and other produce) pass its inspection.

FRANCE

The various organisations include the blanket **Fédération Européenne des Syndicats d'Agribiologistes (FESA)**, using the logo **'Terre et Vie'**; **Lemaire-Boucher** (with **'Terre et Océan'** used as a logo for farms in the process of conversion to organic); **Nature et Progrès**; and **Demeter**, the logo for a biodynamic system based on homeopathy and theories of Rudolph Steiner which require planting and harvest to be in harmony with astral cycles (also in Germany and the UK).

GERMANY

The most commonly seen names are **Bioland** and **Naturland**.

ITALY

Cos'è biologico includes several small organisations, of which **Suolo e Salute** is the best known in the UK.

SPAIN

Vida Sana.

UNITED KINGDOM

The **Soil Association** awards symbols to operations which pass inspection, and also carries out research and various educational projects.

The Vegetarian Society logo is used by some producers to indicate that they have fined without using such animal products as ox blood and sturgeons' swim-bladders.

Many of the producers of organic wines are small estates, where the wines can be essentially hand-made. But that is not crucial to the production of these wines. The largest vineyard in France, that of Listel in the Salins du Midi, is run on fairly organic lines, as are the big Rhône estates of Ch de Beaucastel and Cru de Coudoulet. In the Muscadet region, Alsace and Bordeaux many estates produce organic wines – about 150 in all.

Outside France, producers using organic methods include the Pagliarese and Castellare estates in Tuscany; the Fugazza sisters in Lombardy (Oltrepò Pavese and Gutturnio); and Guerrieri-Rizzardi in the Veneto, as well as Tiefenbrunner in the Alto Adige.

In Germany, we have found wines from producers in Franconia and the Nahe which are available here, and Australian Botobolar St Gilbert from Mudgee made by Wahlquist. England, too, has its organic vineyards at Bewl Valley at Wadhurst and Sedlescombe at Robertsbridge, both in East Sussex.

Even though these organic wines are better for you in the sense that they are more natural products (just as organic foods are 'better' for you than manufactured foods), whether they taste better is much more a matter of opinion. When *Which? Wine Monthly* organised a tasting of organic wines in the summer of 1988, we found that standards and quality had improved dramatically in the two or three years since we had last been tasting these wines. It was particularly noticeable in reds: white wines are more of a problem, simply because their production relies more on sulphur to keep them clean and hygienic and also because a commitment to the organic production of white wines necessitates a heavy expense on modern equipment to compensate for chemicals.

In the end it is a matter of choice. Unless you are an asthmatic (in which case excessive sulphur in wines can cause problems), drinking non-organic wines is going to do no more harm than drinking organic wines. But if you feel strong concern for the environment and dislike the use of artificial fertilisers and chemicals, you may find that organic wines are for you.

Below we list merchants whose entries appear in the WHERE TO BUY section and who stock at least some organically produced wines. Those firms dealing entirely in organic wines are indicated with an 'O'.

Addison Avenue Wine Shop
Adnams
Bedford Fine Wines
Bibendum
Bin Ends
Bordeaux Direct
Bottle and Basket
Cachet Wines
Chaplin & Son
Croque-en-Bouche
Cumbrian Cellar
Curzon Wine Company
C C G Edwards (O)
Ellis Son & Vidler
Alex Findlater
GM Vintners
Great Northern Wine Company
Peter Green
Greens
Hampden Wine Company
Gerard Harris
Hedley Wright
Charles Hennings
High Breck Vintners
George Hill of Loughborough
Jeroboams
S H Jones

Justerini & Brooks
Kurtz and Chan Wine
Lockes
Martinez Fine Wine
Mayor Sworder
Mitchells Wine Bin
Morris & Verdin
Morrisons
Nobody Inn
Oddbins
Oxford and Cambridge Fine Wine
Thomas Panton
Prestige Vintners
Christopher Piper Wines
Raeburn Fine Wines and Foods
Rosetree Wine Company
Paul Sanderson Wines
Sapsford Wine
Sebastopol Wines
Selfridges
Sherborne Vintners
Smedley Vintners
Tanners Wines
J Townend & Sons
Helen Verdcourt Wines
La Vigneronne
Vinceremos (O)

Vintage Roots (O)
Wessex Wines
West Heath Wine (O)
Willoughby's
Windrush Wines
Winecellars
Wine Growers Association

Wine House
Wine Spot
Wines from Paris
Wines Galore
Yapp Brothers
Yorkshire Fine Wines

Pudding wines

Merchants who stock a particularly wide range of sweet dessert wines include:

Barnes Wine Shop
Berry Bros & Rudd
Christchurch Fine Wines
Christopher & Co
College Cellar
Croque-en-Bouche
Eldridge Pope
Alex Findlater
Friarwood
Gerard Harris
High Breck Vintners

S H Jones
Nobody Inn
Thos Peatling
Christopher Piper Wines
T&W Wines
Tanners Wines
Henry Townsend
Valvona & Crolla
La Vigneronne
Peter Wylie Fine Wines

Old and rare wines

Specialist stockists include:

Nigel Baring
Butler's Wine Cellar
Cairns & Hickey
Classic Wines
College Cellar
Eldridge Pope
Farr Vintners
Fine Vintage Wines
Justerini & Brooks

Richard Kihl
Kurtz & Chan Wine
Nickolls & Perks
Orpheus & Bacchus
T&W Wines
Philip Tite Fine Wines
La Vigneronne
Peter Wylie Fine Wines

Special bottle sizes

Half-bottles

Although you may find odd half-bottles at many merchants, the following stockists make a point of carrying a good number. It's a practice we think every merchant should adopt.

Adnams
David Baillie Vintners
Berry Bros & Rudd
Butler's Wine Cellar
D Byrne & Co
Christopher & Co
Curzon Wine Company
Domaine Direct
Eldridge Pope
Peter Green
Douglas Henn-Macrae
Hungerford Wine Company
S H Jones

Richard Kihl
Ingletons Wines
Lay & Wheeler
Lockes
Le Nez Rouge/Berkmann Wine Cellars
Nobody Inn
Christopher Piper Wines
Raeburn Fine Wines and Foods
Paul Sanderson Wines
Edward Sheldon
T&W Wines
Tanners Wines
La Vigneronne

Large bottles

For celebrations or for finer wines which age well in larger bottles, you may find the following stockists' list particularly rewarding.

Adnams
Farr Vintners
Gerard Harris
Hungerford Wine Company
Jeroboams
Justerini & Brooks
Kurtz & Chan Wine
Richmond Wine Warehouse

Edward Sheldon
Stones of Belgravia
T&W Wines
Tanners Wines
La Vigneronne
Peter Wylie Fine Wines
Yorkshire Fine Wines

Part III

Wine away from home

Britain's top fifty wine bars

As in previous years, here is our pick of Britain's top fifty or so wine bars. All have been singled out on the strength of their wines, not on their food or atmosphere – although generally all three are of similar quality.

   Would-be visitors should be aware that although we checked with proprietors before going to press, since the recent changes of licensing laws there is now the option of flexible and longer opening hours.

LONDON

Albertine

1 Wood Lane, W12   TEL 01-743 9593

OPEN Mon–Fri 11–3, 5.30–11   CLOSED Sat, Sun, public holidays
CREDIT CARDS Access, Amex, Diners   UNDERGROUND Shepherd's Bush
WHEELCHAIR ACCESS Yes, not to lavatories   VEGETARIAN DISHES At least
two daily

A busy Shepherd's bush wine bar offering interesting food and a
helpfully annotated list of about a hundred wines, with a useful score
by the half-bottle. House wines are Chanut Frères's red and white

(£5.20/95p); others by the glass include Rioja Berberana 1984, Carta da Plata (£5.80/£1.10). Other names worth noting include Gisselbrecht in Alsace, Duboeuf, Michel Lafarge (Volnay 1982, £15.50) and Dürrbach (stunning Domaine de Trévallon 1981, Coteaux des Baux, £9.75). The New World is also well represented (Edna Valley Pinot Noir 1984, £10.25).

L'Autre

5b Shepherd Street, W1   TEL 01-499 4680

OPEN 12–3, 5.30–11   CLOSED Sat L, Sun, most public holidays
CREDIT CARDS Access, Visa   UNDERGROUND Green Park, Hyde Park Corner
WHEELCHAIR ACCESS Impossible   VEGETARIAN DISHES Usually

Things are less happy at this popular Shepherd Market wine bar: the happy hour is now a genuine hour (5.30–6.30), not two as it was before. But cheer up: as well as Péchereau Champagne Brut dropping from £14.50 to £12.50, you can also enjoy Bruno Paillard Brut 1979 at £19.50 instead of £22.50. Wines by the glass include house Cabernet Sauvignon and Blanc de Blancs (£4.95/£1), Duboeuf Beaujolais Villages 1987 (£6.95/£1.50), Léon Beyer Pinot Blanc 1986 (£6.95/£1.50) and Italian Bollini Chardonnay 1987 (£6.95/£1.50). Bottles are equally intelligently selected: Rosso Cònero DOC 1982 (£6.95); New Zealand Morton Estate Chardonnay 1987 (£9.95), and Ch Millet 1978, Graves (£12.95). The menu is fairly Mexican and fairly fishy.

Balls Brothers

2/3 Old Change Court, St Paul's Churchyard, EC4	TEL 01-248 8697
6/8 Cheapside, EC2	TEL 01-248 2708
42 Threadneedle Street, EC2	TEL 01-628 3850
Bucklersbury House, Cannon Street, EC4	TEL 01-248 7557
Great Eastern Hotel, Liverpool Street, EC2	TEL 01-626 7919
Laurence Pountney Hill, EC2	TEL 01-283 2947
Moor House, London Wall, EC2	TEL 01-628 3944
St Mary at Hill, EC3	TEL 01-626 0321
Fish Restaurant and Wine Bar, Hay Galleria, Tooley Street, SE1	TEL 01-407 4301
Hop Cellars, 24 Southwark Street, SE1	TEL 01-403 6851

OPEN Mon–Fri 11–3, 5–8 (Fish Restaurant & Hop Cellars to 11 pm)
CLOSED Sat, Sun, public holidays   CREDIT CARDS All accepted
VEGETARIAN DISHES Sandwiches; others with prior notice

Half of the Balls Brothers wine bars offer jumbo sandwiches, the remainder more elaborate fare with an English accent. They all share a good and reasonably priced wine list. Least interesting – as so often – are the wines by the glass: La Tour Michèle Bordeaux (£5.65/£1.15), Beaujolais 1986 (£5.65/£1.15), Muscadet de Sèvre-et-Maine 1987

(£5.65/£1.15) and Choix d'Alsace (£5.90/£1.20), with insufficient information to allow an accurate estimate of quality. Once into more serious stuff – although even then too few producers' names are listed – the choice can be made more confidently: as a recent wine of the month, for example, Frescobaldi's Galestro 1987 (£6.50/£1.35). Consider, too, Mâcon-Clessé, Domaine de la Quintaine 1986 (£8.75); Penfold's Semillon/Chardonnay 1985 (£7.80); Château de Juliénas 1987, estate-bottled (£8.50/£4.50 half); Ch de Fonscolombe, Coteaux d'Aix-en-Provence (£5.75); Chilean Concha y Toro Cabernet Sauvignon 1984 (£6.20). Sherries, Ports and Champagnes are well chosen, prices especially kind in Champagne: Laurent Perrier Rosé (£20) and Krug Grande Cuvée (£35), not much more than the 'bargain' prices charged by various wine merchants.

Bleeding Heart

Bleeding Heart Yard, Hatton Garden, EC1   TEL 01-242 8238

OPEN Mon–Fri, 12–3, 6–11   CLOSED Sat, Sun, public holidays
CREDIT CARDS Access, Amex, Diners, Visa   UNDERGROUND Chancery Lane, Farringdon   WHEELCHAIR ACCESS Possible   VEGETARIAN DISHES Good selection

This Dickensian wine bar is worth finding: off Greville Street, between Hatton Garden and Saffron Hill. Nothing is given away in the City, but at least there are some good wines, starting with house red and white (£4.95/95p) and including Barton & Guestier Bordeaux Blanc 1986 (£5.95/£1.25) and Ch Beaulieu 1985, Côtes de Bourg (£6.75/£1.40). Consider also Bulgarian Khan Krum Chardonnay 1984 (£5.45); Montagny Premier Cru 1986, Caves de Buxy (£14.95); Rosemount Chardonnay 1987 (£9.75); Cornas 1982, Paul Jaboulet (£14.50); Sterling Cabernet Sauvignon 1983 (£11.95) from California; and Juliénas 1986, Georges Duboeuf (£10.95). Cavalier Brut sparkling wine is £7.95; there are ten half-bottles; and various Sandeman Ports. Fairly French food.

Boos

1 Glentworth Street, NW1   TEL 01-935 3827

OPEN Mon–Fri 11.30–3, 5.30–8   CLOSED Sat, Sun, public holidays, 3 weeks Sept, 2 weeks Chr   CREDIT CARDS Access, Amex, Diners
UNDERGROUND Baker Street   WHEELCHAIR ACCESS Not possible
VEGETARIAN DISHES Some

The Roses celebrated Boos' tenth anniversary last year by opening up the Fayre Exchange coffee and tea lounge at ground level (Mon–Fri 8.30–4 all year; Sat 10–4 May–Sept) to offer light snacks and a limited range of wines. Down below, things continue as before: comfortable, clubby surroundings, tasty food and carefully chosen and served wines at reasonable prices. The house wines include a good Alsace

Pinot Blanc (£7.50/£1.80) and Penedès Grand Civet 1984 (£6.95/£1.70). The other ten Alsace wines are hard to resist (Riesling Cuvée Emile Willm 1983, Vendange Tardive, £12.75); the clarets include Ch Dutruch Grand Poujeaux 1978 (£10.90) and Ch Cheval Blanc 1971 (£45). Other treasures include Condrieu, Ch du Rozay 1985 (£23.75); Geoff Merrill Semillon 1983 from McLaren Vale (£11.50); Marqués de Griñon Cabernet Sauvignon 1982 from Penedès (£14.50); and Pio Cesare Barolo 1981 (£14.50). A wide range of aperitifs, such as Chambéry vermouth (£1.50); and the Champagnes start off with Barancourt Brut Réserve (£15.95).

Bow Wine Vaults

10 Bow Place Churchyard, EC4   TEL 01-248 1121

OPEN Mon–Fri 11.30–3, 5–7   CLOSED Sat, Sun, public holidays
CREDIT CARDS Access, Amex, Diners, Visa   UNDERGROUND Mansion
House   WHEELCHAIR ACCESS Yes, but not to lavatories
VEGETARIAN DISHES Yes

These vaults near Cheapside house wine merchant, cellars, restaurant, private dining-rooms and two wine bars. As well as blackboard specials, wines by the glass include Jurançon Sec 1986, Domaine Jean Guirouilh (£7.50/£1.35) and Rully 1982, Domaine Daniel Chanzy (£11.05/£2.10). As befits a City wine bar, the list kicks off with a fine range of Champagnes, from the house Private Cuvée (£12.20) to Krug Special Cuvée (£44), via Laurent Perrier, Mumm, Bollinger, Roederer, and so on. They should by now have moved on to 1987 Sauvignon and Muscadet, though the classier Loires age to advantage (Savennières, Ch de Chamboureau 1985, Yves Soulez, £9.75). Alsace is mainly from Willm and Kuentz Bas (Willm Riesling 1985, £8.20); Germans sound distinguished, but lack shippers' names. The reds include strong Beaujolais and Burgundy, clarets spanning Ch du Pont du Roy 1985, Côtes de Bourg (£7.20) and Ch Cissac 1979 (£18.80); and Rhônes such as La Vieille Ferme Rouge 1985 (£6.25) and Côte Rôtie Brune et Blonde 1981, Guigal (£21.45). Plenty from elsewhere also, plus a stunning list of Ports and Madeiras. Snack or banquet, depending on where you perch.

Le Cochonnet

1 Lauderdale Parade, W9   TEL 01-289 0393

OPEN Mon–Sat 11.30–3, 5.30–11   Sun 12–2, 7–10   CLOSED Chr Day
CREDIT CARDS Access, Amex, Diners, Visa   UNDERGROUND Maida Vale
WHEELCHAIR ACCESS Possible   VEGETARIAN DISHES Several

An extrovert local for extrovert locals, handily situated where Lauderdale Road meets Elgin Avenue, with outdoor tables when summer strikes. The list of over 150 wines begins with unspecified house French red and white (£5.95/£1.50) and a good Provençal Rosé, Commanderie de la Bargemone 1986 (£7.75/£1.90). After that there are riches in all directions: Alsace wines from Théo Cattin (Gewürztraminer Bollenberg 1985, £12.95); the English Penshurst Seyval Blanc 1985 (£7.25); Ménétou-Salon, Domaine de la Montaloise 1986 (£9.50); cru Beaujolais from Duboeuf, Paquet and Fessy; interesting red Burgundies and Bordeaux; Bunan's excellent Provençal Cabernet Sauvignon 1984, Vin de Pays de Mont Caume (£8.25); Torres and Raimat from Spain; a wide range of New World wines; Lebanese Ch Musar 1979 (£8.95); ambitious Champagnes; and imaginative dessert wines (Quady Essencia Orange Muscat from California, £15.95/£2.50). Decent food.

Cork & Bottle

44–46 Cranbourn Street, WC2   TEL 01-734 7807

OPEN Mon–Sat 11–3, 5.30–11   CLOSED 25 & 26 Dec, 1 Jan
CREDIT CARDS Amex, Diners, Visa   UNDERGROUND Leicester Square,
Charing Cross   WHEELCHAIR ACCESS Not possible
VEGETARIAN DISHES Always several

Don Hewitson's popular basement wine bar off Leicester Square is often too crowded for comfort, but for good reason. And at least there is now a lunchtime no-smoking section. The food is imaginative and well cooked; the wines are exciting, frequently changing, and reasonably priced. Hewitson's favourite themes recur: Champagne, Beaujolais, Rosé and Alsace all have seasonal promotions. Wines by the quarter-bottle glass vary from week to week, but might include, say, Hugel Pinot Blanc 1986 (£7.50/£1.85) and Sauvignon Trois Mouline 1987 (£6.95/£1.75). The young vines at Ch Labégorce-Zédé in Margaux have produced, thanks to carbonic maceration, a cuvée de la Jeune Vigne NV (£7.95), said to be 'fragrant fruity Cabernet with no tannin'. Other likely Bordeaux include Ch Respide 1983 (£8.50), Ch Fombrauge 1983 (£14.50) and Domaine de Chevalier 1978, Grand Cru Classé Graves (£35). Australia pops up with Marienberg Rhine Riesling 1986 (£7.95), Penfold's Bin 202 Gewürztraminer Riesling 1986 (£8.50), Krondorff Semillon 1987 (£9.95), De Bortoli Cabernet Sauvignon 1985 (£8.95) and Hardy's Cabernet Malbec 1981, Eileen Hardy's Selection (£13.95). And plenty more . . . Good jazz and lots of special events.

Davys of London

Most branches are closed Sat, Sun and public holidays; many close at
about 8 pm on weekday evenings.

Arch 9 Arch 9, Old Seacoal Lane, EC4	TEL 01-248 8991
Bangers 2–12 Wilson Street, EC2	TEL 01-377 6326
Bishop of Norwich 91–93 Moorgate, EC2	TEL 01-920 0857
Bishop's Parlour 91-93 Moorgate, EC2	TEL 01-588 2581
Boot & Flogger 10–20 Redcross Way, SE1	TEL 01-407 1184
Bottlescrue 53–60 Holborn Viaduct, EC1	TEL 01-248 2157
Bung Hole 57 High Holborn, WC1	TEL 01-242 4318
Burgundy Bens 102/108 Clerkenwell Road, EC1	TEL 01-251 3783
Champagne Charlies 325 Essex Road, Islington, N1	TEL 01-226 4078
Chopper Lump 10C Hanover Square, W1	TEL 01-499 7569
City Boot 7 Moorfields High Walk, EC2	TEL 01-588 4766
City Flogger 120 Fenchurch Street, EC3	TEL 01-623 3251
City FOB Lower Thames Street, EC3	TEL 01-621 0619
City Pipe Foster Lane, EC2	TEL 01-606 2110
City Vaults 2 St Martins-le-Grand, EC1	TEL 01-606 6721
Colonel Jaspers 161 Greenwich High Road, SE10	TEL 01-853 0585
Colonel Jaspers 190 City Road, EC1	TEL 01-608 0925
The Cooperage 48–50 Tooley Street, SE1	TEL 01-403 5775
Crusting Pipe 27 The Market, Covent Garden, WC2	TEL 01-836 1415
Davys 10 Creed Lane, EC4	TEL 01-236 5317
Davys Wine Vaults 161 Greenwich High Road, SE10	TEL 01-858 7204
Grape Shots 2/3 Artillery Passage, E1	TEL 01-247 8215
The Guinea Butt White Hart Yard, Borough High Street, SE1	TEL 01-407 2829
Gyngle Boy 27 Spring Street, W2	TEL 01-723 3351
The Habit Fiery Court, 65 Crutched Friars, EC3	TEL 01-481 1137
Lees Bag 4 Great Portland Street, W1	TEL 01-636 5287
The Pulpit 63 Worship Street, EC2	TEL 01-377 1754
Segar & Snuff Parlour 27A The Market, Covent Garden, WC2	TEL 01-836 8345
Shotberries 167 Queen Victoria Street, EC4	TEL 01-329 4759
Skinkers 42 Tooley Street, SE1	TEL 01-407 9189
The Spittoon 15–17 Long Lane, EC1	TEL 01-726 8858
Tappit-Hen 5 William IV Street, WC2	TEL 01-836 9839
Tapster 3 Brewers Green, Buckingham Gate, SW1	TEL 01-222 0561
Tumblers 1 Kensington High Street, W8	TEL 01-937 0393
Truckles of Pied Bull Yard off Bury Place, WC1	TEL 01-404 5334
Udder Place Wine Rooms Russia Court, Russia Row, 1–6 Milk Street, EC2	TEL 01-600 2165
The Vineyard International House, St Katharine's Way, E1	TEL 01-480 6680
Wines Galore 161 Greenwich High Road, SE10	TEL 01-858 6014

Davys continue to burgeon, with 40 or so London wine bars, half of them in the City, and several country branches (see under Exeter and Hythe). Their apparent simplicity – a formula of Dickensian atmosphere enhanced by sawdust floors, casks and candles, plus limited English food and a short wine list – conceals the careful planning and talented wine-buying of John Davy. Read the special offers on the blackboard before consulting the list of 40 or so wines, starting with reliable French Red and White 'Ordnary' No 1 (£5.05/£1.30), taking in BEST Sauvignon 1987 (£6.05/£1.50), Davy's Claret (£6.05/£1.50) and Rioja 1984 (£6.35/£1.60). Other favourites include the Alsace Pinot Blanc (£6.35); Brouilly, Clos de Briante 1986 (£8.35), Ch La Roche Beaulieu 1981, Côtes de Castillon (£8.25), with other good Burgundies and clarets as well. Fly even higher by ordering from the Boot & Flogger's list of fine wines (24 hours' notice required). Good Ports and Sherries by glass and bottle (Fonseca Guimareans 1972 Port, £26/£3.85) and Champagne.

Draycott's

114 Draycott Avenue, SW3   TEL 01-584 5359

OPEN Mon–Sat 11.30–3, 5.30–11   Sun 12–2, 7–10.30   CLOSED 25 & 26 Dec   CREDIT CARDS All accepted   UNDERGROUND South Kensington, Sloane Square   WHEELCHAIR ACCESS Yes   VEGETARIAN DISHES Selection available

The Yuppie branch of the Ebury Wine Company remains popular for its imaginative food, relaxed Sunday brunch (from 11am) and well-chosen wines. House wines start at £5.95/£1.60, and the list encompasses classic regions of France as well as Spain, Italy and Australia (Renmano Fumé Blanc 1985, £9.50). A whole page of Champagnes (house £14.50) with Buck's Fizz and Bellinis too.

Ebury Wine Bar

139 Ebury Street, SW1   TEL 01-730 5447

OPEN Mon–Sat 11–3, 5.30–11   Sun 12 noon–2, 7–10.30   CLOSED 24 & 25 Dec   CREDIT CARDS Access, Amex, Diners, Visa   UNDERGROUND Victoria, Sloane Square   WHEELCHAIR ACCESS No   VEGETARIAN DISHES Very limited selection

The Ebury Wine Company keeps its bar well stocked with fine wines, at prices which seem markedly higher than last year's: most glasses now cost £2 or more, but they include, for example, Muscadet-sur-Lie, Domaine de la Bretonnière 1987 (£7.80/£2.10) when too many bars are still offering *passé* vintages; Ch Bonnet 1985 (£9.50/£2.50); and Ch de Septy Monbazillac 1985 (£8.50/£1.60). Other interesting listings include Inglewood from California, Penfold's from Australia and the appealing English Breaky Bottom Müller-Thurgau 1986 (£8.50). Good Ports,

Sherries and Madeiras; a wide range of Champagnes on the blackboard. Imaginative food.

Hoults

20 Bellevue Road, SW17   TEL 01-767 1858

OPEN Every day 12 noon–2.30, 5.30–11   CLOSED 24–31 Dec
CREDIT CARDS Access, Amex, Visa   UNDERGROUND Balham
WHEELCHAIR ACCESS Possible   VEGETARIAN DISHES Good selection

This rather smart 'wine bar restaurant' on Wandsworth Common has a wine warehouse attached. The ten wines by the glass include Chardonnay di Appiano 1986 (£5.95/£1.20); Bergerac Blanc, Ch de Fayolle 1986 (£5.95/£1.20) and the Australian Cabernet Sauvignon, Hardy's Captain's Selection 1983 (£6.50/£1.30). Other discoveries include Winkeler Hasensprung Riesling Kabinett 1985 (£8.50); Gisselbrecht Pinot Blanc 1985 (£6.50); Ch Patache d'Aux 1982 (£10.50); and Penfold's Bin 389 South Australian Cabernet/Shiraz 1984 (£9.95). Five Taylors Ports by the glass (including the delectable 10-year-old tawny, £2.95), and several half-bottles.

Just Williams

6 Battersea Rise, SW11   TEL 01-228 9980

OPEN Mon–Sat 12–3, 6–11 (Sat 7–11)   Sun 7–10.30   CLOSED Sun L, Chr,
Easter Day   CREDIT CARDS Access, Amex, Visa   BR STATION Clapham
Junction   WHEELCHAIR ACCESS One small step down to bar; lavatories
impossible   VEGETARIAN DISHES A couple each day

Good bistro cooking (less adventurous than the related Pollyanna's next door), a patio and well-chosen wines all make Just Williams a popular neighbourhood spot. As well as basic house red (£4.95/£1), there are a house claret (£5.25/£1.15), Ch de Rivard 1985 (£6.30), and a Bordeaux Supérieur, Ch des Arras 1983 (£6.75) before the 'Connoisseur's Choice', which includes Ch Trimoulet 1979, Grand Cru Classé St-Emilion (£15.50) and Ch Siaurac 1982, Lalande de Pomerol (£17.50). Other French regions are treated equally seriously: Burgundy, for example, ranges from Chanson Mâcon Supérieur Rouge 1984 (£6.75) to Volnay Les Chevrets 1982, Marcel Amance (£19.50). Country wines include the organically made Terres Blanches, Coteaux d'Aix-en-Provence, 1984 red and 1985 white (£8.60). Spain is represented by several good Riojas and the Penedès Marqués de Griñon Cabernet Sauvignon 1984 (£12.50); Portugal by Fonseca Camarate 1982 (£6.52), and the João Pires Dry Moscato 1986 (£5.60); the New World by various impressive names (Carmenet Sauvignon Fumé 1985, from California, £8.25).

Macnab's

43 Balham High Road, SW12   TEL 01-675 5522

OPEN Mon–Sat 12–3, 7–11   12–2, 7–10.30   CLOSED Chr holidays
CREDIT CARDS 'All major'   UNDERGROUND Clapham South
WHEELCHAIR ACCESS Possible   VEGETARIAN DISHES Limited

Bal-ham, gateway to Yuppiedom, has sprouted a smart restaurant and
wine bar in an early 19th-century house. Go quickly: prices have
already risen considerably. Both bar snacks and wines are eclectic:
satay pork kebabs, quiche or samosas, for example, to be washed
down by, say, house red or white – 'the best available', but what? – at
£5.50/£1.10, Cook's 1987 Chardonnay from New Zealand (£9.50),
Duboeuf's Beaujolais Villages 1986 (£8) or Inglenook Zinfandel 1982
(£9.50). Some other good bottles, but none of them the bargain of the
century. Save the 1978 Pomerol, Ch L'Enclos (£25) for something more
restrained in the restaurant.

Methuselah's

29 Victoria Street, SW1   TEL 01-222 0424

OPEN Mon–Fri 11–3, 5.30–11   CLOSED Sat, Sun, public holidays
CREDIT CARDS All accepted   UNDERGROUND St James's Park, Victoria
WHEELCHAIR ACCESS Not possible   VEGETARIAN DISHES Good selection

A member of the Hewitson stable (see under Cork & Bottle), this
Westminster enterprise, with two ground-floor restaurants as well as
the basement wine bar, is crowded at lunchtime, more peaceful in the
evening. It shares the group's lively and reasonably priced wine list,
with special promotions and seasonal events.

Le Métro

28 Basil Street, SW3   TEL 01-589 6286

OPEN Mon–Fri 7.30am–11pm   Sat 7.30am–6pm   Sun 8am–11am
CLOSED Sat & Sun evenings, public holidays   CREDIT CARDS Amex, Visa
UNDERGROUND Knightsbridge   WHEELCHAIR ACCESS Difficult, only from the
rear; lavatories impossible   VEGETARIAN DISHES Some

The Capital Hotel's smart basement wine bar near Harrods remains
popular for its light and elegant food and its impressive range of fine
wines: mouthwatering Burgundies, Loire and Alsace wines leading up
to a sonorous list of mature Bordeaux (for example, Ch Rauzan-Gassies
1973, £13; and Ch Troplong-Mondot 1971, £19). Nothing much under
£6 a bottle, but plenty to think about. And, there's the Cruover
machine offering ten interesting wines by the glass: a summer visit had
five Italian organic wines (Rizzardi Chardonnay 1987, £1.70) and five
New Zealand whites (Babich Gisbourne Semillon Chardonnay 1986,
£2.50). (Note that Sunday morning is alcohol-free breakfast time.)

Odette's

130 Regent's Park Road, NW1　　　　　　　　　TEL 01-586 5486

OPEN 12.30–2.30, 5.30–11　CLOSED Sun, public holidays, 10 days Chr
CREDIT CARDS All accepted　UNDERGROUND Chalk Farm
WHEELCHAIR ACCESS Impossible　VEGETARIAN DISHES A few

Odette's basement wine bar (beneath their busy restaurant) has a computerised list these days, but it still sports too many split vintages and too few producers' names. Tread carefully, therefore – it is worth the effort to find, for example, Alsace wines from Rolly Gassmann (Gewürztraminer 1986, £10.95); Chassagne Montrachet, Morgeot Premier Cru 1985, Berthe Morey (£19.75); Frascati Superiore 1986, Colli di Catone (£7.25); Basedows Semillon 1986, Barossa Valley (£11.25); and the many fine clarets, including Ch Notton 1982 (£15.75). Sparklers include grande marque Champagnes and Varichon et Clerc's attractive méthode champenoise Blanc de Blancs and Rosé (£9.50). Pinot des Charentes (£2.25) as an aperitif; house red and white Domaine de Bresson Vin de Pays Catalan (£6.75/£2.25).

192

192 Kensington Park Road, W11　　　　　　　　TEL 01-229 0482

OPEN Mon–Sat 12.30–3, 5.30–11　Sun 1–3　CLOSED Sun evening, Chr–New Year's Day, some public holidays　CREDIT CARDS Access, Amex, Visa
UNDERGROUND Ladbroke Grove, Notting Hill Gate
WHEELCHAIR ACCESS Yes, not to lavatories　VEGETARIAN DISHES Yes

192 has expanded and now seems even more a restaurant than a wine bar, but it is worth braving the bustle and smoke for their imaginative food (menus change twice daily) and decent wines on a helpfully laid out list. There are 20 by the glass, including the house Cuvée Ste-Anne Blanc de Blancs (£6/£1.25); Carte Noir Rosé de Provence 1986, Maîtres Vignerons de St-Tropez (£8/£1.55); McLaren Vale Cabernet Sauvignon 1985 (£7/£1.40); and the latest Spanish stunner, Tinto Pesquera 1984 (£15.50/£2.80). Delamotte Brut Champagne goes down from £18.50 to £14.50 between 5.30pm and 7.30pm; Laurent Perrier remains at £23.50, with the Rosé version, one of the very best, £26. Many other Corney & Barrow wines worth investigating.

The Pavilion

Finsbury Circus Gardens, Finsbury Circus, EC2　　　TEL 01-628 8224

OPEN Mon–Fri 11.30–3, 5–8　CLOSED Sat, Sun, public holidays
CREDIT CARDS Access, Amex, Visa　UNDERGROUND/BR STATIONS Moorgate,
Liverpool Street　WHEELCHAIR ACCESS Impossible
VEGETARIAN DISHES Salads, cheeses

The bowling-green's former clubhouse feels surprisingly rustic and old-fashioned for a busy spot in the City, but David Gilmour's impressive wine list is up to the minute and exciting. He chooses a theme (region or grape, say) for wines by the glass, changed every two months. House wines include the Pavilion's Hock (£5.90/£1.50), Vin du Pavillon Rouge (£5.90/£1.50) from the co-operative at Oisly-et-Thésée; others by the glass are changed frequently. The list is persuasively annotated to encourage customers to try, for example, Chardonnays from around the world (from Penedès, Jean León 1984, £13.50; from California, Edna Valley 1985, £11); or excellent Zind-Humbrecht Alsace wines (Riesling, Clos Häuserer 1985, £8.75); or red Loires (Chinon, Domaine de la Chapellerie 1985, Olek, £8.70). The Champagnes are varied enough for any City crisis or celebration; there's Mas de Daumas Gassac Rosé 1986 (£8.20); fine mature Burgundies; and half-bottles which include Ch Rayne-Vigneau 1983 Sauternes (£9.20); as well as a wide selection of Sherry, Madeira and Port.

Rebato's

169 South Lambeth Road, SW8   TEL 01-735 6388

OPEN Mon–Fri 12–2.30, 7–11.15   CLOSED Sat lunchtime, Sun
CREDIT CARDS Amex, Diners, Visa   UNDERGROUND Vauxhall, Stockwell
WHEELCHAIR ACCESS Yes; not lavatories   VEGETARIAN DISHES Some

Rebato's combines a successful Spanish restaurant with a crowded tapas bar offering everything from huevos flamenca to stuffed squid. Over 30 Spanish wines include many Torres bottles (let's hope they've moved onto a younger Viña Sol than the 1985 which was still listed as we went to press: £4.95). Even the fabulous Gran Coronas Black Label is there – 1978/79 (£14.50). Good Riojas, too, with a few other Spanish offerings and a page of French, German and sparklers for the unconverted. Don't miss the traditional accompaniment to tapas, Sherry, with several good examples available.

Reynier Wine Library

43 Trinity Square, EC3   TEL 01-481 0415

OPEN Mon–Fri 11.30–3, 5–7.30   CLOSED Sat, Sun, public holidays
CREDIT CARDS Access, Amex, Visa   UNDERGROUND Tower Hill
WHEELCHAIR ACCESS Not possible   VEGETARIAN DISHES Not available (but see below)

Reynier have moved their clubby Wine Library from Fleet Lane, but otherwise things are as before: a choice of about 700 sound wines on the Eldridge Pope/Reynier list in the retail section on the ground floor, and a chance to drink your purchase in comfort in the cellar (£1 corkage charge) along with pâté, cheese, salads and coffee. The list repays leisurely study – luckily there is well-informed advice to hand. France is particularly well covered, from Grand Chevalier vin de table (£2.13) to Bienvenue Bâtard Montrachet 1985, Henri Clerc (£40.37). Don't miss the good range of Champagne, from halves to salmanazars, the California section, and the 'Chairman's Selection' by Christopher Pope, every one a winner.

Shampers

4 Kingly Street, W1 TEL 01-437 1692

OPEN Mon–Fri 11–3, 5.30–11 Sat 11–3 CLOSED Sat evening, Sun, Easter, 25 & 26 Dec CREDIT CARDS All accepted UNDERGROUND Oxford Circus, Piccadilly Circus WHEELCHAIR ACCESS Yes, but not to lavatories VEGETARIAN DISHES Varied selection

Another member of the Hewitson stable (see under Cork & Bottle), this cheerful bar and downstairs brasserie behind Regent Street shares the same interesting and reasonably priced wine list, with special offers and events throughout the year. The brasserie does lunches and acts as a spillover for the wine bar in the evening.

Whittington's

21 College Hill, EC4 TEL 01-248 5855

OPEN Mon–Fri 11.30–3, 5–8 CLOSED Sat, Sun CREDIT CARDS All accepted UNDERGROUND Cannon Street WHEELCHAIR ACCESS No VEGETARIAN DISHES Selection of salads

Dick of That Ilk is said to have owned these ancient cellars before the Great Fire, and they are still popular, whether bar or restaurant. Wines available by the glass include Bordeaux Belair Sauvignon 1987 (£6.55/£1.70); Gisselbrecht Pinot Blanc 1986 (£8.25/£2.10); and house claret (£6.75/£1.70). There are over 50 others to choose from, including Besserat de Bellefon Champagne Rosé (£17); Ch Senailhac 1983 (£9.20); Sancerre Le Paradis 1987, Vacheron (£14.50/£7.75 half); Louis Jadot Pinot Noir 1985 (£11.95); Bardolino Classico 1986, Rizzardi (£6.95); Raimat Chardonnay 1987 (£8.50); Penfold's Koonunga Hill Shiraz/Cabernet 1985 (£10.25); and Ch Musar 1980 (£11.95). The list still needs fewer alternative vintages and more shippers' names.

OUT OF LONDON

BAKEWELL Derbyshire

Aitch's Wine Bar and Bistro

TEL (062 981) 3895

OPEN Mon–Sat 12–2, 7–10.30   Sun (end Easter–end Sept) 6–10   CLOSED Chr
Day   CREDIT CARDS None accepted   WHEELCHAIR ACCESS Yes
VEGETARIAN DISHES Yes

A former clothing factory has been handsomely converted, its oak
beams and trusses still in situ, with potted palms and church pews for
company. The Hattersleys' exotic food is famed countrywide (outside
catering a speciality), and their wines deserve to be better known.
House wines include Cuvée Jean Paul Rouge (£6.60 a litre/85p) and
Sauvignon 1987, Vin de Pays du Jardin de la France (£5.50/95p). Others
include the excellent Alsace wines from the Turckheim co-operative
(Pinot Blanc 1986, £6); Bourgogne Aligoté 1986, Vallet Frères (£8);
Ramage La Batisse 1983 (£9.75); Châteauneuf-du-Pape, Domaine
Chante Cigale 1982 (£9.50); Wynn's Coonawarra Shiraz 1985 (£7.80);
and Portuguese Bairrada 1982 Reserva, Caves Aliança (£6.35). The
sparklers include Bricout Rosé and Carte d'Or (£17.50/£16.50), and
there are decent ports and a Muscat de Rivesaltes by the glass.

BEDALE North Yorkshire

Plummers

North End   TEL (0677) 23432

OPEN Tue–Sat 12–2, 7–10   CLOSED Mon, Sun   CREDIT CARDS Access, Visa
WHEELCHAIR ACCESS Possible with assistance   VEGETARIAN DISHES Yes

A newish wine bar with upstairs restaurant is pleasing locals with its
warm welcome, reasonably priced food (rather smart and eclectic) and
decent wines. By now some of the ageing Sauvignons will surely have
been updated. If not, stick to the grapes which can take it: Hugel's
Alsace Pinot Blanc 1986 (£7.70/£1.50); Australian Jacob's Creek
Semillon 1986 (£5.95/95p); Chablis, Montée de Tonnerre 1985, Premier
Cru, Louis Michel (£18.75). Likely reds include Rioja Gran Reserva
1982, Monte Real (£8.50); Ch Gardéra 1983 (£8.25); Bourgogne Pinot
Noir 1985, Cave de Buxy (£9.50); and Paul Jaboulet Hermitage 1983
(£17.50). House wines are Dourthe Frères red and white Bordeaux
(£5.50/95p) and Chanson red and white Burgundy at the same price.

BILLERICAY Essex

Webber's

2 Western Road   TEL (0277) 656581

OPEN 11.30–2.30, 6–10.30 (Mon from 7, Fri & Sat to 11)   CLOSED Sun, public
holidays L, 1 week Chr, last week July, first week Aug   CREDIT CARDS All
accepted   WHEELCHAIR ACCESS Possible with help
VEGETARIAN DISHES Good selection

First-timers are surprised by what they find in this split-level wine bar
near the station: several hundred wines, with plenty of halves and
magnums, a Wine Machine, an off-sales department, various special
events, and food so popular they take bookings. The Wine Machine
glasses (quarter-bottle size) might include, say, Morey St-Denis 1984,
Domaine Dujac £4.22) and Domaine de Grange Grillard 1983 (£2.64)
from the Jura; several vintage Ports are also kept on the machine (Dow
1966, £6.85). House wines include Geoffrey Roberts reds and white
(£4.60/£1.75) from California and Joly Champagne Brut (£16.35). The
magnums are tempting: house claret from Pierre Lacoste (£15.25);
Côtes du Rhône, Ch du Grand Moulas 1985, Ryckwaert (£15.85); and
the Portuguese Camarate 1980, Fonseca (£15.45). The list, complete
with succinct notes, is worth leisurely study. The Australian section
was expanded to celebrate the Bicentennial, and now includes
everything from Brown Brothers Dry Muscat 1986 (£8.55) to Petaluma
Cabernet Sauvignon 1981 (£16.45), with a half-bottle of Petaluma's
sumptuous Botrytis Riesling 1982 (£15.75) to finish. Clarets go back to
1967 (Ch Cantenac Brown, £19.75), and Rhônes to 1979 (Côte Rôtie
1979, Guigal, £17.45). There is plenty worth drinking at half that price,
too.

CHOBHAM Surrey

Racoons

1 Bagshot Road   TEL (099 05) 8491

OPEN Tue–Fri 12 noon–2.30, 7–10.30   Sat 7–10.30   CLOSED Sun, Mon, public
holidays   CREDIT CARDS Access, Diners, Visa   WHEELCHAIR ACCESS Yes,
but not to lavatories   VEGETARIAN DISHES Some

The Wales family have enlarged their pleasant wine bar: it now seats 60
(you must eat as well as drink on Friday and Saturday evenings – no
complaints). House wines from Eldridge Pope are Grand Chevalier
vins de tables (£5.50/£1.10), plus three others, perhaps a Bordeaux, a
Muscadet and a Nahe (£6.05/£1.20), changed quite frequently. The
whites include some serious wines: Savennières, Clos du Papillon 1986
(£10.10) and Nobilo Gewürztraminer 1986 (£12.50) from New Zealand.
The reds are equally attractive, with, for example, St-Amour, Domaine

des Billards 1986, Loron (£11.60) – and many other fine cru Beaujolais; Châteauneuf-du-Pape, Clos de l'Oratoire 1984, Amouroux (£14.85); and useful half-bottles, including the Chairman's Late-Bottled Port, Eldridge Pope (£7.20).

CIRENCESTER Gloucestershire

Shepherd's

Fleece Hotel, Market Place   TEL (0285) 68507

OPEN 10.30am–11pm   CLOSED 25 Dec   CREDIT CARDS All accepted
WHEELCHAIR ACCESS Yes   VEGETARIAN DISHES Reasonable selection

The old coaching-inn in the square boasts a comfortable, wood-panelled wine bar with a list mainly from Averys of Bristol and some appetising snacks. House claret, Burgundy and Côtes de Duras cost £6.90 (£1.15 the small, £2.30 the large glass). Others available by the glass include Orvieto Classico Secco 1987 (£5.70/95p); Marqués de Cáceres Rioja 1984 (£7.25/£1.25); and Blanquette de Limoux (£9.75/£1.95). Other worthwhile bottles include Rully Varots 1978, Delorme (£11.75); Nobilo's Gisbourne Chardonnay 1986 from New Zealand (£10.95); California Clos du Val Zinfandel 1979 (£9.95); Tyrrell's Long Flat White 1985 (£7.95) and Long Flat Red 1982 (£8.75); and Muga Rioja 1981 (£7.95).

CLACTON-ON-SEA Essex

Nookes & Crannies

1 Carnarvon Road   TEL (0255) 426572

OPEN Mon–Sat 12–2.30, 7–12 (Sun 12 noon–2, 7–10.30)   CLOSED 25 & 26 Dec,
1 Jan   CREDIT CARDS Access, Amex, Visa   WHEELCHAIR ACCESS Yes
VEGETARIAN DISHES Some

The Starrs continue to offer home-cooked food and special wine events (for example, an Italian food and wine evening), as well as sustaining their interesting list of almost 100 wines, over 20 of them by the glass: Côtes de Gascogne Colombard 1987 (£5/£1); Faugères, Val d'Orbieu 1986 (£5/£1). Others worth considering include Alsace Pinot Blanc 1986, Blanck (£6.25); Torres Viña Esmeralda 1987 (£6.25); Gigondas 1982, Vouillard (£7.95); and Lebanese Ch Musar 1980 (£7.50). Note too the useful half-bottles – and the reasonable prices.

Please let us know if you agree or disagree with our choice of Britain's top 50 wine bars.

CONGLETON Cheshire

Odd Fellows

20 Rood Hill   TEL (0260) 270243

OPEN Mon–Sat 12–2.30, 6.45–11   CLOSED Sun, public holidays (except Good
Fri), 25–28 Dec   CREDIT CARDS Access, Amex, Visa
WHEELCHAIR ACCESS Difficult   VEGETARIAN DISHES Wide selection

The enthusiastic Kirkhams continue to burst out in all directions: nooks
and crannies on several floors provide bistro, business seminar room
and wine bar. Hearty home-made food is ballast for the 150 or so
wines, which include a special 'wine of the week' by glass or bottle.
Paul Boutinot house wines are £5.95 a litre (90p a glass). Other
Boutinot trophies include the excellent Alsace wines from the
Turckheim co-operative (Pinot Blanc 1986, £6.35), Ch Ramage La
Batisse 1983 (£11.45) and Bricout Carte Noir Champagne (£15.95). Two
new sections cover French country wines and 'end of meal' wines, the
latter including Eldridge Pope's Chairman's Selection Dessert Wine
and Port. The wine list's new design and more restrained prose make it
a pleasure to read.

CROYDON Greater London

Pearls

34 Surrey Street   TEL 01-686 0586

OPEN Mon–Fri 12–3, 5.30–11   CLOSED Sat L, Sun, public holidays, 25 & 26
Dec   CREDIT CARDS All accepted   WHEELCHAIR ACCESS Impossible
VEGETARIAN DISHES Good selection

This rather smart wine bar underneath its parent restaurant, 34 Surrey
Street ('The UK's largest selection of fish') is worth a visit for its
extensive range of California wines: pale-pink White Zinfandel 1987,
Santa Barbara Winery (£9.95), Mirassou Fumé Blanc 1986 (£13.50), Clos
du Bois Chardonnay 1986 (£11.50), and plenty more. Some decent
French at fairly stiff prices, lip-service to other wine-growing countries.
What a pity the only wines by the glass are the house Cuvée Hébrard
(£4.95/£1) and Mirassou Pastel 1987 (£8.95/£1.50), a pink blend of wine
and grape juice. Evening meals are now available.

Please write to tell us about any ideas for features you would like to see in
next year's edition or in *Which? Wine Monthly*.

Doric Tavern

15 Market Street   TEL 031-225 1084

OPEN Mon–Wed 12 noon–1am (Thur–Sat to 2am) CLOSED Sun, 25 Dec, 1
Jan CREDIT CARDS Access, Amex, Visa WHEELCHAIR ACCESS Impossible
VEGETARIAN DISHES Always some

A cheerfully informal first-floor wine bar overlooking Waverley station
and Princes Street, with freshly cooked food (fish good) and a serious
wine list (supplemented by some real bargains on the blackboard).
House wines include Bulgarian Chardonnay/Aligoté (£5.65/£1.05);
André Simon Claret (£5.85/£1.10); and Hardy's Australian Cabernet
Sauvignon/Shiraz 1986 (£7/£1.20). The list is less relentlessly
'international' than before, with the main strength still lying in France:
for example, Ch Chasse-Spleen 1979 (£14.35); Hugel Riesling 1983
(£8.85); Fleurie 1986, Paul Sapin (£7.75); and Hautes Côtes de Nuits
1978, Dufouleur (£7.95). Others worth considering include the Torres
Spanish wines, the Wehlener Sonnenuhr Riesling Auslese 1975 from
Licht-Bergweiler (£10.75) and the Portuguese Colares 1981 (£6.35).
Impressive list of single malts, including the unpronounceable – but
delicious – Auchentoshan and Bruichladdich (£1.05 a glass).

Handsel's Wine Bar

22 Stafford Street   TEL 031-225 5521

OPEN Mon–Sat 10–11 CLOSED Sun CREDIT CARDS Access, Amex, Diners,
Visa WHEELCHAIR ACCESS Yes, but not to lavatories
VEGETARIAN DISHES Only by request (not on menu)

Handsel's remains a good, stylish restaurant with a good, stylish
wine-bar at ground-floor level. They serve coffee and tea as well as
lunch and dinner: interesting, light modern food. (Book if you want
lunch.) There are about 40 wines, at least half of them by the glass, and
with a good selection of half-bottles as well. Their basic French whites
should have advanced a year by now: too many 1986s still hanging
around. However, Muscadet-sur-Lie, Domaine du Grand Frère, André
David is 1987 (£6.90), as are the Australian RF Chardonnay, Orlando
(£7.30/£1.65), and Thomas Hardy 'Bird' series Bone Dry White
(£6.75/£1.50) and Chardonnay (£8.65). The reds start with Leith Claret
1985 (£6.10/£1.45) and take in, for example, Henri Jayer Bourgogne
Passetoutgrain 1986 (£9.40); Wyndham Estate Shiraz Bin 555 1984
(£6.60/£1.50) and the Chilean Cousiño Macul Cabernet Sauvignon 1981
(£7.35).

Whighams Wine Cellars

13 Hope Street   TEL 031-225 8674

OPEN 11am–midnight (Fri to 1am)   CLOSED Sun, 25 & 26 Dec, 1 Jan
CREDIT CARDS Visa   WHEELCHAIR ACCESS Impossible
VEGETARIAN DISHES Several

An attractive and busy semi-basement bar just round the corner from
the west end of Princes Street, offering interesting food to go with the
fine wines on the list, which is still rather terse. About 20 of the 50 or so
wines are available by the glass: for example, Ch Canteloup 1985
(£5.95/£1.15), Corbières Blanc de Blancs 1986 (£4.95/95p), and Lilliano
Chianti Classico 1985 (£5.95/£1.15). House wines start at £4.65/95p, and
into double figures are some excellent mature clarets and burgundies.
(The wine bar is not connected with Whighams, the wine merchants
listed on page 250.)

EPWORTH Humberside

The Epworth Tap

9–11 Market Place   TEL (0427) 873333

OPEN Tue–Sat 7.30–12   CLOSED All lunchtimes, Sun, Mon, 1st 2 weeks Aug,
25 Dec–1 Jan   CREDIT CARDS Access   WHEELCHAIR ACCESS Yes, but not to
lavatories   VEGETARIAN DISHES Occasionally on menu, special dishes by
arrangement

The Tap is so popular that it is best to book for the good home-cooking
and spectacular wines. John Wynne's enthusiasm is now matched by
such knowledge that anyone, beginner or sophisticate, could spend
happy and instructive visits here for months, even years. John accepts
that his list is indigestible for most people but enjoys the fact that he is
often asked for advice and can gently guide them with realistic
suggestions. It is hard to quote anything in the face of so many
hundreds: clarets start modestly with Ch Patache d'Aux 1982 (£11.50)
or 1983 (£8.95) and wander through the great estates, taking in, for
example in St-Emilion, styles as different as Ch Tertre Rôteboeuf 1984
(£10.50) and Ch Ausone 1979 (£45). (If they are not thought ready to
drink, either they are in the cellar but not on the list, or a terse 'NFS'
lets you know it might be worth being patient and making a return
visit.) There are also mature Cahors (Clos La Coutale 1981, £7.95), a
dozen cru Beaujolais from 1983 and 1985, pages and pages of superb
Burgundies and Rhônes (Chave Hermitage 1981, £20; Clape Cornas
1979, £17.50). He also has Mas de Daumas Gassac 1983 at a modest
£12.50 and Opus One 1982 at a reasonable £50. Whites are no less
impressive, with a run of premier and grand cru Chablis (1983
Fourchaume, Pic, £16.95) and opulent white Burgundies – and of
course, Ch Fuissé, Vieilles Vignes 1983, Vincent (£22) is amongst

them. There are good white Graves (Ch Olivier 1982, £9.99), and Rhônes (Guigal's 1982 Condrieu, £15); and a wealth of New World wines, including Delegat's distinguished New Zealand Chardonnay 1985 (£12.50). Sweet wines are inventive, international, and mostly available in useful half-bottles: from Mondavi's Moscato d'Oro 1986 (£5.95) to Ch Monbazillac 1981 (£5.50), Brown's Brothers Orange Muscat 1985 (£5.95) and Nackenheimer Schmittskapellchen Beerenauslese 1976, Mann (£12). House wines are changed from time to time, but as we went to press included the Plaimont co-operative Colombard 1987 (£5.95/£1) and Ch du Grand Moulas Côtes du Rhône 1986 (£6.95/£1). Service is thoughtful, there are suggested wines on the Saturday night menu, and courses on wine appreciation are held from time to time.

ETON Berkshire

Eton Wine Bar

82/83 High Street   TEL (075 38) 54921
OPEN Mon–Sat 12–3, 6–11   Sun 12–2   CLOSED 5 days Chr, Easter Sun
CREDIT CARDS Access, Visa   WHEELCHAIR ACCESS Possible
VEGETARIAN DISHES Good selection

The Gilbey family continue to run a smoothly efficient wine bar, offering a good range of wine by bottle, half-bottle and glass at ungrasping prices. Each section is arranged by style of wine and, within that, in ascending order by price. Thus 'dry whites' run from Gros Plant-sur-Lie 1986, Poiron (£5.95) to Chassagne-Montrachet Les Verges 1985, Premier Cru, Lamanthe (£32.25). Chanut house wines are £5.25 (£1.55 a glass). Note the Rutherford & Miles Madeira, Barbadillo Sherries. Pineau des Charentes. and Muscat de Lunel, all available by the glass. Interesting food.

EXETER Devon

Bottlescrue Bills

White Hart Hotel, South Street   TEL (0392) 37511
OPEN Mon–Sat 12–2, 7–10 (to 10.30 Fri & Sat)   CLOSED Sun, public holidays
CREDIT CARDS All accepted   WHEELCHAIR ACCESS Yes
VEGETARIAN DISHES With notice

A link in John Davy's chain (see under Davys in the London section), this attractive old inn has the added advantage of a summer barbecue. Don't miss the blackboard special wines which supplement the sound, modestly priced basic list: French 'Ordnary' white or red (£4.95/£1.30), Pinot d'Alsace 1985 (£6.25/£1.60). Champagne, Port, Sherry and Madeira are also available by glass, pint jug or tankard, as appropriate.

HARROGATE North Yorkshire

William & Victoria

6 Cold Bath Road   TEL (0423) 506883

OPEN Mon–Sat 12 noon–3, 6.30–11   CLOSED Sun, Chr
CREDIT CARDS Access   WHEELCHAIR ACCESS No
VEGETARIAN DISHES Available

Downstairs at Will and Vic's pleases its regulars with good Yorkshire food and French-accented wines. House red and dry white are changed frequently (£5.50/95p); house claret is from Henri Rodier (£5.95/£1); house hock from Carl Reh (£5.50/95p). Higher flyers might consider Ch Senailhac 1983, Bordeaux Supérieur (£7.35/£4.75 half); Fleurie, Domaine des Roches des Garants 1986, Sarrau (£9.95); Chablis, Mont de Milieu 1986, Premier Cru, Dauvissat (£15.50); Opus One 1982, Rothschild-Mondavi (£46), first fruits of the famous partnership in California; and Ch de Malle 1981, Grand Cru Sauternes (£9.95 a half). There are also blackboard specials.

HUNGERFORD Berkshire

The Galloping Crayfish

Courtyard, 24 High Street   TEL (0488) 84008

OPEN Tue–Sat 12–2.30, 6–11   Sun 12–2 (summer only), 7–10.30
CLOSED Mon, Chr Day, Boxing Day   CREDIT CARDS Access, Visa
WHEELCHAIR ACCESS Yes   VEGETARIAN DISHES Always at least two

This relaxed bistro/wine bar, in a pretty courtyard behind the Hungerford Wine Company (see the WHERE TO BUY section), continues to please with its imaginative, freshly cooked food and good range of wines, 20 of them on tap on the Wine Machine. Quarter-bottle-sized glasses have recently included Gisselbrecht Muscat d'Alsace 1985 (£9.95/£2.50); Petersons Chardonnay 1985 (£17.95/£4.50) from Australia; CVNE Imperial Reserva 1978 (£11.95/£3); Ch Lasserre 1983 (£9.50/£2.50); and the sweet Ockfener Geisberg Riesling Auslese 1983 (£3.50 a large glass, £1.90 small). The list groups wines by style – light-bodied, robust reds, and so on – with lively tasting notes as an additional aid. 'Oak-aged Chardonnay dry whites' puts together Mâcon Peronne 1985, Domaine Rousset (£11.50); William Wheeler's Chardonnay 1984, Napa Valley (£15.95); and Matua Valley's Chardonnay 1986, Yates Estate (£16.50). There are a few tables in the courtyard; and tutored tastings on Monday evenings in winter.

Please let us know if you agree or disagree with our choice of Britain's top 50 wine bars.

LLANGOLLEN Clwyd

Gales

18 Bridge Street   TEL (0978) 860089

OPEN (May–Sept) Every day 12–2, 6–10.15 CLOSED (Oct–April) Sun pm,
Mon, Chr and New Year CREDIT CARDS Not accepted
WHEELCHAIR ACCESS Difficult VEGETARIAN DISHES Limited selection

Gales, though small, has a list of over 80 wines at ungrasping prices,
starting with house Cuvée André Côtes du Ventoux 1986, Salavert
(£4.75/85p) and Akerman Rosé d'Anjou 1986 (£4.75/85p). Bordeaux
includes three fine 1983s (Ch Monbousquet, St-Emilion Grand Cru,
£12.95) as well as the modest Charles Prince Médoc 1985 (£6.55); the
Salavert Rhônes include Crozes-Hermitage 1985 (£6.95); the Loire
offers Ackerman's Vouvray 1986 (£6.25) as well as a couple of ageing
Muscadets. Italians include Chianti Classico 1986, Rocca delle Macie
(£6.85); the Californians have several Mondavi wines (Sauvignon Blanc
1986, £7.95); and the Australians have a couple of excellent Peter
Lehmann bottles (Semillon 1984, £6.70). With notice, mature claret,
Burgundy and Port can be summoned from the cellar. Well-cooked
food, and a bed if you don't drink and drive.

OXFORD Oxfordshire

The Crypt

Frewin Court, off Cornmarket   TEL (0865) 251000

OPEN Mon–Sat 11.30–2.30, 6–10.30 (Fri 6–11, Sat 7–11) CLOSED Sun, public
holidays CREDIT CARDS All accepted WHEELCHAIR ACCESS Impossible
VEGETARIAN DISHES Some available

The John Davy formula (see under Davys in the London section)
furnishes these 'wine and steak vaults' with lots of Victorian
atmosphere, sawdust floors and wine paraphernalia. The wine list, as
always in the chain, offers over 30 reliable and modestly priced bottles,
from red and white French 'Ordnary' No 1 (£4.85/85p) to Chablis 1985,
Jean-Claude Simmonet (£12.50) and Ch de Terrefort-Quancard 1983
(£7.35). The Davy's Hock and Pinot Blanc d'Alsace remain favourites,
as does the Piper Heidsieck Champagne (£16.95/£2.75/£4.75 a tankard).
Don't miss the blackboard specials and the many fine Sherries, Ports
and Madeiras.

Find the best new wine bargains all year round with our newsletter, *Which?
Wine Monthly*, available for £15 a year from: Dept WG89, Consumers'
Association, FREEPOST, Hertford SG14 1YB – no stamp is needed if posted
within the UK.

ROSSETT Clwyd

Churtons Wine & Food Bar

Machine House, Chester Road   TEL (0244) 570163
OPEN Mon–Sat 12 noon–2, 7–10   CLOSED Sun, public holidays, 24 Dec–2/3
Jan   CREDIT CARDS Access, Amex, Diners, Visa   WHEELCHAIR ACCESS With
assistance   VEGETARIAN DISHES A selection

You have to pick your way carefully through the list in this attractive
converted barn: split vintages occur all too often, whereas shippers'
names, especially important in Germany and Italy, for example, are all
too often missing. That said, there are many fine bottles in both
sections: the list divides into wines under £9 and those above that
figure. In the cheaper section, for example, consider the Boeckel Alsace
wines (Muscat Réserve 1985, £8.10); Sauvignon de St-Bris 1986, Tabit
(£7.80); Ch Haut-Sociando 1983 (£6.50); Campo Viejo Rioja Gran
Reserva 1978 (£8.20) and João Pires Tinto da Anfora 1982 (£6.95). In the
higher price bracket, choose from Kaseler Nies'chen Riesling Kabinett
1985, Deinhard (£10.25); Rosemount Show Reserve Chardonnay 1987
(£10.50); Marcilly Monthélie 1983 (£12.75); and the many sturdy
Bordeaux. There is an adjacent delicatessen and wine shop, and
another Churtons wine bar in Tarporley, Cheshire (run on similar
lines, but closed on Monday).

ROSS-ON-WYE Hereford & Worcester

The Wine Bar

24 High Street   TEL (0989) 67717
OPEN Mon–Sat 11–2.30, 7–11   Sun (public holidays only) 7–10.30
CLOSED Sun (except public holiday evenings), 25 & 26 Dec, 1st two weeks Feb
CREDIT CARDS Access, Visa   WHEELCHAIR ACCESS Yes, but not to
lavatories   VEGETARIAN DISHES Always several

A 17th-century building is the home of the Bennetts' wine bar, behind
a beamed coffee shop. Their inventive menu is supplemented by
special evenings (Beaujolais Nouveau, New Year's Eve, and so on).
The wines are well chosen, carefully annotated and reasonably priced:
house Bordeaux Blanc (£4.25/85p); Ch La Tour St-Bonnet 1983 (£8.95);
Hautes Côtes de Beaune 1985, Michel Plait (£8.25); Bulgarian Cabernet
Sauvignon 1980, Oriahovitza (£5.50); Alsace Riesling 1985, Pfaffenheim
(£6.45); and Villa Antinori Bianco 1986 (£6.45). There are several useful
half-bottles.

Send us your views on the report forms at the back of the book.

SOUTHEND-ON-SEA Essex

The Pipe of Port

84 High Street   TEL (0702) 614606

OPEN Mon–Fri 11–2.30, 6–11 (Sat 7–11)   CLOSED Sun, public holidays
CREDIT CARDS Access, Diners, Visa   WHEELCHAIR ACCESS Impossible
VEGETARIAN DISHES Some

Last year we reported that a Le Cruvinet (Cruover-style) machine was
being installed in this old casks-and-sawdust bar. That is now in full
flood and this year's innovation is a computerised list which allows
Steve Jones to offer a more varied selection of wines. From Le
Cruvinet, you can choose eight wines at under £2 a glass, perhaps
including Rosemount Fumé Blanc 1987 and Ch Lamothe Côtes de
Bourg 1982. A 'special' dégustation offers tastings of all eight, plus a
tasting sheet (£3.85). House wines are from Loron (£4.95/£1.25) and
Rudolf Müller (£5.40/£1.40); others by the glass include Davy's claret
(£5.95/£1.50), CVNE Rioja (£5.95/£1.50) and Varichon et Clerc
sparkling Blanc de Blancs (£9.75/£1.85). Thereafter the range is wide
and worth serious study: it includes some fine older wines, such as
Ch L'Angélus 1978, Grand Cru St-Emilion (£18). Food with an English
accent.

SOUTHWOLD Suffolk

The Crown

High Street   TEL (0502) 722275

OPEN Mon–Sat 10.30–2.30, 6–11   Sun 12 noon–2, 7–10.30
CREDIT CARDS Access, Amex, Visa   WHEELCHAIR ACCESS Yes
VEGETARIAN DISHES Some

The Crown continues to combine old-fashioned comforts with
innovative food, a dazzling list of over 250 wines, a Cruover machine
to allow posh tasting by the glass and, the most recent addition, a
Cellar & Kitchen Store behind the inn. See the WHERE TO BUY section
for an evaluation of the full wine list: with prior notice you can
summon its treasures to drink in the bar. Last summer, the Cruover
yielded, among others, Bernkasteler Kurfurstlay 1986 (£4.30/£1.10);
Domaine du Bosc Rosé 1986, Vin de Pays de l'Hérault (£5.35/£1.10);
and ten 'Californian Classics', including Trefethen Chardonnay 1981
(£18.40/£4.60) and Clos du Bois Merlot 1985 (£9.15/£2.30). The 20-page
list demands leisurely study: 12 Rhônes (Guigal Hermitage 1980,
£15.25); another dozen red Burgundies (Bourgogne La Digoine 1983,
Aubert de Villaine, £10); over 30 clarets, starting with Pierre Coste's
Bordeaux 1986 (£6.05) and soaring to Ch Latour 1961 (£170), with many
interesting steps en route. Simon Loftus's interest in Italian wines is

revealed by such listings as Teroldego Rotaliano 1983, Conti Martini (£9.50): 'Italian equivalent of Pomerol? Blackberries and gamey generosity.' Whites begin with the Plaimont co-operative's Côtes de St-Mont (£4.65), wander through all the classic French regions (don't miss the outstanding Alsace wines from Blanck), Italy, California, New Zealand (is there any left of the superb Cloudy Bay Sauvignon Blanc 1987, £10.60?), and Germany. Dessert wines are treated seriously: Bordeaux from a modest Ch des Tours, St-Croix du Mont 1979 (£10.25) to Yquem 1976 (£65); interesting Loires, including Moulin Touchais and Anjou Rablay 1928, Caves de la Maison Prunier (£30); and others from Italy, Germany, Hungary and the New World. A special offer provides three glasses of wine for £6 to go with the menu (generally a rosé, a red or white, and a pudding wine).

STAMFORD Lincolnshire

The George at Stamford

St Martins   TEL (0780) 55171

OPEN Mon–Sat 11–3, 6–11   Sun 12–2.30, 6.30–10.30   CREDIT CARDS All accepted   WHEELCHAIR ACCESS Limited   VEGETARIAN DISHES Yes

The George's Garden Lounge continues to offer airy comfort as a setting for a generous buffet and sensible range of hot dishes to enjoy along with 20 good Italian wines chosen by Ivo Vannocci, a Poste Hotels director. A Wine Machine allows all but the sparklers to be offered by glass as well as bottle: for example, Bollini Chardonnay 1986 (£8.25/£1.70) and Rosso Cònero 1984 (£7.45/£1.50).

TAUNTON Somerset

Porters

49 East Reach   TEL (0823) 256688

OPEN Mon–Fri 12 noon–2.30, 7–11   Sat 7–11   CLOSED Sun
CREDIT CARDS Access, Visa   WHEELCHAIR ACCESS Possible
VEGETARIAN DISHES Selection available

The Porters run an appealingly friendly wine bar, popular locally for its home-cooked food on a daily-changing menu and its interesting and reasonably priced wines. House wines include Côtes du Ventoux (£5/90p); Chenin Blanc de Blancs (£5/90p); and others by the glass, for example, New Zealand Montana Sauvignon Blanc (£1) and Lageder Pinot Grigio (£1.20). Vintages and shippers are still not always listed, but where they are, they are carefully chosen. The 70 or so wines include, in reds, Loron Mâcon Rouge 1985 (£6.60); Gevrey Chambertin 1982, Louis Trapet (£14.50); Jaboulet's Crozes-Hermitage 1985 (£9.50); Antinori's Chianti Classico Riserva 1982 (£8.50); and Bulgarian

Cabernet Sauvignon and Merlot, both 1981 (both £5). Whites include Vouvray Demi-Sec 1985 from the excellent co-operative (£7.30); four good Dopff & Irion Alsace wines (Gewürztraminer 1985, Seigneur d'Alsace, £8.50); Tyrrell's Vat 47 Chardonnay (£11); and the good local Staplecombe English Table Wine (£5.80). Check the blackboard specials and bin-ends.

THAXTED Essex

The Cuckoo

36 Town Street   TEL (0371) 830482

OPEN Tue–Sat 12–2.30, 7–11   CLOSED Mon (except bank holidays, 1–2 weeks Jan   CREDIT CARDS Access, Diners, Visa   WHEELCHAIR ACCESS Difficult, not to lavatories   VEGETARIAN DISHES Several

The Cuckoo sounds as if it is getting too big for its nest, what with a separate restaurant with a menu as big as a table for two, and a separate fine wines list as well as the good basic one of about 70 wines. Choose a snack in the bar, or order from the à la carte menu if you wish. House wines (£4.50/85p) include Fleur de Lys white and Barton & Guestier's Partager red. Others available by the glass include Gatão Vinho Verde (£5.30/£1.05), and Rioja Berberana 1985, Carta de Plata (£5.85/£1.15). Weightier bottles include Ch Clos des Jacobins 1978, Grand Cru Classé St-Emilion (£19.95); St-Joseph 1983, Delaunay (£9.45); Chianti Classico Riserva 1982, Castello di Volpaia (£11.15); Ménétou-Salon 1985, Jacky Rat (£8.70); and Brown Brothers Semillon 1984 (£9.20).

English vineyards
open to the public

ENGLAND

AVON

Avonwood (1 acre)
Dr J D Minors, Seawalls Road,
Sneyd Park, Bristol
(0272) 686635
VA VS

BERKSHIRE

Ascot (3 acres)
Col A R Robertson, Ascot Farm,
Winkfield Road, Ascot
(0990) 23563
V WTF VS CP+M/BA

The Holt (1 acre)
Brigadier W G R Turner CBE,
Woolton Hill, Newbury
(0635) 253680
VA

Joyous Garde (2½ acres)
D T Dulake, Crazies Hill, Wargrave
(073 522) 2102
VD OD WTF VS

Thames Valley (17 acres)
J S E Leighton, Stanlake Park,
Twyford
(0734) 340176
CP/BA VA VS

Westbury (12½ acres)
B H Theobald, Westbury Farm,
Purley on Thames, Nr Reading
(073 57) 3123
VA WTC VS CP+M/BA TC

BUCKINGHAMSHIRE

Wickenden (4 acres)
R H Lock, Wickenden, Cliveden
Road, Taplow
(0628) 29455
CP/BA VA WTC VS S

CAMBRIDGESHIRE

Chilford Hundred Vineyard
(18 acres)
S Alper, Chilford Hall, Balsham
Road, Linton, Nr Cambridge
(0223) 892641
CP/BA OD VA WTC M VS

DEVON

Highfield (3 acres)
Ian & Jennifer Fraser, Long Drag,
Tiverton
(0884) 256362
V OD VS WTF M/BA

Loddiswell (7 acres)
R H Sampson, Lilwell, Loddiswell,
Kingsbridge
(0548) 550221
V CP OD WTC VS S TC

**Whitmoore House Vineyard and
Orchid Nursery** (2 acres)
Richard and Ann Trussell, Ashill,
Cullompton
(0884) 40145
VA (winter) WTF CP/BA VS

Whitstone (1½ acres)
George and Laura Barclay, Bovey
Tracey, Nr Newton Abbot
(0626) 832280
OD VA WTF VS

ESSEX

Nevards (1 acre)
W Hudson, Boxted, Colchester
(0206) 230 306
VA

GLOUCESTERSHIRE

Deerhurst Wines (3 acres)
P Hall, The Vineyard, Wells Farm,
Apperley
(045 278) 435
CP/BA VA VS (by the case)

St Anne's (2 acres)
A V & B R Edwards, Wain House,
Oxenhall, Newent
(098 982) 313
CP/BA WTF V VS S/BA

Three Choirs (32 acres)
T W Day, Rhyle House, Welsh House
Lane, Newent
(053 185) 223/555
V CP/BA WTF VS

HAMPSHIRE

Aldermoor (5 acres)
M F & W A Baerselman, Aldermoors,
Picket Hill, Ringwood
(04254) 472912
V VA CP WTF

Beaulieu (6 acres)
The Hon Ralph Montagu, John
Montagu Buildings, Beaulieu, Nr
Brockenhurst
(0590) 612345
VA CP VS

Holly Bush (4 acres)
C & E Landells, Holly Bush Farm
(A337), Brockenhurst
(0590) 23054
V CP/BA

Lymington (6 acres)
C W & M M R Sentance, Wainsford
Road, Pennington, Lymington
(0590) 72112
V WTC VS

Meon Valley (8 acres)
C J Hartley, Hillgrove, Swanmore,
Southampton
(0489) 877435
VA CP/BA VS WTF VS (by the case)

HEREFORD & WORCESTER

Astley (5 acres)
R M & C B Bache, The Crundels,
Astley, Stourport-on-Severn
(02993) 2907
CP VA VS

Broadfield (12 acres)
Mr & Mrs K R H James, Broadfield
Court Estate, Bodenham
(056 884) 483/275
CP/VA OD/VA WTC VS S

Croft Castle Vineyard (½ acre)
The Hon Mrs F Uhlman, Croft Castle,
Nr Leominster
(056 885) 560
V CP/BA

HERTFORDSHIRE

Frithsden (3 acres)
Peter and Anne Latchford,
Frithsden, Nr Hemel Hempstead
(0442) 57902
CP/BA WTF V/BA VS

ISLE OF WIGHT

Adgestone (23 acres)
K C Barlow (and others), Upper
Road, Adgestone, Sandown
(0983) 402503
V WTF VS

Barton Manor (8½ acres)
Mr & Mrs A H Goddard,
Whippingham, East Cowes
(0983) 292835
CP WTC VS S

Cranmore (6½ acres)
N & A Valentine, Solent Road,
Cranmore, Nr Yarmouth
(0983) 761414
VA WTC

Hamstead (4 acres)
T J Munt, Hamstead Vineyard,
Yarmouth
(0983) 760463
VA OD VS WTC

Morton Manor (1¾ acres)
J A J Trzebski, Morton Manor
Vineyard, Brading
(0983) 406168
VA WTC CP/BA M S VS

KENT

Bardingley (2 acres)
H B Smith & I Winter, Babylon Lane,
Hawkenbury, Staplehurst
(0580) 892264
V VS WTC

Biddenden (22 acres)
R A Barnes, Little Whatmans,
Biddenden
(0580) 291726
V CP/BA WTF VS

Chiddingstone (12 acres)
J M & D Quirk, Vexour Farm,
Chiddingstone, Edenbridge
(0892) 870277
VA OD

Conghurst (¾ acre)
Miss J Helen Bridgwater, Conghurst
Oast, Conghurst Lane, Hawkhurst
(05805) 2634
WTF VA VS

Elham Valley (3 acres)
Mrs J V Allen & Mr P W Warden,
Breach, Barham, Canterbury
(0227) 831266
VA WTC VS OD

Harbledown & Chaucer (2 acres)
A G Fisher & L C W Rea, Isabel Mead
Farm, Upper Harbledown,
Canterbury
(0227) 463913
WTC VA

Harbourne (2½ acres)
L S Williams,
Vineyard: High Halden,
Nr Tenderden
Winery & Wine Shop: Wittersham,
Nr Tenterden
(07977) 420
V VS WTF

Lamberhurst (55 acres)
K McAlpine, Ridge Farm,
Lamberhurst, Nr Tunbridge Wells
(0892) 890844 & 890286
CP/VA V CP WTF VS S M

Leeds Castle (2¾ acres)
Leeds Castle,
Maidstone
(0622) 65400
CP OD S VS

Penshurst (12 acres)
D E Westphal, Grove Road,
Penshurst
(0892) 870255
CP/BA WTF V VS OD M/S

St Nicholas of Ash (2 acres)
J G Wilkinson, Moat Lane, Ash,
Canterbury
(0304) 812670
CP/BA WTF V VS S

Staple (7 acres)
W T Ash, Church Farm, Staple,
Canterbury
(0304) 812571
CP/BA V (except winter) WTC OD VS
S/BA TC

Tenterden (18 acres)
W Garner & D Todd, Spots Farm,
Small Hythe, Tenterden
(05806) 3033
V CP WTF VS M TC

Three Corners (1½ acres)
Lt Col C S Galbraith, Beacon Lane,
Woodnesborough
(0304) 812025
VA VS

NORFOLK

Elmham Park (7 acres)
R S Don, Elmham House, North
Elmham, Dereham
(036 281) 571 or 363
CP VA WTF TC

Heywood (2 acres)
R C Aikman, Heywood, Holly Farm,
The Heywood, Diss
(0379) 642461 & 01-340 9635
OD VA

Lexham Hall (8 acres)
W R B Foster and Partners, Lexham
Hall, Nr Litcham, Kings Lynn
(0328) 701288
CP/BA OD VA VS TC

Pulham (6 acres)
P W Cook, Mill Lane, Pulham
Market, Diss
(037 976) 342 and 672
CP VA WTC VS

NOTTINGHAMSHIRE

Eglantine (3⅓ acres)
A M & V Skuriat, Ash Lane, Costock,
Nr Loughborough
(050 982) 2386/(0509) 852386
VA WTF VS

OXFORDSHIRE

Bothy (3 acres)
R & D B Fisher, Frilford Heath,
Abingdon
(0491) 681484
VA VS WTF

Chiltern Valley (3 acres)
D J Ealand, Old Luxters Farm,
Hambleden, Nr Henley
(049163) 330
OD WTF CP/BA V VS

SOMERSET

Brympton D'Evercy (1 acre)
Charles E B Clive-Ponsonby-Fane,
Yeovil
(093 586) 2528
V CP VS S

Castle Cary (6 acres)
Mr & Mrs P C Woosnam Mills,
Honeywick House, Castle Cary
(0963) 50323
V VS WTF

Cheddar Valley (3 acres)
N A & P K McDonald, Stoneleys,
Hillside, Axbridge
(0934) 732280
CP/BA WTF V VS

Coxley (4 acres)
W Austin, Coxley Vineyard, Coxley,
Nr Wells
(0749) 73854
WTF V VS CP/BA M

H R H Vineyard (& English Basket
Centre) (8 acres)
Nigel Hector, Alastair Reid, Derek
Hector, The Willows, Curload, Stoke
St Gregory, Taunton
(0823 69) 418
V

Moorlynch (12 acres)
Mr & Mrs T Rees, Moorlynch,
Bridgwater
(0458) 210393
CP/BA V WTF VS S

Pilton Manor (22 acres)
J M Dowling, Pilton Manor, Shepton
Mallet
(074 989) 325
CP OD V VS M/S TC

Staplecombe (4 acres)
M M Cursham, Burlands Farm,
Staplegrove, Taunton
(082 345) 217
VA WTF

Whatley Vineyard & Herb Garden (4 acres)
M J E Witt, Old Rectory, Whatley, Nr Frome
(037 384) 467
V CP + M/BA VS WTC S

Wootton (6 acres)
C L B Gillespie, North Wootton, Shepton Mallet
(074 989) 359
V CP VS

Wraxall (5½ acres)
A S Holmes and Partners, Shepton Mallet
(074 986) 486 and 331
V CP/BA WTC VS M B&B

SUFFOLK

Brandeston Priory (5½ acres)
H P B Dow, The Priory, Brandeston, Woodbridge
(072 882) 462
V WTF CP VS (+ picnic area and gardens)

Broadwater (3½ acres)
A W & S F Stocker, Broadwater, Framlingham
(0728) 723645
CP V WTF VS

Bruisyard (10 acres)
Mr & Mrs I H Berwick, Church Road, Bruisyard, Saxmundham
(072 875) 281
CP/BA WTF V VS (+ herb and water garden)

SUSSEX

Arundel (1½ acres)
J & V Rankin, Church Lane, Lyminster Road, Nr Arundel
(0903) 883393
V WTF VS OD TC/BA M

Berwick Glebe (2 acres)
Jane Broster & Doreen Birks, Frensham Cottage, Berwick, Nr Polegate
(0323) 870361
VA VS WTC

Bookers (5 acres)
J M & R V Pratt, Foxhole Lane, Bolney
(044 482) 575
VA VS

Breaky Bottom (4 acres)
Peter Hall, Northease, Lewes
(0273) 476427
V WTF CP/BA VS M

Carr Taylor (21 acres)
David and Linda Carr Taylor, Westfield, Hastings
(0424) 752501
V WTF VS CP + M or S/BA

Chilsdown (10½ acres)
Ian Paget, The Old Station House, Singleton, Chichester
(0243 63) 398
V CP/BA VS WTF

Downers (7 acres)
Commander & Mrs E G Downer, Downers, Clappers Lane, Fulking, Henfield
(079 156) 484
V VS WTF

English Wine Centre (1 acre)
Christopher & Lucy Ann, Drusillas Corner, Alfriston
(0323) 870532
CP/BA M S OD VA VS WTF

Flexerne (5 acres)
Peter & Brenda Smith, Fletching Common, Newick
(082 572) 2548
V A

Hooksway (3 acres)
S R Moore, c/o Lares, Bepton Road, Midhurst
(073 081) 3317
VA WTF VS (by the case)

Leeford (34 acres)
J P Sax, Leeford Vineyard, Whattlington, Battle
(04246) 3183
WTF VA VS

Lurgashall (Winery only)
Virginia & Jerome Schooler,
Windfallwood, Lurgashall,
Nr Petworth
(0428 78) 292 or 654
CP/BA WTF VA VS

Nutbourne Manor (14 acres)
J J Sanger, Nutbourne Manor,
Nr Pulborough
(07983) 3554
OD V VS WTC + S or M/BA CP/BA

Rock Lodge (10 acres)
Norman Cowderoy, Scaynes Hill
(044 486) 224
WTC VS S/BA

St George's (20 acres)
Gay Biddlecombe, Waldron,
Heathfield
(043 53) 2156
M/S V WTF OD VS CP/BA

Seymours (2 acres)
Mr & Mrs H McMullen, Forest Road,
Horsham
(0403) 52397
CP/BA VA OD VS WTF

Steyning Vineyard – Nash Wines
(3 acres)
Joyce Elsden, Nash Hotel, Horsham
Road, Steyning
(0903) 814988
CP/BA VS WTC V S/BA

Swiftsden House (3½ acres)
William & Moira Gammell, Swiftsden
House, Hurst Green
(058 086) 287
VA VS WTF

WILTSHIRE

Chalkhill (6½ acres)
D Mann, Knowle Farm,
Bowerchalke, Salisbury
(0722) 780041
VA WTF

Elms Cross (3 acres)
A R Shaw, Elms Cross,
Bradford-on-Avon
(022 16) 6917
V VS

Fonthill (13 acres)
C P M Craig-McFeeley &
J F Edginton, The Old Rectory, Rye
Close, Fonthill Gifford, Tisbury
(0747) 870231 (retail sales – 0747
871230)
VA VS WTF CP/BA

Sherston Earl (3 acres)
Norman Sellers, Sherston,
Malmesbury
(0666) 840716
V VS WTF

Stitchcombe (5 acres)
N Thompson, Stitchcombe,
Nr Marlborough
(0672) 52297
V CP/BA OD VA VS S

WALES

GLAMORGAN

Croffta (3 acres)
J L M Bevan, Groes-Faen, Pontyclun
(0443) 223876
VA VS WTC

GWENT

Tintern Parva (5 acres)
Martin & Gay Rogers, Parva Farm,
Tintern, Nr Chepstow
(029 18) 636
CP/BA VS V WTF

CHANNEL ISLANDS

La Mare (6 acres)
R H and A M Blayney, St Mary,
Jersey
(0534) 81491
CP/BA V WTC VS M (Light)

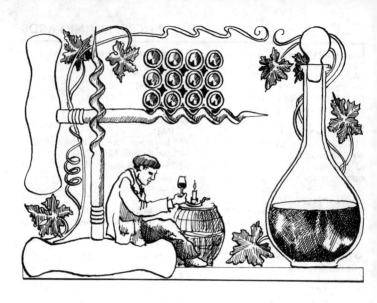

Serving wine

Temperature Port, and medium-bodied and heavier reds, need to be served warm enough for their aromas to evaporate; chilling white, rosé, light red, sweet or sparkling wines in the fridge for a couple of hours adds to their freshness, while chilling any poor wine will help disguise its defects. A good, full-bodied white such as a California or Australian Chardonnay, a fine white Burgundy or a fino Sherry needs less chilling – just an hour in the fridge is enough, or the aromas will not be released.

If you're caught short of cold wine, ten minutes in the freezer will certainly do the wine no harm – but beware of lollipops in broken bottles. In desperation, for a not particularly fine wine, ice cubes are the other obvious solution – though it's a shame to water down a *good* wine. Once your bottle is cool, good alternatives to the ice bucket are the widely available plastic insulating sleeves, and insulated portable bottle-bags useful for picnics.

It's more difficult to warm up a bottle of red instantly without overheating parts of the bottle and risking spoiling the wine's aromas. Be gentle. Pour it into a warm, not hot, decanter, or, better still, just wait for it to warm up in the glass – cupping in your hands will help.

Glasses To taste a wine at its best and to catch all the aromas, use a glass that curves in at the upper edges and is big enough to hold a reasonable amount. The thinner and finer the glass, the finer the wine will taste: experiment and see. Any engraving, and particularly smokiness or colour in the glass, will of course make it impossible to inspect the wine's colour and clarity properly. Filling the glass just half to two-thirds full leaves an air-space into which the aromas can evaporate and remain trapped until sniffed out. It also leaves scope to swirl the wine around the glass without putting tablecloth or carpet at risk. Nowadays the flat coupe-shaped Champagne glasses are fortunately less common: they are hopeless, allowing expensive bubbles to escape in a flash from their enormous surface. Best are the tall, thin Champagne flutes, with only a tiny surface area, but there's nothing wrong with using an ordinary large wine glass for Champagne and other sparkling wines. For Sherry, use a copita – a tulip-shaped glass – and avoid the narrow-waisted Elgin glass.

Opening Remove the foil or plastic capsule completely, or cut it well underneath the bottle lip, so that it cannot possibly come into contact with the wine: this would be just messy with modern aluminium foil or plastic, potentially poisonous in the long term if it's the old-fashioned lead variety! If the cork won't budge, hold the neck for a minute or so under fairly hot running water and try again. For corks that drop into the bottle, there's a long spindly-legged plastic gadget called a 'Decorker'; you may have to resort to a coffee filter or a sieve if you make unacceptable quantities of cork crumbs.

Champagne corks Twist the bottle by holding it firmly at the base: don't twist the cork or it may break. Hold the top firmly and be careful where you point the bottle: people have lost eyes through flying corks. If the mushroom top breaks off as you twist the bottle, carefully use a corkscrew. Always disturb the bottle as little as possible beforehand, and keep a glass on hand to catch accidental fountains.

Checking the quality Pour some for *yourself* first to check that it is sound before serving your guests; and don't forget to check subsequent bottles. There may be a difference between two bottles of a quite simple wine, so make sure that any wine connoisseurs among your guests have finished up the dregs of one bottle in their glass before serving them from the next; they may be deeply shocked if you mix bottles, especially of different wines! Non-winos will think this nonsense – so just top them up.

Unfinished bottles Still wines can just be recorked, or poured into a smaller bottle for better keeping. Special clamp tops are available for stopping half-drunk Champagnes or sparkling wines.

Decanting

There are no hard and fast rules about whether to decant or not. It's a favourite subject for argument in the wine magazines – especially in the letters columns. But a consensus does emerge about when it can be an advantage.

- When a bottle of wine has a sediment in the bottom, decanting is essential unless you want to end up with the last glasses full of unpleasant black sludge.

- Strong red wines, which may have spent some time in wood before bottling – Barolo, some Portuguese reds, Gran Reserva Rioja or Rhônes, for example – will benefit from some decanting, especially if they are quite young.

- Conversely, old vintages of any wine will suffer positive harm if decanted – the remains of the fruit will combine with oxygen and the whole delicious fragrance of mature wines will disappear.

- The only reason for decanting everyday reds will be to get rid of some of the sulphury smells that may still linger in the bottle. A few minutes in a glass will achieve the same effect.

- Some whites – particularly those which have been in wood and are still quite young – will benefit from an hour in a decanter before serving. Make sure the decanter is cool before pouring the wine in and then keep it in a cool place or in the fridge.

The only time when care needs to be taken over decanting is when the wine has thrown a sediment and the purpose of decanting is to leave this in the bottle and the clear wine in the decanter. Before decanting, stand the bottle upright for two or three hours to allow the deposit to collect in the bottom. Draw the cork and pour the wine carefully into the decanter. If the bottle is dusty from the cellar, a light shining through from below will help identify when the sediment reaches the neck of the bottle. If you're at all worried about letting the sediment pass into the decanter, despite all your efforts, a coffee filter paper should solve the problem.

Keeping wine fresh

If you don't want to drink a bottle of wine in one session, keeping white wine in the fridge helps, or you could decant wine of either colour into two half-bottles as soon as it is opened.

Alternatively, various devices are available which keep the wine fresh either by creating a vacuum in the bottle or by pumping a layer of inert gas on top of the wine.

The cheapest is the Vacu-Vin (which sells for about £6.99 in many off-licences and wine merchants). This system consists of rubber stoppers and a small plastic pump which pumps the air out of the bottle, creating a vacuum. Wine treated this way should stay pretty fresh for three or four days, and, depending on how full the bottle is, up to a week.

Another system is more elaborate and expensive. It consists of pumping inert gas from a cylinder into the wine through a special stopper. Although it is effective and can keep wine fresh for longer than the Vac-u-Vin, its price, we feel, makes it unnecessary for the normal wine drinker at home.

A third system, the Wine Preserver, consists of a gas squirted from a canister on to the open bottle of wine. In some cases the canisters have exploded. We suggest you avoid this system.

How the law can help you

If you buy a bottle that is bad or isn't what the label says it is, the law offers you some protection and redress. Barrister JENI MCCALLION *sets out just what the law can do to assist you.*

In the eyes of the Law, if not the connoisseur, wine is any liquor obtained from the alcoholic fermentation of fresh grapes or the must of fresh grapes. Wine can, of course, be made from other fruits or vegetables, but in this case an indication of the type of fruit or vegetable used must appear on the label immediately before the word wine: Apple wine or Elderberry wine, for example.

There are a number of laws which protect you when you buy and drink wine. Civil laws cover things like getting a bottle of Burgundy when you ask for a bottle of Bordeaux. It's generally necessary to enforce your civil rights through court action if necessary. Criminal offences include selling adulterated wine and false or misleading labelling – and are matters for your local trading standards department. Some things may infringe both the Criminal and Civil law. So if the pickled remains of a snail drop into your glass as you drain the last of your bottle of Châteauneuf-du-Pape, and you are violently ill as a result, the seller may be guilty of a criminal offence, under the Food Act, and you might also be able to sue the seller or the manufacturer for damages.

Here are some of the things that you might need to know:

1 *You notice a bottle of 'de-alcoholised' wine on sale in your local off-licence. This seems to be a bit of a contradiction in terms – is it legal?*

Yes. As long as the product is made from fresh grapes or fresh grape must and has been fermented, the fact that the alcohol is then removed doesn't prevent it from being called wine. The term 'non-alcoholic wine', on the other hand, should be used only to describe a drink made from unfermented grape juice which is intended exclusively for communion or sacramental use – and it must be clearly labelled as such. You're unlikely to find this in your local supermarket.

2 *You see a very attractive wine offer in a magazine. A delivery time of 28 days is given and you send off your order, along with a cheque for the full amount. Your cheque is cashed, but six weeks later you're still waiting for the wine to arrive. What should you do?*

Write to the company concerned giving them an ultimatum – either they deliver within the next, say, 14 days, or you will consider the order cancelled. If you get your wine within the specified time, all well and good; if not, you should write to the advertising manager at the publication in which the advertisement appeared. The advertising manager should see that your complaint is investigated. Your legal rights when buying goods by mail order are the same as those when buying from a shop. So if the company fail to deliver the goods, you are entitled to your money back, plus any additional cost in getting the same wine elsewhere.

3 *You buy a bottle of inexpensive red wine at a local supermarket. It tastes like vinegar and is quite undrinkable.*

It's usually true that you get what you pay for – and there's a world of difference between a good bottle of St-Emilion and a litre of vin de table. Leaving aside the finer distinctions that exist between a good and a mediocre bottle of wine, the Law says that wine must be of 'merchantable quality' and that it must be 'fit for human consumption'. So even the cheapest plonk must be drinkable – but you can't reasonably expect the same standard, say, from a bottle of cheap sparkling wine as from a much more expensive vintage Champagne.

4 *You buy a bottle of wine which, when opened, turns out to be way past its best. What can you do?*

Not much, apart from putting it in the boeuf bourguignonne. Unlike some foods, the law doesn't insist that wine bottles be labelled with a 'sell by' or 'best before' date.

5 *You buy a bottle of wine and share it with friends. The next day all who indulged are violently ill – suggesting that the wine may have been contaminated.*

It is a criminal offence to sell or to offer for sale any food or drink which is intended for human consumption, but which is unfit. If you suffer as a result, inform your local trading standards department who will consider bringing a prosecution. As the actual buyer of the wine, you are entitled to redress for a breach of contract. Until recently, the unfortunate consumer who suffered injury as a result of faulty goods, but didn't actually buy them, could only get compensation if he or she could prove negligence. The Consumer Protection Act 1987 should make things easier. Under this Act, your friends wouldn't have to prove negligence, only that the wine was defective and that they were ill as a result.

6 *You're looking for something festive to take to a special celebration. The Champagne is a bit pricy, but you notice a bottle of 'German Champagne' at a price you can afford.*

The Courts have decided on a number of occasions that the word 'Champagne' can be given only to wine which originates in the Champagne district of France – so you shouldn't see German, Spanish or Australian Champagne around. The same goes for 'Champagne Perry' or 'Champagne Cider'. The term 'méthode champenoise' is now on its way out as well, following pressure from Champagne producers. So although you will still see 'méthode champenoise' on bottles of Saumur or Spanish Cava for a while, producers of sparkling wine made by the Champagne method will have to dream up a new term to distinguish their product from cheaper sparkling wines. American producers sometimes use the phrase 'wine fermented in this bottle'.

7 *You buy a bottle of '1868 Vintage Port' at auction, but you subsequently discover that it's really an injudicious mixture of supermarket vintage character Port and Lambrusco-style home brew. What can you do?*

Deliberately setting out to fake something (be it a bottle of vintage Port or a Constable painting) and then passing it off as the real thing, is fraud and the seller will be liable to criminal prosecution. But in sales by auction (as opposed to buying from a wine merchant), any undertaking as to merchantable quality or conformity with description or sample can be excluded. It's also worth noting that your rights are generally against the seller rather than the auctioneer, which could make it difficult to get redress if the wine does happen to be faulty in some way (although, as we suggest in the section on buying wine at auction, most auction houses will help in negotiations with the seller).

8 *You go to a restaurant and order a bottle of house red. You are disappointed to find that it yields six smaller glasses than usual. You inspect the bottle, and find that it is labelled as having 70cl instead of the 75cl that you are familiar with. You note that the wine list makes no mention of the bottle size.*

70cl bottles of wine are now illegal in the EEC, but the phasing-out period runs until 31 December 1988. So, until then, it's still legal to sell 70cl bottles – and there is no legal obligation on a restaurant or shop to state the bottle size.

9 *You're having a quick lunch-time drink at a local wine bar, so you order by the glass, rather than the bottle. Your second glass of house white is noticeably smaller than the first, but you're charged exactly the same. Is it legal?*

Unfortunately, the Law is extremely slack on wine glass measurements. At the moment, there are no standard quantities for wine, unlike those for beer and spirits. There is, however, a purely voluntary code which says, among other things, that quantities of wine should be given alongside prices, and that no bar or restaurant should sell wine by the glass in more than two measures and that the difference between these two measures should be at least two fluid ounces (or 50ml). However, few wine bars or restaurants seem to follow this voluntary code.

10 *You order a bottle of 1985 Chablis Premier Cru at a local restaurant. The waiter brings the bottle to your table, and allows you a cursory glance before opening it. When you taste the wine, you realise immediately that you're drinking a lesser quality 1987 Petit Chablis. What should you do?*

Strictly speaking, the fact that you had an opportunity to inspect the label before the bottle was opened might weaken your legal position and your right to insist on getting exactly what you ordered. But in most cases, a bar or restaurant should exchange without too much hassle. If you proceed to consume the whole bottle before noticing the difference, you can't then complain and reasonably expect to get your original order.

11 *What do you do if you think you've been over-charged for a bottle of wine?*

A restaurant must display a menu and a wine list outside, or immediately inside the entrance. Wine lists containing six or fewer items must state the price (inclusive of VAT) for each wine available. Establishments with a larger selection must show at least six items, but they don't have to display a comprehensive list. You should always check your bill carefully and query anything which doesn't add up.

Sour grapes? – how to complain

The Criminal Laws mentioned above are usually enforced by public authorities. So if you've been sold a bottle of wine which contains something unpleasant or positively harmful to health, you should report the matter to the environmental health department of your local authority. False or misleading descriptions are a matter for the trading standards department of your local authority. If you want to bring a civil action for damages, you should seek legal advice.

Find out more about wine

For those smitten with a fascination for wine, plenty of things are happening – organised and happily disorganised – to help you find out more. They include wine clubs up and down the country which either sell wine (often specialising in one area) or organise wine tastings. Or there are special wine courses, many run by the top people in the wine trade, where you can learn more intensively. And there are also holidays to wine regions where, apart from learning, you can meet some of the friendliest people – wine producers – and see some beautiful parts of the world.

WINE CLUBS

Les Amis du Vin

19 Charlotte Street, London W1P 1HB   TEL 01-636 4020
Life membership £15. Discounts: five per cent off all wines, ten per cent off unmixed cases, free delivery for 2+ cases or over £75. Priority booking for tastings. Regular newsletter and special offers including en primeur. (See also the WHERE TO BUY section under Christopher & Co.)

Christchurch Fine Wine Co

1–3 Vine Lane, High Street, Christchurch, Dorset
BH23 1AE   TEL (0202) 473255
Membership costs £5, which is refunded upon the purchase of one case
of wine. Members receive a monthly newsletter, invitations to tutored
tastings and five per cent discount off the basic wine list.

Coonawarra Club

Mike McCarthy (secretary), 224 Minard Road, Catford, London
SE6 1NJ   TEL 01-828 2216 (work), 01-698 2504 (home)
This club was set up by Mike McCarthy, who also runs the Zinfandel
Club (see below). Membership £5, renewal £2 per annum. Tastings of
Australian wines, sometimes tutored. Occasional dinners with
appropriate wines.

Howells of Bristol Limited Bin Club

Creswicke House, 9 Small Street, Bristol, Avon BS1 1DB
TEL (0272) 277641   TELEX 449443 (CRES HO)
This club, run by Jim Hood and Rodney Holt, specialises in the laying
down of wines 'under the ideal conditions of Howells' fine old cellars,
so that customers can buy wines at opening prices, gradually build
up a cellar and then enjoy their wines at a later date when they are
properly mature'. There is a once-only membership fee (£15) and then
payment is made by monthly subscription (min £30). On joining, a
cellar book is provided and cellars cards follow each purchase of wine.
Offers are sent to all members twice yearly in the spring and autumn
and, in addition, en primeur offers of new vintages of clarets,
Burgundies and Ports. Included with each offer are notes on the wine
and recommended 'ready for drinking' dates. When maturity dates are
reached, the wines are reviewed and members kept advised of the
development of their wines. Statements of account are sent with the
spring and autumn offers, showing the amount of credit accumulated
and offering advance credit calculated at three times the monthly
contributions. There is a storage charge (currently 17 pence per case
per month) and all wines are insured against fire, flood and theft.

The International Wine & Food Society

108 Old Brompton Road, London SW7 3RA   TEL 01-370 0909
Director Hugo Dunn-Meynell. Enrolment fee £4.60. Membership £16
single, £22 joint, £8.70 young members (under 25). President Michael
Broadbent MW. London HQ with library and worldwide contacts.
Regional branches organise dinners, tastings, lectures, visits. Annual
journal *World Gastronomy* free of charge.

Lay & Wheeler

6 Culver Street West, Colchester, Essex CO1 1JA
TEL (0206) 67261
A series of popular wine workshops held in the Colchester Garrison officers' Club: during 1988 three important German wine producers presented a selection of their wines. Monthly workshops are also held at Lay & Wheeler's Gosbecks Road Wine Market in Colchester: subjects in 1988 included wines of the Te Mata estate in New Zealand, and wines of Australia and the Loire. (See also the WHERE TO BUY section.)

Lincoln Wine Society

12 Mainwaring Road, Lincoln, Lincs LN2 4BL   TEL (0522) 42077
Chairman Christine Austin. Monthly talk and tasting sessions, sometimes with guest speakers. Fine Wine evenings held three times a year, regular newsletters and an annual trip to a wine region. Membership £5 annually (£8 joint membership).

Methuselah's

29 Victoria Street, London SW1H 0EU   TEL 01-222 0424/3550
Annual subscription £15. Tutored tastings usually held every first Monday of the month. Priority bookings for events. Two-course dinner with coffee at £8.50 a head available after tastings. (Part of Don Hewitson's Cork & Bottle wine bar chain – see under WINE BARS.)

Martin Mistlin's Fine Wine Dining Club

41 Kingsend, Ruislip, Middlesex HA4 7DD
TEL 01-427 9944 (day)
The Club specialises in wine and food events such as tastings, dinners, wine tours, etc. The subscription for 1988 was £7.50 (may be increased for 1989).

Le Nez Rouge Wine Club

Berkmann Wine Cellars, 12 Brewery Road, London N7 9NH
TEL 01-609 4711
Manager Philip Macgregor. Annual membership £11.75. Reduced prices, special offers, regular tastings, dinners, etc. Members are sent the Club's wine list twice a year. (See also the WHERE TO BUY section.)

North East Wine Tasting Society

Terry Douglas (Secretary), 3 Bemersyde Drive, Jesmond, Newcastle-upon-Tyne, Tyne & Wear NE2 2HL   TEL 091-281 4769
Monthly tastings held in Newcastle, some of them tutored. Annual membership £10.

Northern Wine Appreciation Group

D M Hunter, 21 Dartmouth Avenue, Almondbury, Huddersfield,
West Yorkshire HD5 8UR TEL (0484) 531228
Weekly meetings in West Yorkshire from September to June, 'to taste,
assess and extend the members' experience of wine and food'. The
relationship between food and wine leads to the planning of the meals
which form part of the group's activities. Graded tutored tastings are
held for new members.

Ordre Mondial des Gourmets Dégustateurs

Details from: Martin Mistlin, 41 Kingsend, Ruislip, Middlesex
HA4 7DD TEL 01-427 9944
This is a French wine guild with a British chapter. The headquarters are
in Paris. Its aims are the promotion of the knowledge of good wines
and spirits. Varied regular tastings and dinners are held with access to
meetings abroad.

Helen Verdcourt Wines

Spring Cottage, Kimbers Lane, Maidenhead, Berkshire SL6 2QP
TEL (0628) 25577
Two local clubs meet monthly, one in Maidenhead, the other in
Englefield Green, for tastings tutored by Helen Verdcourt. Other clubs
meet occasionally. No membership fees, tastings charged at cost.
(See also the WHERE TO BUY section and WINE TOURS.)

La Vigneronne

105 Old Brompton Road, London SW7 3LE TEL 01-589 6113
The tutored tastings of fine and rare wines held every Monday and
Thursday (and occasionally on Wednesdays) are very popular.
No membership fee. (See also the WHERE TO BUY section.)

Vintner Wine Club

Winefare House, 5 High Road, Byfleet, Surrey KT14 7QF
TEL (09323) 51585
Initial enrolment fee and annual membership £12. Club secretary:
Deborah Morgan. Quarterly newsletter. Comprehensive list of 300
wines and individual tasting notes. Members can get a discount on
single bottles at every Arthur Rackhams. Gastronomic programme of
monthly tutored tastings and dinners in West End and Surrey
restaurants. La Grande Taste – weekend members' tastings at Arthur
Rackhams. The Vintner Festival at the Savoy Hotel (London) every
October. (See also Arthur Rackhams in the WHERE TO BUY section.)

The Wine Club

New Aquitaine House, Paddock Road, Reading, Berkshire
RG4 0JY   TEL (0734) 481713
Also known as The Sunday Times Wine Club. Mail order only.
President Hugh Johnson, Secretary Hilary Penrose. Annotated list,
tastings, tours, Vintage Festival, and a lively quarterly-journal, *Wine
Times*. Tours vary from long weekends to six-day tours of other
European wine-growing regions. (See also Bordeaux Direct in the
WHERE TO BUY section.)

The Wine & Dine Society

96 Ramsden Road, London SW12 8QZ   TEL 01-673 4439
Weekly tastings of wines from all over the world, including fine and
rare bottles. Guest speakers. Dinners in London follow an ethnic
theme.

Wine and Gastronomic Societies (WAGS)

Martin Mistlin, 41 Kingsend, Ruislip, Middlesex HA4 7DD
TEL 01-427 9944 (day)
This newly formed society comprises the Alsace Club of Great Britain
(President Hugh Johnson), the Cofradia Riojana and the Gallo Nero
Club of Great Britain (President The Hon Rocco Forte). A joining fee of
£12 and no annual subscription allows members to attend tastings and
dinners featuring wines from these regions plus occasional events
based on other wine regions. Wine tours abroad and wine weekends in
the UK will feature in the club's activities.

Wine Mine Club

Peter Dominic, Vintner House, River Way, Harlow, Essex
CM20 2EA   TEL (0279) 416291
Membership £5 per annum (on receipt of which members receive a £5
wine voucher to spend in any Peter Dominic shop). The club provides
a basic information service, organises tastings, makes special offers
(eg en primeur claret and Port) and distributes a quarterly newsletter.
(See also Peter Dominic in the WHERE TO BUY section.)

The Wine Society

Gunnels Wood Road, Stevenage, Hertfordshire SG1 2BG
TEL (0438) 741177; DELIVERIES (0438) 741010; FAX (0438) 741392;
ORDER OFFICE (0438) 740222 or 01-349 3296; TELEX 826072 (IECWS)
53 Bolsover Street, London W1P 7HL   TEL 01-387 4681
See the WHERE TO BUY section.

The Winery

4 Clifton Road, Maida Vale, London W9 1SS   TEL 01-286 6475
Manager Marcus Titley. Offers a large selection of fine wines,

particularly from the New World. Tastings are organised by Les Amis du Vin (see above).

The Winetasters

P N Beardwood (Secretary), 44 Claremont Road, London
W13 0DG   TEL 01-997 1252
Annual subscription £3 (£1.50 if you live more than 50 miles from London). Non-profit-making club which organises tastings, seminars, dinners and tours (next major tours in 1989 to Italy, and in 1991 – destination not yet fixed). The club grew out of the Schoolmasters' Wine Club.

Winewise

Michael Schuster, 107 Culford Road, London N1 4HL
TEL 01-254 9734
Set up in early 1987 to promote all aspects of tasting, understanding and appreciating wines and spirits. The current tastings comprise two wine courses: a Beginners' Course (£60 for six evenings) and an Intermediate Course (£100 for eight evenings). Each course is limited to 16 participants. Other types of tastings are held on individual properties, vintages or comparisons of interesting wines from around the world, including blind tastings. Workshops are also held, normally on Saturday mornings.

Zinfandel Club

Mike McCarthy (Secretary), 224 Minard Road, Catford, London
SE6 1NJ   TEL 01-828 2216 (work), 01-698 2504 (home)
Membership fee £5. Sporadic meetings to taste California wines, sometimes tutored. Occasional dinners with appropriate wines.

WINE COURSES

David Baillie Vintners School of Wine

The Sign of the Lucky Horseshoe, 86 Longbrook Street, Exeter, Devon
EX4 6AP   TEL (0392) 221345
This West-country wine merchant (see the WHERE TO BUY section) plans to repeat his School of Wine course in 1989. The course is run twice a year at Exeter University, and comprises seven three-hour evening sessions of tastings and lectures given by experienced members of the Wine Trade, with an optional exam at the end, leading (for those who pass) to a Certificate from the David Baillie School of Wine. Cost in 1989, £100.

Christie's Wine Course

63 Old Brompton Road, London SW7 3JS   TEL 01-581 3933
Principals Michael Broadbent MW and Steven Spurrier, Secretary
Caroline de Lane Lea. Christie's run two wine courses: Part 1 is an
introduction to wine tasting through the principal wines of France and
is run four to five times a year; Part 2 consists of specialised tastings of
Burgundy, Bordeaux, Port and Madeira, and is run once or twice a
year. Both courses take place on five consecutive Tuesday evenings,
lasting roughly two hours, for 45 students. Discussion and tasting are
conducted by top wine experts (in 1988 the roll included Michael
Broadbent MW, Serena Sutcliffe MW, David Peppercorn MW, Pamela
Vandyke Price and Steven Spurrier). Part 1 costs £115 and Part 2
£143.75, but the latter can be taken as five separate evenings, each at
£30.

Ecole du Vin, Château Loudenne, Bordeaux

Valerie Sargent, Ecole du Vin, IDV, Gilbey House, Fourth Avenue,
Harlow, Essex CM20 1DX   TEL (0279) 635771
Six-day courses (starting on Monday) are held for a dozen students five
times a year at Gilbey's Ch Loudenne, under the direction of Charles
Eve MW. Accommodation and cuisine of very high standard in the
château. Aimed at the public and professionals in the trade, the
lectures and tastings cover all aspects of viticulture and vinification.
Visits are arranged to other Bordeaux areas and châteaux. Cost (in
1988) £825, exclusive of travel to France.

German Wine Academy

PO Box 1705, 6500 Mainz, Federal Republic of Germany
A 12th-century monastery is the setting for courses (delivered in
English), which include lectures by wine experts, vineyard visits and
tastings. The basic seven-day course is run throughout the year
(DM 1640 in 1988) and is supplemented by more advanced courses.

Leith's School of Food and Wine

21 St Alban's Grove, London W8 5BP   TEL 01-229 0177
Some of Leith's wine courses are for students of the School only, as
part of their food and wine studies. However, at least two are available
to others: five two-hour evening sessions starting on 31 January 1989,
leading to the Leith's Certificate (if you pass the exam, that is); and a
ten-session course (also two-hour evening sessions) starting in
October, leading to Leith's Advanced Certificate of Wine, examined by

Leith's Master of Wine, Richard Harvey. This is roughly analogous to the Wine and Spirit Education Trust's Higher Certificate, without the sessions on licensing and labelling laws, and with particular stress on tasting. Cost £130 and £225 respectively. Other courses, such as specialist evenings, are also sometimes available.

The Lincoln Wine Course

Christine Austin, 12 Mainwaring Road, Lincoln, Lincs LN2 4BL
TEL (0522) 42077
A series of 20 evenings (2 terms) held at Yarborough Adult Education Centre, Lincoln, on Tuesdays starting in September each year. The course is for both public and trade and covers all aspects of wine and tasting. It can lead to the Certificate and Higher Certificate examinations of the Wine and Spirit Education Trust for trade students.

Sotheby's

Wine Evenings with Sotheby's, 34–35 New Bond Street,
London W1A 2AA   TEL 01-408 5272
A series of six evenings held twice a year in the spring and autumn, tutored by experts (John Avery, Harry Eyres, Michael Schuster, Patrick Grubb, David Molyneux-Berry were among the names in 1988). A relaxed atmosphere is encouraged by an aperitif at 6.45pm, with the tasting running from 7pm to 8.30pm. The series of six tastings cost £130 in 1988 (individual evenings £17–£29.75). Subscribers to Sotheby's wine catalogues are entitled to a 15 per cent discount on wine evenings. Contact Jane Swallow for further details.

Tante Marie School of Cookery

Woodham House, Carlton Road, Woking, Surrey GU21 4HF
TEL (048 62) 26957
Conal Gregory MW, MP, organises wine appreciation courses, generally during autumn and winter, on three weekday evenings (lasting two hours), aimed at those with modest knowledge and including extensive tutored tastings.

WINE TOURS

Abreu Travel Agency

109 Westbourne Grove, London W2 4UL   TEL 01-229 9905
Organises two or three tours of the Portuguese wine areas every year. In 1988 tours included the vineyards of northern Portugal, starting from Oporto and taking a trip up the Douro Valley by train; and a visit to the cellars of J M da Fonseca. Costs for each trip were just under

£400. The tours are linked whenever possible with restaurants specialising in regional food.

Arblaster & Clarke Boo's Breaks

104 Church Road, Steep, Petersfield, Hampshire GU32 2DD
TEL (0730) 66883
This is a small family-run specialist tour operator in its third year. In 1988 short breaks were offered to Champagne, the eastern Loire, Beaujolais and Bruges; also a week in Portugal. Prices ranged from £149 (2 nights in Bruges) to £435 (7 nights in Portugal). Clients are escorted personally and 'stay in friendly hotels, eat in popular local restaurants and visit the best wine addresses, tasting lots of great wines'.

Australian Tourist Commission

Heathcoat House, 20 Savile Row, London W1X 1AE
The Tourist Commission can provide information on tours and holidays available through Australian travel firms. For more specific information on wine tours, contact South Australia House, 50 Strand, London WC2N 5LW TEL 01-930 7471, and see also Victour and World Wine Tours below.

Blackheath Wine Trails

13 Blackheath Village, London SE3 9LD   TEL 01-463 0012
In 1988, nine wine tours were offered: northern Portugal, Burgundy and Beaujolais, Champagne, Beaujolais Nouveau, Madrid and Rioja, Seville and Jerez, Tuscany, Piedmont and the Madeira Wine Festival, ranging from four to eight days. All were air/coach (except Champagne which was ferry/coach).

DER Travel Service

18 Conduit Street, London W1R 9TD   TEL 01-408 0111
As well as Rhine and Mosel cruises, DER arranges accommodation in German and Austrian hotels, guest houses or apartments, some of them in wine-growing areas: with your own car you would be free to visit vineyards. In 1988 'The Connoisseur Collection' holidays included 'The Wine Lover's Holiday', based in the village of Erbach in the Rheingau. The cost in 1988 was £395 for seven nights.

English vineyards

Many English vineyards are open to the public offering guided tours, tastings and sales. For further information see the ENGLISH VINEYARDS section.

Eurocamp

Edmundson House, Tatton Street, Knutsford, Cheshire WA16 6BG
TEL (0565) 3844
(Reservations only: 28 Princess Street, Knutsford, Cheshire WA16
6BG)
Eurocamp arrange self-drive camping and mobile home holidays at 150
sites in Europe, many of which are 'almost among the grapes – and the
more well-known grapes at that'. These include the Gironde, Saumur,
Meursault, Bergerac, Cahors and the Mosel.

European Canal Cruises

79 Winchester Road, Romsey, Hampshire SO51 8JB
TEL (0794) 514412
The *Royal Cognac II* spends a week (6 nights) exploring the Charente,
with appropriate visits. It sleeps eight and has available a mini-bus and
bicycles. Cost in 1988 was £750 per person.

Francophiles

Ron and Jenny Farmer, 66 Great Brockeridge, Westbury-on-Trym,
Bristol, Avon BS9 3UA   TEL (0272) 621975
The Farmers offer France 'lovingly packaged' on their personally
accompanied holidays of discovery in the wine-growing regions. Their
customers are 'not usual coach holiday travellers' who appreciate
in-depth, unhurried visits and structured tastings. In 1989 they offer
Portrait of Alsace, Loire Valley and 'Vive le Beaujolais', plus general
interest holidays with wine appeal.

KD German Rhine Line

G A Clubb Rhine Cruise Agency, 28 South Street, Epsom, Surrey
KT18 7PF   TEL (037 27) 42033
In 1988, a week-long cruise left from Cologne, visited vineyards on the
Rhine, the Mosel and in Alsace, and included lectures and tutored
tastings by Dr Hans Ambrosi, Director of the Eltville State Vineyards.
This 'floating wine seminar' ended in Basle.

Moswin Tours

PO Box 8, Oadby, Leicestershire LE2 5WX
TEL (0533) 719922
Tours of the Mosel Valley range from four to fifteen days and include
sightseeing excursions, wine-tastings and visits to vineyards in the
autumn. Travel by air or coach. Holidays staying with a wine farmer
(May to Oct) can be arranged. Moswin Tours also tailor individual
wine and gourmet tours and wine seminars (as part of a tour or
separately), not only to the Mosel Valley, but also to other
wine-growing regions of Germany and France.

Rosecourt Fine Wine

Wine Warehouse, Unit 5/7, Osborne's Court, High Street South,
Olney, Buckinghamshire MK46 4LA   TEL (023 471) 3077
Specialised educational tours relating to winegrowers in France,
Germany and Austria. Plans for tours to Italy, Portugal, Spain and
Sicily as well in 1989.

Special Interest Tours

1 Cank Street, Leicester, Leicestershire LE1 5GX   TEL (0533) 531373
Coach tours (with convenient joining points: Leicester, Birmingham,
Coventry, Sheffield, London etc) visit French wine regions for five, six
and seven days tours, which include tastings.

Helen Verdcourt Wine Tours

Spring Cottage, Kimbers Lane, Maidenhead, Berkshire SL6 2QP
TEL (0628) 25577
A 22-day round-the-world trip to the Australian vineyards is the tour
on offer for 1989. Places to be limited to a maximum of 30 people. Final
details and price had yet to be finalised as we went to press.

Victour

Tourist Office, Victoria House, Melbourne Place, Strand, London
WC2B 4LG   TEL 01-836 2656
The Victoria Tourism Commission produce a good wine and food
guide to Victoria with helpful notes on wineries and ideas for self-drive
visits. They also have details of various rail and coach tours including
brochures for Australian Wine Tours, Peter Heath's Unique Winery
Tours and Winery Walkabout. (See also World Wine Tours Below.)

Vintage Wine Tours

8 Belmont, Lansdown Road, Bath, Avon BA1 5DZ
TEL (0225) 315834/315659
Concentrates on designing tours for groups (10–40 people) by air and
coach, and will 'custom make' tours to any destination, including
gourmet meals, sightseeing excursions and any special requirements.
A brochure is available to spark off ideas.

Wessex Continental Travel

13 Old Town Street, Plymouth, Devon, PL1 1DA
TEL (0752) 228333/225572
The Wine Tour programme has been devised and will be presented by
Helen Gillespie-Peck. Regions on offer in 1988 were the Dordogne,
Alsace and Champagne, Burgundy, Bordeaux, Spain and Portugal.

World Wine Tours

4 Dorchester Road, Drayton St Leonard, Oxfordshire
OX9 8BH   TEL (0865) 891919

World Wine Tours, run by Liz and Martin Holliss, offer a wide range of quality wine tours, each lasting from four to eight days, most of which are led by a Master of Wine. Tours in 1989 will run throughout the year and will include: Alsace, Australia (they are the sole agent for packaged Australian Wine Tours), Bordeaux, Burgundy, Champagne, Germany, the Loire Valley, Madeira, Penedès, Portugal, the Rhône Valley, Rioja and Tuscany. Inclusive prices range from £325 to £850 per person. Some combined tours are planned, such as Wine and Golf in Portugal and Wine and Opera in Italy. Specially tailored tours can be arranged for private groups. Also: stays in private châteaux in France; self-catering holidays in Tuscany; cruises in luxury barges on French canals. Two Fine Wine Weekends based in the UK have also been planned for 1989.

Wine Bookshelf

While fewer wine books have been published over the past year, there are still plenty coming off the presses. This is a selection from the past three years which we have found most interesting and useful.

General

The Wine Companion – Hugh Johnson (Mitchell Beazley, £14.95)

A complete revision of the widest-ranging guide to wine regions of the world and the producers who work in them. Essential reference.

Webster's Wine Guide (1989 edition) – edited by Oz Clarke (Webster's, £8.95)

A paperback guide to the price you should expect to pay for wine at merchants and in the supermarkets, coupled with brief articles on the state of the market in the regions of production.

Pocket Wine Book (1989 edition) – Hugh Johnson (Mitchell Beazley, £5.95)

The annual update of the book most wine merchants stick in their pockets when they travel or even when they meet customers.

The World Atlas of Wine – Hugh Johnson (Mitchell Beazley, £22.50)

A revision of the best-selling book which now includes greater detail on the New World wine areas as well as Italy and Spain.

Vines, Grapes and Wines – Jancis Robinson (Mitchell Beazley, £16.95)

A book that goes back to origins – the vine – and explores the character of each vine and the types of wine it produces. Beautiful line drawings.

The Demon Drink – Jancis Robinson (Mitchell Beazley, £9.95)

This is a book for wine lovers, because it shows how wine and health go together, if both are treated in the right way. It's full of scholarly research and information about the way alcohol affects us. Essential reading.

Drilling for Wine – Robin Yapp (Faber Paperback, £6.95)

Dentist-turned-wine-merchant Robin Yapp (of Yapp Brothers) relates the stages of his conversion in witty, elegant prose. Some very good portraits of wine producers in the Loire and the Rhône enliven the proceedings still further.

The Taste of Wine – Emile Peynaud (Macdonald Orbis, £14.95)

Professor Peynaud, guru and adviser to many of the great Bordeaux châteaux, writes on the art and science of wine appreciation. It's fairly technical stuff – and the language is pretty dense – but a little burrowing reveals a coherent view of why and how wine tastes as it does.

The Pocket Guide to Non-Alcoholic Drinks – Jill Cox (Mitchell Beazley, £5.95)

A worthy interloper on our Wine Bookshelf, this is a guide to the wide variety of drinks and flavours that are based on fruits, vegetables, waters, dairy products and herbs. A look at what other cultures enjoy, plus lists and plans for entertaining.

Sainsbury's Book of Wine – Oz Clarke (Websters/Sainsbury's, £5.95)

Terrific value for a well-written, beautifully produced guide to the world's wines. Plenty of information and plenty of opinions.

Specialist

AUSTRALIA

The Wines of Australia – Oliver Mayo (Faber and Faber, £12.95)

Published in 1986, this may be a little out of date, but it still has fascinating sections on the history of Australian wine and the way different areas developed.

CHILE

Chilean Wines – Jan Read (Sotheby's, £19.95)

The first English book on the wines from this exciting wine country. Jan Read – an expert on Spanish wines – gives a wide-ranging portrait of Chilean wine history, present conditions and producers.

FRANCE — GENERAL

French Wine Atlas – Hubrecht Duijker and Hugh Johnson (Mitchell Beazley, £16.95)

A complete and well-written guide to visiting French vineyards: route maps, lists of producers, where to eat and drink, where to stay, places of interest. To read at home as well as useful for taking with you.

The Pocket Book of French Regional Wines – Roger Voss (Mitchell Beazley, £4.95)

In the familiar Pocket Book format, a guide to the wines and producers of all the regions of France apart from Bordeaux, Burgundy and Champagne. Tasting information and vintage reports, plus detailed information on all the AC and VDQS areas of France.

The Wine Lovers' Guide to France – Michael Busselle (Michael Joseph, £14.95)

Beautiful photographs of the vineyard areas, but also useful information for tours and visits (including details from *Michelin* maps).

Eperon's French Wine Tour – Arthur Eperon (Pan, £6.95)

A tour of French vineyards, with maps, information on where to stay and eat, a description of the wines and advice on where to taste and buy them.

The Vineyards of France – Don Philpott (Morland Publishing, £7.95)

Rather less glossy than the Eperon book above, but still with useful information on who to visit and where to stay when visiting French vineyards.

The Macdonald Guide to French Wines – André Vedel (Macdonald Orbis, £17.50)

Over 5,000 tasting notes on French wines. A formidable work, provided you can cope with French tasting notes which tend to the flowery and vague.

FRANCE — BORDEAUX

Pocket Guide to the Wines of Bordeaux – David Peppercorn (Mitchell Beazley, £4.95)

Following the standard Pocket Book style, this covers the whole of Bordeaux with a tightly written guide to the main areas and estates. Tasting notes cover recent vintages.

The Wines of Bordeaux (revised edition) – Edmund Penning-Rowsell (Penguin, £12.95)

Anybody who knows how comprehensive and useful previous editions of this guide to Bordeaux were will want to buy this latest edition.

Bordeaux – The Definitive Guide – Robert Parker (Dorling Kindersley, £12.95)

Despite its aggressive title, this is a major guide to Bordeaux, packed full of Robert Parker's tasting notes on individual châteaux.

The White Wines of Bordeaux – William Bolter (Octopus Books, £4.95)

Part of a new series of guides to the wines and producers, containing a regional description plus a guide to producers.

The Red Wines of Bordeaux – William Bolter (Octopus Books, £4.95)

Companion volume to the above.

FRANCE – BURGUNDY

Pocket Guide to the Wines of Burgundy – Serena Sutcliffe (Mitchell Beazley, £4.95)

A guide to the minefield of Burgundy, based on the Pocket Book formula, with directory-style entries for producers and villages. Plenty of opinions, too.

The White Wines of Burgundy – Jasper Morris (Octopus Books, £4.95)

Information about the region, plus guided tours of each village and the best producers. Illustrated with maps and photographs.

The Red Wines of Burgundy – Mark Savage (Octopus Books, £4.95)

Companion volume to the above.

FRANCE – CHAMPAGNE

Champagne – Tom Stevenson (Sotheby's, £19.95)

An authoritative guide to everything there is to know about Champagne – the producers, the villages, the history, the taste, the vintages, how to drink and store it.

The Story of Champagne – Nicholas Faith (Hamish Hamilton, £17.95)

The fascinating history of Champagne is told with scholarship and style. There's nothing romantic about this view, either – there are warts a-plenty among the Champenois. Details on the way Champagne is made and a directory of producers follow.

FRANCE – RHÔNE AND PROVENCE

The Wines of the Rhône Valley and Provence – Robert Parker (Dorling Kindersley, £14.95)

A guide to the producers in both regions, accompanied by copious tasting notes. Plenty of reputations are pricked here, but there are also exciting discoveries.

GERMANY

Atlas of German Wines – Hugh Johnson and Ian Jamieson (Mitchell Beazley, £14.95)

A guide to the German vineyards, with listings of all the different estate names and regions. Good for touring (if a bit big) and for reference.

WINE BOOKSHELF

ITALY

Life Beyond Lambrusco – Nicolas Belfrage (Sidgwick & Jackson, £7.95)

Full of information on Italian wines with easy cross-referencing and plenty of background. Wines and producers are described, the main styles are analysed and what each area produces is listed.

PORTUGAL AND SPAIN

Rich, Rare and Red – Ben Howkins (Christopher Helm/Wine Appreciation Society, £5.95)

A revised edition of this guide to Port which first appeared six years ago. History, geography, plus profiles of the Port houses and anecdotes from someone closely connected with the Port wine trade.

The Wine and Food of Spain – Jan Read and Maite Manjon (Weidenfeld and Nicolson, £12.95)

The top experts on Spanish food and wine cover the country, looking at the different regions, their wine, the local cuisine. Includes information on restaurants and hotels.

The Wines of Spain and Portugal – Charles Metcalfe and Kathryn McWhirter (Salamander Press, £7.99)

A region-by-region view of the wine regions of the two Iberian countries, liberally illustrated with maps and colour photographs.

The New Wines of Spain – Tony Lord (Christopher Helm, £12.95)

A review of the rapid developments that have taken place in Spain over the past few years, plus a regional guide to who is doing what where.

SPARKLING WINES

Pocket Guide to Champagne and Sparkling Wines – Jane MacQuitty (Mitchell Beazley, £4.95)

Exhaustive guide to the sparkling wines of the world – from New Zealand to Oregon and Champagne to Chile. Directory-style entries, full of tasting notes and opinions.

SWEET WINES

Liquid Gold, Dessert Wines of the World – Stephen Brook (Constable, £14.95)

The first book ever devoted entirely to sweet wines. Covers the world, but devotes most detail to France and Germany. Well written, with good profiles of producers and a detailed study of the way the wines are made.

Index

This index covers the WHAT TO BUY section only. Names from the lists of 'Who's Who' in each country have been indexed only if they also appear in the main text. Maps have not been indexed.

Report to the Editor *Which? Wine Guide*

This report is

a new recommendation ☐

a comment on existing entry ☐ *please tick as appropriate*

name of establishment

address

tel no:

please continue overleaf

date of most recent visit

signed

I am not connected directly or indirectly with the management or proprietors

name   *in block letters, please*

address

Send to: Which? Wine Guide, Freepost, London NW1 4DX
(please note: no postage required within UK)

Report to the Editor *Which? Wine Guide*

This report is

a new recommendation ☐

a comment on existing entry ☐

please tick as appropriate

name of establishment

address

tel no:

please continue overleaf

date of most recent visit
_____

signed
_____

I am not connected directly or indirectly with the management or proprietors

name   *in block letters, please*
_____

address
_____

_____

Send to: Which? Wine Guide, Freepost, London NW1 4DX
(please note: no postage required within UK)